Global Legal Insights
Blockchain & Cryptocurrency Regulation
Regulation

2019, First Edition
Contributing Editor: Josias Dewey
Published by Global Legal Group

GLOBAL LEGAL INSIGHTS – BLOCKCHAIN & CRYPTOCURRENCY REGULATION
2019, FIRST EDITION

Editor
Josias Dewey, Holland & Knight LLP

Production Editor
Andrew Schofield

Senior Editors
Suzie Levy
Caroline Collingwood

Group Consulting Editor
Alan Falach

Publisher
Rory Smith

We are extremely grateful for all contributions to this edition.
Special thanks are reserved for Josias Dewey for all his assistance.

Published by Global Legal Group Ltd.
59 Tanner Street, London SE1 3PL, United Kingdom
Tel: +44 207 367 0720 / URL: www.glgroup.co.uk

ISBN 978-1-912509-35-5
ISSN 2631-2999

Printed and bound by CPI Group (UK) Ltd, Croydon, CR0 4YY
September 2018

CONTENTS

Country chapters

PREFACE

Over the last two years, an obscure technology once associated only with the virtual currency Bitcoin, has become one of the most important technologies under development today. No longer known only as the technology on which Bitcoin was built, it has either been deployed or is under active development in virtually every industry. Financial services, healthcare, energy, capital markets, and many other industries are seeing legacy technology challenged by proposed blockchain-based solutions.

Blockchain has also exploded in terms of its geographic impact. Once a novelty that was only familiar to people in a handful of countries, the technology is now relevant to the global economy. In some countries, like Venezuela, virtual currency has taken a prominent role in the day-to-day lives of ordinary citizens. Yet, for all of the interest, popularity and media attention, many, including lawyers, struggle to understand the underpinnings of the technology and its implications for policymakers and other officials. This difficulty is compounded by the extraordinarily broad application of the technology across numerous industries. Certain implementations of the technology look very little like others. Some seek to supplement or replace traditional fiat currency, while others have no native virtual currency at all. Some are accessible by anyone with a computer or smart phone, while others are only accessible by those having credentials. This diversity of implementations and use cases, together with misguided statements espousing "absolute truths" about the technology, lead to confusion for most trying to tackle blockchain.

While blockchain has taken a much more prominent role in society, it remains a relatively nascent technology, having existed for less than ten years. This brief history has caused tension when the technology has been deployed in areas traditionally subject to extensive regulation, such as capital-raising and money transmission. Policymakers and other officials have often struggled to apply laws crafted decades ago, in many cases, built on assumptions now being challenged by the technology. In part, this continues to be driven by the technology's ability to disintermediate market participants, many of whom have traditionally been relied upon as unofficial gatekeepers in certain industries. No consistent policy has yet to evolve, with numerous states within the U.S. taking very different approaches to the technology, while the U.S. government has relied on its agencies to navigate the myriad of issues. The picture is no clearer on the international stage, where some nations have sought to foster the growth of the technology, and others have sought to eliminate the technology from their jurisdiction. This uncertainty has contributed to the lack of commercially deployed blockchain solutions, and many of the following chapters focus on these grey areas where much work remains to be done.

Our hope is that this publication will provide the reader with an understanding of some of the most critical issues facing practitioners and others involved in this area of technology and policy. The diversity of jurisdictions covered by this publication also provides a glimpse into how various governments have approached regulating this technology. Many have tried to balance their desire to foster innovation and the development of the technology in their country, while protecting their citizens from fraud or other harm. There is no doubt that this debate has only just begun, but we believe readers of this publication will be able to follow this debate in the future, regardless of what policymakers ultimately decide.

Josias Dewey
Holland & Knight LLP

FOREWORD

Dear Industry Colleagues,

On behalf of the Enterprise Ethereum Alliance ("EEA"), I would like to thank Global Legal Group ("GLG") for bringing to life an explication of the state of regulation in the blockchain sector, with first edition publication of *GLI – Blockchain & Cryptocurrency Regulation*. GLG has assembled a remarkable group of leaders in the legal industry to analyse and explain the environment in front of us, and EEA members were pleased to contribute to the publication.

We stand at the beginning of an industry, and the depth and breadth of the contributors from leading law firms across the world shows the interest and fascination with the ideas around blockchain technology. We thank each of the authors for taking the time to compose their chapters and for the expertise they demonstrate. We hope readers will find this publication useful.

The EEA is the industry's first global standards organisation to deliver an open, standards-based architecture and specification to accelerate the adoption of Enterprise Ethereum. The EEA's world-class Enterprise Ethereum Client Specification and forthcoming testing and certification programs will ensure interoperability, multiple vendors of choice, and lower costs for its members – more than 550 of the world's largest enterprises and most innovative startups. For additional information about joining the EEA, please reach out to: membership@ entethalliance.org.

Our next global event is Devcon 4, taking place in Prague, Czech Republic from October 30–November 2, 2018. For more information on the EEA and its events, head to: https://entethalliance.org.

Sincerely,

Aaron Wright

Chairman, EEA Legal Advisory Working Group

GLOSSARY

Alice **decision**: a 2014 United States Supreme Court decision about patentable subject matter.

Cryptocurrencies: a term used interchangeably with virtual currency, and generally intended to include the following virtual currencies (and others similar to these):

- Bitcoin
- Bitcoin Cash
- Ether
- Ethereum Classic
- Litecoin
- Monero
- NEO
- Ripple's XRP
- DASH
- Dogecoin
- Zcash

Cold storage: refers to the storage of private keys on an un-networked device or on paper in a secure location.

Copyleft licence: the practice of offering people the right to freely distribute copies and modified versions of a work with the stipulation that the same rights be preserved in derivative works down the line.

Cryptography: the practice and study of techniques for secure communication in the presence of third parties, generally involving encryption and cyphers.

DAO Report: report issued in July, 2017 by U.S. Securities and Exchange Commission, considering and ultimately concluding that The DAO (*see below*) was a security.

Decentralised autonomous organisation ("The DAO"): a failed investor-directed venture capital fund with no conventional management structure or board of directors that was launched with a defect in its code that permitted someone to withdraw a substantial amount of the $130,000,000 in Ether it raised.

Decentralised autonomous organisation ("a DAO"): a form of business organisation relying on a smart contract (*see below*) in lieu of a conventional management structure or board of directors.

Digital assets: anything that exists in a binary format and comes with the right to use, and more typically consisting of a data structure intended to describe attributes and rights associated with some entitlement.

Digital collectibles: digital assets that are collected by hobbyists and others for entertainment, and which are often not fungible (e.g., CryptoKitties) (*see* **Tokens**, non-fungible)

Digital currency: a type of currency available only in digital form, which can be fiat currency or virtual currency that acts as a substitute for fiat currency.

Digital currency exchange: a business that allows customers to trade cryptocurrencies or digital currencies for other assets, such as conventional fiat money, or one type of cryptocurrency for another type of cryptocurrency.

Digital/electronic wallet: an electronic device or software that allows an individual to securely store private keys and broadcast transactions across a peer-to-peer network, which can be hosted (e.g., Coinbase) or user managed (e.g., MyEtherWallet).

Distributed ledger technology (DLT): often used interchangeably with the term *blockchain*, but while all blockchains are a type of distributed ledger technology, not all distributed ledger technologies implement a blockchain style of achieving consensus.

Fintech: new technology and innovation that aims to compete with traditional financial methods in the delivery of financial services.

Initial coin offering: a type of crowdfunding using cryptocurrencies in which a quantity of the crowdfunded cryptocurrency is sold to either investors or consumers, or both, in the form of "tokens".

Initial token offering: See *Initial coin offering.*

Internet of Things: a system of interrelated computing devices, mechanical and digital machines, objects, animals or people that are provided with unique identifiers and the ability to transfer data over a network without requiring human-to-human or human-to-computer interaction.

Licences, software: the grant of a right to use otherwise copyrighted code, including, among others:

- Apache
- GPLv3
- MIT

Mining, cryptocurrency: the process by which transactions are verified and added to the public ledger known as the blockchain, which is often the means through which new units of a virtual currency are created (e.g., Bitcoin).

Money transmitter (U.S.): a business entity that provides money transfer services or payment instruments.

Permissioned network: a blockchain in which the network owner(s) decides who can join the network and issue credentials necessary to access the network.

Platform or protocol coins: the native virtual currencies transferable on a blockchain network, which exist as a function of the protocol's code base.

Protocols: Specific code bases implementing a particular blockchain network, such as:

- Bitcoin
- R3's Corda
- Litecoin
- Ethereum
- Hyperledger Fabric

Private key: an alphanumeric cryptographic key that is generated in pairs with a corresponding public key. One can verify possession of a private key that corresponds to its public key counterpart without exposing it. It is not possible, however, to derive the private key from the public key.

Private key storage:

- *Deep cold storage*: a type of cold storage where not only bitcoins are stored offline, but also the system that holds the bitcoins is never online or connected to any kind of network.

- *Hardware wallet*: an electronic device capable of running software necessary to store private keys in a secure, encrypted state and structure transactions capable of being broadcast on one or more blockchain networks. Two popular examples are Ledger and Trezor.

Public network: blockchain which anyone can join by installing client software on a computer with an internet connection. Best known public networks are Bitcoin and Ethereum.

Qualified custodian: a regulated custodian who provides clients with segregated accounts and often places coins or tokens in cold storage (See above).

Robo-advice/digital advice: a class of financial adviser that provides financial advice or investment management online, with moderate to minimal human intervention.

Sandbox (regulatory): a programme implemented by a regulatory agency that permits innovative start-ups to engage in certain activities that might otherwise require licensing with one or more governmental agencies.

Security token: a token intended to confer rights typically associated with a security (e.g., stock or bond), and hence, generally treated as such by regulators.

Smart contract: a piece of code that is written for execution within a blockchain runtime environment. Such programs are often written to automate certain actions on the network, such as the transfer of virtual currency if certain conditions in the code are met.

Tokens: a data structure capable of being fungible (ERC-20) or non-fungible (ERC-721) that is capable of being controlled by a person to the exclusion of others, which is typically transferable from one person to another on a blockchain network.

Utility token: a token intended to entitle the holder to consume some good or service offered through a decentralised application (Dapp).

Vending machine (Bitcoin): an internet machine that allows a person to exchange bitcoins and cash. Some Bitcoin ATMs offer bi-directional functionality, enabling both the purchase of Bitcoin as well as the redemption of Bitcoin for cash.

Promoting innovation through education:

The blockchain industry, law enforcement and regulators work towards a common goal

Jason Weinstein, Alan Cohn & Chelsea Parker
The Blockchain Alliance

Criminal use of technology

When many people think of "bitcoin" or other cryptocurrencies, they often think of crime, because of "Silk Road" and other high-profile examples of people exploiting cryptocurrencies for unlawful purposes.

But for the entrepreneurs, engineers, venture capitalists and bankers who are pouring their time, energy, and money into bitcoin- and other cryptocurrency-related businesses, it's the underlying "blockchain" technology that is the real attraction. And contrary to popular belief, this technology is friendlier to law-enforcers than it is to law-breakers.

Blockchain technology uses cryptography to verify and confirm all transactions and then records those transactions on a searchable public ledger. Bitcoin and other cryptocurrencies represent just the first "app" for blockchain technology. There are endless other possibilities for that technology – from securities and commodities trading, to supply chain, to IP rights, to identity management and security, to real estate to government services, just to name a few – that could transform the way the world does business, much like the internet did over 20 years ago.

It's a fact of life in law enforcement that criminals are always among the first adopters of any novel technology that works. And law enforcement has a long history of adapting in order to pursue criminals who use "new school" technology to commit "old school" crimes. From beepers to email to online chat to Skype to social networking, law enforcement consistently has had to evolve as new technology designed for legitimate purposes is used to facilitate criminal activity. Bitcoin and other cryptocurrencies represent just the latest example.

While there is unquestionably criminal activity taking place via the internet, we don't think of the internet as the "computer network of criminals". That's because the vast majority of commercial activity over the internet is legitimate, whereas illicit activity facilitated by the web represents just a small portion of what happens on the internet every day. Similarly, bitcoin and other cryptocurrencies should not be thought of as "currencies of criminals", because illicit transactions, while they exist, account for only a minute portion of the activity involving this new technology.

Proactive engagement by industry

Recognising a shared interest in helping combat criminal exploitation of this revolutionary technology, the blockchain and cryptocurrency industry proactively approached law enforcement and regulatory agencies and offered to help educate these agencies about how cryptocurrencies work, provide technical assistance, and foster an open dialogue about issues of common concern. Under the leadership of the Chamber of Digital Commerce and Coin Center, the industry established the Blockchain Alliance, a non-profit organisation that serves as a forum for engagement between the blockchain industry and law enforcement and regulatory agencies. Since the Blockchain Alliance was founded in 2015, it has grown to include over 100 blockchain and cryptocurrency companies and law enforcement and regulatory agencies in the U.S. and around the world, including Europol and Interpol and authorities in Europe, Latin America, Africa, Asia, and Australia.

Through the Blockchain Alliance, some of the brightest minds in the industry are working with law enforcement and regulatory agencies to combat criminal activity involving this new technology, in an effort to promote public safety and a pro-innovation regulatory environment. The Blockchain Alliance convenes regular calls to discuss trends in the industry and tools for combating criminal activity. Among other activities, the Alliance has conducted educational programs for nearly 700 law enforcement officers and regulators from more than 35 countries. These educational programs cover a range of topics from the basics of the technology, to tracing tools, to privacy coins.

Tracing the flow of funds

One of the main misconceptions Blockchain Alliance members have worked to correct is that bitcoin transactions are anonymous. The reality is that the technology has significant benefits for investigators seeking to "follow the (digital) money". Having a public, traceable, immutable, borderless ledger of every bitcoin transaction ever conducted allows law enforcement to trace the flow of funds involving an investigative target anywhere in the world in a way that would not be possible with cash or many other types of financial instruments. And industry has developed software tools for connecting bitcoin addresses to a particular user – similar to the challenge law enforcement has faced for years trying to identify anonymous hackers and other cybercriminals – and those tools are continually improving. Those same types of tools allow cryptocurrency exchanges to better identify suspicious actors and transactions as part of their anti-money laundering compliance programs. Under the circumstances, criminals should be running, not walking, away from using bitcoin and other types of cryptocurrencies.

Impact of regulation

While it is often said that cryptocurrencies and blockchain technology are unregulated, nothing could be further from the truth. Numerous federal and state agencies in the United States, as well as agencies in other countries, regulate applications for this technology in some fashion. But the disparate approaches taken by different countries, or even by different agencies within the U.S., have led to confusion on the part of blockchain companies about the jurisdictions and regulatory regimes to which their products and services will be subject.

An analysis of illicit laundering of bitcoin found regional differences in volume, part of which may be explained by the different approaches to regulation. The Foundation for Defense of Democracies' Center on Sanctions and Illicit Finance, along with Elliptic, a cryptocurrency analytics provider, researched the illicit flows of bitcoin through conversion services, or platforms where users can exchange cryptocurrency to fiat, and cryptocurrency to cryptocurrency, or send cryptocurrency to other users.[1] Researchers found that the second-highest amount of illicit bitcoin flowed through conversion services located in Europe, second only to those conversion services where the operating jurisdiction could not be identified.

While Europe has now adopted regulation to include cryptocurrency companies like exchanges within the scope of the 5th Anti-Money Laundering Directive, these regulations were not in place during the period of study, 2013 to 2016. Many jurisdictions, even within the U.S., regulate cryptocurrency activities like the exchange of cryptocurrency to fiat, or cryptocurrency to cryptocurrency, differently. Some exchanges offering services that do not clearly fit in the current regulatory regime have voluntarily developed robust procedures in order to verify their customers' identity and the source of funds. However, clear regulations and guidelines on AML and know-your-customer policies can help reduce the criminal activity flowing through exchanges and other cryptocurrency companies. It is important to note that while Europe saw the second-highest exposure to laundering in bitcoin, this illicit activity made up only a small portion of the overall bitcoin volume received by conversion services.

Moving forward through continued engagement

In order to ensure the growth of the industry while also protecting consumers and preventing money laundering, a pro-innovation approach to regulation is needed. Positive and proactive engagement by industry with law enforcement and regulators, through the Blockchain Alliance and otherwise, has been critical to the growth of this sector to date. Continued engagement of this type will be equally important going forward, as industry seeks to foster an approach to lawmaking and rule-making that encourages, rather than stifles, innovation. Only then can the full potential of blockchain technology be realised.

* * *

Endnote

1.   Yaya J. Fanusie & Tom Robinson, *Bitcoin Laundering: An Analysis of Illicit Flows into Digital Currency Services* (2018), http://www.defenddemocracy.org/content/uploads/documents/MEMO_Bitcoin_Laundering.pdf.

Jason Weinstein, Director
Tel: +1 202 429 8061 / Email: jweinstein@steptoe.com
Jason Weinstein is Partner at Steptoe & Johnson LLP, co-chair of the firm's Blockchain and Cryptocurrency practice, and Director to the Blockchain Alliance. He has represented just about every type of participant in the blockchain ecosystem and is widely recognised as an authority on legal and regulatory issues involving digital currencies and blockchain technology. Jason previously served as deputy assistant attorney general in the Department of Justice's Criminal Division, where he supervised the computer crime and organised crime sections, and oversaw numerous investigations involving the use of digital currencies. Jason serves on the advisory boards of Coin Center and the Chamber of Digital Commerce. He also serves as an advisor to BitFury, the leading full-service blockchain technology company and one of the largest private infrastructure providers in the industry.

Alan Cohn, Counsel
Tel: +1 202 429 6283 / Email: acohn@steptoe.com
Alan Cohn is Of Counsel at Steptoe & Johnson LLP, co-chair of the firm's Blockchain and Cryptocurrency practice, and counsel to the Blockchain Alliance. Alan counsels companies on cybersecurity, blockchain and distributed ledger technology, and national security issues. He previously served in senior policy and management positions at the U.S. Department of Homeland Security for almost a decade, most recently as the Assistant Secretary for Strategy, Planning, Analysis & Risk and second-in-charge overall of the DHS Office of Policy. Alan serves as an advisor to several blockchain companies, including companies focused on blockchain transaction analysis, identity validation, enterprise blockchain applications, and device authentication for the Internet of Things.

Chelsea Parker, Director of Operations
Tel: +1 202 778 3573 / Email: cparker@steptoe.com
Chelsea Parker is the Director of Operations for the Blockchain Alliance. Chelsea manages the day-to-day operations of the Blockchain Alliance and our 100 members consisting of blockchain and cryptocurrency companies and law enforcement and regulatory agencies. Chelsea is also the Blockchain Industry Analyst at Steptoe & Johnson LLP where she manages business development, marketing, and operations of the Blockchain and Cryptocurrency practice. She plays an active role in all aspects of client engagement and assists companies and investors with technology-specific questions related to the adoption and use of blockchain technology and cryptocurrencies.

The Blockchain Alliance

1330 Connecticut Avenue, NW, Washington, DC 20036, USA
URL: www.blockchainalliance.org

The loan market, blockchain, and smart contracts: The potential for transformative change

Bridget Marsh, LSTA
Josias Dewey, Holland & Knight LLP

Introduction

The Loan Syndications and Trading Association ("LSTA") is the trade association in the United States for the corporate loan market. We promote a fair, orderly, and efficient loan market and actively seek ways in which we can achieve that. During the past couple of years, the LSTA has considered how blockchain and distributed ledger technology ("DLT") will impact the industry and believes that this new technology can propel the syndicated loan market forward and help address some of its current challenges.

This article provides a brief description of the loan market and its participants to put our conversation in context, sets out the basics of blockchain and DLT, reviews the concept of "smart contracts", and examines how the primary and secondary loan markets can benefit from these new technologies.

U.S. loan market and loan market participants

There is no single regulatory authority charged with the responsibility of regulating the syndicated loan market in the United States. Of course, most loan market participants are regulated institutions that have one or more regulators overseeing their activities, but the loan market itself is not regulated. The LSTA is, therefore, the entity to which loan market participants turn for standard forms, best practices, and general assistance with primary loan market activities and secondary market loan trades.

The LSTA maintains a suite of documents that can be used by market participants in the origination, servicing, and trading of loans. Since its formation nearly 25 years ago, the LSTA has published standard agreements, forms, and best practices for use in the primary loan market which have been widely adopted by market participants. The LSTA's comprehensive suite of secondary trading documents are used by all loan market participants to evidence their loan trades and then settle those transactions.

At its most basic, in the primary loan market, there are several interested parties involved in the origination of any large syndicated loan, the terms of which are documented in a credit agreement. There must be: (i) a borrower to which the loan is made and which is responsible for principal and interest payments under the terms of the credit agreement; (ii) one or more lenders in the syndicate, each of which owns a portion of the outstanding loan; and (iii) an administrative agent which is responsible for the ongoing administration of the loan until its maturity date. Although complex deal terms may vary from deal to deal, the basics of each loan will generally operate the same way. In the secondary loan market, each loan trade will, of course, include a selling lender and a legal entity buying the loan, an administrative agent who must acknowledge or consent to the loan assignment, and a borrower whose consent to the loan trade is also typically required. The buyer and seller of the loan execute an LSTA Par/Near Par Trade Confirmation ("LSTA Confirm") to evidence their loan trade, and the relevant form of assignment agreement pursuant to which the loan is then assigned to the buyer. Finally, the administrative agent updates the register of lenders to reflect the loan assignment.

For the trading of performing loans ("par trades") where the borrower is making timely loan payments in accordance with the terms of the credit agreement and neither the borrower nor the applicable industry is in any type of financial distress or experiencing any type of turmoil, most of the steps outlined above have become standard practice in the U.S. loan market, and LSTA trading documentation is used uniformly by all participants. After the relevant consents are obtained, those par trades are typically settled on an electronic platform with little or no lawyer involvement and few, if any, modifications. Instead, market participants expect the LSTA to provide the market with trading documents that are periodically updated to reflect current market practices, legal developments, and the latest deal trends.

Because there is no (or very limited) tailoring of documents in the trading of par loans and with practices being quite streamlined and uniform, distinct elements of this market seem ideally suited for the implementation of new blockchain technology.

Blockchain basics

The terms blockchain and DLT are often used interchangeably by those in financial services, and both terms seem to be used as acceptable nomenclature for this new technology. Although there is a technical distinction between a blockchain and a DLT, for the purposes of our discussion, the terms will be used interchangeably, although it seems that the term blockchain has, in recent months, again become the favoured term by those in financial services.

Perhaps surprising to some is that the technology underlying blockchain is actually a collection of technologies that has been used for quite some time. Blockchain is a decentralised peer-to-peer network that maintains a ledger of transactions (e.g., a transfer of an asset from one party to another party) that uses cryptographic tools to maintain the integrity of transactions and the integrity of the ledger itself, and a protocol-wide consensus mechanism that verifies the data and determines if, when, and how to update the ledger. The decentralised network makes this technology distinct from a traditional centralised database that has one authoritative database maintained by a trusted third party. For example, central banks around the world serve as that trusted third party for a state's banking system; similarly, for a syndicated loan, the administrative agent is the trusted third party that maintains the register of lenders, administers the loan, and keeps a record of all loan positions, including related interest and principal payments. Lenders in the syndicate must reconcile their own records with those of the administrative agent whose entries in the register are conclusive, absent manifest error. Without a trusted party to maintain a ledger, by contrast, in a blockchain, the cryptographic tools (e.g., a public or private encryption key) keep the information secure, for they are used to control the ownership of and/or the right to access the information on the ledger.

A blockchain is often considered to be immutable or tamper-proof because of the technology used to maintain the integrity of the ledger. Although there have been a few examples of hacking of digital currencies that rely on this technology, the unique way in which the information is stored and updated does make it incredibly secure. For example, to create each "block" in a blockchain, transactions are aggregated together and, using the appropriate protocol (a protocol can be thought of as software or a set of rules for a particular system), subjected to a special mathematical algorithm. The calculation results in an alphanumeric string that is put on the next block, and those two blocks are now inextricably chained together or "cryptographically linked". The process is then repeated for each bundle of transactions that are aggregated together; the number of blocks will increase, and the chain will continue to grow over time. To tamper or attempt to hack into or change some of the stored information would be nearly impossible and incredibly expensive. Because a new entry on a blockchain ledger is verified by a consensus mechanism at the time of entry and updated across all computers simultaneously, the computers rely on and trust this single source of truth. One of the enormous benefits of this technology is the potential for cost savings because separate reconciliation efforts will no longer be needed. (This alone makes it incredibly attractive technology for the loan market.)

Public or permissioned ledger

Distributed ledger technology can be implemented with or without access controls, depending on whether an open, public network is used or a restricted, permissioned network is chosen. The decentralised digital currency, Bitcoin, is likely the most well-known example of an open, public network where anyone can query the ledger and broadcast transactions without any authorisation (assuming, of course, the individual has the proper computer equipment and software). In a public blockchain, ledgers are replicated across many computers referred to as "nodes", which are connected to a common network over the internet. Those operating the nodes are referred to as "miners". In contrast, a closed, permissioned network is restricted to certain individuals who have been given permission and the necessary credentials to access the ledger by a trusted third party.

It is not surprising that the financial services industry is currently favouring the implementation of permissioned networks. Because of anti-money laundering ("AML"), know-your-customer ("KYC"), and privacy considerations (discussed more fully below), public networks are not really feasible in financial services at this time. A Bitcoin miner that is anonymous on a public network should be subject to the requirements of the Bank Secrecy Act and a financial institution's own KYC program as if it were to be involved in a similar function in the financial services industry for a bank Thus, it is understandable that given current frameworks, a bank's systems cannot be integrated with public networks, but as technology develops this, too, could change.

Each member of a permissioned network knows the identity of the counterparty on the other side of a transaction. Being able to identify a counterparty is important for many reasons in a transaction, including KYC and AML. For financial transactions, in particular, it provides parties with a way to make formal demands against each other in the event of nonperformance by one of them. Similarly, if the nonperforming party fails to cure a default, the other party may file a lawsuit and exercise its rights and remedies under the transaction documents. By contrast, on public networks, people are often transacting anonymously or with those who have not disclosed their true identity.

Smart contracts

The term "smart contracts" can be misleading especially for lawyers who have a definite idea of what must be shown for there to be a binding legal agreement between parties. At a minimum, a contract requires there to be an offer by one party, an acceptance by another party, and some form of consideration to exist. When the term is used by software engineers, it means computer code that is self-executing (the type of code will depend on the protocol on which the code is implemented). I think a more useful structure for the loan market is a hybrid legal contract that has certain parts of it coded and other parts that remain in human prose. The term "smart legal agreements" has been used to describe this type of hybrid legal contract, and this combination of a legal agreement with a smart contract would be most useful for financial instruments. One could envision how the LSTA Confirm could become a smart legal agreement with certain provisions remaining in human prose; for example, the reference to LSTA Arbitration Rules could remain as text while provisions relating to the calculation of the loan purchase price could be coded and thus become self-executing.

There is an aspect of utilising smart legal agreements which does increase the risk of error or corruption and should, therefore be highlighted – the management of information that is drawn from an external source referred to as an "oracle" in the blockchain nomenclature. Because smart contracts are programmed to be self-executing, some information may need to be pulled in from an external source, and therefore it is essential that this information from the oracle be accurate. For example, pursuant to the terms of the LSTA Confirm, if a trade does not timely settle, then upon settlement the buyer is credited for certain interest payments made by the borrower, but it must also pay the seller the interest that would accrue at one month LIBOR for deposits in the applicable currency as set by the ICE Benchmark Administration on the amount equal to the purchase price. If the LIBO Rate, an oracle, is corrupted for any reason, then of course there will be repercussions for trades settling on the blockchain, where the Confirm has been turned into a smart legal agreement with certain elements of it coded and thus self-executing.

Smart contracts build on the innovation of blockchain technology and have the potential to allow parties to structure and effectuate transactions in a more efficient and secure manner than traditional contracts; however, there are still challenges and obstacles that must be overcome before smart legal agreements become commonplace. Although we recognise that the technology remains in its infancy and is not a panacea for all our market's present challenges, we remain confident that smart contracts and blockchain technology will ultimately transform our market.

Blockchain, smart contracts and the loan market

There is enormous potential for the marriage of blockchain technology and smart contracts to result in incredible strides forward for the loan market. Although the typical syndicated loan agreement is a complex instrument that cannot be reduced simply to computer code, there are aspects of it which do lend themselves to becoming coded and, where a legal agreement has been standardised for a particular market or asset, then it can be more easily coded and efficiently implemented.

In the context of the loan market, the origination of a syndicated loan – from the time the credit agreement is drafted and the loan funded – could be made using distributed ledger technology (and in fact, there is already an example of a large loan being done on a blockchain in Europe). In today's market, a credit agreement is typically drafted by legal counsel based on deal terms that have been emailed to them. The lawyers then prepare the draft credit documentation based on that information. This approach introduces the risk of manual transcription errors, and validation rules will not have been applied to the information included in the credit agreement. By using document-automation tools, together with a distributed ledger, the credit agreement can be generated from data stored on the ledger that has already been validated. Although this can, of course, be accomplished without a blockchain, in the absence of a distributed ledger there is no single source of validated data. Having a single source of truth as to the ownership of a syndicated loan ultimately will eliminate the redundant, time-consuming, and costly exercise of multiple parties manually processing and accounting for primary allocations, payments and assignments.

In today's loan market, the closing of primary trades is a time-consuming and slow process. After initial funding of the loan by the administrative agent, each party with a primary market allocation must then fund its portion of the loan and execute an assignment agreement to evidence the settlement of their primary trade. With the disparate systems used by loan market participants today, each party is likely still emailed a PDF or another form of the executed agreement, and from those documents it must then extract the relevant information and manually input that information into its own back office system (with all the human touchpoints, there is a greater risk of error and delay with this type of process).

With a blockchain, the credit agreement and related documents could be digitally signed and delivered electronically at closing, thus allowing the deal terms, including information about loan positions, automatically to populate on the network's ledger – the same ledger accessed by all lenders. Think how a DLT network with the applicable credit agreement, assignment agreement and Confirm, all structured as smart legal agreements, could implement identical functionality in a way similar to today's loan operations – but one where the contracts are self-executing and the database replicated across an entire network of computers. Although the computers in the network (assuming a permissioned network is used) will be controlled by potentially hundreds of lenders in the syndicate, the integrity of the data across the network will be assured by the integration of a protocol-wide consensus mechanism.

A blockchain platform for a syndicated loan could also track a loan's interest rate, interest and principal payment dates, and any other data fields relevant to the life cycle of the loan. In a typical syndicated loan, many different parties, each storing information about a syndicated loan, have to continually reconcile all information they receive against their own internal databases. A blockchain platform could eliminate the need for, or significantly reduce the time spent on, reconciling data across the market. That alone could save the loan market an enormous amount of time and money. In addition, other aspects of a credit agreement could also be coded. For example, when a borrower submits periodic financial reports to the syndicate, certain data from those reports could be extracted, thus allowing financial covenants in the credit agreement automatically to be tested.

Secondary market trades in the loan market are memorialised by the parties executing an LSTA Confirm. Settlement of the trade – when the seller's legal ownership of the loan is transferred to the purchaser, and the purchaser pays the purchase price to the seller – typically occurs days or even weeks after the trade is entered into by the parties. It is easy to imagine how the transfer of this asset could be done far more seamlessly and efficiently on a blockchain, with smart legal agreements self-executing and data being updated on the ledger automatically. In this way, one can imagine lenders in the syndicate on a permissioned ledger using private keys digitally to execute the LSTA Confirm and applicable assignment agreements. When the assigning lender digitally signs the Confirm and relevant assignment agreement (and any other consents have been obtained), the register of lenders (assuming existing nomenclature is retained) will be updated automatically to reflect the assignee's account being credited by the amount of the loan transferred to it, and a corresponding debit to the assignor's account. No-one will need to reconcile their own positions because they will all have access on the permissioned ledger to the same information.

Although the adoption of blockchain will shorten the settlement times for loan trades, the payment of the loan purchase price will likely occur outside of blockchain networks for some period of time. Although it is not currently possible to transfer U.S. dollars across a distributed ledger, in the future, a central bank-issued digital currency could make settlement on the blockchain seamless. Until then, the payment method of a loan trade purchase price will need to rely on processes external to any blockchain to initiate payment. Reliance on such external processes may be acceptable on a permissioned blockchain network, where the identity of parties are known to each other and regulated financial institutions are involved.

AML and KYC issues

An appropriately built blockchain solution for the loan market would meet both KYC and AML requirements, and in so doing, would likely improve both the speed of implementation and accuracy of a financial institution's compliance program while satisfying any legal and regulatory requirements. The LSTA's 2017 Guidelines for the Application of Customer Identification Programs, Foreign Correspondent Account Due Diligence, and Other Considerations ("LSTA CIP Guidelines") serve as a comprehensive report outlining the specific due diligence and other compliance work required to engage in primary and secondary loan market transactions in the United States. The LSTA CIP Guidelines, which accurately set forth what is required for different primary and secondary loan market transactions and relationships between loan market participants, can be embedded in the smart legal agreement implementing the framework.

Because the KYC and AML requirements would be incorporated in this way, there would no longer be any need to have a separate stream of compliance work to satisfy a bank's KYC requirements and AML diligence in any syndicated loan that is processed through the framework. For example, perhaps checking the sanctions lists on the U.S. Department of the Treasury's Office of Foreign Assets Control website to ensure that a counterparty is not on any of the lists, which is typically the only due diligence required under U.S. law, could be like an "oracle", with the diligence thereby completed seamlessly and without any delays. This would result in huge cost savings for our market and would likely also lead to much shorter loan-trade-settlement times.

Regulators could also benefit greatly from the adoption of blockchain in the loan market. Because blockchains contain a complete history of all transactions that have taken place on the network, including a time stamp for all such transactions, internal auditing would be much simpler, and regulators could be granted access to the ledger to confirm that all related transactions are consistent with the stated intentions and information provided by customers. The ability to see transactions in real time would also be beneficial to regulators, who could monitor the transactions and more easily detect and identify illicit activities.

Competition law issues and corporate governance matters

There are, of course, competition law considerations that must be taken into account when considering the implementation of this new technology, and as a trade association we are acutely aware of these. During the process of selecting the appropriate DLT, there will be collaborative efforts necessary to implement the chosen DLT to the particular use case within the loan market. This collaboration and the development of a technological solution raise intellectual property concerns that the parties should seek to address. Although the task of identifying the correct technology may be challenging, once common ground is reached by market participants on that issue, the focus should then turn to internal governance matters, and the relative rights and obligations of the participants.

These efforts are complicated by the ever-present need to ensure compliance with applicable antitrust law, an issue that requires continuing diligence and vigilance amongst industry participants. We would caution consortium participants about anti-trust issues which may arise in such circumstances, and to seek advice from counsel where appropriate. The exchange of specific data on current and future prices and competitive activities – as opposed to aggregated past information – is likely to attract the greatest antitrust scrutiny. Thus, participants in blockchain consortia should take care to ensure that they are not, or could not be perceived to be, agreeing to eliminate their independent decision-making as to any aspect of the prices they charge or markets they serve.

Loan market developments

Several promising protocols are under active development in the U.S. loan market. In April 2018, Finastra launched LenderComm, which is underpinned by R3's Corda, a distributed ledger designed specifically for financial services that permits lenders to view their current loan positions and related information without agent involvement. IHS Markit's STAX is a private blockchain that creates a distributed ledger of all cash movement in the industry, providing parties with an encrypted record of their transactions. Synaps, a joint venture between Ipreo and Symbiant, is currently working on another blockchain-based product to distribute loan information across a network of computers. Although certain aspects of these technologies are not true blockchain technologies, they are definitely far more advanced than the loan market's existing platforms and services, and we welcome and encourage such investments and strides for our market.

Conclusion

The LSTA is optimistic about the potential for blockchain, or any type of advanced technology, to have a positive effect on the US loan market. At its simplest, blockchain is an efficient way to transfer any asset, including a loan, and the current systems and practices of the US syndicated loan market could benefit enormously from this technology. The LSTA is well-placed to lead the legal, technological, operational and business efforts to develop a general framework for implementing solutions that address the lifecycle of a loan from origination to repayment. Our market participants should understand not only the potential benefits of blockchain but the challenges to its adoption. This suggests that a sustained educational initiative targeting all loan market participants is necessary, and the LSTA is committed to offering that. The LSTA has been following developments around blockchain and providing educational resources to its members for a couple of years and will continue to be a resource as its members navigate many of these challenges and, in some cases, take a leading role in helping to craft standards that facilitate the efficient deployment of the technology. Forging consensus within an entire industry about standards, best practices and other uniform approaches and protocols is challenging, as we know, but the LSTA is well-placed to lead these efforts.

Although blockchain technology will not eliminate all inefficiencies in the loan market, it seems very likely that blockchain technology will eventually bring about fundamental change in how syndicated loans are originated, administered and traded in today's loan market.

Yet, there is much work to be done before this can be achieved. Computer software engineers, finance professionals, lawyers, and operational personnel will need to work together to analyse all of the processes used in the loan market, loan administration, and secondary loan trading. Policy, legal, and regulatory issues will need to be addressed thoughtfully, and we must always balance our desire to promote innovation with the need for a strong, stable, and reliable loan market.

Bridget Marsh
Tel: +1 212 880 3004 / Email: bmarsh@lsta.org
Bridget Marsh is Executive Vice President and Deputy General Counsel of the Loan Syndications and Trading Association (LSTA). Bridget heads the LSTA's Primary Market Committee and Trade Practices and Forms Committee and leads the legal projects for the development and standardisation of the LSTA's documentation.
Prior to joining the LSTA, Bridget practised as a corporate finance attorney at Milbank, New York, and as a lawyer in the corporate/M&A department of Simmons & Simmons, London, and completed a judicial clerkship for The Honorable Justice Beaumont of the Federal Court of Australia. She is a Regent of the American College of Commercial Finance Lawyers and a Fellow of the American Bar Foundation.
Bridget received a B.A. *magna cum laude* from Georgetown University, a law degree with first class honors from Sydney Law School, University of Sydney, and a Masters in Political Science from the University of New South Wales. She is admitted as an attorney in New York, England & Wales, and New South Wales, Australia.

Josias N. Dewey
Tel: +1 305 374 8500 / Email: joe.dewey@hklaw.com
Joe Dewey is a financial services and real estate partner in Holland & Knight's Miami office and is considered a thought leader on blockchain technology. Mr Dewey regularly represents banks and other financial institutions across the entire spectrum as measured by assets and scale, from community to global money center banks. Mr Dewey spends a considerable amount of time at the convergence of human prose legal contracts, as well as computational contracts, based primarily on computer code. This includes smart contracts that can be implemented on Hyperledger Fabric (or IBM's Blockchain service), Ethereum (both public and permissioned versions) and R3's Corda platform. Mr Dewey spends a considerable amount of his practice in this space assisting clients in identifying optimal distributed ledger use cases and developing proof of concept applications. He can assist in the transition from proof of concepts (PoCs) to production systems built by our clients' primary technology solutions providers.

Loan Syndications and Trading Association (LSTA)

366 Madison Avenue, 15th Floor, New York, NY 10017, USA
Tel: +1 212 880 3000 / Fax: +1 212 880 3040 / URL: www.lsta.org

An overview of the Wall Street Blockchain Alliance

Ron Quaranta
Wall Street Blockchain Alliance

The first decade

As we approach an almost full decade since the release of Bitcoin to the world, and the underlying blockchain technology that makes it possible, industries, businesses, entrepreneurs and governments across the globe are still working to not only understand its impact, but to enable applications that take full advantage of the benefits of this technology. Benefits such as *decentralization*, which removes the need for intermediaries to validate transactions; *immutability*, which makes data changes extremely difficult; and *transparency*, which makes the secure data set available to all network participants, are among the most significant of these. And to participants in the blockchain world, the cost savings possible because of these benefits are quite clear. Given this, it is the hope of blockchain and cryptoasset advocates that this innovation may fundamentally reinvent the economic models upon which much of the world is built.

Since 2009, we have seen a proliferation of technology solutions which are based in whole or in part on the original Bitcoin blockchain technology. Solutions and capabilities such as Ethereum,[1] Hyperledger,[2] Quorom,[3] Stellar[4] and more have been launched to offer the world blockchain capabilities across multiple industries. And it is not only the universe of startups that are involved. Indeed, some of the biggest names in technology, including Microsoft, IBM, SAP and others have entered the arena. This is to say nothing of the biggest banks, supply chain companies, securities exchanges, healthcare companies, media corporations and many more, vying to grab hold of this innovation. In conjunction with the rise of cryptoassets and smart contracts, all are endeavouring to pave a path towards a future in a blockchain world. Add to this the increasing scrutiny from governments and regulators worldwide, and it is easy to see the growing importance and urgency of blockchain technology for the future.

Foundation of the WSBA

In the midst of all of this change, the *Wall Street Blockchain Alliance (WSBA)* was founded in 2015 by a gathering of attorneys, bankers, trading experts, financial technology executives and others, all focused on the important work needed to shepherd the adoption of blockchain technology and cryptoassets across our relevant industries. Today, with membership representing more than 270 companies and organizations around the world, the WSBA is an industry-leading, non-profit, trade association with a global mission to advocate, guide and promote comprehensive adoption of blockchain technology and cryptoassets across global markets. The WSBA stands as a neutral, unbiased steward of education and co-operation between our global member firms. We do this by engaging with market participants, regulators, policymakers and technology innovators through direct communication, comment letters, studies and more to guide the public dialogue about blockchain, cryptoassets and smart contract technology, so that the global markets can realize the full potential of these capabilities.

Working groups

Like all trade associations, the WSBA has a wide range of tools available to its members to guide and serve its mission. One of the most important tools that we have are the WSBA Working Groups. WSBA Working Groups (WGs) are the mechanisms by which our members can directly interact with the WSBA itself, with other WSBA members and with industry participants, all in pursuit of learning about blockchain, and advocating for solutions relevant to their businesses and industry segments. Working Groups now include the Cryptoassets WG, Technology WG, Cybersecurity WG, Research and Innovation WG and many more. One of our largest, the WSBA Legal Working Group, which is chaired by Joshua Ashley Klayman of the boutique law firm of Klayman LLC, is composed of over 75 attorneys from around the world, all of whom we are privileged to have as WSBA members. These members of the Legal WG represent more than 50 law practices. Many are contributing authors to this publication. Their firms all have blockchain and cryptoasset practices or thought leaders in place, and are working towards solutions that will impact everything from security tokenization to cryptoasset custody, to blockchain use in the legal practice, to governmental regulation and much more.

Likewise our Cryptoassets Working Group, chaired by financial markets veteran and best-selling author Jack Tatar,[5] focuses on the important initiatives needed to help the world of institutional investors evolve in a cryptoasset future. Discussions such as how cryptoassets should be valued, the challenges and work associated with the launch of cryptoasset-based exchange traded funds (ETFs), and the regulatory questions that need to be answered to enable acceptance of cryptoassets, are all part of the ongoing dialogue and WG efforts.

Alliances and partnerships

One of the WSBA's most important features is its policy of global partnership with an assortment of other non-profit trade associations across many important industries. For example, in November of 2017, the WSBA entered a partnership with the Association of International Certified Professional Accountants (AICPA) and its technology arm, CPA.com. This partnership will allow both organizations to work together to define the impact of blockchain technology for the global accounting profession, and advance the profession's interests regarding rulemaking and standard-setting in this area. As part of this collaboration, the AICPA will administer the WSBA's working group on tax and accounting, a focal point for advocacy and education on blockchain adoption within the profession. For a global profession built on confirmation and verification, blockchain technology will have a profound impact on accounting and finance in the future, and it is important that adoption develops in a way that is in the best interest of the public and global financial markets. The working relationship between both organizations will help further that goal.

Similarly, in February of 2018, the WSBA entered into a partnership with the Blockchain in Transport Alliance (BiTA), the principal trade association focused on the development of blockchain standards and education for the freight and transport industries. Both organizations will co-develop materials related to the financing of the global physical supply-chain, and leverage the industry knowledge and resources from member participants to develop risk-management and supply-chain finance conferences, certifications and educational initiatives.

All of these partnerships, plus the new partnerships planned for the future, highlight a philosophy of cooperation and engagement that is a fundamental part of the Wall Street Blockchain Alliance. As new technologies and advances develop in the future, it is our core belief that cooperative engagement at all levels is the best path towards a future which realizes the full benefits of global innovation and enterprise.

Global outreach

Since our founding, we have often been asked the not wholly unexpected questions regarding why our Board and members had made the decision to form a non-profit trade association. Our answer is simple: a non-profit trade association can act in a non-partisan way. Since the WSBA neither develops nor sells software, we can work with and represent our members in an objective way that furthers their businesses. We can collaborate with other trade associations across a multitude of industries around the world to further joint missions in an efficient and effective manner. We can reach out to and engage governmental organizations and regulators around the globe, speaking with the unified voice of our members to make sure that laws safeguard people and organizations, while not letting those same laws stifle growing innovation. And ultimately, we can operate as an ecosystem for all of our members and partners to share and learn from each other, even if some compete with each other on the world stage.

As we look back on what blockchain technology is meant to accomplish, namely the decentralization of engagement between entities, it is our core belief that "co-opetition", which can be loosely defined as the "collaboration between business competitors, in the hope of mutually beneficial results",[6] is a fundamental element of the WSBA's mission. The future in a blockchain world will need this type of co-operation, and the Wall Street Blockchain Alliance is proud to be at the centre of it all.

* * *

Information about the Wall Street Blockchain Alliance can be found at www.wsba.co, or by email to info@wsba.co.

Endnotes

1. https://ethereum.org.
2. https://www.hyperledger.org.
3. https://www.jpmorgan.com/country/US/en/Quorum.
4. https://www.stellar.org.
5. https://www.amazon.com/Cryptoassets-Innovative-Investors-Bitcoin-Beyond/dp/1260026671/.
6. https://en.wikipedia.org/wiki/Coopetition.

Ron Quaranta
Tel: +1 908 415 9027 / Email: ron@wsba.co
Ron Quaranta possesses over 27 years of experience in the financial services and technology industries. He currently serves as Chairman of the Wall Street Blockchain Alliance, the leading non-profit trade association promoting the comprehensive adoption of blockchain technology and cryptoassets across global markets. Prior to this, Ron served as CEO of DerivaTrust Technologies, a pioneering software and technology firm for financial market participants. He is a sought-after speaker and writer regarding financial technology and innovation, and serves as advisor to multiple startups and corporations focused on Fintech innovation and blockchain technology.

Wall Street Blockchain Alliance

Tel: +1 908 415 9027
URL: www.wsba.co

Blockchain and intellectual property: A case study

Joshua Krumholz, Ieuan G. Mahony & Brian J. Colandreo
Holland & Knight LLP

Introduction

As discussed elsewhere in this book, blockchain has the potential for transformational change. Like most transformational technologies, its development and adoption are laden with intellectual property ("IP") issues, concerns and strategies. Further, given the potentially wide-ranging impact of blockchain technology, the public and private nature of its application, and the prevalent use of open source software, blockchain raises particularly unique IP issues.

The purpose of this chapter is to help the practitioner identify some of the issues that may affect blockchain development and adoption. We address these issues as they may relate to a company's creation of its own IP, and as they may relate to efforts by others to assert their IP against a company. We discuss the issues in the context of the hypothetical scenario discussed below.

The hypothetical transaction

Although many sectors stand to benefit from the use of blockchain technology, the financial and supply chain management sectors may be among the first to benefit. For purposes of discussion, this chapter focuses on the financial sector, and in particular the following hypothetical:

> *A U.S. company is building a new platform using distributed ledger technology for its syndicated loan transactions. Many participants are involved in a typical transaction serviced by the platform, including borrowers, lenders, an administrative agent, credit enhancers and holders of subordinated debt. The platform that the company is building employs smart contracts to effectuate the functionality over a permissioned (private) network with several hundred nodes in the network.*

Our hypothetical company, as noted, has chosen to deploy its solution via a permissioned network. A blockchain developer has two broad options in this regard. First, the developer could select a public blockchain network for its platform. In a public network, each node contains all transactions, the nodes are anonymous, and participants are unknown to each other. Second, the developer could select a permissioned network (as our hypothetical company has). In a permissioned network, the network owner vets network members, accepts only those that it trusts, and uses an access control layer to prevent others from accessing the network. Unlike the nodes on a public network, the nodes on a permissioned network are not anonymous. In addition, a permissioned network can be structured so that specified transactions and data reside only on identified nodes, and are not stored on all nodes in the network.[1] In certain commercial transactions, participants must be known to each other in order to meet regulatory requirements, such as those designed to prevent money laundering. In these situations, a network of anonymous nodes would not be compliant.

Our hypothetical company has selected a permissioned network, we can assume, to obtain these benefits. This selection comes with costs, however, and the company will lose the benefit, for example, of validating a transaction over the full multitude of distributed nodes in a public blockchain network, and the assurances of immutability that that provides.

The blockchain patent landscape

Since Satoshi Nakamoto published the Bitcoin whitepaper in 2008,[2,3] the number of blockchain patent applications has steadily risen. In 2016, applicants filed 521 patents related to blockchain technologies in the United States.[4] In 2017, the number of filings rose to 602.[5] Notably, Chinese entities filed the greatest number of U.S. blockchain patent applications in 2017, accounting for 56% of all filed applications.[6] Applications for blockchain patents filed by U.S. entities accounted for 22% during that same period.[7]

The United States Patent and Trademark Office has begun to issue blockchain patents based on these filings. Below is a breakdown of the largest holders of blockchain patents as of early 2018.[8]

Entity	Industry	No. of blockchain patents
Bank of America	Finance	43
MasterCard	Finance	27
IBM	Technology	27
Fidelity	Finance	14
Coinbase	Finance	13
World Award Foundation / World Award Academy / AMobilePay, Inc.	IP holding	12
TD Bank	Finance	11
402 Technologies S.A.	IP holding	10
Accenture	Technology	9
Dell	Technology	8

Because blockchain technology assists in the efficient and secure transfer of assets, it is no surprise that the financial industry currently dominates the blockchain patent space. Technology companies like IBM[9] and Dell[10] also are utilising blockchains to improve existing technologies and processes, including supply chain and digital rights management. The IP holding companies, meanwhile, presumably seek patents solely to monetise them.

What can be protected?

Only new and novel ideas may be patented

Ideas that already are in the public domain may not be patented, and much of blockchain technology falls into that category. As discussed elsewhere in this book, a blockchain is a distributed ledgering system that allows for the memorialising of transactions in a manner that is not easily counterfeited, is self-authenticating, and is inherently secure. The basic concept of a blockchain may not be patented. A ledgering system that records such transactions, employs multiple identical copies of the ledgers, and maintains them in separate and distinct entities, similarly may not be patented as a new and novel idea. Blockchain technology also uses cryptography. Known cryptography techniques, even if used for the first time with blockchain, also are not likely to be patentable unless the combination resulted from unique insights or efforts to overcome unique technical problems.

Anyone is generally free to use these concepts and, as such, they are not patentable. So what is left that can be protected? Only novel and non-obvious ways to use the above-described blockchain distributed ledger system may be protected. For example, the traditional banking industry utilises central banks and clearing houses to effectuate the transfer of money between entities, which often results in significant delay to complete the transactions. With access to overnight shipping, real-time, chat-based customer service, and social networks allowing for the live-video conferencing of multiple parties positioned around the globe, it is understandable that today's consumer could be disillusioned with the pace at which financial transactions move through the traditional banking industry.

Accordingly, various companies and entities are devoting considerable time and resources to refining and revising the manner in which the traditional banking industry effectuates such monetary transactions. Entrepreneurial companies are inventing unique systems for effectuating asset transfers between banking entities that are memorialised via the above-described blockchain distributed ledgering system, as well as unique systems for expanding the utility of distributed ledgers via remote (and cryptographically-secured) content defined within the distributed ledgers. These improvements, as a general proposition, build and improve upon the foundational blockchain technology. Such an improvement could take the form, for example, of an application deployed on the "foundation" of the Hyperledger platform, and designed to verify the identity of participants in the hypothetical company's permissioned network, or to create audit trails for transactions on this network. It is these incremental improvements that potentially may be patentable. And it is in this area that our hypothetical company should be focusing its patenting efforts.

The *Alice* decision

Obtaining a patent by our hypothetical company also faces another obstacle. As explained by the Supreme Court in *Alice Corp. v. CLS Bank Int'l*, to be patentable, a claimed invention must be something more than just an abstract idea.[11] Rather, it must involve a technical solution to a specific problem or limitation in the field. In the *Alice* case, for example, a computer system was used as a third-party intermediary between parties to an exchange, wherein the intermediary created "shadow" credit and debit records (*i.e.*, account ledgers) that mirrored the balances in the parties' real-world accounts at "exchange institutions" (*e.g.*, banks). The intermediary updated the shadow records in real time as transactions were entered, thus allowing only those transactions for which the parties' updated shadow records indicated sufficient resources to satisfy their mutual obligations.

The Supreme Court held that, "[O]n their face, the claims before us are drawn to the concept of intermediated settlement, *i.e.*, the use of a third party to mitigate settlement risk." The Court went on to explain that "[T]he concept of intermediated settlement is a fundamental economic practice long prevalent in our system of commerce." The Court then explained that such basic economic principles could not be patented, even if implemented in software or in some other concrete manner, because abstract ideas are not themselves patentable. Allowing patents on abstract ideas themselves, the Supreme Court explained, would significantly restrict and dampen innovation.

The following flowchart defines the manner in which the patentability of subject matter should be analysed with respect to the *Alice* decision:

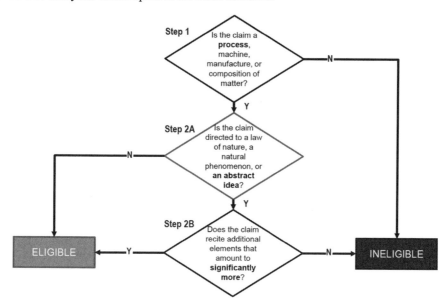

As such, basic concepts, even as they relate to blockchain, may not be patentable. So our hypothetical company must present more than just basic, economic principles in order to get a patent. It must, for example, claim specific improvements to the functioning of a computer, improvements to other, related technology, effect a transformation of a particular article to a different state or thing, add a specific implementation that is not well-understood, routine or conventional, or add unconventional steps that confine the claim to a particular useful application.

The following flowchart may be utilised when assessing the patentability of subject matter with respect to the *Alice* decision:

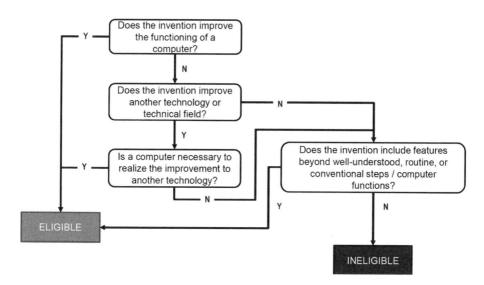

If the *Alice* decision taught practitioners anything, it is that IP law is continuously changing. Accordingly, just as a sound investment plan requires a diversified securities portfolio, a sound IP strategy requires a diversified IP portfolio. Therefore, companies should not put all of their proverbial eggs into one IP basket. For example, if a company was in the "intermediated settlement" space and all they owned were U.S. utility patents, the *Alice* decision would have been devastating to it.

Accordingly, companies should include utility patents in their IP portfolio. But the prudent company also would include design patents (for protecting, *e.g.*, user interfaces); trade secrets (for protecting, *e.g.*, backend algorithms that are not susceptible to reverse engineering); trademarks (for protecting the goodwill associated with the products produced by the company); service marks (for protecting the goodwill associated with the services provided by the company); copyrights (for protecting software code, and/ or the expression of a concept or an idea); and various IP agreements (*e.g.*, employment agreements, development agreements, and licensing agreements). The best IP portfolio for our hypothetical company, therefore, should resemble a quilt that is constructed of various discrete components (utility patents, design patents, trade secrets, trademarks, service marks, copyright, and IP agreements) that are combined to provide the desired level of IP coverage.

The assertion and defence of patent litigation

The threat of patent litigation

Just a few years ago, patent litigation was ubiquitous. Identifying an unique market opportunity, non-practising entities ("NPEs"), also known as "patent trolls", sprung up, aggregated patents, targeted specific industries, and monetised those patents either through threats of litigation or actual lawsuits. One sector that was the subject of this attack was the telecommunications industry. Beyond a number of competitor-versus-competitor suits (such as *Apple v. Samsung*), large, sophisticated NPEs also arose that did not make a product or sell a service. Rather, they purchased telecom patents, created portfolios, and engaged in litigation campaigns to force companies to pay royalties on those patents. Often, if a NPE had a large enough portfolio, a telecom company would enter into a licence agreement to license that portfolio for a defined period of time, often five years.

In the last few years, patent litigation has waned. Due to Congress's creation of *inter parties review* ("IPR") proceedings, stricter requirements on proving damages, member organisations that acquire patents and offer licences to their members, restrictions on where patent lawsuits may be filed, and new defences that allow patents to be invalidated more easily in the early stages of litigation, patent litigation is no longer the economic opportunity it once was. While competitors still will engage in patent litigation to preserve (or attack) their relative positions in the marketplace, NPEs have found that this changing landscape has made patent litigation financially less rewarding. To be sure, such patent litigation still exists. Indeed, new lawsuits are filed daily. The number and threat of those lawsuits has greatly diminished, however, and the value of patents generally has diminished as well.

Market changes, of course, can create new incentives for initiating patent litigations, and the increased role of blockchain technology is likely to bring about one of those changes. To the extent blockchain technology becomes prevalent, it is likely to result in substantially increased patent litigation, both between competitors and between NPEs and practising companies. The reasons for this potential change are several:

- In a competitive landscape, certain companies – specifically those technology companies solely directed toward creating blockchain products – must use their patents to keep competitors out of the marketplace.

- Blockchain is ushering in a new set of patents, based on new technology, that have not been licensed.

- Blockchain technology will be used in lucrative fields which, by association, will make blockchain patents more valuable.

- Blockchain technology likely will be used as fundamental building blocks, making the technology more valuable and damages more lucrative.

Certainly, NPEs see the opportunity. Eric Spangenburg, a well-known founder of NPEs, has set up "IPwe" to collect and exploit blockchain patents, and Intellectual Ventures, a well-known and well-financed NPE, similarly is seeking to acquire and exploit patents in this area.[12] And our hypothetical transaction platform reflects this opportunity. If our hypothetical company builds blockchain technology into the basic building blocks of its transactions, and its transactions form the basic building blocks of its business, then it stands to reason that the technology underlying those activities has significant value.

Offensive and defensive uses of patent rights

When entering into this new technical field, therefore, it is critical that our hypothetical company understand the patent landscape. Are there so many patents that they create a barrier to entry? Are other companies actively applying for patents? If so, are they doing so to block others or require licensing fees, or are they doing so merely for defensive purposes? Understanding and properly predicting this landscape may be the difference between a successful and a failed endeavour.

Broadly speaking, the strategic use of patent rights can be categorised as offensive or defensive (or a mix of the two). These strategies are discussed in greater detail below.

- *Offensive uses of patent rights*

  From an offensive perspective, the holder of a patent gains the right to exclude others from making, using or selling the invention.[13] An offensive patent holder therefore has the ability to block all others from utilising its patented inventions. In an emerging technical field like blockchain, patent-filers typically have a more open landscape of new solutions to discover and claim. Because of the patent holder's right to exclude, each solution it is able to patent can block competitors from utilising that solution in their own products or services, unless granted permission.

  For our hypothetical company, if the patented technology allows for a more efficient and secure transaction, our hypothetical company may want to exclude others from using that technology, giving the hypothetical company a competitive advantage in the marketplace. If our hypothetical company does not wish to exclude competitors, it may instead allow other companies to use its patented technology, but demand that they pay reasonable royalties for that use, perhaps to help defray research-and-development costs or to create an alternative revenue stream.

  It is not enough, however, for the offensive patent holder to file and receive issued patents. The offensive patent holder must affirmatively enforce its patent rights, and make sure that those patent rights are not encumbered by open source licences, *per* our discussion below in "The impact of open source software", or by FRAND licensing obligations, *per* our discussion below in "The role of industry standards". Enforcement requires monitoring for activities that may infringe the patent holder's claims, demanding that others halt infringing activities and, if necessary, instituting litigation to halt the activities by and/or receive reasonable compensation for those activities.

Our hypothetical company also may seek to develop income streams from its patent portfolio. By enforcing its patent rights, the offensive patent-holder may force competitors to take and pay for licences. These licences may provide income to the offensive patent-holder as a single lump sum, where the licensee pays for its license upfront, or as a running royalty, where the licensee pays a percentage of the revenue generated by its products in the marketplace.

- *Defensive uses of patent rights*

  Rather than affirmatively asserting patents, the defensive patent-holder uses them as a hedge against other potential claims against it. Thus, in our hypothetical, where the hypothetical company is building a platform and cannot have that platform's use interrupted, the hypothetical company needs to build up as many defences against a claim of patent infringement as possible. By having its own portfolio, our hypothetical company may be able to deter competitors from a lawsuit against it, because that competitor knows that it may face claims against it if it brings a patent infringement action.

  A defensive strategy, if timely performed, also can block others from securing patents that later can be asserted against it. That is, in fact, the precise strategy of Coinbase's patent filings. By filing for as many patents as possible in the blockchain field, Coinbase hopes to take away patent rights from non-practising entities, which they could otherwise assert against Coinbase.[14]

  Ultimately, as blockchain matures, players in the field will tend to take several forms. Patent leaders will emerge, and to avoid mutual destruction, they will enter into cross-licences with each other. Other companies will try to enter the industry without a proper patent portfolio, and may find significant barriers to entry if the patent leaders seek to assert their right to exclude those other companies from using their patented technology. And then there will be companies that simply acquire patents for the purpose of asserting them. They will create transaction costs, but should not bar entry into the marketplace.

* * *

So, for our hypothetical company, it needs to look at the long-term. Is it creating a platform of critical importance, but leaving itself vulnerable to its competitors? Is it fully taking advantage of its hard work and innovation by protecting the original and novel concepts that it created? Will it find itself blocked by aggressive competitors that are aggregating important patents? All of these questions must be addressed at the same time that our hypothetical company is investing in its technological improvements, and seeking to attract entities and (perhaps) developers to join and participate in its newly created blockchain network.

Strategies for limiting patent litigation exposure

The threat of patent litigation in the blockchain field is real. So how can our hypothetical company limit potential liability? There are several steps that it can take:

- **Open source defences**. At a minimum, if a claim is asserted, our hypothetical company needs to consider whether that claim is blocked or barred by open source restrictions. In addition, our company also should be deliberating carefully on its own open source strategy, and how the use of open source software impacts its potential defences and assertion rights.

- **Actively enter into cross-licence agreements**. If our hypothetical company has acquired a significant patent portfolio, then it may want to approach other major players in the blockchain field and seek to enter into cross-licences with those companies. This approach allows companies to compete based on the quality of their product or service, rather than engage in a damaging patent war.

- **Join patent pools**. In certain industries, particularly telecommunications, companies have arisen to help combat NPEs. These companies are membership-based organisations, whereby companies pay a fee for a licence to all patents held by the company. The company's typical approach is to acquire patents, or take licences on patents, for the benefit of its members. The goal of these organisations is to charge a reasonable fee for a licence to a broad-based portfolio.

- **Monitoring patent application and allowed patents**. While there are many blockchain patents and patent applications, they number in the hundreds, not the thousands. As such, if committed, our hypothetical company can review patent applications as they are published (18 months after filing) and when patents issue. Doing so allows a company to identify potentially problematic patents. The downside of such an approach, however, is that such monitoring may become discoverable in a patent litigation, and perhaps can be used as evidence of knowing (wilful) infringement.

- **Consider design arounds where available**. To the extent our hypothetical company identifies potentially problematic patents or applications, an option for it is to "design around" the problematic patent. In other words, our hypothetical company can analyse the particular elements that make up the invention, and eliminate one or more of those elements in its product in order to avoid practising the patent.

- **Be prepared to file IPRs**. If our hypothetical company finds a problematic patent, one option is to file an IPR with the Patent Office to try to invalidate the patent. Our hypothetical company can take that step even if no lawsuit has been filed against it. Deciding to do so requires an assessment of the likelihood that the patent can be invalidated and the cost associated with that process, but that cost will always be substantially less than the cost of patent litigation.

- **Be prepared to attack the patents on *Alice* grounds**. If our hypothetical company ends up in litigation, it still may be able to terminate that litigation early by filing an Alice motion, discussed more fully in the section, "Defensive uses of patent rights", above. The concept of blockchain itself is an abstract idea, and not patentable as such. To have a valid blockchain patent, the claimed idea must identify some technical problem in the field and provide some specific technical solution to that problem. Without providing something sufficiently concrete, our hypothetical company may be able to invalidate the asserted patent early in the litigation process.

- **Assert counterclaims**. As discussed above, it is important for our hypothetical company to acquire its own patent portfolio. If successful in doing that, and if sued by a practising company, our hypothetical company may be able to assert its own claims of patent infringement. Doing so typically makes it easier to resolve a dispute in its early stages.

The impact of open source software

The term "open source software" refers to software that is distributed in source code form. In source code form, the software can be tested, modified, and improved by entities other than the original developer. The term "proprietary" software refers to software that, in contrast, is distributed in object code form only. The developer of proprietary software protects its source code as a trade secret, and declines to allow others to modify, maintain, or have visibility into its software code base. Proponents of open source software state that the structure fosters the creation of vibrant – and valuable – developer communities, and leads to a common set of well tested, transparent, interoperable software modules upon which the developer community can standardise.

Open source software is ubiquitous in blockchain platforms. The software code bases for Bitcoin,[15] public Ethereum,[16] and Hyperledger,[17] and portions of the software code bases for Enterprise Ethereum[18] and Corda,[19] all consist of open source software. Bitcoin and Ethereum are the leading public blockchain platforms, and Hyperledger, Corda, and Enterprise Ethereum are the "big three" leading commercial, permissioned blockchain platforms.[20] Accordingly, if our hypothetical company wishes to leverage solutions that rely on software from any of these leading platforms, it must consider the impact of the licences that govern this software.

The open source community has developed a number of licences, and these range from: (a) permissive licences, that allow licensees royalty-free and essentially unfettered rights to use, modify, and distribute applicable software and source code;[21] to (b) restrictive, so-called "copyleft" licences, that place significant conditions on modification and distribution of the applicable software and source code. Two open source licences are particularly relevant to our hypothetical company: the General Public License version 3 ("GPLv3"),[22] because this licence (and variants) governs large portions of the Ethereum code base,[23] and the Apache 2.0 licence (the "Apache License"),[24] because this licence governs open source software provided via the Hyperledger, Corda, and Enterprise Ethereum platforms.[25] Each of these licences embodies a "reciprocity" concept that our hypothetical company must consider.

GPLv3 is known as a "strong" copyleft licence. The licence functions as follows: assume a developer is attracted to a software module subject to GPLv3, and incorporates this module into proprietary software that he or she then distributes to others. To the extent the developer's proprietary software is "based on" the GPLv3 code,[26] the developer is required to make his or her proprietary code publicly available in source code form, at no charge, under the terms of GPLv3. This requirement will remove trade secret protection embodied in the proprietary code, as well as the developer's ability under copyright law to control the copying, modification, distribution, and other exploitation of its software.[27] This licence, therefore, has a significant impact on the developer's trade secret and copyright portfolios.

GPLv3 also has a significant impact on the developer's patent portfolio. The licence obligates the developer to grant to all others a royalty-free licence to patents necessary to make, use, or sell the Derivative Code.[28] Finally, simply by distributing GPLv3 code, without modification, the developer agrees to refrain from bringing a patent infringement suit against anyone else using that GPLv3 code.[29] In sum, the structure of GPLv3 reflects a strong "reciprocal" concept: if a developer wishes to incorporate open source software into its code base, it must reciprocate by contributing that code base (and all needed IP rights) back to the community. As noted above, the Ethereum code base is licensed predominantly under GPLv3. Therefore, our hypothetical company should use caution in relying on Ethereum code.

Our hypothetical company should also consider the impact on its IP portfolio of relying on Hyperledger, Corda, and Enterprise Ethereum code. The Apache licence (or an equivalent) governs large portions of these code bases. For our hypothetical company, although the Apache licence has reciprocal features, it is considerably more flexible than GPLv3. The

Apache licence impacts a developer's rights to its software under patent, trade secret, and copyright law in a manner similar to GPLv3;[30] however, these impacts only arise where the developer affirmatively contributes its software to the maintainer of the Apache code at issue. The structure functions with respect to patents as follows: if a patent owner contributes software to an Apache project, the Apache licence restricts the owner from filing a patent infringement claim against any entity based on that entity's use of the contributed software. If the owner does bring such a suit, the owner's licence to the Apache code underlying its contribution terminates.[31] The licence thus has a reciprocal structure: a patent owner cannot benefit from Apache-licensed software while suing to enforce patents that read on its contributions to the Apache software community. If the developer, however, decides not to contribute its code to an Apache project, the developer remains free to incorporate Apache code into its proprietary code base, and commercialise this code without obligation to the Apache open source community. The Apache licence, therefore, provides developers with considerable flexibility.[32]

This flexibility may present strong value to our hypothetical company. It would permit the company, for example, to leverage existing Apache-licensed software from the Hyperledger, Corda, and Enterprise Ethereum code bases in order to develop its new platform and applications, and would give the company full control over whether and to what extent it wishes to encumber its intellectual property portfolio with open source obligations.

Based on the above, it might appear that our hypothetical company would take extreme steps to avoid GPLv3 code (or other strong copyleft code) and would never contribute code to an Apache project. This, however, has not been the case. A number of entities have contributed code under the Apache licence, for example, in order to encourage developers and users to adopt the permissioned commercial network that implements this code.[33] Our hypothetical company will similarly want to consider the potential benefits of seeking to create a vibrant developer and user community using an "open" approach to its intellectual property portfolio, and potentially contributing code under an appropriate open source software licence. In any event, open source software licences and licensing techniques play a key role in blockchain technology, and our hypothetical company will want to carefully consider these licences and techniques in its IP strategy.

The role of industry standards

Background

Industry standards refer to a set of technical specifications that a large number of industry players agree upon to use in their products.[34] Industry players collaboratively develop these technical specifications in a Standards Setting Organization (or "SSO"). Periodically, the SSO will hold meetings where participants, often scientists and engineers, representing industry players will propose and debate differing proposals regarding how a technology should operate. Decisions regarding proposals, and the final technical specifications that stem from them, are reached by consensus by the participants.

Current efforts to standardise blockchain technology

Several organisations have begun standardising a variety of blockchain technologies:

- The International Standards Organization ("ISO") has formed Technical Committee 307 ("ISO/TC 307") to consider blockchain and distributed ledger technologies.[35]
- The Institute of Electrical and Electronics Engineers ("IEEE") has formed two blockchain groups: (1) Project 2418 to develop a standard framework for the use of

blockchain in Internet-of-Things applications;[36] and (2) Project 825 to develop a guide for interoperability of blockchains for energy transaction applications.[37]

- The Blockchain in Transportation Alliance ("BiTA") is focused on the use of blockchain in freight payments, asset history, chain of custody, smart contracts and other related goals.[38]

- Hyperledger is a blockchain standard project and associated code base hosted by the Linux Foundation that focuses on finance, banking, Internet-of-Things and manufacturing.[39]

- The Enterprise Ethereum Alliance recently released an architecture stack designed to provide the basis for an open-source, standards-based specification to advance the adoption of Ethereum solutions for commercial, permissioned networks (referred to as "Enterprise Ethereum").[40]

Advantages and disadvantages of standards

- *Advantages of using and contributing to industry standards*

  There are several advantages to using standards that benefit an industry at-large:

  - **Ensures product compatibility** – With a standard in place, any vendor can develop a product that will be compatible with other products in the industry.

  - **Stronger technology** – Technical specifications created with the input of many industry players tend to result in stronger overall technologies. In theory, the best ideas should emerge from the process and become industry standards that benefit both vendors and consumers.

  - **Shifts competition from the standardised technology to implementation** – Standardisation allows industry players to avoid competition with regard to the standardised technology, and instead shift their focus to developing the best implementation of the remaining technology. Entities that participate in the standard-setting process are obligated to disclose patents that are essential for implementing the standard, and to provide licences to these patents on fair, reasonable, and non-discriminatory terms (so-called "FRAND" terms). These FRAND obligations ensure that all implementers bear the same licensing burden as regards patents essential to the standard.

  - **Greater likelihood of wide adoption** – Approval by many industry players makes the standardised approach a "safer bet" for technology adopters and investors.

  Contributing to SSOs also yields several benefits to individual participants. First, a participating company gains visibility into what comes next in their industry. For example, a software vendor for a syndicated loan blockchain platform could observe the emerging form and content of the blockchain's smart contracts and begin to steer its internal development toward efficiently processing those contracts. Second, a participating company has the opportunity to guide the standardisation process. For example, steering the SSO toward smart contracts that reference cloud-based digital documents would be advantageous for a vendor with a strong cloud-based solution in place.

- *Disadvantages of using and contributing to industry standards*

  There are disadvantages to employing industry standards as well. First, a company loses control over certain aspects of the technology. Instead of developing technology in isolation, our hypothetical company could be at the whim of the industry and its own competitors. Second, a company could develop its own technology that wins over others' in the marketplace. Good-faith participation in an SSO implies that a company will contribute its best, most valuable ideas to the SSO instead of applying them solely to its own products. But the prize for developing better technology than the SSO's participants, and not contributing it, is alluring: a lucrative monopoly on the best technology. Third, an SSO is less nimble than an individual company because changes to industry standards takes consensus of many parties, which in turn takes time. Finally, by participating in the SSO process, the company will place FRAND obligations on any patents in its portfolio that are essential for purposes of implementing the standard.

Lessons from wireless telecommunications industry standards

Blockchain technology is a relatively new field, and SSOs are only starting to form to develop blockchain standards. Many companies are now deciding whether to join a blockchain SSO or pursue their own solutions. Another technical field, telecommunications, and the history of its standardisation activities, provides a good example of the advantages and disadvantages of pursuing industry standards or deciding to go it alone.

In order for a phone to access a carrier's wireless network, it must know how to communicate with the carrier's network. Telecommunications standards dictate how that communication proceeds. By adhering to the telecommunications standard, a manufacturer can ensure that its phone can operate on any carrier's wireless network that also follows that standard.

In the 1980s, the European "first generation" wireless telecommunications market was fractured by a handful of standards marked by national or regional boundaries. Scandinavia used a standard called "NMT"; Great Britain used "TACS"; Italy used "RTMS" and "TACS"; France used "RC2000" and "NMT"; and Germany used "C-Netz".[41] Using this hodgepodge of telecommunications standards meant that a German's phone would not work during her vacation to France, and an Englishman's phone would not work in Scandinavia.[42] Manufacturers for both phones and network infrastructure were likewise geographically constrained. These manufacturers would typically only research and develop products for specific European regions. What resulted were regional monopolies for those manufacturers, but with low subscriber rates and little opportunity to compete in foreign markets where their technology would be inoperable.[43]

Mindful of these issues with the first generation wireless telecommunications standards, phone and infrastructure manufacturers from around Europe (and indeed around the world) came together to develop a pan-European, "second generation" standard within the European Telecommunications Standards Institute ("ETSI") SSO. These manufacturers sent their best scientists and engineers to ETSI to ensure that this emerging standard would meet wireless subscribers' and carriers' needs. The result of their work was the Global System for Mobile communications ("GSM"), which was the *de facto* wireless standard throughout Europe and parts of the United States from 1992 through 2002. During that period, manufacturers would compete to develop better phones or network equipment, all the while maintaining compliance with the GSM standard. As a result, equipment developed in Sweden or Finland could be sold throughout Europe. This open market brought the price of wireless technology down, increased subscriber bases and, by adoption of a similar approach in the United States, ushered in today's ubiquitous smartphones and wireless networks.

Analogies can be drawn to current trends in blockchain standardisation. Blockchain is based on networks that are large enough – i.e. have enough nodes – to create reliability. As such, interoperability and scalability are important. Standardisation of blockchain elements can be an important tool in achieving those goals. But the standardisation process often involves competing visions. Certain companies will advance one approach, and other companies will advance a different approach. That advocacy typically is based on a good faith belief, but it also arises from investments that companies make in their technology.

A meaningful standardisation process contains both risk and opportunity for our hypothetical company. No company wants to make the wrong bet and become the Betamax of blockchain technology. Companies therefore need to be thinking hard about the competing standards that are being created and what role they wish to play in that creation. An entirely passive role could result in other thought leaders seizing the marketplace, but too aggressive a role could lead to massive investments that are not adopted by the marketplace as a whole. Ultimately, every company needs to think about the role that they wish to play on that spectrum.

Acknowledgment

Jacob W.S. Schneider

The authors would like to thank Jacob Schneider, partner in Holland & Knight's Boston office, for his contribution to this chapter.

* * *

Endnotes

1. There are a range of other differences between public and permissioned networks as well. For example, a permissioned network can be structured with different consensus rules that reduce the resource requirements (including electricity requirements) needed on a public network such Bitcoin. There are also a range of gradations between fully public and fully private blockchain networks. The Enterprise Ethereum Alliance, for example, is designed to permit operation on a public network, but to restrict the nodes on that public network that receive the data at issue. *See* I. Allison, Enterprise Ethereum Alliance Is Back – And It's Got a Roadmap (May 2, 2018), located at https://www.coindesk.com/enterprise-ethereum-alliance-isnt-dead-got-roadmap-prove/.
2. Nakamoto, Satoshi, *Bitcoin: A Peer-to-Peer Electronic Cash System* (Oct. 31, 2008) (available at https://bitcoin.org/bitcoin.pdf).
3. 2008 is not the earliest disclosure of blockchain-like solutions. *See* Stuart Haber and W. Scott Stornetta (1991) and Bayer, Haber and Stornetta (1992).
4. https://blogs.thomsonreuters.com/answerson/in-rush-for-blockchain-patents-china-pulls-ahead.
5. https://blogs.thomsonreuters.com/answerson/in-rush-for-blockchain-patents-china-pulls-ahead.
6. https://blogs.thomsonreuters.com/answerson/in-rush-for-blockchain-patents-china-pulls-ahead.
7. https://blogs.thomsonreuters.com/answerson/in-rush-for-blockchain-patents-china-pulls-ahead.
8. http://patentvue.com/2018/01/12/blockchain-patent-filings-dominated-by-financial-services-industry.
9. https://www.ibm.com/blockchain.
10. https://www.delltechnologies.com/en-us/perspectives/tags/blockchain.
11. *Alice Corp. v. CLS Bank Int'l*, 134 S. Ct. 2347 (2014).
12. Certain industry participants have been working to place restrictions on key patents, to prevent them from being acquired by NPEs. *See* Michael del Castilloite, Patent Trolls Beware: 40 Firms Join Fight Against Blockchain IP Abuse (March 16, 2017) located at

https://www.coindesk.com/40-blockchain-firms-unite-in-fight-against-patent-trolls/.

13. 35 U.S. Code § 154(a)(1) ("Every patent shall . . . grant to the patentee, his heirs or assigns, of the right to exclude others from making, using, offering for sale, or selling the invention throughout the United States or importing the invention into the United States . . .").

14. https://blog.coinbase.com/how-we-think-about-patents-at-coinbase-26d82b68e7db.

15. *See* http://www.Bitcoin.org.

16. L. Zeug, "Licensing" (September 4, 2016), located at https://github.com/ethereum/wiki/wiki/Licensing.

17. "About Hyperledger," located at https://www.hyperledger.org/about.

18. Enterprise Ethereum Alliance Specification Clears the Path to a Global Blockchain Ecosystem (May 16, 2018), located at https://entethalliance.org/enterprise-ethereum-alliance-specification-clears-path-global-blockchain-ecosystem/.

19. "Contributing to Corda," located at https://github.com/corda/corda/blob/master/CONTRIBUTING.md; Downloads: DemoBench for Corda 3.0, located at https://www.corda.net/downloads/.

20. R. Brown, "Corda: Open Source Community Update" (May 13, 2018) located at https://medium.com/corda/corda-open-source-community-update-f332386b4038.

21. Bitcoin software, for example, is licensed under the permissive, MIT Licence. *See* http://www.Bitcoin.org; https://opensource.org/licenses/MIT.

22. GPLv3 license, located at https://www.gnu.org/licenses/gpl-3.0.en.html.

23. L. Zeug, "Licensing" (September 4, 2016), located at https://github.com/ethereum/wiki/wiki/Licensing. *See, e.g.*, Ethereum-sandbox License, located at https://github.com/ether-camp/ethereum-sandbox/blob/master/LICENSE.txt.

24. Apache 2.0 license, located at https://www.apache.org/licenses/LICENSE-2.0.

25. For Corda, *see* R. Brown, "Corda: Open Source Community Update" (May 13, 2018) located at https://medium.com/corda/corda-open-source-community-update-f332386b4038; "Contributing to Corda," located at https://github.com/corda/corda/blob/master/CONTRIBUTING.md. For Hyperledger, *see* Brian Behlendorf, "Meet Hyperledger: An 'Umbrella' for Open Source Blockchain & Smart Contract Technologies" (September 13, 2016) located at https://www.hyperledger.org/blog/2016/09/13/meet-hyperledger-an-umbrella-for-open-source-blockchain-smart-contract-technologies. Code contributed to the Enterprise Ethereum Alliance is generally made available under an open source license that mirrors the Apache 2.0 license, *see* Enterprise Ethereum Alliance Inc. Intellectual Property Rights Policy, available at https://entethalliance.org/join/.

26. In defining the key term "based on", GPLv3 largely relies on copyright law rules governing derivative works. Courts generally rule that two copyrighted works are distinct (and one is not derivative of the other), if "they can live their own copyright life;" in other words, the test focuses on whether each expression "has an independent economic value and is, in itself, viable." *E.g., Columbia Pictures Indus. v. Krypton Broad. of Birmingham, Inc.*, 259 F.3d 1186, 1192 (9th Cir. 2001); *Lewis Galoob Toys, Inc. v. Nintendo of America, Inc.*, 964 F.2d 965, 969 (9th Cir. 1992).

27. For convenience, the code the developer is required to open-source in this manner is referred to as "Derivative Code".

28. GPLv3, sec. 11 (Patents).

29. GPLv3, sec. 10 (Automatic Licensing of Downstream Recipients).

30. The maintainer of the relevant Apache code at issue, through the Apache Software

Foundation, has the ability to set downstream terms for the contributed software.

31. Apache 2.0, sec. 3 (Grant of Patent License).

32. Our hypothetical company will also need to consider "compatibility" issues between various open source licences. The Hyperledger platform, for example, was unable to assimilate Ethereum code due to incompatibility between the Apache licence and strong copyleft licences, and the resulting need to obtain permissions from copyright owners to "re-license" the Ethereum code at issue. *See* J. Manning, Hyperledger Fails Ethereum Integration Due To Licensing Conflicts (February 3, 2017), located at https:// www.ethnews.com/hyperledger-fails-ethereum-integration-due-to-licensing-conflicts; J. Buntinx, Ethereum app Developers may Face Licensing Issues Later on (December 6, 2017), located at https://www.newsbtc.com/2017/12/06/ethereum-app-developers-may-face-licensing-issues-later/.

33. IBM, for example, has contributed code under the Apache licence to the Hyperledger platform, and in turn is providing commercial Blockchain-as-a-Service (BaaS) offerings based on this platform using IBM's cloud infrastructure. *See IBM Blockchain, The Founder's Handbook: Your guide to getting started with Blockchain* (Edition 2.0) located at https://www-01.ibm.com/common/ssi/cgi-bin/ssialias?htmlfid=28014128USEN. Microsoft has similar commercial offerings, based on Azure and the Enterprise Ethereum platform. *See* M. Finley, Getting Started with Ethereum using Azure Blockchain (January 24, 2018), located at https://blogs.msdn.microsoft.com/premier_developer/2018/01/24/getting-started-with-ethereum-using-azure-blockchain/.

34. A simple example is the shape and voltage of a wall power outlet. Because the power outlet is standardised among geographic regions, an appliance maker can ensure that its coffee maker will work (and can be sold) anywhere within a given region.

35. https://www.iso.org/committee/6266604.html.

36. http://standards.ieee.org/develop/project/2418.html.

37. http://standards.ieee.org/develop/project/825.html.

38. https://bita.studio.

39. https://www.hyperledger.org.

40. Enterprise Ethereum Alliance Advances Web 3.0 Era with Public Release of the Enterprise Ethereum Architecture Stack (May 2, 2018), located at https://entethalliance. org/enterprise-ethereum-alliance-advances-web-3-0-era-public-release-enterprise-ethereum-architecture-stack/; https://entethalliance.org/wp-content/uploads/2018/05/EEA-TS-0001-0-v1.00-EEA-Enterprise-Ethereum-Specification-R1.pdf.

41. Funk, Jeffrey L., GLOBAL COMPETITION BETWEEN AND WITHIN STANDARDS: THE CASE OF MOBILE PHONES at 39 (New York, Palgrave, 2002); Garrard, Garry A., CELLULAR COMMUNICATIONS: WORLDWIDE MARKET DEVELOPMENT (Boston, Artech House, 1998).

42. Gruber, Harald, THE ECONOMICS OF MOBILE TELECOMMUNICATIONS (Cambridge University Press, 2005) at 35.

43. *Id.*

Joshua Krumholz
Tel: +1 617 573 5820 / Email: Joshua.Krumholz@hklaw.com
Josh Krumholz is a partner in Holland & Knight's Boston office. A trial
attorney and the national Practice Group Co-Leader for the firm's Intellectual
Property Group, Mr Krumholz focuses primarily upon intellectual property
litigation, with a particular focus on patent litigation. His practice covers a
variety of technologies and jurisdictions. Mr Krumholz has successfully taken
cases to jury verdict in the Eastern District of Texas, Illinois, Massachusetts,
New York and New Jersey, among other jurisdictions. Technologies that
Mr Krumholz handles include telecommunications, software, hardware,
electronics and consumer goods. Mr Krumholz represents leading companies
across a range of industries, including Ericsson Inc., T-Mobile, Inc., Verizon
Corp., Avaya Inc., Acushnet Company and Hasbro, Inc., among others.

Ieuan G. Mahony
Tel: +1 617 573 5835 / Email: Ieuan.Mahony@hklaw.com
Ieuan Mahony is a partner in Holland & Knight's Boston office. He
concentrates his practice in intellectual property (IP) licensing and
development, data privacy and security, and information technology (IT).
Mr Mahony combines his transactional and compliance work with dispute
resolution and litigation matters. His substantial background in transactional
and litigation practice areas helps clients receive high-quality advice in the
dynamics of reaching an agreement as well as the realities of combating an
adversary. Mr Mahony is a member of the firm's three-partner Information
Technology Governance Committee.

Brian J. Colandreo
Tel: +1 617 305 2143 / Email: Brian.Colandreo@hklaw.com
Brian Colandreo is a partner in Holland & Knight's Boston office. Mr
Colandreo serves as the National Patent Practice Leader and is a member of
the Intellectual Property Group. A registered patent attorney, Mr Colandreo
focuses his practice on client management, general intellectual property
prosecution, transactional work, litigation support, due diligence work, and
utility and design patent opinion work. Prior to entering law school, Mr
Colandreo worked as a systems/software engineer for Johnson Controls.

Holland & Knight LLP

800 17th Street N.W., Suite 1100, Washington, DC 20006, USA
Tel: +1 202 955 3000 / Fax: +1 202 955 5564 / URL: www.hklaw.com

Initial Coin Offerings:

A comparative overview of securities regulatory environments in the US, UK and Asia Pacific

Justin Cooke, Richard Cohen & Jason Denisenko
Allen & Overy LLP

Introduction

Distributed ledger technology, and particularly applications of blockchain, are poised to revolutionise a range of industries, from financial services to supply chain management. Initial coin offerings (**ICOs**) – sales of blockchain-based "coins" or "tokens" that may be exchanged for products, services or fiat currency – have become a powerful and seemingly efficient new means for blockchain-related businesses to raise capital, bypassing more traditional funding through venture capital firms, institutional investors or regulated securities markets. However, the seeming ease of ICOs has led many sponsors – even those acting with good intentions – to engage in activities that may violate securities regulations in various jurisdictions.

Securities law compliance is particularly challenging in the context of blockchain-based instruments because they are decentralised, liquid and transferable across regulatory borders virtually with the click of a button. Furthermore, existing securities regulatory frameworks were not designed to address the novel features of these emerging technologies, which often leads to uncertainty and inconsistency in the ways regulators across jurisdictions characterise them.

This article is intended to provide a very high-level overview of the securities regulatory environments for ICOs in the United States, the United Kingdom and Asia Pacific. It concludes with a discussion of general considerations for ICOs of non-security utility tokens. The regulations discussed herein are nuanced – one size does not fit all – and they are just some of the many legal hurdles an ICO sponsor may need to address before commencing an offering.[1] Sponsors should engage sophisticated counsel in key jurisdictions well in advance of any offering to evaluate their commercial objectives relative to applicable legal regimes.

United States

Is the token a security?

In the United States, the threshold questions an ICO sponsor should ask is whether its token constitutes a security under U.S. securities law, and, if so, whether it is prepared to invest the time and resources needed to comply with the applicable U.S. legal regimes.

Under the U.S. Securities Act of 1933 (the **Securities Act**) and the Securities Exchange Act of 1934 (the **Exchange Act**), the term "security" is defined broadly to include not only financial instruments that are easily identifiable as securities (for example, stocks and bonds), but also any "investment contract." That term has been interpreted very broadly by the U.S. Supreme Court and the U.S. Securities and Exchange Commission (the **SEC**) to include many financial and commercial arrangements, including the types of arrangements that have been the subject of numerous ICOs.

In 1946, the Supreme Court developed, in its seminal case *SEC v. W.J. Howey & Co*,[2] the so-called "*Howey* Test" for determining whether a transaction is an investment contract and in turn a security. *Howey* and cases that followed it defined an investment contract as (i) an investment of money, (ii) in a common enterprise, (iii) with the expectation of profits, (iv) through the efforts of others. Many commentators have argued for a distinction, based on the *Howey* Test, between cryptocurrencies that represent an investment in the underlying blockchain protocol or enterprise (**security tokens**) and cryptocurrencies that provide access to a service or network (**utility tokens**). Under this logic, a token that provides rights to dividends from a business operated by the ICO sponsor would clearly be a security, whereas a token that only allows network participants to access a service (e.g., computer processing power or storage space) may, under the right circumstances, not be a security.

The SEC has not issued any official guidance that clearly distinguishes tokens that are securities from those that are not, and it is unlikely to do so in the near future. However, various informal, non-binding statements by the Chairman of the SEC and members of the SEC's Staff indicate they recognise there is a continuum spanning from security tokens to utility tokens, and that tokens may move along this continuum during their lifecycle.[3] These statements have suggested several factors that market participants may consider in determining whether or not a token is a security. For example, a token granting access to a fully operational blockchain protocol is less likely to be considered a security token than one issued in order to raise funds for the development of a new blockchain protocol, because the latter relies more heavily on the efforts of the founders. On that basis, William Hinman, the Director of the SEC's Division of Corporation finance, has suggested the SEC would likely not deem Ether, in its present form, to be a security token, although it may have taken a different view at the time of Ether's ICO.[4] It is critical to emphasise that regulators and courts will look past the purported form of a token and examine its substance: labelling a blockchain instrument a "utility token" will not insulate it from security classification if it functions economically as a security.

Regulation of security tokens

The Securities Act is drafted very broadly to require any offer of a security to be registered with the SEC, or rely on an available exemption from registration. This requirement applies extraterritorially to both initial sales by an issuer and subsequent resales by holders in the secondary market. Accordingly, it is very important for ICO sponsors to consider the potential impact of U.S. securities regulation even if they do not plan to offer tokens directly in the United States or to U.S. investors: resales to U.S. investors of tokens initially sold outside the United States may give rise to regulatory action or private litigation. Among other concerns for sponsors, sales of securities in violation of the Securities Act are subject to a statutory right of rescission in favour of the purchaser under Section 12 of the Securities Act (such that purchasers will have been sold "put" rights along with the security).[5]

Registration under the Securities Act and ongoing compliance with post-registration reporting obligations is complicated and expensive, even for established businesses that have a solid financial track-record and are offering traditional securities. Accordingly, most sponsors of security token ICOs focus on two exemptions from the SEC registration requirements: Regulations S for offshore sales,[6] and Regulation D for private placements to accredited investors.[7]

Regulation S effectively creates a safe harbour from the extraterritorial reach of the Securities Act if certain conditions are satisfied. In the case of a first-time non-U.S. issuer, those conditions are that (i) each offer and sale is made in an "offshore transaction,"[8] and (ii) no "directed selling efforts"[9] are made in the United States. Under those circumstances, Regulation S does not expressly restrict resales in the United States of securities initially sold outside the United States. However, significant "flowback" of those securities to the United States (other than in transactions that rely on an available exemption from registration) could undermine the issuer's reliance on Regulation S.

Rule 506(c) of Regulation D permits an issuer to sell its securities to an unlimited number of verified "accredited investors",[10] including through the use of "general solicitation and general advertising," (e.g., websites, advertisements or media interviews). Rule 506(c) includes significant conditions, including that: (i) each purchaser must be an accredited investor; (ii) purchasers' accredited investor status must be verified;[11] (iii) the issuer must not be subject to "bad actor" disqualifications;[12] and (iv) the issuer must file a Form D with the SEC to report the sale.[13]

Any securities sold in reliance on Rule 506(c) (or other private offering exemptions) are "restricted securities" that are not freely sellable by the holder into the secondary market. Accordingly, any ICO sponsor planning to sell securities in reliance on Regulation D should discuss with experienced counsel how those restrictions will impact its marketing efforts and the operation of its platform. In light of these resale restrictions, and the "flowback" concerns that arise under Regulation S, it is important for ICO sponsors to apply appropriate contractual transfer restrictions and to implement technological systems and procedures to prevent resales that may violate the Securities Act.

Security tokens that constitute "equity securities",[14] including those that provide any right to participate in profits, face additional regulatory challenges in the United States. An issuer of any equity security is required to file a detailed registration statement with the SEC (and comply with related governance and accounting rules) under the Exchange Act, and thereafter file periodic reports with the SEC like a U.S.-listed public company, if: it has more than $10 million in assets and the class of equity securities is held of record by 2,000 or more persons, or 500 or more persons who are not accredited investors[15] (and, in the case of any "foreign private issuer",[16] at least 300 of whom are residents of the United States).[17] The extensive ongoing reporting and other obligations that accompany Exchange Act registration would prove far too burdensome for the typical ICO issuer. Accordingly, those ICO sponsors who sell tokens that are equity securities must take particular care to avoid these ownership triggers.

In addition to these threshold considerations under the Securities Act and the Exchange Act, any ICO sponsor should consult with counsel to ensure that its offering and ongoing operations will comply with, among others, broker-dealer and securities exchange regulations under the Exchange Act; the Investment Company Act of 1940; the Investment Advisers Act of 1940; and any state "blue sky" or "bitlicense" laws, each of which may present considerable challenges.

United Kingdom

Is the token a security?

Unlike the *Howey* Test under U.S. law, neither English nor European law contains a generalised test to define a security. Accordingly, ICO sponsors must look to the definitions under the UK and EU rules. These rules contain definitions of many types of instruments that would constitute a security and prospective ICO issuers should consider each of these to assess whether or not the token being issued may be a security. While these will be fact-specific and so must necessarily be done on a case-by-case basis, the key ones to assess are as follows:

- shares or stock in the share capital of a body corporate or any unincorporated body under English law (i.e., if they have any capital, voting, dividend, governance or similar rights or entitlements in the issuer);

- debentures, debenture stock, loan stock, bonds, certificates of deposit, any other instrument creating or acknowledging indebtedness, or an alternative finance investment bond;

- instruments that entitle the holder to subscribe for, or confer property rights in, any of the above; and

- units in a Collective Investment Scheme (**CIS**) or an Alternative Investment Fund (**AIF**).

Generally speaking, tokens issued as part of an ICO fall into one of the following categories:

- tokenised shares – these are tokens representing the ordinary share capital of a company and carry the rights to voting and dividends (if they are declared) that one would normally associate with shares;

- tokenised equity interests – these are tokens which do not function like ordinary shares, they have no voting rights, but carry rights to equity style payouts. These may be discretionary dividends or fixed payouts linked to a certain percentage of revenue or profit;

- tokenised debt securities – these function just like ordinary bonds, structured products or derivatives but are settled using a blockchain infrastructure;

- tokenised funds – these are essentially units in a fund represented by a token on a blockchain and would be deemed to be one, or more likely both, of a CIF and an AIF; or

- utility tokens – these are tokens issued by a particular platform that may be used as a means of payment on that platform but carry no rights to any payouts and cannot be redeemed. They function very much like air miles or loyalty points but with the key difference that it is possible to trade them with others and thereby potentially sell them on at a profit without ever making use of the offered utility.

Of the above tokenised shares, equity interests, debt securities and funds all constitute securities and will be regulated as such in the UK. Utility tokens, however, do not clearly fall within any of the existing definitions of a security: while the ability to trade and profit from investments in them is leading U.S. regulators to classify them as securities under the *Howey* Test, their position under English and European law is not so clear cut.

It seems reasonably clear that utility tokens should not be classified as shares, equity interests or debt securities, but their position in relation to the CIS regime does carry more risk that issuers should be aware of. There are reasonably good arguments that the issuer of utility tokens or the utility tokens themselves should not be classed as a CIS but, as there is no judicial or regulatory guidance under the CIS regimes in relation to utility tokens, there is a risk that a UK court could conclude that the CIS regimes applies. If the issuer of utility tokens or the utility tokens themselves were classified as a CIS, then they could only be marketed to institutional investors and certain limited types of retail investors (i.e. certified high-net-worth persons).

There is also a risk that the UK Financial Conduct Authority (**FCA**) (or a UK court on behalf of the FCA) or disgruntled token-holders (either individually or in a class action) may take a substance-over-form approach and interpret the legislation as broadly as possible so as to regulate utility tokens or their promotion if it feels that (as a policy matter) holders of utility tokens (whether retail or professional) need greater protection. Because of the vagueness of the definitions, if a regulator were looking to bring the issuance of utility tokens into its regulatory scope, then it could seek to use the regulatory provisions to fulfil this purpose. The current approach of the FCA is to assess tokens on a fact-specific basis, but it has said that the current ambit of regulation is sufficient to cover digital assets. Accordingly, each proposed transaction must be specifically assessed by issuers and counsel to establish whether a regulatory regime applies, or the risks of it doing so.

Security tokens

Security tokens will be regulated as securities in the UK; indeed, the only difference from any other securities is that they are settled and owned via a blockchain infrastructure.

There are some key consequences of this. Dealing in securities, promoting and otherwise offering a security to persons in the UK is regulated by the FCA under the terms of the FCA Handbook and the Financial Services and Markets Act 2000 (**FSMA**). Of particular relevance to issuers of security tokens are the two broad prohibitions in the FSMA:

(a) section 19 of the FSMA provides that no person may carry on a regulated activity in the UK (or purport to do so) unless that person is authorised or exempt; and

(b) section 21 of the FSMA provides that a person must not, in the course of business, communicate an invitation or inducement to engage in investment activity unless the promotion has been made or approved by an authorised person, or it is exempt. If the security is a unit in a CIS or AIF, there are also other restrictions on its promotion that will apply.

There is also a prohibition, under Directive 2003/71/EC (as amended) (the **Prospectus Directive**) (as implemented in the UK), on offering transferable securities to the public in the UK unless an approved prospectus has been made available to the public before any offer is made. Breach of these regulatory restrictions could result in civil or criminal liability in the UK.

Accordingly there are three main issues to manage: (i) conducting regulated activities by arranging transactions; (ii) making financial promotions; and (iii) the requirement to produce a Prospectus Directive-compliant prospectus. There are, of course, many other issues to consider too but these are beyond the scope of this article. Issuers should consider each of these issues and whether any exemptions might apply.

Conducting regulated activity

Any entity which is arranging securities transactions, namely introducing investors to issuers, is likely to be conducting regulated activity under section 19 and therefore needs to be authorised; it is unlikely that any exemptions will apply.

Financial promotions

Under section 21 of the FSMA, financial promotions will be exempt if they are made, or can reasonably be regarded as being made, to investment professionals. Financial promotions can also be exempt if made to certain high-net-worth individuals and high-net-worth companies if certain conditions are met.

Prospectus requirements

Assuming that the security tokens are not going to be listed on a regulated market (and to date, none have been), then there are exemptions available from the requirement to produce a Prospectus Directive-compliant prospectus. Of these exemptions, the key ones are: (i) offers that are addressed solely to qualified investors (essentially professional investors); (ii) offers to fewer than 150 natural or legal persons per Member State; and (iii) offers of securities where the minimum denomination is at least €100,000 or its equivalent.

There is also an exemption for offers of less than €8,000,000 (or its equivalent) in any 12-month period, which may suit some token issuers.

Accordingly most security token offerings are being structured to comply with the above exemptions, and are therefore being directed only at professional investors, which may also include high-net-worth individuals who opt to be professional investors. Issuers need to take active steps to ensure that tokens are only being offered and sold to such persons; these should include appropriate website blockers and disclaimers, obtaining relevant representations and warranties from investors, and a technological solution which profiles investors and, through restrictions in the smart contract, only allows persons who fall within an exempt category to purchase tokens. While there is no legal requirement to produce a prospectus if one of the exemptions is being met, issuers should still produce an information memorandum which will be similar to a prospectus. The information memorandum should contain a formal set of risk factors highlighting the risks of purchasing the tokens, properly drafted disclosure of the project, detailed sections setting out the sale process, and appropriate disclaimers.

Asia Pacific

Australia

The Australian Securities and Investments Commission (**ASIC**) takes a relatively broad approach to regulating ICOs. ASIC has emphasised that the structure and operation of an ICO determines its legal status.[18] Therefore, ICOs that are financial products will be subject to general laws as well as the Australian *Corporations Act 2001* (Cth) (**Corporations Act**). For example, ICOs may constitute an offer of securities, an interest in a collective investment scheme, a derivative, or a non-cash payment facility under the Corporations Act. Conversely, ICOs that are not financial products will still be subject to general laws and Australian consumer laws.

Collective investment schemes generally arise where people contribute money or assets, which are pooled or used in a common enterprise to produce financial benefits in circumstances where the participants do not have active control over the operation of the scheme.[19] This test is similar in formulation, if not application, to the *Howey* Test in the United States. A token offering that has these characteristics may constitute a regulated collective investment scheme, and the promoter of the tokens will be subject to a range of obligations pertaining to product disclosure, licensing and registration (with some concessions for offers to high-net-worth or institutional investors).

Alternatively, an ICO may constitute an offer of securities where it has rights which are typically associated with those attaching to shares in a company. These include rights pertaining to ownership, voting dividends and residual assets. If these rights are attached to a token, it will likely fall within the definition of a share under the Corporations Act, requiring the issuance of a prospectus.[20]

A token may be characterised as a derivative where it is priced and based on either another financial product, underlying market indices, or assets resulting in a payment as part of rights or obligations attached to the token.[21] For example, this could include payment arrangements associated with changes in the token value.

On the other hand, non-cash payment (**NCP**) facilities involve an arrangement through which payments are made by means other than physical delivery of currency.[22] While it is unlikely that tokens under an ICO will constitute an NCP facility, they may be a form of value used to make payment.

There are also separate market operator rules which can apply to platforms or trading venues that enable tokens to be traded.

The Australian Competition and Consumer Commission (**ACCC**) has delegated power to ASIC to take action against potential misleading or deceptive conduct in relation to token offers.[23] In practice, this means that irrespective of whether the token is characterised as a financial product, it will be subject to prohibitions against misleading or deceptive conduct in relation to marketing or selling it under the Corporations Act and the Australian Consumer Law.

Hong Kong

Similar to Australia, the Hong Kong Securities and Futures Commission (**SFC**) does not specifically regulate ICOs, unless the tokens constitute "securities" as defined in the *Securities and Futures Ordinance* (**SFO**).[24] Accordingly, ICOs falling within this definition will be subject to securities laws in Hong Kong. For example, tokens offered in an ICO may be regarded as shares, debentures or collective investment schemes (**CIS**) (and regarded as securities for SFO purposes).

Tokens that represent ownership interests or equity in a corporation may be regarded as shares. This is likely the case where token holders are provided shareholder rights, for example, receiving dividends. Alternatively, tokens used to establish a debt or liability owned by the respective issuers may be treated as debentures. For example, interest may be paid to token holders after an issuer repays the token holders the principal of their investment upon redemption. Additionally, ICOs may fall within the SFO definition of CIS (and thus the securities definition); tokens may be managed collectively by ICO operators to invest in projects, allowing token holders to obtain shares of the returns.

Where it can be established that tokens fall within this definition of securities schemes, it can likely be ascertained that the dealing, advising, managing or marketing of ICOs constitutes a "regulated activity".[25] Accordingly, this will trigger SFC licensing requirements on parties engaging in the relevant activity as a business in Hong Kong (or hold themselves out as doing so). The SFC has openly announced its tight monitoring of ICOs, particularly in relation to licensing requirements.[26] Consumer protection legislation may also apply to ICOs to prevent unfair trade practices.

Furthermore, the offer of "securities" to the public in Hong Kong will generally require a prospectus to be registered (in the case of shares or debentures)[27] or offering documents authorised (in the case of CIS),[28] unless an exemption applies.

Singapore

The Monetary Authority of Singapore (**MAS**) takes a very similar approach to the SFC in Hong Kong. The MAS confirmed that it currently does not regulate virtual currencies *per se*,[29] however, tokens offered in an ICO that are considered an offer of shares or units in a collective investment scheme under the Securities and Futures Act (**SFA**) will be regulated.[30] For example, where the use of a token offered in an ICO relates to an interest in, or ownership of, the issuer's assets or property, it may constitute an offer of shares or units in a collective investment scheme under the SFA. Additionally, a token that represents a debt owed by an issuer may constitute a debenture is therefore subject to these requirements under the SFA.

Issuers of ICOs are required to lodge and register a prospectus with MAS if the tokens constitute securities, unless specifically exempted. The SFA prescribes a number of exemptions from the prospectus requirements, for example, offers made to institutional investors are exempted, and offers made to accredited investors may instead be accompanied by an information memorandum. There may also be a requirement for issuers and intermediaries to obtain a licence under the SFA and the Financial Advisors Act (**FAA**). This includes any platform facilitating secondary trading of ICOs. The MAS announced its strict monitoring of digital token exchanges, including releasing eight official warnings in respect of MAS authorisation.

China

The People's Bank of China (**PBOC**) explicitly banned the use of ICOs in China. Additionally, the PBOC made an official order to banks to stop opening accounts for virtual fundraisers, and will further increase regulatory pressure on cryptocurrency trading by targeting online platforms which offer exchange-like services and ICOs. However, the ban on ICOs does not mean that China has a final ban on cryptocurrencies. Officials have suggested that a new licensing regime will be introduced.[31]

Indonesia

Bank Indonesia currently does not recognise cryptocurrencies as legal payments, and has issued a press release to warn the public not to sell, buy or trade virtual currency.[32] This statement was also mentioned by the Minister of Finance who, in the press conference on 23 January 2018, warned that virtual cryptocurrencies are a high-risk and speculative investment.[33] Despite the debate among the government institutions, in June 2018, the Indonesian Trade Ministry Futures Exchange Supervisory Board[34] signed a decree to legalise cryptocurrency as a tradable commodity in the future exchanges.[35] The Indonesian Government is expected to issue several regulations to regulate cryptocurrency-exchange companies and related taxation, money-laundering and terrorism-financing regulations.

Japan

The Japanese Financial Services Agency (**FSA**) released proposed guidelines to legalise and regulate ICOs, including providing regulatory definitions and approvals.[36] The proposed guidelines also provide a means to prevent money laundering and restrict unfair trade practices. Interestingly, the guidelines do not identify ICOs as financial securities. The FSA highlighted that businesses launching an ICO may fall within the *Payment Services Act* or the *Financial Instruments and Exchange Act*. In doing so, cryptocurrency exchanges providers must be registered with each Local Finance Bureau.

Korea[37]

The Korean Financial Services Commission (**FSC**) has banned ICOs in Korea. The FSC issued a statement detailing its intention to ban all future ICOs in Korea due to concerns over the highly speculative nature of virtual currency trading.[38] The FSC has also warned issuers that they may be involved in an unauthorised public offering of securities for ICOs that constitute a "financial investment instrument" or a "security" under the *Financial Investment Services and Capital Markets Act* (**FISCMA**), although the status of a broad range of coins/tokens that are being purchased by Korean investors as "security" under the FISCMA remains unclear.

Philippines[39]

The Philippine Security and Exchange Commission (**SEC**) on 2 August 2018 released the draft Rules on Initial Coin Offerings in the Philippines and has invited interested parties to make submissions on the proposed rules no later than 31 August 2018.[40] The proposed rules cover the conduct of an ICO where convertible security tokens are issued by corporations targeting Philippine residents through online platforms. The rules provide that corporations offering coins in the Philippines have the burden of proving that the tokens being offered are not security tokens.

Thailand

The Thailand Security Exchange Commission (**SEC**) released a framework regulating ICOs in Thailand, which falls under the *Emergency Decree on Digital Asset Businesses*. The SEC identified that tokens may be treated in the same way as securities under the *Securities and Exchange Act*.[41] This requires issuers to comply with applicable regulatory requirements, including approval from the SEC. In order to seek SEC approval, the issuer must obtain approval from an ICO portal before applying with the SEC.

Considerations for utility tokens

Where an ICO sponsor determines that the tokens it is offering do not constitute "securities" in applicable jurisdictions, its initial impulse may be to sell its tokens to the general public without producing any prospectus or similar disclosure document. However, we suggest that sponsors take a cautious approach in light of the risks of categorisation highlighted above, by adopting certain best practices from the securities market. We encourage issuers of utility tokens to produce not just a white paper highlighting the potential benefits of the project, but also a much fuller information memorandum similar to that customary for security token offerings, including risk factors that may adversely impact the project.

We also encourage token issuers to consider whether it is appropriate to market their tokens to the general public, as opposed to a more refined base of sophisticated users who will understand the risks associated with the platform. As would be the case for a securities offering, utility token sales should also be underpinned by properly drafted subscription agreements, and a token instrument constituting the token and containing its terms. These will detail the rights and obligations of both the issuer and purchasers, such that those rights can be enforced through the courts, as opposed to through "smart contracts", which may not constitute binding legal obligations under applicable law. Issuers adopting this approach may also benefit from their ability to demonstrate to regulators or courts they have followed a responsible and diligent course of action, highlighting the risks to purchasers and giving them all material information.

* * *

Acknowledgments

Special thanks and recognition to the partners and staff of our respective offices for their contributions to this article including: Oystein Lokken in New York; Philip Smith and Simon Toms in London; Charlotte Robins and Michael Jacobs in Hong Kong; Shuhui Kwok and Yu Jia Ang in Singapore; Harun Reksodiputro and Raditya Putra in Indonesia; Stephen

Jaggs, Peerajit Chanmolee and Anchalee Limviriyalers in Thailand; Jane Jiang and Jason Song in China; and Nick Wall and Tokutaka Ito in Japan.

* * *

Endnotes

1. Numerous regulatory regimes affecting cryptocurrencies are outside the scope of this article, including securities exchange regulation, KYC and AML requirements, money service business regulation, and state securities and "bitlicense" regimes.

2. *Securities and Exchange Commission v. W. J. Howey Co.*, 328 U.S. 293 (1946).

3. See CoinCenter.org, "SEC's Clayton: Use of a token can evolve toward or away from being a security"(April 12, 2018), available at https://coincenter.org/entry/sec-s-clayton-use-of-a-token-can-evolve-toward-or-away-from-being-a-security.

4. See William Hinman, Director of the SEC Division of Corporation Finance, Remarks at the Yahoo Finance All Markets Summit: Crypto (June 14, 2018), available at https://www.sec.gov/news/speech/speech-hinman-061418.

5. Although beyond the scope of this article, actions against ICO sponsors by the SEC and private plaintiffs have ramped up significantly in the past year. After pursuing various regulatory actions against allegedly fraudulent ICOs in the fall of 2017, the SEC expanded the scope of its enforcement actions to non-fraudulent ICOs when it issued a cease-and-desist order to Munchee Inc. in December 2017. Although the SEC did not suggest that Munchee had engaged in fraudulent activities, it concluded that Munchee's ICO constituted an unregistered offer and sale of securities. The SEC has since pursued several enforcement actions against both fraudulent and non-fraudulent unregistered ICOs. In addition to regulatory actions by the SEC, the U.S. plaintiffs' bar sees potential windfalls in private class action lawsuits against ICO sponsors. Most prominently, several class action lawsuits have been filed by various purchasers of the cryptocurrency Tezos. Most recently, Irish cryptocurrency company Cloud With Me Ltd. has become the target of a proposed class action lawsuit in Pennsylvania federal court for failure to register with U.S. regulators.

6. 17 C.F.R. §§ 230.901-905.

7. 17 C.F.R. §§ 230.500-508.

8. For the purposes of this article, an "offshore transaction" is one in which (i) no offer is made to a person in the United States, and (ii) at the time the buy order is originated, the buyer is outside the United States, or the seller and any person acting on its behalf reasonably believes that the buyer is outside the United States.

9. "Directed selling efforts" include activity undertaken for the purpose of, or that could reasonably be expected to have the effect of, conditioning the market in the United States for an offering of securities. This includes sending promotional materials to US investors, holding promotional seminars for US investors, and placing advertisements in publications with a general circulation in the US or having contacts with the press in the U.S.

10. Accredited investors are defined in Rule 501 to include many institutional investors; businesses with total assets in excess of $5 million; natural persons whose net worth (individually or with that person's spouse, but excluding the person's primary residence),

exceeds $1 million; and natural persons whose individual income exceeds $200,000 (or $300,000 jointly with that person's spouse), in each of the two most recent years, with a reasonable expectation of reaching the same income level in the current year.

11. Regulation D does not prescribe specific means of verification. However, sufficient steps may include verifying income (through a review of IRS tax returns) or net worth (through a review of bank, brokerage and other documents) or obtaining a written confirmation from a registered broker-dealer, an SEC-registered investment adviser, a licensed attorney or a certified public accountant that it has taken reasonable steps to verify that the purchaser is an "accredited investor".

12. Generally, these disqualify the issuer if a director, officer, promoter or beneficial owner of 20% or more of the voting securities of the issuer has been the subject of a "disqualifying event," such as an order from a regulatory agency barring that person from engaging in the business of securities or a conviction of a felony or misdemeanor related to securities transactions.

13. The Form D must be filed within 15 days of the first sale, is public and requires the issuer to establish filing codes with the SEC.

14. Equity securities include stock, partnership interests and similar securities, but also more broad categories, including any "participation in any profit sharing agreement," and any securities convertible into such securities.

15. 17 C.F.R. § 12g-1.

16. The term "Foreign private issuer" includes any non-U.S. company unless it meets the following conditions as of the last business day of its most recently completed second fiscal quarter: (i) more than 50% of the outstanding voting securities of the issuer are directly or indirectly owned of record by residents of the United States; and (ii) any of the following: (A) The majority of the executive officers or directors are United States citizens or residents; (B) more than 50% of the assets of the issuer are located in the United States; or (C) the business of the issuer is administered principally in the United States.

17. 17 C.F.R. § 12g-3-2(a).

18. *Corporations Act 2001* (Cth) Ch 5C.

19. Ibid Ch 6D.

20. ASIC, *Information Sheet 225: Initial Coin Offerings and Crypto-Currency* (May 2018).

21. ASIC Corporations (Non-cash Payment Facilities) Instrument 2016/211.

22. ASIC, *Information Sheet 225: Initial Coin Offerings and Crypto-Currency* (May 2018).

23. Hong Kong Securities and Futures Commission (SFC), *Statement on Initial Coin Offerings* (September 2017) available at https://www.sfc.hk/web/EN/news-and-announcements/policy-statements-and-announcements/statement-on-initial-coin-offerings.html.

24. *Securities and Futures Ordinance* (HK) Sch 5 Pt 1.

25. Hong Kong Securities and Future Commission (SFC), '*SFC Warns of Cryptocurrency Risks*' (February 2018) available at https://www.sfc.hk/edistributionWeb/gateway/EN/news-and-announcements/news/doc?refNo=18PR13.

26. The prospectus regime under Part II and Part XII of the Companies (Winding Up and Miscellaneous Provisions) Ordinance.

27. Under Part IV of the SFO.

28. However, this position is proposed to change as the MAS is currently consulting on an omnibus Payment Services Bill.

29. Monetary Authority of Singapore (MAS), *'MAS clarifies regulatory position on the offer of digital tokens in Singapore'* (August 2017) available at http://www.mas.gov.sg/News-and-Publications/Media-Releases/2017/MAS-clarifies-regulatory-position-on-the-offer-of-digital-tokens-in-Singapore.aspx.

30. See e.g. Coin Telegraph, *'China ban on ICO is temporary, licensing to be introduced: official'* (September 2017) available at https://cointelegraph.com/news/china-ban-on-ico-is-temporary-licensing-to-be-introduced-official.

31. Bank Indonesia, *Statement of Bank Indonesia Related to Bitcoin and Other Virtual Currency* (February 2014) available at http://www.bi.go.id/en/ruang-media/siaran-pers/Pages/SP_160614.aspx.

32. Minister of Finance Republic of Indonesia, *'Bitcoin Is Not In Line With Law'* (January 2018) available at http://www.kemenkeu.go.id/en/publications/news/minister-of-finance-bitcoin-is-not-in-line-with-law/.

33. See *Badan Pengawas Perdagangan Berjangkla Komoditi Kementerian Perdagangan.*

34. See e.g. The Jakarta Post, *'Cryptocurrencies decided as future trading commodity'* (June 2018) available at http://www.thejakartapost.com/news/2018/06/04/cryptocurrencies-decided-as-future-trading-commodity.html.

35. See e.g. https://investasi.kontan.co.id/news/bappebti-resmi-tetapkan-uang-kripto-sebagai-subjek-perdagangan-berjangka.

36. Center For Rule-Making Strategies (Tama University), *Call for Rule-Making on ICO* (April 2018) available at https://www.tama.ac.jp/crs/2018_ico_en.pdf.

37. With thanks to Nelson K. Ahn of Lee & Ko for their assistance and contribution.

38. Korean Financial Services Authority (FSC), *Joint TF for Virtual Currency-Related Institutions* (September 2017) available at http://www.fsc.go.kr/info/ntc_news_view.jsp?bbsid=BBS0030&page=1&sch1=&sword=&r_url=&menu=7210100&no=32085.

39. With thanks to John Paul V. De Leon of Sycip Salazar Hernandez & Gatmaitan for their assistance and contribution.

40. See http://www.sec.gov.ph/wp-content/uploads/2018/08/MC-Rules-for-ICOs.pdf.

41. Thailand Securities and Exchange Commission (SEC), *SEC Thailand's Viewpoint on ICOs* (September 2017) available at https://www.sec.or.th/EN/Pages/FinTech/ICO.aspx.

Justin Cooke
Tel: +1 212 610 6351 / Email: justin.cooke@allenovery.com

Justin is a partner in the International Capital Markets practice group in the firm's New York office. Justin specialises in securities offerings, financial transactions and corporate governance and has extensive experience representing issuers, sponsors and underwriters in a wide range of domestic and cross-border capital markets transactions, including SEC-registered and private offerings of debt and equity securities. In the process, Justin has guided businesses through transformative transactions, including IPOs, public and private spin-offs, recapitalisations and corporate reorganisations. Justin's experience includes advising financial institutions, fintech companies and entrepreneurs on their development/adoption of capital markets technology platforms and distributed ledger technologies. He has counselled a number of ICO sponsors on structuring their offerings to accomplish their commercial objectives while complying with U.S. securities laws.

Richard Cohen
Tel: +44 20 3088 2130 / Email: richard.cohen@allenovery.com

Richard acts for both managers and issuers and specialises in straight-debt (Regulation S and Rule 144A standalone issues, LPNs, MTN programmes, CP, CDs), covered bonds and liability management transactions. He combines his debt capital markets practice with a focus on fintech and blockchain advisory work in the context of the optimisation of securities issuance and as part of Allen & Overy's Markets Innovation Group.

Richard recently assisted Nivaura to facilitate the issuance of the world's first fully automated, cryptocurrency-denominated bond that was also cleared, settled and registered on a public blockchain infrastructure. As part of the FCA's sandbox Richard also assisted Nivaura to facilitate the issuance of a sterling denominated bond where fiat currency was successfully digitised on a public blockchain infrastructure. Richard has spent time on secondment at a major investment bank and is a regular speaker at the Euromoney School of International Financial Law held at Oxford University.

Jason Denisenko
Tel: +612 9373 7809 / Email: jason.denisenko@allenovery.com

Jason is an expert on financial services regulatory matters including financial services licensing, marketing and distribution of financial products, payment arrangements and fintech initiatives across a range of products and services. Jason also advises on the structuring and provision of a wide range of financial products and services to wholesale and retail clients. He is a leading investment funds partner who advises major fund managers on the structuring, establishment and promotion of listed and unlisted funds and in relation to capital raisings and fund restructures. He also advises Australian and foreign institutional investors on their participation in a wide range of collective investment schemes and investment arrangements as well as custody, investment management and similar arrangements.

Allen & Overy LLP

1221 Avenue of the Americas, New York, NY 10020, USA
Tel: +1 212 610 6300 / Fax: +1 212 610 6399 / URL: www.allenovery.com

The custody of digital assets

Jay G. Baris
Shearman & Sterling LLP

Introduction

The growing fascination with digital assets, including cryptocurrencies and tokens, presents legal and operational challenges to investors, entrepreneurs and service providers, not to mention the regulators who oversee them. Perhaps no cryptocurrency issue presents more challenges than custody: how do individuals, broker-dealers, investment advisers, private funds and registered investment companies legally and effectively safeguard digital assets?

On the surface, the answer is simple: individuals can store their cryptocurrencies in digital wallets. Private funds managed by registered investment advisers can store their cryptocurrencies with "qualified custodians." Registered investment companies can store their cryptocurrencies only with custodians that meet additional statutory requirements.[1]

But alas, as is often the case with digital assets, it is not so simple. In reality, the operational and regulatory issues are more complicated, including whether the custody arrangements meet regulatory requirements, and whether they provide adequate safeguards, regardless of regulatory requirements.

This chapter examines the custody requirements that apply to various industry players under U.S. investment management laws and regulations, and analyses the challenges that they and the regulators face in evaluating arrangements for safeguarding digital assets.[2]

<u>Terminology</u>

Before we examine the legal requirements for custody, it is helpful to ensure that we use consistent terminology.

For the purposes of this chapter, "cryptocurrencies" refer to digital assets that function as a digital representation of a store of value, such as Bitcoin or Ethereum. Cryptocurrencies are not issued or backed by a central government, and thus are not legal tender. Alternatively we refer to cryptocurrencies as "digital currency" or "virtual currency."

"Utility tokens" refer to coins or tokens that serve a particular (non-incidental) function, or give the holder rights or access to goods, licences or services. A common form of utility token may give the holder the right to use a computer program that provides a kind of service for a defined period of time. Some refer to utility tokens as "app coins," "app tokens," or "utility coins." Some utility tokens may be securities, others are not. As we will see later, whether or not a utility token is characterised as a security becomes critical in evaluating what custody rules apply.

"Securities tokens" or "investment tokens" are tokens or coins that are securities for purposes of federal securities laws. The status of a token as a security token may be intentional or unintentional. Some utility tokens may start out as securities and at some point morph into non-securities, depending on their usage, how they are sold, and the expectations of the holders of those tokens.

Simply labelling a digital asset as a utility token, however, does not mean that the digital asset is not a security.[3] The analysis of whether or not a utility token functions as a security token, or when a security token transforms into a utility token is beyond the scope of this chapter, but, again, the distinction is relevant for purposes of the custody analysis.

Legal requirements for custody of digital assets

Background

The safeguarding of client assets has long been a priority of Congress and the Securities and Exchange Commission (the SEC). The legislative history of the Investment Company Act of 1940 (the ICA), and, by implication, its companion statute, the Investment Advisers Act of 1940 (the Advisers Act), shows that Congress was clearly concerned with the potential for abuses or misappropriation of client assets held in investment trusts and managed by investment advisers:[4]

> *That investors in investment trusts and investment companies are subject to substantial losses at the hands of unscrupulous persons is obvious from the very nature of the assets of such companies. Their assets consist almost invariably of cash and marketable securities. They are liquid, mobile, and easily negotiable. These assets can be easily misappropriated, 'looted,' or otherwise misused for the selfish purposes of those in control of these enterprises. In the absence of regulating legislation, individuals who lack integrity will continue to be attracted by the opportunity available for personal profit in the control of the liquid assets of investment trusts and investment companies.[5]*

The Senate had similar concerns:

> *Basically the problems flow from the very nature of the assets of investment companies. The assets of such companies invariably consist of cash and securities, assets which are completely liquid, mobile and readily negotiable. Because of these characteristics, control of such funds offers manifold opportunities for exploitation by the unscrupulous managements of some companies. These assets can and have been easily misappropriated and diverted by such types of managements, and have been employed to foster their personal interests rather than the interests of public security holders. It is obvious that in the absence of regulatory legislation, individuals who lack integrity will continue to be attracted by the opportunities for personal profit available in the control of the liquid assets of investment companies and that deficiencies which have occurred in the past will continue to occur in the future.[6]*

These issues made national headlines in December 2008, when Bernard L. Madoff admitted to perpetrating a massive Ponzi scheme in which he convinced his clients that they owned securities that did not exist. For years, he evaded regulatory scrutiny until the scheme began to unravel. This scandal prompted the SEC to take actions to reduce the chance that a Madoff-style fraud would occur or go undetected in the future.[7] While the SEC took steps to bolster its oversight and enforcement functions, it focused on rules designed to enhance the custody rules for investment advisers and broker-dealers. In December 2009, the SEC amended Rule 206(4)-2 (the "custody rule"), which was designed to provide greater assurance that investors' accounts contain the funds that their account statements say they contain.

Among other things, the rule encouraged advisers to maintain their clients' assets with independent custodians. For investment advisers who can control their clients' assets, the rules require enhanced procedures, such as surprise asset-counts, third-party reviews and audited financial statements. To be sure, when the U.S. Congress enacted the ICA and the Advisers Act, it clearly did not contemplate, or could even dream of, how the law would apply to digital assets such as cryptocurrencies or utility tokens. But the basic concerns of preventing fraud or misappropriation are just as valid today as they were in 1940. The only difference, of course, is that we are now attempting to apply 80-year-old laws designed to protect assets consisting of cash and securities to an entirely new class of digital assets created by a technology that did not exist at the time the laws were written.

What is "custody"?

Rule 206(4)-2 under the Advisers Act defines custody to mean "holding, directly or indirectly, client funds or securities, or having any authority to obtain possession of them." The regulation provides that you have custody of an asset "if a related person holds, directly or indirectly, client funds or securities, or has any authority to obtain possession of them, in connection with advisory services you provide to clients."

Rule 206-4(2) defines custody of an asset to include:

• possession of client funds or securities;

• any arrangement (including a general power of attorney) under which you are authorised or permitted to withdraw client funds or securities maintained with a custodian upon your instruction to the custodian; and

• any capacity (such as general partner of a limited partnership, managing member of a limited liability company or a comparable position for another type of pooled investment vehicle, or trustee of a trust) that gives you or your supervised person legal ownership of or access to client funds or securities.

A threshold question is whether the SEC's custody rule applies to digital assets? The answer depends on the facts and circumstances.

The SEC's Division of Investment Management has said that Rule 206(4)-2 does not apply to an adviser to the extent that it manages assets that are "not funds or securities."[8] Does this mean that advisers to clients or funds that invest in Bitcoin are free to hold these assets in personal digital "wallets" without regard to federal regulation? If not, to what standard will an adviser be held? Again, it depends. In light of the legislative history, which makes the protection of investors' assets a priority, it is possible that most, if not all, digital assets would be considered "funds or securities" for the purposes of the Advisers Act and the custody rule. The matter is not free from doubt.

What are the legal custody requirements for an investment adviser?

The first step in analysing the legal requirements for the custody of assets is to determine the nature of the investment adviser. The two threshold questions are:

• What law applies? That is, is the adviser an "investment adviser" as defined in the Investment Advisers Act of 1940, as amended (the "Advisers Act")?

• If yes, is the adviser registered or required to be registered under the Advisers Act?

Next, we examine the nature of the assets and the nature of the entity that holds them.

What law applies?

To determine what law applies, we must look at the nature of the person or entity that holds or proposes to hold a digital asset. The holder of a digital asset can be:

- a natural person, directly or in a managed account;
- a pooled investment vehicle that is not publicly offered in the U.S., such as a hedge fund, private equity fund, or other private fund;
- a pooled vehicle that is registered as an investment company;
- a regulated entity such as a broker-dealer, bank or investment adviser;
- an operating company; or
- other pooled investment vehicles which might be commodity pools that otherwise would be investment companies but for an exemption under the 1940 Act.

Our focus here will be investment advisers and their clients, including natural persons, private funds and investment companies. We first discuss investment advisers and then registered investment companies.

What is an investment adviser?

Section 202(a)(11) of the Advisers Act defines an investment adviser as a person or entity that:

- engages in the business of advising others, directly or indirectly,
- as to the value of securities or as to the advisability of investing in securities,
- for compensation.

If you satisfy each of these three elements, you are an investment adviser for purposes of federal law.

Investment advisers who satisfy each of these three elements will be investment advisers for the purposes of federal securities laws, unless they fall within one of the statutory exemptions.[9]

This analysis is important, because whether a person falls within the statutory definition of an investment adviser determines whether (a) the person is subject to regulation by the SEC, and (b) the person is subject to the substantive provisions of the Advisers Act and its rules, including Rule 206(4)-2 (the SEC rule that applies to the custody of client assets, if the person is required to register as an investment adviser).

Is the adviser providing advice to anyone about *securities*? For example, an adviser that solely provides investment advice about a "pure cryptocurrency," such as Bitcoin or Ethereum, is not an investment adviser, because these cryptocurrencies are not securities.[10] The answer will be different if the adviser is providing advice about a derivative, the reference asset of which is a cryptocurrency. In that case, the advice may relate to a security (e.g., a structured note that links a return to a benchmark reference cryptocurrency or shares of a trust that holds cryptocurrency) or a commodity-related instrument that is regulated under the Commodity Exchange Act (e.g., a forward, future, put, call, straddle, swap, etc. relating to a cryptocurrency).

If the person is providing advice with respect to securities, the person may have to register with the SEC, depending on whether the person: (a) meets the statutory thresholds that permit registration; (b) is required to register by the Advisers Act; or (c) is eligible for status as a an "exempt reporting adviser."[11]

Investment advisers not required to register under the Advisers Act

The Advisers Act provides several voluntary exemptions from registration, including, among others:

- intrastate advisers, that is, advisers whose clients all reside in the state in which the adviser maintains its principal place of business;
- advisers to insurance companies;
- "foreign private advisers," which generally are advisers that (a) have no place of business in the U.S., (b) have fewer than 15 clients and investors in private funds in the U.S., (c) have less than $25 million in assets under management attributable to those clients and investors; and (d) do not hold themselves out as investment advisers in the U.S.;
- charitable organisations and plans;
- commodity trading advisers;
- private fund advisers, which generally are advisers solely to private funds that have less than $150 million in assets under management in the U.S.;
- venture capital fund advisers; and
- advisers to small business investment companies (SBICs).

Advisers that rely on the private fund adviser exemption and the venture capital fund exemption are considered "exempt reporting advisers." Exempt reporting advisers must file with the SEC certain disclosures on Form ADV, but generally they are not subject to the substantive rules of the Advisers Act, including the custody rule (discussed below).

Exempt reporting advisers, and investment advisers that fall within the definition but are not required to register are, however, nonetheless subject to the anti-fraud provisions of the Advisers Act, not to mention their fiduciary obligations to those clients under federal law. This includes state-registered investment advisers and investment advisers that are not required to register anywhere. While these advisers are not subject to the custody rule, it is reasonable to presume they still must exercise care and prudence in maintaining or arranging for the custody of their clients' digital assets, including a responsibility to disclose related risks.

We discuss some of the challenges that they face in maintaining custody of digital assets below.

Investment advisers required to register under the Advisers Act

Rule 206(4)-2, the custody rule under the Advisers Act, applies to investment advisers registered, or required to be registered, with the SEC (RIAs) and their related persons that have "custody" of client funds or securities.

As noted, an RIA is deemed to have "custody" of client assets if the RIA (or its related person) directly or indirectly holds client funds or securities, or has any authority to obtain possession of them.[12] This authority can arise out of custodial or advisory arrangements. For example, an adviser that has access to a client's private key to a cryptocurrency holding could be deemed to have access to the client's asset, even if the same key is held by a third-party custodian. Depending on the facts and circumstances, the SEC staff has said, "custodial agreements could impute advisers with custody they otherwise did not intend to have."[13] Other arrangements in which an RIA is presumed to have custody of client assets include when an RIA or an affiliate acts as general partner or managing member to a private fund.

Put another way, it would be difficult for an RIA to avoid having custody of client funds and securities unless an RIA neither holds, nor has authority to obtain possession of, client funds and securities, including cryptocurrencies. When an RIA or its related person is deemed to have custody of client funds or assets, it must comply with certain requirements under Rule 206(4)-2(a), unless an exception in Rule 206(4)-2(b) applies. Unless the RIA qualifies for such an exception, an RIA that fails to comply likely violates the anti-fraud provisions of the Advisers Act.[14]

What does the custody rule require of RIAs? Unless an exemption applies, if an RIA or its "related person" has custody of a client's assets (including funds and securities), Rule 206(4)-2(a)(1) requires the RIA to use a "qualified custodian" to maintain those client funds and securities:

- in a separate account for the client under the client's name; or
- in accounts that contain only the client's funds and securities, under the RIA's name as agent or trustee for the client.

Qualified custodian. A "qualified custodian" includes:

- many federal and state chartered banks;
- registered broker-dealers holding client assets in customer accounts;
- registered futures commission merchants holding client assets in customer accounts (but generally only with respect to futures contracts and other securities incidental to transactions in futures and related options); and
- foreign financial institutions that customarily hold financial assets for customers, provided that they keep advisory clients' assets in customer accounts segregated from its proprietary assets.[15]

Notice, Account Statement and Examination Requirement. Rules 206(4)-2(a)(2), (a)(3) and (a)(4) impose certain notice, account statement, and examination requirements on RIAs if RIAs or their "related persons" have custody of client funds or securities, unless an exemption is met. These requirements are relatively burdensome.

Notice to clients requirement. When an adviser opens an account with a qualified custodian on the client's behalf, Rule 206(4)-2(a)(3) requires the RIA to notify the client *in writing* of the qualified custodian's name, address, and the manner in which the custodian maintains the funds or securities in the account, promptly when the account is opened and following any changes to this information.

Account statement requirement. Rule 206(4)-2(a)(3) requires that the qualified custodian send account statements to each client for which it maintains funds or securities, unless an exemption applies. The statements, which must be sent at least quarterly, must identify the amount of funds and each security in the account at the end of the period, and all transactions during the period. RIAs must "have a reasonable basis, after due inquiry" for believing that the qualified custodian has sent the required account statements. This necessarily entails due diligence. Advisers have the option of sending their own account statements to their clients, in addition to those required to be sent by the qualified custodian. In this event, the notice to clients (summarised above) must include a statement "urging the client to compare the account statements from the custodian with those from the adviser."[16]

When the RIA (or a related person of the RIA) serves as general partner or the equivalent of a pooled investment vehicle, the qualified custodian must send the account statement to each beneficial owner of the fund.[17] This is so unless the audit exception for pooled investment vehicles (described below) applies.

Surprise audit requirement. Under Rule 206(4)-2(a)(4), at least once during each calendar year, RIA and "related person" custodied funds and securities must be verified by actual examination in a "surprise audit," unless an exemption applies. The surprise audit – which is really a securities count and not a traditional "audit" of financial statements – must be conducted by an independent public accountant and must be chosen by the accountant without prior notice or announcement to the RIA and that is irregular from year to year.

The surprise audit must be subject to a written agreement. The written agreement must provide for an initial surprise examination within six months of becoming subject to the surprise audit, except that if the RIA is a "qualified custodian," then the agreement must provide for the first surprise audit to commence not later than six months after the adviser obtains an "internal control report" as described below.

The written agreement must require the independent public accountant to: (a) file a certificate on Form ADV-E within 120 days of the examination date, stating that it has examined the funds and securities, and describing the nature and extent of the examination; (b) notify the SEC within one business day of any findings of "material discrepancies" during the examination; and (c) notify the SEC by filing Form ADV-E accompanied by certain statements regarding the registration if the independent public accountant resigns, or is dismissed, removed or terminated.[18]

Surprise audits of cryptocurrency assets may pose significant challenges for independent auditors, who must validate that the private key actually represents ownership of a cryptocurrency without the benefit of traditional ownership indicia supported by securities registrars, control practices associated with regulated securities intermediaries, known and trusted parties to receive verification requests, etc.

Pooled investment vehicles. When the RIA (or a related person of the RIA) serves as general partner (or the equivalent) of a pooled investment vehicle, it can satisfy the notice, account statement and surprise audit requirements described with respect to the fund that is subject to an annual audit:

(a) if at least annually, the fund sends its audited financial statements, prepared in accordance with generally accepted accounting principles, to all limited partners (or members or other beneficial owners) within 120 days of the end of its fiscal year;

(b) by an independent auditor that is registered with and subject to regular inspection as of the commencement of the engagement, and as of each calendar year-end, by the Public Company Accounting Oversight Board (PCAOB) in accordance with its rules; and

(c) upon liquidation, and distributes its audited financial statements prepared in accordance with generally accepted accounting principles (GAAP) to all limited partners (or members or other beneficial owners) promptly after the completion of the audit.

Similar asset verification challenges to those described above apply during the audit process.

Independent advisers or related parties acting as qualified custodians. RIAs that maintain custody of client funds or securities, directly or through a related person that has actual rather than deemed custody (i.e., those acting as a qualified custodian) "in connection with" advisory services, must comply with two requirements that require the use of independent public accountants.[19]

First, a PCAOB-registered and inspected independent public accountant must satisfy the surprise audit requirement (discussed above). RIAs must obtain, or receive from their related person, a written internal control report *within six months of becoming subject to such requirement and at least once per calendar year.*

Second, the internal control report must be prepared by an independent public accountant. The internal control report must include an opinion of a PCAOB-registered and inspected independent public accountant "as to whether controls have been placed in operation as of a specific date, and are suitably designed and are operating effectively to meet control objectives relating to custodial services, including the safeguarding of funds and securities held by either the RIA or a related person on behalf of the RIA's advisory clients, during the year." The independent public accountant must verify that the funds and securities are reconciled to a custodian other than the RIA or its related persons. A copy of any internal control report obtained or received is subject to record-keeping requirements.[20]

Non-U.S. advisers. Generally, non-U.S. RIAs with a principal place of business outside of the U.S. are not subject to the custody rule with respect to their non-U.S. clients. This includes a client that is a non-U.S. fund (organised outside the U.S.), whether or not the fund has U.S. investors.[21]

Registered investment companies

Section 17(f) of the Investment Company Act, as amended ("1940 Act") governs how registered investment companies must maintain custody of their assets.[22] This section requires a registered fund to maintain its securities and other investments with certain types of custodians under conditions designed to assure the safety of the fund's assets.[23] While the section addresses custody of fund assets by certain banks, broker-dealers and futures commission merchants (FCMs), as well as securities depositories, unsurprisingly it does not specifically address custody of digital assets.

Notably, Section 17(f)(1) refers to "securities and similar investments," which is a broader category of assets than covered the custody rule under the Advisers Act.

Section 17(f)(1) provides that every registered management company shall place and maintain its securities *and similar investments* in the custody of:

- a bank;
- a company that is a member of a national securities exchange, subject to the SEC's rules; or
- the investment company itself, subject to the SEC's rules.

When Congress enacted Section 17(f), of course, no-one anticipated how it would apply to digital assets. The term "and similar investments," however, can readily be read to include digital currencies.

Rule 17f-1 under the 1940 Act governs custody of investment company assets maintained by broker-dealers that are members of a national securities exchange. Among other things, Rule 17f-1 requires that the securities *and similar investments* held in such custody shall at all times be individually segregated from the securities and investments of any other person and marked in such manner as to clearly identify them as the property of such registered management company, both upon physical inspection thereof and upon examination of the books of the custodian. The rule, however, is a bit dated if its terms are to be taken literally: "The physical segregation and marking of such securities and investments may be accomplished by putting them in separate containers bearing the name of such registered management investment company or by attaching tags or labels to such securities and investment."

Rule 17f-2 governs custody by the investment company itself or by a bank.

Rule 17f-2(a) provides that "[t]he securities and similar investments of a registered management investment company may be maintained in the custody of such company only in accordance with the provisions of this section." While the rule is deemed largely unworkable by the industry, it is in any event not clear how an investment company itself could take custody of cryptocurrencies without running afoul of the other provisions of the 1940 Act.

This section also addresses custody by banks:

> *Except as provided in paragraph (c) of this rule, all such securities and similar investments shall be deposited in the safekeeping of, or in a vault or other depository maintained by, a bank or other company whose functions and physical facilities are supervised by Federal or State authority. Investments so deposited shall be physically segregated at all times from those of any other person and shall be withdrawn only in connection with transactions of the character described in paragraph (c) of this rule.*

Rule 17f-4 allows investment companies to maintain custody of assets with a securities depositary or intermediate custodian, subject to certain conditions.

Rule 17f-6[24] generally provides that investment companies may "place and maintain cash, securities, and similar investments with a Futures Commission Merchant in amounts necessary to effect the Fund's transactions in Exchange-traded futures contracts and commodity options," subject to certain conditions to safeguard the assets.

In sum, a registered investment company can comply with the requirements of Section 17(f) by placing cryptocurrencies in the possession of a bank, a broker-dealer that is a member of a national securities exchange, or a securities depository.

Funds that utilise derivatives related to cryptocurrencies (e.g., swaps, futures, options) can maintain custody with the futures commission merchant, but the custody arrangements present challenges when the derivative calls for physical settlement of the underlying asset, which we discuss below.

Other custody considerations for registered investment companies include oversight by chief compliance officers and the fund's board of directors.

Funds that invest in cryptocurrencies directly or indirectly through derivatives must ensure that their compliance policies and procedures address the attendant risks.

Legal and practical custody challenges faced by investment advisers and investment companies with respect to digital assets

Investment advisers, whether or not they are registered with the SEC, and investment companies, face challenges when designing a custody arrangement that meets the regulatory requirements as well as protecting the client's assets.

How does an investment adviser maintain custody of a digital asset? To start, an investment adviser can satisfy the custody rule by maintaining the digital assets with a "qualified custodian." To be sure, some qualified custodians have begun to accept digital asset custody accounts, and more are expected to enter that business.

Arguably, that is the easy part. Now comes the challenge: how does the qualified custodian maintain custody of digital assets in a way that satisfies regulatory scrutiny and provides adequate safeguards for the client or fund's assets? How much protection against fraud can a qualified custodian of digital assets really provide, and what liability would it be willing to accept by contract?

In the final analysis, cryptocurrencies exist merely as computer-coded entries on a digital ledger, or blockchain, visible to and verifiable by all "nodes." Ownership is reflected in a string of numbers on a distributed ledger, accessible only by a public key and a private key, much the same way access to a safe deposit box is accessible by the bank's key and the depositor's private key.

A custodian, for example, can take physical possession of a stock certificate. It also can take "possession" of an uncertificated stock certificate, because the custodian's name is registered on the books of the issuer. Cryptocurrencies, which are recorded in digital form on the distributed ledger, reflect the transfer of ownership, but not necessarily who is the record owner of the cryptocurrency. Whoever has possession of the private key has access to that asset.

To satisfy regulatory requirements, a custodian could hold a "private key" and a "public key" to the digital asset. But what steps can a custodian take to ensure that the private key cannot be misappropriated? A custodian can maintain private keys in digital form on a computer hard drive unconnected from the internet and protected by layers of cybersecurity. Or, the custodian can place a piece of paper (or hard drive) containing the private key and lock it in a physical vault encased in concrete and (to wax metaphorically) surrounded by an alligator-filled moat. In any event, the technology used for safeguarding digital assets is emerging.

Moreover, cryptocurrencies are essentially bearer assets. In general, a bad actor who obtains possession of the private key can, in theory, misappropriate the asset, no matter where the private key maintained. Some industry participants have addressed this risk by proposing to obtain insurance against loss or theft of the cryptocurrency. While insurance may address some of the counterparty and custody risks associated with cryptocurrencies, it may be costly and may not completely cover potential risks.

As already suggested, there also are other practical considerations that apply to the auditors of accounts holding cryptocurrency. For example, how will independent auditors verify ownership of the cryptocurrency? To whom would they send the audit letter requesting confirmation?

Registered funds must also ensure that that the board of directors has sufficient information to provide meaningful oversight of the fund's custody arrangements. Among other things, fund directors must approve the compliance policies of the investment company and its investment adviser, and also must approve of contractual arrangements with fund custodians. While some qualified custodians are willing to take custody of cryptocurrencies held by registered investment companies, they may face some challenges. For example, will the fund directors be satisfied that the custodian has adequate safeguards in place to protect the assets? Will the custodian's limitations on liability be acceptable to the directors? Will the directors conclude that the cost of cryptocurrency custody is reasonable?

The staff of the SEC raised these issues in a letter dated January 18, 2018 by Dalia Blass, Director of the Division of Investment Management:[25]

> *The 1940 Act imposes safeguards to ensure that registered funds maintain custody of their holdings. These safeguards include standards regarding who may act as a custodian and when funds must verify their holdings. To the extent a fund plans to hold cryptocurrency directly, how would it satisfy the custody requirements of the 1940 Act and relevant rules? We note, for example, that we are not aware of a custodian currently providing fund custodial services for cryptocurrencies. In addition, how would a fund intend to validate existence, exclusive ownership and software functionality of private cryptocurrency keys and other ownership records? To what extent would cybersecurity threats or the potential for hacks on digital wallets impact the safekeeping of fund assets under the 1940 Act?*

These custody issues carry over to settlement of cryptocurrency-related derivatives. That is, when a fund holds derivatives that are based on the value of an underlying cryptocurrency, the futures commission merchant, which holds the derivative position for the benefit of the fund, will satisfy the qualified custodian requirements. But a fund that takes a long position in a Bitcoin futures contract may be required to accept Bitcoin when the contract matures, or to deliver Bitcoin to a futures commission merchant upon settlement of a short position. The Blass Cryptocurrency Letter noted the challenges that registered funds will face when taking positions in cryptocurrency-based derivatives:

> *While the currently available bitcoin futures contracts are cash settled, we understand that other derivatives related to cryptocurrencies may provide for physical settlement, and physically settled cryptocurrency futures contracts may be developed. To the extent a fund plans to hold cryptocurrency-related derivatives that are physically settled, under what circumstances could the fund have to hold cryptocurrency directly? If the fund may take delivery of cryptocurrencies in settlement, what plans would it have in place to provide for the custody of the cryptocurrency?*

These challenges are just some of the issues facing the industry and its regulators as RIAs and registered investment companies begin to invest in digital currencies.

To be sure, however, the current environment of persistent uncertainty cannot last; as the markets for cryptocurrencies and other digital assets mature, so too will custody standards. Custodians, auditors and other trusted parties that comprise the infrastructure for reliable custody in the securities markets will develop a battery of tailored procedures appropriate to this new and growing asset class.

Acknowledgments

The author gratefully acknowledges the contributions and insights provided by Nathan J. Greene, Partner, and Andrew J. Donohue, Of Counsel, of Shearman & Sterling LLP.

* * *

Endnotes

1. Broker-dealers, commodity pool operators, commodity trading advisors and advisers to certain retirement plans are subject to separate requirements, which are not the subject of this chapter.
2. For a general discussion of blockchain issues for investment managers, see Jay G. Baris and Joshua Ashley Klayman, "Blockchain Basics for Investment Managers: A Token of Appreciation," 51 *The Review of Securities and Commodities Regulation* 67 (Mar. 21, 2018), available at https://www.shearman.com/-/media/Files/Perspectives/2018/03/ Baris_Klayman_RSCR_Final_1.pdf?la=en&hash=4CD602B56ED60D38CB5EAC23 2EF3D80981026B0F.
3. William Hinman, Director SEC Division of Corporate Finance, Digital Asset Transactions: *When Howey Met Gary (Plastic)*, Remarks at the Yahoo Finance All Markets Summit: Crypto (June 14, 2018), available at https://www.sec.gov/news/ speech/speech-hinman-061418.
4. The Advisers Act does not specifically address custody of clients. Rather, the SEC addressed this issue in the Rule 206(4)-2 under the Advisers Act (the "custody rule"), which is discussed below.
5. H.R. Report No. 76-2639 (1940).

6. Senate Report No. 76-1744 (1940).

7. The Securities and Exchange Commission Post-Madoff Reforms, available at https://www.sec.gov/spotlight/secpostmadoffreforms.htm.

8. The SEC staff has taken the position that if an adviser manages client assets that are not funds or securities, the custody rule does not require the adviser to maintain the assets with a qualified custodian. Question II.3, *Staff Responses to Questions About the Custody Rule* (online FAQ), available at https://www.sec.gov/divisions/investment/custody_faq_030510.htm. The issue now presented is whether the SEC staff considers cryptocurrencies to be "funds or securities" for purposes of the custody rule.

9. For example, family offices, banks, insurance companies and broker-dealers that provide advice incidental to their brokerage business, among others, are excluded from the definition of an investment adviser under the Advisers Act.

10. We are assuming that at least these two cryptocurrencies are not "securities" for purposes of the federal securities laws. The analysis of whether a particular digital asset is a security is beyond the scope of this chapter.

11. The provisions of the Advisers Act relating to whether an adviser is required to register are beyond the scope of this chapter.

12. Advisers Act Rule 206(4)-2(d)(2).

13. SEC Division of Investment Management Guidance Update No. 2017-01 February 2017, available at https://www.sec.gov/investment/im-guidance-2017-01.pdf.

14. One notable exemption is that Rule 206(4)-2 does not apply with respect to mutual fund accounts of the RIA. *See* Rule 206(4)-2(b)(5).

15. Advisers Act Rule 206(4)-2(d)(6).

16. Advisers Act Rule 206(4)-2(a)(2).

17. Advisers Act Rule 206(4)-2(a)(5).

18. Advisers Act Rule 206(4)-2(a)(4)(iii).

19. Advisers Act Rule 206(4)-2(a)(6).

20. Advisers Act Rule 204-2(a)(17)(iii).

21. Exemptions for Advisers to Venture Capital Funds, Private Fund Advisers With Less Than $150 Million in Assets Under Management, and Foreign Private Advisers, SEC Release No. IA-3222 (Jun 22, 2011) at note 515, available at https://www.sec.gov/rules/final/2011/ia-3222.pdf: "[W]e do not apply most of the substantive provisions of the Advisers Act to the non-U.S. clients of a non-U.S. adviser registered with the Commission." See also Robert E. Plaze, *Regulation of Investment Advisers by the U.S. Securities and Exchange Commission*, at note 374 (June 2018), available at: https://www.proskauer.com/report/regulation-of-investment-advisers-by-the-us-securities-and-exchange-commission-june-2018.

22. Investment Company Act of 1940, 15 U.S.C. § 80a (1958).

23. See generally Securities and Exchange Commission, Custody of Investment Company Assets with a Securities Depository, Release No. IC-25934 (Feb. 13, 2003), available at https://www.sec.gov/rules/final/ic-25934.htm.

24. Final Rule: Custody of Investment Company Assets with Futures Commission Merchants and Commodity Clearing Organizations, Release No. IC-22389 (Dec. 11, 1996), available at https://www.sec.gov/rules/final/ic-22389.txt.

25. SEC Staff Letter: *Engaging on Fund Innovation and Cryptocurrency-related holdings* (Jan. 18, 2018), *available at* https://www.sec.gov/divisions/investment/noaction/2018/cryptocurrency-011818.htm (the "Blass Cryptocurrency Letter").

Jay G. Baris
Tel: +1 212 848 4000 / Email: jay.baris@shearman.com
Jay G. Baris is a partner in the Investment Funds practice and has practiced in
the asset management area for more than 35 years.

Jay is widely recognised for his breadth of experience representing registered
funds, investment advisers, financial institutions, broker-dealers and
independent directors on the full spectrum of financial services regulation,
transactions and governance matters. Jay's work with registered funds spans
mutual funds, closed-end funds, exchange-traded funds (ETFs) and business
development companies (BDCs). He has extensive experience advising on
the regulatory aspects of fund and investment advisory operations, and has
represented numerous clients on mergers and acquisitions, reorganisations,
compliance, exemptive applications and compliance issues. He also advises
operating companies on "status" issues that arise under the Investment
Company Act of 1940. More recently, he has been advising Fintech clients on
cryptocurrency issues.

An active speaker and writer on issues concerning investment management
and the regulation of financial institutions, Jay has been published in a variety
of trade and general interest publications, *Insights: The Corporate & Securities
Law Advisor, The New York Times, The Wall Street Journal, The Review of
Securities & Commodities Regulation, Fund Action, The Review of Banking &
Financial Services, Fund Directions* and *Fund Board Views.*

Educated at Hofstra University, J.D. and Stony Brook University, B.A., Jay is
admitted to the Bars of New York, District of Columbia and New Jersey.

- Chair of the ABA Task Force on Blockchains, Cryptocurrencies and
  Investment Management of the ABA Subcommittee on Investment
  Companies and Investment Advisers.
- Co-Chair of the Task Force on Investment Company Use of Derivatives
  and Leverage of the Committee on Federal Regulation of Securities of the
  ABA's Business Law Section.
- Previously, vice chair of the Committee on Federal Regulation and
  chair and vice chair of the Subcommittee on Investment Companies and
  Investment Advisers of the ABA's Business Law Section.
- Member of the Advisor Panel of *Blockchain, Virtual Currencies and
  ICOs – Navigating the Legal Landscape* (Wolters Kluwer 2018).
- Member of the Board of Advisors of The Review of Securities &
  Commodities Regulation.
- Member of the Advisory Board of the Mutual Fund Directors Forum.
- Member of the Advisory Board of BoardIQ.
- Ranked in "Band 2" in *Chambers USA* 2018 for Nationwide: Investment
  Funds: Registered Funds.
- Recognised as a "Leading Lawyer" and "Hall of Fame" by *The Legal 500*
  US (2018).
- Listed in *Best Lawyers in America* for his work in corporate law, mutual
  funds law and financial services regulation law (2008–2019).

Shearman & Sterling LLP

599 Lexington Avenue, New York, NY 10022, USA
Tel: +1 212 848 4000 / URL: www.shearman.com

Mutually assured disruption: The rise of the security token

Joshua Ashley Klayman[1]

Klayman LLC / Inflection Point Blockchain Advisors, LLC

Introduction

The advent of blockchain technology, with all of its promise for disrupting existing business, economic, and even governmental and social models, more immediately has disrupted traditional models of capital markets activity, as well as the sleep of many a securities regulator. Initial coin offerings (also known as ICOs, token sales, token generation events, or TGEs)[2] are increasingly displacing venture capital fundraising and initial public offerings as a favoured means of raising capital and funding the development of product and service offerings. Whether driven by well-intentioned technologists, financial professionals or scammers, burgeoning technological capabilities and the ability to build and leverage network effects have frequently outpaced legal understanding and compliance.

While the earliest token sale occurred in 2013,[3] it was 2016 and 2017 that brought ICOs into the mainstream media focus.[4] Many of those selling or otherwise distributing digital tokens to fund project development, drive network adoption and monetise goodwill believed that they had created something new, that fell entirely outside of existing United States securities laws – token sales were sales of software, after all.

However, long before the U.S. Securities and Exchange Commission (the "SEC") made clear that token sales could be sales of securities, experienced securities lawyers counselled that this likely was the case. Indeed, months before the SEC provided formal guidance on the topic (via *The DAO 21A Report*),[5] blockchain industry pioneer Emma Channing had already structured as a sale of securities the Blockchain Capital token sale, which, among other things, was conducted pursuant to Regulation D and Regulation S, in each case, of the Securities Act of 1933, as amended (the "Securities Act"). Launched from Singapore, the Blockchain Capital token sale is believed by many to be the first self-described security token offering.

This chapter is titled "The Rise of the Security Token," and not "The Birth of the Security Token," because, while popular belief within the blockchain community at one time bifurcated the universe of ICO tokens into broad categories of so-called "utility tokens," purported not to be securities, and tokens with securities-like features that were understood to be securities, it now is widely recognised that, in the eyes of U.S. federal securities regulators, sales of tokens to U.S. persons in ICOs generally have been sales of securities all along. In other words, with limited exceptions, utility tokens sold to U.S. persons via ICOs were born as securities after all, by virtue of the investment contracts through which they were marketed or sold. While applicable law and interpretive guidance remain scant, it also now appears that certain of those tokens might one day, as a legal matter, "morph" into non-securities, as in the case of Ethereum (as discussed below).

Even if it is presumed that all token sales to U.S. persons are sales of investment contracts and, hence, securities, for token sellers and their counsel, there remain many unanswered questions, particularly in the cases of tokens that have a "consumptive" use. Not only is it unclear how and when a token may be said no longer to be a security under U.S. securities laws, but issuance of a token as a security raises questions under *existing* U.S. securities laws. For instance, certain unresolved issues include the requirement to file periodic reports with the SEC under Section 12(g) of the Securities Exchange Act of 1934, as amended (the "Exchange Act"), flowback of tokens into the United States from regulated and unregulated exchanges around the world, broker registration requirements and the risk of inadvertent status as an investment company under the Investment Company Act of 1940, as amended (the "40 Act").

This chapter provides a brief review of the nature of a blockchain token (alternately referred to as a token or digital token),[6] and highlights some of the most prominent U.S. federal securities law guidance[7] and market developments that have led to practitioners' current understandings. Finally, it explores some of the key unanswered legal questions being wrestled with by market participants, their counsel and regulators alike.

Part 1: What are digital tokens?

Despite regulatory uncertainty and pronounced market volatility, digital token sales have emerged as an important capital markets activity. According to some estimates, more than US $10 billion in the aggregate was raised via token sales during the first half of 2018 alone,[8] with token sales increasingly rivalling traditional IPO and venture capital markets:

> *"The initial coin offering (ICO) market – defined as capital raised on open blockchains via token sales – was 45% and 31% of the traditional IPO and venture capital markets during Q2 2018, respectively, up from 40% and 30%, during Q1 2018. ICO volume during Q2 2018 was approximately $7.2 billion, according to Coindesk, while the US IPO market raised $16.0 billion (as reported by PwC), and US venture capital markets raised $23 billion (as reported by CB Insights and PwC) during the same period."[9]*

But what are these digital tokens? At core,

> *"digital tokens are no more or less than numbered entries on a blockchain-based electronic ledger. These ledger entries may indeed be structured to look very much like traditional 'securities'– representing promises to pay amounts in the future, ownership, or other interests in an entity, etc. However, digital tokens can also represent units of value, which may make them look more like commodities; they can function as property records or warehouse receipts; they can entitle owners to the right to use a software system, which makes them look more like licenses. Some digital tokens may simply represent data points in a larger data structure. This is what many lawyers and others mean when they caution that there is no single type, nor set of clear categories, of digital tokens. There is tremendous flexibility in how to structure digital tokens and what those digital tokens may represent."[10]*

If, rather than imagining a token as a physical coin, one thinks of a digital token as more akin to a credit card number, one can begin to see how there may be no single "paradigmatic" token, as well as why U.S. regulators may, at various times and sometimes at the same time, view a token alternatively as property (the IRS), a commodity (the CFTC), money (FinCEN) or a security (the SEC). For instance, when a user purchases computer software, upon installation, she may be prompted to enter in a licence key, typically a string of letters or numbers. In an alternative model, each person who holds a string of numbers issued by a company or project could have the right to receive $5, or a specified percentage interest in the company's or project's economic returns, or the right to vote on certain activities or developments of the company or project. Alternatively, each string of numbers could entitle the holder to entrance to a particular members-only event, with the lowest number being the first in line. In another of endless potential examples, one could identify individual items of personal property, such as a treasured watch or ring, or authenticate a legal document by specifying a string of numbers that corresponds to it.

As one lawyer noted while reflecting on 2017, in his view:

> "[....] most blockchain tokens are something very different from traditional securities. Rather than representing fungible contractual rights or claims, such as the right to receive dividends or a residual claim on the assets of a corporation, in the case of stock, or the right to payments of principal or interest in the case of debt instruments, they are particularized digital assets, each immutably tied to a specific cryptographic key. It is not financial sophistication that is needed to understand these assets but rather technological sophistication and [....] a healthy amount of imagination as to what the future will look like and the types of products and services that will be appealing to people."[11]

This tremendous variability in token characteristics has led many individuals and certain nations[12] to posit that sales of certain tokens that have nonincidental utility[13] or consumptive use (in the nature of tokens at a laundromat or video game arcade) are not sales of securities. Over the past couple of years, some in the crypto community have referred to such tokens alternatively as utility tokens, consumer tokens or consumptive tokens, in an attempt to distinguish them, categorically, from tokens that are securities.[14]

Notwithstanding such terminology, U.S. securities regulators have made clear that even if an individual token is not structured to have characteristics of traditional debt or equity securities, an initial token sale may be – and in most cases, almost certainly is – a sale of an investment contract, and, therefore, a security, under U.S. securities laws.[15]

Part 2: The rise of the security token

The DAO report: ICOs may be sales of securities

The most famous, or infamous, token sale of 2016, The DAO, now stands as a cautionary example of how not to conduct a token sale.

The DAO,[16] a "decentralised autonomous organisation" that sought to be a virtual venture fund, has been described as a token sale where the project's marketing efforts were superior to its smart contracts. The DAO token generation event, launched from Switzerland by a Swiss foundation, was wildly successful, rapidly raising some $150 million to $250 million[17] in digital currency, depending on the date of calculation. However, due to a vulnerability in the smart contract code, a bad actor was able to remove roughly US$50 million shortly thereafter. This caused a heated debate in the blockchain community, with some taking the position that "code is law", and that, essentially, it is rightful to exploit a software design flaw, while others argued that "code is code" and "law is law", and that no-one who participated in The DAO crowdsale would have done so with the expectation that their contributions would be removed in such a way. The ensuing struggle led to the so-called "hard fork" of Ethereum, which resulted in a new blockchain diverging from the then-existing Ethereum blockchain. On what is now referred to as "Ethereum," an earlier block was appended to the blockchain, essentially resulting in those who contributed to The DAO crowdfund being "refunded" the digital tokens that they had donated, so that no-one was harmed. On the legacy blockchain, now called "Ethereum Classic," the original transaction by the bad actor was not "erased" and lives on.

Understanding the story of The DAO is important for multiple reasons.

First, in 2016, The DAO initially was viewed – by token sellers and investors alike – as a success story, a model of how to conduct a token offering (other than with respect to the smart contract vulnerabilities).

> "*The DAO was launched on April 30, 2016, at 10:00am GMT/UTC (by several "anonymous" submissions associated with DAOhub, who executed the open source bytecode on the Ethereum blockchain), with a set funding or "creation" period of 28 days (A2be, 2016). As the funding period came to a close (concluding May 28, 2016), The DAO went live with the equivalent of about US$250m[illion] in funding, breaking all existing crowdfunding records. Some 10,000 to 20,000 (estimated) people invested in The DAO, contributing 11,994,260.98 Ethereum tokens (known as ether, or ETH), which amounted to about 14% of the total ETH supply.*"[18]

When certain lawyers, including the author of this chapter, raised U.S. securities law concerns, responses from certain token sellers often approximated, "Well, The DAO did it, and no one is going after them." Despite many of the same lawyers noting that The DAO likely ran afoul of myriad laws around the world, some organisations and individuals were unpersuaded. In fact, anecdotally, some token sellers may have decided to follow The DAO's Swiss foundation token-generation model at the specific behest of potential contributors. Why? While reasons may vary, some token generators (and contributors) evidently believed that a non-profit entity could not issue securities,[19] as well as that the term "foundation" would sound trustworthy to prospective purchasers or contributors.[20]

Second, because all of those who had contributed money to The DAO token generation event had been refunded and The DAO itself had been disbanded, it gave the SEC a strong, useful opportunity for a "teachable moment" to warn the blockchain and crypto community, and their lawyers, that digital token sales may be sales of securities, without the backdrop of continuing harm requiring practical redress. In July 2017, the SEC's Division of Enforcement published a "report of investigation" ("The DAO Report") making clear that The DAO violated U.S. federal securities laws when it sold tokens with the goal of funding certain projects without registering the offering.[21,22] The DAO fundraising had been a sale of securities under U.S. federal securities laws.

In The DAO Report, the SEC emphasised that sales of digital tokens may be "investment contracts," and, therefore, securities. In doing so, the SEC applied the so-called *Howey* test, an over 70-year-old, four-prong, facts-and-circumstances test that asks whether there has been (i) an investment of money, (ii) in a common enterprise, (iii) with a reasonable expectation of profit, (iv) with such profit being solely or primarily based on the managerial or entrepreneurial efforts of others.[23]

The DAO Report didn't stop there, however. The SEC also indicated that, because The DAO Tokens were securities, the platforms on which The DAO Tokens were bought, sold or traded were securities exchanges, which meant that The DAO platform needed to register as a national securities exchange, or avail itself of an exemption from registration, such as by registering as an alternative trading system or broker-dealer.[24] This had follow-on implications for the many unregulated crypto exchanges around the world serving U.S. persons, of which the SEC reminded exchanges in 2018.[25]

In a footnote to The DAO Report, the SEC raised the possibility that The DAO also may have been an investment company but noted that, because The DAO had never commenced its business operations funding projects, the SEC declined to conduct such analysis.[26]

Some other key takeaways from The DAO Report included the following:

- No matter where in the world one launches a token sale from, a token issuer must comply with U.S. securities laws if tokens are being marketed, issued or sold to U.S. persons. Indeed, the fact that The DAO was a Swiss foundation did not exempt it from compliance with U.S. federal securities laws.

- The SEC will disregard form and focus on substance when it comes to sales of digital tokens. Notwithstanding the creation of new technology and new terminology, the principles-based U.S. securities laws are intended to be broad enough to contemplate such innovations. For instance, although The DAO involved a decentralised autonomous organisation, the SEC still found that there was an "issuer" as contemplated by U.S. securities laws. And although contributions were made to The DAO in digital tokens, including Ethereum, which the SEC referred to in The DAO Report as a "virtual currency," the SEC found that there had been an investment of money.

However, while informative, and while it confirmed the views of many responsible securities lawyers,[27] The DAO Report left many questions unanswered. As noted previously, The DAO was a virtual venture fund. It was an example of a digital token that in many ways looked just like a traditional security. While the SEC made clear that a token that looked just like a security was in fact a security, it did not provide guidance as to the facts and circumstances under which a token would not be a security. For instance, if a token had a consumptive use, or some non-incidental utility, what were the boundaries for when a sale of such a token was not a sale of a security? While The DAO Report provided clear guidance based on its idiosyncratic facts, it did not provide much clarity in other contexts.

A brief word on why it matters at all if a token sale is a sale of securities. With roots in the stock market crash of 1929 – the culmination of a period rife with speculation, poor investor disclosure and rampant fraud – the mandate of U.S. securities regulators is investor protection. Many investors lack the sophistication, experience, savings cushion or income level to appreciate the risks inherent in investments in securities, or to bear the risk of a failed investment. For that reason, sales of securities are required to comply with robust disclosure requirements (including disclosure of things that are likely to be material to a purchase decision, such as information about the issuer and the proposed use of proceeds) that sales of software typically do not include, as well as explicit descriptions of potential investment risk factors. As evidenced by the tremendous variability among token project white papers, some of which may contain false promises, little to no description of the team, nearly incomprehensible token and network descriptions, or mere marketing fluff, full and fair disclosure is a goal that likely would be helpful, even if tokens were deemed not to be securities.[28]

Notably, the SEC had focused on The DAO and not on Ethereum (or, Ethereum Classic). Had Ethereum been deemed to be a security, presumably the entire economy of ERC-20 and, later, ERC-721 and other tokens, built on the Ethereum blockchain, would have been in legal peril. The SEC could have cut off at the knees nearly the entire token sale industry, but it chose not to.

Searching for solutions

By autumn 2017, the *Howey* test was being quoted (*ad nauseum*) at cocktail parties by lawyers, technologists and investors alike. Industry groups, such as the Wall Street Blockchain Alliance Legal Working Group and Wharton Reg@Tech, among others, were wrestling actively with the application of *Howey* and its progeny on token sales, trying to develop a common view of situations in which an initial token sale was unlikely to be a sale of securities.

Many in the community drew a distinction between those tokens that were being sold for consumptive use (albeit usually at an uncertain future date) and those that were being sold for investment purposes. However, the growing popularity of token sales and interest by traditional accredited investors, including VC funds, high-net-worth individuals, and certain family offices, in purchasing or pre-purchasing digital tokens (sometimes for a deep discount and little to no lockup) appeared in some ways at odds with the assertion that a given token was being sold other than as an investment. Often, those traditional investors had little interest in actually using the purchased tokens, or purchased or pre-purchased tokens in a quantity that such investors were unlikely to use.

In the background, many of these digital tokens were being traded around the world on unregulated token exchanges, many of which were accessible to U.S. persons, whether accredited or "Main Street" (i.e., "mom-and-pop") investors. While some in the crypto community pointed to the importance of such exchanges for helping to get tokens in the hands of potential users worldwide and amplifying a "network effect" and demand to access a particular token ecosystem, others acknowledged that unregulated exchanges were critical for driving appreciation of the token's price. Intentionally or not, the existence of the secondary market for digital tokens contributed to the expectation of profit by token purchasers.

Unfortunately for investors, if a token were deemed to be a security, The DAO Report made clear that such token could not trade on a platform accessible by U.S. persons, unless such platform registered as a national securities exchange or as an alternative trading system or broker-dealer (with attendant significant compliance requirements). Many unregulated exchanges did not want to register as such, and some therefore attempted to restrict access by U.S. persons to such exchanges, or limited listed tokens to those that they were confident – or had been advised by lawyers or token sellers – were less likely to be securities. Unfortunately, even if one were to acknowledge that a given token sale was a sale of securities, no alternative trading systems then existed on which such tokens could be traded.[29]

Moreover, if token sales were sales of securities, then such sales would need to be registered pursuant to U.S. securities laws (perhaps on a Form S-1) or be effected pursuant to an exemption from registration, such as Regulation D (accredited investors), Regulation S (non-U.S. persons), Regulation A+ (mini-IPO) or Regulation CF (crowdfunding capped at US$1,070,000), in each case, under the Securities Act. For token sellers that wished to sell tokens to U.S. persons who were *not* accredited investors[30] – which arguably may have included some of the very people who most wanted to purchase tokens for their intended consumptive use – some of the most convenient exemptions from registration, such as conducting a private placement under Regulation D, generally would not permit that.

And even for U.S. accredited investors, if tokens were securities and were sold pursuant to Regulation D, there would be corresponding compliance requirements, such as significant transfer restrictions (typically one year for companies that are not already SEC reporting companies) and, for Rule 506(c) offerings, a statutory requirement to take reasonable steps to verify that the token purchasers were, in fact, accredited.[31]

If tokens were securities, then there would be potential follow-on effects for nearly the entire universe of crypto market participants. Those marketing token sales risked becoming unregistered broker-dealers and unlicensed investment advisors, and transaction-based pricing for token transactions (whether or not paid in tokens) risked raising broker-dealer issues. Investment company and investment advisor rules and regulations would be implicated for funds investing in tokens. The domino effects would be significant for the nascent and burgeoning cryptocurrency community.

However, as significant funds were being raised by token sellers in presales, sometimes long before the tokens or the token networks were created, to fund the projects' development, could anything be done to stop the resulting tokens – which presumably were intended for consumptive use – from being deemed securities?

The SAFT

Enter the SAFT Project.[32] Introduced as a proposal for discussion and further iteration, the SAFT (Simple Agreement for Future Tokens) was embraced quickly by a market hungry for a solution. Based generally on a SAFE (Simple Agreement for Future Equity), SAFTs were not invented by the creators of the SAFT Project, but they were made immensely popular by it. At its most basic, the SAFT white paper proposed that a SAFT, an executory contract for the future sale of tokens, was itself a security but that the resulting token – to be delivered at a time when the token and network were "functional" – would not be a security. By conceptually bifurcating the presale of a token from the token itself, one purportedly could sell a SAFT to accredited investors, pursuant to Regulation D, who were purchasing the SAFT for investment, yet allow such investors ultimately to receive a token that was not a security. The rationale was that before the network and token were "functional," purchasers of "pre-functional" tokens would bear enterprise risk, while, once the token was "functional," token purchasers would bear product risk.[33] The form of SAFT proposed by the SAFT white paper expressly stated that purchasers of the SAFT were purchasing the SAFT solely for investment, rather than for use, and did not describe the terms or minimum characteristics of the tokens ultimately to be delivered.

Many in the market began using SAFTs, including the verbatim form of SAFT attached as a discussion piece to the SAFT white paper, sometimes without even engaging legal counsel. Some reportedly created SAFTs without consulting non-U.S. lawyers, sometimes resulting in non-U.S. entities (such as Swiss foundations) being obligated to do things that they simply could not do under their applicable jurisdiction of formation's laws. Critics of the SAFT spoke out, identifying limitations in the proposed form of SAFT and potential weaknesses in the underlying legal rationale. Among them, the Cardozo Blockchain Project released "Not So Fast – Risks Related to the Use of a 'SAFT' for Token Sales" (the "Cardozo Blockchain Report").[34] The Cardozo Blockchain Report argued, among other things, that conceptually separating the SAFT from the underlying token was an artificial distinction, and if a significant percentage of those tokens were being presold by the token seller to persons who had expressly represented that they were purchasing the tokens for investment and not for use, that could make it more, rather than less, likely that the tokens themselves were being sold as investment contracts. Moreover, the Cardozo Blockchain Project asserted that the line between when software is "pre-functional" versus "functional" is not bright. It also raised policy questions regarding whether sales of software should be limited to accredited investors.

In some ways, it seemed that opinions for or against the SAFT white paper divided traditional VCs and other accredited investors, who looked to SAFTs as a way to facilitate investment in the space and help technologists fund the building of token ecosystems, and decentralisation purists, who stressed that many of those most likely to use tokens for their intended purpose were not accredited investors, and that classifying tokens as securities would cause them to be more difficult to obtain and more complicated to use. Today, with the benefit of regulatory hindsight, some in the market continue to use pre-sale documents, including some executory contracts that may be called "SAFTs," but often with the assumption that the underlying token will at all times be a security and employing substantially different substantive terms from the SAFT Project's illustrative starting point.

While the SAFT framework continues to be a lightning rod for strong opinions, and ongoing debate ensues regarding whether the overall SAFT model is, or should be, dead[35] or alive,[36] one of the underlying themes raised in the SAFT white paper – the importance of token functionality to the securities law analysis – appears to have been validated by certain regulators. Notably (and irrespective of whether one believes that software functionality is a grey area), in 2018, certain governmental bodies, including Switzerland's Financial Market Supervisory Authority ("FINMA")[37] and, more recently, SEC Director Hinman,[38] have referenced the "pre-functional" versus "functional" distinction as a factor when assessing whether the sale of a token with a consumptive use would be a sale of a security (or jurisdictional equivalent).[39]

Indeed, to some, an October 2017 quote from one of the crypto industry's most ardent and vocal supporters of the SAFT framework may now sound almost prescient:

> "*I think almost all pre-functional tokens result in a security per U.S. law,*" says [Marco] *Santori, noting that this is a controversial stance in a world in which so many token sales occur before the issuers have launched a network. "Just because utility tokens will one day have a consumptive use, does that remove them from security status prior to that use? On its face, the answer is no.*"[40]

Chairman Clayton and "Hallmarks of a Security"

Despite regulatory uncertainty, initial token sales continued to accelerate as 2017 wore on. SEC Chairman Jay Clayton's bold statement, "I have yet to see an ICO that doesn't have a sufficient number of hallmarks of a security," demonstrated the SEC staff's concern that, notwithstanding The DAO Report, non-compliant token sales were continuing.[41] Chairman Clayton also targeted unregulated token exchanges, noting, "In addition to requiring platforms that are engaging in the activities of an exchange to either register as national securities exchanges or seek an exemption from registration, the Commission will continue to seek clarity for investors on how tokens are listed on these exchanges and the standards for listing; how tokens are valued; and what protections are in place for market integrity and investor protection."[42]

Munchee and manner of sale

In the months after The DAO Report was released, the SEC announced[43] its new Cyber Unit focused on the token sale space, cracked down on ICO-related scams and frauds[44] and engaged in educational outreach to potential token purchasers.[45] Many founders, lawyers and others in the space concentrated on devising tokens with a consumptive use, trying to "fail" the *Howey* test. While the term "utility token" had existed prior to The DAO Report, post-DAO Report, the term was used so frequently and in so many situations as to make the label nearly meaningless. As one industry reporter noted in 2017, "Recently, terms like 'app coin,' 'app token,' 'utility token' and 'utility coin' have seemed to proliferate. But, what they all have in common is this: people use them interchangeably to mean 'a token that is not a security.'"[46]

One hurdle with the *Howey* test related to its "reasonable expectation of profits" prong, and whether that should be a subjective or objective test. If it were a subjective test, it could result in different outcomes, depending on the individual purchaser. For instance, one could purchase Ethereum with the intent to use it as "gas"[47] to execute smart contracts on the Ethereum blockchain. Alternatively, one could purchase Ethereum for investment purposes, as a store of value, with the expectation that its value likely would increase over time.

If the "reasonable expectation of profits" were an objective test, one would look to the actions of the token seller and its agents to see whether they had given purchasers a reasonable expectation of profits. To some lawyers in the crypto space, this seemed to be a more appropriate and consistent method of determining whether a token sale was a sale of securities. It also found support in the line of cases that followed *Howey*, including *Glenn W. Turner*,[48] which focused on the manner of sale of the token seller – namely, that by marketing a token as an investment, one could create a security, even if the token characteristics, on their face, would not appear to be those of a security.

At the time, seemingly countless, carefully structured "utility" tokens were being marketed by those promising returns on investment or network growth, whether by token sellers or by those promoting token sales. Indeed, some token sellers offered "bounties" to token purchasers[49] who encouraged their friends to purchase tokens, without policing the sales activities of the individual promoters. In many cases, the token sellers and others in the space were well intentioned and not fraudsters; however, they still may have been selling unregistered securities without availing themselves of an exemption from registration.[50]

In December 2017, the SEC announced its next warning to the token industry, when it published a Cease and Desist Order (the "Munchee Order") issued to a California corporation, Munchee, Inc. ("Munchee"), halting an ongoing token sale for the MUN Token and requiring the token seller to return funds to those who already had purchased tokens.[51]

The Munchee Order was notable because it reportedly was the first time that the SEC had stopped a token sale without any allegations of fraud. The MUN Token was a self-described "utility token" that would be used in connection with an iPhone app to rank restaurant meals, and Munchee's white paper referenced having received legal guidance that the MUN Token was not a security under the *Howey* test, although it did not include such legal analysis in the white paper.

Nonetheless, the SEC found that the MUN Token sale was a sale of securities, because, among other things, Munchee's and its agents' marketing and sales activities primed MUN Token purchasers to have a reasonable expectation of profit.[52] In other words, those lawyers who had cautioned of the importance of "manner of sale" had been correct. It really did matter – and it mattered a lot.

In the Munchee Order, the SEC detailed a number of activities that promoted a reasonable expectation of profit by token purchasers:

- Although the restaurants were to be located only in the United States, Munchee had marketed the MUN Token to potential purchasers worldwide.

- Rather than marketing the MUN Token to those interested in the restaurant industry who might use the MUN Token, Munchee had marketed to those in Bitcoin chat rooms, who were interested in investing in digital tokens.

- The MUN Token white paper contained a flow-chart illustration showing that as market adoption increased, the value of the MUN Token was likely to increase. While this objectively may have been a true statement, the SEC said that it gave potential purchasers an expectation of an increase in value of their investments.

- Munchee noted that it would promote secondary market liquidity and expected to have the MUN Token listed on unregulated token exchanges.[53]

The SEC's Cyber Unit had also scoured social media and cited evidence of a YouTube video in which a person unrelated to the Munchee team had been predicting great increases in the value of the MUN Token, which Munchee evidently had "liked" or linked to, arguably endorsing those statements.[54]

The SEC did not stop there, however. Instead, the SEC cautioned that even if the MUN Token had had a "practical use at the time of the offering" (which it did not), that still would not have insulated the MUN Token from being a security.[55]

Moreover, the SEC emphasised that "[w]hether or not a particular transaction involves the offer and sale of a security – regardless of the terminology used – will depend on the facts and circumstances, including the economic realities of the transaction." In other words, merely referring to a token as a "utility token" would not make its sale not a sale of securities.

While the MUN Token sale provided the SEC with a virtual treasure trove of "what not to do" examples, similar to The DAO Report guidance, the Munchee Order left many unanswered questions. For example, had Munchee and its agents not marketed the token sale as a sale of securities, would the outcome had been different? Or did the "economic realities" that the value of the token would be based on the efforts of others – in this case, Munchee – and the mere existence of a robust secondary market mean that all initial token sales were, nearly by definition, sales of securities? Unfortunately, no definition of "economic realities" was given in the Munchee Order, leaving many technologists' and their lawyers' hunger for bright-line guidance unsated.

Post-Munchee, many responsible lawyers took the position that the window for determining which initial token sales to U.S. persons, if any, were not sales of securities had become exceedingly narrow. In turn, many adopted the conservative view that any initial token sale to U.S. persons should be conducted as a sale of securities, absent express SEC guidance to the contrary.

SEC Chairman Clayton's call to gatekeepers and joint statement by SEC and CFTC Chairmen

On the day of the Munchee Order's publication, SEC Chairman Clayton issued a powerful reminder to "gatekeepers," such as lawyers, exchanges, accountants, broker-dealers and consultants involved in the token sale space, of their obligations to exercise their judgment and expertise with the goal of investor protection. Some in the market viewed this as a criticism by the SEC Chairman of market participants who may have encouraged "utility token" sales without considering manner of sale or economic realities.[56] In the same piece, Chairman Clayton cautioned retail (i.e., "Main Street") investors to pose extensive and tough questions to token sellers and to be sure that such investors understand and appreciate the risks of purchasing digital tokens prior to purchasing them.

One month later, in an op-ed published in the *Wall Street Journal, portions of which were published on the SEC's website*, Chairman Clayton and J. Christopher Giancarlo, the Chairman of the CFTC, said that the risks of ICOs are high and that "[c]aution is merited."[57]

> "The two Chairmen described the challenges that they face in attempting to monitor and regulate cryptocurrency activities. For example, they noted that federal authority to apply anti-money laundering rules to these activities is clear, but the ability to regulate other aspects of this market is 'murkier.' Acknowledging that distributed

ledger technology 'may in fact be the next great disruptive and productivity-enhancing economic development,' the regulators made it clear that they 'will not allow it or any other advancement to disrupt our commitment to fair and sound markets.'"[58]

Litigation and enforcement activity

The intensification of ICO activity in 2017 and 2018 saw a concomitant rise in private securities litigation against ICO issuers and promoters, as well as regulatory enforcement activity (including, notably, by the SEC). Of particular note, in late 2017, multiple class action lawsuits were filed against the founders and issuer of the US$232 million Tezos ICO (one of the largest ICOs completed during the recent market cycle).[59] With the benefit of hindsight in the form of the Munchee ruling and other SEC pronouncements that, in many cases, was unavailable to token sellers and their legal counsel at the time of the ICOs themselves, plaintiffs' lawyers may be well positioned to identify securities law compliance deficiencies in a number of completed ICOs.

At the time of this writing, litigation activity can be expected to continue, particularly in the face of an arguable cryptocurrency bear market, and as some blockchain projects may fail to realise the visions of their respective white papers. It is important to distinguish, however, between fraudsters and scammers, on the one hand, and those technologists and founders that have proceeded in good faith to develop their projects[60] and may have sought, and followed, the advice of their legal counsels. Similarly, given the volatility of the crypto markets, it is key to distinguish those token purchasers who may have been defrauded from those who may merely regret having used one form of token, such as Bitcoin or Ethereum, to obtain in an ICO a different kind of digital token – particularly if, as sometimes was the case in the latter part of 2017, the value of the Bitcoin or Ether later rose, while the value of the purchased token may have fallen.[61] This is similar to the famous "Bitcoin Pizza Day" purchaser, who likely wishes that he could return the two Papa John's pizzas that he purchased in 2010 for 10,000 Bitcoins (then equal to about US$25.00).[62]

For its part, the SEC has clearly marked ICO activity as a high enforcement priority, including by taking enforcement action to halt fraudulent ICO schemes[63] and, in a likely harbinger of future significant enforcement action, issuing subpoenas to dozens of ICO issuers and their advisors.[64]

A new asset class?

Even as U.S. securities regulators continued to characterise tokens sold to U.S. persons as securities and flexed enforcement muscles, prominent voices in the crypto community opined that the token sale space had contributed to the emergence of not just a new method for distribution and sale of software and project fundraising, but, potentially, a new asset class. Unlike traditional securities, such as equity or debt, many tokens had – and, in fact, were intentionally designed to have – consumptive uses, entitling the holder to purchase goods or services or granting access rights to a blockchain platform or decentralised application. Shoehorning such tokens into a rigid U.S. securities law framework might work, if imperfectly, for governance of initial sales and resales but, almost paradoxically, would not likely work in any logical or efficient manner for purchasers who actually had purchased such consumptive tokens for such tokens' intended uses.

In March 2018, the Wyoming Blockchain Coalition, led by Caitlin Long and Wyoming House Representative Tyler Lindholm,[65] among others, celebrated the successful passage by the State of Wyoming of five popular new blockchain-related laws, including House Bill 70,[66] which exempted from Wyoming state securities and money transmitters laws a category of consumptive tokens. Taking the position that consumptive blockchain tokens constituted a new asset class, and that property typically is the purview of state, rather than federal, law, House Bill 70 was loosely modelled on token classifications promulgated by FINMA (the Swiss securities regulator)[67] and provided exemptions for what it defined as "open blockchain tokens" that are not marketed as investments and that are exchangeable for goods or services.

SEC staff express openness to technological innovations

By early May 2018, SEC Commissioner Hester Peirce had delivered "Beaches and Bitcoin: Remarks before the Medici Conference,"[68] a contemplative speech that examined different types of tokens and invited questions about whether traditional U.S. federal securities law exemptions, such as Regulation D, worked well for token sales. Peirce's remarks were well received by many in the crypto community who appreciated that the regulator appeared to understand that tokens' innovative and flexible structuring might cause existing U.S. securities to fit imperfectly or be inappropriate. Commissioner Peirce lauded so-called "regulatory sandboxes" as a means of testing new technology without a heavy yoke of regulation and, extending the analogy, likened the appropriate role of a regulator to that of a lifeguard on a beach. Of particular note, Commissioner Peirce posited that all ICOs are not necessarily securities offerings: "Given the undeveloped nature of this area, I am wary of any blanket designation for all ICOs. Instead, the best path forward, at least for the time being, is to evaluate the facts and circumstances of each offering."

In June 2018, the SEC announced that Valerie Szczepanik had been named Associate Director of the SEC's Division of Corporation Finance, and Senior Advisor for Digital Assets and Innovation for Division Director, Bill Hinman.[69] Noting that it had newly created such advisory position, the SEC explained that "[....] Szczepanik will coordinate efforts across all SEC Divisions and Offices regarding the application of U.S. securities laws to emerging digital asset technologies and innovations, including Initial Coin Offerings and cryptocurrencies." Previously Assistant Director in the SEC's Division of Enforcement's Cyber Unit, and, currently, Head of the SEC's Distributed Ledger Technology Working Group, Co-Head of its Dark Web Working Group, and a member of its FinTech Working Group, Szczepanik's thought leadership within, and comprehension of, the crypto space made her appointment heartening to many in the blockchain community.[70]

> "[....] Not only is her promotion a sign that the Feds are ready to tackle crypto regulation in earnest, but also a hint that they are willing to cooperate meaningfully with the blockchain industry. Recognized as someone who roots for the healthy balance between investor protection and facilitating technology development, she is well-situated to reconcile the two to the extent it is possible at all. [....]"[71]

Later that month, in an interview with CNBC, SEC Chairman Clayton appeared to draw a distinction[72] between cryptocurrencies, such as Bitcoin, which he characterised as being a substitute for dollars or yen, and which he indicated was not security, with tokens sold pursuant to initial token sale to fund a venture, which he described as being securities. While Chairman Clayton reiterated that most ICOs involve an offering of securities, and indicated that the SEC would not change the definition of a security to suit the ICO community, he did acknowledge that blockchain technology has "incredible promise," and "can drive efficiencies not only in the financial markets but in a lot of markets."[73]

Director Hinman's speech: present-day Ethereum sales are not sales of securities

In a move that was celebrated by many in the crypto community, on June 14, 2018, William Hinman, Director for the Division of Corporation Finance for the SEC, gave a landmark speech[74] (the "Hinman Speech") that appears to have settled, at least unofficially, an enduring and troubling securities law question for the token sale industry: What about sales of Ethereum?[75] Were they sales of investment contracts?

Born via a token generation event using a Swiss foundation structure not unlike the one employed by The DAO, Ethereum had since attained broad adoption and use as "gas" by developers wishing to build and run smart contracts on the Ethereum blockchain, including other tokens or decentralised applications (dApps). The native token of Ethereum was also purchased in the secondary market by many who hoped that it would increase in value. Ethereum was also accepted as payment by numerous token generators, including The DAO, in their token offerings. Indeed, in The DAO Report, the SEC had referred to Ethereum as a "virtual currency."

Unlike Bitcoin (which SEC Chairman Clayton had clarified was not a security),[76] which relies upon a "proof of work" consensus model pursuant to which miners can be awarded an intentionally finite number of Bitcoin (capped by its creator(s), Satoshi Nakamoto, at 21 million),[77] the Ethereum Foundation originally had held an ICO for a then "pre-functional" token. However, was anyone really thinking about the Ethereum Foundation's 2018 activities, if any, when determining the value of Ethereum? Were accredited investors or retail purchasers thinking about the Ethereum Foundation at all when making purchasing decisions? Would it make sense to restrict Ethereum purchases by computer programmers, who might have PhDs and understand precisely how the tokens worked, yet not qualify as accredited investors, while permitting token purchases by those who had sufficient wealth or income, yet no comprehension of the technology?

If the SEC were to say that Ethereum was an illegally issued security, it arguably would have been perilous for the entire crypto industry. And to what avail? In 2018, was any token issuer in a position to provide periodic reporting under the Exchange Act? Would purchasers be better served by requiring that Ethereum be traded on alternative trading systems or by requiring developers to employ a brokerage account in order to use Ethereum for its intended purpose? Arguably, if Ethereum were determined to be a security, would that help protect those vulnerable investors whom U.S. regulators wanted to protect, or would it, in fact, cause the very economic harm that the SEC and other regulators were trying to avoid?

The Hinman Speech was striking because it addressed head-on a token-related situation that was neither a scam, nor an obvious sale of securities. The facts of Ethereum did not add up clearly to a lesson in what not to do, unlike The DAO or Munchee. There was no easy answer for the SEC.

It is difficult to prove a negative. The Hinman Speech arguably marked the first time that the SEC said that a specific token born from an ICO was not a security. In doing so, however, Hinman did not say that the initial Ethereum Foundation crowdfund, of the token now known as Ethereum Classic, had not been a sale of securities. In fact, Hinman specifically declined to comment on whether Ethereum had been born as a security, stating: "[P]utting aside the fundraising that accompanied the creation of Ether . . . current offers and sales of Ether are not securities transactions."

By making such a distinction, Hinman built on concepts raised by Commissioner Peirce's speech and introduced the concept that a token's status as a security need not be fixed at the moment of its sale, stating that the securities law analysis is "not static and does not strictly inhere to the instrument." Instead, the attributes of a particular token that cause it to be a security may evolve over time, and that such evolution ultimately may cause such token, or a subsequently issued token, no longer to be a security.

Importantly, Hinman drew a nuanced distinction between a digital token itself, and the way that such token is sold, stating:

> "[....] Returning to the ICOs I am seeing, strictly speaking, the token – or coin or whatever the digital information packet is called – all by itself is not a security, just as the orange groves in Howey were not. Central to determining whether a security is being sold is how it is being sold, and the reasonable expectations of purchasers. When someone buys a housing unit to live in, it is probably not a security.[6] But under certain circumstances, the same asset can be offered and sold in a way that causes investors to have a reasonable expectation of profits based on the efforts of others. For example, if the housing unit is offered with a management contract or other services, it can be a security.[7] Similarly, when a CD, exempt from being treated as a security under Section 3 of the Securities Act, is sold as a part of a program organized by a broker who offers retail investors promises of liquidity and the potential to profit from changes in interest rates, the Gary Plastic case teaches us that the instrument can be part of an investment contract that is a security.[8]

> The same reasoning applies to digital assets. The digital asset itself is simply code. But the way it is sold – as part of an investment; to non-users; by promoters to develop the enterprise – can be, and, in that context, most often is, a security – because it evidences an investment contract. And regulating these transactions as securities transactions makes sense."[78]

Decentralisation, according to Hinman, is a key determinant of whether a sale or resale of a given token was likely to be a sale of securities, and decentralisation could develop over time, even after an ICO. Indeed, Hinman stated, "[I]f the network on which the token or coin is to function is sufficiently decentralised – where purchasers would no longer reasonably expect a person or group to carry out essential managerial or entrepreneurial efforts – the assets may not represent an investment contract."

Just as purchasers of Ethereum may be unlikely to look to the Ethereum Foundation to carry out managerial or entrepreneurial efforts concerning Ether, Hinman indicated that it may be possible for certain tokens sold to U.S. accredited investors via SAFTs ultimately to no longer be securities, if they one day become part of a sufficiently decentralised token ecosystem. This fluid and ongoing analysis was heartening to many in the market who feared that a token born as a security via an ICO or purchase via a SAFT would forever after remain a security, even in subsequent secondary market transactions. Indeed, some legal practitioners had lamented that "Wall Street plumbing,"[79] and periodic reporting and other traditional U.S. federal securities law requirements, would not work for and would, in fact, thwart the use of consumptive tokens, as well as stymie network growth.

Why would sufficient decentralisation be a meaningful distinction that would enable certain consumptive token sales no longer to be classified as sales of securities, meaning that purchasers would no longer have the benefit of certain protections afforded by the U.S. federal securities laws? The Hinman Speech reminded listeners that the "impetus of the Securities Act is to remove the information asymmetry between promoters and investors," by requiring that sellers of securities make certain disclosures and engage in periodic reporting. This disclosure may be critical when a purchaser must rely on a seller's entrepreneurial or managerial efforts to develop and promote a project, in order for the value of a token to be maintained or increased. "When the efforts of the third party are no longer a key factor for determining the enterprise's success, material information asymmetries recede. As a network becomes truly decentralised, the ability to identify an issuer or promoter to make the requisite disclosures becomes difficult, and less meaningful."

Hinman advised those in the market, including lawyers, to "consider whether a third party – be it a person, entity or coordinated group of actors – drives the expectation of a return" when assessing whether a given token sale may be a sale of securities. To help guide this facts-and-circumstances analysis, Hinman suggested a non-exhaustive list of considerations:

"1. Is there a person or group that has sponsored or promoted the creation and sale of the digital asset, the efforts of whom play a significant role in the development and maintenance of the asset and its potential increase in value?

2. Has this person or group retained a stake or other interest in the digital asset such that it would be motivated to expend efforts to cause an increase in value in the digital asset? Would purchasers reasonably believe such efforts will be undertaken and may result in a return on their investment in the digital asset?

3. Has the promoter raised an amount of funds in excess of what may be needed to establish a functional network and, if so, has it indicated how those funds may be used to support the value of the tokens or to increase the value of the enterprise? Does the promoter continue to expend funds from proceeds or operations to enhance the functionality and/ or value of the system within which the tokens operate?

4. Are purchasers "investing," that is, seeking a return? In that regard, is the instrument marketed and sold to the general public instead of to potential users of the network for a price that reasonably correlates with the market value of the good or service in the network?

5. Does application of the Securities Act of 1933's protections make sense? Is there a person or entity others are relying on that plays a key role in the profit-making of the enterprise such that disclosure of their activities and plans would be important to investors? Do informational asymmetries exist between the promoters and potential purchasers/investors in the digital asset?

6. Do persons or entities other than the promoter exercise governance rights or meaningful influence?"

Director Hinman also focused on whether a token may, in certain circumstances, cease to be a security, emphasising "contractual or technical ways to structure digital assets so they function more like a consumer item and less like a security."

Noting that the SEC staff "would look to the economic substance of the transaction," Hinman asked that token "promoters and their counsels" consider the following questions, among other possible features:

"1. Is token creation commensurate with meeting the needs of users or, rather, with feeding speculation?

2. Are independent actors setting the price or is the promoter supporting the secondary market for the asset or otherwise influencing trading?

3. Is it clear that the primary motivation for purchasing the digital asset is for personal use or consumption, as compared to investment? Have purchasers made representations as to their consumptive, as opposed to their investment, intent? Are the tokens available in increments that correlate with a consumptive versus investment intent?

4. Are the tokens distributed in ways to meet users' needs? For example, can the tokens be held or transferred only in amounts that correspond to a purchaser's expected use? Are there built-in incentives that compel using the tokens promptly on the network, such as having the tokens degrade in value over time, or can the tokens be held for extended periods for investment?

5. Is the asset marketed and distributed to potential users or the general public?

6. Are the assets dispersed across a diverse user base or concentrated in the hands of a few that can exert influence over the application?

7. Is the application fully functioning or in early stages of development?"

In a footnote to the Hinman Speech, Director Hinman expressly declined "to opine on the legality or appropriateness of a SAFT," and reminded listeners that "[b]ecause the legal analysis must follow the economic realities of the particular facts of an offering, it may not be fruitful to debate a hypothetical structure in the abstract." Yet, the Hinman Speech arguably provided the possibility of a path forward for those who may have been parties to certain SAFTs, whether as token sellers or purchasers, and had sought ultimately to sell or purchase "functional" tokens that were not securities. For instance, the Hinman Speech identified the question of an application's stage of functionality (e.g., "fully functioning" *vs.* "early stages of development") as one of several factors for consideration when determining whether a given consumptive token was a security.[80] In addition, Director Hinman continued in a footnote, "From the discussion in this speech, however, it is clear I believe a token once offered in a security offering can, depending on the circumstances, later be offered in a non-securities transaction. I expect that some, perhaps many, may not. I encourage anyone that has questions on a particular SAFT structure to consult with knowledgeable securities counsel or the staff."

While groundbreaking in its assertion that certain consumptive tokens sold pursuant to an initial token sale might someday morph into non-securities, the Hinman Speech did not provide a clear roadmap pursuant to which token sellers, other market participants and their lawyers could objectively identify a consumptive token that was sufficiently decentralised as to no longer be a security, or how a token that initially may have been expressly issued as a security might extricate itself from securities law requirements, including any ongoing reporting requirements.[81]

Subsequent to the Hinman Speech, SEC Chairman Clayton made public statements in support of the points raised by the Hinman Speech,[82] and many legal practitioners expect during the second half of 2018 to participate in ongoing discussions in working groups and with regulators to elucidate the markers of sufficient decentralisation.

Tomahawk: Token giveaways as sales of securities

Even as the SEC continued to reinforce that tokens sold to U.S. persons through ICOs were very likely to be sales of securities, some in the crypto space continued to believe that token give-aways were different. Perhaps taking the view that the Howey test's "investment of money" prong would not be implicated if tokens were gifted or made available for no monetary consideration, rather than being "sold" pursuant to an ICO, some believed that token give-aways provided a method to allow both retail and accredited investors to receive tokens that were not securities.

While certain legal advisors had long cautioned token issuers that giving away a particular token, whether through "bounties" or so-called "air-drops," could still be a sale of securities,[83] the SEC had not addressed this issue directly in the digital token context. On August 14, 2018, that changed, when the SEC published a cease-and-desist order (the "Tomahawk Order")[84] focusing, among other things, on a token issuer that had instituted a token bounty program to promote its ICO. While the issuer, Tomahawk, "did not raise any money through" and, ultimately, abandoned its planned ICO, Tomahawk nonetheless issued, pursuant to its "Bounty Program," more than 80,000 TOM tokens to third parties who had assisted in marketing the token, whether using social media or otherwise.

Having first determined that the TOM token was an equity security,[85] the SEC stated that "[t]he ICO and Bounty Program constituted an offer of securities" under the Securities Act, "because it involved 'an attempt or offer to dispose of, or solicitation of an offer to buy, a security or interest in a security, for value.'" Moreover, the SEC's analysis clarified that the token giveaway was, in fact, a sale of securities, stating: "the distribution of TOM pursuant to the Bounty Program constituted sales under Section 2(a)(3) of the Securities Act, which applies to "every disposition of a security or interest in a security, for value.'"

Explaining that "a 'gift' of a security is a 'sale' within the meaning of the Securities Act when the donor receives some real benefit," the SEC made clear that "the lack of monetary consideration for 'free' shares does not mean there was not a sale or offer for sale for purposes of Section 5 of the Securities Act." Rather, the analysis turns on whether the token issuer received real benefit or value.

The SEC determined that Tomahawk "received value in exchange for the bounty distributions, in the form of online marketing," as well as "in the creation of a public trading market" for the TOM tokens. Specifically, the SEC stated that "[d]istribution of tokens that are securities in exchange for promotional services to advance the issuer's economic objectives or create a public market for the securities constitute sales" for purposes of both the Securities Act and the Exchange Act (including Rule 10b-5 thereunder).[86]

In the case of Tomahawk, an ICO had been planned and substantially pursued. But in the absence of any proposed ICO (or follow-on sale in exchange for fiat or digital currency), or under circumstances in which the token recipients had not provided promotional support, would the mere creation of a market or demand for the TOM token be sufficient "value" to constitute a sale of securities? In other words, had Tomahawk merely delivered the TOM token to wallet addresses with no action being taken whatsoever by token recipients, could that have constituted a securities sale? If the particular token is a security, the SEC's answer appears to be yes. Citing *SEC v. Sierra Brokerage Services, Inc.*,[87] which the SEC noted supports its view that "where a 'gift' disperses corporate ownership and thereby helps to create a public trading market it is treated as a sale," the Tomahawk Order suggests that mere creation of a public market for a security token, such as on token exchanges, would suffice.

The Tomahawk Order reminded market participants and their lawyers that purported gifts of securities may, in fact, be deemed securities sales, which is consistent with SEC guidance dating from the early internet days relating to equity give-aways in exchange for recipients providing personal information (such as email addresses) that was of value to the equity issuer.[88] However, it is notable that the SEC did not say that by virtue of a token giveaway, the particular token *became* a security. Rather, the token first was determined to be a security. Both Tomahawk and the early internet cases focused on an established security (e.g., equity or an equity-linked token). Conversely, in the case of a token that the SEC determines not to be a security, such as present-day Ethereum or Bitcoin, it would seem that a token give-away may not in fact necessarily be a sale of securities. As a legal matter, not every freely distributed item of potentially consumptive value (such as a coupon in a newspaper) necessarily is a security. Importantly, however, "manner of sale"-related factors described in both the Munchee Order and the Hinman Speech (for instance, whether the token issuer suggests or promises that a given token will increase in value) would seem to continue to have relevance to the then-current analysis of whether such a give-away may constitute an investment contract and, therefore, the sale of a security.

While providing useful guidance concerning token give-aways, the Tomahawk Order raises at least one thorny related question: Where is the line between a token recipient doing work to "earn" a token, on the one hand, and providing value or benefit to a token issuer, on the other hand? At first glance, the concepts would seem to go hand in hand, yet potentially pull in opposite directions when analysing whether a sale of securities has occurred. Some believe that when token recipients do work to "earn" a token (such as through "mining"), rather than relying on the entrepreneurial or managerial efforts of others, the delivery of that token is less likely to be an investment contract, and, hence, a sale of securities, because the *Howey* test's "efforts of others" prong would be less likely to be implicated. By contrast, looking from the perspective of a token seller, a token recipient doing work to earn a token may provide value to the token seller, for instance, by creating a market for the token, by validating transactions or by creating demand for the application itself. Based on *Tomahawk*, that would seem to suggest that a "sale" had occurred, particularly if the value derived is meaningful.

So does a token recipient doing work in order to receive a token make it more or less likely that a sale of securities has occurred?

Perhaps one way to navigate this conceptual tangle is to reflect upon the Hinman Speech and its concept of decentralisation. Rather than "going down the rabbit hole" of trying to distinguish between the concepts of "doing work" *vs.* "providing value," or between different kinds or "work" or degrees of "benefits," instead, one might ask who is receiving the benefit of the work? Is there a central promoter or recognisable "issuer" that is deriving benefit or value from the work of the token recipients? Or is it more like the Bitcoin blockchain, where miners earn tokens, but there is no "issuer" or central beneficiary? Perhaps Director Hinman's decentralisation framework may not only be critical for determining whether a given token is a security, but also of heuristic use in distinguishing when a "gift" of tokens is, in fact, a "sale." Maybe if a token is sufficiently decentralised as to no longer be a security, there no longer would be a true "who" receiving value for token recipients' work. And alternatively, as noted above, if the token itself were deemed not to be a security, perhaps one may not need to assess the work *vs.* value question at all.

Part 3: Current challenges with security tokens

While crypto thought-leaders, regulators and others in the token sale space grapple with the circumstances under which a security token may in the future evolve from a security to a non-security, token sellers that wish to affirmatively issue and sell their tokens as securities in compliance with U.S. federal securities laws face challenges of their own.

Unfortunately, as noted earlier in this chapter, opting into the securities law framework[89] may be an imperfect fit at best for token sellers, particularly in the case of tokens that have a consumptive use and have not been structured to resemble traditional debt or equity securities. Even once security token platforms, such as tZERO and Templum, are capable of permitting secondary market sales of security tokens, aspects of U.S. federal securities laws may not quite fit.

It is beyond the scope of this particular article to identify and solve all of the potential U.S. securities law pinch points. However, below is a non-exclusive list of issues for consideration, which relate to some of the more popular exemptions from registration under U.S. securities laws for securities offerings. (The below are intended to be in addition to the reporting requirement questions identified by Hinman's speech.)

Two of the arguably more favored, and potentially less expensive, exemptions from registration under U.S. securities laws are Regulation D and Regulation S, in each case, of the Securities Act, neither of which generally requires pre-sale interaction with the SEC. Below is a brief summary each:

Regulation D is an exemption available for private placements (transactions not involving a public offering). Under Rule 506 of Regulation D, two exemptions from registration are available, without any limitation on the amount of money raised.[90] Under Rule 506(b), a "safe harbour" under Section 4(a)(2) of the Securities Act, an issuer need not register securities so long as specified criteria are met, including that no general solicitation or advertising has been used to market the securities, and that there are no more than 35 non-accredited investors. By contrast, under Rule 506(c), an issuer may engage in broad solicitation and general advertisements of the offering so long as, among other things, all investors meet accreditation criteria (which the issuer has taken reasonable steps to verify, such as through review of W-2s, tax returns and the like). Companies that elect to comply with Rule 506(b) or 506(c) are required to file an electronic notice (Form D) with the SEC.[91]

Regulation S is an exemption available for offers and sales made outside of the United States, to non-"U.S. persons" (as that term is defined in the Securities Act). At its base, the Regulation S exemption may be an acknowledgment that U.S. securities regulators may be less concerned about protecting the interests of potential purchasers that are not U.S. persons, than such regulators would be about protecting those who are U.S. persons. Although frequently combined with Regulation D sales to accredited investors pursuant to Rule 506(b) or Rule 506(c), when used by itself, Regulation S prohibits any "directed selling efforts" from being made in the United States.

While the contours of Regulation D and Regulation S are familiar to securities lawyers, and while their effective use manifestly does avoid registration under the Securities Act, particular characteristics of ICOs may continue to pose challenges under U.S. federal securities laws even for issuers squarely fitting into these exemptions. Notable issues include:[92]

- Issues under Section 12(g) of the Exchange Act: In connection with the JOBS Act liberalisations to the U.S. federal securities laws, the Exchange Act was amended in 2016.[93] Section 12(g) of the Exchange Act specifies the thresholds that trigger the requirement that an issuer register with the SEC a class of securities. Under Section 12(g), an issuer of securities that is not a bank, bank holding company or savings and loan holding company, is required to register a class of equity securities under the Exchange Act if the issuer has more than US$10 million of total assets; and the securities are "held of record" by either 2,000 persons, or 500 persons who are not accredited investors, subject to certain exceptions.[94] While, depending on the facts and circumstances, tokens may not be "equity securities," the widespread holding by persons of digital tokens could trigger Exchange Act registration and corresponding ongoing reporting requirements (*i.e.*, the filing of annual reports on Form 10-K and quarterly reports on Form 10-Q, which would necessitate public disclosure tantamount to that of any public company).[95] To compound matters, it can be extraordinarily difficult to ascertain the number of holders of record of a token, where holders are pseudonymous and a single holder may have numerous digital wallets. One possible solution is to programmatically limit the number of holders (or digital wallets) within the blockchain protocol. (The alternative of aggregating multiple holders within a single "street name" holder would seem to be at odds with the ethos of decentralisation.)

- Flowback issues: While there are multiple categories of issuers under Regulation S, foreign issuers must reasonably believe at the commencement of a securities offering under Regulation S that there is no "substantial U.S. market interest" in the securities being sold. With respect to debt securities, for example, "substantial U.S. market interest" may be satisfied, among other things, by 300 or more U.S. persons being holders of record of such securities. In the context of global markets and unregulated exchanges that may list tokens of their own accord, even a token seller that carefully polices its ICO could nonetheless end up with tokens that, without the token seller's participation or encouragement, are sold in the secondary market to U.S. persons. While some posit that tokens' smart contracts may be programmed to require know your customer/anti-money laundering checks prior to each resale, the current market reality appears to be that some unregulated token exchanges do not or cannot effectively prevent U.S. persons from accessing such exchanges and purchasing tokens that may have been issued pursuant to Regulation S. And while a substantial portion of many tech startups' compensatory packages includes equity incentives, reliance on Regulation S could tend to preclude compensating domestic employees with tokens.

• Broker registration requirements: If a token issuer engages a third party to find U.S. investors or to act as a placement agent in connection with a token offering, that party generally would be required to register as a broker (or be acting on behalf of a registered broker), with attendant compliance requirements.[96] To date, many traditional broker-dealers have been averse to facilitating ICO activity, and, at present, few service firms within the blockchain space have sought broker-dealer registration.[97]

• Investment Company Act issues: ICO issuers typically receive digital tokens in consideration for the tokens issued by them, and may hold a substantial amount of their own tokens. Accordingly, in certain circumstances, an ICO issuer could inadvertently become an "investment company" under the Investment Company Act of 1940, and thereby be subject to regulation as a mutual fund, if the issuer is deemed to hold "investment securities" with a value exceeding 40% of its total assets.[98]

Conclusion

As of August 2018, the date of this chapter, when it comes to ICOs, particularly in the case of tokens designed to have a consumptive use, there appears to be no "perfect fit" within U.S. federal securities laws for issuances to U.S. persons. As regulators, thought leaders,[99] other legal practitioners active in the space actively identify and try to reconcile friction points between existing laws and emerging technologies, the markets continue to move forward and grow. In a sense, there may be "mutually assured disruption," as technological development, legal understanding and compliance best practices grow together. The token sale genie is not going back in the bottle,[100] and moving forward with a goal to promote investor and consumer protection is critical, no matter what we ultimately may call a given token.

Acknowledgments

The author thanks David M. Adlerstein of Wachtell, Lipton, Rosen & Katz for his review and comments on this chapter. His meaningful contribution is deeply appreciated. The author thanks James Fitzpatrick, of Fordham Law School, for his assistance with this chapter. The author also thanks Drew Hinkes, Marco Santori, David H. Klayman and Jay Baris, respectively, for their important feedback concerning certain aspects of this chapter's subject matter, as well as Ron Quaranta, Joel Telpner, Jason Nagi, Mark Wojciechowski and the members of the Wall Street Blockchain Alliance Legal Working Group and Wharton Reg@ Tech, respectively, for their enthusiasm and varied perspectives more generally.

The author is beyond grateful to Gregory Fullerton Klayman and Lubos Kuzar for their priceless support always.

Finally, the author thanks the many, many colleagues and friends in the space with whom she has been traveling this exciting blockchain and crypto path, some of whom are named or cited in, and several of whom kindly provided an advance read of, this chapter. "As soon as I saw you, I knew a grand adventure was about to happen." — A.A. Milne (*Winnie-the-Pooh*).

Endnotes

1. While this chapter attempts to provide a comprehensive view of the United States securities law guidance concerning digital tokens, this chapter does not exhaustively describe developments within the space. The views expressed in this chapter reflect the author's own views and may not necessarily reflect the views of any other person, any entity or any regulator. Nothing in this chapter is intended to be, and nothing should be relied upon as, legal advice or investment advice.

2. This chapter uses the term "ICO" for consistency. More recently, terms such as "security token offering" and "STO" have grown in popularity.

3. Buterin, Vitalik, *Mastercoin: A Second-Generation Protocol on the Bitcoin Blockchain*, BITCOIN MAGAZINE (Nov. 4, 2013), available at https://bitcoinmagazine.com/articles/mastercoin-a-second-generation-protocol-on-the-bitcoin-blockchain-1383603310/.

4. *See, e.g.*, Channing, Emma, *State of the ICO Market – A GC's View*, CHAMBERS AND PARTNERS PROFESSIONAL ADVISORS FINTECH GUIDE 2018, (2017), available at https://www.chambersandpartners.com/state-of-the-ico-market ("2017 was the year that Initial Coin Offerings ('ICOs') broke onto the wider public consciousness (not to-date, assisted by the fact that ICO is a misnomer for digital token offerings in every single way conceivable).").

5. *See infra* Part 2: The rise of the security token.

6. This chapter presumes a background understanding of blockchain, smart contracts and digital tokens. For foundational information on the topics of blockchain, smart contracts and digital tokens, *see* Baris, Jay G. & Klayman, Joshua Ashley, *Blockchain Basics for Investment Managers: A Token of Appreciation*, 51 Nos. 6 and 7 THE REVIEW OF SECURITIES AND COMMODITIES REGULATION 68 (Mar. 21, 2018), available at https://www.shearman.com/-/media/Files/Perspectives/2018/03/Baris_Klayman_RSCR_Final_1.pdf?la=en&hash=4CD602B56ED60D38CB5EAC232EF3D80981026B0F.

7. For purposes of this chapter, we generally will not consider U.S. state securities laws, alternative tests that have arisen under case law for whether something may be a security under U.S. law, such as the "family resemblance test" or the "risk capital test," or legal requirements apart from securities regulation.

8. Lewitinn, Lawrence, *Study Rings Alarm Bells on Some of the Biggest ICOs*, MODERN CONSENSUS (Jul. 20, 2018), *available at* https://modernconsensus.com/cryptocurrencies/alt-coins/icos-code-white-paper-penn-study/ ("The analysis in 'Coin-Operated Capitalism' calculates some $3.8 billion went to 200 ICOs in 2017. 'By July of 2018, an additional 430 ICOs had raised almost $10 billion,' it said."), citing Coney, Shaanan; Hoffman, David A.; Sklaroff, Jeremy; & Wishnick, David A., *Coin Operated Capitalism* (Jul. 17, 2018; last rev. Aug. 7, 2018), *available at* https://papers.ssrn.com/sol3/papers.cfm?abstract_id=3215345 ("This Article presents the legal literature's first detailed analysis of the inner workings of Initial Coin Offerings").

9. Long, Caitlin, *ICOs Were 45% of IPOs in Q2 2018, As Cryptos Disrupt Investment Banks*, FORBES (July 22, 2018), *available at* https://www.forbes.com/sites/caitlinlong/2018/07/22/icos-were-45-of-ipos-in-q2-2018-as-cryptos-disrupt-investment-banks/#2f9a4d8a794c.

10. Klayman, Joshua Ashley; Cohen, Lewis Rinaudo; & Sosnow, Robin, *There are Two Sides to the Initial Coin Offering Debate*, CROWDFUND INSIDER (Oct. 31, 2017), *available at* https://www.crowdfundinsider.com/2017/10/123863-perspective-two-sides-initial-coin-offering-debate/.

11. Cohen, Lewis, *A Crypto-Capital Markets Lawyer Looks Back on 2017*, Medium (Mar. 19, 2018), *available at* https://medium.com/@nycryptolawyer/a-crypto-capital-markets-lawyer-looks-back-on-2017-d5eb2123e570.

12. FINMA, GUIDELINES FOR ENQUIRIES REGARDING THE REGULATORY FRAMEWORK FOR INITIAL

Coin Offerings (ICOS)(Feb. 16, 2018), available at https://www.finma.ch/en/~/media/finma/dokumente/dokumentencenter/myfinma/1bewilligung/fintech/wegleitung-ico.pdf?la=en&hash=9CBB35972F3ABCB146FBF7F09C8E88E453CE600C   (the "FINMA Guidelines").

13. An example of incidental (*vs.* non-incidental) utility for a particular user may be the right to vote at the annual stockholders' meeting of a large public company. Ownership of a single share of that stock may entitle the purchaser to vote at the annual meeting – which may mean that such share has utility – but that right to vote likely may not be the real impetus for purchasing the share of stock. In that sense, the share of stock could be said to have non-incidental utility. *See, e.g.*, A Securities Law Framework for Blockchain Tokens, Coinbase, Coin Center, Union Square Ventures & Consensys (Dec. 7, 2016), *available at* https://www.coinbase.com/legal/securities-law-framework.pdf (the "Securities Law Framework").

14. Bennington, Ash, *Utility Coins or Crypto Assets? Token Terminology Is One Big Gray Area*, Coindesk (Sept. 5, 2017), *available at* https://www.coindesk.com/utility-coins-cryptoassets-token-terminology-one-big-gray-area/.

15. Jurisdictions around the world have reached a variety of different conclusions, with some, including Switzerland, Gibraltar, Singapore and Malta, determining that certain token sales and token generation events are not sales of securities.

16. *See* DuPont, Quinn, *Experiments in Algorithmic Governance: A History and Ethnography of "The DAO," a Failed Decentralized Autonomous Organization*, Bitcoin And Beyond: The Challenges and Opportunities of Blockchains for Global Governance, 157 (Malcolm Campbell-Verduyn ed., Routledge 2018); *See generally The DAO (organisation)*, Wikipedia, *available at* https://en.wikipedia.org/wiki/The_DAO_(organization).

17. Dupont, *supra* n.16, at n.1 ("Values and dates for The DAO were initially collected through online sources, but later confirmed and adjusted to correspond with internal data provided by Stephan Tual of Slock.it. The largest discrepancy between publicly-reported [*sic*] values and internal values is the maximum USD-converted monetary value of The DAO, which online sources claimed reached a maximum of $150m. Using historical market data, Slock.it's internal data showed a maximum of $250m, from 11,944,260.98 ETH. Due to wild ETH price swings during this period, the USD-converted monetary value changed rapidly.")

18. *Id.* at 158.

19. Horner, Timothy L. & Makens, Hugh H., *Securities Regulation of Fundraising Activities of Religious and Other Nonprofit Organizations*, 27 Stetson L. Rev. 473, 473 (Fall 1997) ("There is a common misconception that religious and other nonprofit organisations are exempt from compliance with the securities laws. They are not.").

20. Others may have believed that, if an ICO were launched from Switzerland using a Swiss Foundation model and in compliance with Swiss law, that U.S. securities laws would not be implicated, even if U.S. persons were contributors.

21. *See* SEC, *Report of Investigation Pursuant to Section 21(a) of the Securities Exchange Act of 1934: The DAO*, Release No. 81207 (July 25, 2017), *available at* https://www.sec.gov/litigation/investreport/34-81207.pdf (hereinafter, The DAO Report).

22. *See* Baris & Klayman, *supra* n.6, at 75-76.

23. *45 SEC v. W.J. Howey Co.*, 328 U.S. 293, 301 (1946). Notably, a well-known crypto industry memorandum dated December 5, 2016, titled Securities Law Analysis of Blockchain Tokens (and informally referred to as the "Debevoise memo" or the "Lee Schneider memo") had asserted that the Howey test should be applied. *See* the Securities Law Framework, *supra* n.13, at Part 3.

24. *See* The DAO Report, *supra* n.21 at 16-17 ("[....]The DAO arrangement involved a platform that provided users with 'an electronic system that matched orders from multiple parties to buy and sell DAO Tokens for execution based on non-discretionary methods.' This activity, the SEC said, also required The DAO to register as a national securities exchange because, among other things, it created an exchange for 'securities.' On the same day that it published the DAO Report, the SEC published an Investor Bulletin, cautioning investors about the risks of investing in initial coin offerings (ICOs), and suggesting questions to ask before investing.")

25. SEC, Statement on Potentially Unlawful Online Platforms for Trading Digital Assets (Mar. 7, 2018), *available at* https://www.sec.gov/news/public-statement/enforcement-tm-statement-potentially-unlawful-online-platforms-trading.

26. The DAO Report, *supra* n.21 at n.1. See also Baris & Klayman, *supra* n.6 at 81.

27. *See* the Securities Law Framework, *supra* n.13.

28. Adlerstein, David M., *The ICO Governance Deficit*, COINDESK (Sep. 10, 2017), *available at* https://www.coindesk.com/ico-governance-deficit.

29. Templum and tZERO are among those that are trying to provide platforms for trading security tokens. *See* Dale, Brady, *ICOs Iced: A 12-Month Freeze on US Token Trading May Just Be Beginning*, COINDESK (Mar. 19, 2018), available at: https://www.coindesk.com/icos-iced-12-month-freeze-us-token-trading-just-beginning/.

30. "An accredited investor, in the context of a natural person, includes anyone who:
    • earned income that exceeded $200,000 (or $300,000 together with a spouse) in each of the prior two years, and reasonably expects the same for the current year, OR
    • has a net worth over $1 million, either alone or together with a spouse (excluding the value of the person's primary residence).

    On the income test, the person must satisfy the thresholds for the three years consistently either alone or with a spouse, and cannot, for example, satisfy one year based on individual income and the next two years based on joint income with a spouse. The only exception is if a person is married within this period, in which case the person may satisfy the threshold on the basis of joint income for the years during which the person was married and on the basis of individual income for the other years.

    In addition, entities such as [certain] banks, partnerships, corporations, nonprofits and trusts may be accredited investors." SEC Investor Bulletin, Accredited Investors, SEC Pub. No. 158 (Sept. 2013), *available at* https://www.sec.gov/files/ib_accreditedinvestors.pdf.

31. For a discussion of Regulation D in greater detail, *see infra* Part 3: Current challenges with security tokens.

32. Batiz-Benet, Juan; Clayburgh, Jesse; & Santori, Marco, *The SAFT Project: Toward a Compliant Token Sale Framework*, THE SAFT PROJECT (Oct. 2, 2017), *available at* https://saftproject.com/static/SAFT-Project-White paper.pdf.

33. *See* Shin, Laura, *Are ICOs for Utility Tokens Selling Securities? Prominent Crypto Players Say Yes*, FORBES (Oct. 2, 2017), *available at* https://www.forbes.com/sites/laurashin/2017/10/02/are-icos-for-utility-tokens-selling-securities-prominent-crypto-players-say-yes/#155bbb4734fa.

34. *Cardozo Blockchain Project Research Report #1, Not So Fast—Risks Related to the Use of a "SAFT" for Token Sales*, CARDOZO BLOCKCHAIN PROJECT (Nov. 21, 2017), *available at* https://cardozo.yu.edu/sites/default/files/Cardozo %20Blockchain%20Project%20-%20Not%20So%20Fast%20%20SAFT%20Response_final.pdf.

35. *See*, e.g., Zeoli, Anthony, *Initial Coin Offerings: Why the SAFT is Dead*, CROWDFUND INSIDER (Mar. 26, 2018), available at https://www.crowdfundinsider.com/2018/03/131044-initial-coin-offerings-why-the-saft-is-dead/; *see* Telpner, Joel, LINKEDIN (Aug. 2018), *available at* https://www.linkedin.com/feed/update/urn:li:activity:6433027407199903744

("Great pleasure participating in last night's panel on SAFTs. May they Rest in Peace"); *see* Kaplan, Aaron, *SEC Subpoenas Show the SAFT Approach to Token Sales is a Bad Idea*, VENTUREBEAT (March 3, 2018), *available at* https://venturebeat.com/2018/03/03/sec-subpoenas-show-the-saft-approach-to-token-sales-is-a-bad-idea/ ("The proposition that utility tokens are not securities, as posited by the SAFT White Paper, is nonsense."); see BlockWorks Group, Everything You Need to Know About the SAFT (And Why It's Already Dead), YOUTUBE (Aug. 28, 2018), *available at* https://www.youtube.com/watch?v=ZDykAgigcvs (video of Aug. 7, 2018 panel discussion moderated by Michael Ippolito, featuring Joshua Ashley Klayman, Joel Telpner & Stephen Wink); *c.f.* Shin, Laura, *How Crypto and Blockchain Technology Should Be Regulated*, FORBES (Dec. 12, 2017) (Laura Shin moderating a debate by Joshua Ashley Klayman and Marco Santori regarding the utility and viability of the SAFT framework), *available at* https://www.forbes.com/sites/laurashin/2017/12/12/how-crypto-and-blockchain-technology-should-be-regulated/#62fe51d467ba, podcast *available at* http://unchainedpodcast.co/how-crypto-and-blockchain-technology-should-be-regulated.

36. *See* Crea, Robert M.; Nolan, Anthony R.G.; & Rohrer, Eden L., *Metamorphosis: Digital Assets and the U.S. Securities Laws*, K&L GATES LLP (Jun. 27, 2018), *available at* http://www.klgates.com/metamorphosis-digital-assets-and-the-us-securities-laws-06-27-2018 ("Director Hinman's theory of decentralisation as a means to morph a security into a non-security also might restore some credibility to the "simple agreement for future tokens" or "SAFT" as a technique to insulate tokens from being deemed securities."); *see* Dale, Brady, *After Millions Raised, the SAFT Is Alive, But Who Knows How Well*, COINDESK (Apr. 27, 2018), *available at* https://www.coindesk.com/saft-alive-knows-well ('If you want non-dilutive financing, your choices are a SAFT or try to stay outside of the US.') (quoting Mark Radcliffe, a partner at the law firm DLA Piper).

37. *See* *Switzerland's Financial Regulator Clears the Path for ICOs*, MME (Feb. 28, 2018), *available at* https://www.mme.ch/fileadmin/files/documents/MME_Compact/2018/180228_Swiss_Financial_Regulator_clears_the_Path_for_ICOs.pdf.

38. *See* Hinman, William, SEC Div. of Corp. Fin. Director, Digital Asset Transactions: When Howey Met Gary (Plastic) (June 14, 2018), *available at* https://www.sec.gov/news/ speech/speech-hinman-061418.

39. As discussed later in this chapter, SEC Director Hinman declined to opine about the legality or appropriateness of a SAFT. *Id.*

40. Shin, *supra* at n.33.

41. Michaels, David & Vigna, Paul, *SEC Chief Fires Warning Shot Against Coin Offerings*, WALL STREET JOURNAL (Nov. 9, 2017), *available at* https://www.wsj.com/articles/sec-chief-fires-warning-shot-against-coin-offerings-1510247148.

42. Clayton, Jay, SEC Chairman, Remarks at the PLI 49th Annual Institute on Securities Regulation (Nov. 8, 2017), *available at* https://www.sec.gov/news/speech/speech-clayton-2017-11-08.

43. SEC Announces Enforcement Initiatives to Combat Cyber-Based Threats and Protect Retail Investors, SEC Press Release 2017-176 (Sep. 25, 2017), *available at* https://www.sec.gov/news/press-release/2017-176.

44. *See, e.g.*, SEC Emergency Action Halts ICO Scam, SEC Press Release 2017-219 (Dec. 4, 2017), *available at* https://www.sec.gov/news/press-release/2017-219; Spotlight on Initial Coin Offerings and Digital Assets, SEC ICO Updates, *available at* https://www.sec.gov/spotlight-initial-coin-offerings-and-digital-assets.

45. *See, e.g.*, Investor Alert: Celebrity Endorsements, Investor.gov (Nov. 1, 2017) *available at* https://www.investor.gov/additional-resources/news-alerts/alerts-bulletins/investor-alert-celebrity-endorsements. This investor educational outreach continues in 2018. See, e.g., The SEC Has an Opportunity You Won't Want To Miss: Act Now!, Investor.

gov (May 16, 2018), *available at* https://www.investor.gov/additional-resources/news-alerts/press-releases/sec-has-opportunity-you-won't-want-miss-act-now.

46. Bennington, Ash, *Utility Coins or Crypto Assets? Token Terminology Is One Big Gray Area*, COINDESK (Sept. 5, 2017), *available at* https://www.coindesk.com/utility-coins-cryptoassets-token-terminology-one-big-gray-area/.

47. Satis Group (Satis Group research team led by Sherwin Dowlat, assisted by Michael Hodapp), *Cryptoassset Market Coverage Initiation: Network Creation*, BLOOMBERG LP [US] (Jul. 11, 2018), *available at* https://research.bloomberg.com/pub/res/d28giW28tf6G7T_Wr77aU0gDgFQ, at 5.

48. *SEC v. Glenn W. Turner Enterprises, Inc.*, 348 F. Supp. 766 (1972).

49. The SEC subsequently directly addressed "bounties" in its August 14, 2018 guidance. See *Tomahawk Exploration LLC and David Thompson Laurance*, Securities Act of 1933 Release No. 10530 (Aug. 14, 2018); *see also* Securities Exchange Act of 1934 Release No. 83839 (Aug. 14, 2018) (the "Tomahawk Order").

50. Baris & Klayman, *supra* n.6, at 79.

51. *Munchee, Inc.,* Securities Act of 1933 Release No. 10455 (Dec. 11, 2017), *available at* https://www.sec.gov/litigation/admin/2017/33-10445.pdf (the "Munchee Order").

52. For an analysis of the Munchee Order, see Klayman, Joshua Ashley & Baris, Jay G., *Food for Thought: SEC Turns Up the Heat on Utility Token Sales*, CROWDFUND INSIDER (Dec. 18, 2017), *available at* https://www.crowdfund insider.com/2017/12/126033-food-for-thought-the-sec-cyberunit-halts-munchee-token-sale/.

53. Munchee Order, *supra* n.51, at 6-7.

54. *See id.* at 6, which states,

"In addition, Munchee made public statements or endorsed other people's public statements that touted the opportunity to profit. For example, on or about October 25, 2017, Munchee created a public posting on Facebook, linked to a third-party YouTube video, and wrote '199% GAINS on MUN token at ICO price! Sign up for PRE-SALE NOW!' The linked video featured a person who said 'Today we are going to talk about Munchee. Munchee is a crazy ICO. If you don't know what an ICO is, it is called an initial coin offering. Pretty much, if you get into it early enough, you'll probably most likely get a return on it.' This person went on to use his 'ICO investing sheet' to compare the MUN token offering to what he called the 'Top 15 ICOs of all time' and 'speculate[d]' that a $1,000 investment could create a $94,000 return."

55. Some believe this to have been a direct statement concerning the SAFT white paper, interpreting the SEC's use of the term "practical use" to mean token functionality or usability (whether full or partial) at the moment of sale. Id. This is not a uniform view, however, and certain SAFT supporters hold the view that the SEC specifically declined to use the term "functionality" and that "practical use" focused on the labelling of the token as a "utility token." *See id.* at 9. Paragraph 35 of the Munchee Order reads:

"Even if MUN tokens had a practical use at the time of the offering, it would not preclude the token from being a security. Determining whether a transaction involves a security does not turn on labelling – such as characterizing an ICO as involving a 'utility token' – but instead requires an assessment of 'the economic realities underlying a transaction.' [United Housing Found, Inc. v.] Forman, 421 U.S. [389, 849 (1975)]. All of the relevant facts and circumstances are considered in making that determination. See Forman, 421 U.S. at 849 (purchases of "stock" solely for purpose of obtaining housing not purchase of "investment contract"); see also SEC v. C.M. Joiner Leasing Corp., 320 U.S. 344, 352-53 (1943) (indicating the 'test . . . is what character the instrument is given in commerce by the terms of the offer, the plan of distribution, and the economic inducements held out to the prospect')."

56. Clayton, Jay, SEC Chairman, Statement on Cryptocurrencies and Initial Coin Offerings (Dec. 11, 2017), *available at* https://www.sec.gov/news/public-statement/statement-clayton2017-12-11.

57. Baris & Klayman, *supra* n.6, at 77 (citing Clayton, Jay & Giancarlo, J. Christopher, Regulators Are Looking at Cryptocurrency, WALL STREET JOURNAL (Jan. 24, 2018), *available at* https://www.wsj.com/articles/regulators-arelooking-at-cryptocurrency-1516836363.)

58. *Id.* (*citing* SEC Public Statement, Statement by SEC Chairman Jay Clayton and CFTC Chairman J. Christopher Giancarlo: Regulators are Looking at Cryptocurrency (Jan. 25, 2018), *available at* https://www.sec.gov/news/public-statement/statement-clayton-giancarlo-012518.)

59. *See* Lewis-Kraus, Gideon, *Inside the Crypto World's Biggest Scandal*, WIRED (Jun. 19, 2018), *available at* https://www.wired.com/story/tezos-blockchain-love-story-horror-story/.

60. *Id.*

61. Klayman, Joshua Ashley, *The Token Sale Sky is Not Falling, Unless We Cause It To.*, CROWDFUND INSIDER (Nov. 5, 2017), *available at* https://www.crowdfundinsider.com/2017/11/124118-token-sale-sky-not-falling-unless-cause.

62. Caffyn, Grace Bitcoin Pizza Day: Celebrating the Pizzas Bought for 10,000 BTC, COINDESK (May 22, 2014), *available at* https://www.coindesk.com/bitcoin-pizza-day-celebrating-pizza-bought-10000-btc.

63. *See, e.g.*, Press Release, SEC, Halts Alleged Initial Coin Offering Scam (Jan. 30, 2018), *available at* https://www.sec.gov/news/press-release/2018-8.

64. Popper, Nathaniel, *Subpoenas Signal S.E.C. Crackdown on Initial Coin Offerings*, The NEW YORK TIMES (Feb. 28, 2018), *available at* https://www.nytimes.com/2018/02/28/technology/initial-coin-offerings-sec.html. ("Nick Morgan, a former lawyer in the SEC's enforcement division, said that according to his contacts in the industry, the subpoenas had gone out to as many as 80 companies and individuals.")

65. Long, Caitlin & Lindholm, Tyler, *A Haven for Blockchain: The Case for Wyoming*, COINDESK (January 27, 2018), *available at* https://www.coindesk.com/haven-blockchain-case-wyoming.

66. Open blockchain tokens-exemptions, H.B. 70, 64th Leg., Budget Sess. (Wyo. 2018), *available at* https://legiscan.com/WY/bill/HB0070/2018.

67. *See generally* FINMA, *supra* n.12.

68. Peirce, Hester, SEC Commissioner, Beaches and Bitcoin: Remarks before the Medici Conference (May 2, 2018), *available at* https://www.sec.gov/news/speech/speech-peirce-050218.

69. SEC Names Valerie A. Szczepanik Senior Advisor for Digital Assets and Innovation, SEC Press Release 2018-102 (Jun. 4, 2018), *available at* https://www.sec.gov/news/press-release/2018-102.

70. *See*, e.g., Roberts, Jeff John, *SEC's 'Crypto Czar' Says Smart Contracts Can Help Regulation,* FORTUNE, THE LEDGER (Jun. 7, 2018), *available at* http://fortune.com/2018/06/07/valerie-szczepanik-sec/.

71. Bryanov, Kirill, *What Do We Know About Valerie Szczepanik, the First Crypto Czar,* CoinTelegraph (Jun. 12, 2018), *available at* https://cointelegraph.com/news/what-do-we-know-about-valerie-szczepanik-the-first-crypto-czar.

72. Haan, Cali, *SEC Boss Jay Clayton Says Crypto Tokens Traded and Used to Fundraise are ALWAYS securities and Thus Regulated*, CROWDFUND INSIDER (June 7, 2018), *available at* https://www.crowdfundinsider.com/2018/06/134623-sec-boss-jay-clayton-says-cryptocurrency-used-to-fundraise-traded-are-always-securities-and-thus-regulated (citing a CNBC interview with Bob Pisani).

73. *Id.*

74. See the Hinman Speech, *supra* n.38.

75. While the native token of the Ethereum blockchain often is referred to as "Ether" or "ETH," for purposes of this chapter, the token will be referred to as "Ethereum".

76. Haan, *supra* n.72.

77. Nakamoto, Satoshi, *Bitcoin: A Peer-to-Peer Electronic Cash System* (2008), *available at* https://bitcoin.org/bitcoin.pdf.

78. See the Hinman Speech, *supra* n.38.

79. Long, Caitlin; Cohen, Lewis; Tinianow, Andrea; & Slater, Rich, *A Ray of Hope for Utility Tokens*, COINDESK (Feb. 27, 2018), *available at* https://www.coindesk.com/ray-hope-utility-tokens/.

80. Certain supporters of the SAFT framework have taken the position that this in some ways parallels or supports the "functionality" distinction raised by the SAFT Project. *See* Marco Santori (@msantoriESQ), TWITTER (Jun. 14, 2018), *available at* https://twitter.com/msantoriESQ/status/1007317386721218560; *see also* Roberts, Jeff John, *The SEC's Big Cryptocurrency Speech: 5 Things to Know*, FORTUNE (Jun. 15, 2018), *available at* http://fortune.com/2018/06/15/sec-ethereum/.

81. *See, e.g.,* Crea, Nolan & Rohrer, *supra* n.36; de Martino, F. Dario, Gault-Brown, Susan I., Kahan, Daniel R., Klayman, Joshua Ashley, Klein, Spencer D., Silva, Alfredo B.D. & Wojciechowski, Mark, *The Journey from Security to Non-Security: SEC Director Comments on Mutability of Token Treatment*, MORRISON & FOERSTER LLP (Jun. 19, 2018), *available at* https://media2.mofo.com/documents/180619-sec-mutability-token.pdf.

82. "While Hinman's remarks are not the official view of the SEC, Commissioner Clayton gave testimony June 21, 2018, before the Committee on Financial Services of the U.S. House of Representatives where he noted Hinman's framework is 'the approach staff takes to evaluate whether a digital assetis a security.'" Lom, Andrew & Browndorf, Rachael, *SEC's Jay Clayton and Willliam Hinman reiterate Howey Is Here To Stay*, FINANCIAL SERVICES: REGULATION TOMORROW (Jun. 22, 2018), *available at* https://www.regulationtomorrow.com/us/secs-jay-clayton-and-william-hinman-reiterate-howey-is-here-to-stay/, (citing Testimony on "Oversight of the U.S. Securities and Exchange Commission" by SEC Chairman Jay Clayton, *available at* https://www.sec.gov/news/testimony/testimony-oversight-us-securities-and-exchange-commission.)

83. Baris & Klayman, *supra* n.6, at 76.

84. *See generally* Tomahawk Order, *supra* n.49.

85. While it is beyond the scope of this chapter, it should be noted that the TOM token was convertible into an equity security and that the SEC's cease-and-desist order was not limited to the Bounty Program analysis, see Telpner, Joel S.; Kaufman, Scott,; & Tomunen, Mari, *Low Risk, High Potential Rates of Return are Achievable*, SULLIVAN & WORCESTER LLP (Aug. 16, 2018), *available at* https://blog.sandw.com/financialservicesspotlight/low-risk-high-potential-rates-of-return-are-achievable.

86. As noted by the Tomahawk Order, "Section 10(b) of the Exchange Act and Rule 10b-5 thereunder prohibit fraud in connection with the purchase or sale of securities. Specifically, Rule 10b-5(b) prohibits making untrue statements of material fact or omitting to state a material fact necessary to make statements made not misleading in connection with the purchase or sale of any security. Violations of Section 10(b) and Rule 10b-5(b) require a showing of scienter", *supra* n.49, at 8.

87. 608 F. Supp. 2d 923, 940 (S.D. Ohio 2009).

88. *See Loofbourrow*, Securities Act of 1933 Release No. 7700 (July 21, 1999), *available at* https://www.sec.gov/litigation/admin/34-41631.htm (finding defendant offered free stock to investors via misleading websites); see also Sotirakis, Securities Act of 1933 Release No. 7701 (July 21, 1999), *available at* https://www.sec.gov/litigation/admin/33-7701.

htm (finding that for a short period of time the defendant offered unregistered free stock to people who registered on a website); *see also Web Works Marketing.com, Inc.*, Securities Act of 1933 Release No. 7703 (July 21, 1999) *available at* https://www.sec.gov/litigation/admin/34-41632.htm (finding that defendant offered unregistered free shares via misleading website); *see also WowAuction.com Inc.*, Securities Act of 1933 Release No. 7702 (July 21, 1999), *available at* https://www.sec.gov/litigation/admin/33-7702.htm (finding that defendant offered unregistered free stock via online auctioneer).

89. It should be noted that some securities lawyers may question whether one could choose to "opt into" the U.S. federal securities law framework (and afford purchasers the attendant securities law protections) if a particular token otherwise would not be a security. That consideration is beyond the scope of this chapter.

90. Apart from Regulation D, other exemptions permitting domestic offerings of securities include Regulation A and Regulation Crowdfunding. (*See Regulation A*, SEC, *available at* https://www.sec.gov/smallbusiness/exemptofferings/rega) ("Regulation A has two offering tiers: Tier 1, for offerings of up to $20 million in a 12-month period; and Tier 2, for offerings of up to $50 million in a 12-month period"); *See also Regulation Crowdfunding: A Small Entity Compliance Guide for Issuers*, SEC (May 13, 2017) (updated Apr. 6, 2017), *available at* https://www.sec.gov/info/smallbus/secg/rccomplianceguide-051316.htm ("[An Issuer] is permitted to raise a maximum aggregate amount of $1,070,000 in a 12-month period"). Tokens sold pursuant to Reg A+ and Reg CF may be purchased by both accredited and unaccredited investors, however, Reg A+ requires that the token issuer be a U.S. or Canadian entity, while Reg CF requires that the issuer be a U.S. entity. Notably, while numerous would-be token issuers reportedly have pursued Reg A+ offerings, as of the date this chapter is written, the SEC has not yet qualified any Reg A+ offerings of tokens.

91. Failure to timely file a Form D will not cause the exemption to be unavailable. *See Securities Act Rules*, SEC (updated Nov. 6, 2017), *available at* https://www.sec.gov/divisions/corpfin/guidance/securitiesactrules-interps.htm.

92. Prudent issuers will consider a range of legal matters separate and apart from securities law compliance, including (to name but a few) compliance with Bank Secrecy Act and anti-money laundering requirements, compliance with money transmittal law and regulation, secure and legally compliant custodianship, and compliance with any state licensure requirements. *See generally* Shin, Laura, *Crypto Industry Frustrated by Haphazard Regulation*, the New York Times / Dealbook (Jun. 27, 2018), *available at* https://www.nytimes.com/2018/06/27/business/dealbook/crypto-industry-regulation.html (discusses various relevant U.S. regulators); Alois, JD, *FinCen Director Kenneth Blanco Addresses Tough Topic of Cryptocurrency, Attorney Joshua Klayman Adds Insight to Topics Discussed*, Crowdfund Insider (August 10, 2018), *available at* https://www.crowdfundinsider.com/2018/08/137683-fincen-director-kenneth-blanco-addresses-tough-topic-of-cryptocurrency-attorney-joshua-klayman-adds-insight-to-topics-discussed/.

93. *Changes to Exchange Act Registration Requirements to Implement Title V and Title VI of the JOBS Act*, SEC (May 24, 2016), *available at* https://www.sec.gov/info/smallbus/secg/jobs-act-section-12g-small-business-compliance-guide.htm.

94. "[...] In calculating the number of holders of record for purposes of determining whether Exchange Act registration is required, your company may exclude persons who acquired their securities in an exempt offering:
   - under an employee compensation plan;
   - under Regulation Crowdfunding if the issuer:
      - is current in its ongoing annual reports required pursuant to Rule 202 of Regulation Crowdfunding;
      - has total assets as of the end of its last fiscal year not in excess of $25 million; and

- has engaged the services of a transfer agent registered with the Commission pursuant to Section 17A of the Exchange Act; or
- as a Tier 2 offering under Regulation A if the issuer:
  - is required to file and is current in filing annual, semiannual and special financial reports under Securities Act Rule 257(b);
  - had a public float of less than $75 million as of the end of its last semiannual period, or if it cannot calculate its public float, had less than $50 million in annual revenue as of the end of its last fiscal year; and
  - engaged a transfer agent registered pursuant to Section 17A of the Exchange Act." *Exchange Act Reporting and Registration*, SEC, *available at* https://www.sec.gov/smallbusiness/goingpublic/exchangeactreporting.

95. Depending on the facts and circumstances of how a blockchain token is administered, a requirement to file periodic reports under the Exchange Act could also implicate transfer agent registration requirements under Section 17A(c)(1) of the Exchange Act, under which it is unlawful for a "transfer agent" to perform any "transfer agent function" unless the transfer agent is registered with an appropriate regulatory authority.

96. *Guide to Broker-Dealer Registration*, SEC (Apr. 2008), *available at* https://www.sec.gov/reportspubs/investor-publications/divisionsmarketregbdguidehtm.html.

97. In June 2018, both Coinbase and Circle Internet Financial Ltd., respectively, reportedly announced plans to become among the first crypto broker-dealers. *See, e.g.,* Katz, Lily, *Coinbase Says It Won Approval for Trio of Acquisitions*, Bloomberg (Jul. 16, 2018), available at: https://www.bloomberg.com/news/articles/2018-07-16/coinbase-says-it-has-green-light-to-lost-coins-deemed-securities; Georgiev, Georgi, *Coinbase to Become First Broker-Dealer to Offer SEC-Regulated Crypto Securities*, Bitcoinist.com (Jun. 6, 2018), *available at* https://bitcoinist.com/coinbase-to-become-first-broker-dealer-to-offer-SEC-regulated-crypto-securities.

98. Section 3(a)(1)(A) of the Investment Company Act of 1940. For more information about regulation of investment companies, see Baris & Klayman, *supra* n.6, at 80-82.

99. *See e.g.,* Chambers and Partners, *Legal: Blockchain & Cryptocurrencies – Global-wide*, CHAMBERS AND PARTNERS PROFESSIONAL ADVISORS: FINTECH GUIDE 2018, (2017), *available at* https://www.chambersandpartners.com/15649/2804/editorial/49/1 (first-ever Chambers and Partners' list of top 12 Global-Wide Blockchain & Cryptocurrency Lawyers, including Grant P. Fondo, Joey Garcia, Reuben Grinberg, Dax Hansen, Joshua Ashley Klayman, Brian Klein, Richard B. Levin, Luka Müller-Studer, Patrick Murck, Marco Santori, Lee Schneider, & Carol van Cleef); *Blockchain for Wall Street Presents a Brains Trust of Experts on Blockchain and Cryptoassets in the Financial Markets – Annual Education Day Will Provide Answers to Pressing Blockchain, Smart Contracts, Cryptoasset and ICO Questions and Concerns*, MONDOVISION (Jul. 11, 2017), *available at* www.mondovisione.com/media-and-resources/news/blockchain-for-wall-street-presents-a-brains-trust-of-experts-on-blockchain-and/; Alois, JD, *Legal Guidance on ICOs? Wall Street Blockchain Alliance Will Publish Recommendations Soon*, CROWDFUND INSIDER (Sep. 19, 2017), *available at* https://www.crowdfundinsider.com/2017/09/122014-legal-guidance-icos-wall-street-blockchain-alliance-will-publish-recommendations-soon/; https://zicklincenter.wharton.upenn.edu/regtech/ (Wharton Reg@Tech: https://zicklincenter.wharton.upenn.edu/wp-content/uploads/2018/06/Reg@Tech-March-2018-participant-list-1.pdf); Morris, Angela, *BigLaw Firms Are Working Together to Influence How Blockchain Technology Will Operate in the Future*, ABA JOURNAL (Aug. 2018), *available at* www.abajournal.com/magazine/article/biglaw_cryptocurrency_blockchain_smart_contracts/.

100. *See* Klayman, Joshua Ashley, *A Legal Renaissance, Blockchain Style*, COINDESK (Jan. 7, 2018), *available at* https://www.coindesk.com/2017-legal-renaissance-blockchain-style/.

Joshua Ashley Klayman
Tel: +1 917 565 0645 / Email: josh@klaymanllc.com

Joshua Ashley Klayman is one of the best-known blockchain and cryptocurrency lawyers in the world. Recognized by *Chambers and Partners* as one of the top 12 Blockchain and Cryptocurrency lawyers globally, Ms. Klayman is the Managing Member of Klayman LLC, a boutique blockchain law firm based in New York, and the CEO of Inflection Point Blockchain Advisors, LLC, a blockchain strategy consulting firm. Ms. Klayman also is a consultant to global elite law firm, Shearman & Sterling.

Active in the community, Ms. Klayman chairs the prominent Wall Street Blockchain Alliance Legal Working Group and is a member of the global Wharton Reg@Tech think tank. In addition to serving on the State of Delaware's Blockchain Strategy Committee, she speaks frequently with regulators and other government leaders from around the world regarding blockchain- and digital asset-related matters. Committed to promoting diversity, Ms. Klayman is a co-founder of Diversity in Blockchain, Inc. and a founding member of Collective Future. She collaborates with blockchain leaders from across the community to advance the industry, anticipate and address regulatory concerns and seize strategic opportunities. *Chambers and Partners*' inaugural *Professional Advisers: FinTech* (2018) edition called Ms. Klayman "[....]an up-and-coming star in the blockchain space. One highly regarded contemporary described her as being 'very good – very thoughtful and with the appropriate talents. She deserves a lot of credit.'" Additionally, *Chambers and Partners*' *State of the ICO Market – A GC's View*, by Emma Channing, CEO & General Counsel of Satis Group, deemed her "highly talented."

Ms. Klayman was named to *Super Lawyers*' New York Metro Area "Rising Star" and "Top Women Attorneys" list(s) in 2015, 2016 and 2017, in the areas of Securities & Corporate Finance; Banking; and Business/Corporate Law. *The Information* named her one of six "Lawyers Calling the Shots in the Crypto World," and she is one of only two lawyers in private practice included in BCB Group's "Women to Watch in Crypto & Blockchain." *Decade of Women* named Ms. Klayman one of the "Top 10 Frontier Women in Blockchain and Digital Assets" in connection with the UN's "Decade of Women" launch, and she is a founding member of the Digital Future Council.

A recognized thought leader in the blockchain space, Ms. Klayman is a globally sought-after writer and speaker. She has appeared on television, including on Bloomberg TV and *Today's Verdict with David Lesch*, and has been featured in podcasts, including Forbes' *Unchained* podcast, Law.com's *Unprecedented* podcast, and *The Third Web* podcast, and on radio. Ms. Klayman's writings have been featured in major publications, including *Forbes*, *Coindesk* and *Crowdfund Insider*, and she is quoted regularly in the press, ranging from the *Wall Street Journal* and the *New York Times* to blockchain industry publications. Nicknamed the "Mother of Blockchains," Ms. Klayman is the mother of five children. Before founding her own firm, she co-founded, and led for over two years, a global law firm's 70+ person Blockchain + Smart Contracts Group.

Klayman LLC / Inflection Point Blockchain Advisors, LLC

20 E. 74th Street, NY, NY 10021, USA / 1700 Broadway, New York, NY 10019, USA
Tel: +1 917 565 0645 / URL: www.klaymanllc.com / www.inflectionpointblockchain.com

Cryptocurrency and other digital assets for asset managers

Gregory S. Rowland & Trevor I. Kiviat
Davis Polk & Wardwell LLP

Introduction

In 2008, an unknown author publishing under the name Satoshi Nakamoto released a white paper describing Bitcoin, a peer-to-peer version of electronic cash, and the corresponding software that facilitates online payments directly between counterparties without the need for a financial intermediary. In the decade that has followed, Bitcoin and countless other open-source, decentralised protocols inspired by Bitcoin (for example, Ethereum and Monero) have come to represent a $300 billion-plus market of alternative assets, commonly referred to as "digital assets", which are typically traded over the internet using online exchange platforms.

Digital assets can serve several functions. Although the following categories are not independent legal categories under U.S. law, such distinctions are helpful for understanding and crafting various investment strategies involving these assets. Some digital assets, such as Bitcoin or Litecoin, are widely regarded as decentralised stores of value or mediums of exchange due to certain common economic features that support these functions; these are sometimes referred to as "pure cryptocurrencies". Other digital assets, such as Monero or Zcash, are a subset of pure cryptocurrencies that also possess certain features designed to enhance transaction privacy and confidentiality (**"privacy-focused coins"**).

Beyond pure cryptocurrencies and privacy-focused coins, there exists a broad array of general purpose digital assets (**"platform coins"**), such as Ethereum, NEO and Ravencoin, which are designed to facilitate various peer-to-peer activity, from decentralised software applications to "smart" contracts to digital collectibles, such as CryptoKitties. Platform coins also enable the creation of new digital assets called "tokens", which are typically developed for a specific purpose or application – for example, (1) "utility tokens", which generally are designed to have some consumptive utility within a broader platform or service, or (2) "security tokens", which are designed to represent more traditional interests like equity, debt and real estate with the added benefit of certain features of the digital asset markets, such as 24/7 operations, fractional ownership and rapid settlement.

The digital asset market extends beyond the assets themselves. Other participants, including online exchanges, payment processors and mining companies, compose the broader digital asset industry. And as this industry continues to grow, it has captured the attention of retail and institutional investors alike, including asset managers seeking to develop investment strategies and products involving these emerging assets and companies. Some strategies resemble early-stage growth strategies, featuring long-term investments either directly in certain digital assets or in start-up ventures developing complementary goods and services for the industry. Other strategies include hedge fund strategies, such as long/short funds, which often use derivatives, or arbitrage strategies, which seek to capitalise on the price fragmentation across the hundreds of global online exchanges.

This chapter outlines the current U.S. regulatory framework applicable to cryptocurrency and other digital asset investment funds (**"digital asset funds"**) offered to U.S. investors and how those regulatory considerations affect fund structuring decisions.

The U.S. regulatory framework generally

Digital asset funds operated in the United States or offered to U.S. investors must contend and comply with a complex array of statutes and regulations. These include the Securities Act of 1933 (the **"Securities Act"**), which regulates the offer and sale of securities; the Investment Company Act of 1940 (the **"1940 Act"**), which regulates pooled investment vehicles that invest in securities; the Commodity Exchange Act (the **"CEA"**), which regulates funds and advisers that trade in futures contracts, options on futures contracts, commodity options and swaps; and the Investment Advisers Act of 1940 (the **"Advisers Act"**), which governs investment advisers to such funds. Additionally, many fund-structuring decisions are driven by tax considerations. This section sets out the current U.S. regulatory framework applicable to digital asset funds managed in the United States or offered to U.S. investors and explores how those regulatory considerations affect fund structuring decisions.

Offering of fund interests

Interests in investment funds are securities. Under the Securities Act, an offering of securities must be registered with the SEC or made pursuant to an exemption. While there are a few possible exemptions, the most common exemption that private funds rely upon is Regulation D, which provides two alternative exemptions from registration: Rule 504 and Rule 506. Because most private investment funds intend to raise more than $5 million, Rule 506, which provides no limit on the amount of securities that may be sold or offered, is the exemption under Regulation D most commonly relied on by such funds, and consequently, this discussion of Regulation D is limited to offerings made under Rule 506.[1] In order to offer or sell securities in reliance on Rule 506 of Regulation D, an investment fund must:

- limit sales of its securities to no more than 35 non-accredited investors (unless the offering is made pursuant to Rule 506(c), in which case all purchasers must be accredited investors), although securities may be sold to an unlimited number of accredited investors;

- ensure that all non-accredited investors meet a sophistication requirement by having such knowledge and experience in financial and business matters that they are capable of evaluating the merits and risks of the prospective investment;

- refrain from general solicitation or advertising in offering or selling securities (unless the offering is made pursuant to Rule 506(c));

- comply with the information disclosure requirements of Rule 502(b) with respect to any offering to non-accredited investors. There are no specific information requirements for offerings to accredited investors;

- implement offering restrictions to prevent resales of any securities sold in reliance on Regulation D; and

- file a Form D notice of the offering with the SEC within 15 calendar days of the first sale of securities pursuant to Regulation D.

There are also some important limitations on the scope of the Regulation D exemption. For example, Regulation D only exempts the initial transaction itself (i.e., resales of securities acquired in an offering made pursuant to Regulation D must be either registered or resold pursuant to another exemption from registration). Furthermore, Regulation D is not available for any transaction or series of transactions that, while in technical compliance with Regulation D, is deemed to be part of "a plan or scheme to evade the registration provisions of the [Securities] Act".

The regulatory treatment of cryptocurrencies and other digital assets

As discussed above, interests in investment funds themselves are securities; however, these funds may hold a variety of different assets in pursuing their respective strategies – from digital assets (e.g., Bitcoin and Ether) to derivatives instruments (e.g., Bitcoin futures contracts) to securities (e.g., equity in an emerging growth company or interests in another digital asset investment fund). This section provides an overview of the regulatory treatment of such assets, particularly with respect to the definitions of "securities" under the U.S. securities laws and "commodity interests" under the CEA, before explaining how these characterisations impact structuring decisions. Although some generalisations may be inferred about the possible treatment of certain assets based on common features and fact patterns, there is no substitute for a careful case-by-case analysis of each asset, in close consultation with counsel.

In July 2017, in a release commonly referred to the DAO Report,[2] the SEC determined that certain digital assets are securities for purposes of the U.S. federal securities laws. The DAO Report was published in response to a 2016 incident in which promoters of an unincorporated virtual organisation ("The DAO") commenced an initial coin offering (an "ICO"), a term that generally refers to a sale of tokens to investors in order to fund the development of the platform or network in which such tokens will be used. The DAO was created by a German company called Slock.it, and it was designed to allow holders of DAO tokens to vote on projects that The DAO would fund, with any profits flowing to token-holders. Slock.it marketed The DAO as the first instance of a decentralised autonomous organisation, powered by smart contracts on a blockchain platform. The DAO's ICO raised approximately $150 million (USD) in Ether.

In the DAO Report, the SEC reasoned that The DAO tokens were unregistered securities because they were investment contracts, which is one type of security under the U.S. securities laws. Though it declined to take enforcement action against The DAO, the SEC used this opportunity to warn others engaged in similar ICO activities that an unregistered sale of digital assets can, depending on the facts and circumstances, be an illegal public offering of securities. The SEC has relied on similar reasoning in subsequent actions taken against token issuers that deem certain other digital assets sold in ICOs to be securities (such securities, "DAO-style tokens").[3] Many DAO-style tokens are branded by their promoters as utility tokens to convey the idea that such tokens are designed to have some consumptive utility within a broader platform or service. But as noted above, this terminology does not have any legal consequence under the U.S. securities laws. Instead, a proper inquiry must examine the facts and circumstances surrounding the asset's offering and sale, including the economic realities of the transaction.[4] Key factors to consider include: (1) whether a third party – be it a person, entity or coordinated group of actors – drives the expectation of a return; and (2) whether the digital asset, through contractual or other technical means, functions more like a consumer item and less like a security.[5]

In addition to DAO-style tokens, some digital assets are explicitly designed to be treated as securities from the outset and are meant to represent traditional interests like equity and debt, with the added benefit of certain features of the digital asset markets, such as 24/7 operations, fractional ownership and rapid settlement. These digital assets are securities by definition, and although they represent an innovation in terms of how securities trade, clear and settle, they are not necessarily a new asset class.

Any cryptocurrencies or other digital assets that are not deemed to be securities under the U.S. securities laws may be considered "commodities" under the CEA, due to the broad definition of the term.[6] For example, the Commodity Futures Trading Commission ("**CFTC**") appears to be treating Bitcoin as an exempt commodity under the CEA, a category that includes metals and energy products,[7] but does not include currencies or securities, which are classified as excluded commodities.[8] In addition, the CFTC recently permitted the self-certification of futures contracts and binary options on Bitcoin by futures exchanges under its rules for listing ordinary futures contracts.[9] And although the SEC has not taken any action with respect to Bitcoin specifically, SEC Chairman Jay Clayton recently acknowledged, and appeared to accept as correct, the CFTC's designation of Bitcoin as a commodity over which the CFTC has anti-fraud jurisdiction.[10] Finally, to the extent that a digital asset is a commodity, any derivatives offered on that commodity – for example, Bitcoin futures contracts and binary options – fall squarely within the definition of commodity interests under the CEA.

Possible obligations of the manager under the Advisers Act or the CEA

The question of whether a digital asset fund manager must comply with additional regulations under either, or both of, the Advisers Act and the CEA turns primarily on the characterisation of the assets its funds hold. First, a manager is deemed an "investment adviser" under Section 202(a)(11) of the Advisers Act, and thus is subject to the rules and regulations thereunder, if it "for compensation, engages in the business of advising others, either directly or through publications or writings, as to the value of securities or as to the advisability of investing in, purchasing, or selling securities", or "for compensation and as part of a regular business, issues or promulgates analyses or reports concerning securities". So to the extent that a manager of a cryptocurrency or other digital asset fund is advising on "securities" – for example, because its funds hold DAO-style tokens or security tokens – it must register as an investment advisor with the SEC unless such individual or entity qualifies for an exclusion from the definition or an exemption from the registration requirement.[11]

Registration under the Advisers Act subjects advisers to a host of rules and regulations, including those governing advertising, custody, proxy voting, record keeping, the content of advisory contracts and fees. For example, the Advisers Act custody rule[12] (the "**custody rule**") has detailed provisions applicable to any SEC-registered investment adviser deemed to have custody, as defined under the rule. Among other things, it requires use of a "qualified custodian" to hold client funds or securities, notices to clients detailing how their assets are being held, account statements for clients detailing their holdings, annual surprise examinations and additional protections when a related qualified custodian is used. For example, investment advisers dealing in digital assets may need to consider whether a bank, registered broker-dealer, or other firm that meets the definition of a qualified custodian, is willing to take custody of the digital assets.

Second, managers of private funds that invest or trade in "commodity interests", whether as an integral part of their investment strategy or only in a limited capacity, for hedging purposes or otherwise, are subject to regulation under the CEA and the rules of the CFTC thereunder ("**CFTC Rules**"). Commodity interests generally include: (1) futures contracts and options on futures contracts; (2) swaps; (3) certain retail foreign currency and commodity transactions; and (4) commodity options and certain leveraged transactions. So to the extent that the activities of a manager of a cryptocurrency or other digital asset fund include trading in commodity interests – for example, because it holds Bitcoin futures contracts or binary options – it will be subject to registration and regulation as a commodity pool operator ("**CPO**") or commodity trading advisor ("**CTA**"), unless it qualifies for an exemption or exclusion under the CEA or the CFTC Rules.

If the activities of an investment fund bring it within the definition of a "commodity pool" under the CEA, the manager is required to register as a CPO with the CFTC, unless such person otherwise qualifies for an exclusion from the definition of CPO or an exemption from the registration requirement. The CEA also provides for the registration of CTAs, which is in some respects analogous to the treatment of investment advisers under the Advisers Act. It should be noted, however, that numerous requirements under the CEA and the CFTC Rules apply to all CPOs and CTAs, even those that are exempt from registration.

<u>Possible obligations of the fund under the 1940 Act or CEA</u>

Similarly, the fund itself may be subject to additional regulations under either, or both of, the 1940 Act and the CEA, an analysis that, again, turns primarily on the assets the fund holds. An investment company is defined under Section 3(a)(1)(A) of the 1940 Act as any issuer that "is or holds itself out as being engaged primarily, or proposes to engage primarily, in the business of investing, reinvesting or trading in securities". This subjective test is based generally on how a company holds itself out to the public and the manner in which it pursues its business goals, and is designed to capture traditional investment companies that are deliberately acting in that capacity. Additionally, Section 3(a)(1)(C) of the 1940 Act sets forth an objective, numerical test that applies to companies that hold a significant portion of their assets in investment securities, even if they do not hold themselves out as traditional investment companies.

Companies that fall within one of these definitions of an investment company must either satisfy an exemption from the 1940 Act or register under it. The 1940 Act is a comprehensive statutory regime that imposes strict requirements on registered investment companies' governance, leverage, capital structure and operations. Consequently, most private equity funds, hedge funds and other alternative investment vehicles, which fall squarely within the definition of "investment company," are structured to satisfy an exemption from the 1940 Act.

The 1940 Act provides specific exemptions from the definition of "investment company" for privately offered investment funds and certain other types of companies. For example, Section 3(c)(1) exempts a private investment fund from registration if the outstanding securities of such fund (other than short-term paper) are beneficially owned by not more than 100 persons and such fund does not presently propose to make a public offering of its securities. Further, Section 3(c)(7) excludes an entity from registration as an investment company if all of the beneficial owners of its outstanding securities are "qualified purchasers" and the entity does not make or propose to make a public offering of its securities, and it does not limit the number of beneficial owners.

The CEA defines "commodity pool" as any investment trust, syndicate or similar form of enterprise operated for the purpose of trading in commodity interests. The CFTC interprets "for the purpose" broadly and has rejected suggestions that trading commodity interests must be a vehicle's principal or primary purpose. As a result, any trading by a private fund in swaps, futures contracts or other commodity interests, no matter how limited in scope, and regardless of whether undertaken for hedging or speculative purposes, generally will bring a private fund within the commodity pool definition.

According to the CFTC, a fund that does not trade commodity interests directly but invests in another fund that trades commodity interests would itself be a commodity pool. Thus, in a master-feeder fund structure, a feeder fund will be considered a commodity pool if the master fund is a commodity pool. Similarly, a fund of funds that invests in commodity pools may itself be considered a commodity pool.

Finally, an investment vehicle can be both an "investment company" under the 1940 Act and a "commodity pool" under the CEA, and an exception from the registration requirements of the 1940 Act does not generally imply an exception from CPO registration under the Commodity Exchange Act (or vice versa). Similarly, an exception from registration under the Advisers Act does not generally imply an exception from CTA registration (or vice versa). Furthermore, interests in commodity pools are "securities" under the Securities Act, and therefore the Securities Act applies to the offer and sale of interests in a commodity pool to the same extent as it applies to any other type of security. Accordingly, offering of interests in a private fund that is a commodity pool generally will be structured to meet the requirements of a Securities Act exemption (e.g., Regulation D, as discussed above).

Applying this framework to digital asset funds

Given the regulatory minefield laid out above, managers face a multitude of structuring decisions in conceiving and launching digital asset funds aimed at U.S. investors. These decisions will often influence, and be influenced by, the manager's investment strategy – particularly as it relates to the types of assets the fund should be permitted to hold. This section explores some common structures and the strategies they support. In each of these cases, one should keep in mind that interests in the digital asset fund itself are securities, as noted above, that must be offered and sold pursuant to an exemption, such as Regulation D, except in the case of registered (i.e., public) funds, which are offered and sold in fully-registered securities offerings.

First, the manager may decide that the fund should have flexibility to invest in securities. It may want to invest in "traditional" securities like equity or debt in a company within the digital asset industry (including through tokenised securities), or DAO-style tokens and other digital assets at risk of being deemed investment contracts. In this case, the adviser will likely need to register under the Advisers Act and comply with the host of rules and regulations thereunder, including those governing advertising, custody, proxy voting, record-keeping, the content of advisory contracts, and fees. Non-U.S. advisers, however, can potentially rely on Advisers Act Rule 203(m)-1 (the "**private fund adviser rule**").[13]

Custody poses unique questions in the digital asset context, and it is not clear in all cases whether digital assets would be viewed as funds or securities, such that the custody rule would apply. Currently, most qualified custodians do not offer custody services for digital assets. In any case, the manager should familiarise itself with the operational considerations of digital asset custody. First, what does it mean to have custody of an asset that is not physical and even in digital form, does not exist on a centralised database, but instead on one that is universal and distributed? For example, one cannot physically move units of Bitcoin off of the Bitcoin blockchain and store them elsewhere. However, in order to exercise control over one's Bitcoins, one needs a private and a public key. These keys are a series of hexadecimal characters (e.g., 1A1zP1eP5QGefi2DMPTfTL5SLmv7DivfNa), which must be stored carefully. The public key is the identity of the address on the network that has ownership and control of those Bitcoins – this key can be shared with anyone, and in fact, it must be shared in order to receive Bitcoins. The private key is essentially a password, and Bitcoins can be transferred out of a particular address by anyone with possession of that address's corresponding private key. So in the case of a blockchain-based asset like Bitcoin, control of the private key may be tantamount to custody. As there is simply no recourse to retrieve Bitcoins when a private key is lost or stolen, a critical operational point for managers is safe and secure private key storage, for example through "deep cold" storage.[14]

If the manager believes the digital asset fund may invest in securities, the fund itself would likely be structured so as to meet one of the various registration exemptions for entities that would otherwise be classified as "investment companies" under the 1940 Act.[15] For offshore funds, the requirements of Sections 3(c)(1) and 3(c)(7), which are discussed above, generally only apply to U.S. investors.

Alternatively, the manager may decide that the fund should be a registered investment company. In fact, there have been a number of requests to list on national securities exchanges the shares of such funds. The SEC has repeatedly denied such requests, and in January 2018, the SEC's Division of Investment Management outlined several questions that sponsors would be expected to address before it would consider granting approval for funds holding "substantial amounts" of cryptocurrencies or "cryptocurrency-related products."[16] The questions, which focus on specific requirements of the 1940 Act, generally fall into one of five key areas: valuation, liquidity, custody, arbitrage and potential manipulation. And although such funds alternatively could potentially be offered to the public as non-investment companies (to the extent they do not hold significant amounts of securities) under the Securities Act, the SEC has indicated that significant, similar questions exist there also.[17]

Second, the manager may decide that the fund should have flexibility to invest in commodity interests, such as futures contracts or binary options, either for hedging or speculative purposes. Any such trading by a private fund, no matter how limited in scope, and regardless of the purpose, would generally make such fund a "commodity pool," as discussed above. In this case, the manager may be required to register as a CPO or CTA with the CFTC, although certain exemptions exist for non-U.S. managers and for funds that invest in only limited amounts of commodity interests. Even if the manager decides that such fund should only invest in commodity interests and not securities, interests in commodity pools are "securities" under the Securities Act, and therefore, the fund would generally be structured to meet the requirements of a Securities Act exemption (e.g., Regulation D, as discussed above).

Finally, the manager may decide that the fund should hold neither securities nor commodity interests – in other words, a fund that holds only commodities, or "pure cryptocurrencies," such as Bitcoin, and no commodity interests. Because this category does not have independent legal significance under U.S. law, such determinations regarding the risk that a given digital asset could be deemed a "security" for U.S. securities laws purposes should be made carefully and together with legal counsel. In this case, the fund would not be governed by the 1940 Act, and the manager's activities with respect to the fund would not be governed by the Advisers Act, as both of these regimes are premised upon the fund holding securities, as discussed above. Further, because the fund does not hold commodities interests, it would likely not be considered a "commodity pool", and the manager would likely not be required to register as a CPO or CTA with the CFTC. However, the fund and the manager in this case would not be entirely unregulated. As noted above, interests in the fund are securities (regardless of the underlying assets that the fund invests in), the offer and sale of which must comply with U.S. securities laws. Additionally, the CFTC has some, albeit limited, jurisdiction over the spot market for commodities pursuant to its anti-fraud and manipulation authority.[18] Moreover, the manager of such a fund would likely be considered a common law fiduciary to such a fund and thus subject to fiduciary duties in its management of the fund.

While beyond the scope of this paper, many fund-structuring decisions are driven by U.S. federal income tax considerations. For example, many private investment fund structures typically consist of at least two investment vehicles: a vehicle that is organised in the United States and is treated as a partnership for U.S. federal income tax purposes (the "Onshore Fund"); and a vehicle that is organised in a tax haven jurisdiction, such as the Cayman Islands or the British Virgin Islands, and is treated as a corporation for U.S. federal income tax purposes (the "Offshore Fund"). U.S. taxable investors generally invest in the Onshore Fund. Because of the transparency of partnerships for U.S. federal income tax purposes, the U.S. investors are generally treated as if they directly derived their shares of the Onshore Fund's items of income, gains, losses, and deductions. The Offshore Fund is a passive foreign investment company ("PFIC"), for U.S. federal income tax purposes.

Conclusion

Over the past decade, digital assets have come a long way – from Satoshi's original Bitcoin white paper to today's broad universe of 1,600-plus digital assets trading across hundreds of online trading platforms. As this market and the surrounding industry matures, asset managers will likely continue to identify opportunities to either deploy novel investment strategies or adapt their tried-and-true strategies in this new context. As set out above, such managers face a complex array of statutes and regulations in offering digital asset funds to U.S. investors. These considerations, together with the investment strategies that the manager desires to pursue, affect fund structuring decisions, and accordingly, are best addressed together with counsel.

* * *

Endnotes

1. Historically, issuers and any persons acting on their behalf were prohibited from engaging in any form of general solicitation or general advertising in Rule 506 offerings. However, in July 2013, the SEC adopted final rules to permit general solicitation and general advertising in Rule 506 offerings under new Rule 506(c). Additional requirements apply to Rule 506(c) offerings, including the requirement to take reasonable steps to verify an investor's accredited investor status. Under Rule 506(b), an investment fund may offer securities pursuant to Rule 506 without complying with these additional requirements if it does not use general solicitation. Currently, most private funds offered in the United States choose not to use general solicitation.

2. SEC Release No. 81207, *Report of Investigation Pursuant to Section 21(a) of the Securities Exchange Act of 1934: The DAO* (Jul. 25, 2017).

3. *See, e.g.*, SEC Release No. 10445, *In the matter of Munchee, Inc.* (Dec. 11, 2017).

4. This includes, for example, (1) whether the investor's fortunes are interwoven with those of other investors or the efforts of the promoter of the investment, and (2) whether the investor's expectation of profits are based predominantly upon the entrepreneurial

or managerial efforts of the promoter or other third parties. *See SEC v. W.J. Howey Co.*, 328 U.S. 293, 301 (1946).

5. Director William Hinman, Remarks at the Yahoo Finance All Markets Summit, *Asset Transactions: When Howey Met Gary (Plastic)* (Jun. 14, 2018), *available at* https://www.sec.gov/news/speech/speech-hinman-061418. Further, the speech indicates that a digital asset that was originally offered in a securities offering may later be sold in a manner that does not constitute an offering of a security, in limited circumstances, where: (i) there is no longer a central enterprise being invested in; and (ii) the asset is only being sold to end users who will purchase a good or service available through a network. This also raises a counterfactual question – that is, whether a token network that was once decentralised could "centralise", such that it would fall within the scope of the securities laws.

6. *See* 7 U.S.C. § 1a(9).

7. *See* 7 U.S.C. § 1a(20) (defining exempt commodity to mean any commodity that is not an agricultural commodity or an excluded commodity; excluded commodity is defined in Section 1a(19) of the CEA to include any "interest rate, exchange rate, currency, security, security index" and other financial rates and assets).

8. *See In re Coinflip, Inc.*, CFTC No. 15-29, 2015 WL 5535736 (Sept. 17, 2015). In this order, the CFTC found that Coinflip's Bitcoin options were offered in violation of CFTC regulation 32.2, which governs commodity option transactions. The CFTC noted that the options "were not conducted pursuant to [CFTC] Regulation 32.3", the so-called "trade option exemption", which permits trading of commodity options on exempt and agricultural commodities, but not on excluded commodities such as securities, currencies, interest rates and financial indices. The CFTC, in describing why the trade option exemption was not available for Coinflip's options, focused on requirements under CFTC regulation that the options must be offered by eligible contract participants to commercial users of the underlying commodity, and not on the classification of Bitcoin as an excluded commodity.

9. *See* CFTC Release pr7654-17, CFTC Statement on Self-Certification of Bitcoin Products by CME, CFE and Cantor Exchange (Dec. 1, 2017). *See also* CFTC Backgrounder on Oversight of and Approach to Virtual Currency Futures Markets (Jan. 4, 2018) (describing the CFTC's authority with respect to virtual currency and the "heightened review" employed during the Bitcoin futures self-certification process).

10. SEC Chairman Jay Clayton, Statement on Cryptocurrencies and Initial Coin Offerings, at n. 2 (Dec. 11, 2017) ("The CFTC has designated Bitcoin as a commodity. Fraud and manipulation involving Bitcoin traded in interstate commerce are appropriately within the purview of the CFTC, as is the regulation of commodity futures tied directly to [B]itcoin."); *see also* CNBC, *SEC Chief Says Agency Won't Change Securities Laws to Cater to Cryptocurrencies* (Jun. 6, 2018) ("'Cryptocurrencies: These are replacements for sovereign currencies, replace the dollar, the euro, the yen with [B]itcoin,' Clayton said. 'That type of currency is not a security.'").

11. Investment advisers not registered with the SEC may be subject to registration with U.S. states.

12. 17 U.S.C. § 206(4)-2.

13. For an adviser that has its principal office and place of business outside of the United States, an Advisers Act registration exemption is available under the private fund

adviser rule, so long as: (i) the adviser has no client that is a U.S. person (generally as defined in Regulation S under the Securities Act) except for "qualifying private funds" (as defined in the rule); and (ii) all assets managed by the adviser at a place of business in the United States are solely attributable to private fund assets with a value of less than $150 million. Advisers relying on this exemption are still required to file certain information with the SEC.

14. Cold storage refers to the process of storing digital assets, such as bitcoins, offline (i.e., storing the private keys on a device not connected to the internet). However, the private keys associated with this process may have been exposed to the internet at some time during the generation of the signing process. Deep cold storage, however, is a type of cold storage where not only are the digital assets stored offline, but also the private keys associated with those assets are generated in offline systems, and the signing process of the transactions is also made in offline systems. The systems used in this type of storage never touch the internet; they are created offline, they are stored offline, and they are offline when signing transactions.

15. *See* 1940 Act § 3(c)(1)-(7).

16. SEC, Staff Letter: Engaging on Fund Innovation and Cryptocurrency-related Holdings (Jan. 18, 2018), available at https://www.sec.gov/divisions/investment/noaction/2018/cryptocurrency-011818.htm (the "**Letter**").

17. On March 23, 2018, the SEC issued an order instituting proceedings to determine whether it will approve a proposal by NYSE Arca to list two ProShares-sponsored Bitcoin futures-backed exchange-traded funds ("**ETFs**"). On April 5, 2018, the SEC published a second order instituting proceedings relating to a rule-change proposal by Cboe BZX Exchange, Inc. that would allow for the listing of two GraniteShares-sponsored ETFs that invest in Bitcoin futures contracts (both orders together, the "**Orders**"). The Orders ask for comments on many of the same issues raised in the Letter and institute a new period of review for such products, including a request for public comment on 12 areas of interest. These areas include concerns relating to: (1) such ETFs' investment practices; (2) the underlying spot and futures markets for Bitcoin; and (3) how such markets may in turn affect ETFs that invest in Bitcoin futures. For example, the SEC requests comments on the ETFs' valuation policies (e.g., how would such policies account for the possibility of a hard fork), including how such policies relate to the underlying Bitcoin spot markets, their potential for manipulation and what, if any, effect these factors could have on the ETFs' net asset value. On July 26, 2018, the SEC issued an order disapproving a rule-change proposal by Bats BZX Exchange, Inc. that would have allowed for the listing of the Winklevoss Bitcoin Trust.

18. *See* CFTC Rule 180.1.

Gregory S. Rowland
Tel: +1 212 450 4930 / Email: gregory.rowland@davispolk.com
Gregory S. Rowland is a partner in Davis Polk's Corporate Department, practising in the Investment Management Group. He focuses on providing transactional, regulatory and compliance advice relating to investment advisers, mutual funds, closed-end funds, business development companies, private equity funds and hedge funds. He devotes a large portion of his practice to the structuring, launch and operation of registered investment companies and hedge funds and to the sales, acquisitions and restructurings of asset management firms.

Mr Rowland advises financial institutions, technology companies and asset managers in connection with transactional, regulatory and compliance issues concerning digital currency and blockchain activities, including digital currency fund formation. In addition, he advises financial institutions, fund sponsors, corporations, employees' securities companies, and other entities regarding exemptions under the Investment Company Act and Investment Advisers Act.

Trevor I. Kiviat
Tel: +1 212 450 3448 / Email: trevor.kiviat@davispolk.com
Trevor I. Kiviat is an associate in Davis Polk's Investment Management Group. His practice focuses on advising clients on the formation and operation of private investment funds, including private equity funds and hedge funds. He also regularly provides regulatory and compliance advice to his private fund clients.

In addition, Mr Kiviat wrote the first widely read and cited academic paper distinguishing Bitcoin from blockchain technology. He has been cited in the media as an expert on blockchain technology and digital assets and has lectured on related topics at Duke University's law school and business school. He advises clients on the novel strategic, operational and regulatory issues relating to digital asset-based businesses.

Davis Polk & Wardwell LLP

450 Lexington Avenue, New York, NY 10017, USA
Tel: +1 212 450 4000 / Fax: +1 212 701 5800 / URL: www.davispolk.com

The yellow brick road for consumer tokens: The path to SEC and CFTC compliance

David L. Concannon, Yvette D. Valdez & Stephen P. Wink
Latham & Watkins LLP

Developing a framework for consumer tokens

With the rapid growth in the development of blockchain technology, virtual currencies and token sales (sometimes referred to as initial coin offerings, or ICOs) in 2017 and beyond, ICOs came under increased regulatory scrutiny, particularly in the United States. The question on the minds of many entrepreneurs and their counsel during this period, has been whether the issuance and sale of "consumer" or "utility" tokens – those designed for use by consumers on a distributed platform and not intended to constitute securities – is possible in the United States.[1] Based on recent statements of senior officials at the US Securities and Exchange Commission (the SEC), it appears there may be a viable regulatory path to the issuance of consumer tokens that would not necessarily be viewed as "securities" subject to SEC oversight. In this chapter, we discuss the legal issues surrounding such issuances under the US federal commodities and securities laws.

Existing frameworks

The securities law framework

The initial inquiry is whether the token sale would be considered an offer or sale of a security under the US federal securities laws. The SEC's approach to whether a digital asset is a security derives from its application of the test set forth in *SEC v. W.J. Howey Co.* (the *Howey* Test).[2] The *Howey* Test determines whether an asset constitutes an "investment contract," one of the enumerated types of instruments defined in the securities laws.[3] The test states that an investment contract involves (i) an investment of money, (ii) in a common enterprise, (iii) in which the investor is led to expect profits, (iv) derived from the entrepreneurial or managerial efforts of one or more third parties.[4] If the test is satisfied, it is immaterial whether the enterprise is speculative or non-speculative, or whether there is a sale of property with or without intrinsic value.[5] In short, the heart of the analysis is to focus on the economic reality of the arrangement in question.

In July 2017, the SEC applied the *Howey* Test to digital assets for the first time, and arrived at the conclusion that the sale of Decentralized Autonomous Organization tokens (DAO tokens), a digital asset, was an unregistered securities offering that proceeded without a valid exemption from Section 5 of the Securities Act of 1933 (the Securities Act). The SEC observed that the DAO tokens satisfied the four prongs of the *Howey* Test, including that they were designed to provide holders with a return on their investment.[6] The SEC made clear that to the extent instruments have the indicia of investment contracts, they should be offered and sold in compliance with the securities laws, and any intermediaries for such sales, including exchanges on which such instruments were traded, would likewise need to comply with the registration and compliance requirements of these laws. While this was not an unexpected outcome for practitioners,[7] the report served as a helpful reminder to this nascent market that the securities laws apply regardless of the form in which the securities are created and sold.

On December 11, 2017, the SEC issued an order instituting cease-and-desist proceedings with respect to an offering by Munchee Inc. (Munchee).[8] At the time the order was issued, Munchee was in the process of offering digital tokens (the MUN Tokens) to investors through an ICO.[9] In the order, the SEC concluded the ICO was an unregistered offering of securities without an available exemption, despite Munchee's argument that the MUN Tokens served a utility function. Indeed, many practitioners believed at the time that the MUN Tokens had much of the requisite indicia that could lead to their characterisation as utility or consumer tokens, rather than securities. Nonetheless, the MUN Tokens were classified as securities, in large measure because they were marketed as investments amid a substantial marketing blitz that bypassed Munchee's actual user base, focusing instead on regular purchasers of digital assets. A key lesson of the *Munchee* order was that despite the utility design features of the MUN Tokens, the nature of the offering and the presence of investment intent will constitute material factors for the SEC in determining whether a particular transaction may be subject to the securities laws.[10]

William Hinman, Director of the SEC's Division of Corporation Finance, recently indicated a possible path for token transactions to no longer be characterised exclusively as securities transactions.[11] He began by querying whether "a digital asset offered as a security can, over time, become something other than a security." Director Hinman offered two answers to this question. On the one hand, he posited that a digital asset representing a set of rights giving the holder a financial interest in an enterprise would remain a security. On the other hand, he reasoned that a digital asset that, for example, is used to purchase goods or services within a sufficiently decentralised ecosystem, could evolve such that it would cease to be classified as a security under US securities laws.

Director Hinman emphasised that, similar to the assets in *Howey* (which involved assets that were clearly not securities, but fruit trees), digital assets are not necessarily securities. Rather, in addition to the underlying rights associated with such assets, the manner of sale and the reasonable expectations of the purchasers help determine whether a particular digital asset is a security. This is underscored by Director Hinman's reference to *Gary Plastic Packaging v. Merrill Lynch, Pierce, Fenner, & Smith Inc.*,[12] in which the Second Circuit held that transactions in instruments that themselves are not securities can still be subject to the securities laws, when such instruments animate a broader investment contract. There, the court found that the establishment of a secondary market as a critical part of an issuer's marketing efforts for what was otherwise not a security (specifically, certificates of deposit), coupled with the potential for investment profits, rendered the application of the securities laws necessary. In the case of nascent platforms and networks, digital tokens sold in an offering by promoters to "develop the enterprise" will most often constitute securities because the entrepreneurial efforts of the enterprise's promoters will be the primary source of value creation in the token. According to Director Hinman, applying the securities laws in such cases is important because they help mitigate informational asymmetries that exist between issuers and investors. But, if the network on which the token functions is sufficiently decentralised – that is, "where purchasers would no longer reasonably expect a person or group to carry out essential managerial or entrepreneurial efforts" – there is less of a public policy need to correct the informational asymmetries the securities laws aim to prevent.

The commodities law framework

The US Commodity Futures Trading Commission (the CFTC) regulates the swaps (*i.e.*, the CFTC's term for derivatives) and futures markets and retains general enforcement authority to police fraud and manipulation in cash or "spot" commodities markets.[13] In 2014, then-CFTC Chairman Timothy Massad observed that what the CFTC has referred to as virtual currencies are "commodities" subject to provisions of the Commodity Exchange Act, as amended (the CEA).[14] Since 2015, the CFTC has been active in bringing enforcement actions when virtual currency enterprises run afoul of regulatory requirements[15] and in the enforcement against fraud and manipulation in the virtual currency "spot" markets.[16]

Pre-functional consumer token sales[17]

Sales of tokens to fund a promoter's development of a token-based network have long been considered to constitute investment contracts, regardless of the form of instrument evidencing the sale. That is, the efforts of the promoter remain central to the value of the instrument being sold, thus satisfying the *Howey* Test as an investment contract. As a result, in an effort to separate the pre-functional sale and the underlying consumer token, new financing instruments – including the Simple Agreement for Future Tokens (the SAFT)[18] and other similar token presale instruments – were designed. While such instruments attempted to solve the securities law issues with presales, they raised significant other concerns.[19]

Securities law issues

These instruments commonly fail to address the status of the underlying tokens and the impact of the presale offering on the marketing of the underlying tokens. That is, by marketing the token presale as an investment opportunity, these instruments were implicitly marketing the investment value of the underlying token. As a general matter, such instruments have been and continue to be marketed to purchasers with investment intent, such as hedge funds, venture capital funds and others, and, in at least some cases, purchasers are required to represent that they are purchasing for investment purposes.[20] In addition, settlement of these instruments contemplates delivery of the token at network launch,[21] and thus, at least with respect to the initial iteration of these instruments, the delivery of tokens for consumptive use will occur contemporaneously, or at least nearly so, with the delivery of tokens to purchasers who were investors. This would seem to argue in favour of the proposition that a token launch with delivery of tokens in settlement of these instruments is not directed solely to consumers, and, under the logic of *Gary Plastic* and the *Munchee* order, is a securities transaction, not a consumer token launch.[22]

While recent iterations of these instruments have begun to acknowledge that issuances of the underlying tokens could be securities transactions, they continue to subject issuers and purchasers to significant risks by potentially increasing the likelihood that the underlying tokens will be deemed to be securities. This does not represent a viable outcome for many token-based networks, which require the free transfer of tokens on the network as part of their necessary function, because the US securities laws often require the existence and registration of an intermediary in securities transactions (*i.e.,* the transfer of tokens deemed to be securities). Accordingly, an issuer or platform may be required to register as a broker-dealer or exchange (or alternative trading system)[23] to permit the functioning of its token-based network,[24] which would render many token-based networks unusable. Although recent statements indicate an acceptance of the notion that a digital asset originally issued as a security could subsequently cease to be a security once the network is sufficiently decentralised,[25] the uncertainty that remains regarding the viability and timing of the consumer token sale raises challenges for appropriate disclosures to investors and potential liability for issuers. This is particularly the case when the entire investment decision is based on the availability and functionality of the underlying token, and it would seem to be challenging to craft sufficient disclosure in such a circumstance where the entire investment proposition is subject to this level of uncertainty.

Commodities law issues

Beyond the securities law concerns, the SAFT, and more recent iterations of the SAFT and similar presale instruments, also raise commodities laws concerns. Because cryptocurrencies are commodities,[26] a presale of consumer tokens through an instrument that provides the right to receive tokens in the future, or confer the right to exchange or convert such instrument into tokens that are not securities, may be a forward contract for the sale of a commodity or a commodity option, and subject to regulation by the CFTC as a swap, if an exemption is not available.

(a) *Commodity forward contracts*

Forward sales of commodities fall within the CEA's broad definition of "swap," which encompasses numerous types of derivatives, and are subject to regulation by the CFTC absent an applicable exclusion.[27] Notably, the sale of a non-financial commodity for deferred shipment or delivery is excluded from the swap definition, so long as it is intended to be physically delivered,[28] but provided such forward contract also qualifies as a commercial merchandising transaction (Non-Financial Forward Contract Exclusion).[29] If such instruments are purchased by investors or speculators, they will not satisfy the requirement of the Non-Financial Forward Contract Exclusion because the purchasers are not "commercial market participants."[30] The CFTC has expressly stated that hedge funds, acting in their capacity as investors, are not commercial market participants.[31] The SAFT is effectively a prepaid forward contract of a commodity whereby parties have agreed a price or percentage discount on the token to be delivered at a later date. As discussed above, the SAFT was (and continues to be) largely marketed to investors and not commercial market participants;[32] SAFT investors would not be eligible for the Non-Financial Forward Contract Exclusion.

(b) *Commodity options*

Later versions of the SAFT and similar presale instruments have also included convertible features, which provide investors or the issuer, as applicable, a call or put right to deliver tokens upon the consummation of a token sale at an agreed price or discount. Such an instrument may constitute a commodity option and would be subject to CFTC regulation as a swap,[33] unless an exemption applies. Trade options are generally exempt from regulation by the CFTC, other than certain large trader reporting requirements and the CFTC's general anti-fraud and anti-manipulation enforcement authority (the Trade Option Exemption).[34] In order to qualify as a trade option and benefit from the Trade Option Exemption,[35] the commodity option in question must be: (i) intended to be physically settled if exercised; (ii) entered into with an offeror who is either an ECP[36] or a producer, processor or commercial user of, or merchant handling, the commodity (or products or by-products thereof) that is the subject of the option, and such offeror is offering to enter into such option solely for the purposes related to its business as such; and (iii) entered into with an offeree who is either a producer, processor or commercial user of, or merchant handling, the commodity (or products or by-products thereof) that is the subject of the option, and such offeree is entering into such option solely for the purposes related to its business as such.

Unfortunately (as stated above in connection with the Non-Financial Forward Contract Exclusion), many of the SAFT and similar presale instruments are not offered to commercial market participants who would satisfy the "offeree" prong, even if the issuer of the instrument could satisfy the "offeror" prong. Additionally, even if such instruments are offered to "consumers" they would not necessarily satisfy the "offeree" prong of the Trade Option Exemption, unless such consumer could establish a nexus to a business activity. Accordingly, SAFT investors are unlikely to qualify for the Trade Option Exemption.

(c) *Hybrid instrument exemption*

Furthermore, since the SAFT and similar presale instruments may constitute or contain a commodity forward contract or commodity option and may not otherwise qualify for the Trade Option Exemption or the Non-Financial Forward Contract Exclusion, we also consider whether such instruments would meet the Hybrid Instrument Exemption (defined below) and, as a result, be exempt from commodities law regulation. Under CFTC Rule 34.2(a), a "hybrid instrument" is defined to include an equity or debt security with "one or more commodity-dependent components that have payment features similar to commodity futures or commodity options contracts or combinations thereof."[37] Under Section 2(f) of the CEA, a hybrid instrument that is "predominantly a security" is exempt from the provisions of the CEA if, among other things, the instrument is not marketed as a contract of sale of a commodity for future delivery (or option on such a contract) subject to the CEA (the Marketing Condition) (such exemption being the Hybrid Instrument Exemption).[38]

We believe that the SAFT and similar presale instruments likely do not meet the Marketing Condition of the Hybrid Instrument Exemption, given that investors in such instruments are motivated to purchase the instrument solely for the potential of receiving the underlying commodity (*i.e.,* the token) in the future. Modified versions of such instruments – including iterations convertible into either the issuer's equity or tokens – also could be subject to regulation by the CFTC because it may be challenging to successfully argue that such instruments are predominantly securities that satisfy the conditions of the Hybrid Instrument Exemption (and, in particular, the Marketing Condition).[39]

(d) *Consequences of CFTC regulation*

Because such presale instruments may have an embedded swap, which does not qualify for an exemption from regulation by the CFTC (as discussed above), such presale instrument would be subject to the full swaps regulatory framework applicable to such instruments. In particular, in order to trade over-the-counter, swaps must be entered into between eligible contract participants (ECPs).[40] While some investors may qualify as ECPs, token issuers typically are early stage companies that may not have at least $10 million gross assets, and as a result, would not satisfy the ECP test. A swap entered into by parties who are not ECPs would be in violation of the CEA and CFTC regulation and both parties could face penalties and sanctions for such actions.

Potential solutions available through traditional financing instruments

Traditional early-stage financing structures, such as preferred stock and convertible promissory notes,[41] are "tried and true" structures that generally exhibit the necessary flexibility to address the needs of early stage companies/token issuers and token platforms. We believe these structures can be augmented to address investor demand for exposure to consumer tokens, while enabling the parties to comply with applicable securities and commodities laws. This can be achieved by providing investors with various combinations of token-related purchase, economic and voting rights.

First, the conversion and exchange rights featured in currently popular presale instruments could be replaced with appropriately limited token sale participation and economic rights that reduce the regulatory risks associated with consumer token sales discussed above. For instance, the purchase right would not represent a conversion or exchange of the security, but would include these rights in addition to the rights granted to the holder of the securities. The exercise of such token sale participation rights could be limited to sales or distributions of the consumer tokens that would not be deemed to be securities transactions, such as when the network had achieved sufficient decentralisation (although the challenges in defining an objective standard for this trigger may reduce the practicality of this option). The participation rights could also be limited to purchases for actual use, or limit the consumer tokens reserved for distribution or sale to investors, and require that any distributions or sales thereof occur in a manner that supports the broader consumer token-based network.

Instead of the inclusion of pre-negotiated token prices in such instruments, which – from a commodities law point of view – may increase the risk of being considered a commodity option because such pre-agreed price could be seen as a strike price, the participation rights could be coupled with "most favoured nation" pricing provisions, guaranteeing certain investors the best token sale and distribution terms offered by the issuer to any other third party. These rights could also be supplemented with token economic rights that could be triggered in lieu of participation in the consumer token sale. For example, preferred stock could be issued with various rights tied to consumer token sales, such as pre-negotiated dividend or redemption rights, or a convertible promissory note under which the issuer pays a multiple of the note's aggregate principal amount or the note converts into preferred stock with dividend or redemption rights. Such token economic rights would have the goal of providing the investor with a similar economic outcome of participating in the consumer token sale. As a result, the careful balancing of such token sale participation and economic rights could provide issuers the flexibility to allow for the participation of investors eager to receive token economics while protecting the development of the underlying network and consumer tokens from the application of the securities laws.

Second, because consumer tokens and the corresponding network protocol often represent a significant portion of the value proposition associated with investing in such platforms, investors can reasonably expect to receive voting rights with respect to the creation and distribution of tokens by the issuer, including the right to approve the initiation of any offerings or distributions.[42] Eventually, as the pathway for consumer token sales becomes more clear, voting rights grants may be more narrowly tailored to only apply when such a sale does not meet certain specifications. In addition, investors may seek additional protections to prevent potential uses of the issuer's token-based network that circumvent their consumer token-related economic and participation rights.

Finally, these preferred stock and convertible promissory note structures may also be preferable because they more directly address the commodities law issues discussed above. First, conferring future participation rights on an investor to participate in a token sale, or conferring economic rights to an investor in respect of future distributions, is arguably not a swap subject to CFTC regulation. There is no strike price or final price differential that creates market risk that the CFTC would necessarily be incentivised to regulate in the commodity options market. Separately, if a swap were deemed to exist, in such structures where the conditions of the Hybrid Instrument Exemption other than the Marketing Condition are satisfied, one could argue that – despite the associated consumer token rights – such instruments are "predominantly securities" and unlikely to run afoul of the Marketing Condition, because the commodity forward or option would be a small portion of the value of the instrument. Accordingly, it would be much harder to argue that such instrument was marketed as a swap or purchased by investors solely for the purpose of receiving the value provided by the swap component. That is, because the predominant value of the instrument is a traditional security providing specific rights with respect to the issuer – such as traditional preferred stock rights (*e.g.,* liquidation preference, dividends, anti-dilution protection) or traditional promissory note rights (*e.g.,* returns of principal, potential conversion into equity) – such consumer token presales could arguably fall outside some (if not all) of the CFTC regulatory regime by qualifying for the Hybrid Instrument Exemption or being excluded entirely from the swap definition.[43] Of course, while each instrument would need to be analysed on its own merits, we believe this alternate structure has great promise for addressing commodities law issues.

These structures are also preferred from a securities law perspective for many similar reasons – because the investor is receiving a more traditional security, the various rights they are purchasing are far less ambiguous, and appropriate disclosures regarding the material aspects of the investment are more easily crafted.

Enabling true consumer token sales

Once a platform and token protocol has been developed, the question remains whether a viable consumer token sale may be accomplished. Director Hinman identified a number of factors centering around two main inquiries to help distinguish when digital assets transactions may be characterised as securities transactions.[44] First, he emphasised the role of the promoter or enterprise and the corresponding expectation of profits therefrom. Critical in this inquiry is the nature of the marketing of the consumer token and its platform, and the nature of the purchasers. Second, Director Hinman indicated the design of tokens and their economies should be free of the characteristics of a security.

We believe we can draw several inferences from Director Hinman's remarks that bear upon this analysis. First, tokens offered in a manner intended to appeal to an investor's investment intent will trigger the application of the securities laws. Second, when the token-based network has developed to an extent that the value of the tokens is no longer dependent upon the entrepreneurial or managerial efforts of such network's promoters, token trading on that network will not be considered securities transactions. Third, offerings of tokens with utility on a functioning token-based network that are specifically directed solely to users of that network may be conducted in a manner that renders the securities laws inapplicable.

Features of established non-security virtual currencies

Two of the most widely held and well-known digital assets – Bitcoin and Ether – provide good examples of digital assets that Director Hinman expressly posited no longer constitute securities primarily due to the decentralised nature of their use.[45] The "efforts of others" prong of the *Howey* Test requires that such efforts must be "undeniably significant ones, those essential managerial efforts which affect the failure or success of the enterprise."[46] Two seminal cases provide guidance on this prong for instruments traded in well-developed markets such as Bitcoin and Ether.[47] In both *Noa v. Key Futures* and *SEC v. Belmont Reid & Co.*, the Ninth Circuit applied the *Howey* Test to the sale of precious metals, finding that the *Howey* Test is not satisfied if the expectation of economic return is based on market forces, and not on the efforts of a promoter. Thus, the applicability of these cases to the analysis of Bitcoin and Ether within this prong of the *Howey* Test (and therefore the analysis of whether either Bitcoin or Ether is a security) depends on the existence of an established, decentralised market where the spot price is determined by ordinary market forces.

What is the role of the promoter or enterprise? Decentralised networks

As discussed above, the SEC's emerging regulatory framework for consumer tokens appears focused on a threshold question derived from the fourth prong of the *Howey* Test: is the token-based network sufficiently decentralised/independent of the entrepreneurial efforts of the promoter? There are several factors underlying this inquiry and each case requires careful analysis, and, without further guidance from the SEC, it is difficult to predict the appropriate weighting of such factors.

(a) *Ongoing development and maintenance of the network*

For a token-based network to be truly decentralised, no single enterprise should have the ability to significantly and directly influence the value of the consumer tokens exchanged on the network. This implicitly includes ongoing efforts to develop and maintain the network. In his discussion of the Bitcoin and Ether analysis, Director Hinman stated:

> *[W]hen I look at Bitcoin today, I do not see a central third party whose efforts are a key determining factor in the enterprise. The network on which Bitcoin functions is operational and appears to have been decentralised for some time, perhaps from inception. . . . And putting aside the fundraising that accompanied the creation of Ether, based on my understanding of the present state of Ether, the Ethereum network and its decentralised structure, current offers and sales of Ether are not securities transactions. And, as with Bitcoin, applying the disclosure regime of the federal securities laws to current transactions in Ether would seem to add little value.*

Open source projects, where a variety of parties may contribute to the ongoing development of the network, clearly have a greater chance of meeting this requirement.

(b) *Use of token sale proceeds*

Similarly, the expected use of proceeds from a related token sale can impact whether a related token-based network is sufficiently decentralised. For example, a use of proceeds that involves further development and maintenance of the network could lead to a conclusion that the efforts of the issuer remain central to the value of the token, and hence, Director Hinman's focus on this characteristic.[48] This further supports the use of traditional financing instruments, coupled with economic rights in future token offerings. Issuers utilising such instruments would be able to fund the development of their network from the investments received pursuant to such instruments and would, subsequently, be able to use the proceeds from token sales to deliver a return of capital to investors, thereby clearly distinguishing early stage investments from token purchases and supporting the position that the tokens themselves should not be deemed to be securities.

(c) *Network governance*

The SEC also indicated that a token-based network's governance structure will be considered when determining whether such network is decentralised.[49] In its most simple form, a decentralised governance structure would provide token holders the ability to directly determine matters relevant to the network's development. On the other hand, voting rights are an attribute of equity securities, and thus can militate toward a conclusion that the tokens are securities. In any event, the retention of governance rights by the promoter is relevant to its ability to impact the value of the potential investment. Director Hinman specifically noted that it should be considered whether "persons or entities other than the promoter exercise governance rights or meaningful influence."[50]

(d) *Robust token economy*

The value of tokens on certain token-based networks is driven by a robust token economy pitting a number of different forces with different operating incentives against each other. These competing elements will be ascendant, and have a corresponding impact on the token value, at differing times. Courts have reasoned that this sort of market valuation mechanism is critical to distinguish a commodity from a security, as the value in the instrument is created by these broad market forces rather than the efforts of others.[51] Filecoin[52] is an apt example of a robust economic structure that helps ensure market forces drive token values independent of the promoter's efforts. The Filecoin network involves three network participants: (i) clients, who pay to store and retrieve data; (ii) storage miners, who provide data storage to the network; and (iii) retrieval miners, who provide data retrieval to the network.[53] As a result, the competing activities of these three groups create the value of a Filecoin token through the creation of supply and demand economics. This also means the success of the Filecoin network hinges upon a sufficient number of market participants contributing to the network simultaneously, which is a premise reflected in the high proportion of Filecoin tokens allocated to miners in exchange for storage and retrieval services.[54]

There are numerous token-based networks and token economy models that similarly promote the development of a robust economic structure. The success of most decentralised token-based marketplaces, whether for data storage, artificial intelligence, real estate or intellectual property, is dependent on market participants driving the value of the networks and its corresponding tokens. As a result, these marketplaces, like those for Bitcoin and Ether (which rely on market participants to record transactions on their respective blockchains), have a market valuation mechanism that is helpful in distinguishing a commodity from a security.

Is the asset designed for consumptive purposes? Consumer tokens and consumer token sales

Numerous consumer token and consumer token sale features warrant consideration in furthering the consumer token analysis to determine whether the securities laws may apply.

(a) *Functioning network*

A factor closely related to the role of the promoter discussed above, though distinct, is the question of whether the token-based network is "fully functioning or in the early stages of development."[55] A common feature of many early token sales was that they were commenced before the consumer could actually utilise the token. While some consumer goods are purchased in this manner (*e.g.,* concert tickets or a new Tesla car), consumer token presales complicate the analysis of whether "the primary motivation for purchasing the digital asset is for personal use or consumption."[56] As a result, issuers should, to the extent possible, launch their token-based network prior to initiating consumer token sales.

(b) *Secondary markets and transferability*

In February 2018, SEC Chairman Jay Clayton testified before the US Senate Committee on Banking, Housing and Urban Affairs, in part sharing his particular concern for ICO issuers and emphasising the secondary market trading potential of the tokens offered for sale.[57] This line of thinking clearly follows the *Gary Plastic* case, where the marketing of a non-security investment (*i.e.,* bank certificates of deposit) that included the promise of a secondary market transmutes the certificates of deposit into investment contracts.[58] Accordingly, the marketing of a token based on the ability to quickly sell the token in a secondary market strongly supports the view that such token is a security. However, the mere availability of a secondary market developing following a token sale arguably should not be dispositive and, perhaps, should not matter at all. Again, *Gary Plastic* stands for the notion that it is the *marketing* of the "investment" based on the potential of the secondary market that is what makes the instrument a security. Of course, there are many everyday commodities for which secondary markets regularly develop – in fact, Ebay has built a robust business on this basis – and the mere existence of such markets do not transmute the instruments into securities.

For example, a large number of active market participants is critical to the success of Filecoin's network. It is difficult to imagine a scenario where it could achieve the critical mass of network participants necessary if such network participants were restricted from exchanging in some way their Filecoin tokens with other participants for other digital assets or tokens as part of continually broadening the universe of token holders. In order for a network to work under isolated conditions, where such transfers were not permitted, not only would suppliers have to consume the resources created by the network, but maintaining a balance among suppliers and producers would be exceedingly difficult. The secondary market transactions accordingly act to balance the various economic demands without any one actor having to play all roles. Otherwise, for Filecoin, a miner would need to both provide and consume storage and retrieval services, because consumption would be the only way to realise the economic gain in exchange for providing such services. As a result, there would be little incentive for the miner to participate on such a network. A similar case can be made for any network that includes both suppliers/producers of goods or services and consumers of goods or services. Furthermore, supply on any such market would decrease rapidly if the inputs required to produce the supply of goods and services were not principally derived from the tokens received upon sale, or if an insufficient number of other goods and services were available to enable suppliers to consume all of the tokens they earn within such marketplace. Given the negative effect on network participation that limiting secondary market activity would have, it is likely that overly broad restrictions would impede competition and that only the largest and most established marketplaces would succeed.

Because of the foregoing, a measured approach to addressing secondary market activity and transferability is advisable. Fortunately, the flexibility available with second and third generation blockchain technologies provide companies with several options. First, purchasers of consumer tokens in a consumer token sale could be required to agree to a lockup mechanism, whereby a smart contract prevents the purchaser from selling their tokens for a certain period of time or until they participate on the network in the required manner. That is, they could be unlocked initially only in the event they were utilised on the platform itself first, and thereafter could be traded in the secondary market. Second, a tiered transfer fee or other incentive structure could be implemented, whereby the fees (or other similar incentives) for tokens transferred in connection with participation on the token-based network could be lower than the fees for transfers to non-network participants. In each of these cases, initial purchasers would not have the same profit motive in seeking secondary market for token sales as they may have in a typical ICO. Director Hinman appears to have suggested as much in his enumerated factors.[59]

(c) *Inflationary issuances*

Another aspect of consumer token sale structures that warrants discussion is the impact of inflationary/deflationary pressures in token economies. Depending on the token structure, there are a number of scenarios in which subsequent issuances of tokens in exchange for contributions to the economy of the network can simultaneously facilitate network growth while limiting the immediate speculative potential of the token. For example, Filecoin's token allocation design made 70% of the total Filecoin tokens available for miners in exchange for data storage and retrieval services. As those tokens will be subsequently distributed and "earned" by miners, the Filecoin token purchasers are "diluted" in an inflationary sense. However, unlike in the context of an equity security where dilution is significant because the valuation of the interest is always proportionate to the relative interest in the enterprise value, here the value of the token is based on the value of the goods and services that may be received in exchange, and the market supply and demand for such goods and services. Thus, the impact of dilution on a true consumer token is quite different and the value of the token should correspond more directly to the value to the consumer of the applicable goods and services. As a result, consideration should be given to the supply dynamics of a token economy.[60] Ultimate control over dilutive issuances is also a factor in network governance, which may impact the analysis above regarding the decentralisation of a given network.

(d) *Token retention*

To date, a common feature of ICOs has been the retention of the tokens by issuers for distribution to founders, employees, advisors and investors. In instances where there are reasonable and justifiable grounds to believe that these individuals can and will consume these tokens through their own market participation and will thus assist in the seeding of the network, then consumer token issuers should not be dissuaded from including the retention of consumer tokens in their allotment strategy. However, issuers should exercise caution in doing so, particularly in cases where the products and services offered on an issuer's network or the number of tokens retained could not reasonably be consumed by its founders, employees, advisors and investors. In such instances, it would be difficult to make a credible argument to the SEC that such tokens are not being held for investment purposes.[61] In addition, such retention of tokens also makes it more difficult for the token issuer to demonstrate that the tokens are "[d]ispersed across a diverse user base[,]" rather than being "[c]oncentrated in the hands of a few that can exert influence[.]"[62]

As a result, companies who wish to reward their teams for the successful development of a token-based network giving rise to a consumer token sale should look to traditional equity compensation methods, which can be augmented by consumer tokens to the extent a viable use case can be established. Additionally, selling restrictions with respect to both timing and price of tokens by such holders could be adopted to bolster the argument that such grants were not made to persons with an investment intent.

(e) *Token sale legal documentation*

Another means of discouraging purchasers of consumer tokens from an expectation of profit could be found in the documentation used in sales of tokens by issuers. Such agreements could include representations and warranties requiring purchasers to state that their intention is to use such consumer tokens on the issuer's network. As discussed above, such documentation could also include lockup mechanisms, whereby the purchaser's tokens could be "locked" using a smart contract for a specified period. Furthermore, instruments could grant issuers a first refusal with respect to any purchaser's tokens, whereby the issuer would be entitled to repurchase the tokens held by a user if the user had determined not to use them on the issuer's network. In many respects, this could be functionally similar to rights of return that are commonly provided by retailers with respect to tangible consumer goods, and issuers may be well advised to allocate a small percentage of any consumer token sales for such repurchases. While on most networks the issuer will only ever have privity of contract with the initial purchasers of consumer tokens, utilisation of these mechanisms could substantially reduce the risk of such purchasers having an expectation of requiring the protection of securities laws. However, establishment of valuation protocols and resale price, as well as the potential of a withdrawal of cash from an issuer, may detract from the attractiveness of this alternative.

Seeding network activity

Based on the foregoing considerations, issuers who both operate decentralised networks featuring tokens designed for consumption, and sell such tokens in a manner designed to dissuade purchases for investment, should be capable of avoiding the application of securities laws to such token sales under the *Howey* Test. However, this current paradigm appears to create a paradox, given that the process of creating a decentralised and functional network on which consumer tokens can be utilised necessitates that issuers first seed network activity by issuing consumer tokens in transactions that do not trigger the application of securities laws.

As a result, issuers may seek to seed their network through the distribution of consumer tokens via "airdrops" and other distributions to affiliates, vendors and community members. Such distributions promote network activity, facilitate the implementation governance procedures and enable network testing prior to full launch. The information garnered from this process enables developers to resolve potential issues and simultaneously enhances the credibility of the project both within and outside its community. Furthermore, such activity can help consumers better understand the value of the overall network and each consumer token, which ultimately promotes market efficiency. The benefits of such seed activity extend to consumer token issuances targeting strategic partners, who may also assist with the development of the network prior to launch. In addition, this seed activity permits the nascent token economy of the platform to grow, allowing forces beyond those of the initial promoter to begin to determine the value of the token. As a result, this activity directly addresses several of the factors identified by Director Hinman and can strengthen the case that a particular token is a consumer token.[63]

Nonetheless, issuers need to be aware that the SEC may take the view that the securities laws apply to airdrops of tokens, even though no money or digital currency funds is given by airdrop recipients. For example, in the early days of the internet, some issuers sought to issue free shares of common stock to registered website users, as part of a broader promotion to attract traffic to the website and promote brand awareness and loyalty. The SEC took the view that the free distribution of shares was a "sale" of securities.[64] Similarly, the SEC has taken the view that the spin-off of shares of a subsidiary as a free stock dividend to an issuer's shareholders can be a sale of securities.[65] As a result, unless and until the SEC gives more lenient guidance, airdrops should be considered and conducted in the same manner as token offerings, generally, as discussed above.

Conclusion

Much has been made of the need for certainty, and perhaps even innovation, in the application of various laws, including the US securities and commodities laws, to commercial activities relating to blockchain, cryptocurrencies and related technologies. After all, the applicable federal securities statute is 85 years old, and the seminal case, *Howey*, is more than 70 years old. That said, the SEC has not retreated from the application of existing precedent when examining token transactions. Nevertheless, given the underlying principles, and the SEC's public statements, there is some reason for optimism that the existing framework will permit at least some transactions in tokens – consumer token launches – to be executed without the application of the federal securities laws. We suggest, however, that it continues to be prudent for interested parties to seek guidance directly from the SEC staff before proceeding.

* * *

Acknowledgments

In addition to the co-authors listed below, the authors gratefully acknowledge the invaluable contributions of Naim Culhaci, Cameron Kates, and J. Ashley Weeks.

Paul M. Dudek

Tel: +1 202 637 2377 / Email: paul.dudek@lw.com

Paul Dudek is a counsel in the Washington, D.C. office of Latham & Watkins. From 1993 to 2016, he was Chief of the Office of International Corporate Finance in the US Securities Exchange Commission's (SEC) Division of Corporation Finance. Mr Dudek has deep experience in SEC registrations, and his practice covers all aspects of cross-border capital market transactions involving non-US companies and sovereigns, as well as related regulatory matters. In his previous role, Mr Dudek oversaw the Office's efforts to develop and implement rulemaking initiatives and interpretive policies pertaining to US public and private offerings, listings and other transactions and periodic reporting by foreign private issuers in the US and multinational offerings by foreign and domestic issuers.

Miles P. Jennings

Tel: +1 650 463 3063 / Email: miles.jennings@lw.com

Miles Jennings is an associate in the Silicon Valley office of Latham & Watkins. Mr Jennings represents public and private technology, life science, cryptocurrency and other growth companies, as well as the entities that finance them. His practice focuses on general corporate counseling, venture capital financings, cryptocurrency offerings, mergers and acquisitions, and public offerings. Mr Jennings' general company representation includes assistance with formation issues, employment matters, equity incentives, securities law compliance, negotiation of license agreements, and advising boards of directors regarding corporate governance matters.

* * *

Endnotes

1. The Digital Asset Taxonomy published by ConsenSys, a leader in the blockchain field, defined "consumer tokens" as "inherently consumptive in nature, which means that their intrinsic features and primary use are to represent, or facilitate the exchange of or access to, a limited set of goods, services, or content. The term "consumer" here refers to the consumptive nature of the relevant goods, services, or content, which businesses as well as individual users may ultimately use or consume[.]" DIGITAL ASSET TAXONOMY: FROM THE PERSPECTIVE OF GLOBAL FRAMEWORKS FOR SECURITIES AND FINANCIAL INSTRUMENTS, https://thebkp.com/token-taxonomy/ (last visited July 26, 2018).

2. *SEC v. W.J. Howey Co.*, 328 U.S. 293 (1946).

3. 15 U.S.C. §§ 77b(a)(1), 78c(a)(10).

4. *See Howey* at 301.

5. *See id.*

6. *See* SEC Release No. 34-81207, Report of Investigation Pursuant to Section 21(a) of the Securities Exchange Act of 1934: The DAO, 17-18 (July 25, 2017), https://www.sec.gov/litigation/investreport/34-81207.pdf.

7. *See* Latham & Watkins, SEC: Certain Initial Coin Offerings Are Securities Offerings, Client Alert No. 2187 (July 27, 2017), https://www.lw.com/thoughtLeadership/SEC-certain-initial-coin-offerings-securities.

8. *In re Munchee Inc.*, Order Instituting Cease-and-Desist Proceedings pursuant to Section 8A of the Securities Act of 1933, Making Findings, and Imposing a Cease-and-Desist Order, SEC Administrative Proceeding File No. 3-18304 (Dec. 11, 2017), https://www.sec.gov/litigation/admin/2017/33-10445.pdf [hereinafter Munchee Order].

9. For a helpful overview of ICOs, see the SEC's Investor Bulletin on the subject. SEC Investor Bulletin, Initial Coin Offerings (July 25, 2017), https://www.investor.gov/additional-resources/news-alerts/alerts-bulletins/investor-bulletin-initial-coin-offerings.

10. *See* Latham & Watkins, SEC Takes Enforcement Action against Utility Token ICO, Client Alert No. 2257 (Dec. 20, 2017), https://www.lw.com/thoughtLeadership/SEC-vigorously-police-utility-token-ICO.

11. *See* William Hinman, Dir., Div. Corp. Fin., Sec. & Exch. Comm'n, *Digital Asset Transactions: When Howey Met Gary (Plastic)* (June 14, 2018), https://www.sec.gov/news/speech/speech-hinman-061418 [hereinafter Hinman Speech].

12. *Gary Plastic Packaging v. Merrill Lynch, Pierce, Fenner, & Smith Inc.*, 756 F.2d 230 (2d Cir. 1985).

13. *See, e.g.,* 7 U.S.C. §§ 6c(a), 9, 12(a)(5), 15; 17 C.F.R. § 180.1; *see also* Prohibition on the Employment, or Attempted Employment, of Manipulative and Deceptive Devices and Prohibition on Price Manipulation, 76 Fed. Reg. 41398 (July 14, 2011), https://www.gpo.gov/fdsys/pkg/FR-2011-07-14/pdf/2011-17549.pdf.

14. Timothy Massad, Chairman, Commodity Futures Trading Comm'n, Testimony of Chairman Timothy Massad before the U.S. Senate Committee on Agriculture, Nutrition & Forestry (Dec. 10, 2014), http://www.cftc.gov/PressRoom/SpeechesTestimony/opamassad-6 [hereinafter 2014 Massad Senate Testimony].

15. During this time, the CFTC has settled enforcement actions with exchanges, stressing a distinct aspect of its jurisdictional oversight in each: from establishing that virtual currencies are "commodities," to applying the retail commodity rules to leveraged virtual currency transactions, to asserting jurisdiction over virtual currency derivatives. *See* Latham & Watkins, CFTC Brings Significant Enforcement Action Against Online Cryptocurrency Exchange, Client Alert No. 1980 (June 20, 2016), https://www.lw.com/thoughtLeadership/CFTC-brings-significant-enforcement-action-against-online-cryptocurrency-exchange;

Latham & Watkins, Enforcement Trends in Cryptocurrency, Client Alert No. 1904 (Dec. 9, 2015), https://www.lw.com/thoughtLeadership/lw-enforcement-trends-cryptocurrency; Latham & Watkins, Cryptocurrencies Are Commodities: CFTC's First Bitcoin Enforcement Action, Client Alert No. 1874 (Sept. 21, 2015), https://www.lw.com/thoughtLeadership/LW-CFTC-first-bitcoin-enforcement-action.

16. *See, e.g.,* CFTC Release PR7714-18, CFTC Charges Multiple Individuals and Companies with Operating a Fraudulent Scheme Involving Binary Options and a Virtual Currency Known as ATM Coin (April 18, 2018), https://www.cftc.gov/PressRoom/PressReleases/7714-18; CFTC Release PR7614-17, CFTC Charges Nicholas Gelfman and Gelfman Blueprint, Inc. with Fraudulent Solicitation, Misappropriation, and Issuing False Account Statements in Bitcoin Ponzi Scheme (Sept. 21, 2017), http://www.cftc.gov/PressRoom/PressReleases/pr7614-17.

17. The following discussion of consumer token presales only seeks to address fundraising instruments utilised for pure consumer token issuances and not instruments utilised for pure security token issuances, which often have similar terms. We note that the presale of a token designed to be a security is a far easier analysis, as each of the instruments should be offered and sold in compliance with securities law requirements and ordinary corporate finance practices.

18. *See, e.g.,* Juan Batiz-Benet, Jesse Clayburgh & Marco Santori, The SAFT Project: Toward a Compliant Token Sale Framework (Oct. 2, 2017), https://saftproject.com/static/SAFT-Project-Whitepaper.pdf [hereinafter SAFT Whitepaper].

19. In addition to the securities law issues and commodities law issues discussed below, the SAFT and similar presale instruments can raise tax concerns in light of the uncertainty regarding their treatment for US federal income tax purposes. It is possible that an issuer could be subject to US federal income tax on proceeds from SAFT sales on a current basis, particularly where the underlying tokens are consumer tokens.

20. *Id.* (Section 5(c) of the SAFT, which is included as Exhibit 1 to the SAFT Whitepaper): "(c) The Purchaser has no intent to use or consume any or all Tokens on the corresponding blockchain network for the Tokens after Network Launch. The Purchaser enters into this security instrument purely to realise profits that accrue from purchasing Tokens at the Discount Price."

21. Defined in the SAFT as "a *bona fide* transaction or series of transactions, pursuant to which the [issuer] will sell the Tokens to the general public in a publicised product launch." Simple Agreement for Future Token, https://saftproject.com/static/Form-of-SAFT-for-token-pre-sale.docx (last visited July 29, 2018).

22. We note that some practitioners have proposed that if the network launch occurs more than six months after the SAFT sale, they should constitute two distinct plans of financing and thus would not be integrated in accordance with the safe harbor of Rule 502 under the Securities Act. In this regard, we would consider the concurrent settlement to negate this proposition. Similarly, the SAFT itself may constitute an offering of the underlying token that is continuous until delivery. In any event, we would expect that the tokens received by SAFT investors would nevertheless constitute securities on the date of delivery given the nature of the SAFT offering and the delivery of tokens to investors, unless the network has become sufficiently decentralised in the interim such that the "efforts" prong of the *Howey* Test was no longer satisfied.

23. It is worth noting, however, that the US House of Representatives recently passed several bills aimed at improving capital formation for smaller companies. For example, the Main Street Growth Act would amend the Securities Exchange Act of 1934, as amended, to allow registration of venture exchanges that would provide trading venues tailored for smaller companies, such as blockchain-based start-ups, whose securities are

considered less liquid than those of larger companies. Main Street Growth Act, H.R. 5877, 115th Congress (as passed by House, July 10, 2018), https://www.congress.gov/bill/115th-congress/house-bill/5877; *see* Tom Zanki, *House Passes Bill to Allow Venture Exchanges,* LAW360 (July 11, 2018), https://www.law360.com/articles/1062096/house-passes-bill-to-allow-venture-exchanges.

24. *See* 15 U.S.C. § 78c(a)(4)(A) (defining "broker" as "any person engaged in the business of effecting transactions in securities for the account of others"); 15 U.S.C. § 78c(a)(5)(A) (defining "dealer" as "any person engaged in the business of buying and selling securities . . . for such person's own account"); 15 U.S.C. § 78c(a)(1) (defining "exchange" as "any organization, association or group of persons, whether incorporated or unincorporated, which constitutes, maintains or provides a marketplace or facilities for bringing together purchasers and sellers of securities or for otherwise performing with respect to securities the functions commonly performed by a stock exchange as that term is generally understood, and includes the market place and the market facilities maintained by such exchange.").

25. *See* Hinman Speech.

26. *See, e.g.,* 2014 Massad Senate Testimony.

27. *See* 7 U.S.C. § 1a(47)(A)(ii) ("the term 'swap' means any agreement, contract, or transaction . . . that provides for any purchase, sale, payment, or delivery . . . that is dependent on the occurrence, nonoccurrence, or the extent of the occurrence of an event or contingency associated with a potential financial, economic, or commercial consequence."). Swap contracts are subject to a myriad of CFTC regulations under the CEA, as amended by the Dodd-Frank Wall Street Reform and Consumer Protection Act of 2010 (the Dodd-Frank Act), including the requirement that over-the-counter (OTC) swap counterparties be "eligible contract participants." *Id.* § 1a(18) (defining eligible contract participants (ECPs)). An individual can only qualify as an ECP if such person has amounts invested on a discretionary basis, the aggregate of which is in excess of US$10 million; or US$5 million and enters into swaps in order to manage the risk associated with an asset owned or liability incurred (or reasonably likely to be owned or incurred) by such person. *Id.* § 1a(18)(A)(xi). If one or both of the parties to a swap transaction are non-ECPs, the swap must be executed on a CFTC-registered designated contract market. *Id.* § 2(e).

28. Both the CEA and CFTC regulations thereunder have long recognised a forward contract exclusion from futures contracts. *See* 7 U.S.C. § 1a(27) ("The term 'future delivery' does not include any sale of any cash commodity for deferred shipment or delivery."). Following enactment of the Dodd-Frank Act in 2010, the sale of a non-financial commodity for deferred shipment or delivery was also excluded from the definition of "swap" in Section 1a(47) of the CEA under the Non-Financial Forward Contract Exclusion. *Id.* § 1a(47)(B)(ii).

29. *See* Further Definition of "Swap," "Security-Based Swap," and "Security-Based Swap Agreement"; Mixed Swaps; Security-Based Swap Agreement Recordkeeping, 77 Fed. Reg. 48208, 48228 (Aug. 13, 2012), https://www.gpo.gov/fdsys/pkg/FR-2012-08-13/pdf/2012-18003.pdf [hereinafter *Products Release*].

30. As the CFTC has noted, "the underlying postulate of the [forward] exclusion is that the [CEA's] regulatory scheme for futures trading simply should not apply to private commercial merchandising transactions which create enforceable obligations to deliver but in which delivery is deferred for reasons of commercial convenience or necessity." *Id.* at 48228.

31. The CFTC drew a clear distinction between commercial market participants and investors in the Products Release, stating that "[a] hedge fund's investment activity is not commercial activity within the CFTC's longstanding view of the Brent Interpretation." *Id.* at 48229. The "Brent Interpretation" refers to the CFTC's 1990 interpretation of the

application of the forward contract exclusion from the definition of "future delivery" in the context of "book-outs" transactions, which the CFTC extended in the Products Release to apply to the forward contract exclusion from the swap definition for non-financial commodities. Statutory Interpretation Concerning Forward Transactions, 55 Fed. Reg. 39188 (Sept. 25, 1990), https://cdn.loc.gov/service/ll/fedreg/fr055/fr055186/fr055186.pdf.

Moreover, the CFTC continued to elaborate on its discerning view of "commercial" in the Products Release, stating that "an investment vehicle taking delivery of gold as part of its investment strategy would not be engaging in a commercial activity within the meaning of the Brent Interpretation." Products Release at 48229. However, if the investment vehicle were to own a chain of jewelry stores and would purchase gold on a forward basis to provide raw materials for the jewelry store, the CFTC would consider such activity to fall within the forward contract exclusion under the Brent Interpretation. *Id.* Notably, the CFTC stated in the Products Release that, for purposes of the "swap" definition, the Non-Financial Forward Contract Exclusion will be interpreted in a manner consistent with the CFTC's historical interpretation of the existing forward exclusion with respect to futures. As a result, the Brent Interpretation analysis is applicable for purposes of evaluating the Non-Financial Forward Contract Exclusion as it pertains to the "swap" definition. *Id.* at 48227-48228.

32. *See Id.*; *supra* text accompanying note 20.

33. 7 U.S.C. § 1a(47)(A)(i) ("the term 'swap' means any agreement, contract, or transaction . . . that is a put, call, cap, floor, collar, or similar option of any kind that is for the purchase or sale, or based on the value, of 1 or more . . . commodities").

34. *See* 17 C.F.R. § 32.3(c).

35. *See* 17 C.F.R. § 32.3(a).

36. *See supra* text accompanying note 27.

37. 17 C.F.R. § 34.3(a).

38. Under Section 2(f) of the CEA, a hybrid instrument is "predominantly a security" and exempt from the provisions of the CEA if:

   (i)   the hybrid instrument issuer receives payment in full of the hybrid instrument's purchase price, substantially contemporaneously with delivery of the hybrid instrument;

   (ii) the hybrid instrument purchaser/holder is not required to make any payment to the issuer in addition to the purchase price described above, whether as margin, settlement payment or otherwise, during the life of the hybrid instrument or at maturity;

   (iii) the hybrid instrument issuer is not subject by the instrument's terms to mark-to-market margining requirements; and

   (iv) the hybrid instrument is not marketed as a contract of sale of a commodity for future delivery (or option on such a contract) subject to the CEA.

   7 U.S.C. § 2(f)(2).

39. This discussion assumes that prongs (i) – (iii) of the Hybrid Instrument Exemption are met with respect to any such presale instrument. Any such presale instrument must meet all four prongs of the exemption.

40. *See supra* text accompanying note 27; 7 U.S.C. § 2(e).

41. Such securities offerings are almost exclusively accomplished through the use of an exemption from registration, such as in a private placement that is limited to participants who are "accredited investors," as defined in 17 C.F.R. § 230.501, either under the more traditional style private placement of Regulation D, Rule 506(b), or the crowdfunding

compatible, Regulation D, Rule 506(c). Issuers may also consider utilising Regulation CF or Regulation A, which permit sales to non-accredited investors after making certain filings with the SEC. For additional information, see Latham & Watkins, SEC Adopts Final Crowdfunding Rules, Client Alert No. 1893 (Nov. 10, 2015), https://www.lw.com/thoughtLeadership/lw-sec-adopts-crowdfunding-rules; Stephen P. Wink and Brett M. Ackerman, Crowdfunding Under the SEC's New Rules, 49 Rev. of Sec. & Commodities Reg. 267 (Dec. 21, 2016), https://www.lw.com/thoughtLeadership/crowdfunding-SEC-new-rules-2016.

42. While issuers should be cautious when granting such rights, generally the enterprise and its investors are best served when their interests align. In consumer token sales, the parties share a direct interest in ensuring the offering or distribution complies with applicable securities and commodities laws. In addition, all participants should share a similar interest in the maturing of the market for token presales, as in the traditional venture capital space, to attract capital from investors that have yet to approach the sector due to regulatory risks.

43. A discussion of the types of structures that may so qualify and the nature of the availability of the possible exemptions is beyond the scope of this chapter.

44. *See* Hinman Speech; *see also* Latham & Watkins, A Path Forward for Consumer Tokens, Client Alert No. 2336 (June 27, 2018), https://www.lw.com/thoughtLeadership/lw-a-path-forward-for-consumer-tokens.

45. *See* Hinman Speech.

46. *SEC v. Glenn W. Turner Enterprises Inc.*, 474 F.2d 476, 482 (9th Cir. 1973) ("[T]he fact that the investors here were required to exert some efforts if a return were to be achieved should not automatically preclude a finding that the Plan or Adventure is an investment contract. To do so would not serve the purpose of the legislation. Rather we adopt a more realistic test, whether the efforts made by those other than the investor are the undeniably significant ones, those essential managerial efforts which affect the failure or success of the enterprise."); *see United Housing Found., Inc. v. Forman*, 421 U.S. 837, 855 (1975) (the "efforts of others" prong of the *Howey* Test requires that investors have a reasonable expectation of profit derived from the efforts of others).

47. In *Noa v. Key Futures, Inc.*, the Ninth Circuit held that if the expectation of economic return from an instrument is based solely on market forces, and not on the efforts of a promoter, then the instrument does not satisfy this prong of the *Howey* Test. *Noa v. Key Futures, Inc.*, 638 F.2d 77 (9th Cir. 1980). The scheme in *Noa* involved the sale of silver bars through high-pressure sales efforts, and the Ninth Circuit's decision rested primarily on the existence of a separate market for the instrument that the investor could sell into, such that the economic return was driven by the market price and not the efforts of the promoter: "Once the purchase of silver bars was made, the profits to the investor depended upon the fluctuations of the silver market, not the managerial efforts of Key Futures. The decision to buy or sell was made by the owner of the silver." *Id.* at 79.

SEC v. Belmont Reid & Co. involved a promoter that was involved in a gold mining operation who obtained prepayments from investors for the purchase of gold coins that would be obtained as a result of the mining operation. *SEC v. Belmont Reid & Co,* 794 F.2d 1388 (9th Cir. 1986). While the purchaser's return was highly dependent on the ability of the promoter to successfully mine and deliver the gold coins, the Ninth Circuit reasoned that the same non-performance risk exists in the context of any sale-of-goods contract in which the buyer pays in advance, and therefore that such a dependence on the promoter's efforts could not itself satisfy the *Howey* Test without making any such sale-of-goods contract a security. Instead, the Ninth Circuit held that the *Howey* Test was not satisfied in *Belmont Reid & Co.*, because the purchasers who prepaid for the gold coins: "[H]ad as their primary purpose to profit from the anticipated increase in the world price of gold . . . In short, the purchaser[s] were speculating in the world gold market . . . To the extent the purchasers relied on the managerial skill of [the promoters] they did so as an ordinary buyer, having advanced the purchase price, relies on an ordinary seller." *Id.* at 1391.

48. *See* Hinman Speech ("Has the promoter raised an amount of funds in excess of what may be needed to establish a functional network, and, if so, has it indicated how those funds may be used to support the value of the tokens or to increase the value of the enterprise? Does the promoter continue to expend funds from proceeds or operations to enhance the functionality and/or value of the system within which the tokens operate?").

49. *See id.*

50. *Id.* ("Do persons or entities other than the promoter exercise governance rights or meaningful influence?").

51. *See supra* text accompanying note 47.

52. Please note that we have chosen Filecoin in this example in part because we have no connection to its activities.

53. Protocol Labs, FILECOIN: A DECENTRALIZED STORAGE NETWORK (Aug. 14, 2017), https://filecoin.io/filecoin.pdf.

54. CoinList, FILECOIN TOKEN SALE ECONOMICS, https://coinlist.co/assets/index/filecoin_index/Filecoin-Sale-Economics-e3f703f8cd5f644aecd7ae3860ce932064ce014dd60de115d67ff1e9047ffa8e.pdf (last visited July 26, 2018).

55. Hinman Speech; *see* Munchee Order; Jay Clayton, Chairman, Sec. & Exch. Comm'n, Statement on Cryptocurrencies and Initial Coin Offerings (Dec. 11, 2017), https://www.sec.gov/news/public-statement/statement-clayton-2017-12-11.

56. Hinman Speech.

57. Jay Clayton, Chairman, Sec. & Exch. Comm'n, Chairman's Testimony on Virtual Currencies: The Roles of the SEC and CFTC, (Feb. 6, 2018), https://www.sec.gov/news/testimony/testimony-virtual-currencies-oversight-role-us-securities-and-exchange-commission ("In short, prospective purchasers are being sold on the potential for tokens to increase in value with the ability to lock in those increases by reselling the tokens on a secondary market or to otherwise profit from the tokens based on the efforts of others. These are key hallmarks of a security and a securities offering.").

58. *See Gary Plastic* at 240–241.

59. *See* Hinman Speech ("Are the tokens distributed in ways to meet users' needs? For example, can the tokens be held or transferred only in amounts that correspond to a purchaser's expected use? Are there built-in incentives that compel using the tokens promptly on the network, such as having the tokens degrade in value over time, or can the tokens be held for extended periods for investment?").

60. *See id.* ("Is token creation commensurate with meeting the needs of users or, rather, with feeding speculation?").

61. *See id.* ("Has this person or group retained a stake or other interest in the digital asset such that it would be motivated to expend efforts to cause an increase in value in the digital asset?").

62. *Id.*

63. *See id.* ("Are the assets dispersed across a diverse user base or concentrated in the hands of a few that can exert influence over the application?").

64. Simplystocks.com, SEC No-Action Letter (Feb 4, 1999).

65. SEC Staff Legal Bulletin No. 4 (Sept 16, 1997), https://www.sec.gov/interps/legal/slbcf4.txt.

David L. Concannon
Tel: +1 212 906 1389 / Email: david.concannon@lw.com
David Concannon is a partner in the New York office of Latham & Watkins where he is a member of the firm's Emerging Companies Practice. Mr Concannon is among a select few lawyers in New York whose practices focus exclusively on emerging companies, representing both clients as company counsel and venture capital firms as investor counsel. He advises emerging companies through their entire lifecycle, from formation through growth stages and exits. Mr Concannon spends substantial time advising market participants regarding cryptocurrencies and initial coin offerings, and serves as a Co-Chair of the firm's Blockchain and Cryptocurrency Task Force.

Yvette D. Valdez
Tel: +1 212 906 1797 / Email: yvette.valdez@lw.com
Yvette Valdez is a partner in the New York office of Latham & Watkins and a member of the Derivatives Practice, Financial Institutions Group, and FinTech Industry Group. Ms Valdez advises emerging companies, financial institutions, and investment managers on complex regulatory challenges in the development of bespoke financial crypto-asset and cryptocurrency technologies, including token sales, market infrastructure, trading, clearing, and settlement solutions on distributed ledger technology. She also advises clients on domestic and cross-border fintech initiatives in the derivatives markets. Ms Valdez also has significant experience representing dealers, intermediaries, and end-users in connection with derivatives (swaps and futures) legal and regulatory matters under the Dodd-Frank Act, the Commodity Exchange Act, as well as related CFTC, SEC, and prudential regulation.

Stephen P. Wink
Tel: +1 212 906 1229 / Email: stephen.wink@lw.com
Stephen Wink is a partner in the New York office of Latham & Watkins and a member of the Financial Institutions Group and FinTech Industry Group. Mr Wink is Co-Chair of the firm's Blockchain and Cryptocurrency Task Force. His practice focuses on advising a wide range of market players, including fintech companies, cryptocurrency issuers and platforms, investment banks, hedge funds, private equity firms, trading platforms, and other financial institutions. Mr Wink has in-depth knowledge and broad experience advising institutions on regulatory and related matters, gained in part from a decade as general counsel of a full-service investment bank.

Latham & Watkins LLP

885 Third Avenue, New York, New York 10022, USA
Tel: +1 212 906 1200 / Fax: +1 212 751 4864 / URL: www.lw.com

Custody and transfer of digital assets: Key U.S. legal considerations

Michael H. Krimminger, Colin Lloyd & Sandra Rocks
Cleary Gottlieb Steen & Hamilton LLP

Introduction

Particularly since 2017, cryptocurrencies, initial coin offering ("ICO") tokens, and other similar financial assets ("Digital Assets") have drawn increased interest and participation from institutional investors. As with other financial assets, investors in Digital Assets face the risk of theft or loss of their holdings. This risk can be especially pronounced in connection with Digital Assets because transfers may not be easily reversible, intermediaries can be lightly capitalised, and other market participants are frequently anonymous or pseudonymous. These market characteristics underscore the importance of effective practices for the custody and transfer of Digital Assets. Unfortunately, the legal framework for such custody and transfer is evolving and not always well understood.

This chapter summarises that legal framework as it currently stands within the United States ("U.S.").[1] First, it describes certain aspects of how distributed ledgers operate, which are relevant to the mechanics for holding or transferring Digital Assets. It then describes the U.S. commercial and insolvency law considerations relevant to custodial relationships and transfers involving Digital Assets. Next, it summarises the key U.S. regulatory frameworks currently applicable to Digital Asset custodians. Finally, it describes the proposed Uniform Regulation of Virtual-Currency Businesses Act (the "URVCBA"), which would make certain reforms in these areas.

Operation of distributed ledgers

The ownership and transfer of a Digital Asset is commonly recorded on a "blockchain" or other distributed ledger. Typically, distributed ledgers operate through the use of public and private keys.[2] The distributed ledger shows which public key owns each Digital Asset. To effect a transfer of a Digital Asset, the transferor needs to enter the private key that corresponds to the public key that the ledger shows as the owner of the Digital Asset. Private keys are created in mathematical relation to their public key pair and are unmodifiable. Participants in the distributed ledger validate transactions by confirming that the transfer has been authorised by the private key associated with the relevant public key.

Through the possession and use of a private key to validate Digital Asset transfers, every asset recorded on a specified distributed ledger may be transferred between different public keys. Without a public key's private key match, however, no assets held in connection with a public key may be transferred at all. As a result, Digital Asset investors must be able to effectively retain and protect such private key information, and thus control over all attached Digital Assets to protect their investments. Without security and control over all private key information, investors are susceptible to both malicious attacks intended to obtain access to their private key – resulting in a malicious actor gaining the ability to transfer their Digital Assets and often leaving investors without recourse – and to losing possession of the private key, and the ability to transfer their Digital Assets to or from any other person's public key in the future.

On a rudimentary level, Digital Asset investors have often looked to solve this problem with what are referred to as "wallets," which hold a private key for those investors and often require the use of a "passphrase" to subsequently access their private keys to transfer any Digital Assets. If investors choose to store their private keys in a "hot" wallet that is connected to the internet, they face an increased risk of cyber-attack – but may more quickly transfer Digital Assets to other parties. By contrast, maintaining private keys in an offline, hardware-based "cold" wallet protects against cyber-hacking risks, but requires an investor's continued maintenance and possession of the hardware. Given some of the difficulties that investors may face in sufficiently managing all of these risks on their own, Digital Asset investors have frequently looked to some form of centralised custodian to hold their assets.

Many investors have stored Digital Assets directly with the exchanges through which they trade. Many exchanges maintain those assets in pooled, "hot" wallets that always remain connected to the internet. While such storage solutions provide for faster access when an investor is looking to execute Digital Asset transactions on the exchange, hackers have increasingly succeeded in capitalising on exchanges' vulnerabilities, including hot wallets' connections to the internet, to steal large quantities of pooled Digital Assets from such exchanges. In those instances, investors have faced challenges in recouping their assets from the exchanges or otherwise. Other exchanges maintain both hot wallets for immediate transactions, and cold wallets for longer-term custody. The cold wallets are usually wholly disconnected from the internet and provide far superior security.

Market participants have attempted to address these issues by providing Digital Asset custody services.[3] Such services often primarily or exclusively use cold storage wallets, holding all Digital Asset private keys in pooled accounts that are entirely offline until an individual investor wishes to withdraw or transfer their Digital Assets. This model provides investors with increased assurances in the safety of their private keys and Digital Assets, while also removing the additional work required of investors if they were to protect this information themselves.

Key U.S. commercial and insolvency law considerations

Custodial relationships

The characterisation of the relationship between a holder of a Digital Asset and its custodian is a question of state law. Some key factors that may affect the characterisation of the relationship include:

- What service is the custodian providing?
  - Is the custodian holding the holder's private key or the Digital Asset itself?
  - Has the custodian established a "multi sig" arrangement (*i.e.* an arrangement in which more than one key is required to authorise a Digital Asset transaction)? If so, does the custodian have all of the keys that are needed to allow the Digital Asset transaction to take place?

- How does the parties' agreement (if any) describe the relationship?
  - Does it call the relationship a bailment or another similar relationship such as some form of an agency?
  - Does the documentation transfer any ownership of the private key or Digital Asset to the custodian or does the customer retain all right, title, and interest in the private key or Digital Asset?
  - Does the custodian have the right to reuse the custodial assets?
  - Is there an agreement to treat the private key or Digital Asset as a "financial asset"?

A custodial relationship may take many different forms, and the questions to consider will depend on the facts at hand. While the documentation will likely be crucial, it is not necessarily determinative.

Bailment or similar relationship. One possible way to frame the relationship between an owner of a Digital Asset and its custodian is as a bailment or similar relationship such as some form of an agency. A number of Digital Asset market participants have characterised their relationship as a bailment or similar agency relationship in order to ensure the application of certain rights and duties, discussed in greater detail below. A written or express agreement, however, is not necessarily required for a bailment or agency to be created. A court may conclude that the facts and circumstances demonstrate that a bailment or agency relationship was created. Such characterisations are more likely when the owner does not transfer to the custodian its rights in the private key or Digital Asset.

If the custodian is recognised as the bailee or agent of the customer, then the custodian would owe certain duties to the bailor or principal. Such duties include, if the custodian is recognised as a bailee, a duty to exercise ordinary care in keeping and safeguarding property of the bailor and (if instead the custodian is recognised as the customer's agent), then the duties of obedience, loyalty, and care.

Although the rules governing the distribution of custodial assets upon the custodian's insolvency will depend on the applicable insolvency regime, many U.S. regimes, including the U.S. Bankruptcy Code, look to state law in the first instance to see whether the property is considered property of the custodian or instead property of the customer. If the latter, the assets will generally not be subject to claims of the custodian's general creditors. The way state law views property held subject to a bailment or similar relationship will depend on whether the property is fungible or not. For non-fungible property, the assets would be considered property of the customer and therefore, as long as the customer can substantiate the bailment or similar relationship and identify the relevant assets, its claim for the return of the asset will not be subject to the claims of the custodian's general creditors. State law also provides that fungible property held subject to a bailment or similar relationship is the property of the bailor, but that if there is a shortfall in the amount of a particular fungible asset relative to the claims of all bailors, the bailors will share *pro rata*.

While it appears unlikely that private keys would be considered fungible assets, the analysis is less clear for the Digital Assets themselves. For example, Digital Assets carried on particular blocks that make them sufficiently non-interchangeable may be non-fungible. However, if a custodian were to hold the Digital Assets in bulk with each customer owning a portion thereof, such Digital Assets could be considered fungible.

Securities intermediary-entitlement holder relationship. Another possible way to describe the customer-custodian relationship is as one between an entitlement holder and its securities intermediary within the purview of Article 8 of the Uniform Commercial Code as in effect in the applicable state ("UCC").

In the U.S., the relationship between securities broker-dealers and their customers in respect of the customers' securities is generally subject to Article 8 of the UCC. However, a broader range of relationships can fall within the scope of Article 8 if the asset being maintained is a "financial asset." An ICO token would likely be a financial asset by virtue of its status as a security.[4] Article 8 also allows parties to agree to treat an asset that is not a security as a financial asset so long as it "makes sense to apply the [duties in Part 5 of Article 8 of the UCC ("Part 5 duties")] to the relationship."[5] It is likely appropriate to apply the Part 5 duties to the custody of cryptocurrencies. For other assets recorded on a distributed ledger, one would have to analyse whether it would make sense to apply the Part 5 duties to the relationship based on the nature and properties of the asset, including whether the asset is transferable, generates payments or distributions, or provides holders with certain rights such as voting rights.

Overall, the benefit of electing to treat custodial assets as "financial assets" and thereby subject to Article 8 is that parties would then be able to have their relationship governed by a well-established legal regime that governs a very large market.

If the custodial relationship is subject to Article 8, then Part 5 of Article 8 imposes certain duties on the custodian as the securities intermediary, including: a duty to maintain a sufficient quantity of the custodial assets to satisfy customer entitlements; a duty to comply with a customer's instructions; and a prohibition on granting security interests in the custodial assets without consent. In the absence of an agreement between the custodian and its customer as to which standard applies to the custodian in the exercise of its Part 5 duties, the custodian must exercise "due care in accordance with reasonable commercial standards."[6]

As in the context of a bailment or similar relationship, the rights of a customer in the event of the custodian's insolvency will depend on the applicable insolvency regime.[7] As mentioned above, most U.S. insolvency regimes look to state law to determine who has an interest in certain assets. However, the Securities Investor Protection Act ("SIPA"), which will likely govern the insolvency of a securities broker-dealer, provides that a securities customer will have a claim against the debtor based on its "net equity," which generally reflects all of the customer's securities positions and associated customer cash. To the extent this distribution rule applies, which it may in the case of ICO tokens held with a broker-dealer, a Digital Asset customer's claim for the return of its securities will share ratably with the claims of other securities customers and in priority to the broker-dealer's general creditors.

In the event the SIPA distribution rules do not apply and the insolvency regime points to state law, Section 8-503 of the UCC provides that financial assets held by a securities intermediary are not property of the securities intermediary and Section 8-511 of the UCC provides that the claims of entitlement holders would have priority over creditors except when the creditors have "control" over the financial asset. Section 8-503(b) further provides that each entitlement holder's property interest is a *pro rata* property interest in all interests of the securities intermediary in the particular type of financial asset that is being held for the entitlement holder by the securities intermediary.

Other relationship characterisations. If there is no bailee-bailor or similar relationship and no securities intermediary-entitlement holder relationship, then there might only be a contractual relationship. In the context of such other relationships, the custodian may not have any special duties, and if it enters into insolvency proceedings, the customer might only have an unsecured monetary claim (and not a claim to the actual custodial assets). However, this does not exclude the possibility that there are other relationships with legal import that might exist between the custodian and its customer.

Transfers of Digital Assets to third parties

In addition to determining the rights and obligations of a custodian of a Digital Asset and the Digital Asset owner, how a Digital Asset is held and the agreement governing the Digital Asset may have significant implications for the rights of any transferee of the Digital Asset. This is because the UCC's rules concerning perfection and priority differ for different asset categories and the nature and documentation of the custodial relationship may dictate which category a Digital Asset falls into. Most notably, while many Digital Assets would, absent an agreement to the contrary, likely be considered "general intangibles" for purposes of Article 9 of the UCC, an effective agreement between a custodian and customer to treat a Digital Asset as a financial asset would cause such asset to be "investment property" under Article 9, which is subject to very different priority and perfection rules.

Pledging. Perfecting a security interest in a general intangible requires filing a UCC financing statement, and the pledgee must be the first to file in order for its security interest in the Virtual Asset to have priority over the rights or interests of most third parties. In contrast, a security interest in investment property can be perfected by "control," and control affords enhanced priority. A secured party can obtain control by: (1) becoming the entitlement holder; (2) being the securities intermediary; or (3) entering into a control agreement.[8]

Sales. Whereas there are no commercial rules that provide for adverse claim cutoff protection for general intangibles in the context of sales, Sections 8-502 and 8-510 of the UCC provide that if a transferee of a financial asset gives value, acquires its interest without notice of any adverse claims and obtains "control," it will acquire its interest free of adverse claims.

Key U.S. regulatory considerations

Analysing the regulatory status of a Digital Asset custodian begins with a categorisation of the underlying Digital Asset. Generally speaking, as a matter of U.S. federal law, Digital Assets are viewed as either "securities" (as appears to be the case with most ICO tokens),[9] and thus subject to regulation by the Securities and Exchange Commission ("SEC"), or non-security "commodities" (as appears to be the case with Bitcoin and certain other cryptocurrencies),[10] and thus subject to regulation by the Commodity Futures Trading Commission ("CFTC"). In addition, certain state laws may apply to Digital Asset custodial activities.

Federal Securities Law considerations

The Securities Exchange Act of 1934 (the "Exchange Act") generally requires any person engaged in the business of effecting transactions in securities for the account of others (a "broker") to register with the SEC as a broker-dealer.[11] The SEC views handling customer funds or securities as a type of brokerage activity.[12] Accordingly, a person acting as custodian for Digital Assets that are securities typically must register with the SEC as a broker-dealer. Among other regulations, registered broker-dealers are subject to extensive requirements related to the handling of customer funds and securities (which would include these Digital Assets), maintenance of minimum net capital, creation and maintenance of books and records, and anti-money laundering requirements.[13]

An exception from broker-dealer registration exists, however, for certain federal or state chartered or licensed banks engaged in custody or safekeeping activities.[14] These custodians are instead subject to banking law regulation of their custodial activities. Banking regulation for custodial or fiduciary activities by state and federal banks and trust companies, whether insured by the Federal Deposit Insurance Corporation ("FDIC") or not, is designed to preserve the customer's interest in the property held by the bank or trust company for safekeeping. The trust departments of banks and trust companies are examined by the appropriate supervisory agency in order to require segregation and recordkeeping for trust assets, and those assets are treated exclusively as customer assets even in a failure of the bank or trust company.

In addition, federal securities law regulation of investors can obligate them to use certain regulated institutions as custodians for client assets. For example, Rule 206(4)-2 (the "Custody Rule") under the Investment Advisers Act of 1940 (the "Advisers Act") generally requires SEC-registered investment advisers that have custody[15] of client funds or securities[16] to maintain such funds or securities with a "qualified custodian," such as a bank or broker-dealer.[17] The qualified custodian must maintain an adviser's client funds and securities either in a separate account for each client in the client's name, or in one or more accounts containing only funds and securities of the client in the name of the investment adviser as agent or trustee for the client. Also, as investment advisers must have a "reasonable basis, after due inquiry, for believing that the qualified custodian sends an account statement, at least quarterly"[18] to each of the adviser's clients, such account statements are implicitly demanded of qualified custodians as well.[19]

The Custody Rule does not apply to accounts of SEC-registered investment companies.[20] Rather, a separate set of requirements under Section 17(f) of the Investment Company Act of 1940 (the "Investment Company Act") and related rules governs how assets of SEC-registered investment companies must be held. Like the Advisers Act, the Investment Company Act requires either that registered investment companies use a regulated intermediary as a custodian, or that they self-custody assets. Self-custody subjects registered investment companies to significant additional regulatory burdens, including surprise physical inspections by an independent public account, and procedures that must be followed for the deposit and withdrawal of securities,[21] as well as recordkeeping requirements and the need to develop systems to facilitate trading. Section 17(f) of the Investment Company Act and the related rules allow registered investment companies to use, among other custodians, U.S. banks,[22] certain foreign banks,[23] and members of national securities exchanges.[24]

Federal Commodities Law considerations

Unlike the federal securities laws, the Commodity Exchange Act ("CEA") generally does not impose registration or licensing requirements on intermediaries, including custodians, providing services in connection with cash commodities, including Digital Assets traded on a spot or forward basis. Instead, substantive regulation under the CEA and CFTC rules thereunder typically extends solely to parties transacting in commodity-related derivatives, with CFTC jurisdiction over cash commodity market participants mostly limited to the enforcement of anti-fraud and anti-manipulation provisions of the CEA.[25]

Aspects of a custodial arrangement for Digital Assets can affect whether the CFTC views transactions in the Digital Asset to be cash market transactions or derivatives. For example, in the retail context, the CFTC has proposed to treat certain leveraged or margined transactions as a type of derivative if certain liens or transfer restrictions apply to the Digital Asset.[26] The CFTC has not finalised this interpretation, however, and a recent court decision (currently on appeal) casts doubt on it.[27] The CFTC has also not yet addressed how its other precedents distinguishing cash market transactions from derivatives apply to Digital Asset transactions.[28]

CFTC regulations can also apply to the custody of Digital Assets if they serve as collateral for CFTC-regulated derivatives. In particular, a party accepting customer funds or other property (such as Digital Assets) to secure a CFTC-regulated derivatives (other than an uncleared swap) typically must register with the CFTC as a futures commission merchant and satisfy CFTC customer segregation rules.[29] These segregation rules, in turn, require the futures commission merchant to deposit its customer's funds or other property in a segregated account held by a permissible depository, such as a bank, trust company, another futures commission merchant, or a derivatives clearing organisation.[30]

State law considerations

At the state level, many jurisdictions similarly require that custodial services for customers' financial assets can only be provided by certain regulated persons. Many states similarly require some form of a bank, trust company, or other fiduciary charter to act as a fiduciary in performing such custodial duties. Additionally, many state laws limit such fiduciary powers either to federally-chartered entities or to entities chartered or regulated by that state. While reciprocity may be provided to out-of-state trust companies for certain activities, the regular conduct of custodial and fiduciary activities typically requires separate licensing by the state where the customers reside.

In addition, New York requires licensing and oversight for custodial activities through the relatively extensive "BitLicense" framework introduced in 2015 or through its oversight of banks and trust companies. Persons who are "storing, holding, or maintaining custody of virtual currency on behalf of others" within the New York market are conducting "virtual currency business activity" within the jurisdiction,[31] and must either obtain a BitLicense from the New York Department of Financial Services ("NYDFS"), or otherwise fit an exemption by being chartered under New York Banking Law and approved by NYDFS to engage in such activity.[32] Persons operating as BitLicensees (as opposed to exempt, chartered institutions) are required to maintain a trust account with a "qualified custodian" – defined to extend only to a broad number of federal and New York banking entities in the state's relevant regulations – and must also hold Digital Assets of the same type and amount as any "owed or obligated" to another person for whom it is providing such custodial services. Thus, for any person seeking to provide Digital Asset custodial services of any kind involving New York markets, this additional regulatory hurdle is imposed.

In addition to state laws governing custodial relationships, it is important to note the central role played to date by state money transmitter laws in governing transactions in Digital Assets. State money transmitter licensing is frequently required for many Digital Asset activities, particularly for serving as an intermediary in fiat currency, virtual currency, and related transactions. While custodial activities may not be subject to the money transmitter laws, it is important to carefully consider the applicable statutory and regulatory language as well as any interpretative rulings by individual state regulators to define what is within the ambit of that state's money transmitter law.

Looking Ahead: the URVCBA and UCC Article 8 Companion Act to the URVCBA

The URVCBA and the UCC Article 8 Companion Act to the URVCBA (the "Companion Act") are an initiative of the Uniform Law Commission intended to provide a state-level regulatory framework similar to that created by state money transmitter laws for entities that offer virtual currency[33] transfer, exchange, or storage services. The URVCBA has not yet been enacted by any state, although it has been introduced in Connecticut, Hawaii, and Nebraska.

The URVCBA

In order for a person to exchange, transfer or store a virtual currency for purposes of the URVCBA, such person must have "control" over that virtual currency, which means the "power to execute unilaterally or prevent indefinitely a virtual-currency transaction."[34] In the context of a "multi sig" arrangement, a custodian may only have one of several private keys that are needed to effectuate a transaction in the relevant virtual currency, in which case such custodian would not have "control" over such virtual currency for the purposes of the URVCBA. However, certain entities are exempt from the URVCBA's requirements, including: (1) federally- or state-chartered depository institutions; (2) broker-dealers or futures commission merchants provided that their virtual currency activities are ancillary to their securities or commodities business and they comply with Section 502 of the URVCBA (discussed below); and (3) governments.

A person within the scope of the URVCBA needs to obtain a licence from state authorities if the value of such person's virtual currency business activities exceeds a $5,000 *de minimis* threshold. The URVCBA, however, also creates an "on-ramp" or "lite" regime for entities whose virtual currency business activity is below a $35,000 threshold. Such persons still need to register with the relevant authorities, but are subject to less onerous licensing requirements.

Obligations applicable to licensees and registrants are similar to those imposed under money transmitter laws and include recordkeeping, disclosure, and business continuity planning obligations. Unlike money transmitter laws, however, Section 502 of the URVCBA requires licensees and registrants that have "control" over customers' virtual currencies to "maintain an amount of each type of virtual currency sufficient to satisfy the aggregate entitlements of the persons to each type of virtual currency for the benefit of its resident customers." While this obligation is similar to that imposed on securities intermediaries under Part 5 of Article 8 of the UCC, Part 5 permits a securities intermediary and its customer to agree that a different rule will apply and also provides that this obligation will be displaced to the extent addressed by another statute or regulation. Section 502 also provides that virtual currency held by a licensee or registrant for a customer is not property of the licensee or registrant and will not be available to satisfy the claims of such licensee's or registrant's creditors. Customers will share *pro rata* in the virtual currencies to which they are entitled.

The Companion Act

The Companion Act requires entities subject to the URVCBA to agree with their customers that virtual currencies controlled by such entities for such customers are to be treated as financial assets, which would mean that the commercial law rules for financial assets discussed above would apply to such virtual currencies. Notably, the Companion Act also provides that the agreement between a licensee or registrant and their customers cannot provide for a standard for the licensee or registrant to comply with its Part 5 duties that is less protective of the customer than the standard that applies under Part 5 when there is no agreement between the parties as to which standard applies (i.e., "due care in accordance with reasonable commercial standards"). The Companion Act further requires that the agreement between a licensee or registrant and its customer must state that the licensee or registrant will not grant a security interest in the virtual currency it is maintaining on behalf of its customer.

Conclusion

As with many issues involving Digital Assets, the laws and interpretations governing their custody and transfer continue to evolve. Current law generally was not designed to address Digital Assets and, as a result, is being adapted to fit this new asset class that, in some areas, fits imperfectly within existing legal frameworks and interpretations. Perhaps the only sure prediction is that the law will continue to evolve and, less certainly, continue to develop to promote greater certainty as Digital Assets themselves continue to evolve and play an increasingly significant role in the markets.

The views expressed in this chapter are solely those of the authors and do not necessarily represent the policies or views of Cleary Gottlieb or any of its partners. © 2018 Cleary Gottlieb Steen & Hamilton.

Acknowledgment

The authors gratefully acknowledge the contribution of Marc Rotter, Brandon Hammer, Reshama Patel, and Jim Wintering to this chapter.

* * *

Endnotes

1. This chapter reflects legal developments as of July 31, 2018.
2. This chapter describes the typical operation of publicly accessible distributed ledgers, such as the blockchain used for Bitcoin. Other distributed ledger technologies, especially permissioned (*i.e.*, "private") blockchains, can involve different mechanics for recording the ownership and transfer of Digital Assets.
3. *See, e.g.,* Olga Kharif and Sonali Basak, *Regulated Crypto Custody Is (Almost) Here. It's a Game Changer*, Bloomberg (June 18, 2018), https://www.bloomberg.com/news/articles/2018-06-18/regulated-crypto-custody-is-almost-here-it-s-a-game-changer.
4. UCC § 8-102(a)(9) defines a "financial asset" as, in relevant part, "(i) a security; [or] "(ii) an obligation of a person or a share, participation, or other interest in a person or in property or an enterprise of a person, which is, or is of a type, dealt in or traded on financial markets, or which is recognized in any area in which it is issued or dealt in as a medium for investment."
5. *See* UCC § 8-102 cmt. 9.
6. *See* UCC §§ 8-504(c)(2), 8-505(a)(2), 8-506(2), 8-507(a)(2) and 8-508(2).
7. *See* UCC § 8-503 cmt. 1.
8. *See* UCC §§ 8-106(c), 9-106(a).
9. *See Virtual Currencies: The Oversight Role of the U.S. Securities and Exchange Commission and the U.S. Commodity Futures Trading Commission*, 115th Cong. (Feb. 6, 2018) (Testimony of Chairman Clayton before the Senate Committee on Banking, Housing, and Urban Affairs, Washington D.C.) ("I believe every ICO I've seen is a security.")
10. *See In re Coinflip, Inc.*, CFTC Docket No. 15-29 (Sep. 17, 2015) ("Bitcoin and other virtual currencies are encompassed in the definition [of commodity under Section 1a(9) of the CEA] and properly defined as commodities."). Questions have been raised, however, regarding whether all Digital Assets qualify as commodities, or just those (such as Bitcoin) that underlie listed futures contracts. *See e.g.* Defs.' Opp'n. to Pl.'s Mot. for Prelim. Inj., *CFTC v. My Big Coin Pay, Inc.*, 1:18-cv-10077-RWZ at 7-10 (D. Mass. Apr. 3, 2018).
11. Section 15(a)(1) of the Exchange Act.
12. *See* Definition of Terms in and Specific Exemptions for Banks, Savings Associations, and Savings Banks Under Sections 3(a)(4) and 3(a)(5) of the Securities Exchange Act of 1934, SEC Release No. 34-44291 (May 11, 2001).
13. The application of these regulations to Digital Assets is not clear in many cases. For a high-level summary, *see* Financial Industry Regulatory Authority, *Distributed Ledger Technology: Implications of Blockchain for the Securities Industry*, https://www.finra.org/sites/default/files/FINRA_Blockchain_Report.pdf.
14. *See* Section 3(a)(4)(B)(viii) of the Exchange Act. Although most U.S. depository institutions clearly qualify for this exception, the status of other types of banks, such as state-licensed, non-depository trust companies, is not as clear in all cases.
15. Custody is broadly defined as "holding, directly or indirectly, client funds or securities, or having any authority to obtain possession of them," and includes (i) possession of client funds or securities, (ii) any arrangement under which an adviser is authorized or permitted to withdraw client funds or securities held by a custodian upon instruction to

the custodian, and (iii) access to client funds by virtue of an adviser's dual role as both general partner and investment adviser to a limited partnership or other such capacity. Rule 206(4)-2(d)(2) under the Advisers Act.

16. The SEC has not yet addressed whether or under what circumstances Digital Assets that are not securities remain subject to the Custody Rule as "funds."

17. The term "qualified custodian" is defined in the Custody Rule to include: banks or savings associations with deposits insured by the FDIC; broker-dealers registered with the SEC; futures commission merchants registered with the CFTC; and non-U.S. financial institutions that customarily hold financial assets for their customers, so long as they keep the advisory assets separate from their own.

18. Rule 206(4)-2(a)(3) under the Advisers Act.

19. Additionally, investment advisers that also serve as qualified custodians themselves must be subject to an annual surprise examination from an independent public accountant that is registered with and regularly inspected by the Public Company Accounting Oversight Board. Furthermore, that adviser must also obtain or receive from its affiliate an annual report prepared by such an accountant that covers all internal controls the adviser uses relating to providing custody services for client assets.

20. Rule 206(4)-2(b)(5) under the Advisers Act.

21. Rule 17f-2 under the Investment Company Act.

22. Section 17(f)(1) if the Investment Company Act.

23. Rule 17f-5 under the Investment Company Act.

24. Rule 17f-1 under the Investment Company Act. In addition, SEC-registered investment companies are able to deposit securities in securities depositories that meet certain requirements and hold assets with futures commission merchants and commodity clearing organisations in amounts necessary to effect certain types of transactions. *See* Rules 17f-4, 17F-6, and 17f-7 under the Investment Company Act.

25. For example, CFTC Regulation § 180.1 prohibits fraud and manipulation in connection with any contract of sale of any commodity in U.S. interstate commerce.

26. *See* Retail Commodity Transactions Involving Virtual Currency, 82 Fed. Reg. 60335 (Dec. 20, 2017).

27. *Commodity Futures Trading Comm'n v. Monex Credit Co.,* 311 F. Supp. 3d 1173 (C.D. Cal. 2018).

28. For example, some of this precedent depends on whether a commodity is "nonfinancial," which in turn depends on whether ownership of the commodity can be conveyed in some manner and the commodity can be consumed. *See* Further Definition of "Swap," "Security-Based Swap," and "Security-Based Swap Agreement"; Mixed Swaps; Security-Based Swap Agreement Recordkeeping, 77 Fed. Reg. 48208, 48233 (Aug. 13, 2012). However, this precedent was intended to address environmental commodities, such as emission allowances, that do not provide good analogies for many Digital Assets.

29. *See* Section 4d of the CEA and CFTC Regulations §§ 1.20-1.30 (futures segregation rules), 30.7 (foreign futures segregation rules) and Part 22 (cleared swaps segregation rules).

30. *See* CFTC Regulations §§ 1.20(b), 22.4, and 30.7(b).

31. 23 NYCRR § 200.2(q).

32. *See* 23 NYCRR § 200.3(a)-(c).

33. The URVCBA uses the term "virtual currency" throughout, which is very broadly defined. *See* URVCBA § 102(23).

34. URVCBA § 102(3)(A).

Michael H. Krimminger
Tel: +1 202 974 1720 / Email: mkrimminger@cgsh.com
Michael H. Krimminger is a partner based in the Washington, D.C. office of Cleary Gottlieb Steen & Hamilton LLP. Mr Krimminger advises domestic and international banking and financial institutions, as well as a variety of clients on fintech and related regulatory issues. Mr Krimminger joined Cleary Gottlieb in 2012 after serving for more than two decades with the Federal Deposit Insurance Corporation (FDIC), including as its General Counsel.

Colin Lloyd
Tel: +1 212 225 2809 / Email: clloyd@cgsh.com
Colin Lloyd is a partner based in the New York office of Cleary Gottlieb Steen & Hamilton LLP. He advises on securities and derivatives regulatory, legislative, transactional and enforcement matters. Mr Lloyd frequently counsels U.S. and non-U.S. broker-dealers, swap dealers, investment managers and other clients, as well as technology companies, on the application of U.S. securities and derivatives regulations to new technologies, including cryptocurrencies and distributed ledgers.

Sandra Rocks
Tel: +1 212 225 2780 / Email: srocks@cgsh.com
Sandra Rocks is counsel based in the New York office of Cleary Gottlieb Steen & Hamilton LLP. She advises on commercial and insolvency law in the context of financial market transactions, with a focus on the development and analysis of arrangements designed to mitigate credit risk and minimise adverse regulatory capital implications of various products, including digital assets.

Cleary Gottlieb Steen & Hamilton LLP

2000 Pennsylvania Avenue, NW, Washington, D.C. 20006, USA
Tel: +1 202 974 1500 / Fax: +1 202 974 1999 / URL: www.clearygottlieb.com

An introduction to virtual currency money transmission regulation

Michelle Ann Gitlitz & Grant E. Buerstetta
Blank Rome LLP

Introduction

The proliferation of virtual currencies, and activities relating to this new asset class, including how businesses are looking to incorporate blockchain payments to quickly and seamlessly effectuate remittances to locations around the world, raises significant compliance issues with respect to money transmission laws and regulations. This treatise chapter examines when businesses in the virtual currency arena may be obligated to comply with both U.S. federal and state money transmission laws and regulations.

On the federal level, the Financial Crimes Enforcement Network ("FinCEN"), a division of the U.S. Department of the Treasury, exercizes regulatory authority pursuant to the Currency and Financial Transactions Reporting Act of 1970, as amended by Title III of the USA PATRIOT Act of 2001 and other legislation, which legislative framework is commonly referred to as the Bank Secrecy Act ("BSA").[1] The BSA is a comprehensive federal anti-money laundering ("AML") and counter-terrorism financing ("CTF") statute. FinCEN is charged with protecting the financial system from being used for money laundering and to prevent terrorism financing. Accordingly, the federal government is primarily concerned with preventing criminals from laundering money or otherwise participating in illegal financial activities. The laws are in place to allow FinCEN to manage the collection, processing, storage, dissemination, and protection of data filed pursuant to its reporting requirements in order to monitor personal information or transactional data.

The data is analysed by FinCEN, which allocates its resources to the areas that pose the greatest financial crime risk. FinCEN also shares information with foreign financial intelligence unit counterparts on AML and CTF efforts. Specifically, FinCEN recently announced that it is sharing its experience on virtual currency with foreign partners through the Egmont Group of Financial Intelligence Units ("FIU") and other international forums. The goal is to help FIUs better advise reporting entities on what to report about virtual currency transactions or activity and other relevant information for revealing important methods and constituents involved in financing illicit activities.

In addition to the federal regime, any entity operating in the virtual currency arena must also consider the intricate (and often confusing) web of state money transmission laws with which they may have to comply. State money transmission regulations are not aimed at protecting against money laundering and terrorist financing; they focus on consumer protection to ensure that a money transmitter will not lose, steal, or misdirect the consumer's money. Virtually every state has its own money transmission licensing regime, which is inefficient, particularly in the context of virtual currency businesses whose technologies and products may operate fluidly across state lines.

The maze of state licensing regulations, paired with FinCEN's federal requirements, demand thoughtful consideration of legal compliance for any person or business who operates in the virtual currency industry and may be considered a money transmitter.

Federal virtual currency money transmission

The BSA requires that "financial institutions," businesses offering a wide array of broadly-defined financial services, surveil their customers and provide information about those customers to FinCEN.[2] Financial institutions must take a number of precautions against financial crime, including establishing Know Your Customer ("KYC") and AML programs and the filing of Suspicious Activity Reports ("SARs") and Currency Transaction Reports ("CTRs") that are used in criminal, tax, and regulatory investigations and proceedings and certain intelligence and counter-terrorism matters.[3]

"Financial institution" includes any bank, broker or dealer in securities, money services business, telegraph company, casino, card club, or a person subject to supervision by any state or federal bank supervisory authority, and that status is determined based on the type of activities in which that person or entity engages.[4] A "money services business," which includes a money transmitter, is the financial institution most relevant to this treatise.

The definition of money transmitter for purposes of BSA regulations includes:

(a) [a]ny person, whether or not licensed or required to be licensed, who engages as a business in accepting currency, or funds denominated in currency, and transmits the currency or funds, or the value of the currency or funds, by any means through a financial agency or institution, a Federal Reserve Bank or other facility of one or more Federal Reserve Banks, the Board of Governors of the Federal Reserve System, or both, or an electronic funds transfer network; or

(b) [a]ny other person engaged as a business in the transfer of funds.[5]

Whether a person is a money transmitter, including those operating in the virtual currency arena, is a matter of facts and circumstances.[6] The term "money transmission services" means "the acceptance of currency, funds, or other value that substitutes for currency from one person and the transmission of currency, funds, or other value that substitutes for currency to another location or person by any means."[7] In 2011, FinCEN issued a final rule amending definitions and other regulations relating to money services businesses to provide that money transmission covers the acceptance and transmission of value that substitutes for currency.[8] Simply put, when a person accepts and transmits anything of value that substitutes for currency, that person is deemed a money transmitter. The regulations specifically exempt from money transmitter status a person who only provides the delivery, communication, or network data access services used by a money transmitter to supply money transmission services; for example, when the only type of brokerage services offered by a person are those in which the buyer makes payment directly to the seller.[9]

FinCEN virtual currency guidance

FinCEN issues guidance on various issues that arise under FinCEN regulations (hereinafter, collectively, the "Guidance"), which is intended to clarify issues or respond to questions of general applicability.[10] FinCEN first addressed rulemaking authority over virtual currency in March 2013, clarifying that it would regulate transmitters of virtual currency in the same manner as transmitters of fiat currency.[11]

Under FinCEN regulations, fiat currency (also referred to as "real" currency) is defined as "the coin and paper money of the United States or of any other country: [i] that is designated as legal tender; [ii] that circulates; and [iii] is customarily used and accepted as a medium of exchange in the country of issuance."[12] "'Virtual' currency is a medium of exchange that operates like a currency in some environments, but does not have all the attributes of real currency."[13] The Guidance issued in March 2013 addressed "convertible virtual currency," which is defined as either having "an equivalent value in real currency, or acts as a substitute for real currency."[14] FinCEN regulations cover both transactions where the parties are exchanging fiat and convertible virtual currency, as well as transactions from one virtual currency to another virtual currency. Businesses providing anonymizing services (also known as "mixers" or "tumblers"), which attempt to conceal the source of the transmission of virtual currency, are money transmitters when they accept and transmit convertible virtual currency and, therefore, have regulatory obligations under the BSA.[15]

The convertibility of the virtual currency is an important distinction. If a virtual currency cannot be converted to or sold for real currency and does not have any monetary value on the open market, then it does not implicate federal money transmission laws.

The Guidance refers to three categories of participants in the virtual currency ecosystem: users, exchangers, and administrators as explained below.[16]

- **User**: a person who obtains virtual currency to purchase goods or services.[17] In January 2014, this definition was expanded to also include businesses that are strictly investing in convertible virtual currency for their own account and not for any other party.[18] Under the current Guidance, it would appear that institutions investing in virtual currencies such as co-mingled investment funds are considered users.

- **Exchanger**: a person *engaged as a business* in the exchange of virtual currency for real currency, funds, or other virtual currency. Note that a person must be engaged in a business; thus, trading simply for personal investment purposes does not qualify one as an exchanger. In addition, one must accept *and* transmit virtual currency from one person to another or to another location, such as a brokerage service or trading platform. Mere acceptance of virtual currency in exchange for providing a good or service does not make a person a money transmitter.

- **Administrator**: a person engaged as a business in issuing (putting into circulation) a virtual currency, and who has the authority to redeem (to withdraw from circulation) such virtual currency.[19]

Users are not considered money transmitters, and thus are not required to register with FinCEN. Exchangers or administrators may operate as money transmitters and may be required to register with FinCEN depending on the specific facts and circumstances.

Since issuing the Guidance in March 2013, FinCEN has issued other Guidance and rulings on virtual currency that further inform the application of existing money transmission regulations: *Application of FinCEN's Regulations to Virtual Currency Software Development and Certain Investment Activity*, FIN-2014-R002 (Jan. 30, 2014) (the "2014 Software and

Investment Guidance"); *Application of FinCEN's Regulations to Virtual Currency Mining Operations*, FIN-2014-R001 (Jan. 30, 2014) (the "2014 Mining Guidance"); and *Request for Administrative Ruling on the Application of FinCEN's Regulations to a Virtual Currency Payment System*, FIN-2014-R012 (Oct. 27, 2014) (the "2014 Payment System Ruling").

Classification of persons and entities conducting virtual currency business activities for money transmission purposes

The aforementioned Guidance provides insight into how to apply the FinCEN standards of when registration is necessary to various players in the virtual currency market. How FinCEN's Guidance might apply to these persons and entities is set forth below:

- **Software developer**: The production and distribution of virtual currency-related software, in and of itself, are not money transmission services and the entity engaged in the activity is not a money transmitter, even if the purpose of the software is to facilitate the sale of virtual currency.[20]

- **Miners**: Miners play a vital role in allowing many decentralized blockchain-based virtual currency systems to operate properly. Mining is important because virtual currencies or tokens such as Bitcoin are initially acquired through mining; unlike paper money, decentralized virtual currencies do not have a central government to issue the currency. This provides a somewhat controlled way to distribute tokens and creates a real incentive for miners to enter the market. Miners also play another vital role; in the traditional banking system, banks maintain an accurate record of parties and details of each transaction; however, since there is no central regulator for decentralized virtual currencies, the miners assume this role.

  Those who mine virtual currencies, whether by "earning," "harvesting," "creating," or "manufacturing," are all classified as users and not money transmitters. Once the virtual currency is mined, a miner, depending on how he/she uses the convertible virtual currency and for whose benefit, may potentially become a money transmitter.[21] Just because the miner acquired the tokens directly by mining them, rather than purchasing or being given them, his/her status as a user is unaffected. Miners may use their mined tokens or currencies to purchase goods, and until they engage in activities that would qualify them as a transmitter, they remain a user.

- **Centralized virtual currencies**: A convertible virtual currency that has a centralized repository is a centralized virtual currency ("CVC"). The repository of a CVC is a money transmitter to the extent that it allows transfers of value between persons or from one location (i.e., a user's account in New York) to another (i.e., that user's account in California). In addition, if the CVC repository accepts currency or its equivalent from a user and privately credits the user with an appropriate portion of the repository's own convertible virtual currency, and then transmits that internally credited value to third parties at the user's direction, the CVC repository is a money transmitter.[22]

- **Decentralized virtual currencies**: A decentralized virtual currency ("DVC") is a virtual currency that has no central repository and no single person who has the ability to issue or redeem the virtual currency. Persons may obtain the virtual currency through their own computing or mining effort or by purchasing the currency. A person who creates units of a DVC and uses it to purchase real or virtual goods and services is a "user" of the convertible virtual currency and is not subject to regulation as a money transmitter. By contrast, a person who creates units of a DVC, and sells those units to another person for real currency or its equivalent and is engaged in that transfer as a business, is a money transmitter to the extent that he/she is transferring it from one person or location to another person or location. A person who accepts and transmits real currency to one person in exchange for a DVC, but is arguably engaged in the business of providing goods and services, may have a valid argument that he/she is not a money transmitter. The exact scope of the regulation in this context is currently unclear.[23]

- **Wallets**: are secure virtual currency storage systems used to hold and potentially send or receive virtual currency. Most virtual currencies have official or suggested wallets and the use of a wallet is necessary. The wallet contains a public and private key for each virtual currency address. The private key is a secret number that allows the virtual currency to be spent. The public key is used to ensure the wallet holder is the owner of the wallet address and can receive funds. The public key is mathematically derived from the private key. The status of a wallet as a money transmitter is primarily determined by whether or not the wallet company has custody of the private keys for the virtual currency.

  - **Custodial wallets**: Custodial wallet companies are likely money transmitters. They typically accept virtual currencies for users and transmit them when the currencies need to be moved. The custodial wallet is in full control of the transaction and the user could not facilitate the transaction without the participation and action of the wallet provider. Examples of custodial wallet companies include Bitfinex, Bitthumb and Coinbase.

  - **Non-custodial wallets:** Non-custodial wallet companies are likely *not* money transmitters. These wallets never accept or transmit virtual currencies; they are a software tool. The user facilitates the transaction and neither the wallet nor the keys are ever in the possession of the non-custodial wallet company. This entity can be thought of as merely a developer of software used to aid the customer in facilitating his/her own transactions. Examples of non-custodial wallet companies include Jaxx, BitGo and Mycellium.

- **Custodial exchanges**: are virtual currency exchange platforms on which users are able to buy and sell virtual currencies. What distinguishes this type of exchange as custodial is the fact that the exchange is in control of a user's funds, or in other words, the exchange is the custodian of the private keys for the virtual currencies or tokens. Examples of these types of exchanges include Coinbase, GDAX, Kraken, and Bitfinance. Custodial exchanges are money transmitters because they are both buying and selling, and accepting and transmitting virtual currencies.

- **Non-custodial exchanges**: are virtual currency exchange platforms on which users are able to purchase and sell virtual currencies. What makes the non-custodial exchange different from the custodial exchange is that the exchange never takes possession of the user's virtual currency or private keys. Examples include Shape Shift and Evercoin. Non-custodial exchanges are likely not money transmitters. They are merely a source to help connect potential buyers with potential sellers, similar to a message or classifieds board like Craigslist. Because they are never in possession of the currency or private keys, they are never accepting or transmitting, and they are not buying or selling.

- **Token developers**: are the individuals who create a token platform and the virtual currency. Satoshi Nakamoto, the creator of Bitcoin, was the first to develop and release to the public a peer-to-peer digital currency platform. A token developer who either gives away his/her tokens or allows mining is simply distributing his/her software and, absent other facts, is not a money transmitter.[24] These token developers never accept and transmit tokens, but rather are simply developing and distributing the software in order to allow other users to operate peer-to-peer. Whether token developers are subject to regulation depends on the business they are engaged in and whether they are a DVC or CVC, as discussed above.

A token developer who sells virtual currency or tokens to users, rather than giving them away or allowing users to mine currency, is more complex. A miner who sells the currency he has mined and a developer who sells currency he has created should be treated the same. At the outset, the Guidance does not address these scenarios and there is not yet any case law in the area. However, in FinCEN's first civil enforcement action against a virtual currency exchanger, Ripple Labs Inc., FinCEN alleged that Ripple Labs' currency, XRP, made the developer an exchanger subject to BSA regulation.[25]

Ripple Labs settled, agreeing to a $700,000 penalty and to take certain remedial measures. This settlement is not precedential because it was a negotiated agreement. However, the allegations seemingly contradict the 2014 Software and Investment Guidance and make the treatment of token developers planning to sell their tokens somewhat unclear.

- **Token issuers:** Although no official guidance has been issued, FinCEN has indicated that those who raise money through an Initial Coin Offering ("ICO") may also have to register as money transmitters. A February 13, 2018 letter from FinCEN to U.S. Senator Ron Wyden of the Senate Committee on Finance (the "FinCEN Letter") states that FinCEN is working with the SEC and CFTC to enforce AML obligations of businesses engaged in ICOs.[26] FinCEN was careful to note that not all ICO issuers must register with FinCEN. Instead, whether an issuer must register depends on the nature of the financial activity involved.[27] The FinCEN Letter further states that a developer that sells convertible virtual currency such as Bitcoin (which has an equivalent value in fiat currency and can be exchanged back and forth for fiat currency), including in the form of an ICO, in exchange for another type of value that substitutes for currency, is a money transmitter and must comply with AML requirements. On August 9, 2018, FinCEN Director Kenneth A. Blanco stated in a speech that "[w]hile ICO arrangements vary and, depending on their structure, may be subject to different authorities, one fact remains absolute: FinCEN, and our partners at the SEC and CFTC, expect businesses involved in ICOs to meet all of their AML/CFT obligations."[28]

- **Payment systems**: Virtual currency payment processing systems typically process payments and assist in executing transactions by accepting cash from the buyer, keeping that cash, and then paying the seller with the approximate market value of a virtual currency, or vice versa. By keeping a large reserve of virtual currency at all times, the payment processer is able to act as his/her own currency exchange to supply equivalent virtual currency for the cash supplied by the buyer.

According to FinCEN, payment processing systems that accept and convert both real and virtual currencies are money transmitters because they are exchangers and, therefore, must register.[29] "An exchanger will be subject to the same obligations under FinCEN regulations regardless of whether the exchanger acts as a broker (attempting to match two (mostly) simultaneous and offsetting transactions involving the acceptance of one type of currency and the transmission of another) or as a dealer (transacting from its own reserve in either convertible virtual currency or real currency)."[30]

There is, however, a carve-out from registration for payment processors when four conditions are met:

(a) the entity providing the service facilitates the purchase of goods or services, or the payment of bills for goods or services (other than money transmission itself);

(b) the entity operates through clearance and settlement systems that admit only BSA-regulated financial institutions;

(c) the entity provides the service pursuant to a formal agreement; and

(d) the entity's agreement must be at a minimum with the seller or creditor that provided the goods or services and receives the funds.[31]

Meeting this exemption requirement can prove difficult.

- **Bitcoin ATMs:** Generally, a fiat currency automated teller machine ("ATM") is not subject to FinCEN regulation as a money services business or money transmitter.[32] Fiat ATMs simply allow a consumer to access his/her own account and his/her own fiat currency. There is no exchange because most fiat ATMs are unable to transmit funds to third parties or accounts at other financial institutions.[33] Bitcoin ATMs, however, are not merely an intermediary between a consumer and his/her personal bank. Bitcoin ATMs function as either one-way (converting fiat currency to Bitcoin) or two-way (converting fiat currency to Bitcoin and Bitcoin to fiat currency) machines. In both instances, these machines may act as intermediaries between buyers and sellers, more as a broker than as a teller. Therefore, Bitcoin ATM operators generally must register with FinCEN as money transmitters.

Registering as a money services business

Once established, money services businesses have 180 days to register with the United States Secretary of the Treasury.[34] Any company or individual serving as a money services business must file a FinCEN Form 107, along with an estimate of business volume for the coming year, information related to the business' ownership and control, and a list of its authorized agents.[35] FinCEN Form 107 requires money services businesses to identify the states in which they have agents and branches, the type of money services activities they plan to carry out (i.e., money transmitter, currency dealer or exchanger, check casher), the number of agents they have authorized to carry out each activity, and the location (financial institution and account number) of their primary transaction account.[36] If accepted, registration must be renewed every two years. If there is any change in ownership or control, transfer of a 10% voting or equity interest, or more than a 50% increase in authorized agents, then the business must re-register.[37]

Money services businesses must comply with recordkeeping, reporting and transaction monitoring requirements under FinCEN regulations. Examples of these requirements include the filing of reports relating to currency in excess of $10,000 received in a trade or business whenever applicable,[38] general recordkeeping maintenance,[39] and, to the extent any transactions constitute "transmittal of funds" under 31 C.F.R. § 1010.100(ddd), then the money services business must comply with the "Funds Transfer Rule" (31 C.F.R. § 1010.410(e)) and the "Funds Travel Rule" (31 C.F.R. § 1010.410(f)). These requirements apply to both domestic and foreign-located convertible virtual currency money transmitters, even if the foreign-located entity has no physical presence in the United States, as long as it does business in whole or substantial part within the United States.[40] Compliance requirements may vary depending on whether or not the business is a peer-to-peer exchange or a large, high-volume exchanger.[41]

Failure to comply with these requirements, including submission of false or materially incomplete information, can result in fines up to $5,000 per violation, or per day of a continued violation, and imprisonment of up to five years.[42] While registration is relatively easy, once registered, the compliance obligations are burdensome.

No action letters/Requests for rulings to federal or state regulators

If a person or entity is clearly a money transmitter, then federal registration with FinCEN is required, as is potential state licensing as discussed below. However, there may be situations in which it is unclear whether a person or entity must register as a money transmitter. In such a circumstance, it is possible to use "no-action" letters or "requests for rulings" from federal and state regulators. These letters allow a person or entity to explain their business activity to the federal or state regulators to address unclear areas of the law, and to clarify whether particular business activities subject the person or entity to registration or licensing requirements under the federal or state regulatory regimes.

State virtual currency money transmission

State money transmission, unlike federal money transmission, requires licensure, not registration. As a pre-requisite to receiving a licence and/or in connection with maintaining a licence, states generally require some combination of: payment of licensing costs; bonding (or other security device); minimum net worth requirements; disclosure of applicant employment history; submission to investigations or examinations; audited financials and periodic financial reporting to the state; prior money transmission or financial services business experience; disclosure of litigation and bankruptcy proceedings; and fingerprinting and background checks. Even if a person or entity is not a money transmitter under the BSA, they may be a money transmitter in any number of states, or vice versa.

A licence is required in any state where the person or company does business, or solicits citizens, regardless of whether or not he/she has any physical presence in the state. Thus, any entity that is planning a global or nationwide rollout of its virtual currency business must satisfy state licensing requirements regardless of where it is physically located. This is particularly onerous to comply with for virtual currency businesses, because virtual currency is a borderless medium of exchange.

States where money transmission licensing or other requirements are necessary for virtual currency activities

Alabama: requires a licence to transmit virtual currencies.[43]

Alaska: requires that a licensee or applicant who requests approval of a licence to provide transmission of virtual currency enter into a Limited Licence Agreement with the Alaska Department of Commerce, Community and Economic Development, Division of Banking and Securities.[44]

Connecticut: requires the licensing of virtual currency storage and transmission.[45]

Georgia: requires a licence to transmit virtual currencies.[46]

Hawaii: requires a licence and fiat reserves equal to the value of virtual currency held for clients.[47]

Idaho: virtual currency exchangers that accept legal tender (e.g., government backed/issued "fiat" currencies) for later delivery to a third party in association with the purchase of a virtual currency must be licensed as a money transmitter with the Department of Finance.[48] Idaho exempts the sale of virtual currency via Bitcoin ATMs from licensing.[49]

New York: a BitLicense is required by the New York State Department of Financial Services to engage in any "Virtual Currency Business Activity," which is broadly defined under the regulations.[50]

North Carolina: requires virtual currency transmitters to obtain a licence and additional insurance. The law provides several exemptions, including for miners, software companies implementing blockchain services such as smart contract platforms, smart property, multi-signature software and non-custodial and non-hosted wallets.[51]

Oregon: the state recently amended the definition of "money" in its money transmission statute (Or. Rev. Stat. §§ 717 *et seq.*) to include virtual currency. In addition, the state requires virtual currency exchanges to be registered as money transmitters.

Vermont: requires virtual currency transmitters to obtain a money transmission licence.[52]

Virginia: requires virtual currency transmitters to obtain a money transmission licence.[53]

Washington: virtual currency transmitters must obtain a money transmission licence. For companies that store virtual currency on behalf of others, there must be a third party security audit, a money transmitter bond which is calculated on the basis of the transmitter's dollar volume and payment's dollar volume from the previous year, and the company must provide certain disclosures to consumers.[54]

Wisconsin: state law does not currently give the Department of Financial Institutions the authority to regulate virtual currency. Therefore, Wisconsin is unable to license or supervize companies whose business activities are limited to those involving virtual currency. However, should the transmission of virtual currency include the involvement of sovereign currency, it may be subject to licensure in Wisconsin depending on how the transaction is structured. Wisconsin encourages companies to consult with legal counsel to determine whether the business activities they plan to conduct meet those defined in Chapter 217, the "Seller of Checks" law, as requiring licensure.[55]

<u>States that have enacted friendly virtual currency licensing regulations or have taken no position on virtual currency activities</u>

Arizona: the state has taken no position on virtual currency money transmission as of the date of publication of this treatise. Some virtual currency businesses have obtained a traditional money transmitter licence from the Arizona Department of Financial Institutions pursuant to Ariz. Rev. Stat. § 6-1201 *et seq.*

Arkansas: the state has taken no position on virtual currency money transmission as of the date of publication of this treatise. Some virtual currency businesses have obtained a traditional money transmitter licence from the Arkansas Securities Division pursuant to the Arkansas Uniform Money Services Act, Ark. Code Ann. §§ 23-55-101 *et seq.*[56]

California: the state has taken no position on virtual currency money transmission as of the date of publication of this treatise, but proposes licensing all "digital currency businesses."[57]

Colorado: the state has taken no position on virtual currency money transmission as of the date of publication of this treatise. Some virtual currency businesses have obtained a traditional money transmitter licence from the Colorado Division of Banking pursuant to the Colorado Money Transmitters Act, Colo. Rev. Stat. §§ 11-110-106 *et seq.*

Delaware: the state has taken no position on virtual currency money transmission as of the date of publication of this treatise. Some virtual currency businesses have obtained a traditional money transmitter licence from the Delaware Office of the State Bank Commissioner pursuant to 5 Del. Code §§ 2301 *et seq.*

District of Columbia: the district has taken no position on virtual currency money transmission as of the date of publication of this treatise. Some virtual currency businesses have obtained a traditional money transmitter licence from the District of Columbia Department of Insurance, Securities, and Banking Bureau pursuant to D.C. Law §§ 26-1001 *et seq.*

Florida: the state has taken no position on virtual currency money transmission as of the date of publication of this treatise, but prohibits the laundering of virtual currency.[58] Some virtual currency businesses have obtained a traditional money transmitter licence from the Florida Office of Financial Regulation pursuant to Fla. Stat. §§ 560.101 *et seq.*

Indiana: the state has taken no position on virtual currency money transmission as of the date of publication of this treatise.

Illinois: the state has no virtual currency money transmission-specific regulations. The Illinois Department of Financial and Professional Regulation has issued Digital Currency Regulatory Guidance stating that virtual currencies are not "money" under the Transmitters of Money Act and exempting the exchange of "digital currencies" from "money transmission" licensing requirements. Some virtual currency businesses have obtained a money transfer licence from the Illinois Department of Financial and Professional Regulation pursuant to 205 Ill. Comp. Stat. 657.

Iowa: the state has taken no position on virtual currency money transmission as of the date of publication of this treatise. Some virtual currency businesses have obtained a money services licence from the State of Iowa Division of Banking pursuant to Iowa Code §§ 533C.201 *et seq.*

Kansas: The Kansas Office of the State Bank Commissioner issued guidance regarding the applicability of the Kansas Money Transmitter Act to people or businesses using or transmitting virtual currency.[59] Virtual currency is not considered "money" for the purposes of the Kansas Money Transmitter Act and a person or business engaged solely in transmitting virtual currency is exempt from licensing.[60] Some virtual currency businesses have obtained a traditional money transmitter licence from the Kansas Office of the State Bank Commissioner pursuant to Kan. Stat. Ann. §§ 9-508 *et seq.*

Kentucky: the state has taken no position on virtual currency money transmission as of the date of publication of this treatise. Some virtual currency businesses have obtained a traditional money transmitter licence from the Kentucky Office of Financial Institutions pursuant to KY. Rev. Stat. §§ 286.11.0001 *et seq.*

Louisiana: the state has taken no position on virtual currency money transmission as of the date of publication of this treatise. Some virtual currency businesses have obtained a traditional money transmitter licence from the Commissioner of Financial Institutions pursuant to La. Rev. Stat §§ 6:1031 *et seq.*

Maine: the state has taken no position on virtual currency money transmission as of the date of publication of this treatise. Some virtual currency businesses have obtained a traditional money transmitter licence from the Maine Department of Professional and Financial Regulation, Bureau of Consumer Credit Protection pursuant to Title 32 Me. Rev. Stat. §§ 6101 *et seq.*

Maryland: the state has taken no position on virtual currency money transmission as of the date of publication of this treatise, but the Maryland Department of Labor, Licensing and Regulation has advized consumers that under the federal paradigm, an "administrator" or "exchanger" must register with FinCEN.[2] Some virtual currency businesses have obtained a traditional money transmitter licence from the Maryland Department of Labor, Licensing and Regulation pursuant to Md. Code Ann., Fin. Inst. §§ 12-401 *et seq.*

Massachusetts: the state exempts Bitcoin ATMs from "financial institution" and bitcoins from foreign currency transmission regulations.[61] Businesses involved in the dissemination of virtual currencies on the internet are "market place facilitators" subject to sales or use tax collection.[62] Some virtual currency businesses have obtained a traditional money services business licence from the Massachusetts Office of Consumer Affairs and Business Regulation, Division of Banks, pursuant to 209 CMR 45 *et seq.*

Michigan: the state has taken no position on virtual currency money transmission as of the date of publication of this treatise. Some virtual currency businesses have obtained a traditional money transmission licence from the Michigan Department of Licensing and Regulatory Affairs Office of Financial and Insurance Regulation pursuant to the Money Transmissions Services Act, Mich. Comp. Laws §§ 487.1001 *et seq.* Virtual currency transactions are exempt from sales tax and retailers are required to instantly convert the value of the virtual currency to USD as of the day and the exact time of the transaction.[63]

Minnesota: the state has taken no position on virtual currency money transmission as of the date of publication of this treatise. Some virtual currency businesses have obtained a traditional money transmission licence from the Department of Commerce Division of Financial Examinations pursuant to Minn. Stat. §§ 53B.01 *et seq.*

Mississippi: the state has taken no position on virtual currency money transmission as of the date of publication of this treatise. Some virtual currency businesses have obtained a traditional money transmitter licence from the Mississippi Department of Banking and Consumer Finance pursuant to Miss. Code Ann. §§ 75-15-1 *et seq.*

Missouri: the state has taken no position on virtual currency money transmission as of the date of publication of this treatise except that it exempts Bitcoin ATM transactions from sales tax.[64] Some virtual currency businesses have obtained a traditional money transmitter licence from the State of Missouri, Division of Finance pursuant to Mo. Rev. Stat. §§ 361.700 *et seq.*

Montana: the state is notable as being one of the only states not to have enacted a money transmission statute.

Nebraska: the state has taken no position on virtual currency money transmission as of the date of publication of this treatise. In an administrative release, the Nebraska Department of Revenue found that the term "currency" does not include Bitcoin or other virtual currency. Proposed legislation, L.B. 691, which was introduced in the legislature in January 2018, would amend the state's money-laundering statutes to account for virtual currencies. Proposed legislation LB 987 establishes regulations focused on businesses engaging in "virtual currency business activity," and creates a tiered system of registration and licensure for companies that want to do business using virtual currencies. Some virtual currency businesses have obtained a traditional money transmitter licence from the Nebraska Department of Banking and Finance pursuant to the Nebraska Money Transmitters Act, Neb. Rev. Stat. §§ 8-2701 *et seq.*

Nevada: the state has taken no position on virtual currency money transmission as of the date of publication of this treatise. Some virtual currency businesses have obtained a traditional money transmitter licence from the Nevada Department of Business and Industry, Financial Institutions Division, pursuant to Nev. Rev. Stat. Ann. §§ 671.010 *et seq.*

New Hampshire: the state amended its Money Transmitter statute (N.H. Rev. St. Ann. § 399-G:3) to exempt "persons who engage in the business of selling or issuing payment instruments or stored value solely in the form of convertible virtual currency or receive convertible virtual currency for transactions to another location" from the state's money transmission regulation.[65]   Some virtual currency businesses have obtained a traditional money transmitter licence from the New Hampshire Banking Department.

New Jersey: the state has taken no position on virtual currency money transmission as of the date of publication of this treatise.   Some virtual currency businesses have obtained a traditional money transmitter licence from the New Jersey Department of Banking and Insurance pursuant to N.J.S.A 17:15C-1 *et seq.*

New Mexico: the state enacted its Uniform Money Services Act (§§ 58-32-301 (A)(1) *et seq.*) effective January 1, 2017, but the application to virtual currencies is currently unknown.   The definition of "money" does not include virtual currencies.

North Dakota: the state has taken no position on virtual currency money transmission as of the date of publication of this treatise.   Some virtual currency businesses have obtained a traditional money transmitter licence from the North Dakota Department of Financial Institutions pursuant to N.D. Cent. Code §§ 13-09-01 *et seq.*

Ohio: the state has taken no position on virtual currency money transmission as of the date of publication of this treatise.   Some virtual currency businesses have obtained a traditional money transmitter licence from the Ohio Division of Financial Institutions pursuant to Ohio Rev. Code §§ 1315.01 *et seq.*

Oklahoma: the state has taken no position on virtual currency money transmission as of the date of publication of this treatise, but subordinates the rights of merchants accepting Bitcoin to the rights of any security interest in the Bitcoin (traditional money transfers are free and clear of any security interest).[66]   Some virtual currency businesses have obtained a traditional money transmitter licence from the Oklahoma Office of the State Bank Commissioner pursuant to 6 Okla. Stat. §§ 1511 *et seq.*

Pennsylvania: the state has taken no position on virtual currency money transmission as of the date of publication of this treatise, but in late 2016, Pennsylvania amended the definition of "money" in its money transmission law to encompass virtual currencies.   Some virtual currency businesses have obtained a traditional money transmitter licence from the Pennsylvania Department of Banking and Securities pursuant to 7 P.S. §§ 6101 *et seq.*

Rhode Island: the state has taken no position on virtual currency money transmission as of the date of publication of this treatise.   Some virtual currency businesses have obtained a traditional money transmitter licence from the Rhode Island Department of Business Regulation pursuant to R.I. Gen. Laws §§ 19-14 and 19-14.3.

South Carolina: the state has taken no position on virtual currency money transmission as of the date of publication of this treatise, but the South Carolina Attorney General has published frequently asked questions that disclose that further guidance with respect to the transmission of virtual currencies will be provided in the "near future."[67]

South Dakota: the state has taken no position on virtual currency money transmission as of the date of publication of this treatise.   Some virtual currency businesses have obtained a traditional money transmitter licence from the South Dakota Department of Labor Regulation, Division of Banking pursuant to S.D. Codified Laws §§ 51A-17-1 and S.D. Admin. R. 20:07:21:01 *et seq.*

Tennessee: the state has issued guidance clarifying that it does not consider virtual currency to be money under its Money Transmitter Act and therefore, no licence is required.[68]   Some virtual currency businesses have obtained a traditional money transmitter licence from the Tennessee Department of Financial Institutions pursuant to Tenn. Code. Ann. §§ 45-7-201 *et seq.*

Texas: in Supervisory Memorandum 1037 issued by the Texas Department of Banking, Texas exempted the exchange of virtual currencies from money transmission licensing requirements because it does not consider virtual currency to be money.[69] Some virtual currency businesses have obtained a traditional money transmitter licence from the Texas Department of Banking pursuant to Tex. Fin. Code § 151.001 and Tex. Fin. Code § 151.301.

Utah: the state has taken no position on virtual currency money transmission as of the date of publication of this treatise. Some virtual currency businesses have obtained a traditional money transmitter licence from the Utah Department of Financial Institutions pursuant to Utah Code Ann. §§ 7-25-101 *et seq.*

West Virginia: the state has taken no position on virtual currency money transmission as of the date of publication of this treatise, but prohibits the laundering of cryptocurrencies.[70] Some virtual currency businesses have obtained a traditional money transmitter licence from the West Virginia Division of Financial Institutions pursuant to W. Va. Code §§ 32A-2-1 *et seq.*

Wyoming: the state amended its Money Transmitter Act to exempt virtual currencies from the Wyoming money transmitter licence and regulations.

Attempts to standardize licensing practices

In an attempt to simplify the process and to create some uniformity and efficiency, seven states – Georgia, Illinois, Kansas, Massachusetts, Tennessee, Texas and Washington – have come together to reach a level of reciprocity. In early 2018, these states agreed that if one party state reviews key requirements of state licensing for a money transmitter applicant, including cybersecurity, background checks, and compliance with the BSA, then the other participating states will accept those findings in their own licensing process. This is the first real step toward an integrated 50-state system of licensure and supervision.[71]

Acknowledgments

The authors acknowledge with thanks the contributions to this chapter by Dennis M.P. Ehling, Gregory Cronin and Justin Porter.

* * *

Endnotes

1. 31 U.S.C. §§ 5311-5332.
2. *Id.* § 5321(a)(2).
3. *See* FinCEN, *BSA Requirements for MSBs*, https://www.fincen.gov/bsa-requirements-msbs.
4. 31 C.F.R. § 1010.100(t).
5. *Id.* § 1010.100(ff)(5).
6. *Id.* § 1010.100(ff)(5)(ii).
7. *Id.* § 1010.100(ff)(5)(i)(A).
8. Bank Secrecy Act Regulations – Definitions and other Regulations Relating to Money Services Businesses, 76 FR 43585 (July 21, 2011).
9. 31 C.F.R. § 1010.100(ff)(5)(ii)(A); *see also Application of FinCEN's Regulations to Persons Issuing Physical or Digital Negotiable Certificates of Ownership of Precious Metals*, FIN-2015-R001 (August 14, 2015).
10. 31 C.F.R. Chapter X (formerly 31 CFR Part 103).

11. *Application of FinCEN's Regulations to Persons Administering, Exchanging, or Using Virtual Currencies*, FIN-2013-G001 (Mar. 18, 2013) ("March 2013 Guidance").
12. *Id.* pg. 1.
13. *Id.*
14. *Id.*
15. *See* https://www.fincen.gov/news/speeches/prepared-remarks-fincen-director-kenneth-blanco-delivered-2018-chicago-kent-block?utm_source=7-28-18+Member+List&utm_campaign=7b8d25b1ba-EMAIL_CAMPAIGN_2018_01_19_COPY_01&utm_medium=email&utm_term=0_e50a6ec6df-7b8d25b1ba-344964271#_ftn1 (last visited on August 11, 2018).
16. *Id.*
17. *Id.* pg. 2.
18. *Application of FinCEN's Regulations to Virtual Currency Software Development and Certain Investment Activity*, FIN-2014-R002 (Jan. 30, 2014).
19. FIN-2013-G001 pg. 2.
20. 2014 Software and Investment Guidance pg. 2.
21. 2014 Mining Guidance.
22. FIN-2013-G001 pg. 4.
23. FIN-2013-G001 pg. 5.
24. *See* 2014 Software and Investment Guidance.
25. *See* FinCEN, *FinCEN Fines Ripple Labs Inc. in First Civil Enforcement Action Against a Virtual Currency Exchanger: Company Agrees to $700,000 Penalty and Remedial Actions*, (May 5, 2015), https://www.fincen.gov/sites/default/files/2016-08/20150505.pdf.
26. The FinCEN Letter is not technically Guidance that must be followed, but the underlying regulations in the FinCEN Letter must be followed.
27. The FinCEN Letter appears to suggest that, at least in certain cases, virtual currency exchanges are subject to the BSA not because they are money services businesses, but because they are broker-dealers.
28. *See* https://www.fincen.gov/news/speeches/prepared-remarks-fincen-director-kenneth-blanco-delivered-2018-chicago-kent-block?utm_source=7-28-18+Member+List&utm_campaign=7b8d25b1ba-EMAIL_CAMPAIGN_2018_01_19_COPY_01&utm_medium=email&utm_term=0_e50a6ec6df-7b8d25b1ba-344964271#_ftn1 (last visited on August 11, 2018).
29. 2014 Payment System Ruling.
30. *Id.*
31. 2014 Payment System Ruling pg. 3.
32. *Application of the Definition of Money Services Business to Certain Owner-Operators of Automated Teller Machines Offering Limited Services*, FIN-2007-G006 (Dec. 3, 2007).
33. *Id.*
34. 31 U.S.C. § 5330.
35. 31 C.F.R. § 1022.380.
36. *See* FinCEN Form 107 (Mar. 2011).
37. 31 C.F.R. § 1022.380(b)(4).
38. *Id.* § 1027.330.
39. *Id.* § 1027.410.
40. FinCEN pursued enforcement action against BTC-e, an internet-based virtual currency exchange and a foreign located money services business, for failing to implement basic

AML controls that enabled criminals to launder proceeds. FinCEN fined BTC-e $110 million and its administrator, Alexander Vinnik, $12 million – the largest individual penalty ever assessed by FinCEN. FinCEN partnered with the Department of Justice, which pursued BTC-e and Vinnik criminally.

41. *See* FinCEN, *BSA Requirements for MSBs,* https://www.fincen.gov/bsa-requirements-msbs.

42. 18 U.S.C. § 1960.

43. Ala. Code § 8-7A-2(8).

44. *See* https://www.commerce.alaska.gov/web/dbs/LimitedLicenseAgreementOrders.aspx (last visited on August 11, 2018). Some virtual currency businesses such as Coinbase and CoinX have also obtained a traditional money transmitter licence from the Alaska Division of Banking and Securities pursuant to AS 06.55.102, which is limited to the transmission of fiat currency. Alaska's legislature has proposed a bill to define virtual currency and broaden the definition of money transmission to include it. H.B. 180, 30th Legislature, First Session (introduced Mar. 14, 2017).

45. Conn. Gen. Stat. § 36a-598. In February 2018, a bill was proposed (H.B. 5001, 2018 Leg., 2018 Feb. Reg. Sess. Gen. Ass. (Conn. 2018)), which would impose fees to trade or transfer virtual currency. Some virtual currency businesses have obtained a traditional money transmitter licence from the Connecticut Department of Banking.

46. Ga. Code § 7-1-680(26); Ga. Code § 7-1-690(b)(1) (authorizes virtual currency transmission regulations to encourage economic development).

47. HI Rev Stat § 489D-1 (2013); *see* Hawaii Division of Financial Institutions Application available at https://cca.hawaii.gov/dfi/files/2018/04/HI-Money-Transmitter-License-Company-New-App-Checklist.pdf (last visited August 12, 2018). Coinbase exited Hawaii in 2017, requiring Hawaiian customers to close their accounts, stating that it would be impossible for Coinbase to operate in the state given the reserve requirement. In early 2017, the Hawaiian Senate introduced Senate Bill 949, which seeks to clarify that decentralized virtual currency activities are *not* subject to the state's Money Transmitters Act, and establishes a Decentralized Virtual Currency Working Group within the state's Department of Commerce and Consumer Affairs to study whether virtual currencies should be regulated under the Act. Two bills, Senate Bill 2853 and Senate Bill 3082, introduced in the Hawaiian Senate in January 2018, aim to define and include virtual currencies under Hawaii's Money Transmitters Act. The bills would mandate that those transmitting virtual currencies in the state obtain a licence to do so, and that these persons or businesses issue a warning to consumers before enabling such transactions.

48. *See* Idaho Department of Finance, Letter Re: Money Transmissions (Dated July 26, 2016), *available at* https://www.finance.idaho.gov/MoneyTransmitter/Documents/NAOP/Digital%20Currency/2016-07-26.pdf (last visited August 11, 2018) ("An exchanger that sells its own inventory of virtual currency is generally not considered a virtual currency transmitter under the Idaho Money Transmitters Act." However, "an exchanger that holds customer funds while arranging a satisfactory buy/sell order with a third party, and transmits virtual currency… between buyer and seller, will typically be considered a virtual currency transmitter.")

49. Idaho Dep't of Finance, No Action Letter (Oct. 10, 2014).

50. 23 NYCRR 200. The New York State regulatory scheme has been the subject of much criticism and has resulted in an exodus of businesses from New York because of the costs and regulatory requirements associated with the BitLicense. As of the date of this treatise, only eight companies have been granted a BitLicense. Assembly Bill

A9899A to amend certain provisions of the BitLicense is pending in the New York State Legislature.

51. N.C. Gen. Stat. § 53-208.41, *et. seq.*
52. 8 Vt. Stat. Ann. §§ 2500, *et seq.*
53. Va. Code § 6.2-1900.
54. Wash. Rev. Code §§ 19.230.010, *et seq.*
55. *See* https://www.wdfi.org/fi/lfs/soc/ (last visited August 11, 2018). Some virtual currency businesses have obtained a money transmitter licence from Wisconsin.
56. Ark. Code Ann §§ 23-55-101 *et seq.*
57. Assembly Bill 1123 has been introduced for the second time into the California assembly, which proposes to enact the Virtual Currency Act to prohibit a person from engaging in any virtual currency business, unless licensed by the Commissioner or Business Oversight, or is exempt from licensure.
58. Fla. Stat. § 896.101.
59. *See* Kansas Office of the State Bank Commissioner, Guidance Document MT 2014-01, Regulatory Treatment of Virtual Currencies Under the Kansas Money Transmitter Act, (June 6, 2014), available at http://www.osbckansas.org/ mt/guidance/mt2014_01_virtual_currency.pdf.
60. *See* Kansas Office of the State Bank Commissioner, Guidance Document MT 2014-01, Regulatory Treatment of Virtual Currencies Under the Kansas Money Transmitter Act, (June 6, 2014), available at http://www.osbckansas.org/mt/guidance/mt2014_01_virtual_currency.pdf (last visited August 11, 2018).
61. *See* Office of the Commissioner of Financial Regulation, Virtual Currencies: Risks for Buying, Selling, Transacting, and Investing - Advisory Notice 14-01, (April 24, 2014), *available at* http://www.dllr.state.md.us/finance/advisories/advisoryvirtual.shtml (last visited August 11, 2018).
62. Mass. Division of Banks, Opinion 14-004 (May 12, 2014).
63. 830 CMRH 1.7(b)(1).
64. *See* Tax Policy Division of the Michigan Dept. of Treasury, Treasury Update, Vol. 1, Issue 1 (November 2015), *available at* https://www.michigan.gov/documents/treasury/Tax-Policy-November2015-Newsletter_504036_7.pdf (last visited August 11, 2018)
65. Missouri Dep't of Revenue, LR 7411, Collection of Sales Tax on Bitcoin Transfers Through an Automated Teller Machine (ATM), (September 12, 2014).
66. *See* H.B. 436, 2017 Leg., 165th Sess. (N.H. 2017).
67. Okla. Stat. § 1-9-332.
68. *See* http://www.scag.gov/money-services-frequently-asked-questions (last visited August 11, 2018).
69. Memo, Tenn. Dep't of Fin. Inst., Regulatory Treatment of Virtual Currencies under the Tennessee Money Transmitter Act (Dec. 16, 2015) *available at* https://www.tn.gov/content/dam/tn/financialinstitutions/new-docs/TDFI%20Memo%20on%20Virtual%20Currency.pdf (last visited August 11, 2018).
70. *See* https://www.dob.texas.gov/public/uploads/files/consumer-information/sm1037.pdf (last visited August 11, 2018).
71. W. Va. Code §§ 61-15-1 *et seq. See* Conference of State Bank Supervisors, "State Regulators Take First Step to Standardize Licensing Practices for Fintech Payments", Feb. 6, 2018, https://www.csbs.org/state-regulators-take-first-step-standardize-licensing-practices-fintech-payments.

Michelle Gitlitz
Tel: +1 212 885 5068 / Email: mgitlitz@BlankRome.com

Michelle Gitlitz is a securities lawyer who represents corporations, individuals, investment companies and funds in corporate, regulatory, and litigation matters. She co-leads Blank Rome's Blockchain Technology & Digital Currencies group and regularly advises companies as they bring blockchain technology applications to market, raise capital through coin/token issuances and digital securities offerings, establish digital currency mining operations, form private investment funds and hedge funds that invest in emerging technologies and digital currencies, and navigate through state and federal money transmission rules and regulations.

Michelle is a frequent presenter on the legal and regulatory aspects of blockchain technology and tokenization. She has participated in MIT's Legal Forum for Artificial Intelligence and Blockchain and has lectured on blockchain and tokenization at MIT's Computational Law Course. Michelle also participated in the United Nations' Blockchain for Impact Global Summit. She is a member of the Wall Street Blockchain Alliance, Chamber of Digital Commerce, Global Legal Blockchain Consortium, and the Accord Project. She is also Vice Chair of Blank Rome's Women's Forum and is the co-founder of a non-profit, Diversity in Blockchain, Inc.

Grant Buerstetta
Tel: +1 212 885 5454 / Email: GBuerstetta@BlankRome.com

Grant Buerstetta represents financial institutions, asset managers, issuers, and investment funds focused on debt and structured securities and serves clients in areas such as: complex structured and asset-backed securities and securitization transactions; alternative investment fund formation and operation; securities issuances in domestic and international capital markets; and blockchain technology and cryptocurrencies. Grant is the Chair of Blank Rome's Finance, Restructuring and Bankruptcy Practice Group and co-leads Blank Rome's Blockchain Technology & Digital Currencies group. Grant has formed and advises numerous alternative investment funds investing in cryptocurrencies and blockchain infrastructure. Grant's experience with and knowledge of various structured credit products and securities law exemptions benefit his clients in structuring and executing transactions. In addition, Grant advises on legal, regulatory and risk management issues surrounding digital securities offerings. Grant also assists in advising clients on money transmission, securities and related regulatory issues. These representations draw on his broader corporate and securities skills as well as in-depth knowledge of complex transaction structuring.

Blank Rome LLP

The Chrysler Building, 405 Lexington Avenue, New York, NY 10174-0208, USA
Tel: +1 212 885 5000 / Fax: +1 212 885 5001 / URL: www.blankrome.com

The rise of the crypto asset investment fund: An overview of the crypto fund ecosystem

Jonathan Cardenas
Yale Law School

Introduction

Cryptocurrency has emerged as a lucrative financial asset class that has captured the attention of investors around the world.[1] Together with its rise as an asset class, investor interest in cryptocurrency has led to the creation of a variety of investment vehicles dedicated exclusively to crypto asset investment.[2] These crypto assets include cryptocurrencies and non-cryptocurrency, blockchain technology-based assets, such as digital tokens generated through initial coin offerings ("ICOs") and pre-ICO token sales, as well as traditional equity investments in blockchain technology startup companies.[3]

Crypto asset investment funds ("crypto funds") have intrigued both private and public sector investors around the world due, in part, to the colossal returns that some crypto fund managers captured in 2017 when Bitcoin reached its all-time high market price of $19,783.06 per coin.[4] Some crypto funds continue to raise significant levels of capital in 2018 despite Bitcoin's price slump.[5] Crypto funds have also attracted international criticism due to extreme volatility, cybersecurity risk, illicit activity, and concern over potential systemic risk that crypto funds could "spawn" in mainstream financial markets.[6]

With the launch of over 100 crypto funds in 2017, and the projected launch of over 150 new crypto funds in 2018,[7] challenging questions arise from regulatory and operational perspectives, as well as from the perspective of legal service providers who will service the emerging international crypto fund market.[8] This chapter will provide an overview of the crypto fund ecosystem, as well as a close look at select crypto investment funds, some of which are projected to become dominant players in the crypto fund market.

Market overview

Terminology

Crypto funds and the crypto assets in which they invest come in a variety of forms. As a preliminary matter, crypto funds (also referred to as cryptocurrency funds, digital asset funds or blockchain funds) can be defined as investment vehicles that raise capital from investors in order to invest in crypto assets for profit. Crypto assets, in turn, can be defined as "digital assets recorded on a distributed ledger".[9] These digital assets include cryptocurrencies and non-cryptocurrency, blockchain technology-based assets, such as digital tokens generated through ICOs and pre-ICO token sales, as well as traditional equity stakes in blockchain technology startup companies. Although there is no universally accepted definition of cryptocurrency (also referred to as virtual currency or digital currency),[10] a cryptocurrency can be conceptualised as an electronic medium of exchange that operates independent of any central or commercial bank.[11]

In contrast to cryptocurrencies, which are intended to serve as a medium of exchange across blockchain applications, digital tokens are intended to provide financing for an early-stage blockchain company's projects by providing investors with future access to that blockchain company's projected goods or services.[12] These tokens can be issued by way of a crowdfunding-style fundraising campaign known as an ICO (also known as an initial token offering), or by way of a pre-ICO token sale, which is generally targeted to specific "angel" investors.

It is worth noting that, to date, there is no harmonised international standard for the treatment and characterisation of crypto assets or related crypto asset transactions, such as ICOs and pre-ICO token sales.[13] Instead, there are conflicting classifications both domestically and internationally. In the U.S., for example, digital tokens have been categorised by federal and state agencies as either securities, commodities, currency or property. Outside of the U.S., financial regulators have taken a variety of approaches to crypto regulation, ranging from complete bans on ICOs in China and South Korea to more permissive forms of regulation, such as that in existence in Switzerland and Singapore. Notwithstanding the current state of international legal fragmentation with respect to crypto assets, private and public sector institutions from the around the world are collaborating vigorously to develop international norms that will enhance, rather than hinder, the growth of the crypto ecosystem.[14]

Market size

At the time of writing, it is estimated that over 460 crypto funds exist worldwide,[15] collectively managing between $7.5–10bn in assets.[16] This figure does not include cryptocurrency investment trusts, such as Grayscale's Bitcoin Investment Trust, or Bitcoin futures traded on Bitcoin futures exchanges, such as the Chicago Mercantile Exchange and Chicago Board Options Exchange, which would otherwise add approximately $2–4bn of crypto fund exposure to crypto assets.[17] The largest crypto funds have over $100m in assets under management ("AUM"), including Arrington XRP Capital, BlockTower Capital and the Logos Fund.[18] Polychain Capital, founded and led by early Bitcoin investor Olaf Carlson-Wee, is estimated to control $1bn in AUM according to recent filings with the U.S. Securities & Exchange Commission ("SEC").[19] Other large crypto funds include Brian Kelly Capital Management, the Galaxy Digital Assets Fund, MetaStable Capital and Pantera Capital.[20] The majority of crypto funds, however, have less than $10m in AUM[21] and fewer than 10 employees.[22]

The crypto fund sector has grown rapidly due, in part, to inflows of investment from institutional investors.[23] Reputable venture capital firms, such as Andreesen Horowitz, Sequoia Capital and Union Square Ventures, have invested heavily in crypto startups, including early-stage crypto funds. Polychain Capital, for example, raised $10m in a round led by Andreesen Horowitz and Union Square Ventures in December 2016.[24] Grayscale Investments has reported that 56% of its incoming capital in the first half of 2018 derived from institutional investors.[25] In addition, research from the Tabb Group indicates that sovereign wealth funds and pension funds have expressed significant interest in cryptocurrency investment.[26] Universities are reportedly also investing in crypto assets with the goal of increasing revenue for their endowments.[27]

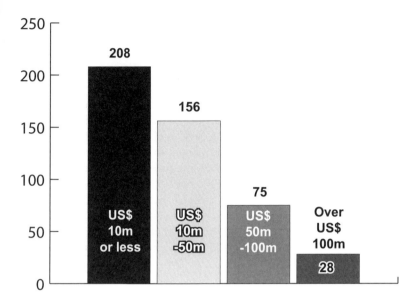

Source: Crypto Fund Research

<u>Geographic location</u>

More than half of all crypto funds are domiciled in the U.S., with the largest concentration located in California and New York. The most favoured cities for crypto funds are San Francisco, New York, London, Singapore, Hong Kong, Zurich and Chicago,[28] all of which have established investment fund communities. Although most crypto funds are U.S.-based, the crypto fund phenomenon is global in nature. As of August 2018, the following number of crypto funds exist in the following jurisdictions: Argentina (1), Australia (12), Bahamas (1), Bermuda (1), Brazil (1), British Virgin Islands (1), Bulgaria (1), Canada (17), Cayman Islands (6), China (16), Cyprus (2), Denmark (1), Estonia (2), Finland (1), France (5), Germany (14), Hong Kong (15), India (4), Isle of Man (1), Israel (3), Japan (4), Jersey (1), Kenya (1), Liechtenstein (1), Lithuania (1), Luxembourg (2), Malta (1), Mexico (2), Monaco (1), Netherlands (2), Nigeria (1), Portugal (2), Puerto Rico (2), Russia (3), Singapore (22), South Africa (1), South Korea (2), Switzerland (19), Taiwan (1), The Netherlands (4), Tortola (2), Turkey (3), United Arab Emirates (1), Ukraine (1), United Kingdom (30), and United States (250).[29]

While many crypto funds are privately held, others have significant levels of public sector involvement. The $1.6bn Xiong'An Global Blockchain Innovation Fund, for example, was launched in April 2018 by Chinese venture capital firm Tunlan Investment, with $400m provided by the Hangzhou city government.[30] In addition, the 10bn yuan Nanjing Public Blockchain Fund, which was launched by the Chinese city of Nanjing in July 2018 to spur public blockchain projects and the development of a "token economy" in China,[31] is believed to have received 30% of funding from the Nanjing government.[32] In addition, the Chinese city of Shenzhen has setup its own 500m yuan blockchain investment fund to invest in local blockchain startups, with 40% of funding provided by the Shenzhen municipal government and the remainder provided by the private sector.[33]

Fund investment strategies

The crypto fund market can be divided into segments based upon the multiple investment strategies that are executed by crypto fund managers. London-based fintech research firm Autonomous NEXT has divided the crypto fund market into seven such segments:[34] (1) liquid venture funds, which invest in early stage blockchain companies, cryptocurrencies and digital tokens; (2) trading funds, which actively trade cryptocurrencies using buy-and-hold, long-short and long-only approaches;[35] (3) artificial intelligence-driven quant funds, such as San Francisco-based Numerai, which use machine learning algorithms to execute statistical arbitrage strategies; (4) token basket funds, in which fund managers invest in baskets of crypto assets (i.e. cryptocurrencies and/or digital tokens),[36] which can be purchased by way of a single basket token, such as the Daily Crypto Basket offered by Flipside Crypto; (5) passively managed index funds, such as Bitwise Asset Management's HOLD 10 Private Index Fund and the Coinbase Index Fund, which invest in indices of top performing cryptocurrencies in exchange for 2–3% annual management fees; (6) crypto funds of funds, such as the Apex Token Fund and Protocol Ventures, which invest in other crypto hedge funds; and (7) crypto credit funds, such as SALT Blockchain Asset Management and Genesis Global Capital, which offer investors crypto asset-backed loan products. As illustrated below, crypto venture funds and crypto trading funds (i.e. crypto hedge funds) are the most popular category of crypto fund and hold the most in AUM, with crypto venture funds holding 56% and crypto hedge funds holding 20% of all crypto fund AUM, respectively.[37] As between crypto venture capital funds and crypto hedge funds, more crypto hedge funds have been launched in 2018 than crypto venture capital funds.[38]

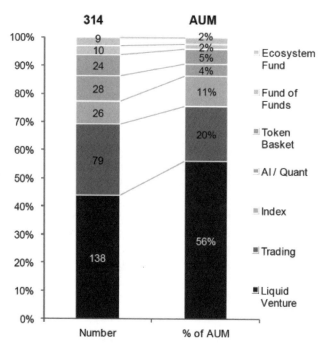

Source: Autonomous NEXT

Crypto asset hedge funds

Overview

Crypto asset hedge funds ("crypto hedge funds") can be defined as open-ended private investment vehicles that actively invest in crypto assets, including both cryptocurrencies, as well as non-cryptocurrency, blockchain technology-based crypto assets, such as digital tokens generated through ICOs or pre-ICO token sales, as well as equity investments in blockchain technology startup companies.[39]

Blockchain technology-based trading of crypto assets is considered revolutionary to the traditional hedge fund industry from an investment standpoint because of the opportunities that crypto investments afford to traditional fund managers from a returns and portfolio diversification perspective.[40] Cryptocurrency-focused hedge funds generated nearly 900% year-to-date returns in 2017, for example.[41] Although crypto hedge fund returns declined by approximately 50% in the first half of 2018,[42] many crypto fund managers remain bullish on crypto asset markets, particularly as certain crypto hedge funds, such as Altana Digital Currency Fund and Amber AI Pivot Digital Trading-2, performed well notwithstanding Bitcoin's price slump.[43] Crypto hedge funds, moreover, are considered to be the fastest-growing segment of the hedge fund industry as a whole.[44] As of August 2018, there are over 250 crypto hedge funds in existence worldwide, with approximately 60 crypto hedge funds launched in 2018.[45]

Multi-asset traditional hedge funds, which are reported to have captured higher net inflows in 2017 than those engaging in single-asset strategies,[46] are the most likely to see crypto assets become an increasingly important component of their multi-asset investment strategies. In this regard, there is growing evidence of increased appetite on the part of traditional hedge fund managers for crypto asset investment. Northern Trust Hedge Fund Services has publicly announced, for example, that it is providing three unnamed "mainstream" hedge funds that have been investing in cryptocurrencies with crypto fund administration services, including crypto asset valuation, anti-money laundering compliance and digital asset validation.[47]

In addition, BlackRock, which is widely regarded as the largest asset manager globally with $6.3tln in AUM as of March 2018,[48] has set up an internal working group to analyse potential future investment into crypto assets.[49] Although BlackRock CEO Larry Fink has publicly stated that he does not foresee massive investor interest in cryptocurrency strategies,[50] major traditional hedge funds like BlackRock can more likely than not be expected to engage in some form of experimentation with crypto asset investment in the near future. In addition, continued interest in crypto asset investment from senior hedge fund managers, such as Steven A. Cohen, who recently invested in crypto hedge fund Autonomous Partners by way of his family office's venture capital division, Cohen Venture Partners,[51] provides further evidence of a growing crypto investment trend in the traditional hedge fund community.

Categories of crypto hedge funds

Broadly speaking, crypto hedge funds can be divided into at least three categories: (1) active trading crypto hedge funds; (2) buy-and-hold crypto hedge funds; and (3) blockchain ecosystem crypto hedge funds.[52]

Active trading crypto hedge funds, such as Arrington XRP Capital, MetaStable Capital and Polychain Capital, trade cryptocurrencies and employ long-only and/or long-short approaches.[53]

Buy-and-hold funds can be divided into public buy-and-hold funds and private buy-and-hold funds.[54] Public buy-and-hold funds include both exchange traded notes ("ETNs") and exchange traded funds ("ETFs"). Examples of ETNs include Grayscale's Bitcoin Investment Trust (symbol: GBTC) and Ethereum Classic Investment Trust (symbol: ETCG), both of whose shares are publicly quoted on the OTC Markets Group's OTCQX market, as well as Jersey-based Global Advisors' Bitcoin Tracker One (symbol: BITCOIN XBT), Bitcoin Tracker Euro (symbol: Bitcoin XBTE), Ether Tracker One (symbol: ETHEREUM XBT) and Ether Tracker Euro (symbol: ETHEREUM XBTE), all of which are listed on the NASDAQ/OMX in Stockholm.[55] Several cryptocurrency ETFs have been proposed to the U.S. SEC for regulatory approval, such as the Winklevoss Bitcoin Trust ETF (symbol: COIN) and VanEck SolidX Bitcoin Trust (symbol: XBTC), but none have received approval to date.[56] Unlike public buy-and-hold funds, private buy-and-hold funds are not listed on publicly traded exchanges. One example of a private buy-and-hold fund is Pantera Capital's Pantera Bitcoin Fund.

Blockchain ecosystem crypto hedge funds invest in non-cryptocurrency assets related to blockchain ecosystem infrastructure, such as emerging blockchain protocols. These funds, which appear to resemble venture capital funds in terms of their early-stage investment targets, invest in ICOs, pre-ICO token sales and/or directly into blockchain startups through equity investments.[57] Pantera Capital's Pantera ICO Fund, for example, was created to invest solely in tokens that power public blockchain protocols.[58] Pantera Capital has also invested in blockchain startup companies including 0x, Abra, Augur, OmiseGO and Ripple.[59]

Crypto venture capital funds

Overview

Venture capital interest in crypto assets has surged in 2018 as a result of the exponential returns that continue to be generated from ICOs.[60] PwC Switzerland, in collaboration with the Swiss Crypto Valley Association, has recently reported that 537 ICOs closed successfully in the first five months of 2018, generating a total of $13.7bn in funds raised, thereby exceeding all pre-2018 ICO fundraising levels combined.[61] The largest ICOs in 2018 have so far included Telegram's $1.7bn ICO and Block.one's $4.1bn EOS protocol ICO.[62] In addition, as illustrated below, annual venture capital activity in the crypto asset market has shown a consistent upward trend in deal flow, amounting to 187 deals closed with a total value of $1.7bn through late-June 2018:

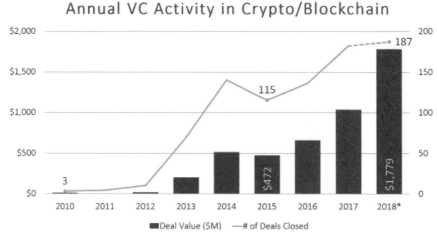

Source: PitchBook

While there has been much debate as to whether or not the ICO model would replace the traditional venture capital fundraising process, it is clear that many traditional venture capital firms have paid close attention to the rapidly evolving crypto asset market and have adapted their strategies accordingly.[63] Union Square Ventures and Andreesen Horowitz, for example, have both made long-term decisions to enter the "potential trillion-dollar" crypto asset market.[64] The Rockefeller family's venture capital firm Venrock Partners has also recently announced that it is entering the crypto startup investment market through a partnership with CoinFund, a New York-based crypto fund.[65] Some traditional venture capital firms, moreover, have been described as "crypto unicorn hunters"[66] due to their investments in several fintech and blockchain startups whose valuations now exceed $1bn, such as Coinbase, Robinhood and Revolut.[67] Ribbit Capital, for example, which is ranked by CB Insights as the most active venture capital fintech unicorn investor, manages a portfolio of 10 fintech unicorns, three of which are crypto unicorns.[68]

Crypto venture capital investment

Venture capital firms that invest in crypto assets do so in at least one of three ways: (1) investment through pre-existing internal funds that are not focused exclusively on crypto assets; (2) investment through separate funds dedicated exclusively to crypto asset investment; and (3) investment into external crypto funds managed by other crypto investment firms.[69]

Dedicated crypto venture capital funds

A crypto venture capital fund can be defined as an investment vehicle dedicated exclusively to investment in crypto assets ("crypto venture fund"). Some traditional venture capital firms in the U.S. have decided to launch separate, dedicated crypto venture funds in order to overcome regulatory obstacles that would otherwise limit the amount of crypto assets that they can invest in and hold. More specifically, U.S.-based venture capital funds that are structured as "Exempt Reporting Advisers" ("ERAs") under the rubric of the Venture Capital Fund Advisers Exemption to registration requirements under the Investment Advisers Act of 1940 can hold no more than 20% of aggregate capital contributions and uncalled capital commitments in "non-qualifying investments",[70] which include liquid assets, such as cryptocurrencies and digital tokens.[71] In order to avoid this 20% limit on crypto asset holdings, crypto venture funds have been structured as "Registered Investment Advisers" ("RIAs"), similar to hedge funds. One preeminent Silicon Valley venture capital firm that has launched a crypto venture fund in this way is Andreesen Horowitz.

In June 2018, Andreesen Horowitz launched a $300m crypto venture fund known as a16z crypto, which is designed to be a long-term, "all weather" fund that will invest aggressively in crypto assets irrespective of their stage of development or geographic location, even if there is another so-called "crypto winter" characterised by extreme price fluctuations.[72] Recognising that crypto is a rapidly evolving open source software movement, a16z crypto was structured as an RIA so as to hold crypto asset investments of greater than 20% for over 10 years.[73] A16z crypto is unique in that it will invest at all stages of the crypto business lifecycle, from pre-launch and seed rounds to investments in later-stage mature blockchain companies.[74] It also will provide operational support to its crypto portfolio companies, including participation in corporate and blockchain network governance, similar to the levels of operational support that it has historically provided to its traditional early stage portfolio companies. With its base of pre-existing equity investments in leading crypto businesses, such as Coinbase, Ripple and Polychain Capital, as well as its current ability to acquire larger crypto asset holdings through its RIA structure, a16z crypto is projected to become one of the largest and most influential investors in the emerging crypto fund market.

Conclusion

The explosive growth of crypto funds in 2017 and 2018 is expected to deepen the existence of the crypto ecosystem by augmenting the ability of investors to trade crypto assets and provide financing to crypto startups. As crypto fund-backed startups, in particular, develop into mature enterprises, these enterprises and their investors will seek to expand through traditional exit strategies, such as merger and acquisition transactions and initial public offerings. The future of the crypto asset market is likely to be one of expansion and increased deal activity, calling for specialised legal services from attorneys who understand the intricacies of the industry and its underlying technologies. Similar to blockchain-based securitisation, which is already recognised as a growth area by major law firms,[75] there is likely to be an increased demand for attorneys who are able to service crypto funds and subsequent transactions involving their portfolio companies. As a result, transactional and regulatory law practitioners should pay close attention to developments in this space.

The views and opinions expressed in this article are those of the author alone, and do not necessarily reflect the views of Yale University, Stanford University, the University of Vienna, nor of the American Bar Association. The material in this article has been prepared for informational purposes only and is not intended to serve as legal advice, nor as investment advice, nor as an endorsement of any entity or crypto asset mentioned in the body of the article.

* * *

Acknowledgment

The author would like to thank the Information Society Project at Yale Law School, the Stanford/Vienna Transatlantic Technology Law Forum, and the Stanford CodeX Blockchain Working Group for their encouragement in the undertaking of comparative and international academic research on blockchain technology and cryptocurrency regulation. The author would also like to thank Preqin, PitchBook, Crypto Fund Research and the Tabb Group for providing access to their high-quality data on cryptocurrency market trends and cryptocurrency investment funds.

* * *

Yale Law School Information Society Project

The Information Society Project ("ISP") is an intellectual centre at Yale Law School, founded in 1997 by Professor Jack Balkin. Over the past 20 years, the ISP has grown from a handful of people gathering to discuss internet governance into an international community working to illuminate the complex relationships between law, technology, and society.

Endnotes

1. vision& (2018), *The Blockchain Story: Birth of a New Asset Class?* Available at: https://www.visionand.ch/wp-content/uploads/2018/03/vision_-_Birth_of_a_new_Asset_Class.pdf [Accessed 14 August 2018].
2. Mokhtarian, E. and Lindgren, A. (2018), *Rise of the Crypto Hedge Fund: Operational Issues and Best Practices for an Emergent Investment Industry,* 23 Stan. J.L. Bus. & Fin. 112 (2018). Available at: https://papers.ssrn.com/sol3/papers.cfm?abstract_id=3055979 [Accessed 14 August 2018].

3.   Ernst & Young (2018), IFRS (#) *Accounting for Crypto-Assets*. Available at: https://
     www.ey.com/Publication/vwLUAssets/EY-IFRS-Accounting-for-crypto-assets/$File/
     EY-IFRS-Accounting-for-crypto-assets.pdf [Accessed 14 August 2018].
4.   Global Advisors Bitcoin Investment Fund, for example, had a net return of 330.08% in
     2017. *See* Preqin (2018), Preqin Special Report: *Top Performing Hedge Funds in 2017*.
     Available at: http://docs.preqin.com/reports/Preqin-Special-Report-Top-Performing-
     Hedge-Funds-in-2017.pdf [Accessed 14 August 2018]. *Fortune*, "Bitcoin Hits a New
     Record High, But Stops Short of $20,000", 17 December 2017. Available at: http://
     fortune.com/2017/12/17/bitcoin-record-high-short-of-20000/ [Accessed 14 August
     2018]. Bloomberg, "Bitcoin Frenzy Helps Crypto Hedge Funds Reap 1,100% Gains,"
     15 January 2018. Available at: https://www.bloomberg.com/news/articles/2018-01-16/
     crypto-hedge-funds-soar-more-than-1-000-as-bubble-debate-rages   [Accessed   14
     August 2018].
5.   Grayscale Investments raised $250m in new assets during first half of 2018. *See*
     Business Insider, "Bitcoin may be down 45% this year, but money is pouring into one
     crypto fund manager at the fastest clip in its history," 18 July 2018. Available at: https://
     finance.yahoo.com/news/bitcoin-may-down-45-money-120000293.html [Accessed 14
     August 2018].
6.   *Forbes*, "Islands No More: Crypto Hedge Funds Bring Cryptocurrency Risk Into
     Mainstream Financial System," 11 October 2017. Available at : https://www.forbes.
     com/sites/angelawalch/2017/10/11/islands-no-more-crypto-hedge-funds-bring-
     cryptocurrency-risk-into-mainstream-financial-system/#7c6d92c25281   [Accessed
     14 August 2018]. Grym, A. (2018), The Great Illusion of Digital Currencies, Bank
     of Finland Economics Review 1/2018.   Available at: https://helda.helsinki.fi/bof/
     bitstream/handle/123456789/15564/BoFER_1_2018.pdf [Accessed 14 August 2018].
7.   Crypto Fund Research (2018), "Cryptocurrency Investment Fund Industry Graphs
     and Charts." Available at: https://cryptofundresearch.com/cryptocurrency-funds-
     overview-infographic/ [Accessed 14 August 2018].   AlphaQ, "Crypto Fund Research
     Reveals Rapid Pace of Fund Launches," 6 June 2018. Available at: https://www.alphaq.
     world/2018/06/06/265017/crypto-fund-research-reveals-rapid-pace-fund-launches
     [Accessed 14 August 2018].
8.   Morgan, N. and Reich, A., *Crypto-Funds and Their Advisers Will Be a Focus of the SEC
     in 2018*, 14 February 2018. Available at : https://www.law.com/therecorder/2018/02/14/
     crypto-funds-and-their-advisers-will-be-a-focus-of/?slreturn=20180615233434
     [Accessed 14 August 2018].
9.   Ernst & Young (2018), IFRS (#) *Accounting for Crypto-Assets*.
10. Dabrowski, M. and Janikowski, L., "Virtual currencies and central banks monetary
     policy: challenges ahead," European Parliament, Monetary Dialogue, July 2018.
     Available   at: http://www.europarl.europa.eu/cmsdata/149900/CASE_FINAL%20
     publication.pdf [Accessed 14 August 2018].   Northern Trust, "Cryptocurrencies:
     What You Need to Know," June 2018. Available at: https://www.northerntrust.com/
     documents/white-papers/asset-servicing/cryptocurrencies-what-you-need-to-know.
     pdf?bc=25551164 [Accessed 14 August 2018].
11. Ernst & Young (2018), IFRS (#) *Accounting for Crypto-Assets*.
12. Ernst & Young (2018), IFRS (#) *Accounting for Crypto-Assets*.
13. Financial Stability Board, "Crypto-Assets: Report to the G20 on work by the FSB and
     standard-setting bodies," 16 July 2018. Available at: http://www.fsb.org/wp-content/
     uploads/P160718-1.pdf [Accessed 14 August 2018].
14. Werbach, K. *et al* (2018), *Regulatory Considerations for Token Offerings*, Spring
     2018 Reg@Tech Token Offerings Workshop Report, Zicklin Center for Business
     Ethics Research, Wharton School, University of Pennsylvania. Available at: https://
     zicklincenter.wharton.upenn.edu/wp-content/uploads/2018/06/June-2018-Regulatory-
     Considerations-for-Token-Offerings.pdf [Accessed 14 August 2018].

15. Crypto Fund Research (2018), "New Crypto Funds Launching at Record Pace." Available at: https://cryptofundresearch.com/new-crypto-funds-launching-at-record-pace/ [Accessed 14 August 2018].

16. Autonomous NEXT (2018), #CRYPTO UTOPIA: The $20 billion Cambrian explosion of tokenized digital assets, and the emerging infrastructure being built to support them. Available at https://next.autonomous.com/crypto-utopia/ [Accessed 14 August 2018].

17. *Id.*

18. Crypto Fund Research (2018), "Cryptocurrency Investment Fund Industry Graphs and Charts."

19. *Fortune*, "Polychain Becomes First $1 Billion Crypto Fund: What Happens Now?," 26 June 2018. Available at: http://fortune.com/2018/06/26/polychain-capital-bitcoin/ [Accessed 14 August 2018].

20. *Id.*

21. Crypto Fund Research (2018), "Cryptocurrency Investment Fund Industry Graphs and Charts."

22. *Id.*

23. *Id.*

24. *CoinDesk*, "A16z, USV Invest $10 Million in Blockchain Token Trading Firm," 9 December 2016. Available at: https://www.coindesk.com/a16z-usv-invest-10-million-blockchain-token-trading-polychain-capital/ [Accessed 14 August 2018].

25. Grayscale Investments, Grayscale Digital Asset Investment Report: H1 2018, July 2018. Available at: https://grayscale.co/digital-asset-investment-report/ [Accessed 14 August 2018].

26. The TABB Group, "Crypto Trading: Platforms Target Institutional Market," 5 April 2018. Available at: https://research.tabbgroup.com/report/v16-013-crypto-trading-platforms-target-institutional-market [Accessed 14 August 2018].

27. Cryptovest Media, "Universities Invest in Cryptocurrency Hedge Funds, Says Lawyer," 5 June 2018. Available at: https://cryptovest.com/news/universities-invest-in-cryptocurrency-hedge-funds-says-lawyer/ [Accessed 14 August 2018].

28. Crypto Fund Research (2018), "Cryptocurrency Investment Fund Industry Graphs and Charts."

29. Crypto Fund Research (2018), Crypto Fund List. Available at: https://cryptofundresearch.com/ [Accessed 14 August 2018].

30. *CoinDesk*, "$1 Billion Blockchain Fund Launches with Chinese Government Backing," 9 April 2018. Available at: https://www.coindesk.com/1-billion-blockchain-fund-launches-with-chinese-government-backing/ [Accessed 14 August 2018].

31. ZDNet, "China's Nanjing launches $1.5 billion blockchain fund," 23 July 2018. Available at: https://www.zdnet.com/article/chinas-nanjing-launches-1-5-billion-blockchain-fund/ [Accessed 14 August 2018].

32. *CoinDesk*, "Another $1 Billion Blockchain Fund to Launch With Government Backing," 24 July 2018. Available at: https://www.coindesk.com/another-1-billion-blockchain-fund-to-launch-with-government-backing/ [Accessed 14 August 2018].

33. *CoinDesk*, "Another Chinese City Is Backing a Big Blockchain Investment Fund," 23 April 2018. Available at: https://www.coindesk.com/another-chinese-city-is-backing-a-big-blockchain-investment-fund/ [Accessed 14 August 2018].

34. Autonomous NEXT (2018), #CRYPTO UTOPIA.

35. Preqin, "The Rise of Cryptocurrency Hedge Funds," 4 May 2018. Available at: https://www.preqin.com/blog/0/22331/rise-cryptocurrency-hedge-fund [Accessed 14 August 2018].

36. *Bitcoin.com News*, "Cryptocurrency Baskets Are Growing in Popularity," 5 June 2018. Available at: https://news.bitcoin.com/cryptocurrency-baskets-are-growing-in-popularity/ [Accessed 14 August 2018].

37. Autonomous NEXT (2018), #CRYPTO UTOPIA.

38. Crypto Fund Research (2018), "Cryptocurrency Investment Fund Industry Graphs and Charts."

39. Preqin, "The Rise of Cryptocurrency Hedge Funds," 4 May 2018.

40. *The Hedge Fund Law Report*, "How Blockchain Will Continue to Revolutionize the Private Funds Sector in 2018," Vol. 11, No. 1, 4 January 2018. Available at: https://www.hflawreport.com/issue/488 [Accessed 14 August 2018]. *See also* Kaal, W. (2017), Blockchain Innovation for the Hedge Fund Industry. Available at: https://medium.com/@wulfkaal/blockchain-innovation-for-the-hedge-fund-industry-cc4ae59eaaf [Accessed 14 August 2018].

41. *Eurekahedge* (2018), 2017 Overview: Key Trends in Global Hedge Funds. Available at: http://www.eurekahedge.com/Research/News/1708/Global-Hedge-Funds-Key-Trends-Overview-January-2018 [Accessed 14 August 2018].

42. CryptoVest Media, "Crypto, Blockchain Focused Hedge Funds Down 50% H1 2018 – HFR Report," 11 July 2018. Available at: https://cryptovest.com/news/crypto-blockchain-focused-hedge-funds-down-50-h1-2018---hfr-report/ [Accessed 14 August 2018].

43. *Bloomberg*, "As Bitcoin Plunged, These Crypto Hedge Funds Kept Making Money," 19 April 2018. Available at: https://www.bloomberg.com/news/articles/2018-04-19/as-bitcoin-plunged-these-crypto-hedge-funds-kept-making-money [Accessed 14 August 2018]. CryptoCoinsNews (CCN), "Prominent Investors Bullish on Bitcoin Reaching $8,100 With Strong Volume," 24 July 2018. Available at: https://www.ccn.com/prominent-investors-bullish-on-bitcoin-reaching-8100-with-strong-volume/ [Accessed 14 August 2018].

44. *Crypto Globe*, "Crypto is The Fastest Growing Segment of The Hedge Fund Industry," 2 July 2018. Available at: https://www.cryptoglobe.com/latest/2018/07/crypto-is-the-fastest-growing-segment-of-the-hedge-fund-industry/ [Accessed 14 August 2018].

45. Crypto Fund Research (2018), Crypto Fund List. *See also* Crypto Fund Research (2018), "New Crypto Funds Launching at Record Pace."

46. *Hedgeweek* (2018), "Multi-Asset Strategies: A Hedgeweek Webinar Report." Available at: https://www.hedgeweek.com/sites/default/files/Hedgeweek_Special_Report_Multi_Asset_Strategies.pdf [Accessed 14 August 2018].

47. *Forbes*, "Northern Trust Opens Doors To Cryptocurrency Hedge Funds As Part Of Pervasive Blockchain Expansion," 31 July 2018. Available at: https://www.forbes.com/sites/michaeldelcastillo/2018/07/31/northern-trust-opens-doors-to-cryptocurrency-hedge-funds-as-part-of-pervasive-blockchain-expansion/#f29546248bce [Accessed 14 August 2018]. CCN, "$10.7 Trillion Custodian Northern Trust Helping Hedge Funds Invest in Bitcoin," 31 July 2018. Available at: https://www.ccn.com/10-7-trillion-custodian-northern-trust-helping-hedge-funds-invest-in-bitcoin/ [Accessed 14 August 2018].

48. BlackRock, "Q1 2018 Earnings: Earnings Release Supplement," 12 April 2018. Available at: http://ir.blackrock.com/Cache/1500109536.PDF?O=PDF&T=&Y=&D=&FID=1500109536&iid=4048287 [Accessed 14 August 2018].

49. Reuters, "BlackRock is evaluating cryptocurrencies, CEO Fink says," 16 July 2018. Available at: https://www.reuters.com/article/us-blackrock-cryptocurrency/blackrock-is-evaluating-cryptocurrencies-ceo-fink-says-idUSKBN1K61MC [Accessed 14 August 2018].

50. *Id.*

51. *Fortune*, "Steven Cohen's Venture Capital Firm Gets Into Crypto With New Partner," 12 July 2018. Available at: http://fortune.com/2018/07/12/steven-cohens-bitcoin-crypto-autonomous-partners/ [Accessed 14 August 2018]. Business Insider, "Steve Cohen has reportedly backed a crypto hedge fund," 13 July 2018. Available at: https://www.businessinsider.com/steve-cohen-crypto-hedge-fund-autonomous-partners-2018-7 [Accessed 14 August 2018].

52. Hedge Fund Research (2018), "HFR Blockchain Indices Defined Formulaic Methodology. Available at: https://www.hedgefundresearch.com/sites/default/files/pdf/HFR_Blockchain_Indices_methodology.pdf [Accessed 14 August 2018].

53. Preqin, "The Rise of Cryptocurrency Hedge Funds," 4 May 2018.

54. Seeking Alpha, "The Cryptocurrency Funds Have Arrived, And They're Bringing Wall Street Money," 6 March 2017. Available at: https://seekingalpha.com/article/4052276-cryptocurrency-funds-arrived-bringing-wall-street-money [Accessed 14 August 2018].

55. CNBC, "What the US can learn from Sweden about how to launch a bitcoin fund," 17 January 2018. Available at: https://www.cnbc.com/2018/01/17/sec-frets-over-bitcoin-etfs-but-swedes-figured-it-out-years-ago.html [Accessed 14 August 2018].

56. CNBC, "Over $9 billion wiped off bitcoin's value after SEC postpones key decision on a cryptocurrency ETF," 8 August 2018. Available at: https://www.cnbc.com/2018/08/08/bitcoin-price-falls-after-sec-postpones-key-etf-decision.html [Accessed 14 August 2018].

57. Hedge Fund Research (2018), HFR Blockchain Indices Defined Formulaic Methodology.

58. *CoinDesk*, "Pantera Capital to Raise $100 Million in Investment for ICO Hedge Fund," 28 June 2017. Available at: https://www.coindesk.com/100-million-pantera-capital-ico-hedge-fund/ [Accessed 14 August 2018].

59. CryptoSlate, "Crypto Investment Fund Pantera Capital Predicts $67,500 Bitcoin in 2019," 30 July 2018. Available at: https://cryptoslate.com/crypto-investment-fund-pantera-capital-predicts-67500-bitcoin-in-2019/ [Accessed 14 August 2018].

60. Bloomberg, "Venture Capital Surges Into Crypto Startups," 26 March 2018. Available at: https://www.bloomberg.com/news/articles/2018-03-26/icos-can-wait-venture-capital-surges-into-crypto-startups [Accessed 14 August 2018].

61. PwC/Strategy & (2018), Initial Coin Offerings: A Strategic Perspective. Available at: https://cryptovalley.swiss/wp-content/uploads/20180628_PwC-S-CVA-ICO-Report_EN.pdf [Accessed 14 August 2018].

62. *Wall Street Journal*, "What Crypto Downturn? ICO Fundraising Surges in 2018," 1 July 2018. Available at: https://www.wsj.com/articles/what-crypto-downturn-ico-fundraising-surges-in-2018-1530466008 [Accessed 14 August 2018].

63. CryptoSlate, "Crypto Funds Explode in 2018 as Venture Capital Attacks the ICO Model," 1 June 2018. Available at: https://cryptoslate.com/crypto-funds-explode-in-2018-as-venture-capital-attacks-the-ico-model/ [Accessed 14 August 2018].

64. CryptoSlate, "Union Square Ventures: Blockchain Might Be Worth Trillions," 2 July 2018. Available at: https://cryptoslate.com/union-square-ventures-blockchain-might-be-worth-trillions/ [Accessed 14 August 2018]. CNBC, "Union Square Ventures is investing in crypto for the long haul, but won't start a dedicated fund," 29 June 2018. Available at: https://www.cnbc.com/2018/06/29/union-square-ventures-is-doubling-down-on-crypto.html [Accessed 14 August 2018].

65. *Fortune*, "It Started With the Rockefellers. Now It's Taking on Crypto," 6 April 2018. Available at: http://fortune.com/2018/04/06/crypto-vc-venrock-coinfund/ [Accessed 14 August 2018].

66. CryptoSlate, "Crypto Unicorn Hunters: The VC Firms Behind Billion-Dollar Crypto Startups," 15 July 2018. Available at: https://cryptoslate.com/crypto-unicorn-hunters-the-vc-firms-behind-billion-dollar-crypto-startups/ [Accessed 14 August 2018]. CB Insights, "Ribbit, Index Lead Fintech Unicorn Hunters," 10 July 2018. Available at: https://www.cbinsights.com/research/fintech-unicorn-top-vc-investors/?utm_term=0_9dc0513989-7abd42b986-87924829&utm_content=buffer5bfe1&utm_medium=social&utm_source=twitter.com&utm_campaign=buffer [Accessed 14 August 2018].

67. CryptoSlate, "Crypto Unicorn Hunters: The VC Firms Behind Billion-Dollar Crypto Startups," 15 July 2018.

68. *CB Insights*, "Ribbit, Index Lead Fintech Unicorn Hunters," 10 July 2018.

69. Recode, "Why are big VCs opening up crypto funds?," 21 June 2018. Available at: https://www.recode.net/2018/6/21/17484524/venture-capital-cryptocurrency-investing -structures [Accessed 14 August 2018].

70. U.S. SEC, Final Rule: Exemptions for Advisers to Venture Capital Funds, Private Fund Advisers With Less Than $150 Million in Assets Under Management, and Foreign Private Advisers, 17 C.F.R. Part 275 (21 July 2011). *See also* U.S. SEC, IM Guidance Update: Guidance on the exemption for advisers to venture capital fund, No. 2013-13, December 2013. Available at: https://www.sec.gov/divisions/investment/guidance/im-guidance-2013-13.pdf [Accessed 14 August 2018].

71. Union Square Ventures, "Investing in Token Focused Funds," 20 June 2018. Available at: https://www.usv.com/blog/investing-in-token-focused-funds [Accessed 14 August 2018].

72. Dixon, C. (2018), "Introducing a16z crypto." Available at: https://a16zcrypto.com/ [Accessed 14 August 2018]. CoinDesk, "Andreesen Horowitz Starts a Crypto Fund," 25 June 2018. Available at: https://www.coindesk.com/andreessen-horowitz-launched-300-million-crypto-fund/ [Accessed 14 August 2018].

73. *Wall Street Journal*, "Andreessen Pure-Play Crypto Fund Won't Have Cap Limiting Most VCs," 25 June 2018. Available at: https://www.wsj.com/articles/andreessen-horowitz-names-katie-haun-as-first-female-gp-closes-300-million-crypto-fund-1529956810 [Accessed 14 August 2018].

74. *Fortune*, "Why the Structure of Andreessen Horowitz's New $300 Million Crypto Fund Matters," 26 June 2018. Available at: http://fortune.com/2018/06/26/andreessen-horowitz-crypto-fund/ [Accessed 14 August 2018].

75. *The American Lawyer*, "Law Firms See Opportunity Pairing Blockchain and Securitization Expertise," 25 June 2018. Available at: https://www.law.com/americanlawyer/2018/06/25/law-firms-see-opportunity-pairing-blockchain-and-securitization-expertise/?slreturn=20180713133521 [Accessed 14 August 2018].

Jonathan Cardenas
Tel: +1 203 432 8464 / Email: jonathan.cardenas@yale.edu
Jonathan Cardenas is a Visiting Fellow at the Information Society Project at
Yale Law School. His research is focused on legal issues surrounding private
equity and venture capital investment in fintech companies. He also serves as
a Fellow with the Transatlantic Technology Law Forum, a joint initiative of
Stanford Law School and the University of Vienna School of Law. He serves
as Founding Chair of the Financial Services Technology Subcommittee within
the Commercial Finance Committee of the American Bar Association Business
Law Section.

Jonathan received his J.D. from the New York University School of Law, where
he was a Jacobson Leadership Program in Law & Business Scholar, and where
he served as a Managing Editor of the *NYU Journal of Law & Business*. He
received an M.Phil. in International Relations from the University of Cambridge, and a B.A. in Political Science, *summa cum laude*, from the University
of Pennsylvania. He is admitted as an attorney in the District of Columbia, the
State of Florida, and the State of New York.

Yale Law School

127 Wall Street, New Haven, Connecticut 06511, USA
Tel: +1 203 432 8464 / URL: www.law.yale.edu

Cryptocurrency compliance and risks: A European KYC/ AML perspective

Fedor Poskriakov, Maria Chiriaeva & Christophe Cavin
Lenz & Staehelin

Introduction

The rapid development, increased functionality, and growing adoption of new technologies and related payment products and services globally continue to pose significant challenges for regulators and private sector institutions in ensuring that these technologies are not misused for money laundering ("**ML**") and financing of terrorism ("**FT**") purposes. The underlying reasons for this are numerous and some of such risks were identified and discussed already in 2013 in the Financial Action Task Force ("**FATF**") NPPS Guidance,[1] even though the said report did not specifically refer to "virtual currencies" at the time.

In the last couple of years, a significant number of virtual currencies ("**VC**") have emerged and at least some of them attracted significant investment in payments infrastructure built on the relevant software protocols. These payment infrastructures and protocols seek to provide a new method for transmitting value over the internet or through decentralised peer-to-peer networks.

As decentralised, convertible cryptography-based VCs and related payment systems are gaining momentum, regulators and financial institutions ("**FI**") around the world are recognising that VCs and the underlying consensus protocols (1) likely represent the future for payment systems, (2) provide an ever-more powerful new tool for criminals, terrorist financiers and other sanctions-evaders to move and store illicit funds, out of the reach of law enforcement, and, as a result, (3) create unique new challenges in terms of ML/FT risks.[2] Although the global volumes and estimates are relatively low, Europol has estimated in 2017 that 3–4% of Europe's crime proceeds were laundered through cryptocurrencies – the proportion will likely continue to increase rapidly[3] due to the rate of adoption of VCs, including by institutional investors and FIs.

Given the trans-jurisdictional (or borderless) nature of the VC phenomenon, major institutions at the international level have all focused on and issued reports addressing VCs and the risks associated with them, including ML/FT risks. FATF and the European Banking Authority ("**EBA**"), in particular, have issued recommendations in this context, concluding that VC exchange platforms allowing the conversion of VC into fiat money (and vice versa) are of particular relevance and must be brought within the scope of the respective national anti-money laundering and counter-financing of terrorism ("**AML/CFT**") frameworks.

Key potential risks

Key definitions and concepts

(a) *Definitions*

There is no single global definition of the term "crypto- or virtual currency". In 2012, the European Central Bank ("**ECB**") defined VCs as "a type of unregulated, digital money, which is issued and usually controlled by its developers, and used and accepted among the members of a specific virtual community".[4] In 2014, The EBA defined VCs as a "digital representation of value that is neither issued by a central bank or a public authority, nor necessarily attached to a [fiat currency], but is accepted by natural or legal persons as a means of payment and can be transferred, stored or traded electronically".[5] Finally, in its 2014 report on key definitions on VCs, FATF gave the following definition: "[T]he digital representation of value that can be digitally traded and functions as: (i) a medium of exchange; and/or (ii) a unit of account; and/or (iii) a store of value, but does not have legal tender status (i.e., when tendered to a creditor, is a valid and legal offer of payment) in any jurisdiction. It is not issued nor guaranteed by any jurisdiction, and fulfils the above functions only by agreement within the community of users of the virtual currency."

In order to provide for a common regulatory approach through the fifth Anti Money Laundering Directive ("**MLD5**", see also "Current legal and regulatory regime, MLD5", below), the EU decided to adopt a definition of VC deriving from the FATF's guidance. According to MLD5, a VC is defined as a digital representation of value that is not issued or guaranteed by a central bank or a public authority, is not necessarily attached to a legally established currency, and does not possess a legal status of currency or money, but is accepted by natural or legal persons, as a means of exchange, and which can be transferred, stored and traded electronically. Given the broad nature of this definition, it is likely that, in practice, most forms of VCs and other transferable cryptographic coins or tokens (as we know them today) fall within the scope of MLD5.

For the purposes of this chapter, we will adopt the definitions and conceptual framework set out in FATF's June 2014 report on virtual currencies.[6] In this respect, we will focus on decentralised convertible VCs and related payment products and services ("**VCPPS**"), to the exclusion of other VC-related securities and/or derivatives products and services, even though these are also relevant for ML/FT risk assessment, in particular crowdfunding methods like ICOs.

(b) *KYC and transaction monitoring*

Know Your Customer ("**KYC**") is the cornerstone of the AML/CFT due diligence requirements that are generally imposed on FIs whose AML/CFT legislation is aligned with international standards. KYC requirements are relatively recent, as they were first implemented in the 70s in both the Swiss and US legislations, before becoming an internationally recognised concept through the issuance of the FATF recommendations.

KYC requires that FIs duly identify (and verify) their contracting parties (i.e., customers) and the beneficial owners (namely when their contracting parties are not natural persons) of such assets, as well as their origin. Together with transaction monitoring, KYC ensures the traceability of assets, as long as those remaining in the financial system (i.e., paper trail) and allow the identification of ML/FT indicia.

Although KYC and transaction-monitoring requirements were globally implemented at a time when VCs did not exist, it appears to be clear today, based on the various initiatives both at the international and national levels, that the application of AML/CFT requirements to VCPPS remains to be clarified.

One of the challenges is that KYC and other AML/CFT requirements were designed for a centralised intermediated financial system, in which regulatory requirements and sanctions can be imposed by each jurisdiction at the level of financial intermediaries operating on its territory (i.e., acting as "gatekeepers"). By contrast, VCPPS rely on a set of decentralised cross-border virtual protocols and infrastructure elements, neither of which has a sufficient degree of control over or access to the underlying value (asset) and/or information, so that identifying a touch-point for implementing and enforcing compliance with AML/CFT requirements is naturally challenging.

Potential AML/CFT risks

It has to be recognised that like any money-transmitting or payment services, VCPPS have legitimate uses, with prominent venture capital firms investing in VC start-ups and developing infrastructure platforms. VCs may, for example, facilitate micro-payments, allowing businesses to monetise very low-cost goods or services sold on the internet. VCs may also facilitate international remittances and support financial inclusion in other ways, so that VCPPS may potentially serve the under- and un-banked.

However, most VCs by definition trigger a number of ML/FT risks due to their specific features, including anonymity (or pseudonymity), traceability and decentralisation. Many of those risks and uses materialise not on the distributed ledger ("**DL**") of the relevant VC, but rather in the surrounding ecosystem of issuers, exchangers and users. Rapidly evolving technology and the ease of new cryptocurrency creation are likely to continue to make it difficult for law enforcement and FIs alike to stay abreast of new criminal uses, so that integrating those in a solid KYC/client due diligence ("**CDD**") framework is a never-ending task.

In addition to potential illicit uses of VCPPS, the use of VCs may facilitate ML by relying on the same basic mechanisms as those used with fiat currency, with a significant potential for abuse of unregulated and decentralised borderless networks underpinning VCs. In a nutshell:

- **Placement**: VCs offer the ability to open a significant number of anonymous or pseudonymous wallets, at no or very low cost, something which is a low-risk method of rapidly placing proceeds of illicit activity.

- **Layering**: VCs enable the source of funds to be obfuscated by means of multiple transfers from wallet to wallet and/or their conversion into different types of VCs across borders. This allows for an easy layering without significant cost or risk, it being understood that recent technological developments such as "atomic swaps" may even further facilitate the misuse of VCs. Incidentally, substantial demand for unregistered ICOs may allow criminals (assuming they control the ICO) to highjack the popular crowdfunding mechanism to convert VC proceeds into other VCs and/or fiat currencies, while adding a seemingly legitimate "front" for the source of funds.

- **Integration**: the use of VC to acquire goods or services, either directly or through the conversion of the VCs into fiat currency, is facilitated by the ever-increasing list of goods and services for which payment in VCs is accepted, as well as the entry into the VC markets of institutional players both for investment and trading (speculation) purposes, providing substantial liquidity in the VC markets and thereby potentially facilitating large-scale integration by abusing unsuspecting institution actors/investors. Likewise, ICOs with below-average KYC requirements may be abused by criminal actors who may be able to convert their illicit VC holdings into other tokens through subscribing to an ICO, and then exiting the investment immediately upon the relevant coins or tokens becoming listed on any VC exchange.

Naturally, AML/CFT risks are heightened among the unregulated sectors of the cryptocurrency markets. Given regulatory pressure to reject anonymity and introduce AML controls wherever cryptocurrency markets interface with the traditional financial services sector, there are new VCs being created to be more compatible with existing regulations.

However, until such time as novel technological solutions are in place, ML/FT risks are typically addressed by imposing strict AML/KYC requirements to "gatekeepers" such as VC exchangers and other FIs. However, according to the Impact Assessment of the European Commission of July 2016,[7] depending on the evolution of the network of acceptance of VCs, there might come a point in time when there will no longer be a need to convert VCs back into fiat currency if VCs become widely accepted and used. This presents a critical challenge in itself, insofar as it will reduce the number of "touchpoints" (i.e., conversion points from VC to fiat, exchangers, etc.) with the traditional intermediated financial services sector and thereby limiting the opportunities for ML/FT risk mitigation through regulation of defined intermediaries.

Anonymity/pseudonymity

By definition, decentralised systems are particularly vulnerable to anonymity risks. Indeed, in contrast to traditional financial services, VC users' identities are generally unknown, although in most cases they are only pseudonymous, and there is no regulated intermediary which may serve as "gatekeeper" for mitigation of ML/FT risks.

The majority of VCs, such as *Bitcoin (BTC)* or *Ether (ETH)*, have anonymity or pseudonymity by design. The user's identity is not linked to a certain wallet or transaction. However, while a user's identity is not visible on the relevant DL underpinning the VC infrastructure, information on transactions, such as dates, value and the counterparties' addresses, are publicly recorded and available to anyone. For the purposes of their investigation and prosecution work, enforcement authorities are therefore able to track transactions to a point where the identity may have been linked to an account or address (e.g., wallet providers or exchange platforms).

Some VCs, such as Dash, Monero or Zcash, even go further, as they are designed to be completely anonymous: wallet addresses, transactions and information on transactions are not publicly recorded on the relevant DL and provide for a complete anonymity, preventing the identification of the legal and beneficial owner of the VCs.

In addition, a number of solutions have emerged that allow a certain enhancement to the anonymity and seek to limit traceability of transactions on otherwise pseudonymous VC networks. For instance, mixing services (also known as *"tumblers"* or *"washers"*) aggregate transactions from numerous users and enable the actual paper trail of the transactional activity to be obscured. However, while the precise trail of individual transactions might be obscured, the fact that mixing activity has occurred is detectable on the relevant DL.

Traceability

Although the anonymous or pseudo-anonymous design of VCs is an obvious risk of ML/FT, the public nature of the DL acts as a mitigant by offering a complete transaction trail. The DL is an immutable, auditable electronic record of transactions whose traceability may, however, be limited due to user anonymity and anonymising service providers that obfuscate the transaction chain (see also "Technological solutions", below).

The traceability or "trail" risks may not be significant when dealing with a single DL or VC protocol. However, the situation becomes much more complex when considering cross-VC exchanges where it may not necessarily be possible to easily trace conversion transactions from one VC/DL to another, given that such tracing may require access to off-chain records of intermediaries or exchangers, which may be unregulated, and located in multiple jurisdictions. Likewise, with the emergence of technological solutions allowing for so-called "atomic swap", or atomic cross-chain trading, traceability will become an even greater challenge. In essence, it will allow users to cross-trade different VCs without relying on centralised parties or exchanges.

Decentralisation

Most VCs are decentralised, i.e., they are distributed on a peer-to-peer basis and there is no need for validation by a trusted third party that centrally administers the system. As noted by FATF, law enforcement cannot target one central location or entity (administrator) for investigative or asset-seizure purposes, and customers and transaction records may be held by different entities, often in different jurisdictions, making it more difficult for law enforcement and regulators to access them.[8]

This problem is exacerbated by the rapidly evolving nature of the underlying DL technology and VCPPS business models. Without proper safeguards in place, transition from a VCPPS to the fiat financial system may be facilitated by unsuspecting VC exchangers and/or abused by complicit VCPPS infrastructure providers who deliberately seek out jurisdictions with weak AML/CFT regimes.

Legal and regulatory challenges

Current legal and regulatory regime

Despite calls for the adoption of global AML standards for VCs, no such uniform rules have yet emerged. However, we have seen some convergence toward the logical FATF view that VCPPS should be subject to the same obligations as their non-VC counterparts. In this respect, the majority of European jurisdictions that have issued rules or guidance on the matter have typically concluded that the exchange of VC for fiat currency (including the activity of VC "exchanges") is or should be subject to AML obligations.

Differences in national regulations include: (1) varying licensing requirements for VC exchangers and wallet services; (2) treatment of ICOs from an AML regulatory standpoint; and (3) the extent to which crypto-to-crypto exchange is treated differently from crypto-to-fiat exchange. In many cases, the regulatory status of these activities is either ambiguous or case-specific, and partially dependent on new legislation or regulation being adopted.

EU

VCs were first addressed at the EU level when the ECB published its VC report in October 2012. The ECB notably acknowledged that the degree of anonymity afforded by VCs can present ML/FT risks. The ECB further suggested that regulation "would at least reduce the incentive for terrorists, criminals and money launderers to make use of these virtual currency schemes for illegal purposes".[9]

In July 2014, the EBA issued a formal opinion on VCs, indicating in particular that VCs present high risks to the financial integrity of the EU, notably due to potential ML/FT risks.

(a) MLD4

   MLD4, namely implementing the FATF recommendations of 2012, was in force between May 20, 2015 and July 9, 2018. It sets minimum standards, which allows

Member States to retain or adopt more stringent AML measures in order to prevent the use of the EU's financial system for ML/FT purposes.

MLD4 is applicable to all FIs, as well as an array of other actors including auditors, notaries, and real estate agents. MLD4 has developed a preventive system whereby these entities and professionals are under, *inter alia*, KYC obligations and are to check the identity of their customers, identify beneficial ownership and ensure ongoing monitoring and third-party equivalence.

However, the topic of VCs came too late in the MLD4 negotiation process to be integrated into this instrument.

(b) MLD5

On July 5, 2016, the European Commission presented a legislative proposal to amend MLD4. The proposal was part of the Commission's Action Plan against FT, announced in February 2016. It also responded to the 'Panama Papers'[10] revelations of April 2016.

MLD5 was adopted by the Parliament in plenary on April 19, 2018 and the Council of the European Union adopted it on May 14, 2018 as well. It was formally published in the EU's *Office Journal* on June 19, 2018, and entered into force on July 9, 2018. Member States will have until January 10, 2020 to amend their national laws to implement MLD5.

Among different objectives, MLD5 expressly aims at tackling FT risks linked to VCs. In this context, VC exchange platforms and custodian wallet providers have been added in the scope of MLD5. In order to allow competent authorities to monitor suspicious transactions involving VCs, while preserving the innovative advances offered by such currencies, the European Commission concluded that it is appropriate to include in the institutions subject to MLD4 ("obliged entities") all gatekeepers that control access to VCs, and in particular, exchange platforms and wallet providers,[11] as recommended by FATF in its guidance (see "Current international initiatives, FATF" below).

(i) *Providers engaged in exchange services*

Interestingly, MLD5 extends EU AML requirements to "providers engaged in exchange services between virtual currencies and fiat currency". As a result, most crypto-to-fiat (or fiat-to-crypto) exchanges will be covered by MLD5. However, crypto-to-crypto exchanges do not seem to be expressly covered by MLD5.

Notwithstanding this, it is still possible that certain crypto-to-crypto exchanges may fall within the scope of MLD5 if their activities are conducted by "obliged entities" for other reasons, such as custodian wallet services (see (b) below). Further, crypto-to-crypto exchanges could still be regulated at Member State level, depending on how each Member State incorporates MLD5's provisions into its national law. Likewise, for the time being, it is not clear whether VC ATMs are covered under MLD5.

(ii) *Custodian wallet providers*

Custodian wallet providers are defined entities that provide services to safeguard private cryptographic keys on behalf of its customers, to hold, store and transfer VCs. The definition appears to only include wallet providers that maintain control (via a private cryptographic key) over customers' wallets and the assets in it, in contrast to pure software wallet providers that provide applications or programs running on users' hardware (computer, smartphone, tablet…) to access public information from a DL and access the network (without having access to or control over the user's private keys).

Switzerland

The Swiss AML legislation does not provide for a definition of VC, relying upon the FATF's definition used in its 2014 Report. That being said, since the revision of the Swiss Financial Market Supervisory Authority ("**FINMA**") AML Ordinance in 2015, exchange activities in relation to VCs, such as money transmitting (i.e., money transmission with a conversion of VCs between two parties), are clearly subject to AML rules. Before this revision took place, both FINMA and the Federal Council had already identified,[12] on a risk-based approach, the increased risks associated with VC exchangers and the necessity for them to be subject to AML requirements. As such, Switzerland was a precursor in the implementation of this rule, which has now become standard.

In a nutshell, the purchase and sale of convertible VCs on a commercial basis, and the operation of trading platforms to transfer money or convertible VCs from a platform's users to other users, are subject to Swiss AML rules. Before commencing operations, a provider of these kinds of services must either become a member of a self-regulatory organisation ("**SRO**") or apply to FINMA for a licence to operate as a directly supervised financial intermediary ("**DSFI**").

Because convertible VCs can facilitate anonymity and cross-border asset transfers, FINMA considers trading in it to have heightened ML/FT risks, requiring strict CDD, particularly as regards client identification, beneficial ownership and source-of-funds analysis.

Managing compliance AML/CFT risks

Although there are developments on the regulatory front in terms of strengthening requirements applicable to VCPPS providers, there has been practically no guidance by regulators to their respective domestic FIs as to how to approach KYC/CDD from an ML/FT risk assessment perspective when dealing with customers exposed to VC and VCPPS risks, other than a recommendation to adopt a prudent, risk-based approach.

In practice, as with any new line of business, type of client or financial transaction, the central AML/CFT compliance questions for FIs will be whether they: (1) understand the relevant risks; (2) can reasonably manage them; and (3) have the knowledge, tools and resources to do so on an ongoing basis (including policies, procedures, training programmes, etc.). FIs that choose to serve the new types of clients in the VC ecosystem should elaborate and put in place specific policies and procedures to ensure that they are able to comply with their AML obligations despite the VC context.

The specifics of each set of requirements will depend on the type of business, client type and jurisdiction, as well as other factors. That being said, the ability of FIs to confirm the identity, jurisdiction and purpose of each customer, as well as the assessment of the source of wealth and funds, is essential to the fulfilment of AML/CFT requirements. VCPPS actors as customers present specific challenges in each of these aspects, so that FIs must ensure that their policies and procedures allow them to perform these core functions with a degree of confidence which is at least equal to that which FIs would require for their traditional financial services.

Given the varying typology of VCPPS service providers, it is virtually impossible to draw up KYC/CDD standards, procedures and checklists that would be applicable universally. It is therefore understandable that regulators have not issued blanket guidance in this space. As the understanding of VCPPS and related AML/CFT risks evolves, it is likely that international standards and recommendations will emerge, and possibly compliance tools which will simplify the implementation thereof by FIs. In this respect, FIs, VCPPS providers, developers, investors, and other actors in the VC space should seek to develop technology-based solutions that will improve compliance and facilitate the integration of VCPPS with the existing financial system.

Possible avenues to address compliance concerns

Current international initiatives

FATF

(a) VCs – Guidance for a risk based approach (June 2015 standards)

In June 2015, FATF issued a specific guidance on VCs, focusing on the points of intersection that provide gateways to the regulated financial system – *Guidance for a Risk-Based Approach: Virtual Currencies* (the "**Guidance**"). This Guidance derives from previous reports of FATF, namely the June 2014 *Virtual Currencies Report* and the FATF NPPS Guidance of June 2013.

In accordance with the cardinal risk-based approach principle, the Guidance provides for a certain number of clarifications on the application of the FATF recommendations to entities involved in VCPPS.

FATF is of the view that domestic entities providing convertible VC exchange services between VC and fiat currency should be subject to adequate AML/CFT regulation in their jurisdiction, like any other FI, and be subject to prudential supervision. In this context, the distinction between centralised and decentralised VCs is a key aspect for the purposes of the risk assessment to be performed. FATF recommends that entities involved in convertible and decentralised VCPPS be subject to an enhanced due diligence process, as such activities are regarded of higher risk due to the inherent anonymity element and challenges to perform proper identification (i.e., the underlying protocols on which the major part of the decentralised VCPPS are currently based do not provide for the participants' identification and verification) (see also "Anonymity/ pseudonymity", above).

It is important to note that FATF does not recommend prohibiting VCPPS. On the contrary, such prohibition could drive such activities underground and lead to a complete lack of visibility and control over them. As a result, in case of prohibition of VCPPS, FATF recommends implementing additional mitigation measures, taking also into account the cross-border element in their activities.

As regards transaction monitoring, FATF is of the view that countries must ensure that originator and beneficial owner information is always included when convertible VC exchangers conduct convertible VC transfers in the form of wire transfers. Certain *de minimis* thresholds may, however, be implemented in order to exclude lower risk transactions. Transaction monitoring remains a key risk mitigant in the convertible VC world, as long as a conversion of VC occurs.

(b) Upcoming binding rules

FATF and the Middle East and North Africa Financial Task Force met between June 24 and 29, 2018 to discuss, *inter alia*, FATF engagement with the fintech and RegTech sectors, as well as the future steps to be undertaken to support innovation in line with effective AML/CFT standards. During this meeting, FATF also discussed its ongoing work to understand the risks associated with VCs for ML/FT, and the action to undertake in order to adopt a consistent regulatory approach. FATF will submit a report for the attention of the G-20 in July 2018, setting out FATF's progress on its work programme addressing the above issues (see "G20", below). An intersessional meeting will take place in September 2018 on how FATF standards apply to VCs.

G-20

Latest discussions and developments

In its communication of March 19 and 20, 2018, the G-20 recalled that technology, including digitalisation, has been reshaping the global economy over the past years and that a common understanding of the changes and the potential implications thereof is to be developed. In G-20's view, although VCs have the potential to improve the efficiency of the financial system and the economy, those raise a certain number of issues, namely with respect to tax evasion, and ML/FT. In this respect, the G-20 committed to implement the FATF standards as they apply to crypto-assets (see "VCs – Guidance for a risk based approach", above). More importantly, it has called on FATF to advance global implementation on this issue. The G-20 further expects that international standard-setting bodies ("**SBBs**") will continue their monitoring of VCs and their risks and assess multilateral responses, if required.

For the moment, the G-20 has not proposed any concrete action and awaits the FATF's report to be submitted to it in July 2018 (see "Upcoming binding rules", above). It is, however, likely that essentially the G-20 will continue to rely upon the FATF's position to ensure that global solutions are implemented at a broader level (through the 37 FATF member States and the nine FATF-Style Regional Bodies).

Creation of specific FIUs

The creation of specific Financial Intelligence Units ("**FIUs**") for VC-related transactions could be one of the measures to be implemented at national level which would have an impact at the international level. The cooperation between such specific FIUs would improve investigatory assistance and international cooperation in this respect (as stated in the Guidance).

Self-regulation & codes of conduct

Like Switzerland, certain jurisdictions attach great importance to self-regulation in the context of AML/CFT. Specific codes of conduct and self-regulations issued by SROs monitoring the compliance of affiliated FIs may be one of the measures that could be taken to address the ML/FT issue in relation to VCs, quickly and efficiently. FIs active in the sector of crypto-currencies, such as VC exchangers, could be specifically targeted by self-regulations adapted to their activities and providing for more clarity on their KYC and due diligence duties. Regulators and/or legislators could issue general guidelines and principles in this area, while specialised SROs could enrich them with detailed and practical recommendations until a consensus is found at the international level.

Central bank crypto-currencies

Based on the various statements and reports on VCs issued by central banks in different jurisdictions, it appears that central banks agree that VCs such as *BTC* and *ETH* are not meant to replace fiat currency. According to the *International Monetary Fund Global Financial Stability Report* dated April 2018, the use of crypto-currencies as a medium of exchange has been limited and their high volatility has prevented them from becoming a reliable unit of account. In this context, VCs do not appear to pose at present macro-critical financial stability risks, although if widely used, the may raise issues about, *inter alia*, ML and investor and consumer protection.

Notwithstanding the above, certain central banks (such as Riksbank, Norges Bank and the Bank of England) are currently contemplating issuing their own central bank cryptocurrencies (the "**CBCC**") in order to take advantage of the dematerialisation of the currency (triggering costs reductions) and facilitate international transactions by avoiding currency exchanges issues and providing for instantaneous transfers.

CBCCs could be viewed as a solution to mitigate the ML/FT risks, as the transactions related thereto would necessarily go through a regulated financial intermediary subject to AML/CFT regulations. This presupposes a new generation of centralised crypto-currencies which will not have the same level of anonymity and transferability as the current crypto-currencies. In this respect, it is worth noting that the Bank for International Settlements indicated in its March 2018 report, *Central bank digital currencies*, that the issuance of CBCCs could come, in addition to more efficient and safer payments and settlement systems, with some benefits from a AML/CFT perspective. To the extent that CBCCs allow for digital records and traces, it could indeed improve the application of rules aimed at AML/CFT. To date, we are not aware of central banks having issued their own CBCCs (with the exception of the specific case of Venezuela which has issued a state crypto-currency backed by the country's oil and mineral reserves (i.e., the petro)).

Technological solutions?

According to certain authors and actors active in the crypto-currency field, the specific features of DL technologies and protocols could be used to mitigate the ML/FT risks in relation to VCs. KYC, beneficial owner and transactional information could be registered and verified on a dedicated DL, in the form of a global network of unalterable information that would be accessible by "gatekeepers" and law enforcement. This solution, although very promising at first sight, would raise significant technical and legal issues. Among the latter, one should mention the legal requirements in terms of data protection and, as the case may be, banking secrecy. Furthermore, the access to information and its use by public authorities such as criminal prosecution authorities would have to be strictly regulated in order to avoid any intervention outside the applicable mutual assistance channels. In this respect, and as one of the main challenges, such a private DL would need to comply with rules enacted at an international level by the jurisdictions whose FIs would be involved in such network. It appears, therefore, that there are a certain number of obstacles as of today to use DL technologies for AML/CFT purposes, especially in the absence, at this stage, of clear guidance and standards at the international level.

As mentioned in the FATF 2015 Report on VCs, other technical solutions may be available. Third party digital identity systems, as well as new business models, could be developed to facilitate customer identification/verification, transaction monitoring and other due diligence requirements. In particular, in FATF's view, application programming interfaces ("**APIs**") that provide customer identification information, or allow FIs to set conditions that must be satisfied before a VC transaction can be sent to the recipient, could be used to reduce the ML/CTF risks associated with a VCPPS. A certain number of fintech companies have already started to develop technological AML solutions.

Conclusion

VCPPS are still in the early stages of development, but are gaining momentum. As adoption increases and innovation relevant to AML/CFT compliance becomes embedded in the VCPPS "genetics", we may witness the emergence of improved existing VC protocols or entirely new VCs, built on fundamentally different underlying principles that could include build-in controls, trusted "gatekeepers", digital identity interfaces and transaction monitoring.

Unfortunately, for as long as consistent and recognised standards and/or compliance tools are lacking, many legitimate actors in the VCPPS space will continue to be denied access to traditional banking services in a number of jurisdictions, and/or be "de-risked" by FIs. To the extent that international standard-setters, national regulators, FIs and VCPPS service providers and innovators recognise the opportunities and benefits of VCPPS globally, they should cooperate to define best practices and standards, as well as training programmes for the next generation of VC "compliance officers". Indeed, applying existing concepts and approaches tailored to an intermediated, centralised financial infrastructure simply does not work when transposed to VC ecosystems which abide by different rules and principles by design.

* * *

Endnotes

1. *Guidance for a Risk-Based Approach to Prepaid Cards, Mobile Payments and Internet-Based Payment Services*, June 2013, http://www.fatf-gafi.org/media/fatf/documents/recommendations/Guidance-RBA-NPPS.pdf.

2. Communication from the Commission of the European Parliament and the Council on an Action Plan for strengthening the fight against FT. Strasbourg, February 2, 2016.

3. Europol, *Drugs and the Darknet – Perspectives for Enforcement, 2017.*

4. European Central Bank, *Virtual Currency Schemes*, October 2012.

5. European Banking Authority, Opinion on virtual currencies, July 4, 2014.

6. Available here: http://www.fatf-gafi.org/media/fatf/documents/reports/Virtual-currency-key-definitions-and-potential-aml-cft-risks.pdf.

7. Impact Assessment accompanying the document Proposal for a Directive of the European Parliament and the Council amending Directive (EU) 2015/849 on the prevention of the use of the financial system for the purposes of ML or FT and amending Directive 2009/101/EC, July 5, 2016 ("**MLD4**").

8. FATF, *Virtual Currencies: Key Definitions and Potential AML/CFT Risks*, June 2014.

9. Report of the ECB on Virtual Currency Schemes, October 2012.

10. The documents, some dating back to the 1970s, were created by, and taken from Panamanian law firm and corporate service provider Mossack Fonseca, and were leaked by an anonymous source.

11. European Commission, *Explanatory Memorandum*, proposal for a Directive of the European Parliament and of the Council amending MLD4.

12. Swiss Federal Council Report on Virtual Currencies, June 25, 2014.

Fedor Poskriakov
Tel: +41 58 450 71 31 / Email: fedor.poskriakov@lenzstaehelin.com
Fedor Poskriakov is a partner at Lenz & Staehelin in the banking and regulatory group in Geneva and specialises in banking, securities and finance law. He regularly advises on various regulatory, contractual and corporate matters. His practice covers banking, investment management and alternative investments, including private equity and hedge funds. He also advises on complex asset structuring and protection for business and private assets. His other practice areas include compliance advisory, internal investigations, private clients and fintech. Highlighted as a "Next Generation Lawyer" (*The Legal 500*, 2017), Fedor Poskriakov "is a highly reputed banking and finance specialist who handles complex matters for Swiss and international clients" (*Who's Who Legal*, 2017). Mr Poskriakov is admitted to the Bar in Geneva. He has a law degree (*lic. iur.*) from the University of Geneva.

Maria Chiriaeva
Tel: +41 58 450 70 00 / Email: maria.chiriaeva@lenzstaehelin.com
Maria Chiriaeva is a senior associate in the Banking and Finance group in Geneva and specialises in banking, securities and finance law. She regularly advises on various regulatory, contractual and corporate matters. Her practice covers banking, investment management and alternative investments. Her areas of expertise also include compliance advisory and internal investigations. Maria Chiriaeva is admitted to the Bar in Geneva. She has a Master's in economic law from the University of Geneva.

Christophe Cavin
Tel: +41 58 450 70 00 / Email: christophe.cavin@lenzstaehelin.com
Christophe Cavin works as an associate in the Geneva office and is a member of the Banking and Finance group and the Investigations group, respectively. His main areas of practice include banking and finance, regulatory, investigations, corporate, commercial and contractual matters. Christophe Cavin is admitted to the Bar in Geneva and New York. He has a Master's in commercial law from the University of Geneva and an LL.M. from the University of Pennsylvania Law School.

Lenz & Staehelin

Route de Chêne 30, CH-1211 Geneva 6 / Brandschenkenstrasse 24, CH-8027 Zurich, Switzerland
Tel: +41 58 450 7000 / +41 58 450 8000 / Fax: + 41 58 450 7001 / +41 58 450 8001 / URL: www.lenzstaehelin.com

Aspects of state securities regulation

Greg Strong & Rodrigo Seira
DLx Law, LLP

Introduction

State securities regulators have been very active in regulating cryptocurrency-related investment products and the sale of digital assets. In May of 2018, state securities regulators announced "Operation Cryptosweep," a coordinated series of enforcement actions and public outreach focused on fundraising schemes often referred to as Initial Coin Offerings ("ICOs") as well as other investment schemes involving digital currencies. The focus of the coordinated action was on protecting main street investors from securities fraud, which state securities regulators have been doing for more than 100 years, and raising public awareness of the risks associated with ICOs and cryptocurrency-related investment products. In this chapter, we examine: how state securities regulators have defined cryptocurrency, digital tokens and related terms; when the offer or sale of digital assets may be considered an offer of securities under state law; and the obligations that flow from that determination from a state law perspective.

State securities laws are generally similar but certain aspects vary significantly across jurisdictions. Many state securities statutes are derived from the Uniform Securities Act, mainly the 1956 version or the 2002 version. This Chapter refers to the most recent version of the Uniform Securities Act from 2002 ("USA 2002") throughout many parts of the discussion to provide examples of certain concepts.

How do state securities regulators define cryptocurrency and digital tokens?

Recent enforcement actions by state securities regulators that include definitions of these terms provide a window into how state securities regulators are thinking about cryptocurrencies and digital tokens. The definitions used across states vary and may refer to definitions of these digital assets used in other parts of the state code outside of the securities laws. Understanding how an individual state regulator defines these terms may be key to determining whether, and to what extent, a digital asset may come within the ambit of that state's securities laws.

Definitions from enforcement actions and investor outreach

The North American Securities Administrators Association ("NASAA") is a voluntary membership organisation of 67 state, provincial, and territorial securities regulators. NASAA has coordinated public outreach and enforcement efforts related to investments involving cryptocurrency or digital tokens. In that context, NASAA described "cryptocurrencies" as follows:

"Cryptocurrencies are a medium of exchange that are created and stored electronically in the blockchain, a distributed public database that keeps a permanent record of digital transactions. Current common cryptocurrencies include Bitcoin, Ethereum and Litecoin. Unlike traditional currency, these alternatives have no physical form and typically are not backed by tangible assets. They are not insured or controlled by a central bank or other governmental authority, cannot always be exchanged for other commodities, and are subject to little or no regulation."[1]

The Texas State Securities Board has been active in investigating and bringing enforcement actions related to investment schemes involving cryptocurrencies or digital tokens, and issued an Enforcement Report ("The Texas Report") on April 10, 2018 detailing widespread fraud uncovered in these offerings. The Texas Report defined cryptocurrency as follows: "a digital currency secured through cryptography, or codes that cannot be read without a key."[2] The Texas Report refers to cryptocurrency and virtual currency interchangeably and considers all digital tokens to be cryptocurrency.[3] Notably, the Texas Report indicates that the Texas State Securities Board is not regulating cryptocurrencies themselves, only the investments that claim to use virtual currencies in an investment program.[4]

The Massachusetts Securities Division has consistently referred to the Financial Action Task Force ("FATF") report *Virtual Currencies, Key Definitions and Potential AML/CFT Risks*, to define "virtual currency" and "cryptocurrency," which they refer to interchangeably, as follows:

"Virtual currency is a digital representation of value that can be digitally traded and functions as (1) a medium of exchange; and/or (2) a unit of account; and/or (3) a store of value, but does not have legal tender status (i.e., when tendered to a creditor, is a valid and legal offer of payment) in any jurisdiction. It is not issued nor guaranteed by any jurisdiction, and fulfils the above functions only by agreement within the community of users of the virtual currency. Virtual currency is distinguished from fiat currency (a.k.a. "real currency," "real money," or "national currency"), which is the coin and paper money of a country that is designated as its legal tender; circulates; and is customarily used and accepted as a medium of exchange in the issuing country. It is distinct from e-money, which is a digital representation of fiat currency used to electronically transfer value denominated in fiat currency. E-money is a digital transfer mechanism for fiat currency—i.e., it electronically transfers value that has legal tender status."[5]

Interestingly, the FATF report distinguishes cryptocurrencies as a subset of virtual currencies that are decentralised, noting that they "are distributed, open-source, math-based, peer-to-peer virtual currencies that have no central administrating authority, and no central monitoring or oversight."[6]

The North Carolina Securities Division recently described a "digital token" as: "a digital asset that entitles its owners to certain rights related to the business underlying the ICO. Such rights could include rights to profits, a share of assets, rights to use certain products or services or voting rights. Tokens can be listed on cryptocurrency exchanges, and they can be used to buy other digital assets or fiat currencies."[7]

Legislative definitions

Legislation has been passed in certain jurisdictions to amend the securities laws to include definitions related to certain digital assets. For example, in Wyoming, first-of-its-kind legislation was recently passed that defines an "open blockchain token."[8] Pursuant to this statute, an "open blockchain token" means a digital unit which is:

(i)   Created:

   (A) In response to the verification or collection of a specified number of transactions relating to a digital ledger or database;

   (B) By deploying computer code to a blockchain network that allows for the creation of digital tokens or other units; or

   (C) Using any combination of the methods specified in subparagraphs (A) and (B) of this paragraph.

(ii) Recorded in a digital ledger or database which is chronological, consensus-based, decentralized and mathematically verified in nature, especially relating to the supply of units and their distribution; and

(iii) Capable of being traded or transferred between persons without an intermediary or custodian of value.[9]

This definition of "open blockchain token" contains several interesting features. First, an open blockchain token must be created in a specific way. Subsection (i)(A) relates to tokens created to reward participants for verifying transactions in blockchain systems such as miners verifying transactions in systems using "proof of work" consensus rules. Open blockchain tokens created pursuant to subsection (i)(B) are those created during a token-generation event in a new blockchain-based platform, presumably for the purpose of selling or distributing the tokens which will be integral components of the operation of that platform.

Second, an open blockchain token must be recorded on a digital ledger that is, among other things, decentralised. Whether and when a blockchain-based platform is or becomes decentralised has been the subject of much recent debate. In a recent June speech, William Hinman, the Director of the Division of Corporation Finance at the U.S. Securities Exchange Commission, discussed the concept of decentralisation in the context of determining when the offer or sale of a digital asset constitutes the offer or sale of a security and is subject to the securities laws.[10] This speech laid the conceptual groundwork for the idea that a digital asset, once sold in a securities transaction, could later be sold in a non-securities transaction, and identified the degree of decentralisation of the blockchain-based platform as a key factor in that analysis.[11] Following this logic, it is possible that a digital asset sold in Wyoming could be sold in a securities transaction at one time, and then later, once the blockchain-based platform has become decentralised and the digital asset meets the definition of an "open blockchain token," sold again in a transaction that does not implicate the Wyoming securities laws.

Arizona has also passed legislation defining "virtual coin" and "virtual coin offering." A "virtual coin" means a digital representation of value that can be digitally traded and that functions as a medium of exchange, unit of account and store of value.[12] A "virtual coin offering":

(a)   means an offer for sale of a virtual coin that either:

   (i)   meets the definition of a security prescribed in this section.

   (ii) the issuer elects to treat as a security by complying with section 44-1844, subsection a, paragraph 22.

(b)   does not include an offer for sale of a virtual coin that both:

   (i)   has not been marketed by the issuer as an investment.

   (ii) grants to the purchaser, within ninety days after the purchaser's receipt of the virtual coin, the right to use, contribute to the development of, or license the use of a platform using blockchain technology as defined in section 44-7061, including a license to use a product or service on the platform or a discount against fees for use of the platform.[13]

Legislation was also introduced in Colorado during the last legislative session that sought to define "open blockchain token" using the Wyoming definition verbatim.[14] This legislation was not passed.

Definitions from other statutes

Many state money transmission statutes also define virtual currency and, in many states, the same office is responsible for both the regulation of money transmission and the regulation of securities. Practitioners seeking to determine how a particular state securities regulator defines virtual currency may also look to state money transmission statutes for guidance. For instance, the Alabama Securities Commission administers and enforces the Alabama Monetary Transmission Act §§8-7a-1 to 8-7a-27. In this statute the definition of "monetary value" includes "a medium of exchange, including virtual or fiat currencies, whether or not redeemable in money," and "money transmission," which requires a licence, and includes receiving "monetary value" for transmission.[15]

Even in states in which an entity other than the securities regulator has jurisdiction over money transmission, state securities regulators may reference the definitions of virtual currency used by those regulators. For example, the New York Attorney General recently launched a Virtual Markets Integrity Initiative which involved sending a survey to virtual currency trading platforms or exchanges, requesting certain information. The information request includes multiple references to the term virtual currency and defines that term by reference to the Department of Financial Services Regulations that define "Virtual Currency":

"Virtual Currency means any type of digital unit that is used as a medium of exchange or a form of digitally stored value. Virtual Currency shall be broadly construed to include digital units of exchange that: (i) have a centralized repository or administrator; (ii) are decentralized and have no centralized repository or administrator; or (iii) may be created or obtained by computing or manufacturing effort. Virtual Currency shall not be construed to include any of the following: (1) digital units that (i) are used solely within online gaming platforms, (ii) have no market or application outside of those gaming platforms, (iii) cannot be converted into, or redeemed for, Fiat Currency or Virtual Currency, and (iv) may or may not be redeemable for real-world goods, services, discounts, or purchases; (2) digital units that can be redeemed for goods, services, discounts, or purchases as part of a customer affinity or rewards program with the issuer and/or other designated merchants or can be redeemed for digital units in another customer affinity or rewards program, but cannot be converted into, or redeemed for, Fiat Currency or Virtual Currency; or (3) digital units used as part of Prepaid Cards."[16]

How regulators define cryptocurrency, virtual currency, and other related concepts will continue to evolve as the regulatory landscape in this area gains clarity. For now, it is clear that there are many variations in the definitions applied to these concepts, and a lack of uniformity in approach.

Does the sale of a digital asset involve the sale of a security?

The threshold question to determine whether state securities laws apply to the offer or sale of a digital asset is whether it involves the offer or sale of a "security." Security is a defined term in all state securities laws, with slight variation across states.[17] For instance, in some states, viatical settlements and variable annuities are specifically included in the definition of security, and in others they are not.

The _Howey_ test

State securities laws specifically include "investment contracts" in the definition of security.[18] At the federal level, an "investment contract" is also specifically enumerated within the definition of security.[19] In _SEC v. W.J. Howey Co.,_[20] the United States Supreme Court developed the test used to determine whether the sale of an interest constitutes an investment contract. The _Howey_ test has several parts, each of which must be met for the transaction in question to involve the offer or sale of an investment contract: an investment of money, in a common enterprise, with an expectation of profit, derived solely, or substantially, from the efforts of others.[21] The majority of states have adopted the _Howey_ test in their own jurisdictions to determine when an investment contract is involved.

As discussed in the introduction, in May of 2018 NASAA announced the results of "Operation Cryptosweep," a coordinated series of investigations designed to identify and address fraud in the offer and sale of cryptocurrency-related investments.[22] A number of consent orders, cease and desist orders, and administrative actions were announced in connection with "Operation Cryptosweep."

In many of these actions, state securities administrators determined that the offer or sale of a digital asset involved the offer or sale of a security by applying the _Howey_ test, either explicitly or implicitly.

The South Carolina Securities Division concluded that the sale of cryptocurrency mining contracts were investment contracts _In the Matter of Swiss Global, Inc._, and thus securities subject to the South Carolina Securities Act.[23] In this matter, _Howey_ is not explicitly discussed, but each of the _Howey_ factors are recited in the findings of fact section of the Order, leading to the conclusion that the offer or sale of the mining contracts involved the offer or sale of investment contracts and, thus, securities and subject to the South Carolina securities laws.[24]

The Colorado Securities Commissioner brought an action against Broad Investments, LLC in connection with a purported token sale. In describing the Commissioner's jurisdiction, the Order to Show Cause filed in this action explicitly cited the Colorado case, adopting the definition of an investment contract set in _Howey_ and noting that an investment contract is a security pursuant to the Colorado Securities Act.[25] The Order goes on to find that the token sale involved the sale of an investment contract and was subject to the Colorado securities laws.[26]

The Securities Commissioner of Maryland brought an action against Browser Labs, LLC in the form of a Summary Order to Cease and Desist and Order to Show Cause. The Commissioner concluded that the contemplated sale of digital tokens by Browser Labs, LLC in an ICO constituted the offer or sale of investment contracts and was subject to the Maryland Securities Act.[27]

The Alabama Securities Commission ("ASC") brought an action against Chain Group Escrow Service ("CGES") in the form of a Summary Order to Cease and Desist. The ASC found that CGES was offering investment contracts, and thus securities, because the "investment plans require investors to invest money into the common investment plan in order to pool their investments with other investors. Investors share and expect a profit, as represented by CGES, and the profit is derived from the managerial efforts of CGES."[28]

In some instances, the interests offered for sale were advertised as investments and the determination that the offer or sale of the interests were securities offerings was more conclusory in nature.[29]

The risk capital test

There are several states that also use an additional test called the risk capital test to determine if the sale of an interest constitutes the sale of a security. The California Supreme Court formulated the risk capital test in *Silver Hills Country Club v. Sobieski*.[30] The test considers whether the scheme "involves an attempt by an issuer to raise funds for a business venture or enterprise; an indiscriminate offering to the public at large where the persons solicited are selected at random; a passive position on the part of the investor; and the conduct of the enterprise by the issuer with other people's money."[31] It was determined that the sale of memberships in a golf course that was not yet built involved the solicitation of the risk capital necessary to develop a business for profit and therefore constituted the sale of a security.[32] Additionally, it was noted that this result could have been reached even in transactions where the purchaser put capital at risk without the expectation of any material benefits.[33]

The risk capital test has since been adopted in a minority of jurisdictions. Some states have passed laws codifying the risk capital test, others have passed regulatory rules, and others have judicial decisions recognising the application of the test. Although the basics are the same in each jurisdiction, the test may vary from state to state. In Washington, for example, the definition of a security includes any "investment of money or other consideration in the risk capital of a venture with the expectation of some valuable benefit to the investor where the investor does not receive the right to exercise practical and actual control over the managerial decisions of the venture."[34]

The risk capital test has not yet been applied in the context of the offer or sale of a digital asset, but it may have broader reach than an investment contract under the *Howey* test. Thus, even sales of digital tokens that do not satisfy the *Howey* test, and are not securities transactions for federal purposes, may nevertheless be deemed securities transactions in states that have adopted the risk capital test.

State legislation

In some states, digital assets have been specifically excluded from the definition of a security through the legislative process. The Wyoming legislation, which defines an "open blockchain token," also specifically excludes an "open blockchain token" from the definition of security.[35] Accordingly, offers and sales of open blockchain tokens in Wyoming are not subject to the Wyoming securities laws because they are not offers or sales of securities.

In the Arizona legislation defining a "virtual coin" and a "virtual coin offering," there is also a provision that excludes from the definition of a "virtual coin offering" the offer or sale of a virtual coin that both: "has not been marketed by the issuer as an investment; and grants to the purchaser, within ninety days after the purchaser's receipt of the virtual coin, the right to use, contribute to the development of or license the use of a platform using blockchain technology . . . including a license to use a product or service on the platform or a discount against fees for use of the platform."[36] This language is evidence of an intent to exclude certain transactions in virtual coins from the definition of virtual coin offerings and, by implication, the definition of a security. Whether it accomplishes this intent is an open question, as it is not clear from a plain reading how this definition was intended to operate.

It is anticipated that more states will consider legislation like the Wyoming and Arizona legislation in the future to promote entrepreneurship and capital access for new blockchain-based platforms.

Interpretive opinions

Finally, it is worth noting that state securities laws provide for no action requests or requests for interpretive opinions. Practitioners may consider submitting a request for no action or an interpretive opinion to assist in determining whether the contemplated sale of a digital asset would be determined to involve the offer or sale of an investment contract and be subject to the securities laws in a particular jurisdiction.[37]

What obligations arise from the determination that the sale of a digital asset involves the sale of a security?

In each of the enforcement actions referenced above, the consequences of selling a security without complying with the applicable state securities laws is set forth and generally includes three categories of violations. First, securities offered for sale must be registered in the state in which they are offered for sale, or exempt from registration, or be federally covered securities. Second, the entities offering the securities for sale may need to be registered as a broker-dealer in each state in which they offer the security for sale. Finally, individuals recruited to sell the securities by the issuer or promoter may also need to be registered as broker-dealer agents or issuer agents in each state in which they offer the securities for sale if they are receiving compensation related to any such sales.

Securities must be registered, exempt from registration, or federally covered

Generally, securities offered for sale in a state must be registered, exempt from registration, or federally covered.[38] Registration of securities at the state level can be done by coordination or qualification and generally requires disclosure similar in nature to the disclosure required by the federal securities laws.[39] Registration by coordination is available where there is registration under the Securities Act of 1933 at the federal level. The state registration is coordinated with review and effectiveness by the Securities and Exchange Commission ("SEC").[40] Registration by qualification is required if an offering is not registered under the Securities Act of 1933, such as an offering exempt from registration under the Securities Act but not exempt from state registration requirements.[41] Either way, the process begins with the filing of the required documents including a registration statement, the disclosure document, and paying the fee.[42]

The review associated with an application for registration can differ significantly depending on the state. Some states are *disclosure review* states, meaning that if the issuer files the required disclosure documents with their application for registration, the application should become effective. Disclosure review does not address the substantive merits of the offering.

Other states conduct *merit review* of applications for registration of securities offerings. These states conduct a substantive review of a registration statement to determine if the offering will be fair to investors in their states. Where it is determined that an offer is unfair in certain respects, the merit review state may issue comments regarding the substance of the offering and can refuse to declare the registration statement effective in their state.

Securities issuers that do not wish to register their offering may rely on an exemption from registration when applicable. Certain types of securities and types of securities transactions are exempt from the general rule that securities offered for sale must be registered.[43] Typical transactional exemptions found in state securities laws include, but are not limited to:

i.   a limited offering exemption to fewer than a threshold number of offerees (typically 25 or less);

ii.   offers to banks, savings institutions, trust companies or other institutional buyers that are sophisticated; and

iii.   transactions between issuers and underwriters.

Finally, states are pre-empted from registering federal covered securities, but retain anti-fraud jurisdiction and may require notice filing and the payment of a fee. Federal-covered securities include:

i.   securities issued by an investment company registered under the Investment Company Act of 1940;

ii.   securities offered or sold to a "qualified purchaser" as that term is defined by the SEC;

iii.   securities offered or sold pursuant to most of the exemptions contained in the Securities Act, Section 3(a) and under Section 4(2);

iv.   federal exemption for crowdfunding offerings under Section 4(a)(6) of the Securities Act and Regulation Crowdfunding; and

v.   offerings under Tier 2 of Regulation A of the Securities Act.

An issuer of a digital asset that is offered in a securities offering will need to comply with the registration requirements in each state in which the issuer intends to offer the digital asset for sale, and either make sure that there is an applicable exemption from registration or issue the digital assets in a federal-covered security. Federal-covered securities include securities offered under Section 4(2) and Rule 506 of Regulation D, and pursuing an offering of digital tokens in this way would allow an issuer to raise an unlimited amount of money selling to accredited investors, and could allow sales to 35 or fewer non-accredited investors depending on the circumstances. Federal-covered offerings of digital tokens pursuant to Tier 2 of Regulation A would permit an issuer to raise up to $50 million and sell to both accredited and non-accredited investors, subject to certain limitations on aggregate purchase amounts for non-accredited investors. Both Regulation D and Regulation A Tier 2 offerings may require notice filings at the state level.

In each of the state enforcement actions referenced in this chapter, the primary cause of action was for the sale of unregistered securities. In each case, the offer or sale of the digital asset in question was determined to be the offer or sale of a security, and in each case none of the securities were registered, exempt from registration, or federally covered.

<u>Registration as a broker dealer; Registration of individuals as agents; Employing unregistered agents</u>

Most of the state actions referenced in this chapter also contain causes of action for acting as an unregistered broker-dealer or agent. Generally, a "broker-dealer" for state securities law purposes is a person engaged in the business of effecting transactions in securities for the account of others or for the person's own account.[44] An "agent" for state securities law purposes is an individual who represents a broker-dealer in effecting or attempting to effect purchases or sales of securities, the issuer's securities or an issuer, in effecting or attempting to effect purchases or sales of the issuer's securities.[45] State securities laws generally provide that it is unlawful for an agent to transact business in the state unless they are registered.[46] There are also a variety of exemptions from registration available to an agent, that vary by state depending on whether the securities laws are based on the Uniform Act of 1956, the Uniform Act of 2002, or otherwise. Generally, the following exemptions are available:

i.   an individual who represents an issuer with respect to an offer or sale of the issuer's own securities or those of the issuer's parent or any of the issuer's subsidiaries, and who is not compensated in connection with the individual's participation by the payment of commissions or other remuneration based, directly or indirectly, on transactions in those securities;

ii.   an individual who represents an issuer and who effects transactions in the issuer's securities that qualify as certain exempt transactions; and

iii. an individual who represents an issuer that effects transactions solely in federal-covered securities of the issuer unless the individual is compensated in connection with the agent's participation by the payment of commissions or other remuneration based, directly or indirectly, on transactions in those securities.[47]

At the federal level there is a similar requirement that brokers, persons engaged in the business of effecting securities transactions for the account of others, register pursuant to §15(a) of the Securities Exchange Act. "Issuers generally are not brokers because they sell securities for their own accounts and not for the accounts of others."[48] To the extent that agents of an issuer could be brokers and required to register, there is an exemption that applies in Rule §240.3a4-1 related to associated persons of an issuer deemed not to be brokers. It is possible that such issuer agents would still need to register at the state level depending on individual state issuer agent registration rules and exemptions.

State securities regulatory authority to enforce the Commodities Exchange Act

State securities regulators have the authority to enforce the Commodities Exchange Act ("CEA").[49] The Commodities Futures Trading Commission ("CFTC") has primary jurisdiction to enforce the CEA. The CFTC has asserted jurisdiction over virtual currencies as commodities subject to regulation pursuant to the CEA.[50] "Section 1a(9) of the Act defines 'commodity' to include, among other things, 'all services, rights, and interests in which contracts for future delivery are presently or in the future dealt in.'"[51] "Bitcoin and other virtual currencies are encompassed in the definition and properly defined as commodities."[52] The CEA provides general anti-fraud and manipulation enforcement provisions with respect to the spot commodities markets, and broad regulatory authority over derivative commodities markets. Accordingly, state securities regulators may bring actions related to virtual currencies for violations of the CEA when there is evidence of fraud in the spot market or more broadly with respect to the derivative markets.

Conclusion

State securities regulators have been very proactive in asserting their authority with respect to the sale of digital tokens and investment schemes involving virtual currency. The enforcement actions to date, including those outlined in this paper, have been focused on protecting retail investors from fraud and have targeted investments in this area that most clearly run afoul of state securities laws – strengthening the crypto ecosystem for all. As the regulatory landscape in this area evolves, it remains to be seen whether state securities regulators will turn their attention towards the regulation of digital assets intended primarily to provide consumer utility and how they will be treated.

If the recent Wyoming legislation provides an indication, we may see more state securities regulators consider exempting the sale of digital assets with certain characteristics from the definition of security. For now, when an instrument is offered for sale that involves virtual currency or a digital asset, care should be taken to determine if the offer constitutes the offer of a security. If it does, compliance with state securities laws in each of the states in which the securities will be offered will be necessary.

Acknowledgments

The Authors would like to thank their colleagues Lewis R. Cohen, Esquire and Jacob Shulman for their editorial contributions to this chapter.

* * *

Endnotes

1. *NASAA Reminds Investors to Approach Cryptocurrencies, Initial Coin Offerings and Other Cryptocurrency Related Investment Products with Caution*, NASAA (January 4, 2018) available at: http://www.nasaa.org/44073/nasaa-reminds-investors-approach-cryptocurrencies-initial-coin-offerings-cryptocurrency-related-investment-products-caution/.

2. *Enforcement Report: Widespread Fraud Found in Cryptocurrency Offerings*, Texas State Securities Board (April 10, 2018) available at: https://www.ssb.texas.gov/sites/default/files/CRYPTO%20SWEEP%20report%20April%2010%202018%20FINAL.pdf.

3. *Id.*

4. *Id.*

5. *FATF Report, Virtual Currencies, Key Definitions and Potential AML/CFT Risks*, Financial Action Task Force (June 2014), available at: http://www.fatf-gafi.org/media/fatf/documents/reports/Virtual-currency-key-definitions-and-potential-aml-cft-risks.pdf. *See, e.g., In the Matter of: Blue Vase Mining*, Consent Order, Docket No. E-2018-0018, available at: http://www.sec.state.ma.us/sct/current/sctbluevase/MSD-Blue-Vase-Consent-Order-E-2018-0018.pdf; *In the Matter of Caviar and Kirill Bensonoff*, Administrative Complaint, Docket No. E-2017-120, available at: https://www.sec.state.ma.us/sct/current/sctbensonoff/Administrative-Complaint-E-2017-0120.pdf.

6. *Id.*

7. *In the Matter of Adosia LLC and Kyle E. Solomon*, Final Consent Order, File No. 18 ADM 007, available at: https://www.sosnc.gov/vs2010/Soskb.Web.Content/media/1614/2018-05-10-adosia-final-consent-order_redacted.pdf.

8. Wyo. Stat. §17-4-206(e).

9. Wyo. Stat §17-4-206(e).

10. William Hinman, Director, Division of Corporation Finance, *"Digital Transactions: When Howey Met Gary (Plastic),"* (June 14, 2018) available at: https://www.sec.gov/news/speech/speech-hinman-061418.

11. *Id.*

12. A.R.S.§44-1801(31) (effective August 3, 2018).

13. A.R.S.§44-1801(32) (effective August 3, 2018). The "blockchain technology," pursuant to section A.R.S. § 44-7061, referenced in this definition, means: "distributed ledger technology that uses a distributed, decentralized, shared and replicated ledger, which may be public or private, permissioned or permissionless, or driven by tokenized crypto economics or tokenless. The data on the ledger is protected with cryptography, is immutable and auditable and provides an uncensored truth."

14. HB18-1426, Colorado General Assembly, Second Regular Session, 71st General

Assembly and SB18-277, Colorado General Assembly, Second Regular Session, 71st General Assembly.

15. *See* §§8-7a-2(8) and 8-7a-2(10).

16. 23 NYCRR §200.2(p).

17. *See e.g.,* §102(28) of the USA 2002.

18. *See* §102(28) of the USA 2002.

19. §2(a)(1) of the Securities Act of 1933; §3(a)(10) of the Securities Exchange Act of 1934.

20. *SEC v. W.J. Howey Co.*, 328 U.S. 293 (1946).

21. *Howey*, at 299-300.

22. *See* State and Provincial Securities Regulators Conduct Coordinated International Crypto Crackdown, NASAA, (May 21, 2018) available at: http://www.nasaa.org/45121/ state-and-provincial-securities-regulators-conduct-coordinated-international-crypto-crackdown-2/.

23. *In the Matter of Swiss Gold Global, Inc. and Genesis Mining, Ltd.* Administrative Order to Cease and Desist, File No. 17021 (Administrative Proceeding Before the Securities Commissioner of South Carolina, March 9, 2018) available at: http://2hsvz0l74ah31vgcm16peuy12tz.wpengine.netdna-cdn.com/wp-content/ uploads/2018/03/01621904.pdf.

24. *Id.*

25. *In the Matter of Broad Investments, LLC and Guoyong Liu*, Verified Petition for Order to Show Cause, Case No. 2018-CDS-021 (Before the Colorado Securities Commission, May 2, 2018) available at: https://drive.google.com/file/d/1mV8IX5Y Kb3Vx4regOG0L77q9PIPxVLfp/view.

26. *Id.*

27. *In the Matter of Browser Labs, LLC*, Summary Order to Cease and Desist and Order to Show Cause, Case NO. 2018-0312 (Maryland Securities Commissioner May 21, 2018) available at: http://www.marylandattorneygeneral.gov/Securities%20Actions/2018/ Browsers_Lab_ICO_SO_OSC_052118.pdf.

28. *In the Matter of Chain Group Escrow Service*, Cease and Desist Order, Administrative Order No. CD-2018-0003, Alabama Securities Commission (April 20, 2018) available at: http://www.asc.state.al.us/Orders/2018/CD-2018-0003.pdf.

29. *See e.g., In the Matter of USI-Tech Limited, et al.*, Order No. ENF-17-CDO-1753 (Texas State Sec. Board, December 20, 2017) available at: https://www.ssb.texas.gov/ sites/default/files/USI-Tech%20ENF-17-CDO-1753.pdf; *In the Matter of BitConnect*, Order No. ENF-18-CDO-1754 (Texas State Sec. Board, January 4, 2018) https://www. ssb.texas.gov/sites/default/files/BitConnect_ENF-18-CDO-1754.pdf; *In the Matter of Caviar and Kirill Bensonoff*, Administrative Complaint, Docket No. E-2017-120, available at: https://www.sec.state.ma.us/sct/current/sctbensonoff/Administrative-Complaint-E-2017-0120.pdf.

30. 55 Cal.2d 811 (1961).

31. *Id.* at 815.

32. *Id.*

33. *Id.*

34. RCW 21.20.005(17)(a).

35. WYO. STAT §17-4-102(a)(xxviii)(F).

36. A.R.S.§44-1801(32) (effective August 3, 2018).

37. *See, e.g.*, §102(28) of the USA 2002.

38. *See* §301 of the USA 2002.

39. *See* §§303 and 304 of the USA 2002.

40. *See* §303 of the USA 2002.

41. *See* §304 of the USA 2002.

42. *See* §305 of the USA 2002.

43. *See* §§201 and 202 of the USA 2002.

44. *See* §102(4) of the USA 2002.

45. *See* §102(2) of the USA 2002.

46. *See* §402(a) of the USA 2002.

47. *See* §402(b) of the USA 2002.

48. *See Investor Publications, Guide To Broker-Dealer Registration, Division of Trading and Markets*, U.S. Securities and Exchange Commission (April 2008) available at: https://www.sec.gov/reportspubs/investor-publications/divisionsmarketregbdguidehtm.html#II.

49. 7 U.S.C. §13a–2 (2012).

50. *See In the Matter of Coinflip, Inc.*, Order Instituting Proceedings, CFTC Docket No. 15-29 (Sept. 17, 2015) available at: https://www.cftc.gov/sites/default/files/idc/groups/public/@lrenforcementactions/documents/legalpleading/enfcoinfliprorder09172015.pdf.

51. *Id.* (*citing* 7 U.S.C. §1a(9)).

52. *Id.*

Gregory Strong, Attorney
Tel: +1 212 994 6845 / Email: greg.strong@dlxlaw.com
Greg is an attorney at DLx Law focused on advising entities regarding legal issues associated with the adoption of distributed ledger technology including blockchain technology. Greg draws on his deep securities and consumer protection regulatory experience to advise companies about compliance with the securities laws and other regulatory laws that may apply to their activity. Prior to joining DLx, Greg worked at the Delaware Department of Justice for close to 15 years. He most recently served as the Director of the Investor Protection Unit for three years and was responsible for administering and enforcing the provisions of the Delaware Securities Act. Prior to his appointment as Director of the Investor Protection Unit, Greg was the Director of the Consumer Protection Unit for three years. Greg has successfully represented the State of Delaware in many complex civil enforcement matters alleging violations of Delaware investor and consumer protection statutes.

Rodrigo Seira, Attorney
Tel: +1 212 994 6845 / Email: rodrigo.seira@dlxlaw.com
Rodrigo is an attorney at DLx Law. He has represented leading financial institutions, global Fortune 500 companies and sovereigns in complex M&A, restructuring, capital markets and corporate governance matters. Rodrigo focuses his current practice on fintech regulation, including token generation events, regulation of digital asset exchanges and investment funds, as well as enterprise Blockchain applications.
Prior to joining DLx Law, Rodrigo was an associate at Cleary Gottlieb and a graduate of Harvard Law School class of 2016.

DLx Law, LLP

4913 43rd St. NW, Washington, D.C. / 114 East 25th Street, New York, NY 10010, USA
Tel: +1 212 994 6845 / URL: www.dlxlaw.com

The regulation of blockchain technology

Joseph F. Borg & Tessa Schembri
WH Partners

Introduction

There is no denying that blockchain and cryptocurrencies have taken the world by storm. Whether or not these innovative technologies will live up to the revolution which they are predicted to create in various economic sectors, it cannot be refuted that the blockchain phenomenon is a reality which will not be disappearing any time soon. But can blockchain technology be regulated? Can we consider blockchain technology without the involvement of cryptocurrencies? These are two fundamental questions that are often brought up when discussing blockchain and cryptocurrency regulation.

The concept of regulating a disruptive technology, is in itself unrealistic and unattainable as a result of the principle of "technological neutrality". Technology changes exponentially, but social, economic and legal systems change incrementally. Therefore, technology will always render regulation outdated, almost immediately. On the other hand, it is the very tendency of technology to evolve that is crucial in justifying legal and regulatory change. The objective of regulation should never be to slow down or delimit technology, as this inevitably leads to stifling innovation. The focus should always be on creating standards as well as ethical and good governance principles as these are essentially the tools required for a new industry to mature, grow and flourish. Without such standards in place, we would not be able to connect one device produced by Company A with another one produced by Company B. Without ethical principles, vulnerable people would continuously be abused and exploited. Without good governance principles, business ventures would not develop into structured, stable and trustworthy entities.

Building a case for regulation

Thus, we must ask ourselves, is there a good case for regulation? In our opinion, yes! Regulation is necessary, but avoiding over-regulation is crucial. The risks for over-regulation are huge, especially when we take look back at the recent history of regulation. Even today, Europe is notorious when it comes to over-regulation. While it is undeniable that these regulations are backed by good intentions, the reality is that many recent European Union directives and regulations are bad for business: they cripple start-ups and limit innovation. It is important to strike the right balance and maintain the focus on the regulatory objectives. The latter should always constitute the basis of any regulation.

Therefore, we deduce that the regulatory objectives at the basis of any form of blockchain regulation should be:

1. the creation of standards that allow interoperability and protect end users;

2. ensuring the protection of vulnerable people and protecting them from criminals; and

3. ensuring good governance to protect investors as well as end users from fraud, mismanagement and gross negligence.

The open source nature of most blockchain projects is in itself achieving the goal of interoperability. However, the key term among the above regulatory objectives is "protection". There is a fine line for governments and regulators between protecting, and taking on a "Big Brother" approach whereby adults are not allowed to take their own informed decisions. From our angle, the best solution for protection is by ensuring transparency and providing the necessary information for an adult to be able to make his/ her own decision.

Financial freedom through blockchain

As readers may have guessed, we are liberals at heart and firm believers in freedom. Blockchain technology is an expression of liberalism and it provides mankind with both freedom and self-sufficiency. If you try to distort this through regulation, blockchain can be dangerous. This technology was applied for the first time, by a revolutionary person or group of persons to create the world's first cryptocurrency – Bitcoin. The aim behind this project was to create a revolution to dethrone the big intermediaries of the financial world, such as banks and other financial institutions. If regulators attempt to decouple blockchain from its intended purpose, blockchain fundamentalists will retaliate by further developing blockchain to satisfy their objective of replacing the financial system as we know it.

As liberals, we sympathise with blockchain fundamentalists, while remaining mindful that liberal fundamentalism is equally as dangerous as authoritarianism. Therefore, a balance needs to be struck. If the financial system is destroyed, civil wars across the globe will follow suit. This should not be something that we want. Blockchain should serve as a tool to reshape what is outdated and does not function properly in the current financial system. As Don Tapscott[1] correctly points out, big financial intermediaries have done a decent job but instead of creating prosperity, they have also created a lot of wealth for themselves. The time has now come for these intermediaries to be controlled, to avoid another financial crisis like the one we experienced in 2008 and to generate prosperity amongst people from all walks of life and from across the globe. Adequate and proportionate regulation over blockchain technology could be the key.

Cryptocurrencies unchained?

Can blockchain exist without cryptocurrencies? The answer very much depends on the type of blockchain which we are considering. A distinction must be made between a public or permission-less blockchain and a private or permissioned blockchain. Bitcoin is the first example of a public, permission-less blockchain. It is a type of Distributed Ledger Technology that is not controlled by a central entity but which relies on the community that is made up of miners, nodes and users. A public blockchain cannot exist without a cryptocurrency or crypto asset, because miners have to get rewarded in cryptocurrencies or crypto assets, and users have to trade in cryptocurrencies or crypto assets to make use of the network.

On the other hand, a private or permissioned blockchain generally comprises a ledger/ database that is built on a decentralised and possibly distributed infrastructure which is controlled by the same entity or a group of entities. The control of the latter type of blockchain is not distributed among the users of the network but is centralised in that entity or those entities which together control that blockchain. Really and truly, this defeats the whole *raison d'etre* of blockchain. While private blockchains may serve as the perfect tools for large entities to collaborate with each other on a project or a number of projects, or for operating entities of one large group to work better together, the reality is that "blockchain" was intended to be an open-source decentralised system.

Horizontal *vs.* vertical regulation

Ultimately, there really is no other way to help an emerging industry to thrive than by introducing a clear regulatory framework. But how can we regulate a technology designed to be decentralised, through a centralised institution? When considering the concept of "cryptocurrency", it is useful to view such assets as a type of "application" using blockchain technology. Therefore, the regulation of blockchain could also be horizontally regulated through concentration on the hierarchy of identifiable layers involved in the technical structure of such applications. These layers include the platform level (the blockchain), the application level (the tools that run on the platform such as cryptocurrencies) and the overall blockchain ecosystem (the ledger or ledgers). Thus, horizontal regulation of blockchain technology would seek to regulate the infrastructure and as such, such a form of regulation is typically met with scepticism and criticism.

There is wide agreement that cryptocurrencies could be brought within the sphere of regulation without regulating cryptocurrencies *per se,* through the vertical regulation of the blockchain market itself. Vertical regulation follows a sectoral approach, establishing vertical lines respectively between the different intermediary services in the targeted ecosystem which build interfaces with traditional financial and economic sectors. Such a form of regulation is further jusitified in view of the reality that a rising number of cryptocurrency transactions are not performed "on-chain", i.e. directly on the blockchain network, but "offchain" via internal logging systems controlled by centralised cryptocurrency exchanges, wallets and payment companies.

Over the last two years, regulators and policymakers around the world have become increasingly interested in bringing cryptocurrencies and blockchain technology within the scope of regulation. When considering the initiatives which are currently being taken in jurisdictions around the globe, we see that the most widespread approach has been the issuance of warnings in relation to the risks inherent to cryptocurrencies and Initial Coin Offerings. While warnings and public statements are effective forms of pre-regulation of new technologies in the short term, the ever-increasing popularity of blockchain technology merits in-depth regulatory guidance to provide legal certainty to blockchain actors and users.

Existing legislation – fit for purpose?

In some countries (mainly in the EU), existing laws such as those tackling money-laundering, investment services and taxatio have been "recycled" to extend to cryptocurrency-related activities. Other countries such as Lithuania, Gibraltar and Switzerland have introduced new rules applicable to certain cryptocurrency activities such as Initial Coin Offerings. The legislators in these countries have acknowledged that certain "new" services which have come to fruition as a result of the capabilities of blockchain technology merit *sui generis* regulation.

Following its history of looking towards the future, the Maltese legislator has been touted for acknowledging emerging industries and embracing new technology and innovation. In fact, over the past 10 years, Malta has become the hub for the online gaming companies in Europe, an industry which is now of fundamental importance to the economy of the country. Now, Malta is proving to be the most ambitious country so far within the sphere of blockchain technology. Apart from issuing new rules applicable to Initial Coin Offerings and the provision of intermediary services incorporating cryptocurrencies, laws have also been introduced which cover the blockchain (Distributed Ledger Technology) sector in general. The latter is an example of the horizontal regulation contemplated above.

Going forward with caution

The blockchain ecosystem welcomes comprehensive regulation without which, people would be able to make ill-use of blockchain technology. The crux will be in the ability of legislators to strike a balance between the need for governance and the avoidance of heavy-handed government intervention which would kill this emerging technology. As with any other innovative technology or its application, one must carefully analyse the functional characteristics of various concepts under consideration and their implications and risks (real, not perceived), so that the introduced regulatory regime provides an appropriate and adequate response to regulatory concerns without over-regulation. We strongly believe that regulatory intervention should be functional, technology-neutral and based on regulatory goals and principles.

Joseph F. Borg
Tel: +356 9943 2727 / Email: joseph.borg@whpartners.eu
Joseph F. Borg is an Advocate and Partner at WH Partners, heading the
Blockchain Advisory and the Gaming and Gambling Advisory sections of
the firm. He also practises in the areas of Esports, Corporate, IT, Telecoms
and Intellectual Property Law. Joe lectures Gaming Law at the University of
Malta. He co-founded and is currently the Vice-President of Bitmalta, which
is a non-profit organisation with a mission to promoting and stimulating
discussion about blockchain technology and cryptocurrencies in Malta.

Tessa Schembri
Tel: +356 209 25100 / Email: tessa.schembri@whpartners.eu
Tessa Schembri is a legal trainee within the Blockchain advisory practice at
WH Partners. She is a Bachelor of Laws (Honours) graduate and is reading
for a Master of Advocacy degree from the University of Malta. Tessa has a
profound interest in Technology, Privacy and Gaming law, and has written an
undergraduate dissertation entitled 'The Legal Status of Cryptocurrencies in
the EU'.

WH Partners

Level 5 Quantum House, 75 Abate Rigord Street, Ta' Xbiex XBX 1120, Malta
Tel: +356 209 25100 / Fax: +356 209 25902 / URL: www.whpartners.eu

Argentina

Juan M. Diehl Moreno & Santiago E. Eraso Lomaquiz
Marval, O'Farrell & Mairal

Government attitude and definition

In Argentina, the government's attitude towards cryptocurrencies has been limited to the issuance of regulations related to their taxation and the prevention of money laundering and financing of terrorism.

The Argentine government has not implemented specific regulations on the exchange, issuance or, in general, the use of such digital assets, adopting an attitude of observation towards the development of the general impact of cryptocurrencies on the Argentine market.

In Argentina, cryptocurrencies such as Bitcoin are defined by the Financial Information Unit (*Unidad de Información Financiera*, "UIF" after its Spanish acronym) as a "digital representation of value that can be digitally traded and functions as a medium of exchange; and/or a unit of account; and/or a store of value, but does not have legal tender status in any jurisdiction and is neither issued nor guaranteed by any government or jurisdiction".

The Argentine Civil and Commercial Code (the "Civil Code") determines that individuals and legal entities are entitled to all the corresponding rights over the assets that are part of their property. In this regard, the Civil Code classifies assets into two categories: (i) tangible; and (ii) intangible.

As opposed to those that have physical entity, intangible assets – such as intellectual property and, in general, rights – do not materialise in the physical sphere. Thus, as a "digital representation of value", cryptocurrencies are intangible assets that are able to form part of individuals' and legal entities' property.

Section 765 of the Civil Code determines that only the Argentine "fiat" currency may be considered as "money" (*dinero*), thus excluding any possibility of including cryptocurrencies in such category.

In connection with the possibility of considering cryptocurrencies as "currency" under Argentine law, section 30 of the Argentine Central Bank's Charter (Law No. 24.144, the "Charter") provides a definition that excludes any type of instruments that: (i) have no legal tender directly or indirectly imposed by its issuer; or (ii) are not issued with nominal values lower than 10 times the amount of the highest national money bill in circulation. Thus, so far, this provision excludes the possibility of considering several cryptocurrencies as "currency" (*moneda*) under Argentine law. Moreover, extensive interpretations of Section 30 of the Charter are prohibited due to its monetary public order nature.

In this regard, the Central Bank issued in May, 2014, a non-binding press communication stating that virtual currencies are neither issued by itself nor any other international monetary authority and, thus, have no legal tender and are not guaranteed by any government.

Nevertheless, we have not yet seen any local precedents or governmental decisions/ communications in connection with any cryptocurrency issued by foreign authorities.

Government backing for cryptocurrencies

In Argentina, there are no cryptocurrencies backed by either the Argentine Government or the Argentine Central Bank.

Cryptocurrency regulation

Cryptocurrencies are not prohibited in Argentina. For the time being, the only specific regulations related to cryptocurrencies are UIF's Resolution 300/2014 (hereinafter, "UIF Resolution"), which implements additional reporting obligations to certain obliged subjects under the Anti-Money Laundering Law No. 25,246 (hereinafter, the "AML Law") (please see "Money transmission laws and anti-money laundering", below), and Law No. 27,430 (hereinafter, the "Tax Reform Law") (please see "Taxation", below).

Sales regulation

There is no specific regulation applicable to the sale of Bitcoin or other tokens under securities laws or commodities laws in Argentina.

Considering the lack of a central issuing authority, bitcoins cannot be classified as securities. Under Argentine law, securities are essentially negotiable instruments to which their issuers incorporate credit rights. Nevertheless, this conclusion may not be extended to other cryptocurrencies (*tokens*) issued by a centralised entity.

Following the example of Securities and Exchange Commissions in other parts of the world, such as of the United Kingdom, the USA, China, Hong Kong and Brazil, the Argentine Securities and Exchange Commission (hereinafter, the "CNV" after its acronym in Spanish), issued a communique on Initial Coin Offerings (hereinafter, "ICOs") to warn investors of the potential risks.

The CNV clarified that ICOs would not, in principle, be subject to capital markets' regulations. Nevertheless, it also stated that certain ICOs may be subject to the control of the CNV, depending on their structure and particular characteristics.

The communique also warned investors about the following potential risks associated with ICOs: (a) lack of specific regulations; (b) price volatility and liquidity risks; (c) probability of fraud; (d) inadequate access to relevant information; (e) early stage of the projects; (f) probability of technological and infrastructure failures; and (g) transnational nature of transactions involving ICOs.

Although the CNV states that ICOs are not – in principle – subject to specific CNV control, the communique clarified that claims may be filed with the CNV in those cases where there is a suspicion that an ICO could be fraudulent.

Taxation

Among the amendments introduced by the Tax Reform Law, the taxable income derived from the commercialisation of "digital currencies" was incorporated to the Income Tax Law (hereinafter, the "ITL"). One of the main objectives of the tax reform is to tax financial income.

Neither the Tax Reform Law nor the ITL provide a definition of digital currencies, or the scope that such concept comprises. Please note the corresponding regulations of the Tax Reform Law have not been issued yet. We understand that the meaning of such concept should be the same as the one of "virtual currencies" defined by the UIF Resolution and, therefore, such Resolution should apply to cryptocurrencies.

The ITL also determined that if the issuer of the cryptocurrencies is domiciled in Argentina, then an Argentine-sourced income would be generated as a consequence of the exchange thereof.

Provided that cryptocurrencies fall within the definition of intangible assets, the exchange of cryptocurrencies should not be impacted by Value Added Tax.

In general, and in addition to the aforementioned examples, cryptocurrencies must be taxed like any other intangible asset.

Money transmission laws and anti-money laundering requirements

The AML Law lists a number of persons – including financial entities, broker-dealers, credit card companies, insurance companies, public notaries, and certain government registries and agencies – that have, among other things, specific reporting obligations under the AML Law (Obliged Subjects) and provides for certain general obligations, including: applying KYC procedures; reporting to the UIF any transaction suspected of money laundering (ML) or terrorism financing (TF); and abstaining from disclosing to their clients or third parties the activities performed in compliance with that statute.

As explained above, one of the few regulations on cryptocurrencies in Argentina is the UIF Resolution, which requires most of the Obliged Subjects under the AML Law to report all the transactions performed with cryptocurrencies, regardless of their amount.

Following the Financial Action Task Force's guidelines, the UIF also warns Obliged Subjects about the risks involved in transactions with cryptocurrencies. In so doing, the UIF also requires the Obliged Subjects listed in the UIF Resolution to strictly monitor any transactions performed with cryptocurrencies by their clients.

Promotion and testing

There are currently no "sandbox" or other programmes intended to promote research and investment in cryptocurrency in Argentina.

Except for the tax (please see "Taxation", above) and anti-money laundering (please see "Money transmission laws and anti-money laundering", above) regulations, Argentine regulatory authorities have adopted a wait-and-see strategy in connection with cryptocurrencies.

Nevertheless, the Argentine Central Bank has created several research groups – among which there is a group specifically dedicated to cryptocurrencies and blockchain technologies – integrated by members of both public and private entities with the aim of analysing potential regulatory modifications to enable the use of new technologies within the financial services industry.

Ownership and licensing requirements

Although there are no specific prohibitions, given the current lack of certainty in connection with the possibility of considering certain cryptocurrencies as securities under the Capital

Markets Law No. 26,831 (hereinafter, the "CML"), regulated entities subject to the CNV's control – such as investment managers, investment advisors and fund managers – tend not to operate with such assets.

Additionally, the formal requirements for the operational activities of such players have not been designed to address cryptocurrencies. Thus, several regulations may act as practical restrictions that hinder the possibility to operate with such digital assets.

Mining

Mining Bitcoin and other cryptocurrencies is permitted in Argentina, although there are currently no specific regulations on such activity.

Border restrictions and declaration

There are no border restrictions or obligations to declare cryptocurrency holdings in Argentina.

Reporting requirements

There are no reporting requirements for cryptocurrency payments made in excess of a certain value.

Currently, the only specific reporting requirements in connection with cryptocurrencies are regulated by the UIF Resolution (please see "Money transmission laws and anti-money laundering", above) and the Tax Reform Law (please see "Taxation", above).

Estate planning and testamentary succession

Following our explanations in "Government attitude and definition" above, cryptocurrencies must be treated as intangible assets for the purposes of estate planning and testamentary succession. Such treatment may potentially change in the future in connection with tokens issued through ICOs, subject to the CNV's view on their legal nature under the CML.

Juan M. Diehl Moreno
Tel: +54 11 4310 0100 ext. 1807 / Email: jd@marval.com
Juan M. Diehl Moreno has been a partner of Marval, O'Farrell & Mairal since 2006. He specialises in foreign investments, M&A, banking, fintech, and capital markets law. Several guides of the legal profession have recognised Mr Diehl Moreno for several years as one of the leading lawyers in his fields of practice in the Argentine legal sector. From 2000 to 2001, he was a foreign associate at Sidley & Austin (New York office). He graduated from the Universidad Católica Argentina in 1993, and he obtained a Master's degree in Business Law from Universidad Austral in 1996 and an LL.M. with honours from Northwestern University School of Law in 2000. He has lectured at several conferences in Argentina and abroad and has published various articles in his field of expertise.

Santiago Eraso Lomaquiz
Tel: +54 11 4310 0100 ext. 1374 / Email: seel@marval.com
Santiago Eraso Lomaquiz joined Marval, O'Farrell & Mairal in 2011 and is currently a member of the Information Technology and Privacy and Intellectual Property departments, where he is in charge of litigation. He has experience advising companies in matters related to Information Technologies and communication, digital and electronic signature, e-commerce, intellectual and industrial property and personal data protection. Santiago specialises in legal and regulatory framework applied to technologies in the financial sector. He graduated with a law degree from the *Universidad Austral* in 2014 and has been a member of the High Technology Law Commission of the *Colegio de Abogados de la Ciudad de Buenos Aires* since 2011. He has been awarded by the *Comité de Abogados de Bancos de la República Argentina* and by the *Colegio de Abogados de la Ciudad de Buenos Aires* for his research work in his specialisation.

Marval, O'Farrell & Mairal

Leandro N. Alem 882, Buenos Aires, Argentina
Tel: +54 11 4310 0100 / Fax: +54 11 4310 0200 / URL: www.marval.com

Australia

Peter Reeves & Georgina Willcock
Gilbert + Tobin

Government attitude and definition

The past few years have seen a sharp rise in the creation and use of cryptocurrencies in Australia, with companies such as Power Ledger and Havven raising millions through their Australia-based initial coin offerings (**ICO**). The Commonwealth Government of Australia (**Government**) has shared a broader commitment to facilitate growth and innovation within the technology and cryptocurrency sector whilst also increasing its regulatory involvement.

To date, the Government has taken a largely non-interventionist approach to the regulation of cryptocurrency, allowing the landscape to evolve at a faster rate than its regulatory response. Australian law does not currently equate digital currency with fiat currency and does not treat cryptocurrency as "money".

The Governor of the Reserve Bank of Australia (**RBA**), Australia's central bank, stated during the 2017 Australian Payment Summit that the RBA has no immediate plans to issue a digital dollar akin to money. Terming it an 'eAUD', the Governor noted that the rise of new technology associated with cryptocurrencies has the capacity to challenge the role of traditional financial institutions with regard to payments, but that there is currently no public policy case for the RBA to issue an eAUD. Despite this, the Governor indicated that the RBA would be continuing to research this area and highlighted an ongoing study of the use of a central-bank issued digital dollar in relation to settlement arrangements.

While the Government has not intervened in cryptocurrencies and related activities to the extent that foreign government bodies have done in jurisdictions such as China or South Korea, there has been general clarification of the application of Australian regulatory regimes to the sector. For example, the Government recently passed the *Anti-Money Laundering and Counter-Terrorism Financing Amendment Act* 2017 (**AML/CTF Amendment Act**), which brought cryptocurrencies within the scope of Australia's anti-money laundering regime. This recognised the movement towards digital currencies becoming a popular method of paying for goods and services and transferring value in the Australian economy, but also posing significant money laundering and terrorism financing risks.

The Government has also been widely supportive of the new technologies in the cryptocurrency space. In November 2017, the Government awarded a $2.57 million grant through its Smart Cities and Suburbs program to a project partly run by Power Ledger. The project is trialling the use of blockchain-powered distributed energy and water systems.

Cryptocurrency regulation

While there have been recent amendments to various pieces of legislation to accommodate the use of cryptocurrencies, these have predominantly focused on the transaction relationships, such as the issuing and exchanging process, rather than the cryptocurrencies themselves.

Australia's primary corporate, markets, consumer credit and financial services regulator, the Australian Securities and Investments Commission (**ASIC**), holds the view that legislative obligations and requirements are technology-neutral. As such, the existing regulatory framework applies irrespective of the mode of technology that is being used to provide a regulated service. Therefore, while there hasn't been any legislation created to deal with cryptocurrencies as a discrete area of law, this does not hinder it from being captured within existing regimes under Australian law. A key example is that cryptocurrency which is characterised as a financial product under the *Corporations Act* 2001 (Cth) (**Corporations Act**) will fall within the scope of Australia's existing financial services regulatory regime. This is discussed in more detail below.

Generally, to the extent that an entity implements blockchain or other distributed ledger technology (**DLT**) in supporting its cryptocurrency, there are various obligations with which to comply. In March 2017, ASIC released an information sheet (*INFO 219 Evaluating distributed ledger technology*), which provides guidance for businesses considering operating market infrastructure, or providing financial or consumer credit services using DLT. There is a general obligation that entities relying on technology in connection with the provision of a regulated service must have the necessary organisational competence, and must have in place adequate technological resources and risk-management plans. While the existing regulatory framework is sufficient to accommodate current implementations of DLT, as the technology matures, additional regulatory considerations will arise.

Various cryptocurrency networks have also implemented 'smart' or self-executing contracts. These are permitted in Australia under the *Electronic Transactions Act* 1999 (Cth) (**ETA**) and the equivalent Australian state and territory legislation. The ETA provides a legal framework to enable electronic commerce to operate in the same way as paper-based transactions. Under the ETA, self-executing contracts are permitted in Australia, provided they meet all the traditional elements of a legal contract.

Sales regulation

The sale of cryptocurrency through an ICO is regulated by Australia's existing financial services regulatory regime. Core considerations for issuers are outlined below.

Licensing

Of particular concern to those dealing with cryptocurrencies is whether a cryptocurrency (including those offered during an ICO) constitutes a financial product and therefore triggers financial services licensing and disclosure requirements. Entities carrying on a financial services business in Australia must hold an Australian financial services licence (**AFSL**) or be exempt. The definitions of 'financial product' or 'financial service' under the Corporations Act are broad and ASIC has indicated in an information sheet issued in May 2018, *INFO 225 Initial coin offerings* (**Info 225**), that cryptocurrency with similar features to existing financial products or securities will trigger the relevant regulatory obligations.

Within INFO 225, ASIC indicated that the legal status of cryptocurrency is dependent upon the structure of the ICO and the rights attaching to the coins or tokens. Depending on the circumstances, coins or tokens may constitute interests in managed investment schemes (collective investment vehicles), securities, derivatives, or fall into a category of more generally defined financial products, all of which are subject to the Australian financial services regulatory regime. Entities offering such coins or tokens will need to comply with the regulatory requirements under the Corporations Act which generally include disclosure, registration and licensing obligations. An entity which facilitates payments by cryptocurrencies may also be required to hold an AFSL and the operator of a cryptocurrency exchange may be required to hold an Australian market licence if the coins or tokens traded on the exchange constitute financial products.

With the exception of China and South Korea, ASIC's regulatory guidance is consistent with the position of other international regulators. For example, the financial regulator in Hong Kong has outlined situations where cryptocurrency may be a financial product. ASIC has also recommended that companies wishing to conduct an ICO contact its Innovation Hub (discussed in detail below, 'Promotion and testing') for informal assistance. This reflects its willingness to build greater investor confidence around cryptocurrency as an asset class. However, to date there has not yet been a regulated financial product ICO in Australia.

Marketing

ASIC's recognition that an ICO may involve an offer of financial products has clear implications for the marketing of an ICO. For example, an offer of a financial product to a retail client (with some exceptions) must be accompanied by a regulated disclosure document (e.g., a product disclosure statement or a prospectus and a financial services guide) that satisfies the content requirements of the Corporations Act and regulatory guidance published by ASIC. Such a disclosure document must set out prescribed information, including the provider's fee structure, to assist a client to decide whether to acquire the cryptocurrency from the provider. In some instances, the marketing activity itself may cause the ICO to be an offer of a regulated financial product.

Under the Corporations Act, depending on the minimum amount of funds invested per investor and whether the investor is a 'sophisticated investor' or wholesale client, an offer of financial products may not require regulated disclosure.

Cross-border issues

Carrying on a financial services business in Australia will require a foreign financial services provider (**FFSP**) to hold an AFSL, unless relief is granted. Entities, including FFSPs, should note that the Corporations Act may apply to an ICO regardless of whether it was created and offered from Australia or overseas. Australia has cooperation (passporting) arrangements with regulators in foreign jurisdictions (including the United States of America and the United Kingdom), which enable FFSPs regulated in those jurisdictions to provide financial services in Australia without holding an AFSL. However, the passporting relief is currently only available in relation to the provision of services to wholesale clients (i.e. accredited investors), and the FFSP must only provide the services it is authorised to provide in its home jurisdiction. The passporting relief is currently under review ahead of its expiry in October 2018.

Foreign companies taken to be carrying on a business in Australia, including by issuing cryptocurrency or operating a platform developed using ICO proceeds, may be required to either establish a local presence (i.e., register with ASIC and create a branch) or incorporate a subsidiary. Broadly, the greater the level of system, repetition or continuity associated with an entity's business activities in Australia, the greater the likelihood that registration will be required. Generally, a company holding an AFSL will be carrying on a business in Australia and will trigger the requirement.

Promoters should also be aware that if they wish to market their cryptocurrency to Australian residents, and the coins or tokens are considered a financial product under the Corporations Act, they will not be permitted to market the products unless the requisite licensing and disclosure requirements are met. Generally, a service provider from outside of Australia may respond to requests for information and issue products to an Australian resident if the resident makes the first (unsolicited) approach and there has been no conduct on the part of the issuer designed to induce the investor to make contact, or activities that could be misconstrued as the provider inducing the investor to make contact.

Design and distribution obligations and product intervention powers

The Government has released an *Exposure Draft of Treasury Laws Amendment (Design and Distribution Obligations and Product Intervention Powers) Bill* 2017 (the **Bill**), which may impact the way cryptocurrencies are structured and ICOs conducted in future. The Bill proposes to introduce new design and distribution obligations in relation to financial products as well as provide ASIC with temporary product intervention powers where there is a risk of significant consumer detriment. The new arrangements aim to ensure that financial products are targeted at the correct category of potential investors. At the time of writing, ASIC has yet to release guidance on the way it might interpret its powers, but it is highly likely to impact marketing and distribution practices in the cryptocurrency sector.

Consumer law

Even if an ICO is not regulated under the Corporations Act, it may still be subject to other regulation and laws, including the Australian Consumer Law set out at Schedule 2 to the *Competition and Consumer Act* 2010 (Cth) (**ACL**) relating to the offer of services or products to Australian consumers. The ACL prohibits misleading or deceptive conduct in a range of circumstances including in the context of marketing and advertising. As such, care must be taken in ICO promotional material to ensure that buyers are not misled or deceived. In addition, promoters and sellers are prohibited from engaging in unconscionable conduct and must ensure the coins or tokens issued are fit for their intended purpose.

The protections of the ACL are generally reflected in the *Australian Securities and Investments Commission Act* 2001 (Cth) (**ASIC Act**), providing substantially similar protection to investors in financial products or services.

ASIC has also recently received delegated powers from the Australian Competition and Consumer Commission to enable it to take action against misleading or deceptive conduct in marketing or issuing in ICOs (regardless of whether it involves a financial product). ASIC has indicated misleading or deceptive conduct in relation to ICOs may include:

- using social media to create the appearance of greater levels of public interest;
- creating the appearance of greater levels of buying and selling activity for an ICO or a crypto-asset by engaging in (or arranging for others to engage in) certain trading strategies;
- failing to disclose appropriate information about the ICO; or
- suggesting that the ICO is a regulated product or endorsed by a regulator when it is not.

ASIC has stated that it will use this power to issue further inquiries into ICO issuers and their advisers to identify potentially unlicensed and misleading conduct.

A range of consequences may apply for failing to comply with the ACL or the ASIC Act, including monetary penalties, injunctions, compensatory damages and costs orders.

Taxation

The taxation of cryptocurrency in Australia has been an area of much debate, despite recent attempts by the Australian Taxation Office (**ATO**) to clarify the operation of the tax law.

For income tax purposes, the ATO views cryptocurrency as an asset that is held or traded (rather than as money or a foreign currency).

Investors and holders of cryptocurrencies

The tax implications for investors or holders of cryptocurrency depends upon the intended use of that cryptocurrency. The summary below applies to investors who are Australian residents for tax purposes.

Investors in the business of trading cryptocurrencies (including funds) are likely to be subject to the trading stock provisions, much like a supermarket treats its goods for sale as trading stock. The gain and losses on the sale of cryptocurrencies will be taxable to such investors on "revenue account".

Otherwise, the ATO has indicated that cryptocurrency will likely be a capital gains tax (**CGT**) asset. The gain on its disposal will be subject to CGT. Capital gains may be discounted under the CGT discount provisions, so long as the investor satisfies the conditions for the discount. It is unresolved in Australia whether cryptocurrencies are eligible to be CGT assets (and subject to the CGT discount) as a matter of law, considering most users of cryptocurrency have a profit-making purpose by way of selling their coins or tokens (i.e., they hold the cryptocurrency on revenue account).

Capital losses made on cryptocurrencies which are "personal use" assets are disregarded. This includes cryptocurrencies acquired or kept for personal use or consumption (i.e., to buy goods or services). Capital gains on personal use assets are only disregarded where the asset was acquired for less than A$10,000.

Issuers of cryptocurrencies

In the context of an ICO, a coin issuance by an entity that is either an Australian tax resident, or acting through an Australian "permanent establishment", will likely be taxable in Australia. The current corporate tax rate in Australia is between 27.5% and 30%. If the issued coins are characterised as equity for tax purposes, the ICO proceeds should not be taxable to the issuer, but all future returns to the token holders will be treated as dividends.

Australian Goods and Services Tax (**GST**)

Supplies and acquisitions of digital currency made from 1 July 2017 are not subject to GST on the basis that they will be input taxed financial supplies. Consequently, suppliers of digital currency will not be required to charge GST on these supplies, and a purchaser would not be entitled to GST refunds (i.e., input tax credits) for these corresponding acquisitions. On the basis that digital currency is a method of payment, as an alternative to money, the normal GST rules apply to the payment or receipt of digital currency for goods and services.

The term "digital currency" in the GST legislation requires that it is a digital unit of value that has all the following characteristics:

*   it is fungible and can be provided as payment for any type of purchase;
*   it is generally available to the public free of any substantial restrictions;
*   it is not denominated in any country's currency;
*   the value is not derived from or dependent on anything else; and
*   it does not give an entitlement or privileges to receive something else.

Enforcement

The ATO has recently announced the creation of a specialist task force to tackle cryptocurrency tax evasion. With the broader regulatory trend around the globe moving from guidance to enforcement, it is likely that the ATO will also begin enforcing tax liabilities more aggressively.

In relation to mining cryptocurrency, the ATO has also released guidance in relation to how these activities will be taxed. This is discussed in 'Mining', below.

Money transmission laws and anti-money laundering requirements

In 2017, the Government passed the AML/CTF Amendment Act, which brought cryptocurrencies and tokens within the scope of Australia's anti-money laundering and counter-terrorism financing (**AML/CTF**) regulatory framework. The amendments came into force on 3 April 2018 and focus on the point of intersection between cryptocurrencies and the regulated financial sector, namely digital currency exchanges. The Australian Transaction Reports and Analysis Centre (**AUSTRAC**) has outlined transitional arrangements for existing and new digital currency exchange (**DCE**) providers.

Broadly, DCE providers are now required to register with AUSTRAC in order to operate, with a penalty of up to two years' imprisonment or a fine of up to A$105,000, or both, for failing to register. Registered exchanges will be required to implement know-your-customer processes to adequately verify the identity of their customers, with ongoing obligations to monitor and report suspicious and large transactions. Exchange operators are also required to keep certain records relating to customer identification and transactions for up to seven years.

Bringing DCE providers within the ambit of the AML/CTF framework is intended to help legitimise the use of cryptocurrency while protecting the integrity of the financial system in which it operates.

Promotion and testing

Regulators in Australia have generally been receptive to fintech and innovation. While there are no programmes specifically promoting research and investment in cryptocurrency, both ASIC and AUSTRAC have established Innovation Hubs designed to assist fintech businesses more broadly in understanding their obligations under Australian law.

ASIC Innovation Hub

The ASIC Innovation Hub is designed to foster innovation that could benefit consumers by helping Australian fintech start-ups navigate the Australian regulatory system. The Innovation Hub provides tailored information and access to informal assistance intended to streamline the AFSL process for innovative fintech start-ups, which could include cryptocurrency-related businesses.

In December 2016, ASIC made certain class orders establishing a fintech licensing exemption and released *Regulatory Guide 257*, which details ASIC's framework for fintech businesses to test certain financial services, financial products and credit activities without holding an AFSL or Australian credit licence by relying on the class orders (referred to as the regulatory sandbox). There are strict eligibility requirements for both the type of businesses that can enter the regulatory sandbox and the products and services that qualify for the licensing exemption. There are restrictions on how many persons can be provided with a financial product or service, and caps on the value of the financial products or services which can be provided. Businesses may only rely conditionally on the relief for 12 months.

The framework relating to ASIC's regulatory sandbox has been subject to review. The Government recently closed its consultation on draft legislation and regulations outlining the framework for an enhanced regulatory framework that allows businesses to test a wider range of products and services for a longer period of time. ASIC has also released a consultation paper suggesting that no changes to its existing fintech licensing exemption will be made.

Beyond this, ASIC has engaged with regulators overseas to deepen its understanding of innovation in financial services, including in relation to cryptocurrencies. ASIC and the United Kingdom's Financial Conduct Authority have signed an Enhanced Cooperation Agreement, which allows the two regulators to, amongst other things, information-share, refer innovative businesses to each regulator's respective regulatory sandbox, and conduct joint policy work. ASIC currently has either information-sharing or cooperation agreements with regulators in Hong Kong, Singapore, Canada, Kenya and Indonesia. ASIC is also a signatory to the IOSCO Multilateral Memorandum of Understanding, which has committed over 100 regulators to mutually assist and cooperate with each other, particularly in relation to the enforcement of securities laws.

AUSTRAC Innovation Hub

AUSTRAC's Fintel Alliance is a private-public partnership seeking to develop 'smarter regulation'. This includes setting up an innovation hub targeted at improving the fintech sector's relationship with the government and regulators. The hub will provide a regulatory sandbox for fintech businesses to test financial products and services without risking regulatory action or costs.

AUSTRAC has also implemented a new dedicated webpage providing information about the AML/CTF regime and AUSTRAC's role to assist businesses wishing to create a new financial service product or to understand their AML/CTF obligations. In its annual report for 2016–17, AUSTRAC noted that the webpage had been successful, garnering over 40 direct enquiries from entities developing innovative new approaches to providing "designated services" as defined under the *Anti-money Laundering and Counter-terrorism Financing Act 2006* (Cth) (**AML/CTF Act**). As discussed above, designated services now include the provision of DCE services, and consequently DCE providers may contact AUSTRAC through the webpage to understand their regulatory obligations.

Ownership and licensing requirements

At the time of writing, there are currently no restrictions on investment managers owning cryptocurrencies for investment purposes.

With respect to investment advice, where a cryptocurrency held is a financial product, investment advisors will be deemed to be providing financial product advice under the Corporations Act and will need to hold an AFSL or be exempt. ASIC has provided significant guidance in relation to complying with the relevant advice, conduct and disclosure obligations, as well as the conflicted remuneration provisions under the Corporations Act.

Against the backdrop of the *Royal Commission into Misconduct in the Banking, Superannuation and Financial Services Industry* and the broader innovation agenda of the Government, Australia has seen a rapidly rising interest in robo-advice or digital advice models. The provision of robo-advice is where algorithms and technology provide automated financial product advice without a human advisor. For investment or fund businesses seeking to operate in Australia by providing digital or hybrid advice (including with respect to investing in cryptocurrencies), there are licensing requirements under the Corporations Act. ASIC has released *Regulatory Guide 255: providing digital financial product advice to retail clients*, which details issues that digital advice providers need to consider generally, during the AFSL application stage and when providing digital financial product advice to retail clients.

Mining

At the time of writing, there are no prohibitions on mining bitcoin or other cryptocurrencies in Australia.

Cryptocurrency mining taxation

The ATO has released some guidance on its approach to taxation in relation to cryptocurrency mining activities. The summary below applies to miners or business owners who are Australian residents for tax purposes.

Income derived by a taxpayer from 'carrying on a business' of mining cryptocurrency must be included in the calculation of their assessable income. Whether or not a taxpayer's activities amount to carrying on a business is "a question of fact and degree", and is ultimately determined by a weighing up of the taxpayer's individual facts and circumstances. Generally (but not exclusively), where the activities are undertaken for a profit-making purpose, are repetitious, involve ongoing effort, and include business documentation, the activities would amount to "carrying on a business".

Cryptocurrency miners would also be subject to tax on any gains or profits derived from transferring cryptocurrency mined to a third party.

Where carrying on a business, outgoing and losses would be deductible to the taxpayer (subject to integrity measures and the 'non-commercial loss' rules).

Whether or not GST is payable by a cryptocurrency miner on its supply of new cryptocurrency (e.g., by way of an ICO) depends on a number of factors, including its specific features, whether the miner is registered for GST, and whether the supply is made in the course of the miner's enterprise.

The specific features of cryptocurrency include it being a type of security or other derivative; it being "digital currency" as defined in the GST legislation (see 'Taxation', above); or it providing a right or entitlement to goods or services. If the cryptocurrency is "digital currency", its supply will not be subject to any GST because it will be an input taxed financial supply (assuming the other requirements are satisfied).

A cryptocurrency miner would generally be required to register for GST if its annual GST turnover is $75,000 or more, excluding the value of its supplies of digital currencies and other input-taxed supplies. However, a miner who does not satisfy this GST registration threshold may nevertheless elect to register for GST in order to claim from the ATO full or reduced input tax credits (i.e., GST refunds) for the GST cost of its business acquisitions (but acquisitions that relate to the sales or acquisitions of digital currencies are *prima facie* non-creditable or non-refundable).

Cybersecurity

More generally, with the rise of cloud-based bitcoin mining enterprises in Australia, mining businesses should carefully consider cybersecurity issues in relation to mining activities. For example, earlier in 2018, employees at the Bureau of Meteorology were investigated after breaching information technology security systems by allegedly mining cryptocurrency using bureau technology.

In its Corporate Plan 2017–18 to 2020–21, ASIC signalled that cyber resilience would be a key focus area for the regulator, and to date has released regulatory guidance indicating its expectations for licensees' cloud computing security arrangements. Two reports, namely 429 *Cyber resilience: Health check* and 555 *Cyber resilience of firms in Australia's financial markets,* examine and provide examples of good practices identified across the financial services industry. The reports contain questions that board members and senior management of financial organisations should ask when considering cyber resilience.

Border restrictions and declaration

There are currently no border restrictions or obligations to declare cryptocurrency holdings when entering or leaving Australia.

The AML/CTF Act mandates that both individuals and businesses must submit reports where physical currency in excess of A$10,000 (or foreign currency equivalent) is brought into or taken out of Australia. Significantly, this requirement has so far been restricted to 'physical currency', which AUSTRAC has defined as being any coin or printed note of Australia or a foreign country that is designated as legal tender, and is circulated, customarily used and accepted as a medium of exchange in the country of issue. Although recent discourse indicates that some governments have created or are attempting to issue official cryptocurrencies, the intangible nature of cryptocurrency seems to remain a bar to cryptocurrency being captured by declaration obligations under the AML/CTF Act.

It should be noted that the AML/CTF Act was recently amended to address some aspects of cryptocurrency transfer and exchange; however, this amendment did not see the scope of AML/CTF regulation widen the border restrictions. At the time of writing, there appears to be no indication that any such further amendment to include border restrictions is being contemplated.

Reporting requirements

The AML/CTF Act imposes obligations on entities that provide 'designated services', including the provision of DCE services. These obligations include record-keeping and reporting requirements. AUSTRAC has released draft AML/CTF rules, which outline reportable details for matters including but not limited to threshold transaction reports (**TTRs**). TTRs will be required to be submitted where transactions over A$10,000 have occurred.

Reportable information includes, among other details, the denomination or code of the digital currency and the number of digital currency units, a description of the digital currency including details of the backing asset or thing (if known), the Internet Protocol address information of the payee, the social media identifiers of the payee, and the unique identifiers relating to the digital currency wallet of the payee.

Consultation on the draft AML/CTF rules closed in February 2018. At the time of writing, no further updates have been released.

Estate planning and testamentary succession

To date, there has been no explicit regulation or case law surrounding the treatment of cryptocurrency in Australian succession law. Generally, if estate plans do not cater for cryptocurrency and steps are not taken to ensure executors can access a deceased's cryptocurrency, it may not pass to the beneficiaries.

A will should be drafted to give the executor authority to deal with digital assets. As cryptocurrencies are generally held anonymously, a will should also establish the existence of the cryptocurrency as an asset to be distributed to beneficiaries. A method must also be established to ensure passwords to digital wallets and external drives storing cryptocurrency are accessible by a trusted representative. Unlike a bank account which can be frozen upon death, anyone can access a digital wallet, so care should be taken to ensure external drives and passwords are not easily accessible on the face of the will. This may include providing a memorandum of passwords and accounts to the executor to be placed in a safe custody facility which remains unopened until a will is called upon.

There may also be tax implications arising for the beneficiaries of cryptocurrencies, which are similar to the tax implications for cryptocurrency holders. See 'Taxation' above, for further details.

Additional authors

Candice Fraser, Marcus Wong, Robert O'Grady, Emily Shen and Hannah Stern.

Peter Reeves
Tel: +61 2 9263 4290 / Email: preeves@gtlaw.com.au
Peter is a partner in Gilbert + Tobin's Corporate Advisory group and is an expert and market-leading practitioner in financial services regulation and digital assets. He leads the Financial Services and fintech practices at G+T. Peter advises domestic and off-shore corporates, financial institutions, funds, managers and other market participants in relation to establishing, structuring and operating financial services sector businesses in Australia. He also advises across a range of issues relevant to the fintech and digital sectors, including platform establishment, payment solutions, blockchain solutions, digital fundraising and digital currencies.

Georgina Willcock
Tel: +61 2 9263 4202 / Email: gwillcock@gtlaw.com.au
Georgina is a lawyer in Gilbert + Tobin's Corporate Advisory group with a focus on the Australian financial services laws, funds management and anti-money laundering regulation.

Georgina has been involved in a range of transactions and advisory matters, including in relation to the establishment and operation of retail and wholesale funds, private mergers and acquisitions, and compliance with the *Corporations Act* 2001 (Cth) and *Anti-money Laundering and Counter-terrorism Financing Act* 2006 (Cth). Georgina has also advised on issues relevant to the fintech and digital sectors, including platform establishment, blockchain solutions, digital fundraising and digital currencies.

Georgina is involved in a number of innovation initiatives co-ordinated by Gilbert + Tobin. She participated in a legal hackathon, which Gilbert + Tobin hosted in conjunction with Westpac and LegalVision in January 2016 and which won the award for Innovation in use of Technology at the *Financial Times* Innovative Lawyers Awards Asia-Pacific 2016.

Gilbert + Tobin

Level 35, Tower Two, International Towers Sydney / 200 Barangaroo Avenue, Barangaroo NSW 2000, Australia
Tel: +61 2 9263 4000 / Fax: +61 2 9263 4111 / URL: www.gtlaw.com.au

Austria

Ursula Rath & Thomas Kulnigg
Schönherr Rechtsanwälte GmbH

Government attitude and definition

The Austrian government closely monitors developments in the area of alternative means of financing through distributed ledger technology and other digital assets, such as initial coin offerings ("ICOs") or initial token offerings ("ITOs"). It tends to apply an open approach to cryptocurrencies, new technologies and fintech, while at the same time stressing that integrity, security and investor protection must not be compromised.

While Austrian law does not prohibit cryptocurrencies such as Bitcoin, Ethereum, Ripple or Litecoin, there is currently no specific legislation applicable to cryptocurrencies either.

Although there is no statutory definition of cryptocurrencies, according to the Austrian regulator – the Austrian Financial Markets Authority (*Finanzmarktaufsicht*; FMA) – cryptocurrencies are typically characterised as follows:

*   they are not issued by any central bank or governmental authority;
*   new units of value are typically created using a predefined procedure within a computer network (commonly referred to as "mining");
*   there is no central authority which verifies or manages transactions;
*   transactions are recorded on a decentralised, publicly held ledger (commonly referred to as "blockchain") and, once executed, cannot be revoked; and
*   electronic wallets may be used to store and manage virtual currencies (commonly referred to as "wallet").

As follows from the above, cryptocurrency is currently not treated as "money" or otherwise given equal status with domestic or foreign fiat currency in Austria.

Likewise, there are not yet any cryptocurrencies which are backed by the Austrian government or the Austrian National Bank.

Cryptocurrency regulation

Since there is currently no specific legislation applicable to cryptocurrencies, the general legal framework also applies to cryptocurrencies and the FMA is known to apply a "technology-neutral" supervisory approach to regulation.

From an Austrian financial services regulatory perspective, cryptocurrencies are currently neither treated as financial instruments (in particular, not as securities or derivatives) nor as currency (domestic or foreign), but as commodities. It is worth noting, however, that derivative instruments referencing cryptocurrencies or tokens will qualify as financial instruments under MiFID II and hence will be covered by financial services regulation under MiFID II/MiFIR.

While commodities as such are not subject to supervision by the FMA, this does not mean that business activities involving cryptocurrencies are entirely outside the Austrian regulatory regime. Depending on their features/content, the operation of various business models based on cryptocurrencies may trigger licensing requirements under the Austrian Banking Act (BWG; *Bankwesengesetz*), the Austrian Alternative Investment Fund Manager Act (AIFMG; *Alternative Investmentfonds Manager-Gesetz*), the Austrian Payment Services Act (ZaDiG; *Zahlungsdienstegesetz*)) and/or prospectus requirements under the Austrian Capital Markets Act (KMG; *Kapitalmarktgesetz*).

The FMA has published further guidance on the regulatory treatment of certain activities around cryptocurrencies, ICOs and ITOs on the fintech navigator section of its website at https://www.fma.gv.at/en/cross-sectoral-topics/fintech/fintech-navigator/.

Key areas to note are the following:

- Purely technical services do not require a licence under financial services regulation. If, however, a technical billing service also includes transfer of funds, this would no longer be considered a purely technical service and would need to be tested against licensing requirements under the Austrian Banking Act, the Austrian Payment Services Act and the Austrian E-Money Act.

- Alternative currencies, payment instruments or means of payment may trigger a licensing requirement if they are intended for payment at third parties, and the network within which they can be used to purchase goods/services is large in terms of geographical reach, type of products/services and/or number of accepting parties (there is a licensing exception for restricted networks, but this has become increasingly strict following the implementation of Directive 2015/2366/EU ("PSD II")). Also, if accounts are operated in connection with currencies, payment instruments or means of payment through which payments are made, the entity holding the accounts may be obliged to become licensed as a payment service provider.

- If capital is raised in order to invest proceeds into cryptocurrencies or mining, this could be regulated as a banking business (deposits business) or as managing an alternative investment fund under the Austrian Alternative Investment Fund Managers Act if funds are invested in accordance with a defined investment strategy, and returns in each case depend on the performance of the underlying investment. If the capital-raising is structured through the issuance of shares or similar participation in a corporation or partnership, this may also trigger prospectus requirements under Austrian securities laws (see "Sales regulation", below).

- Online platforms for acquiring virtual currencies which also settle/process payments in domestic or foreign currency through their own accounts may require a licence under the Austrian Payment Services Act. Generally, if funds pass through the provider's accounts, this will trigger a licence requirement under payment services regulations. Some online service providers therefore cooperate with licensed partners and transfer funds via their accounts.

- Brokers of new or alternative payment methods may need to become licensed if they are considering intermediating deposits or loans/insurance. This would be the case if an app or online platform was linked to a specific deposit/current account. The mere listing of product information, for example, via product comparison portals, would not require a licence.

- While merely buying and selling virtual currencies in one's own name and for one's own account generally does not trigger a licence requirement, the buying and selling of virtual currencies may form part of business models that do require a licence. For instance, the operation of a bitcoin vending machine may trigger a licence requirement, depending on its design. Also, clearing a bitcoin vending machine and subsequently transferring any funds collected to a third party may require a payment services licence for money remittance under the Austrian Payment Services Act.

There is currently no deposit guarantee scheme and no legal investor protection scheme for cryptocurrencies or tokens.

Accordingly, given the diversity, complexity and rapid evolution of business models in the fintech space, the regulatory treatment of any business models involving cryptocurrencies or tokens will need to be assessed on a case-by-case basis. The FMA therefore encourages discussion of the regulatory treatment prior to engaging in any business activity and has set up a dedicated specialist team and contact portal dedicated to those areas.

Sales regulation

There is currently no specific regulation dedicated to the sale of cryptocurrencies or tokens, which are thus covered by general securities and commodities laws.

Depending on a token's precise terms and conditions/features, certain token offerings/sales may be subject to prospectus requirements under Austrian securities laws if no prospectus exemption applies.

It appears that tokens may currently be broadly classified as follows:

- Investment tokens: tokens that represent assets, in particular payment claims against a specific issuer, e.g. to participate in future earnings or cash-flows or tokens that represent membership rights within the meaning of corporate law. A subclass of investment tokens is security tokens, e.g. tokenised stocks or bonds.

- Utility tokens: tokens that confer the right to purchase certain goods (excluding Bitcoin and other cryptocurrencies) or certain services. There are many designs of utility tokens, but these are often comparable to vouchers.

- Payment/currency tokens: tokens that are accepted as means of payment for the purchase of goods or services, or tokens that serve the purpose of transferring money and value but do not confer any claims against a specific issuer (e.g. Bitcoin or Ripple).

- "No rights" tokens: tokens that are neither investment-minded nor convey rights, and that cannot be used for payments. Examples could be tokens serving an identification function (e.g. KYC token) or a token that can only be traded on crypto-trading platforms, but otherwise cannot be used (either factually or legally) for any of the above purposes.

Under Austrian law, the offer of transferable securities (within the meaning of regulation (EU) 2017/1129)) and so-called "CMA investments" are subject to prospectus requirements. CMA investments are a local Austrian securities law concept and refer to property rights for which no securities are issued which arise out of the direct or indirect investments of capital of several investors for their collective benefit/risk, and where management of the capital invested is not overseen by the investors themselves. Accordingly, due to their specific content/features, security tokens and other types of investment tokens will typically be subject to prospectus requirements (unless an exemption applies), while other types of tokens, such as utility tokens, payment/currency tokens or "no rights" tokens, usually will not.

No prospectus will need to be published if a prospectus exemption applies. This will be the case if the respective tokens are only offered to qualified investors, or if the offering is directed to fewer than 150 persons who are not qualified investors per EEA Member State, or if the minimum investment is at least €100,000 per investor.

Besides issuers, platform operators also may have the obligation to publish a prospectus, as they may be considered "offerors" for these instruments under the Austrian Capital Markets Act.

Breaches of the obligation to publish a prospectus are subject to severe sanctions, including under criminal laws.

Finally, as of the time of writing, the government is evaluating proposals to regulate certain forms of ICOs and ITOs. If these proposals are implemented into Austrian law, the securities law treatment of token offerings may change in the future.

Taxation

Income tax treatment of cryptocurrencies

In general, capital gains from the sale of cryptocurrencies held as business assets, and income from commercial activities related to cryptocurrencies (e.g. mining, brokerage), are subject to progressive income tax rates of up to 55% for individuals and 25% for corporations.

Special rules apply to cryptocurrencies treated as investment assets and other (non-business) assets:

* Cryptocurrencies are treated as investment assets in case the taxpayer uses them to generate interest income. In this case, capital gains from a subsequent sale are taxed at 27.5% for individuals (taxation at lower progressive income tax rates optional) or at 25% for corporations.

* In case cryptocurrencies are not used to generate interest income, are only acquired and sold occasionally (private sales) and are not part of a business (non-business assets), capital gains are subject to taxation of up to 55% for individuals only if they are acquired and sold within 12 months. A tax exemption applies if capital gains do not exceed €440 per calendar year. In case cryptocurrencies are held for longer than 12 months, capital gains are not taxable.

VAT treatment of cryptocurrencies

The exchange of cryptocurrencies (e.g. Bitcoin) into fiat currency (e.g. euro) and vice versa is VAT-exempt (CJEU 22 October 2015, C-264/14, Hedquvist; VAT guidelines para. 759). Bitcoin mining as such is not subject to VAT (CJEU 22 October 2015, C-264/14, Hedquvist).

Purchases/supplies of goods or services that are subject to VAT, and which are paid for in cryptocurrency, are treated no differently from payments with fiat currency. The assessment basis for transactions subject to VAT is the fair market value of the units.

Money transmission laws and anti-money laundering requirements

As stated above, money transmission laws may apply to certain business activities involving cryptocurrencies. Cryptocurrencies and tokens used as means of payment may trigger a licensing requirement if they are intended for payment to third parties, and the network within which they can be used to purchase goods/services is large in terms of geographical reach, type of products/services and/or number of accepting parties. Also, if accounts are operated in connection with currencies, payment instruments or means of payment, through which payments are made, the entity holding the accounts may be obliged to become licensed as a payment service provider.

As of today, activities involving cryptocurrencies are only subject to anti-money laundering ("AML") requirements if they require a licence under financial services regulation (e.g. as provision of payment services) or if they are subject to AML requirements under commercial law. Pursuant to the Austrian Trade Code (*Gewerbeordnung*, GewO), commercial operators, including auctioneers, are subject to AML requirements if they make or receive cash payments of at least €10,000.

However, upon implementation of the fifth Anti-Money Laundering Directive, which will amend the current fourth Anti-Money Laundering Directive (2015/849/EU) and will likely enter into force by the end of 2019, custodian wallet providers (i.e. entities providing services to safeguard private cryptographic keys to hold, store and transfer virtual currencies on behalf of their customers) as well as providers of exchange services between virtual currencies and fiat currencies, will become subject to AML obligations, including KYC checks and AML prevention systems.

Promotion and testing

At the time of writing, there are no "sandbox" or other programmes intended to specifically promote research and investment in cryptocurrency in Austria. However, the Austrian government and Austrian regulators are looking into "sandbox" programmes and international best practice in this respect.

Ownership and licensing requirements

Cryptocurrencies are currently treated by the Austrian regulator as commodities for supervisory law purposes (see "Cryptocurrency regulation", above). Applicable law as well as internal investment policies may restrict investment managers of certain investors to own cryptocurrencies for investment purposes. For example, UCITS funds, real estate investment funds pursuant to the Austrian Real Estate Investment Funds Act, or staff provision funds and their managers, may not invest into commodities. Pension funds and insurance companies are subject to qualitative and quantitative investment restrictions which will typically not permit direct investment into cryptocurrencies. Depending on the relevant investment policy, alternative investment funds ("AIF") and their managers may, however, invest in cryptocurrencies.

There are currently no specific licensing requirements imposed on an investment advisor or fund manager holding cryptocurrency, over and above those set out under the general trade law/financial services licensing framework.

Mining

Mining bitcoin and other cryptocurrencies as such is not yet regulated and thus currently permitted. However, raising capital from the public in order to invest proceeds into mining of cryptocurrencies may be regulated (see "Cryptocurrency regulation" and "Sales regulation", above).

Border restrictions and declaration

There are currently no border restrictions or obligations to declare cryptocurrency holdings.

Reporting requirements

There are currently no reporting requirements for cryptocurrency payments made in excess of a certain value under Austrian law.

Estate planning and testamentary succession

There are no specific rules as to how cryptocurrencies are treated for purposes of estate planning and testamentary succession. Accordingly, general civil law rules apply. Cryptocurrencies qualify as (intangible) assets (*unkörperliche Sache*) for civil law purposes and as such can be included in estate planning/testamentary succession, or form part of a deceased person's estate.

Ursula Rath
Tel: +43 1 534 37 50412 / Email: u.rath@schoenherr.eu
Ursula Rath is a partner at Schönherr in its Vienna office, where she specialises in (equity and debt) capital markets transactions, investment funds and financial services regulation and M&A transactions in the financial services industry. For more than a decade, she has advised issuers, selling shareholders, banks and other financial institutions as well as investors on international and local capital markets transactions and on combined bank debt and high-yield bond issuances. She has a broad range of experience in initial public and secondary offerings, stock exchange listings, liability management transactions, notes offerings (in particular, high-yield) and private placements of debt or equity instruments.

Ursula was the lead partner advising: Agrana on its €190m combined rights offering and SPO (2017); ABBAG along with the Republic of Austria on the successful €11.2bn exchange offer of debt instruments issued by former Hypo Alpe Adria Group (2016); the bookrunners on Nabriva Therapeutic AG's US IPO and NASDAQ listing; the first level III sponsored ADR program of an Austrian issuer (2015) and its follow-on rights offering (2016); the Austrian national public broadcasting company on its €180m debut bond issuance (2015); America Movil as shareholder in Telekom Austria's €1bn capital increase (2014); the initial purchasers on various rounds of secured notes issuances of Schaeffler Group (2012–2015); and VSE-listed UNIQA Insurance Group AG on its €757m Re-IPO (2013).

Thomas Kulnigg
Tel: +43 1 534 37 50757 / Email: t.kulnigg@schoenherr.eu
Thomas Kulnigg is a partner with Schönherr, where he specialises in M&A, capital markets transactions and Austrian corporate law. Thomas frequently acts for clients, in particular in the financial services and TMT-industry and in the private equity sector, advising them on their inbound and outbound investments in Austria and CEE. Thomas regularly acts for Austrian clients on general corporate matters. During his secondment to the London office of Wall Street law firm Davis Polk & Wardwell, Thomas gained experience in US Securities Law and capital markets transactions and, among others, advised the underwriters in one of the largest rights issues by volume worldwide by then (Rio Tinto, 2009, US$ 15.2bn).

Prior to joining Schoenherr in 2006, Thomas worked with small to mid-sized Austrian law firms and the European Center for E-Commerce and Internet-Law (E-Center), under the direction of a.o. Univ.-Prof. Dr Wolfgang Zankl. Thomas holds degrees from the University of Vienna (*Magister iuris, doctor iuris*) and is co-author of a civil law textbook (*Zivilrecht* 24, WUV). Thomas has been a member of the Austrian bar association since 2010 and speaks German (native) and English (fluent).

Schönherr Rechtsanwälte GmbH

Schottenring 19, 1010 Vienna, Austria
Tel: +43 1 534 37 – 0 / Fax: +43 1 534 37 – 66100 / URL: www.schoenherr.eu

Belgium

Muriel Baudoncq & France Wilmet
Janson Baugniet

Government attitude and definition

In Belgium, cryptocurrencies are generally not considered to be "money" as they do not fulfil the three criteria by which money is defined (i.e., unit of account, store of value and medium of exchange), or at least not all of them.

Furthermore, cryptocurrencies are generally not considered to be "e-money". According to the second European E-money Directive (Directive 2009/110/EC, dated 16 September 2009 on the taking-up, pursuit and prudential supervision of the business of electronic money institutions) as implemented in Belgian law, e-money is defined as "monetary value as represented by a claim on the issuer which is stored electronically, issued on receipt of funds of an amount not less in value than the monetary value issued, and accepted as a means of payment by undertakings other than the issuer". Cryptocurrencies (such as bitcoins) do not fall under this definition as they do not represent a claim on the issuer, which is not obliged to exchange them back to real money. Furthermore, they are purely digital and not necessarily linked to the real funds upon which they were issued.

The Belgian Minister of Finance (N-VA Johan Van Overtveldt) recently indicated in response to a parliamentary question (press release dated 25 January 2018) that no cryptocurrency platforms are established in Belgium. However, there are a few unregulated distributors of bitcoins, allowing persons having created a crypto wallet abroad to convert euros into bitcoins and to transfer them directly in their wallet. Belgian citizens therefore have to purchase and sell cryptocurrencies through foreign platforms.

The supervision of financial institutions in Belgium is organised according to a "Twin-Peaks" model, by which the competences are shared between two autonomous supervisors: the National Bank of Belgium ("NBB") and the Financial Services and Markets Authority ("FSMA"). Each regulator has a specific set of objectives. The NBB is the principal prudential supervisor for (amongst others) banks, insurance companies, stockbroking firms, payment and e-money institutions, both on a macro- and micro-level. The FSMA is responsible for supervising the financial markets and the information circulated by companies, certain categories of financial service providers (including investment firms and funds management companies) and intermediaries, compliance by financial institutions with conduct of business rules and the marketing of financial products to the public. The Federal Public Services Economy, SMEs, Self-Employed and Energy (FPS Economy) has also certain supervisory powers (consumer credit, payment services).

Together, the NBB and FSMA are monitoring closely the risks associated with cryptocurrencies in cooperation with the European Union ("EU"). In view of the risks associated with cryptocurrencies, they have published several warnings since 2014 to warn

Belgian consumers against the risks related to cryptocurrencies and trading platforms in respect of which they have noted signs of fraud. Furthermore, since 2014, the marketing to retail clients of financial products whose return depends directly or indirectly on a virtual currency is prohibited (see below).

Furthermore, the government is currently working together with the NBB and the FSMA on a new legal framework for cryptocurrency platforms and intermediaries in cryptocurrencies (including distributors) as well as for providers of the virtual wallets in which cryptocurrencies are stored.

It should be noted that such approach on cryptocurrencies does not mean that Belgium is not a "digital friendly" country. Quite the contrary, Belgium takes a positive stance as regards the opportunities of blockchain (the technology underpinning cryptocurrencies).

Cryptocurrency regulation

Cryptocurrencies are currently not regulated under Belgian law. No licence is required to issue cryptocurrencies and they are not subject to regulatory supervision. Virtual money does not benefit from legal protection.

The FSMA has issued several warnings advising the Belgian public against the risks of cryptocurrencies. The most important risks highlighted by the regulator are:

*   The internet environment where virtual money is held and traded entails various risks; for instance, there is the risk that a trading platform or digital wallet may be hacked and the owner may lose his virtual money.

*   The operational reliability of such systems, particularly the risk of fraud, has not yet been formally assessed by the regulators.

*   In contrast to the situation for electronic money, fluctuations in the virtual money exchange rate can result in substantial financial losses. Virtual money therefore entails a serious exchange rate risk: the rate at which virtual money can be exchanged for official currencies (such as the euro) is highly variable. Those variations can take place in a very short time (one day). There is no government supervision of the virtual money exchange rate.

*   In contrast to the situation for electronic money, there is no legal guarantee that virtual money can be exchanged at any time for the original value.

*   Virtual money is not legal tender: no-one is obliged to accept payment with virtual money.

*   In principle, money held in a savings account or invested in savings notes or deposit accounts is protected by the Belgian protection scheme managed by the Guarantee Fund (up to €100,000 per person and per institution). That protection does not apply to investments in virtual money.

Sales regulation

There is a retail product ban in Belgium according to which it is prohibited (amongst others) to market, on a professional basis, to one or more retail clients, any financial product of which the return depends directly or indirectly on a "virtual currency" (Royal Decree dated 24 April 2014 approving FSMA Regulation of 3 April 2014 on the prohibition of the marketing of certain financial products to retail clients). In such context, "virtual currencies" are defined as "any form of unregulated digital currencies which are not legal tender". This definition covers cryptocurrencies.

In the explanatory note joined to its Regulation, the FSMA emphasises that virtual currencies such as Bitcoin are becoming more and more popular and benefiting from increasing press coverage. Although initially, such means of payment could only be used within a small virtual community, certain "traditional" vendors or service providers now also accept such virtual money. Certain persons purchase or sell virtual money for speculative purposes, hoping they will realise significant profits in a short term. The introduction of a retail ban for such products is justified by the considerable risks related to cryptocurrencies.

Furthermore, depending on exactly which activities are performed in Belgium, other securities laws and regulations could be applicable to the sale of cryptocurrencies or cryptoderivatives, requiring a detailed analysis on a case-by-case basis of both: (i) the licensing requirements that could be applicable to the entity issuing, selling, offering, marketing or acting as intermediary in any way in connection with such cryptocurrencies or cryptoderivatives; and (ii) the marketing rules, restrictions or prohibitions that could be applicable to the product itself (such as the laws and regulations provided in: Prospectus Directive/Regulation, Markets in Financial Instruments Directive and Regulation ("MiFID/MiFIR"), European Market Infrastructure Regulation ("EMIR"), Payment Services Directive ("PSD"), Alternative Investment Fund Managers Directive ("AIFMD"), Market Abuse Regulation ("MAR"), Anti-Money Laundering Directive ("AMLD4"), etc). In relation to retail clients or consumers, additional rules and restrictions need to be taken into consideration, amongst others, the protective provisions of the Code of Economic Law.

In the context of Initial Coin Offerings ("ICOs"), the FSMA issued a Communication dated 13 November 2017 addressed to offerors of ICOs and to consumers. The Communication provides an overview of the legislation and regulations that may apply to offerors. In addition, the FSMA draws consumers' attention to the risks associated with investments in ICOs and to signs that may point to fraud.

Given the variety of products involved, any plan to offer, sell or market such products in Belgium needs, therefore, to be carefully analysed. The characteristics of the tokens and the rights associated with them depend on the specific ICO. In light of the great variety of ICOs, the status of tokens, and the responsibilities of the issuing entity under the current financial legislation and regulations, are not entirely clear.

The FSMA endorsed the two statements on ICOs made by ESMA (the European Securities and Markets Authority) on 13 November 2017 on the risks for investors and on the rules applicable to firms involved in ICOs.

As regards ICO activity in Belgium, the FSMA emphasised that depending on how ICOs are structured, various European financial regulations (as implemented under Belgian law) may apply to them, such as: Prospectus Directive, MiFID/MiFIR, AIFMD, MAR, AMLD4, etc. The FSMA also noted that it is possible that other rules may also apply, such as those governing accounting standards, tax obligations, electronic money, or prudential regulations.

In Belgium, the following legislation and regulations may apply in addition to the aforementioned European legislation:

- FSMA Regulation of 3 April 2014 on the ban on marketing of certain financial products to retail clients (see above).

- Act of 16 June 2006 on public offers of investment instruments and on the admission of investment instruments to trading on regulated markets (to be replaced by the Act of 11 July 2018 on the date on which the EU Regulation 2017/1129 on the prospectus to be published when securities are offered to the public or admitted to trading on a regulated market enters into force). This Act requires the preparation of a prospectus to be approved by the FSMA in the event of a public offering of investment instruments within the territory of Belgium, establishes a monopoly on intermediation for the placement of investment instruments within the territory of Belgium, and determines that advertisements used in connection with the public offering must receive prior approval from the FSMA. This is particularly relevant in relation to the White Paper issued with the ICO.

*   Act of 18 December 2016 regulating the recognition and definition of crowdfunding and containing various provisions on finance: this Act sets out the conditions for authorisation as a recognised alternative finance platform (that is, the financial form of crowdfunding) and the rules that apply to the providers of alternative finance service.

The application of the above rules depends on the way in which the ICO is structured, and this must be analysed on a case-by-case basis.

According to the FSMA, specific points that participants in ICOs need to take into consideration are:

*   Depending on their characteristics, ICOs may lie outside of any legal framework. In many cases, there is thus no protection for the consumer/investor.

*   Their (potentially) unregulated and anonymous nature render ICOs susceptible to fraud and illicit practices (such as money laundering and terrorist financing).

*   The generally summary, non-standardised, convoluted, subjective and unaudited information about ICOs makes it difficult to estimate the associated risks. Anyone who is not well acquainted with online technologies may find the technical and detailed information about an ICO incomprehensible.

*   Start-ups are risky, and there is thus a realistic chance of loss of (part of) the capital invested in an ICO.

*   Promotion takes place entirely digitally, and is usually complex. Many things can go wrong, yet there is no recourse in the event of a dispute relating to a transaction.

*   The value of an ICO is determined subjectively and arbitrarily by the developers.

*   There is no guarantee that the project will effectively go to market or that there is a market for that particular proposal.

*   Distributed Ledger Technology which underpins ICOs is still in its infancy and still has flaws. Hacking and phishing may occur in the course of the purchasing process or may target the application developed by the offerors.

*   In the case of most ICOs, would-be participants must first acquire a cryptocurrency in order to be able to obtain tokens. If the price of the cryptocurrencies used should fall sharply, there is the risk that the developers will have insufficient funds to continue developing their project. In that case, the project may come to a halt, and the tokens could lose their value.

Finally, the Communication of the FSMA on ICOs contains a list of signs which may help to identify dubious ICOs:

*   The white paper is of poor quality and has only limited information.

*   "Pump and dump" ICOs where hype is created around the ICO (for example, with a very short period for the ICO, pushy advertisements, campaign by a celebrity).

*   The token is positioned principally as an investment instrument and, for the time being, the platform's sole functionality is for secondary trading in the specific token.

- There are no background checks on the ICO participants.
- The developers are anonymous, the project is still only an idea rather than a product, and no external validation is available.
- There is no access to the smart contract or to the code or technical information about the token creation.
- The project does not use a decentralised network or a DLT application, and the ICO thus serves exclusively to raise funds.
- The project sets out unrealistic objectives (the amount of capital to be raised, for example, is disproportionate to the value that the project will create).

Taxation

There are no specific tax rules regulating the taxation of cryptocurrencies in Belgium but some guidance is available from the European Court of Justice (in respect of VAT), the Belgian Ruling Commission and various papers drafted by legal authors.

Based on this, the below is a brief overview of the current position of the Belgian tax authorities on the tax treatment of cryptocurrencies.

VAT: purchase and sale of cryptocurrencies

In a decision dated 22 October 2015 (case C-264/14, David Hedqvist), the European Court of Justice was asked to consider how an exchange selling bitcoins for traditional currencies (and vice versa) would be taxed. The case at hand concerned Mr Hedqvist, who wished to set up a Bitcoin exchange but first wanted to clarify the VAT position of his new business. This led to the Swedish courts seeking clarification with the European Court of Justice.

The Court of Justice ruled that an exchange of Bitcoin for a traditional currency is a "supply of services". It further concluded that bitcoins (and by analogy, all cryptocurrencies) should be considered "currencies" for VAT purposes and may therefore benefit from the VAT exemption applicable to transactions "concerning currency, bank notes and coins used as legal tender". Given that the only purpose of Bitcoin is to serve as a means of payment, the Court of Justice decided that the "VAT currency exemption" should apply to Bitcoin trading.

This position has consequences for persons who are mining bitcoins. If Bitcoin trading is VAT exempt, this also means that the VAT on the electricity which is necessary to mine the bitcoins cannot be recovered.

Income taxation

A distinction must be made between companies and individuals.

For companies, standard corporate income tax rules will apply. Any activity generating an income (or a loss) from trading or exchanging cryptocurrencies will be taxable under these standard rules. Corporate tax will also be due on gains from transactions relating to cryptocurrencies.

For individuals, cryptocurrency profits may or may not be taxable depending on whether the crypto activity is to be considered as a hobby or a professional activity and whether the investments in cryptocurrencies are made for speculative purposes or not.

As a matter of principle, Belgium does not tax capital gains on personal property. Capital gains on personal assets and investments are tax-exempted if they are obtained by an individual in the framework of the "normal management of his/her personal assets". The "normal management of personal assets" is generally defined as the conservative, risk-averse and unsophisticated management of the private estate. For example, someone who has purchased a few bitcoins a few years ago to diversify his/her investment portfolio and decides to sell them should not be taxed on the capital gain.

However, if the transactions in cryptocurrencies are carried out with a speculative character (for example, buying and selling quickly and repeatedly, borrowing to buy, investing large sums, etc.) the capital gain will be taxable as miscellaneous income to which a flat tax rate of 33% (+ communal tax) will apply.

In addition, if the transactions in cryptocurrencies are carried out on a professional basis, Bitcoin profit will be seen as professional income and Belgian personal income tax will be due. This is relevant, for example, for miners, traders, intermediaries and payment processors and other service providers that are not working through a company. The standard progressive tax rates range between 25% and 50% (+ communal tax). Furthermore, social security contributions may also be due.

The Belgian Ruling Commission (decision 2017.852 dated 5 December 2017) recently analysed the case of an IT student who realised important capital gains by means of an app to buy and sell bitcoins automatically, which he developed for a school project. The Ruling Commission decided that such activity was not a business, as the app was developed in the framework of a school project; therefore, the income generated by this activity was not considered professional income. However, the Ruling Commission considered that the investments in cryptocurrencies made by the student had a speculative character and, therefore, the capital gains linked to such crypto trading were taxable as miscellaneous income.

If capital gains are taxable, they must be reported in the annual tax return as miscellaneous income (if the investments have a speculative character) or as professional income (if the crypto trading is the main activity of the taxpayer).

It should be noted that the Belgian Ruling Commission allows investors to file a ruling in order to determine whether their capital gains are taxable or not (for transactions carried out in 2017 and 2018, as long as the tax return has not been filed). On 7 June 2018, the Ruling Commission released the questionnaire that will be used to assist with its assessment of taxable status and which investors are invited to fill in where they are seeking a ruling. This questionnaire is also interesting for persons who do not ask for a ruling, as the tax authorities are likely to use the same criteria in case of tax inspection.

The questionnaire of the Belgian Ruling Commission includes the following 17 questions:

1. How did you enter into possession of the cryptocurrencies (for example, by heritage, donation, personal savings, re-investment of movable or immovable property, etc.)?

2. For how many years have you been investing in cryptocurrencies?

3. What amount in total have you already invested in cryptocurrencies?

4. What is the frequency of your buy & sell transactions in cryptocurrencies (daily, weekly, monthly, occasionally, only once)?

5. For how long have you owned the cryptocurrencies that you wish to sell or convert?

6. What is your investment strategy in respect of cryptocurrencies (buy & hold, trending, active trading, day trading, scalping, arbitrage, etc.)?

7. Do you carry out mining?

8. Do you buy or sell cryptocurrencies through an automated process or a software program?

9. What is your usual professional activity? What is your educational background? Have you acquired knowledge in cryptocurrencies in the framework of your professional activity?

10. Have you invested in a cryptocurrencies fund?

11. Are you active in the cryptocurrencies community on forums or blogs? Do you speak at conferences on cryptocurrencies?

12. What percentage of your movable assets have you invested in cryptocurrencies? Do you also have other investments (shares, bonds, art works, gold, etc.)?

13. Do you use a specific device to protect your cryptocurrencies (such as a hardware wallet)?

14. Do you also invest in cryptocurrencies for other persons?

15. Have you borrowed money to invest in cryptocurrencies?

16. What is the market value of your cryptocurrencies portfolio?

17. Have you consulted financial or IT specialists in connection with your investments in cryptocurrencies?

In conclusion, the assessment of whether or not a profit or gain is taxable (or loss-allowable) will always depend on the facts and circumstances. Potential investors are strongly advised to seek guidance on whether their trading activities can be considered a professional trade or speculative activity.

Money transmission laws and anti-money laundering requirements

Various regulations apply in Belgium with respect to the prevention of the use of the financial system for the purposes of money laundering or terrorist financing, including the Belgian Act of 18 September 2017 implementing Directive (EU) 2015/849 dated 20 May 2015 on the prevention of the use of the financial system for the purposes of money laundering or terrorist financing ("AMLD4").

The AML Belgian Act prevents the use of the financial system for the purpose of money laundering being defined as:

1. the conversion or transfer of property, knowing that such property is derived from criminal activity or from an act of participation in such activity, for the purpose of concealing or disguising the illicit origin of the property or of assisting any person who is involved in the commission of such an activity to evade the legal consequences of that person's action;

2. the concealment or disguise of the true nature, source, location, disposition, movement, rights with respect to, or ownership of, property, knowing that such property is derived from criminal activity or from an act of participation in such an activity;

3. the acquisition, possession or use of property, knowing, at the time of receipt, that such property was derived from criminal activity or from an act of participation in such an activity; and

4. the participation in, association to commit, attempts to commit and aiding, abetting, facilitating and counselling the commission of any of the actions referred to in points 1, 2 and 3.

The AML Belgian Act imposes customer due diligence measures and, in particular, imposes scrutiny of transactions undertaken throughout the course of the relationship with a client to ensure that the transactions being conducted are consistent with the knowledge of the customer, the business and risk profile to detect unusual activities. Further scrutiny of unusual activities is required to determine if these activities are suspicious transactions related to a criminal activity or terrorist financing. After such review is made (and documented), declaration of suspicious transactions is possibly made to the authorities.

Although investing in cryptocurrencies as such is not prohibited by the AML Belgian Act, transactions in cryptocurrencies whereby funds are paid from or on the bank accounts of the investors fall under the abovementioned scrutiny and any unusual activities must be further investigated by the bank.

Cryptocurrency platforms, intermediaries in cryptocurrencies and providers of virtual wallets are not currently considered as obliged entities under the AML Belgian Act and AMLD4. However, the new AML/CTF EU Directive 2018/843 of 30 May 2018 ("AMLD5"), which has been published in the Official Journal of the European Union on 19 June 2018 and entered into force on 9 July 2018, with effective application from 10 January 2020, targets two new categories of players: (i) exchange platforms that provide virtual currencies against fiat currencies (and vice versa); and (ii) custodian wallet providers (i.e., entities that provide services to safeguard private cryptographic keys on behalf of their customers, to hold, store and transfer virtual currencies). Under AMLD5, "virtual currency" is defined as "digital representation of value that is not issued or guaranteed by a central bank or a public authority, is not necessarily attached to a legally established currency, and does not possess a legal status of currency or money, but is accepted by natural or legal persons as a means of exchange and which can be transferred, stored and traded electronically".

As "obliged entities", exchange platforms and custodian wallet providers will face the same regulatory requirements as banks and other financial institutions. These include obligations to register with national anti-money laundering authorities, implement customer due diligence controls, regularly monitor virtual currency transactions, and report suspicious transactions to government entities.

Furthermore, AMLD5 increases transparency of virtual currency transactions executed without exchange platforms or custodian wallet providers. As highlighted by the Commission, including exchange platforms and custodian wallet providers as obliged entities "does not entirely address the issue of anonymity attached to virtual currency transactions, as a large part of the virtual currency environment will remain anonymous because users can also transact without these providers". As a result, AMLD5 provides that member states must create central databases comprised of virtual currency users' identities and wallet addresses – not just those using exchange platforms or custodian wallet providers – as well as self-declaration forms submitted by virtual currency users. In addition, AMLD5 directs member states to authorise national Financial Intelligence Processing Units – such as the CTIF-CFI (*Cellule de Traitement des Informations Financières / Cel voor Financiële Informatieverwerking*) in Belgium – to access the information in these databases.

Promotion and testing

There is no regulatory sandbox in Belgium. However, both the NBB and the FSMA offer companies the opportunity to enter into direct contact with them through a dedicated "Fintech portal" available on their website. The purpose of the Fintech Contact Point is to support a dialogue between the regulator and Fintech companies whereby the regulator aims to get back to the firms within three business days and assist them in understanding the applicable regulatory framework. This facility can be used, for example, for any project relating to virtual currencies, crowdfunding, distributed ledger technology, APIs or alternative distribution models.

Ownership and licensing requirements

Depending on which activities exactly are performed in Belgium, several securities laws and regulations could be applicable to the sale of cryptocurrencies or cryptoderivatives, requiring a detailed analysis on a case-by-case basis of both: (i) the licensing requirements that could be applicable to the entity issuing, selling, offering, marketing or acting as intermediary in any way in connection with such cryptocurrencies or cryptoderivatives; and (ii) the marketing rules, restrictions or prohibitions that could be applicable to the product itself (such as the laws and regulations provided in: Prospectus Directive/Regulation, MiFID/MiFIR, EMIR, PSD, AIFMD, MAR, AMLD4, etc). In relation to retail clients or consumers, additional rules and restrictions need to be taken into consideration (such as the rules and restrictions provided in: Code of Economic Law, Retail Product Ban, etc. Please refer to section "Sales regulation" above).

For investors, it is currently not possible to purchase cryptocurrencies through Belgian banks or Belgian investment firms.

Provided that they comply with the rules and restrictions generally applicable to the management and investment of their own funds, Belgian banks or investment firms are not prohibited to invest in cryptocurrencies; however, according to the information publicly available, their direct and indirect exposure to cryptocurrencies is currently very limited.

Mining

Mining Bitcoin and other cryptocurrencies is not a regulated activity in Belgium.

For the tax treatment of such activity, please see above (Taxation).

Border restrictions and declaration

There are no foreign exchange or currency control restrictions, nor any obligation to declare cryptocurrency holdings in Belgium.

Reporting requirements

There are no reporting obligations for payments in cryptocurrencies made in excess of a certain value but note the AML and taxation requirements that need to be complied with.

Estate planning and testamentary succession

Cryptocurrencies are a type of asset that can (and should) be covered by the estate plan to ensure that heirs are aware of their existence. Cryptocurrencies are stored in digital wallets that require a private key to gain access. Therefore, heirs should be informed about the login details and private key, otherwise access to the virtual currencies could be impossible. If the cryptocurrencies are held through a wallet provider (such as Coinbase) holding the private keys on behalf of their clients, access to the crypto wallet may be obtained by the heirs using appropriate documentation. However, where the cryptocurrencies are stored offline, they will be inaccessible unless detailed instructions on how to access them are provided in a detailed written document that should be securely stored offline.

In the case of death of a Belgian resident owning cryptocurrencies, his/her heirs will be subject to Belgian inheritance taxes calculated according to progressive rates, which may reach 30% for heirs in direct line or up to 80% in other cases. These rates vary in function of the kinship of the heirs and the region where the deceased was domiciled.

Muriel Baudoncq
Tel: +32 2 675 30 30 / Email: m.baudoncq@janson.be
Muriel is a partner in the banking and finance department of the firm. She is an expert in complex financial regulatory matters. Muriel specialises in a wide range of Belgian and EU regulatory matters, focusing on advising financial institutions on various regulatory issues and questions related to the offering and provision of financial services and marketing of financial products in Belgium. Muriel has also considerable experience in cross-border issues and local conduct of business rules and she regularly writes legal contributions and speaks at conferences on various banking and finance topics, including blockchain and cryptocurrencies.

France Wilmet
Tel: +32 2 675 30 30 / Email: f.wilmet@janson.be
France is a partner in the banking and finance department of the firm. France is assistant professor at the University of Brussels and deputy judge at the court of appeal in Mons (Belgium). France has gained significant experience of business law and contract law working for both Belgian and foreign clients. In particular she specialises in finance (asset management, commodity finance, derivatives, regulatory finance and regulatory insurance).

Janson Baugniet

Chaussée de la Hulpe, 187, B-1170 Brussels, Belgium
Tel: +32 2 675 30 30 / Fax: +32 2 675 30 31 / URL: www.janson.be

Bermuda

Michael Hanson & Adam Bathgate
Carey Olsen Bermuda

Government attitude and definition

The current Bermuda government was elected in 2017 having undertaken to create new economic pillars in Bermuda, identify new opportunities for economic diversification, and seek local and overseas investment to develop new local industry and thereby create jobs in Bermuda. Since its election, it has enthusiastically embraced the financial technology ("**fintech**") sector and the potential it offers, and has repeatedly expressed its intention for Bermuda to be a significant centre for this industry.

In furtherance of this goal, the government is in the process of implementing a comprehensive regulatory regime aimed at providing legal certainty to industry participants and ensuring that business in the sector conducted in or from Bermuda is done in a properly regulated matter, in accordance with the highest international standards. This regulatory regime is described in more detail below, but, in summary:

- a new Digital Asset Business Act has been passed by the Bermuda Parliament and is awaiting royal assent. When passed, this will comprise a regulatory framework for fintech businesses; and
- although not covered by the Digital Asset Business Act, initial coin offerings will be regulated under a separate regime.

The government has also announced that fintech businesses wishing to set up in Bermuda are to benefit from a relaxed work permit policy, and has signed a number of memoranda of understanding with fintech businesses, under which these businesses have committed to establishing operations and creating jobs in Bermuda.

Although digital asset offerings and businesses will be regulated in the manner described in this article, there is no legislation or other provision of Bermuda law affording official or legal recognition of any cryptocurrency or any other digital asset, or conferring equivalent status with any fiat currency. Nor has the government or the Bermuda Monetary Authority (the "**BMA**"), the territory's financial regulator and issuer of its national currency, backed any cryptocurrency itself, and the Bermuda dollar remains the territory's legal tender.

Cryptocurrency regulation

While both the Bermuda government and the BMA are on record as being keen to embrace the potential offered by fintech, both recognise that the industry presents tremendous risk, requiring prudent regulation.

The Financial Action Task Force (the "**FATF**") recommended in its June 2014 report on virtual currencies[1] that regulators, for the time being, focus their efforts on convertible virtual currencies (i.e. those which can be converted into and out of fiat currencies), on the basis that these currencies presented the highest money-laundering risk. This guidance has heavily influenced the BMA in shaping Bermuda's proposed regulatory regime for digital assets.

Digital Asset Business Act

In April 2018, the BMA published a consultation paper on the regulation of digital asset business. This consultation exercise has resulted in the enactment of a new Digital Asset Business Act (the "**DABA**"), which, at the time of writing, had been passed by the Bermuda Parliament and was awaiting royal assent. Once in force, the DABA will be supplemented by rules, regulations, codes of practice, statements of principles and guidance promulgated by the BMA, and so will operate in a similar manner to the regulatory frameworks in place for other financial services regulated by the BMA.

In summary, the DABA will specify the digital asset-related activities to which it applies, impose a licensing requirement on any person carrying on any of those activities, lay out the criteria a person must meet before it can obtain a licence, impose (and permit the BMA to impose) certain continuing obligations on any holder of a licence, and grant to the BMA supervisory and enforcement powers over regulated digital asset businesses.

Scope of the DABA

The DABA will apply to any entity incorporated or formed in Bermuda and carrying on digital asset business (irrespective of the location from which the activity is carried out) and to any entity incorporated or formed outside of Bermuda and carrying on digital asset business in or from within Bermuda. The term "digital asset" in the legislation is defined widely enough to capture cryptocurrencies, representations of debt or equity in the promoter, representations of other rights associated with such assets, and other representations of value that are intended to provide access to an application or service or product by means of distributed ledger technology. "Digital asset business", for the purposes of the DABA, will be the provision of the following activities to the general public as a business:

(a) *Issuing, selling or redeeming virtual coins, tokens or any other form of digital asset*

This is intended to regulate any business providing these services to other businesses or to individuals. It will **not** include initial coin offerings ("**ICOs**") to fund the issuer's or promoter's own business or project. Instead, ICOs will be regulated under a separate regime, on which see below.

(b) *Operating as a payment service provider business utilising digital assets, which includes the provision of services for the transfer of funds*

The term "payment service provider" is used globally in anti-money laundering and anti-terrorist financing ("**AML/ATF**") laws, regulations and guidance, and is defined in Bermuda's Proceeds of Crime (Anti-Money Laundering and Anti-Terrorist Financing) Amendment Regulations 2010 as "a person whose business includes the provision of services for the transfer of funds". The aim here is to ensure that businesses involved in the transfer of digital assets fall within the DABA's ambit.

(c) *Operating as an electronic exchange*

This category will capture online exchanges allowing customers to buy and sell digital assets, whether payments are made in fiat currency, bank credit or in another form of digital asset. Exchanges facilitating the offer of new coins or tokens through ICOs will also be caught.

(d) *Providing custodial wallet services*

This will cover any business whose services include storing or maintaining digital assets or a virtual wallet on behalf of a client.

(e) *Operating as a digital asset services vendor*

This category will regulate a person that, under an agreement as part of its business, can undertake a digital asset transaction on behalf of another person or has power of attorney over another person's digital asset, or a person who operates as a market-maker for digital assets. It is intended to capture any other business providing specific digital asset-related services to the public, such as operating as a custodian of digital assets.

In addition to the above categories, the DABA will include an option for the Minister of Finance, after consultation with the BMA, to be able to add new categories or to amend, suspend or delete any of the categories listed above by order.

The DABA specifically provides that the following activities will not constitute digital asset business:

- contributing connectivity software or computing power to a decentralised digital asset, or to a protocol governing transfer of the digital representation of value (this category will exempt mining from the DABA's scope);

- providing data storage or security services for a digital asset business, so long as the enterprise is not otherwise engaged in digital asset business activity on behalf of other persons; and

- the provision of any digital asset business activity by an undertaking solely for the purposed of its business operations or the business operations of any of its subsidiaries.

Licensing requirement

The DABA will require persons carrying on digital asset business to obtain a licence before doing so, unless that person is subject to an exemption order issued by the Minister of Finance. At the time of writing, the Minister had not announced any proposed exemption orders.

Two classes of licence will be available for applicants:

- The **Class M licence** will be a restricted form of licence, with modified requirements and certain restrictions, and will be valid for a specified period, the duration of which will be determined by the BMA on a case-by-case basis. Following the expiry of this specified period, it is generally expected that the licensee will either have to apply for a Class F Licence (as described in further detail below) or cease carrying on business, although the BMA will have discretion to extend the specified period.

- The **Class F licence** will be a full licence not subject to any specified period, although it may still be subject to restrictions the BMA may deem appropriate in any given case.

The intention behind this tiered licensing regime is to allow start-ups engaging in digital asset business to do so in a properly supervised regulatory environment, and to engage in proof of concept and develop some sort of track record before obtaining a full licence. The restrictions to which a licensee will be subject will depend on the business model of the prospective licensee (and the risks associated with it), but will almost invariably include an obligation to disclose to prospective customers the fact that the licensee holds a Class M licence and certain limitations on the volume of business the licensee is permitted to conduct, along with other restrictions as the BMA may deem necessary or appropriate on a case-by-case basis.

A prospective licensee may not necessarily receive the licence for which it applies: an applicant for a Class F licence may receive a Class M licence if the BMA decides that a Class M licence would be more appropriate in the circumstances. It is also anticipated that the licence will specify the category (or categories) of digital asset business in which the licensee is permitted to engage.

Carrying on digital asset business without a licence will be a criminal offence punishable by a fine of up to US$250,000, imprisonment for a term of up to five years, or both.

Criteria to be met by licensees

The DABA will provide that the BMA may not issue any licence unless it is satisfied that the applicant fulfils certain minimum criteria addressing the fitness and propriety of directors and officers, ensuring business is conducted in a prudent manner, the integrity and skill of the business's management and standards of corporate governance observed by the (prospective) licensee. This is consistent with the position under other regulatory laws applicable to other sectors and is intended to ensure the BMA maintains high standards for the conduct of regulated business. The BMA has also announced an intention to publish a code of practice detailing requirements as to governance and risk management proportionate to the size, complexity and risk profile of a licensee.

The DABA will require licensees to notify the BMA upon changes in directors or officers, and the BMA will have powers to, *inter alia*, object to and prevent new or increased ownership of shareholder controllers and the power to remove controllers, directors and officers who are no longer fit and proper to carry on their role.

Continuing obligations of licence holders

Persons holding a licence issued under the DABA will be subject to several ongoing obligations.

Dissemination of key information to customers: in order to mitigate the high degree of risk for consumers owing to the highly speculative and volatile nature of digital assets, the BMA has announced it will use powers conferred to it under the DABA to require licensees, before entering into any business relationship with a customer, to disclose to that customer: the class of licence it holds; a schedule of its fees; whether it has insurance against loss of customer assets arising from theft (including cybertheft); the extent to which a transfer or exchange of digital assets is irrevocable and any exceptions; and the extent to which it will be liable for an unauthorised, mistaken or accidental transfer or exchange. Draft rules published by the BMA for this purpose also oblige licensees to confirm certain information regarding transactions with clients at the conclusion of each such transaction.

Crisis management programme: the BMA announced in its consultation plans that licensees will be required to develop and implement a comprehensive crisis management, including cybersecurity, programme commensurate to the licensee's nature, size, complexity and risk profile. This programme must be sufficient to enable the licensee to:

- identify internal and external risks;
- protect the licensee's electronic systems and the information stored on them;
- detect systems intrusions and breaches;
- respond to a detected event in order to mitigate negative effects; and
- recover from operational disruption to the normal course of the licensee's business.

Although licensees will be permitted to engage the services of specialist third parties in order to enhance and supplement the strength of their own cybersecurity systems, ultimate responsibility for compliance with these requirements will rest with the licensee.

Custody and protection of consumer assets: licensees will be required to have in place and maintain a surety bond, trust account or indemnity insurance for the benefit of their customers. Any such trust account must be maintained with a "qualified custodian", which the DABA will define as a licensed Bermuda bank or trust company or any other person recognised by the BMA for this purpose. A licensee will, in addition, be required to maintain books of account and other records sufficient to ensure that customer assets are kept segregated from those of the licensee and can be identified at any time. All customer funds must be held in a dedicated separate account and clearly identified as such.

Senior representative: the DABA will impose an obligation on licensees to appoint a senior representative, to be approved by the BMA, who must be resident in Bermuda and who is sufficiently knowledgeable about both the licensee itself and the industry in general. This senior representative will himself be under a duty to report to the BMA certain significant matters, including: a likelihood of the licensee becoming insolvent; breaches by the licensee of any conditions imposed by the BMA; involvement of the licensee in criminal proceedings, whether in Bermuda or elsewhere; and other material developments.

Head office: the DABA also requires licensees to maintain a head office in Bermuda and to direct and manage their digital asset business from Bermuda. The relevant section goes on to list a number of factors the BMA shall consider in determining whether a licensee satisfies this requirement, together with a number of additional factors to which the BMA may (but need not) have regard.

Annual prudential return: a licensee will be obliged to file with the BMA an annual prudential return, with the BMA being granted the power to require more frequent filings or additions to a filing if required in the interest of consumer protection. The standard annual prudential return will include information relating to business strategy and risk appetite, products and services, number of customer accounts and geographical profile of accounts, information on risk and cybersecurity (including a risk self-assessment and policies in these areas), audited financial statements and details on any outsourcing to third parties.

BMA's supervision and enforcement powers

The DABA will grant the BMA wide-ranging powers of supervision and enforcement.

It will have the power to compel production of information and documents (with criminal sanctions for making false or misleading statements), the power to issue such directions as appear to be desirable to it for safeguarding the interests of a business's customers or potential customers, and the power to impose conditions and restrictions on licences. For example, the BMA may:

- require a person or entity to take certain steps or to refrain from adopting or pursuing a particular course of action, or to restrict the scope of its business activities in a particular way;
- impose limitations on the acceptance of business;
- prohibit a person or entity from soliciting business, either generally or from prospective customers;
- prohibit a person or entity from entering into any other transactions or class of transactions; and
- require the removal of any officer or controller.

In more extreme cases, the BMA may revoke a licence altogether and, if it so elects, subsequently petition the court for the entity whose licence it has revoked, to be wound up.

In the event a licensee fails to comply with a condition, restriction or direction imposed by the BMA or with certain requirements of the DABA, the BMA will have the power to impose fines of up to US$10,000,000. Alternatively, it may issue a public censure ("naming and shaming"), issue a prohibition order banning a person from performing certain functions for a Bermuda regulated entity, or obtain an injunction from the court. It is expected that the BMA will issue guidance in the form of a statement of principles setting out how it proposes to use these enforcement powers shortly after the DABA is passed.

ICO regulation

As noted above, the DABA will not apply to any ICO intended to finance the issuer's or promoter's own business. Instead, the Companies and Limited Liability Company (Initial Coin Offering) Amendment Act, 2018 (the "**ICO Act**") will effect amendments to the Companies Act 1981 and the Limited Liability Company Act 2016 which will form a regulatory framework for ICOs. At the time of writing, the ICO Act had been passed by both houses of the Bermuda Parliament and was awaiting royal assent.

The ICO Act will define an ICO as an offer by a company or a limited liability company (a "**LLC**") to the public to purchase or otherwise acquire digital assets and designate any ICO as a "restricted business activity", requiring consent from the Minister of Finance before any ICO may be made to the public. Private sales and offers of further coins or tokens to existing holders of coins or tokens of the same class will be exempted, as will issuances where the offer is made to a limited number of persons (the actual limit depends on the type of company or LLC the issuer is, and will be 35 in most cases).

The application for consent from the Minister will be required to include specific details regarding:

- the persons managing the issuer and the underlying digital asset(s) offered for sale;
- the development and implementation of any product, service or other project related to the ICO, including timelines for completion;
- the target amount to be raised through the ICO;
- rights, features, functionality and intended transferability of the digital asset(s) offered for sale;
- the technology to be used and confirmation of the ability of the technical platform to enable the collection, confirmation and storage of purchaser identity information; and
- compliance and auditing of ICO transactions.

In addition to obtaining consent from the Minister of Finance, a prospective ICO issuer will also have to publish, in electronic form, an offering document and file this with the Bermuda Registrar of Companies. The offering document must contain:

- details regarding any promoter, including its registered or principal office and details of its officers;
- the business or proposed business of the issuer company or LLC;
- a description of the project to be funded by the ICO and the proposed timeline for the project, including any proposed project phases and milestones;
- the amount of money that the ICO is intended to raise;

- disclosure as to the allocation of the amounts intended to be raised amongst the classes of any issuance (pre-sale, post-ICO etc.);
- any rights or restrictions on the digital assets that are being offered;
- the date and time of the opening and closing of the ICO offer period;
- a statement as to how personal information will be used; and
- a general ICO risk warning containing:
  - information regarding any substantial risks to the project which are known or reasonably foreseeable;
  - information as to a person's rights or options if the project which is the subject of the ICO in question does not go forward;
  - a description of the rights (if any) in relation to the digital assets that are being offered; and
  - information regarding any disclaimer in respect of guarantees or warranties in relation to the project to be developed or any other asset related to the ICO.

If an ICO issuer offers digital assets to the public over a period and any of the particulars in its offering document cease to be accurate in a material respect, the issuer must publish supplementary particulars disclosing the material changes and file these with the Registrar.

The promoter must provide an electronic platform to facilitate communication with prospective investors, and the legislation will also grant investors a cooling-off period during which they will be permitted to withdraw an application to purchase the digital assets offered.

Any person who makes or authorises the making of a false statement in an ICO offering document will be guilty of an offence punishable by a fine of up to US$250,000, imprisonment for a term of up to five years, or both, unless the person proves either that the statement was immaterial or that at the time he made the statement he had reasonable grounds to believe it was true. Officers of the issuer and promoters of the ICO will also incur civil liability to any person who suffers loss as a result of false statements in the offering document, subject to certain defences.

Sales regulation

Issuing, selling or redeeming cryptocurrencies will be regulated under the DABA if carried on as a business, and ICOs will be regulated under the ICO Act, in each case in the manner described more particularly above.

Taxation

There are no income, capital gains, withholding or other taxes imposed in Bermuda on digital assets or on any transactions involving them (the potential application of Bermuda's foreign currency purchase tax is discussed below, under "Border restrictions and declaration"). Moreover, exempted companies or LLCs carrying on digital asset business, including ICO issuers, may apply for, and are likely to receive, an undertaking from the Minister of Finance to the effect that, in the event of there being enacted in Bermuda any legislation imposing tax computed on profits or income or computed on any capital asset, gain or appreciation, then the imposition of any such tax shall not be applicable to such company or to any of its operations.

Money transmission laws and anti-money laundering requirements

Operating a payment service business utilising cryptocurrency or other digital assets (including the provision of services for the transfer of funds) or operating a digital exchange will constitute a regulated activity for the purposes of the DABA (on which see above).

Bermuda has a long-established and well-earned reputation as an international financial centre, and a crucial aspect of this is its robust AML/ATF regime. Bermuda is also due to undergo its fourth round mutual evaluation by the FATF in 2018.

As part of its consultation exercise on the DABA, the BMA announced that activities falling within the scope of the DABA will be subject to AML/ATF regulation. Consequently, the DABA contains provisions amending certain provisions of Bermuda's existing AML/ATF laws and regulations in order to ensure that the carrying on of digital asset business is expressly captured. However, the BMA also recognises the need for new AML/ATF guidelines relating specifically to the conduct of digital asset business, and at the time of writing the BMA is engaged in the drafting of these guidelines in collaboration with the National Anti-Money Laundering Committee and the Bermuda government. These draft guidelines will be presented, along with a new consultation paper addressing the AML/ATF aspects of digital asset business, for industry feedback in due course.

A detailed discussion of the requirements imposed by Bermuda's AML/ATF regime is beyond the scope of this chapter, but in short, digital asset businesses will be required to establish policies and procedures to prevent money laundering and terrorist financing. These policies and procedures must cover customer due diligence, ongoing monitoring, reporting of suspicious transactions, record-keeping, internal controls, risk assessment and management, and the monitoring and management of compliance with, and internal communication of, these policies and procedures.

Promotion and testing

As noted at the beginning of this chapter, the Bermuda government is very enthusiastic about the potential offered by fintech for the territory's economy and has launched, or is in the process of developing, a number of initiatives aimed at promoting investment by fintech businesses in Bermuda.

One aspect of this is a new immigration policy for fintech businesses, announced by the Minister of Home Affairs to the Bermuda Parliament in early May 2018. This allows a company operating in the fintech space and which is new to Bermuda to receive immediate approval of up to five work permits for non-Bermudian staff within the first six months of obtaining its business permit. In order to benefit from this, a business must present a plan for the hiring, training and development of Bermudians in entry-level or trainee positions. A business may not, however, apply for a work permit under this policy in respect of any job categories which are closed (i.e. reserved exclusively for Bermudians, their spouses and permanent resident cardholders only) or restricted (in respect of which a permit may only be obtained for one year) under Bermuda's employment legislation, or which are entry-level, graduate or trainee positions.

Throughout 2018, the government has also been busy entering into a series of memoranda of understandings with various digital asset businesses. Under these memoranda:

* Binance Holdings Limited, the parent company of the Binance Group, the world's largest digital exchange, has committed to develop its global compliance base

in Bermuda, creating at least 40 jobs, and to develop a digital asset exchange in Bermuda. It has also undertaken to sponsor university scholarships for Bermudians in blockchain technology development and regulatory compliance, and to make capital available for investment in new Bermuda-based blockchain companies.

- Medici Ventures LLC, a subsidiary of overstock.com (the world's first major enterprise to accept Bitcoin), will create at least 30 jobs in Bermuda over three years, develop a security token trading platform in Bermuda, support the training of Bermudians in software development, and collaborate with government, the BMA and other stakeholders in developing and improving Bermuda's legal and regulatory framework applicable to digital asset businesses.

- Shyft, a blockchain AML/ATF and identity startup, will invest up to US$10 million over the next three years into Bermuda's economy, support the training of Bermudians in blockchain technology and software development, and collaborate in the development and improvement of Bermuda's digital asset legal and regulatory framework. Shyft has also signed a separate MOU with Trunomi, a Bermuda-based consent and data rights platform, which aims to leverage Shyft's blockchain technology with Trunomi's expertise in consumer consent frameworks to support Bermuda in the implementation of an electronic ID scheme.

- Omega One, an agency brokerage for cryptocurrencies, will open an office in Bermuda, hire at least 20 Bermudians over the next three years, and donate 10% of a planned token sale to philanthropic causes (with 10% of the amount donated going to sports and community clubs in Bermuda).

- Arbitrade, a coin and cryptocurrency exchange, is to move its global headquarters to Bermuda.

Ownership and licensing requirements

Under current Bermuda law, and under the ICO Act and the DABA, no licensing requirements are (or will be) imposed on any person merely by virtue of that person holding any form of digital asset, unless that person does so in the course of its business and on behalf of another, in which case that person will likely be regarded as a digital asset services vendor and thus subject to regulation under the DABA.

An investment fund incorporated or formed in Bermuda which proposes to deal in digital assets as part of its investment strategy or programme may fall within the ambit of the Investment Funds Act 2006. This requires open-ended funds, subject to certain exceptions, to apply to the BMA for authorisation prior to commencing business, and subjects such funds to the ongoing supervision of the BMA. It does not apply to closed-ended funds, such as private equity funds.

Mining

Mining is specifically exempted from the scope of the DABA, as currently drafted. It will therefore remain an unregulated activity.

Although mining is not prohibited by any Bermuda law of which we are aware and will not be subject to regulation under the DABA, Bermuda's high energy costs will, it is anticipated, operate as a practical deterrent to the establishment of any mining operations in Bermuda.

Border restrictions and declaration

Bermuda imposes a foreign currency purchase tax of 1% whenever a Bermuda resident purchases a foreign currency from a Bermuda-based bank. This tax will not apply to most (if not all) purchases of cryptocurrency or other digital assets, on the grounds that these are purchased almost exclusively from digital exchanges, whereas the foreign currency purchase tax applies only to purchases from banks in Bermuda. This renders immaterial the question of whether "foreign currency" in this context would include a cryptocurrency (the BMA has not, to date, expressed a view).

There are no other border restrictions on cryptocurrencies or other digital assets; the only obligation to make a customs declaration in respect of any form of money arises in respect of cash or negotiable instruments in excess of US$10,000.

Reporting requirements

Digital asset businesses and their senior representatives will be subject to certain reporting obligations under the regulatory regime to be imposed by the DABA, as described in more detail above. The DABA will not impose any reporting requirements in respect of individual digital asset payments, irrespective of their value.

Estate planning and testamentary succession

There is no particular regime of Bermuda law which deals specifically with the treatment of cryptocurrencies or other digital assets upon the death of an individual holding them. This means that, in principle, digital assets will be treated in the same way as any other asset and may be bequeathed to beneficiaries in a will, or, if a person dies intestate, will fall to be dealt with under the Succession Act 1974.

The main potential difficulty that may arise is practical and is by no means unique to Bermuda; namely that anyone inheriting any kind of digital asset will, on the face of it, only be able to access that digital asset if the beneficiary has, or can obtain or access, the private key to the wallet in which it is stored. Most exchanges have policies in place to transfer digital assets to next of kin but these policies, and the transfer requirements, will vary between the exchanges.

* * *

Endnote

1. *Virtual Currencies: Key Definitions and Potential AML/CFT Risks*, FATF, June 2014.

Michael Hanson
Tel: +1 441 542 4501 / Email: michael.hanson@careyolsen.com

Michael Hanson is the managing partner of Carey Olsen Bermuda. His core practice is centred on human capital and regulatory law where he advises the largest insurance and reinsurance, banks and professional services businesses on the island.

Michael has particular and significant expertise in corporate, employment and regulatory investigations, complex executive disputes, multijurisdictional crisis management and executive benefit and incentive programs.

Michael is ranked as a leading lawyer by *Chambers Global* and *The Legal 500* describing him as "highly rated", "very knowledgeable", and that "his responsiveness is unbelievable!".

Adam Bathgate
Tel: +1 441 542 4500 / Email: adam.bathgate@careyolsen.com

Adam is counsel in the Bermuda office and advises on all aspects of Bermuda corporate law. His particular specialisms lie in debt finance transactions, the formation and maintenance of investment funds, and the fintech sector.

Adam has considerable expertise in the areas of fund finance, leveraged and acquisition finance and general lending, whether secured or unsecured. He has also worked on asset finance and structured finance transactions.

In the funds sphere, Adam's practice is largely focused on the formation and maintenance of private equity, infrastructure and real estate funds, including related downstream deal work, although he also has experience in hedge funds and hybrid funds.

Adam is ranked as a "rising star" in *IFLR1000*.

Carey Olsen Bermuda

Atlantic House, 11 Par-la-Ville Road, Hamilton HM 11, Bermuda
Tel: +1 441 542 4500 / URL: www.careyolsen.com

British Virgin Islands

Clinton Hempel & Mark Harbison
Carey Olsen

Government attitude and definition

The British Virgin Islands ("**BVI**") regulator, the Financial Services Commission ("**FSC**"), recognises Bitcoin- and Ether-focused funds. This has resulted in leading fintech companies such as Bitfinex, Finamatrix and Football Coin being incorporated in the BVI. The primary focus of the service providers in the jurisdiction relates to initial coin offerings ("**ICOs**") and initial token offerings ("**ITOs**"). The challenge for the BVI, along with all other jurisdictions, is how to regulate the fundraising for such offerings. Most ICOs and ITOs established in the BVI use the structure of a business company incorporated under the BVI Business Companies Act 2004 (the "**BCA**"). This provides corporate flexibility, relative free-flow of funds, and low comparative establishment costs associated with a BVI company.

At the present time neither the FSC nor the BVI Government have given any form of regulatory advice or guidance in respect of ICOs or ITOs, nor have they issued any guidance for cryptocurrencies, blockchain or financial technology more generally. The BVI Government has indicated its intention to establish a legal framework that is supportive of the cryptocurrency and financial technology sectors in the BVI, but no draft legislation or consultations have been announced. In the meantime, the consensus view is that the BVI are following a 'wait and see' approach to the development of how ICOs and ITOs will be regulated.

Some ICOs and ITOs have been promoted as an unregulated form of investment, relying on the argument that tokens do not constitute a security for the purposes of the different investor protection laws around the world. As a result, some token issuers have used ICOs and ITOs as a means of avoiding regulation. However, depending on the nature of an investor's rights that attach to a token, it is possible that a token may represent a form of security, particularly if those rights entitle the investor to a share of the profits of the token issuer and the investor is not involved in the day-to-day management and control of the token issuer. Tokens that give investors other rights, such as licences to products and services, could fall outside the scope of being classed as a security. However, token issuers and investors still need to proceed with caution because it is possible that those types of tokens could be classed as a security, depending on the facts and circumstances of each case and the investor protection laws that apply to the tokens. Further, how the gains on tokens are taxed in different countries may also influence how they are recognised for regulatory purposes.

While the consensus is that ICOs and ITOs will not be subject to securities legislation in the BVI, whether or not the legislation applies will be fact-specific and driven by the nature of the underlying assets of the respective offering. In particular, if a company wishes to: (a) collect and pool investor funds for the purpose of collective investment; and (b) issue fund interests that entitle the holder to receive, on demand or within a specified period after demand, an amount calculated by reference to the value of a proportionate interest in the whole or in a part of the net assets of the company, then it will be deemed open-ended and need to be licensed. There are a number of fund options in the BVI, including public funds, professional funds, private funds, approved funds and incubator funds.

With regard to cryptocurrencies, these are not treated as money in the BVI and do not enjoy equal dignity with domestic or foreign fiat currencies. Pursuant to the Legal Tender (Adoption of the United States Currency) Act 1959 and the Coinage and Legal Tender Act 1973, the US dollar is the legal tender of the BVI. BVI legislation is silent regarding the definition of what is money and currency and the existing regulatory framework does not contemplate cryptocurrencies.

There are no government-backed cryptocurrencies and the BVI's constitutional and currency system means it does not have a central bank.

Cryptocurrency regulation

As discussed above, there is no current regulatory framework for cryptocurrencies in the BVI; similarly there is no express prohibition. The government has indicated a willingness to establish a supportive legal framework, but the industry is still in its early stages in the BVI. The regulation of cryptocurrencies, ICOs and ITOs will be determined by how the framework for such transactions fits into the existing regulatory framework in the BVI which, as noted, above was drafted without contemplating cryptocurrencies.

Sales regulation

The Securities and Investment Business Act 2010 ("**SIBA**") regulates, amongst others, the provision of investment services from within the BVI. SIBA provides that any person carrying on, or presenting themselves as carrying on, investment business of any kind in or from within the BVI must do so through an entity regulated and licensed by the FSC (subject to the safe harbours in SIBA). Investment business is widely defined and covers: (i) dealing in investments; (ii) arranging deals in investments; (iii) investment management; (iv) investment advice; (v) custody of investments; (vi) administration of investments; and (vii) operating an investment exchange.

"Investments" is also widely defined and may include: (i) shares, interests in a partnership or fund interests; (ii) debentures; (iii) instruments giving entitlements to shares interests or debentures; (iv) certificates representing investments; (v) options; (vi) futures; (vii) contracts for difference; and (viii) long-term insurance contracts.

Cryptocurrencies in general, and tokens under an ICO or ITO, do not fall immediately within any of the above criteria and therefore do not fall under the SIBA regime. Where they may fall under the SIBA regime is where the token that is subject to the ICO or ITO is viewed as security or derivative. This will be fact-specific to the relevant ICO or ITO that is being undertaken and would require a level of detailed analysis in each case.

Anti-money laundering

BVI AML legislation must be carefully considered with respect to an ICO or ITO. AML legislation primarily focuses on regulated entities in the BVI and requires certain policies and procedures to be established by "relevant persons" conducting "relevant business". Both the terms "relevant persons" and "relevant business" are strictly defined terms. The requirements seek generally to provide for regulatory rules to minimise and eliminate any form of money laundering or terrorist financing through the BVI. If the company is deemed to carry out "relevant business" (e.g. it is a fund, provides money transmission services, advises on money brokering, etc.) then it has to obtain and maintain client KYC and have internal systems and controls and provide the FSC with a copy of such internal policies for approval.

ICOs of standard utility tokens would not be caught within the definition of "relevant business", and therefore the company is unlikely to be a "relevant person". However, the company and its directors should nevertheless be aware of the BVI AML obligations as a way of future-proofing the business.

Taxation

There are no specific taxes levied against cryptocurrencies in the BVI. The BVI is a tax-neutral jurisdiction and does not have any withholding tax, capital gains taxes, income tax or corporate taxes at the time of writing. In the unlikely event that a BVI entity owns BVI situate land, the entity may be responsible for stamp duties.

Where there is an ICO or ITO, the exchange operators will need to be cognisant of the impact of the Foreign Account Tax Compliance Act ("**FATCA**") and Common Reporting Standards, which will be relevant to determining the ultimate beneficial ownership of the BVI entity issuing the ICO or ITO. While these pieces of legislation will not be immediately relevant at the launch of the ICO or ITO, they will need to be considered as the BVI business company acting as the issuer starts to conduct business more generally.

Money transmission laws and anti-money laundering requirements

The relevant money transmittal law in the BVI is the Financing and Money Services Act, 2009 ("**FMSA**") which regulates money services business. FMSA defines money services as including:

* money transmission services;
* cheque exchange services;
* currency exchange services; and
* the issuance, sale or redemption of money orders or travelers' cheques or other such services.

The regime under FMSA is broadly equivalent to the Payment Services Directive. As set out above, the consensus is that for the purposes of BVI legislation, "money" and "currency" refer to fiat currencies rather than cryptocurrencies. It is therefore unlikely that ICO or ITO transactions solely involving cryptocurrency or digital tokens would be viewed as falling with the definition of money services and the FMSA regime. Where a cryptocurrency transaction is used to facilitate currency exchange services, then this may be viewed as the provision of money services and therefore fall within the remit of FMSA.

Promotion and testing

There are no "sandbox" or other programmes intended to promote research and investment in cryptocurrency in the jurisdiction at present.

Ownership and licensing requirements

As discussed above, there are no specific regulatory requirements in respect of cryptocurrencies; set out below is the framework for the approved financial manager regime under BVI law.

For persons wishing to act as an investment manager or investment advisor in the BVI, regulatory approval from the FSC may be obtained under: (1) SIBA; or (2) the Investment Business (Approved Managers) Regulations, 2012 (the "**Approved Manager Regulations**"). The Approved Manager Regulations were implemented in 2012 with a view to offering a significantly simplified approval process and a lighter regulatory framework than that provided under SIBA.

An Approved Manager's licence authorises you to act as manager or advisor to: (1) BVI incubator funds; (2) BVI approved funds; (3) BVI private funds; (4) BVI professional funds; (5) funds domiciled in certain recognised jurisdictions; and (6) closed-ended funds domiciled in the BVI or in certain recognised jurisdictions, if they have the key characteristics of a private or professional fund. However, an Approved Manager cannot offer services to public funds.

The Approved Manager can be set up as a BVI company or a BVI partnership. The Approved Manager licence is fairly easy to obtain, provided that the directors of the Approved Manager can demonstrate expertise and experience in the area of investment business. The main restriction is that an Approved Manager must not manage assets exceeding US$400m if managing regulated investment funds (such as professional and private funds) or US$1bn if managing unregulated funds. The Approved Manager licence can also be used for the provision of asset management to individuals. The limit on assets under management for the provision of asset-management services depends on the type of asset management to be provided, but will not be below US$400m.

There are no capital requirements for the Approved Manager and there is no need to appoint a compliance officer. In contrast, a holder of a licence under SIBA will have to submit audited financial statements, appoint a compliance officer, provide employees with compliance training, etc. That said, the advantage of having a licence under SIBA is that there is no limitation on the value of assets under management. For eligible investment managers or investment advisors, the advantage of becoming licensed as an Approved Manager, as opposed to becoming licensed under SIBA, is that the ongoing obligations owed by an Approved Manager are less onerous than those owed by an investment business licensee under SIBA, namely:

An Approved Manager must:

- at all times have at least two directors, one of which must be an individual. However, directors can be resident in any jurisdiction;
- have an authorised representative appointed;
- submit financial statements annually, which need not be audited; and
- submit an annual return which has to contain certain prescribed information such as that the directors continue to be fit and proper, details of the persons to whom the manager provides service, complaints received, etc.

Mining

Mining Bitcoin in the BVI is permitted and there are no current regulations in respect of mining activity.

Border restrictions and declaration

Further to the earlier distinction between cryptocurrency holdings and fiat currency, there are no border restrictions or obligations currently in place in the BVI in respect of cryptocurrencies.

Reporting requirements

There are no reporting requirements or thresholds for payments made by cryptocurrency currently in place in the BVI. The Beneficial Ownership Secure Search System Act 2017 ("**BOSS**") requires BVI companies and their registered agents to record information about the beneficial ownership of a BVI company on a central government-controlled, but confidential, database. Beneficial ownership is determined by reference to control tests, i.e. share ownership, voting rights, the right to remove a majority of the board of directors, and the exercise of significant influence and control over a company.

Estate planning and testamentary succession

Cryptocurrencies have not been widely used for the purposes of estate planning and testamentary succession under BVI law. If, in the unlikely event that the cryptocurrency is regarded as an asset actually situated in the BVI, then a deceased's cryptocurrency could not be validly transmitted to his/her heirs or beneficiaries until an application is made to the BVI High Court Probate Registry (the "**Registry**"). To deal with the deceased's cryptocurrency, a person would need to be appointed as legal personal representative of the deceased, by obtaining the appropriate grant from the BVI Probate Registry. There are two types of grant that may be obtained: (1) Grant of Probate (where the deceased left a will which expressly deals with the BVI cryptocurrency); and (2) Grant of Letters of Administration (where the deceased did not leave a will expressly covering the BVI cryptocurrency). In respect of the latter, the deceased would be deemed to have died "intestate" in relation to the BVI cryptocurrency – even if they had a valid will covering assets in other jurisdictions.

Clinton Hempel
Tel: +27 76 412 6091 / Email: clinton.hempel@careyolsen.com
Clinton is the managing partner of Carey Olsen's British Virgin Islands practice group.
Clinton has practised law for over 20 years and has significant experience in advising financial institutions, public and private businesses, high-net-worth individuals and their onshore advisers on the laws of the British Virgin Islands. He advises on a wide range of corporate and commercial transactions, financings and investment structures, including takeovers, joint ventures, mergers and acquisitions and public and private equity transactions. Clinton also advises on all aspects of BVI regulatory compliance and risk management.

Mark Harbison
Tel: +1 284 394 4034 / Email: mark.harbison@careyolsen.com
Mark is an associate in Carey Olsen's British Virgin Islands office. Mark focuses on a broad range of corporate, commercial and finance transactions. Mark has acted for a wide variety of clients in respect of mergers and acquisitions, cross-border debt finance, corporate restructurings and voluntary liquidations. Mark has also worked on a number of BVI regulatory compliance projects.

Carey Olsen

Rodus Building, PO Box 3093, Road Town, Tortola, British Virgin Islands
Tel: +1 284 394 4030 / Fax: +1 284 494 4155 / URL: www.careyolsen.com

Canada

Conrad Druzeta, Simon Grant & Matthew Peters
Bennett Jones LLP

Government attitude and definition

The general attitude of the Canadian government (including regulatory agencies) to cryptocurrencies has been a mix of caution and encouragement: caution in terms of protecting investors and the public, but encouragement in its support of new technology. For example, as early as 2015, the Standing Senate Committee on Banking, Trade and Commerce produced a report entitled, "Digital Currency: You Can't Flip This Coin", in which the committee stated:

> ...the Committee strongly believes that a balanced regulatory approach is needed in the digital currency sector. On one hand, the Committee is mindful that the government has the responsibility to protect consumers and root out illegal activity. On the other hand, it is critical that government action does not stifle innovation in digital currencies and its associated technologies that are in an early and delicate stage of development.

> Having completed the study, the Committee is of the opinion that the opportunities presented by digital currencies, technologies and businesses outweigh the challenges. The Committee is confident that the implementation of our recommendations will have positive outcomes for consumers, merchants, digital currency-related businesses, Canada's financial services sector and others. The Committee looks forward to timely government action designed to maximise the opportunities and manage the challenges facing the digital currency sector.

The Canadian government itself is also experimenting with blockchain technology. The National Research Council is testing blockchain to publish research grant and funding information in real time.[1]

For taxation purposes, cryptocurrencies are treated as commodities, not as money. Under securities laws, many cryptocurrencies or "tokens" are classified as securities.

Cryptocurrencies are not treated as legal tender in Canada. According to section 8 of the *Currency Act*, legal tender is coins issued by the Royal Canadian Mint under the *Royal Canadian Mint Act*, and notes issued by the Bank of Canada under the *Bank of Canada Act*.[2]

Despite cryptocurrency not being recognised as legal tender, the Bank of Canada tested Digital Depository Receipts (DDR) as a digital representation of Canadian currency in 2016 and 2017. DDR is a way to transfer central bank money on to a distributed ledger technology platform (DLT, or "blockchain"). DDRs are issued as digital tokens on a blockchain and act as a claim on central bank reserves.[3] This was tested in Project Jasper in the form of "CADcoin" where the Bank of Canada issued DDR, just like it would Canadian currency,[4] "in order to better understand the potential impacts of blockchain technology on Financial Market Infrastructure" ("**FMI**").[5]

Project Jasper was a joint initiative between the public and private sector, conducted by the Bank of Canada and Payments Canada with the help of banks and corporations (such as R3). Together, they built and tested a closed, simulated payment system to better understand the potential for blockchain to augment or displace FMI. Project Jasper marked the first ever DLT experiment in which a central bank partnered with private financial institutions.[6]

There were two phases of the project. Phase One was developed on an Ethereum platform. Ethereum uses Proof-of-Work ("**PoW**") consensus protocol to operationally settle transactions. Phase Two was built on the Corda platform. In this test, the Bank of Canada served as a notary, accessing the entire ledger and verifying the transactions.[7]

The Bank of Canada also considered legal settlement finality. Project Jasper was designed so that a transfer of DDR equalled a full and irrevocable transfer of the underlying claim on central bank deposits.[8] While using DDR requires significant Bank of Canada involvement in a system that many hope will be decentralised, it can provide certainty regarding legal settlement finality rarely found in blockchains.

Cryptocurrency regulation

In Canada, cryptocurrencies are primarily regulated under securities laws as part of the securities' regulators mandate to protect the public.

Sales regulation

In Canada, securities laws are enacted on a provincial and territorial basis rather than federally. The securities rules throughout the provinces and territories have largely been harmonised. The Canadian Securities Administrators (the "**CSA**"), an unofficial organisation, represents all provincially and territorially mandated securities regulators in Canada.

Defining a "security"

The securities laws of a province or territory apply to people and entities: (a) distributing securities in that jurisdiction; or (b) from that jurisdiction. "Security" is broadly defined in Canadian securities legislation and covers various categories of transactions, including "an investment contract".[9] The test for determining whether a transaction constitutes an investment contract, and therefore a security, for the purposes of Canadian securities laws was established by the Supreme Court of Canada, referring to United States jurisprudence.[10] This test, the "**Investment Contract Test**", requires that in order for an instrument to be classified as a security, each of the following four elements must be satisfied:

1. there must be an investment of money;

2. with an intention or expectation of profit;

3. in a common enterprise (being an enterprise "in which the fortunes of the investor are interwoven with and dependent upon the efforts and success of those seeking the investment, or of third parties"[11]); and

4. the success or failure of which is significantly affected by the efforts of those other than the investor.

The application of the Investment Contract Test has been the subject of judicial and regulatory consideration that is beyond the scope of this overview. That being said, where the elements of the Investment Contract Test are not strictly satisfied, securities regulators in Canada are mandated to consider the policy objectives and the purpose of the securities legislation (namely, the protection of the investing public by requiring full and fair disclosure) in making a final determination. This acts a little like a legislative "basket clause". The Supreme Court of Canada has stated that substance, not form, is the governing factor in determining whether a contract (or group of transactions) is an investment contract.[12]

Regulator guidance

In addition to the law in Canada as set out in the Investment Contract Test, certain securities regulators in Canada have issued notices and statements regarding the potential application of securities laws to cryptocurrency offerings ("**ICOs**"). These notices and statements confirm that Canadian securities regulators, while receptive to innovation and development, continue to carefully monitor investment activity in this space.

In March 2017, the Ontario Securities Commission issued a press release[13] warning that ICOs may trigger certain Ontario securities law requirements (including registration or prospectus requirements), even if the coins or tokens do not represent shares or equity in an entity.

In August 2017, the CSA issued Staff Notice 46-307 *Cryptocurrency Offerings* ("**SN 46-307**").[14] Currently, this is the most comprehensive guidance regarding the applicability of existing securities laws to cryptocurrency offerings in Canada. In SN 46-307, the CSA stated that it was aware of businesses marketing their coins or tokens as software products, and taking the position that the offerings are exempt from securities laws, but cautioned that "in many cases, when the totality of the offering or arrangement is considered, the coins/tokens should properly be considered securities", including because they are investment contracts.[15] In line with Canadian jurisprudence and the Investment Contract Test, the CSA affirmed that it will consider substance over form in assessing whether or not securities laws apply to an ICO.

The CSA further cautioned that, depending on the facts and circumstances, coins or tokens may be considered derivatives and subject to applicable legislative and regulatory requirements.

In June 2018, the CSA issued Staff Notice 46-308 *Securities Law Implications for Offerings of Tokens* ("**SN 46-308**").[16] In SN 46-308, the CSA generally reiterated the position it took in 46-307. Importantly, it again confirms that an ICO may involve a distribution of securities not covered by the non-exclusive list of enumerated categories of securities in the OSA if the offering otherwise falls within the policy objectives and purpose of securities legislation. In addition, the CSA indicated that it had found that most offerings of tokens purporting to be utility tokens involved the distribution of a security, and specifically an investment contract.

Securities law requirements

In Canada, absent an available exemption, a prospectus must be filed and approved with the relevant regulator before a person or entity can legally distribute securities. A prospectus is a comprehensive disclosure document which seeks to satisfy the public protection aim of securities laws by disclosing information about the securities and the issuer to prospective investors. Exemptions from the prospectus requirement are principally set out in National Instrument 45-106 – *Prospectus Exemptions* ("**NI 45-106**"). Generally, securities sold pursuant to a prospectus exemption are subject to resale restrictions and, particularly in the case of a non-reporting issuer (i.e. an issuer that is not a public entity and is not subject to ongoing securities compliance and disclosure obligations), may never be freely tradeable. Resale restrictions rules are set out in National Instrument 45-102 – *Resale of Securities* ("**NI 45-102**").

In addition to the prospectus requirement, an individual or entity engaged in the business of distribution of securities, or advising others with respect to securities, is required to register with Canadian securities regulators. The requirements for registration, and exemptions from registration, are set out in National Instrument 31-103 – *Registration Requirements, Exemptions and Ongoing Registrant Obligations* ("**NI 31-103**"). Once registered, the person or entity is subject to various reporting and compliance obligations. NI 31-103 covers various other categories of registration in addition to dealers and advisers, such as investment fund managers.

Legal status of ICOs in Canada

The present Canadian regulatory trend is to apply and adapt existing securities laws, including the Investment Contract Test, to transactions involving blockchain or cryptocurrency which resemble traditional securities, without regard to the use of new technology.[17] In order to make a determination on whether or not an ICO constitutes a distribution of securities, Canadian securities regulators will perform a case-by-case, highly fact-dependent analysis, focusing on the substance and structure of the ICO rather than its form.[18] Even if an ICO cannot be said to fall within the specific definition of a "security" provided by legislation, as discussed above, it may nonetheless be found to involve the sale of securities if it otherwise triggers the policy objectives and purposes of securities legislation.

Applying the investment contract test to ICOs

As discussed above, there is presently no caselaw or legislation in Canada definitively addressing when an ICO or other sale of cryptocurrency will constitute a distribution of securities. However, statements from the CSA offer guidance regarding certain elements of an ICO that may increase the likelihood of the coins or tokens being found to be securities.[19] While each offering of coins or tokens should be analysed based on the particular circumstances of the offering and the features of the coin or token, these statements, together with statements by United States securities regulators on the subject,[20] offer insight into how the Investment Contract Test may be applied to ICOs.

Coins or tokens as securities

If an ICO is found to constitute a distribution of securities, it will trigger Canadian securities law requirements, including prospectus and registration requirements, unless an exemption from the same is available. Individuals or businesses intending to rely on prospectus exemptions in connection with an ICO will need to ensure that they satisfy the conditions for such exemption as set out in NI 45-106, including any applicable resale restrictions in NI 45-102. Resale restrictions will be of particular concern if coins or tokens begin trading on cryptocurrency exchanges or otherwise in the secondary market following their initial sale. Issuers of a cryptocurrency that is found to be a security will also need to ensure that they comply with any applicable registration requirements, including dealer registration, or that the conditions for exemption from registration are fully satisfied. Failure to comply with securities laws may result in regulatory or enforcement action by securities regulators against the parties behind the ICO, including fines and potential incarceration.

Taxation

Characterisation of cryptocurrency for tax purposes

The Canadian tax authorities currently adopt the position that, despite its nomenclature, a cryptocurrency is not a "currency" for income tax purposes. Rather, cryptocurrency is akin to a commodity (albeit an "intangible"), the value of which will fluctuate based on external factors driven largely by investor sentiment and basic supply/demand. In this respect, cryptocurrency could be analogised as the virtual equivalent of a precious metal such as gold or silver.

Accordingly, the acquisition of, and transacting in, cryptocurrencies is generally regarded as the acquisition of, and transacting in, commodities. This characterisation has significantly different tax implications under Canadian tax law as compared to "normal" cash (even foreign currency) transactions.

(a) *Acquisition of cryptocurrency*

The threshold question is whether the initial acquisition of a cryptocurrency is a taxable event that potentially triggers a Canadian income tax liability to the person acquiring the cryptocurrency. The answer depends on the manner, purpose and circumstances in which the cryptocurrency is acquired.

If the cryptocurrency is acquired through "mining" activities of a commercial nature (*i.e.*, mining carried out generally for business purposes or in connection with a business), the current published administrative position of the Canadian tax authorities is that the acquirer will be required to report business income for the year determined with reference to the value of the mined cryptocurrency. For this purpose, the mined cryptocurrency will generally be treated as inventory of the business. Such a holder will have a myriad of tax issues distinct from the acquisition of cryptocurrency from non-mining activities, and must be reviewed on a case-by-case basis.

The acquisition of cryptocurrency as a pure speculative investment, similar to physical gold or a publicly-traded security, is generally not a taxable event to the person acquiring the cryptocurrency. However, the acquisition will establish the holder's "cost" in the cryptocurrency for Canadian tax purposes, which is relevant in the determination of the tax consequences that will be realised later when the cryptocurrency is eventually sold or otherwise exchanged.

This is to be contrasted with the acquisition of cryptocurrency as consideration for the provision of goods or services, or as compensation for some other right of payment. Such transactions are generally governed at this time by the Canadian tax authorities' position regarding "barter transactions", which is described in greater detail below under the heading "*Using cryptocurrencies in business transactions – Barter transaction*".

(b) *Determining a holder's tax cost in cryptocurrency*

Once a cryptocurrency has been acquired, it will be important to determine its cost for Canadian tax purposes, which is a fundamental concept for determining the future income tax consequences on an eventual disposition of the cryptocurrency.

Where a cryptocurrency is purchased in exchange for Canadian currency, the cost of the cryptocurrency for income tax purposes will be equal to the amount of cash paid, plus any directly related acquisition expenses. If foreign currency is used, the holder will generally be required to convert the foreign currency into the Canadian-dollar equivalent at the applicable rate, pursuant to Canadian tax rules.

Cryptocurrencies can obviously be acquired by several alternative means, including commercial business transactions and other forms of "barter" exchanges. The particular facts surrounding any such acquisition could have meaningful distinctions regarding the determination of the holder's tax cost upon the acquisition of the cryptocurrency (see below, under the heading "*Using cryptocurrencies in business transactions – Barter transaction*").

(c) *Tax on disposition of cryptocurrency*

A person will realise taxable income (or loss) on an eventual disposition of a cryptocurrency. This includes a sale of the cryptocurrency for cash and the use of the cryptocurrency to pay for goods or services, or as consideration under other contractual rights/obligations (*i.e.,* a "barter transaction", described below).

If the cryptocurrency has a value at the time of its disposition in excess of its tax cost, it will be critical to determine whether the holder should report such excess as being on capital account (*i.e.,* a capital gain) or whether the proceeds should be reported as business income. This is a material distinction for tax purposes.

Generally, the buying and selling of a commodity can be regarded as being on capital account unless it is carried out in the context of a business of buying and selling such commodities, or such buying and selling otherwise amounts to an "adventure or concern in the nature of trade". This is a factual, case-by-case determination requiring a detailed review of the holder's dealings with such commodities.

If a person acquires cryptocurrency as payment for goods or services in the normal course of the person's business (even if the person is not, *per se*, in the business of buying and selling cryptocurrencies as part of a speculative investment business), there is a risk that any appreciation realised when the person disposes of the cryptocurrency will be fully taxable as business income. Again, this issue is fact-dependent, should be reviewed on a case-by-case basis, and is described in greater detail below.

Using cryptocurrencies in business transactions

(a) *Barter transaction*

A person can accept a commodity in exchange for the provision of a good or service or as consideration for some other form of right of payment, with such transaction being subject to tax treatment under Canada's "barter transaction" tax rules.

In a barter transaction using cryptocurrency, the following must be considered by the person (referred to below as the "provider") that accepts a cryptocurrency as consideration in exchange for a good, service or other right:

- The provider will generally realise business income for Canadian income tax purposes equal to the fair market value of the goods, services or other rights provided (the "**Business Income Inclusion**"). For this purpose (but not for other purposes – see, *e.g.*, the sales tax implications described below), the value of the cryptocurrency at the time of the exchange is generally not the determining factor.

- The provider will generally acquire the cryptocurrency with a cost for Canadian income tax purposes equal to the Business Income Inclusion.

- The provider is now the owner of the cryptocurrency and must (eventually) do something with it, such as sell it to an investor or use it to purchase goods/services/rights in connection with its own business. Any gain or loss realised by the provider on an eventual disposition of the cryptocurrency (*i.e.*, the difference between the provider's cost in the cryptocurrency, and the amount received on the eventual disposition) will be taxable at such time to the provider. The issue then becomes whether such gain/loss is treated as being on full income account or on account of capital (the income tax treatment being materially different as between the two) (see the discussion above under the heading "*Characterisation of cryptocurrency for tax purposes – Determining a holder's tax cost in cryptocurrency*"). Managing the provider's exposure to fluctuations in the value of the cryptocurrency post-acquisition will be a material and practical concern.

Another type of increasingly prevalent transaction (which may or may not be properly characterised as a "business transaction") is the acquisition by a person of one cryptocurrency ("crypto #1") in exchange for a different cryptocurrency ("crypto #2"). Such a transaction will also be considered a barter transaction involving the exchange of one commodity for another commodity. The person will generally be considered to have acquired crypto #1 with a tax cost equal to the fair market value of the crypto #2 given up in exchange, computed as of the time of the barter transaction. The additional complication in this scenario is that the person acquiring crypto #1 will also be considered to have disposed of crypto #2, and will have to report any income/gain in respect of crypto #2 for Canadian income tax purposes (the person must therefore know his/her tax cost in crypto #2, which depends on the manner in which crypto #2 was originally acquired by such person).

(b) *Sales tax implications*

Canada imposes a federal sales tax (the goods and services tax, or "**GST**") on the supply of many goods and services, subject to detailed exemptions. Most Canadian provinces and territories also levy sales tax, which is often "harmonised" with the federal sales tax to effectively create one blended federal/provincial (or territorial) rate. Persons that are required to charge and collect federal GST (or harmonised sales tax) in respect of a business activity can generally claim a rebate in respect of such tax that the person directly incurs in the course of carrying on such business (generally referred to as an input tax credit or "**ITC**"). The ITC mechanism is generally intended to mitigate the duplication of sales tax throughout a supply chain, and is designed to ensure that the cost of sales tax is ultimately borne solely by the end consumer of any particular good or service.

As with any provision of goods or services subject to federal and provincial/territorial sales taxes, a provider of goods/services that accepts cryptocurrency in lieu of government-issued currency must charge, collect and remit the appropriate sales tax. This may prove easier said than done in the context of cryptocurrency.

In this respect, the provider must be careful not to use the Business Income Inclusion amount (which is relevant under the Canadian tax authorities' current administrative policy to determine the provider's income tax associated with the sale) in determining the applicable amount of sales tax. For federal GST purposes, the Canadian tax authorities require that the provider charge, collect and remit GST based on the value of the cryptocurrency at the time of the sale. Presumably, the purchaser would be entitled to claim an input tax credit (if available) in respect of the full GST charged, if incurred in the course of a business activity.

While this may sound manageable at a high level, a few practical issues arise for the provider:

- How does the provider determine the value of the cryptocurrency at the precise moment of sale, particularly when cryptocurrencies are traded in non-traditional marketplaces and the value can swing wildly from day to day (possibly minute-by-minute)? What record-keeping is required by the service provider to justify the amount upon which it charges sales tax?

- How does the provider charge, collect and remit the sales tax in a transaction entirely handled in cryptocurrency, namely where the sales tax portion is also paid in cryptocurrency? The provider must remit to the Canadian tax authorities in Canadian currency (not cryptocurrency), meaning that the provider will be forced to either remit an equivalent amount of cash from other sources, or sell a sufficient amount of the cryptocurrency to generate the cash to satisfy the remittance. Given the volatility of most cryptocurrencies, an inherent risk is borne by the provider in collecting the sales tax in cryptocurrency.

- Corporate directors are personally liable for any deficiencies in collecting or remitting sales tax. It is therefore critical for the provider of goods/services to take reasonable measures to ensure full compliance and mitigate any associated risk.

Money transmission laws and anti-money laundering requirements

Canada was the first country to approve regulation of cryptocurrencies in the context of anti-money laundering. In 2014, the Parliament of Canada passed Bill C-31. This bill amends Canada's *Proceeds of Crime (Money Laundering) and Terrorist Financing Act* to include digital currencies. The bill laid out a framework for regulating entities "dealing in digital currencies", treating them as money services businesses ("**MSBs**"). As MSBs, those dealing in digital currencies are subject to the same record keeping, verification procedures, suspicious transaction reporting and registration requirements as MSBs dealing in fiat currencies.[21] As of July 2018, the amendments resulting from Bill C-31 had not been proclaimed in force.

Promotion and testing

The CSA Regulatory Sandbox was set up to encourage the development of innovative products and services. The Sandbox allows companies engaged in cryptocurrency matters to register or seek exemptive relief (generally on a time-limited basis) in order to test products and services in the Canadian market.

Ownership and licensing requirements

As noted above, an individual or entity engaged in the business of distribution of securities, or advising others with respect to securities, may be required to register with Canadian securities regulators. Similarly, investment fund managers are required to be registered.

On December 11, 2017 the Investment Industry Regulatory Organization of Canada ("**IIROC**"), the organisation that governs persons and companies registered under securities law, issued a notice to its members regarding margin requirements for cryptocurrency futures contracts that trade on commodity futures exchanges. According to the notice, members are required to market and margin crypto futures contracts daily at the greatest of: (a) 50% of market value of the contracts; (b) the margin required by the futures exchange on which the contracts are entered into; (c) the margin required by the futures exchange's clearing corporation; and (d) the margin required by the Dealer Member's clearing broker.

Mining

Because mining converts electrical energy (typically drawn from the power grid or a private power source) into waste heat in proportion to the difficulty of the underlying mathematical problem, it can result in large quantities of power being used for what may be perceived as a socially undesirable purpose. Furthermore, because mining enables the operation of a variety of cryptocurrencies (e.g. Bitcoin), it functions as a convenient point for regulatory intervention. For those reasons, many official bodies have started to explore, or in some cases implemented, laws or policies that contemplate cryptocurrency mining. In Canada, governmental regulators appear to have adopted a largely "hands-off" approach for the time being.

However, Hydro Quebec (a Quebec Crown entity) recently announced the implementation of higher power prices for users involved in cryptocurrency mining, the effect of which may be to discourage such activities in that Province. We expect to see further intervention by government actors, as the quantity of power used by cryptocurrency mining operations, along with the use of various cryptocurrencies to facilitate illegal activities, continues to grow. To counteract the deleterious effects of such regulations on their operations, we additionally expect to see bitcoin miners move to private power sources as time goes on.

Border restrictions and declaration

There are no border restrictions or declaration requirements as such.

Reporting requirements

See "*Money transmission laws and anti-money laundering requirements*", above. MSBs are required to send a large cash transaction report to the Financial Transactions and Reports Analysis Centre of Canada ("**FINTRAC**") upon receipt of an amount of $10,000 or more in cash in the course of a single transaction, or receipt of two or more cash amounts of less than $10,000 each that total $10,000 or more, if the transactions were made by the same individual or entity within 24 hours of each other.

Estate planning and testamentary succession

Canada levies no separate estate tax, unlike many countries. However, a deceased is deemed to dispose of their property on death for its fair market value, which can result in income taxes being payable by the estate. Although it is far from settled, the Canada Revenue Agency currently takes the view that cryptocurrencies are generally commodities rather than currency, and that trading in cryptocurrencies will usually (with some possible exceptions) be regarded as being on capital account. In such circumstances, the estate will have to pay tax on any capital gains accrued as of the date of death. For a more detailed discussion of tax issues, see "Taxation" above.

In terms of estate planning, given the anonymous, decentralised nature of cryptocurrencies held on a blockchain, it will be imperative to include instructions on where to locate a copy of the private key related to the cryptocurrency. It would be unwise to include a private key in the will itself, since wills generally become public documents following probate.

* * *

Endnotes

1. https://globalnews.ca/news/3977745/ethereum-blockchain-canada-nrc/.
2. *Currency Act*, RSC 1985 c. C-52.
3. https://www.bis.org/publ/qtrpdf/r_qt1709f.pdf.
4. https://www.bankofcanada.ca/wp-content/uploads/2017/05/fsr-june-2017-chapman.pdf.

5. https://www.coindesk.com/project-jasper-lessons-bank-of-canada-blockchain-project/.

6. Payments Canada, Bank of Canada, and R3, *Project Jasper White Paper*, June 2017, p.8. https://www.payments.ca/sites/default/files/29-Sep-17/jasper_report_eng.pdf.

7. https://www.bankofcanada.ca/wp-content/uploads/2017/05/fsr-june-2017-chapman.pdf.

8. https://www.bankofcanada.ca/wp-content/uploads/2017/05/fsr-june-2017-chapman.pdf.

9. *Securities Act*, RSO 1990, c S.5 ("**ONSA**"), s. 1(1). See also *Securities Act*, RSA 2000, c S-4 ("**ABSA**"), s. 1(ggg)(ii), (v) and (xiv).

10. *Pacific Coast Coin Exchange v Ontario Securities Commission*, [1978] 2 SCR 112 [*Pacific Coast*].

11. *Ibid.* at p. 129, quoting *SEC v. Glen W. Turner Enterprises, Inc.*, 474 F. 2d 476 (1973) at p.482.

12. Pacific Coin para 43. A flexible approach to defining an investment contract has also been promoted by the Ontario Securities Commission in *Bluestream Capital Corp, Re* (2015), 38 OSCB 2333.

13. See Ontario Securities Commission, News Release, "OSC Highlights Potential Securities Law Requirements for Businesses Using Distributed Ledger Technologies" at http://www.osc.gov.on.ca/en/NewsEvents_nr_20170308_osc-highlights-potential-securities-law-requirements.htm.

14. See Canadian Securities Administrators, Staff Notice 46-307 *Cryptocurrency Offerings* at http://www.osc.gov.on.ca/en/SecuritiesLaw_csa_20170824_cryptocurrency-offerings.htm.

15. See SN 46-307 at 3.

16. See Canadian Securities Administrators, Staff Notice 46-308 *Securities Law Implications for Offerings of Tokens* at http://www.osc.gov.on.ca/en/SecuritiesLaw_csa_20180611_46-308_securities-law-implications-for-offerings-of-tokens.htm.

17. SN 46-307, p.3.

18. *Ibid.*

19. See SN 46-307 and Canadian Securities Administrators, Staff Notice 46-308 *Securities Law Implications for Offerings of Tokens* [SN 46-308].

20. See United Stated Securities and Exchange Commission, *Report of Investigation Pursuant to Section 21(a) of the Securities Exchange Act of 1934: The DAO*, SEC Release No 81207 (July 25, 2017).

21. https://research.osc.gov.on.ca/c.php?g=699050&p=4969862.

Conrad Druzeta
Tel: +1 416 777 7466 / Email: druzetac@bennettjones.com

Conrad Druzeta is a co-head of the Fintech & Blockchain practice group. Conrad practises securities and corporate law, specialising in capital markets transactions, securities regulation, venture capital, private equity, and public and private mergers and acquisitions. He acts for clients in a wide range of industries, including life sciences, blockchain and fintech, mining, architecture and engineering, financial services and energy.

Conrad is experienced assisting clients on both public debt and equity offerings and private placements of securities, asset and share acquisitions, business combinations and reorganisations and project financing. He also advises private and public companies on complex and emerging securities regulation and corporate governance matters.

Simon Grant
Tel: +1 416 777 6246 / Email: grants@bennettjones.com

Simon Grant is a co-head of the Fintech & Blockchain practice group. Simon practises corporate and commercial law, with an emphasis on financing transactions.

Simon routinely acts for lenders, borrowers and sponsors on acquisition financings, mining debt financings, streaming transactions, cross-border loan facilities, project financings, forward sales, debtor-in-possession financings and capital markets transactions. He also advises end-users with respect to ISDA master agreements and related documentation.

Simon first joined Bennett Jones as an associate after summering and articling with the firm. He later re-joined the firm after practising with an international law firm in New York City.

Matthew Peters
Tel: +1 416 777 6151 / Email: petersm@bennettjones.com

Matthew Peters advises clients in various industries, including natural resources, manufacturing, financial services, telecommunications, pharmaceuticals and technology, in connection with international tax planning, domestic and cross-border mergers and acquisitions, corporate reorganisations, corporate finance, executive and employee compensation and various other tax matters. He has also represented clients before the Tax Court of Canada and the Federal Court of Appeal.

Matthew is a frequent speaker on international and domestic tax matters, and has written and presented papers at conferences and seminars across Canada and the United States. He is a member of the Canadian and Ontario Bar Associations, Canadian Tax Foundation, New York State Bar Association, American Bar Association and International Fiscal Association.

Bennett Jones LLP

3400 One First Canadian Place, P.O. Box 130, Toronto, ON, M5X 1A4, Canada
Tel: +1 416 777 4801 / Fax: +1 416 863 1716 / URL: www.bennettjones.com

Cayman Islands

Alistair Russell & Dylan Wiltermuth
Carey Olsen

Government attitude and definition

The Cayman Islands is a leading global financial centre and has, over the course of several decades, developed a reputation as one of the world's most innovative and business-friendly places to operate. The jurisdiction offers a stable society and political system, judicial and legislative links to the United Kingdom, tax neutrality, many sophisticated service providers, and a proportionate regulatory regime that focuses closely on the financial services industry, and in particular those catering to sophisticated and institutional investors based elsewhere.

It is this reputation and these attributes that have helped the jurisdiction become an obvious choice for many of those proposing to establish fintech-related structures, whether it be in the form of a fund vehicle investing into Digital Assets,[1] an exchange for the same, an initial coin offering ("**ICO**"), or otherwise.

Each of the Cayman Islands Government, the Cayman Islands Monetary Authority ("**CIMA**"), and industry bodies such as Cayman Finance, acknowledge the importance of continuing to attract fintech business to the jurisdiction and ensuring the further growth of the sector. They are also aware, however, of the need to balance this approach with maintaining the Cayman Islands' commitment to the highest standards of financial probity and transparency and the specific considerations that can accompany Digital Assets.

Consequently, there has been no precipitous introduction of new regulation of the Digital Asset space, but rather a more judicious review of the sector and existing regulatory framework. Currently, the Cayman Islands Government is in the process of considering the proposals of an industry working group convened by CIMA regarding the adoption of any additional regulatory measures or governance standards for the marketing or trading of Digital Assets within and from the Cayman Islands. It is anticipated that the conclusion of this review will be made public shortly, but our expectation is that the results of the process are unlikely to lead to a wholesale or dramatic change of the current regulatory burdens, and will instead maintain the existing pro-industry approach while providing welcome clarification on certain areas of potential ambiguity.

In advance of the publication of such review and any steps to implement the same, however, this chapter sets out the current legal position in the Cayman Islands.

Cryptocurrency regulation

Save for certain aspects of the Cayman Islands anti-money laundering regime (as further detailed below), the Cayman Islands has not enacted any law or imposed any regulation that specifically targets Digital Assets.

As such, whether any activity involving a Digital Asset is subject to regulation will largely be determined in accordance with: (a) the nature of the activity being conducted; and (b) how the relevant Digital Asset would best be classified within the existing legislative framework.

Although a detailed analysis of each is outside the scope of this chapter, a summary of the statutory regimes that are most likely to be of relevance are as follows:

<u>The Mutual Funds Law</u>

Pursuant to the Mutual Funds Law of the Cayman Islands, an entity formed or registered in the Cayman Islands that issues equity interests and pools the proceeds thereof, with the aim of spreading investment risks and enabling investors to receive profits or gains from the acquisition, holding, management or disposal of investments, may come within the ambit of that statute and be required to obtain a registration or licence from CIMA.[2] The particular nature or classification of the Digital Assets will not generally be of relevance, provided they are being held as an investment.

As such, any pooling vehicle that is investing into the Digital Asset space or accepting Digital Assets by way of subscription and then investing into more traditional asset classes, would be advised to seek Cayman Islands legal advice on the point.

<u>The Securities Investment Business Law</u>

Pursuant to the Securities Investment Business Law of the Cayman Islands, an entity formed or registered in or that is operating from the Cayman Islands which engages in dealing, arranging, managing or advising on the acquisition or disposal of Digital Assets, may come within the ambit of the Securities Investment Business Law and be required to obtain a registration or license from CIMA. This will, however, only apply to the extent that such Digital Assets constitute "securities" for the purposes thereof. The statute contains a detailed list of assets that are considered securities thereunder. Although such list does not currently make specific reference to any Digital Asset, in our view, certain types of Digital Asset are likely to constitute securities. Consequently, consideration will need to be given on a case-by-case basis as to whether the Digital Asset in question falls within one of the existing categories; for example, instruments creating or acknowledging indebtedness, options or futures. Equally, however, it seems clear that certain Digital Assets are likely to fall outside the definition, and thus outside the scope of the law (for instance, pure utility tokens and some cryptocurrencies).

<u>The Money Services Law</u>

Please see below for further details.

<u>Anti-money laundering regulations</u>

Please see below for further details.

Sales regulation

There are no securities or commodities laws in force in the Cayman Islands that apply specifically to Digital Assets (although please see the requirements of the Securities Investment Business Law as detailed above), whether in relation to their marketing and issuance by a Cayman Islands entity (e.g. pursuant to an ICO), or their sale by an existing holder.

In relation to the offering of securities or interests more broadly, where issuances or sales are targeted at investors based outside of the Cayman Islands, Cayman Islands law does not generally impose any prohibition or regulatory burden; it will instead look to the local authorities where such investors are based, to restrict or regulate the same as they see fit. With that said, this is one area in which the Cayman Islands Government's review may lead to further regulation; specifically, in circumstances where structures are established in order to offer Digital Assets to retail investors based elsewhere. Whether or not this is seen as a suitable step will, however, likely depend in part on the speed with which the major on-shore jurisdictions clarify their approach to Digital Assets under their own securities law regimes.

In relation to the offering, sale, or issuance of interests *within* the Cayman Islands, however, certain regulatory provisions should be borne in mind. For example, the Companies Law prohibits any exempted company formed in the Cayman Islands and not listed on the Cayman Islands Stock Exchange from offering its securities to the Cayman Islands public. The Limited Liability Companies Law includes a similar prohibition in relation to LLCs. Even persons based, formed or registered outside the Cayman Islands should be careful not to undertake any activities in relation to a sale or issuance of Digital Assets that would constitute "carrying on a business" in the Cayman Islands. To do so may entail various registration and licensing requirements and financial and criminal penalties for those who do not comply. There is no explicit definition of what will amount to "carrying on a business" for these purposes, and consequently, persons who propose to undertake concerted marketing to the Cayman Islands public, particularly if it involves engaging in any physical activity in the Cayman Islands, are encouraged to seek specific legal advice on the point.

In practice, however, these restrictions do not generally pose much of a practical concern for issuers given that:

(i) the "public" in this instance is taken to exclude other exempted companies, exempted limited partnerships, and LLCs (which together comprise the majority of Cayman Islands entities); and

(ii) issuers' target investors tend not to include other persons physically based in the Cayman Islands themselves.

For completeness, and as detailed further above, Cayman Islands persons, or those operating from within the Cayman Islands, arranging for the sale or issuance of Digital Assets by another, may come within the ambit of the Securities Investment Business Law regardless of where the activity takes place, or the ultimate investors are based.

Taxation

There are no income, inheritance, gift, capital gains, corporate, withholding or other such taxes imposed by the Cayman Islands government, including with respect to the issuance, holding, or transfer of Digital Assets.

Stamp duty may apply to original documents that are executed in the Cayman Islands (or are brought into the Cayman Islands following execution). However, the sums levied are generally of a nominal amount.

Entities formed or registered in the Cayman Islands may also apply for and, upon the payment of a fee of approximately US$1,830, receive a tax exemption certificate confirming that no law enacted in the Cayman Islands after the date thereof imposing any tax to be levied on profits, income, gains or appreciations shall apply to such entity or its operations. Such certificates will generally apply for a period of between 20 and 50 years (depending on the type of entity).

Money transmission laws and anti-money laundering requirements

Money transmission laws

Pursuant to the Money Services Law, any person carrying on a "money services business" in or from the Cayman Islands must first obtain a licence from CIMA. Any breach of this requirement will constitute a criminal offence.

For the purposes of the foregoing, a "money services business" means the business of providing (as a principal business), among other things, money transmission or currency exchange services.

Although there is no clear authority on the extent to which the foregoing would be seen to include such transactions in cryptocurrency or other Digital Assets, a cautious and substantive reading of the statute may, in some cases, warrant it. In particular, if the Digital Assets in question are primarily used to facilitate the transfer of fiat currency from one party to another, or the conversion between fiat currencies, the legislation may well apply. Consequently, persons wishing to establish such businesses are encouraged to consider closely the application of the Money Services Law and consult appropriate advisors.

Although a consideration of the requirements of the licensing application and approval process under the Money Services Law is beyond the scope of this chapter, it will generally require:

(i)   the maintenance of specified capital levels;

(ii) the appointment of approved auditors;

(iii) the provision of audited financials to CIMA;

(iv) the maintenance of proper records; and

(v)   the payment of an annual fee.

Anti-money laundering requirements

The very nature and, in some cases, the intended features of Digital Assets can present heightened compliance risks and, moreover, practical hurdles to addressing the same. Such features may include the lack of a trusted central counterparty, increased anonymity, and ease of cross-border transfer without any gating or restriction.

Consequently, the Cayman Islands authorities have maintained a keen focus on balancing the jurisdiction's long track record of innovation and the promotion of a business-friendly environment with its commitment to the prevention of crime and maintaining robust standards of transparency. To date, this has been done, not by establishing an entirely separate regime for Digital Assets, but by applying the purposive approach enshrined within the existing framework which focuses on the specific activity and the nature of the assets in question so as to properly quantify the risk that the same may be used to facilitate illegal activity. With that said, we anticipate that the Cayman Islands authorities will continue to provide clarifying guidance and updates to address any ambiguities or uncertainties that arise in relation to the current regime.

Pursuant to the provisions of the Proceeds of Crime Law, the Anti-Money Laundering Regulations, and the guidance notes thereon (together the "**AML Laws**"), any persons formed, registered or based in the Cayman Islands conducting "relevant financial business" are subject to various obligations aimed at preventing, identifying, and reporting money laundering and terrorist financing.

"Relevant financial business" is defined in the Proceeds of Crime Law, and encompasses a broad variety of activity, including the following which may be of particular relevance in the context of Digital Assets:

- money or value-transfer services;
- issuing and managing means of payment (specifically including electronic money);
- trading in transferable securities;
- money broking;
- securities investment business; and
- investing or administering funds or money on behalf of others.

As such, the relevant requirements may depend on the type of Digital Asset in question; for instance, whether it can best be classed as a currency or money substitute, a security, a utility token or something else. We would thus generally expect businesses that engage in the operation of cryptocurrency exchanges, cryptocurrency issuances, brokering transactions in cryptocurrency, the trading and management of Digital Assets that are properly classed as securities, and the investment of funds (whether in the form of fiat currency or cryptocurrency) on behalf of others into Digital Assets, to come within the scope of the AML Laws. Notably, Digital Assets that are purely in the nature of utility tokens may fall outside of the ambit of the regime. However, specific legal advice on such distinctions is vital to ensure proper compliance and readers are encouraged to generally adopt conservative approach.

Although a detailed consideration of the specific requirements of the AML Laws falls outside of the scope of this chapter, any person subject to the regime will generally need, among other things, to do the following:

- appoint a named individual as anti-money laundering compliance officer to oversee its adherence to the AML Laws and to liaise with the supervisory authorities;
- appoint named individuals as the money laundering reporting officer and a deputy for the same to act as a reporting line within the business; and
- implement procedures to ensure that counterparties are properly identified, risk-based monitoring is carried out (with specific regard to the nature of the counterparties, the geographic region of operation, and any risks specifically associated with new technologies such as Digital Assets), proper records are kept, and employees are properly trained.

As above, particular practical concerns will often arise in relation to Digital Assets, specifically with regard to the identification of counterparties and the monitoring of source and use of funds. Most, in our experience, will be best advised to consult specialist third party providers to assist with this process.

Promotion and testing

There are currently no 'sandbox' or other similar programmes in place in the Cayman Islands. However, the Cayman Islands Government has been vocal in promoting the Special Economic Zone ("**SEZ**") to those wishing to develop fintech-related products from the jurisdiction.

The SEZ offers businesses focused on the fintech industry the opportunity to establish physical operations within the Cayman Islands in a more streamlined manner. It provides several benefits, including a simpler, more rapid, and cost-effective work permit process, concessions with respect to local trade licences and ownership requirements, the ability to be operational within four to six weeks, and allocated office space.

When coupled with the other benefits of the jurisdiction and its recently updated intellectual property laws, the SEZ has proven highly popular with the fintech industry. To date, over

50 blockchain-focused companies have been established within it and this is expected to continue to grow. The SEZ also hosts a number of industry-focused events and conferences.

Ownership and licensing requirements

The Cayman Islands does not impose any restrictions or licensing requirements that are specifically targeted at the holding, management or trading of Digital Assets, whether by those doing so for their own account, or those doing so as a manager, trustee or advisor for the account of others.

As such, whether or not any such licensing or regulatory requirement is applicable to a particular activity will fall to be determined in accordance with the existing regulatory regimes, such as the Mutual Funds Law or the Securities Investment Business Law (each as further detailed above).

As also outlined further above, investment funds and managers that operate in the Digital Assets space are likely to need to comply with the requirements set out in the AML Laws.

Mining

The mining of Digital Assets is not regulated or prohibited in the Cayman Islands. We would note, however, that the import duties applicable to computing equipment and the high cost of electricity production in the Cayman Islands are likely to present practical deterrents to the establishment of any material mining operations within the jurisdiction. It is possible that the increased availability of renewable energy options, and the falling price of the same, may mitigate this somewhat in the future.

Border restrictions and declarations

The Cayman Islands does not impose any general border restrictions on the ownership or importation of Digital Assets.

As part of the Cayman Islands' commitment to combating money laundering and terrorist financing, the Customs (Money Declarations and Disclosures) Regulations mandate that individuals transporting money amounting to CI$15,000 (approximately US$18,292) or more into the Cayman Islands must make a declaration in writing to customs officers at the time of entry. However, the Customs Law defines "money" as being confined to cash (i.e. bank notes or coins that are legal tender in any country) and bearer-negotiable instruments (i.e. travellers cheques, cheques, promissory notes, money orders). As such, we would not expect such a requirement to apply to Digital Assets. Further, given the nature of Digital Assets, particularly those based or recorded on a distributed ledger, there is also the conceptual question of what would amount to the importation or transportation of the same.

Reporting requirements

There are no reporting requirements in the Cayman Islands specifically targeted at payments of, or transfers in, Digital Assets.

As above, to the extent that such a payment or transfer is made in the context of the conduct of "relevant financial business" for the purposes of the AML Laws, there may of course be an obligation to make certain filings or reports in the event that there is a suspicion of money laundering or other criminal activity.

Estate planning and testamentary succession

There is no particular regime under Cayman Islands law which deals specifically with the treatment of cryptocurrencies or other Digital Assets upon the death of an individual holding them. This means that, in principle, and assuming Cayman law governs succession to the deceased's estate, Digital Assets will be treated in the same way as any other asset and may be bequeathed to beneficiaries in a will, or, if a person dies intestate, will fall to be dealt with under the intestacy rules in the Cayman Islands Succession Law.

Although, as is the case in many jurisdictions beyond the Cayman Islands, there is likely to be some uncertainty as to where the *situs* of a Digital Asset is located (or indeed whether or not a *situs* can be determined at all), to the extent that the asset can be analysed under traditional conflict-of-laws rules as sited in the Cayman Islands, then a grant of representation would be required from the Cayman Islands court to preclude the risk of intermeddling claims in dealing with the asset in the Cayman Islands.

The main potential difficulty that may arise is practical; namely that anyone inheriting a Digital Asset will, on the face of it, often only be able to access that Digital Asset if the personal representative of the deceased or the beneficiary (as the case may be) has or can obtain the information needed in order to gain access and control over that Digital Asset (e.g. a private key to the wallet in which it is stored). Most exchanges have policies in place to transfer Digital Assets to next of kin but these policies, and the transfer requirements, will vary between the exchanges.

* * *

Endnotes

1. For the purposes of this chapter, "Digital Assets" shall be used to include all forms of blockchain-based units, whether in the form of securities-like tokens, utility tokens, cryptocurrencies or otherwise.

2. Notably, if the entity itself is "closed-ended" in nature, it will generally fall outside the scope of the law.

Alistair Russell
Tel: +1 345 749 2013 / Email: alistair.russell@careyolsen.com
Alistair is a partner in the corporate and finance group of Carey Olsen in the Cayman Islands and advises on all aspects of finance, fintech, corporate, investment funds and commercial law.

He has advised clients on a broad range of transactions including financing, fintech, ICOs, private equity, joint ventures, mergers and acquisitions and capital markets, and is described by clients in *IFLR1000* as "the best Cayman lawyer we've ever worked with".

Alistair was formerly with Skadden, Arps, Slate Meagher & Flom and Cleary, Gottlieb, Steen & Hamilton, each in London.

Alistair obtained a Bachelor of Civil Law with distinction from Christ Church, Oxford University, and an LL.B. with first class Honours from King's College London.

Dylan Wiltermuth
Tel: +1 345 749 2010 / Email: dylan.wiltermuth@careyolsen.com
Dylan is a counsel in the corporate and finance group of Carey Olsen in the Cayman Islands and advises on all aspects of on securities, corporate and structured finance and public and private M&A.

He has spent many years advising clients on complex cross-border transactions across a wide range of jurisdictions and has a demonstrable track record of success in mitigating risk and delivering results.

Alistair was formerly with Kirkland & Ellis in London and Freshfields Bruckhaus Deringer in London and New York.

Dylan obtained an LL.B. with first class Honours from Bond University.

Carey Olsen

PO Box 10008, Willow House, Cricket Square, Grand Cayman KY1-1001, Cayman Islands
Tel: +1 345 749 2000 / Fax: +1 345 749 2100 / URL: www.careyolsen.com/locations/cayman-islands

China

Lefan Gong & Luping Yu
Zhong Lun Law Firm

Government attitude and definition

The rise of cryptocurrencies has provoked regulatory concern in China, while the government has also been cautious in its policymaking efforts, with the aim of striking a balance between encouraging innovation and preventing unbridled speculation. In this chapter, we explore the PRC regulations surrounding cryptocurrencies, the regulatory implications and the potential impact.

In mainland China, the primary regulatory body policing cryptocurrencies is the central bank, the People's Bank of China (the "**PBOC**").

In June 2018, China Banking and Insurance Regulatory Commission (the "**CBIRC**") issued a working paper, which stated that "the sovereign cryptocurrency shall be deemed as a legitimate digital currency issued by the PBOC", which "has value as a fiat currency and can be used as a medium of exchange… while the non-sovereign cryptocurrency shall not be regarded as 'currency'; it's merely a digital symbol programmed and issued by market participants with agreed protocols. It is essentially similar to a kind of commodity that can be circulated." (For details, please refer to *The Study of the Development and Regulation of Distributed Ledger, Blockchain and Digital Currency.*)

Bitcoin has not been recognised as a fiat currency by the PRC regulatory authorities, instead, it is being treated as a kind of virtual commodity. This suggests a signal that in China, the cryptocurrency would likely be classified into sovereign cryptocurrency (or "**official cryptocurrency**") and non-sovereign cryptocurrency (or "**private cryptocurrency**"), and they would be treated differently. However, this classification has not officially taken effect yet.

Having that said, for non-sovereign cryptocurrencies such as Bitcoin, the regulatory authorities have expressly prohibited it as a fiat currency and instead explicitly treat and reference it as a virtual commodity, although those regulations do not mention the treatment of other cryptocurrencies such as Ethereum. *The Joint Notice on the Risks Associated with Bitcoin* (the "**PBOC Circular in 2013**") issued by the PBOC together with other authorities in 2013, has defined the nature of Bitcoin:

"Bitcoin has four major features including, (1) no centralized issuer, (2) limited issuance volume, (3) no geographical boundaries, and (4) anonymity. Despite being called "currency", Bitcoin is not a currency in nature because it is not issued by monetary authorities and does not possess the legal status of being compulsorily used and accepted. Judging from its nature, Bitcoin should be regarded as a specific virtual commodity; it does not have the same legal status as a fiat currency, and it cannot and should not be circulated in market as fiat currency."

On September 4, 2017, the PBOC and other state-level government authorities in China issued a joint circular (the "**PBOC Circular in 2017**") which emphasises that Bitcoin shall not serve as a fiat currency and all initial coin offerings ("**ICOs**") should be regarded as "illegal financing activities".

Currently both the PBOC Circular 2013 and Circular 2017 are the two primary government regulations in relation to private cryptocurrencies in China. These two regulations mainly: clarify the nature of Bitcoin, one of the private cryptocurrencies, as a virtual commodity, and impose restrictions on financial institutions and third-party payment agents participating in cryptocurrency transactions; and prohibit ICOs and cryptocurrency transactions via token financing and trading platforms. In the meantime, the authority emphasises that ICOs can trigger criminal liabilities arising from illegal issuance and sale of tokens, illegal issuance of securities, illegal fundraising, financial fraud, or pyramid schemes.

In short, the PRC government seemingly encourages the development of official cryptocurrency to be issued by the PBOC in the future, and has formed a taskforce to conduct research and exploration in technology, theory and standards. In March 2018, according to the PBOC's governor, the bank began exploring an official cryptocurrency called Digital Currency for Electronic Payment ("**DCEP**"). However, given the current development of the financial system in China, there is no timetable set for the launch of DCEP (the official cryptocurrency) yet. As to private cryptocurrencies, the regulatory authorities have defined and referenced Bitcoin only, while the legal status of other cryptocurrencies including Ethereum are still vague, while ICOs are clearly banned within the PRC. In general, the PRC regulators are quite cautious about private cryptocurrencies.

Cryptocurrency regulation

As mentioned above, the PBOC Circular 2013 and Circular 2017 have formed the primary regulatory framework for cryptocurrency, which has banned ICOs with resulting civil, administrative and criminal liabilities. Some of the liabilities are already in place under the existing law. For instance, the conduct of illegal issuance and sale of tokens is specified in *Law of the People's Republic of China on the People's Bank of China* (amended in 2003) and is under the supervision of the PBOC. According to Article 20 of the abovementioned law, "No units or individuals may print or sell promissory notes as substitutes for Renminbi to circulate on the market." Individuals and institutions that issue and sell tokens illegally will be required to cease the illegal act immediately and be imposed with a fine amounting to up to RMB200,000.

The act of illegal issue of securities is proscribed in Securities Law of the People's Republic of China (amended in 2014) and violators will receive administrative penalties from China Securities Regulatory Commission ("**CSRC**"). If an ICO is regarded as illegal fundraising, the issuer could be sentenced to more than 10 years in prison or life imprisonment, and shall pay the fine in the range of RMB50,000 to RMB500,000 or be sentenced to confiscation of property in the meantime. Although there is no specific law governing cryptocurrency in the PRC, the regulatory framework is already in place. Besides the abovementioned laws and regulations, authorities like the PBOC and other financial regulatory bodies have been sending warnings on further regulation and enforcement actions on cryptocurrency in the PRC.

Although ICOs and a trading platform service for cryptocurrency have been prohibited in the PRC, the authority has not forbidden the existence of cryptocurrency itself. As a virtual commodity, there are no specific or explicit restrictions on the acquisition, ownership or trading of the cryptocurrency by individuals.

Sales regulation

As provided in the PBOC Circular 2013 and Circular 2017, token financing and trading platforms are banned, and no financial institutions or third-party payment agents may directly trade or, serving as a central clearance party, indirectly trade Bitcoin. Token financing and trading platforms are not allowed to engage in exchange services, whether between any fiat currency and tokens or between cryptocurrencies, and China has been cracking down on cryptocurrency trading in recent years. However, the authorities do not expressly forbid the trading of cryptocurrency by or among its owners. In practice, many cryptocurrency owners choose to trade the cryptocurrency via offshore token trading platforms.

On January 26, 2018, a quasi-governmental (self-regulatory) organisation known as the National Internet Finance Association of China warned that ICOs may be using misleading information as part of fundraising campaigns, and urged investors to proceed with extreme caution. The organisation, which works with government authorities on regulatory matters, further stated its intention to enhance security measures. Although the warning does not ban overseas cryptocurrency trading itself, we cannot rule out the possibility that policymakers may introduce stricter regulatory measures in the future.

Taxation

Currently there is no express provision of tax specifically applicable to cryptocurrencies. However, if cryptocurrencies are traded as commodities, the transaction may be imposed with value-added tax for the sale of intangible assets; and income tax for the capital gains when the tokens are sold if the transaction is treated as an investment. If tokens are deemed as a payment method for goods or services, then value-added tax for the sale of intangible assets will apply. Therefore, due to unclear taxation in China currently, tax assessment and planning are required before you intend to sell tokens.

Money transmission laws and anti-money laundering requirements

The anti-money laundering ("**AML**") monitoring mechanisms currently in place largely hinge on the Know Your Client ("**KYC**") system, the client ID data and trading records, and the reporting system for transactions involving large amounts of money and for dubious transactions. Use of the financial proceeds of a crime, when identified, can be easily attributed to a particular person, and legal measures can follow accordingly. However, if a transaction is via cryptocurrency, due to lack of measures for client and transaction identification, the existing AML surveillance and enforcement capabilities can hardly take the reins, as the sources of investment in cryptocurrency are anonymous and difficult to detect, which make cryptocurrencies untraceable and easily used as a money-laundering tool. In addition, the cross-border fund flow of cryptocurrencies can bypass the monitoring and approval of the State Administration of Foreign Exchange ("**SAFE**").

The PBOC Circular 2013 has urged financial institutions to strengthen anti-money laundering measures, while the PBOC and its branches are asked to further assess the risks of money laundering and formulate effective measures in response. Unlike the traditional anti-money laundering supervision, cryptocurrency has features of anonymity, encryption and irreversibility, while the ID of the remitter and the amount of the fund are hard to track, which brings formidable challenges for anti-money laundering efforts.

Promotion and testing

The PBOC initiated the research and exploration of the possible issuance of sovereign cryptocurrency as early as in 2014, and assembled a team to study blockchain application and other related technologies. Later in early 2017, the PBOC established a cryptocurrency research institute to study cryptocurrency and its underlying technology blockchain, which aims to harness the potential of blockchain technology to serve the Chinese financial sector to the fullest extent. In February 2017, the trial of a national platform for bank bill transactions was accomplished successfully. However, there has still been no official timetable of the issuance of sovereign cryptocurrency.

Ownership and licensing requirements

The regulations have explicitly provided that no cryptocurrency may be used as investment assets for trusts and investment funds, and no financial institutions or payment-processing agents may use Bitcoin as payment consideration for any products or services. But the law does not require investment advisors or managers to have any licences or permits for holding cryptocurrencies. If someone makes a capital contribution in the form of cryptocurrency, there may be additional legal issues arising, such as the corporate registration authority's acknowledgment of cryptocurrency as registered capital, which is still uncertain given the lack of regulatory provisions.

Mining

Mining is an act of generating cryptocurrencies through specific computer calculations. The PRC government does not expressly ban mining activities of cryptocurrencies in China. However, the authorities have taken measures to restrict mining activities. In 2018, an Official Document (Letter [2018] No. 2) was released by the Office of the Special Rectification Work Leadership Team for Internet Financial Risks. It urges local government authorities to "help" cryptocurrency mining companies to exit their business, such as limiting electricity consumption and increasing land rental to curb mining activities until they shut down the mining business. Thus, although the authorities have not explicitly prohibited "mining" activities, the activities are being monitored and even discouraged by the government. Therefore, counsel's advice should be sought before initiating mining activities in China.

Border restrictions and declaration

Currently, there is no explicit provision requiring individuals or institutions to report or declare cryptocurrency holdings.

Reporting requirements

There is no reporting requirement for cryptocurrency payments in China. The PBOC and other regulatory authorities have denied cryptocurrency as a "legal currency", and it cannot be circulated as a payment intermediary in the market.

Estate planning and testamentary succession

China has not yet promulgated regulations or updated the law on the inheritance of cryptocurrencies. The PBOC Circular 2017 explicitly defines Bitcoin as a virtual commodity, which is deemed as a kind of virtual property protected by law, and subject to inheritance rules in general.

However, there are issues and challenges associated with inheritance of cryptocurrencies. For instance, what if the owner loses his or her password, or the heir cannot access it?

Due to the decentralised nature of the cryptocurrency, only holders of the private key(s) of a cryptocurrency address can gain access to the coins stored. Thus, once the address or password of the account is lost, it is virtually impossible to relocate the coin(s), and this is true for the owner, as well as the owner's heir. Some US insurance companies such as American International Group, have reportedly been adding crypto-coverage into their standard policy forms, although this is not available in China. It remains uncertain how such risks of losing a password, and then the crypto property, can be prevented.

The decentralised nature of the blockchain on which cryptocurrencies operate also means that once a crypto holder dies, his or her coins could potentially be lost forever. A probate court or central agent can hardly adjudicate the matter of recovering the coins owned by a crypto holder who has passed away. If the holder includes the cryptocurrencies in a will, he or she will have to provide the password in a separate note to the person designated in such will to receive such cryptocurrencies.

Legal counsel's advice should be sought as part of the estate planning exercise. For instance, the holder can consider transferring the cryptocurrencies into a trust, so that the probate process can be avoided. And there are offshore trust companies that have accepted cryptocurrencies as trust assets.

Conclusion and outlook of cryptocurrency in mainland China

The regulators are "closely" watching the cryptocurrency and blockchain technology sector. Also, the authorities often have discretion in exercising their power, including interpretation of the laws and regulations. In general, China has been taking more and more actions to clamp down on various activities related to cryptocurrency, ranging from banning ICOs, discouraging bitcoin miners, to a nationwide ban on internet and mobile access to cryptocurrency trading platforms. Of the major economies, China appears to be one of the most stringent regulators regarding cryptocurrencies.

Although the regulators have cracked down on nearly all activities associated with cryptocurrency, disputes and crimes nevertheless keep rising. According to our legal research, we have found that cryptocurrency disputes-related cases have already reached more than 1,000 and counting. Thus, in the current regulatory framework, buyer's discretion is advised, and caution suggests that legal advice be sought before initiating a cryptocurrency project.

Note: The contents of this chapter are intended for general information purposes only and are prepared based on the current PRC laws and regulations in mainland China up to July 2018. The publication should not be construed as legal advice on any specific facts or circumstances. For specific information on recent developments or particular factual situations, the opinion of legal counsel should be sought.

* * *

Acknowledgments

The authors would also like to thank Joanna Jiang (Jiang Lulu), Yancy Chen (Chen Jiayan) and Eric Huang (Huang Tianyu) for their invaluable help in providing support on overall research and editing work, and thank Mark Gao (Gao Rufeng) for his valuable insights on tax-related sections.

Lefan Gong
Tel: +86 21 6061 3608 / Email: lefangong@zhonglun.com
Dr Lefan Gong is a partner in Zhong Lun's Shanghai office. He is recognised by *Chambers* as a recommended lawyer for private equity fund practice, and a "Leading Individual Lawyer" in PRC for M&A by *The Legal 500*. Dr Gong is qualified to practise law in both China and New York.

With profound experience in capital markets and fintech, Dr Gong has been advising many clients in the digital industry and has extensive experience working with both established and emerging businesses in virtually all market segments. For instance, in the blockchain technology sector, he has provided legal services for some clients on the development, assessment and implementation of their projects. In addition, he has represented private equity clients, family offices, Fortune 500 companies, investment banks and major state-owned enterprises in private equity transactions, corporate financing, cross-border mergers and acquisitions, overseas IPOs, joint ventures, and other complex international investment and commercial transactions. He also advises clients on fund formation, establishing red-chip structures, VIE, corporate restructuring, and wealth management-related matters.

Luping Yu
Tel: +86 156 5071 7778 / Email: yuluping@zhonglun.com
In 2016, Luping Yu graduated from Renmin University of China and received the Doctor's Degree of Science of the Environment and Natural Resources Protection Law.

Dr Luping Yu works as a partner of ZhongLun Law Firm in Beijing. Being an expert in Environment and Natural Resources Protection Law, he serves as a member of the investment and financing professional committee, Qingdao Bar Association and a member of the Environment Resources Law Committee of Lawyers of Shandong Bar Association. Besides this, he was appointed as a Master's Supervisor of the Accounting Department of the Management School of Ocean University of China.

He has engaged in both litigation and non-litigation business in the field of fixed-asset investment, and mainly focused on such environmental protection fields as new energy, energy conservation and emissions-reduction, such all-round green legal services as transaction of rights to produce carbon dioxide emissions, clean development mechanism (CDM project), the identification and diagnosis of energy performance contracting (EPC project), investment and financing, implementation and operation.

Zhong Lun Law Firm

8 Century Avenue, IFC 2, 10th and 11th floors, Pudong, Shanghai 200120, People's Republic of China
Tel: +86 21 6061 3608 / Fax: +86 21 6061 3555 / URL: www.zhonglun.com

Cyprus

Karolina Argyridou
K. Argyridou & Associates LLC

Government attitude and definition

In Cyprus, as is likely the case elsewhere, the topics of blockchain and cryptocurrency are at the forefront of the minds of people, and yet both topics are still very much in their infancy. We make this statement both in terms of the opportunities in Cyprus for exploiting the new technologies in these areas, as well as in terms of how virtual currencies and their related dependencies will be treated from a regulatory, legal and tax perspective.

In the context of traditional currency, Cyprus was recently able to exit the EU's euro bailout programme ahead of schedule, having met the *troika*-set conditions to their satisfaction – receiving plaudits from the international financial community for doing so.

Perhaps inevitably, bank customers who had seen their deposits suffer 'haircuts', and in some cases complete loss, turned their thoughts to the possibility that there could be alternatives to holding cash in banks. The subject of cryptocurrencies provided an interesting and innovative possibility, and there were certain noises being made – though not necessarily formally – that the Cyprus authorities could be open to exploring the possibilities blockchain and cryptocurrencies could bring to the island. However, things have not necessarily advanced as might have been hoped by proponents of these new technologies as an alternative to traditional currency, and the current position of the regulatory authorities in Cyprus might best be described as very cautious and non-committal in the immediate term (see below).

Cryptocurrency regulation

In order to understand the current regulatory treatment of cryptocurrency, it is necessary to understand, at least in brief, its evolution:

Subject to what is set out below in respect of contracts for difference (CFDs) on virtual currencies, in Cyprus there are currently no specific references to cryptocurrency in the legal or regulatory framework currently in force and cryptocurrencies are not, *per se*, regulated. However, both the Central Bank of Cyprus and the Cyprus Securities and Exchange Commission (CySEC) had issued warnings to potential investors in cryptocurrencies as well as investment firms looking to deal in them.

Specifically, as early as **7 February 2014** the Central Bank of Cyprus published an announcement entitled '*Attention to the risks associated with virtual currencies*'. In it, it was pointed out that cryptocurrencies are *not 'legal tender'* and that the public should take care, given that '*...there are no specific regulatory protection measures to cover losses from the use of virtual currencies...*'. The Announcement concluded by pointing out risks in cryptocurrencies such as: the lack of a legal obligation for the currency to be reimbursed at face value; high volatility and the potential for the cryptocurrency's value to fall to zero; that merchants only have to accept the virtual currency at their discretion; and the heightened risk of virtual currencies being used for illegal activities.

On **13 October 2017**, CySEC issued Circular 244 to all Cyprus investment firms (CIFs), noting the lack of an EU regulatory framework for virtual currency trading or related CFDs, and neither was there an official position from the European authorities on the applicability of the relevant paragraph of the Markets in Financial Instruments Directive (MiFID) (para 9, Section C, Annex 1) to virtual currency-related CFDs. Under this Circular, CIFs were required to warn clients, amongst other things, of the foregoing as well as the high risk of loss of capital, and that virtual currencies are not suitable for all investors who would not, in any event, have the benefit of the Investor Compensation Fund or any ombudsman to whom a complaint about a CIF's conduct could be made. The Circular also required CIFs to take a series of other steps including to: (i) identify, measure and record risks associated with the activity of virtual currency trading; (ii) use only feed providers that are *"licensed/regulated"* in their jurisdiction of establishment and on whom the CIF conducted regular due diligence; (iii) publicly disclose their bid and ask price calculation methodology; and (iv) limit retail client leverage to 5:1 for trading CFDs relating to virtual currencies.

By an announcement dated **15 November 2017**, CySEC followed Circular 244 with reference to ESMA's 13 November 2017 press release on Initial Coin Offerings (ICOs) and the requirement for firms, depending on how they are structured, dealing with ICOs to comply with the Prospectus Directive1, MiFID2, the Alternative Investment Fund Managers Directive (AIFMD) and the Anti-Money Laundering Directive. Investors in ICOs, on the other hand, are warned of *"(i) vulnerability to fraud or illicit activities, due to the fact that ICOs might not fall under the remit of the legislation, (ii) high risk of losing all of the invested capital, (iii) lack of exit options and extreme price volatility, (iv) inadequate information, and (v) flaws in the technology"*.

However, on **15 May 2018**, CySEC replaced Circular 244 with Circular 268. Circular 268 is notified to all CIFs under the title, *"Introduction of new rules governing derivatives on virtual currencies"*, and is issued further to ESMA's 27 March 2018 Decision including CFDs on virtual currencies as within the remit of its product intervention measures (with the result that CFDs on virtual currencies are considered to be 'financial instruments' under the Cyprus law transposing MiFID II (the Investment Services and Activities and Regulated Markets Law of 2017)).

Circular 268 continues:

"In effect, virtual currencies may constitute an underlying variable in other derivative contracts including CFDs, options and futures (the "Derivative on Virtual Currencies"). To this end, CySEC hereby clarifies the following:

1. Any activity relating to virtual currencies is not currently regulated by CySEC, unless a virtual currency meets the criteria and falls under the existing regulatory framework, as per CySEC's announcement dated 15 November 2017.

2. However, Derivatives on Virtual Currencies are now capable of qualifying as financial instruments under the Law. A "financial instrument" means those instruments specified in Part III of the First Appendix of the Law. Among the financial instruments listed in Part III of the First Appendix of the Law, Derivatives on Virtual Currencies may fall under the following:

    i.   (4): "[…] any other derivative contracts relating to securities […] which may be settled physically or in cash";

ii.   (9): "financial contracts for differences";

iii. (10): "[…] any other derivative contracts relating to assets […] not otherwise mentioned in this Section, which have the characteristics of other derivative financial instruments".

3.   "Therefore, depending on their specific characteristics and use, providing investment services in relation to derivatives on virtual currencies will require specific authorisation by CySEC."

Sales regulation

ICOs have become an increasingly popular way to raise funds. It is quite common for cryptocurrencies such as Bitcoin to be used in an ICO. There is no prohibition on ICOs in Cyprus. It is noted that care needs to be taken in order to ensure that the way in which an ICO is conducted does not cause a breach of the relevant regulatory framework. The Alternative Investment Fund with Limited Number of Investors (AIFLNP) would potentially be an appropriate vehicle for such ICOs in Cyprus, as it has no diversification requirements and is a particularly flexible investment vehicle.

Taxation

Generally, Cyprus has a favourable tax system. The Cyprus corporate tax rate is only 12.5%. Cyprus has about 40 Double Tax Agreements (DTA) signed. We understand that there is at least one tax ruling of the Cyprus Tax Department confirming that the profits made from trading in Bitcoin are taxable to Corporation/Income Tax.

Money transmission laws and anti-money laundering requirements

Currently there is no specific provision in the AML framework regarding Bitcoin. It is noted, however, that dealing in Bitcoin is generally considered as a high-risk activity for AML purposes. As such, Bitcoin activity is subject to increased scrutiny from an AML perspective. The various credit institutions in Cyprus have adopted their own policies as to dealings in cryptocurrencies such as Bitcoin.

Promotion and testing

There are no "sandbox" or other initiatives at the moment intended to promote research and investment in cryptocurrency in Cyprus.

Ownership and licensing requirements

There is no restriction on a party owning virtual currencies in Cyprus.

Mining

There is no specific restriction stated in the law.

Border restrictions and declaration

There is no specific restriction stated in the law.

Reporting requirements

There is no specific obligation stated in the law.

Estate planning and testamentary succession

The legislative framework in respect of estate planning and succession is not drafted in a way which allows clear conclusions as to the treatment of cryptocurrencies. We would expect that the treatment of cryptocurrencies would be the same as the treatment of any other movable property in Cyprus.

Subject to the provisions of the provisions EU Regulation 650/2012 (more commonly known as Brussels IV) (see below),* Cyprus Cap 195 applies to the estate of any person deceasing as a domiciliary of Cyprus, and to all immoveable property located in Cyprus. That is, Cyprus succession laws will apply to moveable and immoveable property of a person domiciled in Cyprus, and to Cyprus-*situs* immovable property irrespective of the deceased's domicile at the time of death.

Cyprus law provides for a form of "forced heirship", by which if a deceased leaves a spouse and child, or spouse and descendant of a child, or no spouse but a child or descendant of a child, then the disposable portion (i.e. that portion that the deceased can freely dispose of by will) must not exceed ¼ of the net value of the estate, the remaining 'statutory portion' being due to the aforementioned close relative(s) of the deceased. Where the deceased leaves no spouse, child or descendant of a child, the rules of forced heirship do not apply and 100% of the estate of the deceased who is domiciled in in Cyprus may be disposed of freely by will.

As a Member State of the European Union, EU Regulation 650/2012 (more commonly known as Brussels IV) was adopted on 4 July 2012 and applies to all deaths after 17 August 2015 in all EU Member States with the exception of the UK, Denmark and Ireland. Amongst other things, Brussels IV provides that:

- *The default position is that the courts of the member state in which the deceased died habitually resident have jurisdiction in succession matters (Article 21).*

- *The courts of the member state of the deceased's nationality may have jurisdiction if the deceased chose to apply the law of the state of his nationality (Article 22).*

- *A European Certificate of Succession can be used to confirm the status and rights of beneficiaries and personal representatives (Article 62).*

Karolina Argyridou
Tel: +357 22 000 408 / Email: karolina@veritalegal.com
Karolina was awarded an LL.B. (First Class Honours) from the University of East Anglia in 2005 and an LL.M. (Distinction) from the London School of Economics and Political Sciences. Karolina is the founding member of K. Argyridou & Associates LLC and specialises in financial regulation and banking and investment services. Karolina's clients include credit institutions, investment firms and various government authorities.

K. Argyridou & Associates LLC

92 Ifigenias Street, 2003, Nicosia, Cyprus
Tel: +357 22 000 408 / Fax: +357 22 000 409 / URL: www.veritalegal.com

Estonia

Priit Lätt & Carel Kivimaa
PwC Legal

Government attitude and definition

According to *Wired* magazine, Estonia is the "most advanced digital society in the world".

The most important Estonian state e-solution is called "X-Road" – the open-source backbone upon which Estonia's entire digital infrastructure runs, allowing the nation's various e-service databases, both in the public and private sector, to link up and operate in harmony. Although X-Road is not based on blockchain and does not use it internally, both blockchain and X-Road use cryptographic hash functions for linking data items to each other. X-Road lacks a centralised or master database; all information is held in a distributed data system and can be exchanged instantly upon request, providing access 24/7. Estonia is probably the only country in the world where 99% of public services are available online 24/7.

The Estonian government has been testing blockchain technology since 2008 (at that time, this technology was called "hash-linked time-stamping"). Since 2012, KSI Blockchain technology, developed by Estonian-based company Guardtime, has been in production use to protect Estonian governmental data registries such as the national health, judicial and legislative systems, with plans to extend its use to other spheres such as personal medicine, cybersecurity and data embassies. Incidentally, KSI is used by NATO and the US Department of Defense.

Nearly every one of the country's 1.3 million citizens has a state-issued digital identity and an ID card, which functions as much more than simply a driver's licence or passport. This eID uses a public key encryption and allows a person to be verified in an online environment. This is what allows a person digital access to things such as the voting system or the ability to fill a pharmaceutical prescription.

Estonia is also a pioneer in e-Residency, which enables people around the world to receive a virtual residency in Estonia, with access to the digital solutions provided by the government.

In 2014, Estonian commercial bank LHV Pank developed and tested a blockchain-based financial product called CUBER (Cryptographic Universal Blockchain Entered Receivables) and mobile app called Cuber Wallet. CUBER is meant to be a building block for various innovative financial products.

Estonia has already enacted specific anti-money laundering (AML)/counter-financing of terrorism (CFT) regulations applicable to services related to cryptocurrencies (custodian wallet service and exchange service), as from November 27, 2017. Thus, Estonia is the first EU member state to follow the approach of the draft Fifth EU Anti-Money Laundering Directive (5AMLD).

Cryptocurrency regulation

Cryptocurrencies do not possess a legal status of currency or money, but they can be accepted by natural and legal persons, as a means of exchange or payment.

Estonia is the first EU country to provide clear regulation of cryptocurrencies, cryptocurrency exchanges and custodian wallet service providers for AML/CFT purposes.

The definition and legal nature of cryptocurrencies (i.e., are they a right, thing or private money) in the civil law is unsettled, and there is no case-law on the subject in Estonia.

Sales regulation

In this section we shall address the sale of cryptocurrency tokens by companies during their professional activities.

In order to assess which laws apply to a certain cryptographic token sale, the type of the token must be identified. There is no official regulation aimed at classification of crypto tokens, therefore it is advisable to involve a legal professional to provide a legal opinion on the classification of the respective token prior to initiating the sales process, as the results of the classification may considerably influence the legal obligations of the seller.

The Estonian Financial Supervisory Authority (EFSA) has published unofficial guidelines for ICO issuers and token traders on how to categorise crypto tokens issued in an ICO, and which laws apply to each category.[1] According to these guidelines, cryptocurrency tokens are divided into two: tokens that grant their owner a reasonable expectation for profit or governance rights (commonly referred to as Security tokens); and tokens that do not promise any profits or monetary claims. The second group is further divided into three: cryptocurrency – payment instruments for products/services (the Payment tokens); charity (the Charity tokens); and tokens that grant access to a platform/system or a right to use a product/service (the Utility tokens).

Security tokens

The EFSA has explained that offering of tokens that fall under the definition of "security" as stipulated in § 2(1) of the Securities Market Act (SMA) brings legal obligations to the issuer/seller, infringement of which may result in considerable fines.

Pursuant to the § 2(1) of the SMA, each of the following applicable proprietary right or contract transferred on the basis of at least unilateral expression of will is a security, even without a document being issued therefor:

i)   a share or other similar tradeable right;

ii)   a bond, convertible security or other tradeable debt obligation issued which is not a money market instrument;

iii)   a subscription right or other tradeable right granting the right to acquire securities specified in clauses i) or ii);

iv)   an investment fund unit and share;

v)   a money market instrument;

vi)   a derivative security or a derivative contract;

vii)   a tradeable depositary receipt; and

viii)   greenhouse gas emissions for the purposes of the Atmospheric Air Protection Act.

In the context of crypto tokens, the most relevant definitions among these are i), ii), iv), v) and vi).

Tokens are shares, if they grant their owners rights to a holding in the company, rights to a share of profit, or voting rights in corporate matters. Under the Estonian Commercial Code (§ 148(5), § 226), shares grant shareholders: the right to participate in the management of the company and in the distribution of profit and of remaining assets on dissolution of the company; the right to participate in the general meeting of shareholders; and other similar rights prescribed by law or the articles of association.

Tokens are *investment fund units or shares*, if they represent a unitholder's share in the assets of a common fund. According to the Investment Funds Act (IFA), a *common fund* is a pool of assets which is established from the money collected through the issue of units or other assets and assets acquired through investment of money, and which is jointly owned by unitholders. An *investment fund* is a legal entity or pool of assets, which involves the capital of a number of investors with a view to investing it in accordance with a defined investment policy for the benefit of the investors in question and in their common interests.

According to § 2(2) of the SMA, a *money market instrument* is an unsecured, transferable and marketable debt obligation, which is traded on the money market, including a treasury debt obligation, commercial paper, certificate of deposit, bill of exchange secured by a credit institution, or other security complying with the aforementioned characteristics, stipulated in Regulation 2017/565 (EU) of the European Parliament and of the Council[2] (EU 2017/565) article 11. According to the aforementioned regulation, the money market instruments shall have the following characteristics: (a) they have a value that can be determined at any time; (b) they are not derivatives; (c) they have a maturity at issuance of 397 days or less.

According to § 2(3) of the SMA, a *derivative instrument* is a tradeable security expressing a right or obligation to acquire, exchange or transfer, the underlying assets of which are securities, or the price of which depends directly or indirectly on: (a) the stock exchange or market price of the security; (b) the interest rate; (c) the securities index, other financial index or financial indicator, including the inflation rate, freight rate, emission allowance or other official economic statistics; (d) currency exchange rates; (e) credit risk and other risks, including climatic variables; or (f) the exchange or market price of a commodity, including precious metal.

The EFSA's position seems to be that the tokens don't have to correspond to these definitions literally in order to be regarded as securities, rather it is sufficient if the token has the overall characteristics of a security (substance-over-form approach). If the token corresponds to any of these characteristics, the offering of it may constitute the issuance of securities and, depending on its exact nature, be governed by the rules of public offering as prescribed in § 12 of the SMA. That being the case, it is required to register a respective prospectus at the EFSA.

The issuance will not be regarded as a public offering and no prospectus is required in the case of:

i)   an offer of securities addressed solely to qualified investors;

ii)   an offer of securities addressed to fewer than 150 persons per Contracting State, other than qualified investors;

iii) an offer of securities addressed to investors who acquire securities for a total consideration of at least €100,000 per investor, for each separate offer;

iv)   an offer of securities with a nominal value or book value of at least €100,000 per security; or

v)   an offer of securities with a total consideration of less than €2,500,000 per all the Contracting States in total, calculated in a one-year period, of the offer of the securities.

Payment tokens

According to the EFSA guidelines, tokens shall be considered as payment tokens if they are also intended for use outside of the respective token issuer's platform as payment instruments for other products and services provided by third persons. *Payment token* directly corresponds to the concept of "virtual currency" as defined in § 3(9) of the Money Laundering and Terrorist Financing Prevention Act (please see below).

Issuing or selling payment tokens to the public may fall under the definition of provision of the custodian wallet service according to the Money Laundering and Terrorist Financing Prevention Act (please see below).

Charity tokens

According to the EFSA guidelines, a fundraising for the development of a business project shall be considered as a donation only under the condition that it does not lead to: (i) a participation in the issuer; or (ii) any obligation to repay the funds, interest, dividend, or any other repayment, or cash flow. In addition, no right of use of a service or product shall arise in connection with the donation. If the issuer is gathering donations in exchange to tokens, the issuer must expressly indicate that the token is a charity token. In such a case, the issuer will only have certain taxation obligations.

Utility tokens

According to the EFSA guidelines, an ICO, where the tokens offered grant their purchasers access to a product or service, is in essence a prepayment for a product or service. Consequently – taking into account that the contracts entered into within an ICO use means of communication (a computer network) – such ICOs are subject to the provisions of the Law of Obligations Act (LOA) regarding the distance contracts entered into through means of communication and computer network.

Utility tokens are essentially commodities and the usual contractual obligations apply. Additionally, various consumer protection obligations must be met if the buyers are natural persons, such as the notification obligation and the obligation to allow the consumer to withdraw from the contract with simplified procedure.

Taxation

Estonia has not enacted any specific tax regulation on ICOs or cryptocurrencies. Estonian tax legislation does not include any special tax rules for income, profits or gains arising from transactions involving cryptocurrencies, or for charges made in connection with cryptocurrencies. Still, Estonian tax authorities have issued formal guidance in relation to VAT and income tax treatment of cryptocurrencies and mining.

Value added tax (VAT)

For the purposes of VAT, cryptocurrencies are considered as the same currency as euros, etc. Thus, the usage of cryptocurrencies as remuneration is equal to the usage of legal tender and therefore out of the scope of VAT.

The supply of services which consist of the exchange of traditional currencies for units of cryptocurrencies and *vice versa*, are financial transactions exempt from VAT. This approach is in line with the ruling C-264/14 of the European Court of Justice.

The services provided by miners are outside the scope of VAT. However, it is still unclear how the VAT treatment of the mining changes if a pool is used. Estonian tax authorities have not clarified VAT treatment of wallet service providers, yet. The standard VAT rate is 20%.

Corporate income tax

Estonia uses a distinctive corporate tax system in which the taxation of corporate profits is deferred until the profits are distributed. Any retained earnings are thus effectively tax-exempt as long as the shareholder(s) can defer profit distributions. Such exemption covers both active and passive types of income.

Corporate profits are subject to taxation upon distribution of dividend or other types of deemed or hidden profit distribution (e.g., liquidation proceeds, capital redemptions, representation expenses, gifts and donations, non-business-related expenses, transfer pricing adjustments).

Distributed profits are generally subject to 20% corporate income tax (20/80 on the net amount of the profit distribution). For example, an Estonian company that has profits of €100 available for distribution can distribute dividends of €80, on which it must pay corporate income tax of €20. Thus, the proceeds from an ICO are not taxed with corporate income tax at the rate of 20/80 until such proceeds are distributed to the shareholder(s).

From 2018, the corporate income tax rate on regular dividends was reduced from 20% to 14% over an ongoing three-year cycle. According to the new rule on regular profit distributions, the payment of dividends in an amount which is below or equal to the amount of average taxed dividends paid during the three preceding years, will be taxed at a rate of 14% (the tax rate on the net amount being 14/86 instead of the regular 20/80). In cases where the recipient of the 14% dividend is either a resident or non-resident individual, a 7% withholding tax rate will apply unless a tax treaty provides for a lower withholding tax rate (5% or 0%). There are also transitional rules. 2018 is the first year to be taken into consideration for the purposes of determining the average dividend.

Personal income tax

For personal income tax purposes, cryptocurrency is treated as property, the alienation and exchange of which gives rise to capital gains. Income from trading in cryptocurrencies is taxed as business income which, in addition to personal income tax, is also subject to social security contributions.

Income received will be taxed at a 20% flat tax rate.

Employee compensation tax issues

It is rather common that employees recruited early on may receive a certain amount of their yearly salary in the form of cryptocurrencies as a means of compensation and encouragement. Such compensation in non-monetary form should be taxed as fringe benefits under Estonian legislation.

Fringe benefits are any goods, services, remuneration in kind or monetarily appraisable benefits which are given to a person in connection with an employment or service relationship, membership in the management or controlling body of a legal person, or a long-term contractual relationship, regardless of the time at which the fringe benefit is granted.

Fringe benefits are subject to 20/80 income tax and 33% social security contributions (on a gross-up basis). The employer must calculate the tax on the total amount of all fringe benefits granted. The tax base for social security contributions purposes includes both the value of the benefit and the income tax paid on this benefit. Fringe benefits received by resident employees are not included in the taxable income in their annual income tax returns.

Example: where the market value of the fringe benefit is 100:

Income tax due is 25 (20/80 × 100) and social security contributions due is 41.25 (0.33 × (100+25)) = total tax of 66.25

Money transmission laws and anti-money laundering requirements

Before 5AMLD, EU financial authorities emphasised that exchanges where virtual currencies are traded and digital wallets used to hold, store or transfer virtual currencies, are unregulated under EU law. However, Estonia regulated virtual currency exchanges already under the AML law, which was in force as from January 2008 until November 27, 2017 (**please see remarks below**). Estonia implemented the 4AMLD (2015/849) and draft 5AMLD (2018/843) into its national law (the Money Laundering and Terrorist Financing Prevention Act, hereinafter **MLTFPA**) by November 27, 2017.

MLTFPA, among other changes, introduced new definitions and provided a clear new regulation for cryptocurrency exchanges and cryptocurrency wallet service providers.

According to MLTFPA:

• *'Virtual currency' means a value represented in digital form, which is digitally transferable, preservable or tradeable and which natural persons or legal persons accept as a payment instrument, but that is not the legal tender of any country or funds for the purposes of Article 4(25) of PSD2 or a payment transaction for the purposes of points (k) and (l) of Article 3 of the same Directive.* It is interesting that the definition in MLTFPA is narrower than the one in 5AMLD. The latter makes it clear that virtual currencies may also be used for other different purposes and find broader applications such as means of exchange, investment, store-of-value products or uses in online casinos.

• *'Virtual currency wallet service' means a service in the framework of which keys are generated for customers or customers' encrypted keys are kept, which can be used for the purpose of keeping, storing and transferring virtual currencies.* This definition is a rather broad one, but it should not extend to non-custodian wallets, where the user (rather than the wallet provider) holds the private key. Thus, if the private key to the cryptocurrency is (also or exclusively) held by the wallet provider, the wallet service provider should be regarded as an obliged entity.

• Providing only exchange of cryptocurrency to cryptocurrency will remain out of scope of the regulation.

According to MLTFPA, an appropriate authorisation must be granted by the Financial Intelligence Unit to:

i) provide a service of exchanging a virtual currency against a fiat currency; and

ii) provide a virtual currency wallet service.

The application for authorisation can be submitted in the Register of Economic Activities accessible through the portal www.eesti.ee, or the webpage at https://mtr.mkm.ee. The state fee payable for the authorisation is €345. The Financial Intelligence Unit reviews the authorisation application no later than within 30 working days following the date of submission of the application. Prior to the grant of the authorisation, no services shall be offered.

Please note that the rules of operating in the relevant fields of activity subject to authorisation obligation have not been harmonised across the EU. An activity licence granted in another state of the European Economic Area does not grant the right to operate in Estonia, and vice versa.

In addition to authorisation, obliged entities under the MTFPA are required to perform AML/CFT due diligence measures in respect to their clients, including identification, verification obligations and monitoring of each of the business relationships.

The main area that will create a struggle for crypto-businesses in Estonia is the banks, i.e.

opening a bank account and operating payments, as the banks are quite sceptical when it comes to cryptocurrency. In order to at least have a chance to open a bank account, a clear and transparent business model, transparent identity of the company (group structure/shareholders, etc.), effective AML/KYC procedures need to be in place. Therefore, the non-regulated cryptocompany should contact its co-operations partners who are obliged persons under MLTFPA (e.g. banks) in advance to ensure that the company can comply with their internal regulations and requirements.

Remark – Estonian case law

In early 2014, the proprietor of Bitcoin trading platform BTC.ee, Otto de Voogd, was ordered by the Estonian Financial Intelligence Unit of Estonia's Police and Border Guard to provide information on all of his clients. The operations of the Estonian version of the site were halted in February 2014, and de Voogd began legal proceedings against FIU in Estonian courts.

Finally, his appeal in cassation was assessed in the country's Supreme Court. The Supreme Court ordered Estonia's Ministry of Finance, Ministry of Interior, the Bank of Estonia and the Financial Supervision Authority to give opinions on the legality of Bitcoin and on de Voogd's case, specifically on the following: whether Bitcoin trading is under the jurisdiction of Estonian AML/CFT regulations and whether Estonian law on money laundering and terrorist financing is in conformity with the EU law (3AMLD) and with the recommendations of FATF, and whether Bitcoin exchange providers are "alternative mean of payment service providers" as defined by the Estonian AML/CFT law effective in 2014.

On April 11, 2016, the Supreme Court confirmed that Bitcoin exchanges are subject to Estonian AML/CFT regulation and supervision as "alternative mean of payment service providers", in particular, the requirement to identify clients where the client turnover is over €1,000 per month. This important ruling clarified the vague definition of "providers of alternative means of payment", and affirmed the applicability of traditional AML/CFT regulations to innovative business models such as crypto exchanges if they operate in Estonia.

Promotion and testing

Public sector

To date, Estonia has no official, state-backed promotional or testing programmes or policies intended for the promotion of cryptocurrencies and blockchain technologies. This, however, doesn't mean that the state authorities are totally passive or oblivious about the benefits and the need to create appropriate conditions for these technologies, in order to gain competitive advantage over other states that wish to stand out and direct crypto-related capital to their jurisdiction. In the past, Estonia has always been very competitive when it comes to gathering recognition with its innovation and technology-friendly approach and legal atmosphere, and this was also the case with blockchain-related technologies at first.

After the 2015 Parliament elections, the new government coalition stated in its action programme that it will develop an official policy for recognition and use of virtual currencies,[3] and the Ministry of Finance even published respective initial analysis by mid-2016.[4] The new coalition that came to power in November 2016 didn't follow such devotion to blockchain-related technologies; respective reference was left out of their action programme, and development of this policy was interrupted. Therefore, currently Estonia has no official policy on promoting and regulating cryptocurrencies or blockchain technologies at the government level. Nonetheless, there have been roundtables and forums on these topics, initiated by ministries. Furthermore, despite respective suggestions by participants of these forums, tangible policies are yet to be developed.

Estcoin

Despite the general complacency of high-level government towards promoting, directing and regulating the field of crypto-technologies, there have been some interesting proposals from slightly lower tiers of the authorities, relating to their implementation by the Estonian state itself. Namely, Mr Kaspar Korjus, the head of Estonia's e-Residency programme, has suggested launching "estcoins", crypto-tokens specifically developed for Estonian e-residents.[5]

Estonian e-Residency is a programme that enables foreign nationals to apply for an e-resident smart card, which allows access to Estonian e-governmental services such as company formation, taxation, digital signatures and others. According to Mr Korjus' suggestion, Estonia could issue estcoins through an ICO, which could be accessed by anyone in the world through Estonia's e-Residency programme. This initial proposal was met with heated debate and also swift opposition from the president of European Central Bank, Mr Mario Draghi, who rejected the idea of Estonia having "... its own currency" separate from the euro.[6] At first, the actual function of suggested estcoins was left very obscure, but at the end of 2017, Mr Korjus proposed three potential functions that estcoins could have and which could be introduced without alarming the European Central Bank:[7]

i)   The community function – Estcoins could be used as incentives for ensuring the growth and promotion of the e-Residency programme by the community.

ii) The identity function – Estcoins would be tokens used for activities within the e-Residency infrastructure for identification purposes.

iii) The euro function – Estcoins would be an alternative currency to euro with 1 estcoin = 1 euro.

Despite these suggestions, the actual implementation of estcoins in the near future is unlikely.

Private sector

One of the most visible private sector organisations when it comes to promoting and raising awareness of blockchain technologies and cryptocurrencies is the Estonian Cryptocurrency Association. Established in October 2014, the Association is a non-profit organisation, the purpose of which is to promote more widespread use of cryptographic resources and make the Estonian cryptocurrency regulatory environment more attractive to investors and crypto-enthusiasts. The Association organises workshops and training on blockchain technologies, instructs people interested in cryptocurrencies, and acts as the main and most active interest group engaging in discussions with the government, supervisory and regulatory bodies.

Ownership and licensing requirements

Specifically for the purposes of cryptocurrencies, there are no restrictions on investment managers owning cryptocurrencies for investment purposes, nor are there any licensing requirements imposed on someone who holds cryptocurrency as an investment advisor or fund manager under Estonian legislation. However, if the crypto-token in question were to be classified as a security token (see above), the same restrictions to ownership of the respective token would apply as for investment managers and advisors providing services in the field of the stock market. These restrictions include the obligation to avoid conflict of interest that, in some cases, could mean restrictions on ownership of certain security tokens.

Mining

Mining is permitted, but Estonia has not enacted any specific legal or tax regulation on mining activities.

EFSA has stated that mining cryptocurrency as a field of activity does not fall under the supervision of the Authority.

When a new block is created by the requisite unique identification process and verification by the network, the miner gets rewarded. In this regard, there is no contractual relationship with the miner and there is no supply for consideration for VAT purposes when the reward is granted. Therefore, there does not seem to be a supply for VAT purposes, and the mining of cryptocurrency is outside the scope of VAT.

Border restrictions and declaration

To date, there are no border restrictions or obligations to declare cryptocurrency holdings pursuant to Estonian legislation.

Reporting requirements

Estonian legislation doesn't stipulate reporting obligations to individuals making payments in excess of a certain value.

However, obliged entities under applicable AML/CFT regulation have the obligation to monitor the business relationships with their clients in order to identify activities that could indicate suspicious money laundering-related activities. In some cases, large transactions may be considered indications of such suspicious activities, especially if it is uncharacteristic to the usual transaction related to the specific client. When the obliged entity identifies suspicious activities that could reference to money laundering or terrorist financing, it should notify the Financial Intelligence Unit.

Estate planning and testamentary succession

Cryptocurrencies are not treated differently from ordinary assets for the purposes of estate planning and testamentary succession under Estonian legislation.

* * *

Endnotes

1. Available online: https://www.fi.ee/index.php?id=22715.
2. Available online: http://eur-lex.europa.eu/legal-content/EN/TXT/PDF/?uri=CELEX:3 2017R0565&qid=1515161142376&from=ET.
3. Governmental action plan for 2015-2019, available at: https://www.riigiteataja.ee/ aktilisa/3030/6201/5006/231klisa.pdf.
4. Analysis on the potentiality of development of a policy of recognition and use of virtual currencies, available at: https://www.rahandusministeerium.ee/system/files_force/ document_files/2016-vv_virtuaalvaaringute_analuus-22-07.pdf?download=1.
5. *Estonia could offer "estcoins" to e-residents*, available at: https://medium.com/e-residency-blog/estonia-could-offer-estcoins-to-e-residents-a3a5a5d3c894.
6. https://www.ecb.europa.eu/press/pressconf/2017/html/ecb.is170907.en.html.
7. *We're planning to launch estcoin – and that's only the start*, available at: https:// medium.com/e-residency-blog/were-planning-to-launch-estcoin-and-that-s-only-the-start-310aba7f3790.

Priit Lätt, Partner
Tel: +372 511 9268 / Email: priit.latt@pwc.com
Priit Lätt, attorney-at-law, heads the intellectual property/IT, public procurement and tax litigation practices at PwC Legal in Estonia.
Priit is a renowned specialist in IP, IT (including IoT, ICO and cryptocurrencies), tax and public procurement law, representing and advising Estonian and international companies and public institutions. Priit also has significant experience in representing clients in complex disputes which have created precedents at the Supreme Court, including the constitutional review chamber. Among other things, Priit has represented a client in Estonia's biggest software dispute and in Estonia's first bitcoin-related regulatory lawsuit. Priit also successfully represented a client in a trademark dispute, in which the Supreme Court declared several provisions of the Code of Civil Procedure and Government Regulations that established limits to legal fees in civil disputes, as invalid and unconstitutional. Priit has advised several ICOs and launches of innovative blockchain projects.
Priit participated as the only attorney in a public and private sector work group, which for the first time in Estonia developed a recommended standard contract for the public procurement of software development.
Major international legal publications (e.g., *Chambers, The Legal 500, WTR1000*) have repeatedly identified Priit as one of top attorneys in the practice areas of IP, IT and tax law.
Priit is the founder of Estonian Cryptocurrency Association (2014) and has been a long-term member of its management board. In addition, he gives lectures on cryptocurrencies and ICOs at the University of Tartu and numerous crypto conferences.
Priit has been a member of Estonian Bar Association since 2001 and he also is a member of the IP/IT commission of the Estonian Bar.

Carel Kivimaa, Attorney
Tel: +372 6141 858 / Email: carel.kivimaa@pwc.com
Carel Kivimaa is an associate at PwC Legal Estonia who specialises mainly in data protection and IT law. Additionally, Carel has extensive experience in court proceedings in civil cases. In the course of his career, Carel has made a significant contribution to the successful implementation of several ICO projects and advised clients in applying crypto-related activity licences in Estonia. Furthermore, he has extensive experience in helping clients in achieving compliance with applicable data protection regulations, including the GDPR.
Carel holds MA degrees in Law and IT Law from the University of Tartu. He has been a member of the Estonian Bar Association since 2017.

PwC Legal

Pärnu mnt 15, 10141 Tallinn, Estonia
Tel: +372 6141 858 / URL: www.pwclegal.ee

France

Christophe Perchet, Juliette Loget & Stéphane Daniel
Davis Polk & Wardwell LLP

Government attitude and definition

Over the past two years, France has been at the forefront of the blockchain revolution in the European Union ("**EU**") and the French government is currently working, together with the players in the French crypto ecosystem, to establish a favourable legal framework for initial coin offerings ("**ICOs**").

As early as April 2016, France became the first country to recognise blockchain technology in the field of cash vouchers, also called "*minibons*", a particular type of promissory note primarily used in crowd-lending transactions, by allowing issuers to register *minibons* directly into the blockchain.

In October 2017, the French Financial Market Authority (the "**AMF**") launched a unique "digital-asset fundraising support and research programme" to support and analyse ICOs, named UNICORN (for "Universal Node to ICO's Research & Network"), operating similarly to a "sandbox" programme (see **Promotion and testing**, below).

In December 2017, France adopted a specific law to become the first country to authorise the registration and transfer of unlisted securities through the use of blockchain technology.

In March 2018, Bruno le Maire, the French Minister of the Economy, declared that he wanted Paris to become the capital of ICOs, through the implementation of a very innovative optional legal framework governing ICOs (see **Sales Regulations**).

In terms of personal taxation, in April 2018, a decision by France's highest administrative court (*Conseil d'état*) resulted in the lightening of the tax burden on profits resulting from cryptocurrency transactions by applying a flat tax rate of 19% (see **Taxation**).

In June 2018, the French Strategy and Prospective General Commission ("*France Stratégie*"), under the auspices of the French Prime Minister, published a 150-page report relating to blockchain and cryptocurrencies and proposing several reforms to enable the sound development of this technology in France.

In short, the French government is working to establish a favourable legal framework, and France currently stands out as a "blockchain/crypto friendly" jurisdiction compared to some others, through its "soft touch" approach favouring innovation and entrepreneurial projects.

However, France still needs to clarify a number of practical aspects of the tax treatment of ICOs if it wishes to attract ICO issuers. Moreover, this friendly position does not mean that France considers cryptocurrencies (which are not located in France, backed by the French government or the European Central Bank) as "real money" or otherwise gives them equal standing with domestic or foreign fiat currencies. In March 2018, the French Central Bank (*Banque de France*) published a paper regarding the main issues, risks and perspectives raised by Bitcoin and other cryptocurrencies, in which it focuses on the reasons why "cryptocurrencies" cannot be qualified as such. As a result, the French Central Bank considered the term "cryptocurrency" to be unsuitable and that the term "crypto-asset" would be preferable instead. Following such publication, the French regulatory authorities have started using the word "crypto-asset" exclusively, delineating the fundamental difference with "real money" or "fiat currencies".

In particular, the French Central Bank explained that "crypto-assets" do not fulfil the customary roles of fiat currencies for the following reasons: (i) they are too volatile to be used as "units of account" (*unité de compte*); (ii) they are not as efficient as fiat currencies (they are difficult to use, there are high transaction fees and there is no guarantee against fraud); and (iii) they have no intrinsic value and hence cannot be used as reserve in value.

The French Central Bank also emphasised that, pursuant to the French financial and monetary code, the only currency in France is the euro and therefore "crypto-assets" may not be considered as either a means of payment or electronic money under French law. This is logical given that "crypto-assets" are not issued against a cash deposit. As a result, under French law, it is impossible to require someone to accept "crypto-assets" as payment, and "crypto-assets" do not carry a repayment guarantee at any time and at face value in the event of unauthorised payment, in each case in contrast to fiat currencies.

Cryptocurrency regulation

As discussed below (see **Sales Regulation**), as of today, there are no specific regulations governing cryptocurrencies as such, unless they fall within the existing legal framework governing securities offering and trading, according to an analysis to be made on a case-by-case basis depending on the rights and obligations conferred by each cryptocurrency. However, this will change with the adoption of the optional clearance for ICOs subject to AMF approval.

Sales regulation

As of today, there are no specific regulations governing fundraising activity based on cryptocurrencies (such as Bitcoin) and blockchain technology. In view of this, in October 2017, the AMF launched: (i) a public consultation on ICOs to gather the views of stakeholders on the different means of supervision; and (ii) a "digital-asset fundraising support and research programme" to support and analyse these transactions, named UNICORN.

As part of this exercise, the AMF carried out an initial high-level study of these transactions and their legal implications and found that while some of the ICOs identified may fall within existing legal provisions (such as the regulation applicable to intermediaries in miscellaneous assets, the public offering of financial securities, or managers of alternative investment funds), most of these issues would, currently under French law, actually fall outside of the scope of any AMF compliance regulation.

According to the AMF, this analysis must be made on a case-by-case basis depending on the rights and obligations attached to each cryptocurrency. In particular, if such rights and obligations prove to be close to those of a security, i.e. because they carry financial and/or political rights, such as dividend and/or voting rights, respectively, the AMF may qualify such cryptocurrency as a security. In such a case, the sale of such cryptocurrency would have to comply with French securities laws, including notably the obligation to publish a prospectus under certain conditions.

Given such uncertainties for issuers, the AMF proposed three options for the supervision of future ICOs: (i) promote best practices without changing existing law; (ii) extend the scope of existing law to treat ICOs as public offerings of securities; and (iii) propose an *ad hoc* regime adapted to ICOs.

In February 2018, the AMF published a summary of the responses received following the public consultation on ICOs, pursuant to which a large majority of respondents expressed strong support for the establishment of an appropriate legal framework for this new type of fundraising method.

Accordingly, as a unique and particularly innovative approach, the AMF decided to work with the French government to introduce optional clearance for ICOs that would be open to companies incorporated in France wishing to ensure that their contemplated ICO will not be subject to the French law regime applicable to public offering of financial securities. In such a situation, solely this optional clearance would be required given that, contrary to the United States, there are requirements arising from commodities law with respect to cryptocurrencies in France.

Under this new legal framework, issuers will be free to decide whether to implement a regulated ICO, subject to AMF approval, or to proceed without the French regulator's approval. In order to obtain AMF clearance, issuers will have to comply with certain obligations which have not yet been released by the AMF but which we expect to be the following:

- provision of an information document to inform buyers of cryptocurrencies which should include, at a minimum: (1) information on the ICO and its progress; (2) the rights attached to the cryptocurrencies and the accounting treatment of the funds raised during the ICO; and (3) the identification of the legal entity responsible for the offer, its managers and founders, and their expertise;

- adopting rules making it possible to ensure the escrow of the funds raised, such as a smart contract escrow or another form of contractual escrow for cryptocurrencies or fiat currencies, respectively, that have been contributed to the issuer during the ICO; and

- setting-up of a mechanism to prevent money laundering and terrorist financing, such as customer verification requirements ("**KYC**").

In order to ensure complete transparency and publicity of this optional clearance, the AMF will make public a "white list" of approved ICOs.

The French government plans to introduce this new legal framework in the upcoming bill known as "*loi Pacte*". As a first step towards adoption by the French Parliament, this bill was presented to the French Ministers Council on June 18, 2018, and is expected to be discussed in September 2018 and ultimately passed by the end of 2018. Implementation of this new framework should occur soon after this adoption.

However, the EU may cast a shadow over such an innovative approach: on November 13, 2017, the European Securities and Markets Authority ("**ESMA**") published a warning to firms involved in ICOs on the potential qualification that cryptocurrencies could receive, pursuant to which these firms could be involved in offering "transferable securities" to the public. This qualification of "transferable securities" would trigger the application of the EU securities laws and regulations, such as the Prospectus Directive, the Markets in Financial Instruments Directive, the Alternative Investment Fund Managers Directive and the fourth Anti-Money Laundering Directive. However, to date, ESMA has not published any further information regarding the qualification of cryptocurrencies. If ESMA eventually decides to adopt a different approach, the AMF, as well as other EU regulators (including Malta, for instance) would necessarily have to re-examine their attitude towards cryptocurrencies to align with the EU approach.

Taxation

The accounting and tax treatment of ICO proceeds in France is unclear. To improve legal certainty, the French National Accounting Standards Authority (*Autorité des Normes Comptables* or "**ANC**") is currently working closely with the French government and the French tax administration to release specific public guidance before the end of this year.

As of today, the market accounting treatment of ICO proceeds seems to have evolved towards their registration under the category of "deferred revenues" (*produits constatés d'avance*) when looking at "utility tokens". As a result, ICO proceeds would be subject to French corporate tax, the rate of which is currently 33.33% plus surtaxes of 3.3% (to be progressively reduced to 25% plus surtaxes in 2022 as a result of the French government tax reform). Such tax is payable during the financial year immediately following the closing (i.e., between 1 and 12 months following the ICO in most cases, and up to 18–24 months for a newly incorporated ICO issuer).

Under the same interpretation, the sale of cryptocurrencies would qualify as a "sale of goods and/or services" under Directive 2006/112/EC on valued-added tax ("**VAT**"), transposed into each EU domestic law, and therefore the sale of cryptocurrencies to EU purchasers will be subject to VAT, the rate of which is currently 20% in France.

However, this treatment does not appear in our view to be relevant for cryptocurrencies which qualify or could be qualified as "security tokens", which should therefore be subject to the tax regime applicable to the sale of securities, i.e. subject to registration fees only (at a 0.1% rate) and excluded from VAT.

Therefore, we look forward to the ANC public position to obtain a clear view on the accounting and tax treatment of ICOs in France, which we expect before the end of this year.

With respect to personal taxation, despite French tax law remaining silent on the taxation of profits made on the sale of cryptocurrencies by individuals, the French tax authorities published an administrative doctrine back in July 2014, pursuant to which such profits would be subject to French income tax within the category of "industrial and commercial profits", and subject to a progressive tax rate of up to 45%, plus social contributions.

However, several taxpayers concerned with profits made on the sale of bitcoins challenged such doctrine before France's highest administrative court (*Conseil d'Etat*), which, in April 2018, eventually decided to lighten this tax burden by stating that such gains will be subject to French income tax within the category of "movable property" (governing gains made on the sale of cars, bottles of wine, etc.), and subject to a 19% tax rate plus social security contributions at a rate of 17.2%.

However, certain gains will be excluded from this tax treatment and therefore remain subject to income tax within the category of "industrial and commercial profits" or "non-commercial profits" (plus social contributions). These include:

- gains resulting from the taxpayer's participation in the creation and functioning of the Bitcoin system, i.e. gains resulting from "mining" activities; and
- gains resulting from the recurring acquisition and sale of bitcoins, thus materialising the existence of a commercial activity, i.e. gains resulting from professional trading activities.

Although this decision concerns gains made on the sale of bitcoins, this tax treatment is, in our view, applicable to all gains made on the sale of cryptocurrencies.

Money transmission laws and anti-money laundering requirements

Currently under French law, the only anti-money laundering ("**AML**") requirement imposed with respect to cryptocurrency is that applicable to any services platform offering to convert fiat currencies into cryptocurrencies or vice versa (thereby acting as an intermediary between the purchaser and the seller), which is required to obtain approval as a payment services provider and implement customers due diligence controls, including KYC.

In May 2018, the EU Member States adopted an amendment to Directive (EU) 2015/849 of 20 May 2015 on the prevention of the use of the financial system for the purposes of money laundering or terrorist financing (the "**AML Directive**"), to subject cryptocurrency exchange platforms and custodian wallet providers to the AML and terrorism financing obligations (in particular to KYC obligations), in line with traditional financial intermediaries.

This recent amendment will not substantially impact French law since French cryptocurrency exchange platforms are already subject to AML requirements and KYC obligations. However, the amendment to the AML Directive will extend these obligations throughout the EU, ensure the implementation of adequate safeguards and make it impossible for players to perform regulatory arbitrage on this basis within the EU.

Under French and EU law, the AML requirements primarily cover the following:

*   *customer due diligence obligations*: platforms are required to verify the identity and, in certain cases, the "effective beneficiary", i.e. the actual individuals behind a legal entity, whether it is a company, a foundation or a trust, and the origin of the money used through platforms; and

*   *reporting and information obligations*: if the due diligence obligations lead to suspicion about an individual or a legal entity, platforms are required to report the situation to an authority specifically in charge of gathering such reports made by cryptocurrency platforms.

In addition, the French Central Bank (*Banque de France*), in its paper published in March 2018, and together with the French Prudential Authority ("**ACPR**"), proposed the introduction of a new status for "crypto-assets services providers" (*prestataires de services en crypto-actifs*), to: (i) extend to the players offering (x) the exchange of crypto-assets for fiat currencies, and (y) the storage on behalf of private clients of cryptographic keys that can be used to hold, store or transfer crypto-assets, the application of AML requirements and KYC obligations; as well as (ii) submit them to new obligations regarding the security of transactions and the protection of their clients. It has yet to be determined whether the French government will follow the lead of the French Central Bank and the ACPR and create this new status.

Finally, while under French law, there is currently no obligation for ICO issuers to comply with any AML requirements or KYC obligations, such compliance will be required in the context of the upcoming optional clearance for ICOs. In addition, and as a matter of fact, the lack of any AML and KYC actions (which would be applied on a voluntary basis by ICO issuers) would result in important technical difficulties in the exchange of cryptocurrencies received against fiat currencies and/or the retention of such fiat currencies in an account held within the books of a French bank, which would be highly reluctant to receive them.

Promotion and testing

In France, as discussed above, the approach adopted by the AMF is very close to a "sandbox" following the launch, in October 2017, of a public consultation relating to ICOs and the above-mentioned UNICORN programme to support and analyse these transactions (see **Sales regulation**).

As part of this consultation, the AMF organised meetings with several players of the blockchain/crypto ecosystem and received 82 contributions from digital economy players, individuals, finance professionals, market infrastructures, academics and law firms. In February 2018, as part of the UNICORN programme, the AMF announced it had advised about 15 companies during the first two months of the programme, approximately 50% of which related to blockchain-related projects, and that the total amount raised or planned to be raised by these project developers was around €350m.

Overall, the AMF demonstrated an awareness about the importance of these topics and a willingness to get in touch and learn from the ecosystem to shape an *ad hoc,* specifically adapted legal framework.

In addition, at the European level, in April 2018, more than three-quarters of European countries, including France, signed a declaration relating to the establishment of a European Blockchain Partnership, intended to act as a vehicle to foster cooperation among Member States in the exchange of technical and regulatory expertise. This declaration, and the partnership that it creates, follows the launch in February 2018 of the EU Blockchain Observatory and Forum, designed to help cultivate new blockchain opportunities in Europe. The stated goal of the partnership is to ensure that Europe continues to play a leading role in the development and roll-out of blockchain technologies.

France is therefore keen on promoting research and investment in cryptocurrency and blockchain-related projects through specific programmes and actions run by governmental authorities.

Ownership and licensing requirements

Under French law, there are very few investment funds which have invested all or even part of their funds in cryptocurrencies. This is principally explained by the fact that French law in particular, and EU law in general, is not yet well suited to enable investment funds to invest in cryptocurrencies.

Furthermore, French Undertakings for Collective Investment in Transferable Securities ("**UCITS**", otherwise known as *OPCVM* in France), which are open to distribution to retail clients, are constrained by law to invest into a specific restricted list of assets, into which cryptocurrencies do not fall. For this reason, French UCITS cannot invest in cryptocurrencies.

French Alternative Investment Funds ("**AIF**", otherwise known as *FIA* in France), which are open to professional investors only (institutional investors, large firms and investors with sufficient financial experience and competence and also retail clients under certain specific conditions) and therefore are less regulated than UCITS, are less constrained with respect to the assets in which they may invest. However, one of the conditions laid down by the French financial and monetary code is that the title to such asset must be "evidenced by a mechanism that is recognised under French law". In the present case, the fact that the title to cryptocurrency is evidenced by registration into a blockchain is not – yet – recognised under French law and therefore AIF cannot invest in cryptocurrencies. Nevertheless,

French law has already recognised the possibility to register certain assets into a blockchain, namely for cash vouchers, i.e.*"minibons"*, and unlisted securities, and may evolve in the future to also recognise cryptocurrency registered into a blockchain.

The only option left for a French investment fund to invest directly in cryptocurrencies is to use a very specific French vehicle known as "other alternative investment funds" (**"Other AIF"**, otherwise known as *Autres FIA* in France). This vehicle may be either regulated *ex ante* by the AMF and open to both professional and non-professional investors, or merely declared *ex post* to the AMF, in which case it is open to professional investors only. To our knowledge, this structure has been used by Tobam Asset Management, a French investment manager which, in late 2017, announced the launch of the very first French Bitcoin-focused investment fund, "approved" but not "regulated" by the AMF.

In this respect, for an Other AIF to be regulated by the AMF and therefore be open to distribution to both professional and non-professional investors, the Other AIF manager must obtain a portfolio management company licence from the AMF.

An interesting alternative to direct investment in cryptocurrency available under French law may be the use of a structure of "master" funds/"feeder" funds, pursuant to which a French investment fund would invest in a foreign investment fund which would ultimately be investing in cryptocurrencies. This raises the question of whether foreign investment funds are able to invest directly in cryptocurrencies. To our knowledge, a few countries allow the creation of crypto investment funds, including Switzerland, Luxembourg, Canada and the United States of America. However, we do not have any example of the use of such structure and the main weakness of this scenario is that it may be seen as circumventing the rules outlined above.

Finally, this French legal and regulatory framework restricting direct investment by French investment funds in cryptocurrencies may be about to change with the upcoming optional clearance for ICOs subject to AMF approval. During a parliamentary audition held in April 2018, Robert Ophèle, the Chairman of the AMF, explained that it would be appropriate for cryptocurrencies cleared by the AMF to become eligible as assets of French investment funds. However, (i) this would not benefit cryptocurrencies which have already been issued, such as bitcoins or ethers, and (ii) a recent report dated July 4, 2018, submitted by the deputy governor of the French Central Bank, Jean-Pierre Landau, states that banks and asset managers should be strongly discouraged from investing in cryptocurrencies in order to avoid any risk to financial stability.

Mining

"Mining" Bitcoin and other cryptocurrencies is permitted and unregulated under French law. However, the revenues generated by "mining" activities are submitted to a specific taxation regime (see **Taxation**).

Border restrictions and declaration

There is no specific border restriction or obligation to declare cryptocurrency holdings under French law.

Reporting requirements

Under French law, there is no reporting requirement for cryptocurrency payments made in excess of a certain value.

Estate planning and testamentary succession

Under French law, there is no special treatment for cryptocurrencies for the purposes of estate planning and testamentary succession, and cryptocurrencies should be treated like any other assets in such situations.

* * *

Acknowledgment

The authors acknowledge with thanks the contribution to this chapter by Daniel Arroche.

Mr Arroche is an associate in Davis Polk's Corporate Department, practising in the Paris office. Tel: +33 1 56 59 36 82 / Email: daniel.arroche@davispolk.com.

Christophe Perchet
Tel: +33 1 56 59 36 50 / Email: christophe.perchet@davispolk.com
Mr Perchet is a corporate partner in Davis Polk's Paris office. His practice focuses on domestic and cross-border public and private mergers and acquisitions, joint ventures as well as related litigation. Mr Perchet has recently represented major companies in a variety of complex transactions, including Valeo, A.P. Møller – Mærsk and Carrefour.

Juliette Loget
Tel: +33 1 56 59 36 21 / Email: juliette.loget@davispolk.com
Ms Loget is counsel in Davis Polk's Corporate Department, practising in the Paris office. Her practice focuses on domestic and cross-border public and private mergers and acquisitions and includes representing companies and investment banks in domestic and international capital markets transactions. She has recently represented major French and international companies in a variety of complex transactions, including Technip, Valeo, Solvay, Eramet, A.P. Møller – Mærsk and TE Connectivity.

Stéphane Daniel
Tel: +33 1 56 59 36 46 / Email: stephane.daniel@davispolk.com
Mr Daniel is an associate in Davis Polk's Corporate Department, practising in the Paris office.

Davis Polk & Wardwell LLP

121 avenue des Champs-Elysées – 75008 Paris, France
Tel: +33 1 56 59 36 00 / URL: www.davispolk.com

Germany

Dennis Kunschke & Dr Stefan Henkelmann
Allen & Overy LLP

Government attitude and definition

The German government's[1] views on and approach to cryptocurrencies is ambivalent. On the one hand, there is an awareness that the digital age is progressing with an ever increasing dynamic. To reflect these developments, the government has produced a relatively granular digital agenda.[2] On the other hand, there are major concerns that are very much driven by (retail) investor protection considerations, specifically in relation to cryptocurrencies.

The German government has published a warning relating to the unlawful marketing of cryptocurrencies.[3] In this public warning, the government expressly underlines the fact that cryptocurrencies are not legal tender (*gesetzliche Zahlungsmittel*) but merely substitute currencies (*Ersatzwährungen*). The warning also states that cryptocurrencies as such are not problematic in all cases. Rather, the government points out that some related business practices may raise consumer protection and legal concerns or even be of a fraudulent nature, e.g. exhibit features of Ponzi schemes. The warning is broken down into the following areas of concern: (i) risk of (total) loss due to the lack of a protection mechanism at the level of crypto exchanges; (ii) no capital or deposit protection; (iii) lack of consumer protection standards under EU law; (iv) volatility of the instruments and related risk of loss (market risk); and (v) anonymity of counterparties as regards payments and related AML risks. The German government goes on to state that the consumer protection agencies of the German federal state of Hesse have been conducting investigations since February 2018 based on consumer complaints relating to 20 different distributors of six different cryptocurrencies.[4]

The German regulatory authority BaFin has also recently published a public warning relating to the marketing of cryptocurrencies via ICOs.[5] BaFin criticises the use of the term "ICO" as opposed to "IPO" in the securities context, as IPOs can be assumed to be of a highly regulated and transparent nature, almost irrespective of where they take place across the international stage, whereas this is often not the case for ICOs. In its public warning, BaFin also points to the following particular areas of risks identified:

- Tokens are generally assumed to be subject to high volatility. BaFin identifies a general risk that liquid secondary markets are not available, which means that investors risk being ultimately stuck with an illiquid asset.

- BaFin also adopts the view that a substantial number of companies financed via ICOs, i.e. by way of issuing security tokens rather than payment tokens, exhibit underlying business models that are still in an experimental stage, which also generates an underlying business risk. Smart contract elements may be complex, opaque and hard to scrutinise from an investor's perspective. Moreover, Bafin identifies the particular risk that smart contract codes may be subject to successful attacks and therefore open to manipulation by third parties.

- The regulatory authority also raises the general criticism that white papers are often of poor quality from a transparency perspective, and that ICO transparency is not sufficiently regulated. It even identifies the general risk that statements made in white papers may be objectively insufficient, incomprehensible or even completely misleading.

BaFin closes its public warning with the following advice addressed to potential investors:[6]

- Before making any investments in tokens, investors should ensure that they fully understand the related risks and potential rewards. To this end, investors should ask the respective issuers as many questions as necessary in order to achieve an adequate level of transparency. Investors should also try to verify relevant statements via independent sources.

- Investors should ensure that the features of the ICO (including the underlying project, if any) are aligned with their individual investment needs and risk appetite.

While BaFin has expressed the concerns described above in the context of investor protection, BaFin's president *Felix Hufeld* currently does not regard cryptocurrencies as presenting a particular risk from the perspective of financial stability.[7]

The German Bundesbank, whose mandate includes macro-prudential supervision and monetary policy within the ambit of the ECB-led Eurosystem, also regularly publishes opinions and insights into the crypto sector. The attitudes expressed in such publications towards cryptocurrencies vary.[8]

Cryptocurrency regulation

German law does not provide for a general prohibition relating to the issuing, mining nor possession of, nor trading in cryptocurrencies. The same is true for security, asset and utility tokens. However, regulatory licensing and prospectus requirements may be applicable,[9] which means, however, that there are specific hurdles which may be overcome if the respective legal requirements are met.[10]

From a technical legal perspective, cryptocurrencies were classified by BaFin back in 2013 as financial instruments according to Sec. 1(11) of the German Banking Act (*Kreditwesengesetz*).[11] They fall in the sub-category of so-called "units of account" (*Rechnungseinheiten*), which are a specific national category of financial instruments not based on EU law.

Back in 2013, BaFin issued its cryptocurrency guidance in light of the growing significance of Bitcoin. The guidance is, however, also applicable for the general classification of cryptocurrencies. The key issue is that the respective tokens qualify as a substitute for legal tender, as they are accepted for payment based on private law agreements, i.e. in contrast to a public law regulation, which is the core feature of fiat currencies.

In BaFin's view, the decisive question for classification as a unit of account, and thus a financial instrument under the German Banking Act, is whether or not there is a central issuer.[12]

BaFin also states in its guidance that cryptocurrencies do not generally qualify as regulated e-money, since there is no central e-money issuer.[13] Where there is a central issuer, however, an assessment on the basis of the German definition of e-money must be conducted. According to the German Payment Services Supervision Act (*Zahlungsdiensteaufsichtsgesetz*), e-money is defined as any monetary value that is stored electronically, including magnetically, and takes the form of a claim against the issuer which is issued in return for payment of funds in order to make payment transactions within the meaning of Sec. 675f (4), first sentence, of the German Civil Code (*Bürgerliches Gesetzbuch*) and which is accepted by a natural or legal person other than the issuer.

That being said, tokens which exhibit features that go beyond serving as a mere payment substitute, i.e. security, asset and utility tokens in particular, must be classified on a case-by-case basis. They may qualify as securities or even units or shares in investment funds.[14]

In its ICO guidance, which only dates back to February 2018,[15] BaFin explains that tokens may well classify as securities, so-called capital investments or even units or shares in investment funds. BaFin states:

> "*BaFin (WA) determines on a case-by-case basis whether a token constitutes a financial instrument within the meaning of the German Securities Trading Act (Wertpapierhandelsgesetz – WpHG) or the Markets in Financial Instruments Directive (MiFID II), a security within the meaning of the German Securities Prospectus Act (Wertpapierprospektgesetz – WpPG), or a capital investment within the meaning of the German Capital Investment Act (Vermögensanlagengesetz – VermAnlG). BaFin bases its assessment on the criteria set out in the statutory provisions under securities supervision law, i.e. in particular the WpHG, WpPG, Market Abuse Regulation (MAR), VermAnlG as well as other relevant laws and applicable national and EU legal acts in the field of securities supervision.*"

The classification of cryptocurrencies and tokens in a wider sense, i.e. including security, asset and utility tokens, has far-reaching implications for anyone dealing in them on a commercial basis. In its ICO guidance, BaFin explains:

> "*Market participants providing services related to tokens, dealing with tokens or publicly offering tokens must give careful consideration to whether the tokens constitute a regulated instrument, i.e. for instance a financial instrument within the meaning of section 2 (4) of the WpHG, or a security within the meaning of section 2 (1) of the WpPG, so that they can fully comply with any legal requirements. This is also emphasised in the respective warning issued by the European Securities and Markets Authority (ESMA) on 13 November 2017.2 The duty to comply with the legal provisions is particularly relevant with regard to possible authorisation requirements pursuant to the German Banking Act (Kreditwesengesetz – KWG), the German Investment Code (Kapitalanlagegesetzbuch – KAGB), the German Insurance Supervision Act (Versicherungsaufsichtsgesetz – VAG) or the German Payment Services Supervision Act (Zahlungsdiensteaufsichtsgesetz – ZAG). In cases where there is doubt as to whether authorisation is required pursuant to the KWG, KAGB, VAG or ZAG, the competent department at BaFin is the Department for Authorisation Requirements and Enforcement relating to Unauthorised Business (EVG) (part of the Resolution Directorate).*"

In the following paragraphs, the authors will focus on the licensing requirements under financial supervisory law according to the German Banking Act, as well as the resulting AML compliance obligations. For the sake of completeness, it is worth noting that where a security token actually classifies as a security under MiFID II and thus as a security under the German Securities Trading Act (*Wertpapierhandelsgesetz*), there are numerous and complex conduct requirements besides the mere licensing requirements, the details of which go well beyond the scope of this publication. The same is true where the ICO of a security token triggers prospectus requirements under the German Securities Prospectus Act (*Wertpapierprospektgesetz*).

Using cryptocurrencies purely as a substitute for cash or book money in order to participate in the economic cycle in the exchange business is not an activity subject to any licensing requirements under financial supervisory law or other authorisations under German public law. This means that using cryptocurrencies as a means of payment is not a regulated activity, or, in other words, "going shopping" with cryptocurrencies is not a regulated activity for the purchaser, nor is the mere acceptance of cryptocurrencies as a substitute currency by the seller.

Certain commercial dealings in cryptocurrencies and other types of tokens can trigger licensing requirements under financial supervisory law pursuant to the German Banking Act. According to Sec. 32 (1) sent. 1 German Banking Act, anyone wishing to conduct banking business or to provide financial services in Germany on commercial terms, or on a scale which requires commercially organised business operations, requires written authorisation from BaFin. It is important to note in this context that "actively targeting the German market" from abroad is sufficient to trigger the relevant licensing requirements under German law, i.e. a physical presence in Germany is not necessarily required.

Typical business constellations that are subject to authorisation requirements include commercial trading platforms, often called exchanges, if either: (i) those buying and selling cryptocurrency commercially in their own name for the account of others carry out principal broking services; or (ii) the platform is operating a multilateral trading facility. In addition, and depending on the exact circumstances, providers acting as "currency exchanges" offering to exchange legal tender for cryptocurrency or cryptocurrency for legal tender carry out trading for own account, proprietary trading, contract broking or investment broking, which is also generally subject to authorisation in each case. Advising in relation to cryptocurrencies may constitute regulated investment advice. Finally, underwriting an ICO may be "regulated underwriting or placement business" within the ambit of the German Banking Act. Given this magnitude of potentially licensable activities, it is clear that any intention to handle cryptocurrencies on a commercial basis, where such activities are targeted at the German market, must be assessed on a case-by-case basis. The following are definitions of potentially regulated activities that require written authorisation from BaFin:

- <u>Principal broking services</u> are defined as the purchase and sale of financial instruments in the credit institution's own name for the account of others.

- <u>Underwriting business</u> (hard underwriting) is defined as the purchase of financial instruments at the credit institution's own risk for placement in the market or the assumption of equivalent guarantees.

- <u>Investment broking</u> is defined as the brokering of business involving the purchase and sale of financial instruments.

- <u>Investment advice</u> is defined as providing customers or their representatives with personal recommendations in respect of transactions relating to certain financial instruments where the recommendation is based on an evaluation of the investor's personal circumstances, or is presented as being suitable for the investor and is not provided exclusively via information distribution channels or for the general public.

- <u>Operation of a multilateral trading facility (MTF)</u> is defined as operating a multilateral facility which brings together a large number of persons' interests in the purchase and sale of financial instruments within the facility according to set rules in a way that results in a purchase agreement for these financial instruments.

- <u>Placement business</u> (soft underwriting) is defined as the placement of financial instruments without a firm commitment basis.
- <u>Contract broking</u> is defined as the purchase and sale of financial instruments on behalf of and for the account of others.
- <u>Portfolio management</u> is defined as the management of individual portfolios of financial instruments for others on a discretionary basis.
- <u>Proprietary trading</u> is defined (in simplified terms) as the purchase and sale of financial instruments for own account as a service for others.

Sales regulation

As regards the sales regulation for cryptocurrencies, commercial distribution may trigger the aforementioned licensing requirements for distributors under financial supervisory law (e.g. typically at least investment broking) due to the fact that these are financial instruments under the German Banking Act.

Beyond the licensing requirements under financial supervisory law, the legal position becomes very complex. The following are points that need to be considered in any detailed assessment:[16]

(i) While cryptocurrencies are financial instruments (units of account) within the ambit of the German Banking Act, they do not qualify as financial instruments under the German Securities Trading Act (*Wertpapierhandelsgesetz*), i.e. the conduct requirements under German law. The situation is different if tokens go beyond being a mere substitute currency; in such case they may qualify (in particular) as securities according the definitions set out in the German Securities Trading Act, triggering complex conduct regulation of their distribution.

(ii) The test for whether a cryptocurrency qualifies as security considers whether (simplified) securities-like rights are attached to the tokens and whether there is a minimum required fungibility, which can be generally assumed if they are (crypto-)exchange-traded.

(iii) The classification as "security" may also trigger prospectus requirements and where a token sale ICO, is issued to raise funds for a specific purpose, an assessment as to whether the tokens constitute units or shares in investments funds within the ambit of the German Capital Investment Code (*Kapitalanlagegesetzbuch*) must be made. Where an investment fund is in fact established and managed, this constitutes a prohibited activity if no licence under the German Capital Investment Code is obtained, which in turn can have far-reaching criminal and civil liability implications.

Taxation

Handling (in the widest sense) cryptocurrencies may have complex tax implications under German law. In the following paragraphs, one of the most pressing issues is given an overview on, i.e. the classification for VAT-purposes.[17]

On 27 February 2018, the German Ministry of Finance (*Bundesfinanzministerium*) issued its guidance concerning the VAT treatment of certain dealings in cryptocurrencies in light of the decision by the ECJ, dated 22 October 2015 (C-264/14 – *Hedqvist*).[18] The core statements of this guidance are set out below:

(i)   Exchanging cryptocurrency into fiat and *vice versa* is exempted from the VAT regime.

(ii) The mere use of cryptocurrencies as a means of payment is not a taxable transaction for VAT purposes (i.e. the "cash leg" of a sales transaction).

(iii) Mining is not a taxable activity for VAT purposes.

(iv) Offering digital wallet services in return for consideration is a taxable activity for VAT purposes under German tax law where such service is offered in Germany.

(v)   Providing a crypto exchange platform may be a taxable activity for VAT purposes, depending on the precise circumstances.

Money transmission laws and anti-money laundering requirements

German payment services regulation is provided for in the Payment Services Supervision Act (*Zahlungsdiensteaufsichtsgesetz*) which transposes the Second Payment Services Directive (PSD II)[19] as well as the E-Money Directive.[20]

Since cryptocurrencies do not constitute legal tender, "payment accounts", i.e. electronic wallets (hot or cold) where related keys are "stored", do not constitute payment accounts[21] according to Sec. 1 (17) Payment Services Supervision Act. It follows that licensable activities attaching to the opening and operation of payment accounts, such as direct debit business and credit transfer business (involving payment transactions in fiat currency), are not applicable. Due to the fact that fiat currency is not "remitted" outside payment accounts in the legal sense where, for instance, a person exchanges fiat for crypto, transfers the crypto to a third party and this third party (re-)exchanges into fiat, there are very convincing arguments that such activities do not trigger licensable money remittance business according to the Payment Services Supervision Act either, even if they are performed on a commercial business.

That being said, close attention must be paid to the structuring of any "fiat cash legs" involved when structuring a business model that involves transactions in cryptocurrencies, beyond the licensing requirements under financial supervisory law. One criterion that would lead the model to fall outside the ambit of the Payment Services Supervision Act is that no unlicensed administrator receives, stores or manages fiat currency for the account of any customer or any third party. The details need to be analysed on a case-by-case basis.

The mere use of cryptocurrencies and other tokens as a means of payment for goods and services and the sale and exchange of self-procured cryptocurrency does not subject the relevant persons or undertakings to any obligations under the German Anti-Money Laundering Act (*Geldwäschegesetz*).

Where commercial dealing in cryptocurrencies triggers licensing requirements under financial supervisory law according to the German Banking Act, by way of express statutory reference in the German Anti-Money Laundering Act, however, this also means that the person or undertaking becomes an "obliged person" (*Verpflichteter*) for the purposes of German AML law.

The German Anti-Money Laundering Act requires obliged persons (*inter alia*) to have effective risk management systems in place as well as to fulfil general due diligence requirements, including customer and beneficial owner identification and verification duties. The obligations also include monitoring obligations, as well as the implementation of organisational processes for suspicious transaction-reporting to competent authorities.[22]

At the level of European law, the European Parliament and European Council reached an agreement in December 2017 that will extend AML obligations to firms operating centralised cryptocurrency exchanges and custodial wallet providers for cryptocurrencies by adding them to the definition of "obliged entities" contained in the existing directive framework. This means that for such EEA countries where, unlike in Germany, cryptocurrencies do not constitute financial instruments and thus (in an nutshell) commercial dealings in them do not trigger licensing requirements under financial supervisory law, which in turn trigger AML obligations, there will be a minimum harmonisation of AML law in the crypto sector.

Promotion and testing

In Germany, there is no sandbox or any other type of light-touch regulatory regime available for commercial dealing in or handling of cryptocurrencies or any other types of tokens.

This is due to the fact that in Germany there is no legal basis for any light-touch approach, which could potentially include systematic deviation from the principle of equal treatment of the applicants.

The Bundesbank also stresses that, as the German law currently stands, and in contrast to the FCA and the PRA, promotional activities in specific economic sectors are not part of the banking regulators' mission statement.[23] Rather, banking supervisors are, by law, obliged to counteract undesirable developments in the lending and financial services sector which may endanger the safety of the assets entrusted to institutions, impair the proper conduct of banking business or provision of financial services, or entail major disadvantages for the economy as a whole.

That being said, it has been argued that the lack of any sandboxing regimes can also be an advantage, as it fosters the general perception that emerging players are also regulated and supervised in a manner equivalent to those that are already well-established. This trust-building factor may actually induce customers to sign-up to innovative distribution channels and products that are prudentially regulated.[24]

Moreover, there is still a general perception that the German regulatory authorities have become much more "approachable" in light of technological developments, i.e. are open to dialogue as regards explaining licensing and other requirements under financial supervisory law to fintech start-ups. This is reflected, for instance, in initiatives such as the "BaFin Tech 2016" conference.[25]

Ownership and licensing requirements

Where cryptocurrencies are held "for the account of others" on a commercial basis, the respective business model must be assessed on a case-by-case basis. Such activities may, in particular, trigger the regulated activities of: (i) portfolio management; (ii) principal broking services; (iii) contract broking; and/or (iv) investment broking according to the German Banking Act or even constitute managing an investment fund, which is a licensable activity under the German Capital Investment Code.

Mining

BaFin issued public guidance on the regulatory classification of mining back in 2013.[26]

According to this regulatory guidance, the creation of new cryptocurrency by solving complex mathematical computational tasks (i.e. mining) does not constitute a regulated activity under the German Banking Act. In particular, the miner does not underwrite or place financial instruments as a service for another issuer, which might otherwise constitute a regulated activity under the German Banking Act.

Border restrictions and declaration

There is no general prohibition on "importing" cryptocurrencies into Germany or "exporting" them out of Germany.

As regards the calculation of applicable values for the purposes of the Union Customs Code,[27] i.e. in cases where goods are imported from third countries, the legal position is likely to be as follows: According to Art. 69 Union Customs Code, the customs value of goods, for the purposes of applying the common customs tariff and non-tariff measures laid down by Union provisions governing specific fields relating to trade in goods, is to be determined in accordance with Art. 70 and 74 Union Customs Code.

According to Art. 70(1) and (2) Union Customs Code: (i) the primary basis for the customs value of goods is the transaction value, that is the price actually paid or payable for the goods when sold for export to the customs territory of the Union, adjusted, where necessary; and (ii) the price actually paid or payable is the total payment made, or to be made, by the buyer to the seller, or by the buyer to a third party for the benefit of the seller for the imported goods, and includes all payments made or to be made as a condition of sale of the imported goods.

It can likely be derived from Art. 70 Union Customs Code in conjunction with Art. 120 (para. 2 thereof in particular) of the Delegated Regulation[28] that, due to the fact that cryptocurrencies are not legal tender and often subject to major fluctuations, the price conversion into legal tender at the relevant point in time according to Art. 128 of the Delegated Regulation cannot be determined with sufficient accuracy.

Accordingly, the alternative valuation methods according to Art. 74 Unions Customs Code are likely to apply, which (in a nutshell) means that the customs value shall be either of the following: (i) the transaction value of identical goods sold for export to the customs territory of the Union and exported at or about the same time as the goods being valued; or (ii) in case (i) cannot be determined, the transaction value of similar goods sold for export to the customs territory of the Union and exported at or about the same time as the goods being valued; or (iii) in case (ii) cannot be determined, the value based on the unit price at which the imported goods, or identical or similar imported goods, are sold within the customs territory of the Union in the greatest aggregate quantity to persons not related to the sellers. This means that the payment leg of the transaction in question is not the decisive factor, but rather that a valuation cascade is applied in relation to the asset in question.

Reporting requirements

The following paragraphs contain a discussion of some of the core provisions of the German Foreign Trade and Payments Ordinance (*Außenwirtschaftsverordnung*). Cross-border transactions involving cryptocurrencies should be assessed on a case-by-case basis.

According to Sec. 67 (1) Foreign Trade and Payments Ordinance, German residents must notify the Bundesbank, by predefined deadlines, of payments (i) which they receive from foreigners or from residents for the account of a foreigner (incoming payments), or (ii) which they make to foreigners or to residents for the account of a foreigner (outgoing payments).

According to Sec. 67 (2) Foreign Trade and Payments Ordinance, the relevant notifications to the Bundesbank are not required for: (i) payments which do not exceed the amount of €12,500 or the equivalent value in another currency; (ii) payments for the import, export or transfer of goods; or (iii) payments for the granting, receipt or repayment of loans, including the justification and repayment of credit balances, with an originally agreed term or termination deadline of not more than 12 months. Accordingly, the question of whether using cryptocurrencies as an alternative means of payment does not arise within the exemptions set out in Sec. 67 (2) Foreign Trade and Payments Ordinance. In all other cases of cross-border transactions, the legal interpretation of Sec. 67 (3) Foreign Trade and Payments Ordinance is decisive. According to Sec. 67 (3) Foreign Trade and Payments Ordinance, payments within the meaning of the relevant subdivision of the Foreign Trade and Payments Ordinance shall include netting and offsetting and payments handled by direct debit.

Although Sec. 67 (3) Foreign Trade and Payments Ordinance contains a supplementary legal definition for "payments", it does not further specify the core term of "payments" itself. In other words, Sec. 67 (3) Foreign Trade and Payments Ordinance merely expands the definition of "payment" to include other "movements of assets".[29] Hence the concept of payment must be interpreted broadly. According to the prevailing legal view, therefore, the term "payments" within the ambit of Sec. 67 (3) Foreign Trade and Payments Ordinance means "any transfer of means of payment (cash and book money) between two persons".[30]

Despite such very broad definition of "payments", it is very likely that the definition only applies to payments made in fiat currency.[31] As cryptocurrencies are not legal tender, it is very likely that transactions cannot be classified as payments but rather occur within barter transactions which merely contain the economic components of payments in the legal sense.

Accordingly, it is also very likely that "payments" in cryptocurrencies do not constitute payments within the ambit of Sec. 70 Foreign Trade and Payments Ordinance (Reports of the financial institutions). According to Sec. 70 (1) Foreign Trade and Payments Ordinance, domestic financial institutions must report (inter alia) the following to the Bundesbank within predefined deadlines:

(i) payments for the sale or acquisition of securities and financial derivatives which the financial institution sells to foreigners or buys from foreigners on its own or third-party account, and payments which the financial institution makes to foreigners or receives from them in connection with the redemption of domestic securities;

(ii) interest and dividend payments on domestic securities which they make to or receive from foreigners; and

(iii) incoming and outgoing payments for interest payments and similar revenues and expenses, excluding interest on securities received from or made to foreigners on their own account.

Such reporting obligations are not applicable to payments which do not exceed the amount of €12,500 or the equivalent value in another currency.

However, the term "payments" according to the relevant provisions of the Foreign Trade and Payments Ordinance further includes the contribution of objects and rights to companies, branches and permanent establishments.[32] It is very likely that the respective provision applies the concept of payments in fiat currency in an analogous manner to the contribution of objects and rights into companies, branches and permanent establishments located in Germany. It follows that this case-specific sub-definition cannot be taken as a means to argue that transacting in cryptocurrencies is to be generally treated as being equivalent to payments in fiat currency.

However, the question arises as to whether cryptocurrencies, when paid into a German-based undertaking (i.e. by means of a contribution in kind) within the ambit of this definition as a means of raising (equity) capital for such undertaking qualify as "objects" or "rights". While almost all[33] cryptocurrencies are surely not "objects" (*Sachen*), as they do not constitute tangible property (*körperlicher Gegenstand*), cryptocurrencies may from time to time carry rights attached to them or, from a teleological perspective, the factual possibility to effect economic payments via their use, may be construed as being equivalent to being a right within the definition of the term "right" according to Sec. 67 (3) sent. 2 Foreign Trade and Payments Ordinance. Accordingly, where contributions in kind to German-based companies are made in the form of cryptocurrencies, the transactions in questions should be assessed on a case-by-case basis and it may be advisable to seek a common understanding with the competent authorities.

Estate planning and testamentary succession

As regards the question of how cryptocurrencies are treated for the purposes of estate planning and testamentary succession, the rules according to the German Civil Code (*Bürgerliches Gesetzbuch*) are relevant.

Sec. 1922 (1) of the German Civil Code states that upon the death of a person (devolution of an inheritance), that person's property (inheritance) passes as a whole to one or more than one other persons (heirs). This provision of the law codifies the so-called principle of universal succession, which means that the heirs assume the legal positions of the deceased in their entirety.

This principle of universal succession also encompasses the general rule that property relations usually pass to the heirs, and intangible rights expire upon death. Exceptions to this principle require a special statutory provision.[34] Cryptocurrency has the character of a substitute for cash or legal tender. As such, it forms part of the property of the deceased and should pass to the heirs after death according to Sec. 1922 of the German Civil Code (BGB). In a sense, the private key (and the wallet), or such other means that allow for the transfer of a given cryptocurrency, should qualify as forming part of the inheritance within the ambit of Sec. 1922 of the German Civil Code.

It thus follows from this analysis that cryptocurrencies should be subject to all the regular rules of inheritance according to the German Civil Code, including that they can be subject to testamentary succession.

* * *

Endnotes

1. The term "government" in this case also includes regulatory authorities such as the German *Bundesbank* and the German Federal Financial Supervisory Authority (BaFin).

2. For the general digital agenda and related "hightech-strategie" *cf.* the German government's webpage: https://www.bundesregierung.de/Webs/Breg/DE/Themen/Innovationspolitik/_node.html.

3. Public warning dated 2 February 2018, available at: https://www.bundesregierung.de/Content/DE/Artikel/2018/02/2018-02-02-kryptowaehrung.html.

4. For further information on these investigations please refer to the webpage *Marktwaechter*: https://ssl.marktwaechter.de/pressemeldung/kryptowaehrungen-undurchsichtige-geschaefte-rund-um-bitcoin-co.

5. Public warning dated 9 November 2017, available at: https://www.bafin.de/SharedDocs/
Veroeffentlichungen/DE/Meldung/2017/meldung_171109_ICOs.html as well as
further background material dated 15 November 2011 available at: https://www.bafin.
de/SharedDocs/Veroeffentlichungen/DE/Fachartikel/2017/fa_bj_1711_ICO.html.

6. This advice is primarily directed at consumers (*Verbraucher*) but written in a general
"common sense" manner.

7. *Cf.* interview; quotes available at: http://www.faz.net/aktuell/finanzen/digital-bezahlen/
bitcoin-und-co-bafin-stellt-regulierung-in-aussicht-15462114.html.

8. *Cf.* further reference: "Vorteile durch neue digitale Produkte im Zahlungsverkehr"
– Interview in German *Focus*, dated 05.02.2018, available at: https://www.
bundesbank.de/Redaktion/DE/Interviews/2018_02_05_dombret_focus.html?searc
hArchive=0&submit=Suchen&searchIssued=0&oneOfTheseWords=cryptocurren
y%2C+Bitcoin%2C+Kryptow%C3%A4hrung; "Finger weg von Bitcoin!", Guest
commentary in the *Frankfurter Allgemeinen Sonntagszeitung* dated 04.02.2018,
available at: https://www.bundesbank.de/Redaktion/DE/Standardartikel/Presse/
Gastbeitraege/2018_02_04_thiele_fas.html?searchArchive=0&submit=Suchen&searc
hIssued=0&oneOfTheseWords=cryptocurrency%2C+Kryptow%C3%A4hrung%2C+
Bitcoin; "Auswirkungen virtueller Währungen auf die Finanzmärkte", speech at Union
Investment dated 15.01.2018, available at: https://www.bundesbank.de/Redaktion/DE/
Reden/2018/2018_01_15_wuermeling.html?searchArchive=0&submit=Suchen&sear
chIssued=0&oneOfTheseWords=cryptocurrency%2C+Kryptow%C3%A4hrung%2C
+Bitcoin.

9. *Cf.* under "Sales regulation" below for details.

10. E.g. adequate licences are obtained.

11. *Cf.* the public BaFin guidance dated 19 December 2013, available at: https://www.
bafin.de/SharedDocs/Veroeffentlichungen/DE/Fachartikel/2014/fa_bj_1401_bitcoins.
html.

12. Where there is a central issuer, however, detailed analysis must be conducted in order
to assess potential classification as e-money.

13. *Cf.* the public guidance issued by BaFin dated 28 April 2016, available at: https://www.
bafin.de/DE/Aufsicht/FinTech/VirtualCurrency/virtual_currency_node.html.

14. Please refer to further details below.

15. *Cf.* the public guidance issued by BaFin dated 20 February 2018, available at: https://
www.bafin.de/SharedDocs/Downloads/DE/Merkblatt/WA/dl_hinweisschreiben_
einordnung_ICOs.html.

16. For further information on the complex legal implications and classifications, cf.
BaFin's ICO Guidance, available at: https://www.bafin.de/SharedDocs/Downloads/
EN/Merkblatt/WA/dl_hinweisschreiben_einordnung_ICOs_en.html.

17. For further information on taxation of the digital economy, *cf. Troetscher* in: Kunschke/
Schaffelhuber, FinTech, Grundlagen, Regulierung, Finanzierung, Case Studies, (2018),
p. 209 *et seq.*

18. *Cf.* German Ministry of Finance, available at: https://www.bundesfinanzministerium.
de/Content/DE/Downloads/BMF_Schreiben/Steuerarten/Umsatzsteuer/Umsatzsteuer-
Anwendungserlass/2018-02-27-umsatzsteuerliche-behandlung-von-bitcoin-und-
anderen-sog-virtuellen-waehrungen.pdf?__blob=publicationFile&v=1.

19. Directive (EU) 2015/2366 of the European Parliament and of the Council of 25 November 2015 on payment services in the internal market, amending Directives 2002/65/EC, 2009/110/EC and 2013/36/EU and Regulation (EU) No 1093/2010, and repealing Directive 2007/64/EC.

20. Directive 2009/110/EC of the European Parliament and of the Council of 16 September 2009 on the taking up, pursuit and prudential supervision of the business of electronic money institutions amending Directives 2005/60/EC and 2006/48/EC and repealing Directive 2000/46/EC.

21. These are defined as an account held in the name of one or several payment service users and serving the execution of payment transactions.

22. *Cf. Kunschke*, contribution of input for Germany to Holman/Stettner (*et al.*), Chapter "Anti-Money Laundering Regulation of Cryptocurrency: U.S. and Global Approaches" in: The International Comparative Legal Guide to Anti-Money Laundering, (2018), ICLG.

23. *Cf. Niessner/Schlupp* in: Kunschke/Schaffelhuber, FinTech, Grundlagen, Regulierung, Finanzierung, Case Studies, (2018), p. 50 *et seq.*

24. *Cf. Niessner/Schlupp* in: Kunschke/Schaffelhuber, FinTech, Grundlagen, Regulierung, Finanzierung, Case Studies, (2018), p. 50 *et seq.*

25. For further background *cf.* BaFin under: https://www.bafin.de/SharedDocs/ Veranstaltungen/DE/160628_BaFin-Tech2016.html.

26. *Cf.* the public BaFin guidance dated 19 December 2013, available at: https://www. bafin.de/SharedDocs/Veroeffentlichungen/DE/Fachartikel/2014/fa_bj_1401_bitcoins. html.

27. Regulation (EU) No 952/2013 of the European Parliament and of the Council of 9 October 2013 laying down the Union Customs Code.

28. Commission Implementing Regulation (EU) No 2015/2447 of 24 November 2015 laying down detailed rules for implementing certain provisions of Regulation (EU) No 952/2013 of the European Parliament and of the Council laying down the Union Customs Code.

29. *Gramlich* in Hohmann/John § 59 AWV, Rn. 5.

30. *Grämlich* in Hohmann/John § 59 AWV, Rn. 3; *Samm* in: Bieneck, § 21 Rn. 61, und *Contag* in: Schult, § 59 AWV, Rn. 1.

31. On the classification of cryptocurrencies as regards payments *cf.* further *Eckert* in: DB 2013 2108 (2110); Boehm/Pesch MMR 2014, 75 (78); *Spindler/Bille* WM 2014, 1357 (1361).

32. The German original reads: *Als Zahlung gilt ferner das Einbringen von Sachen und Rechten in Unternehmen, Zweigniederlassungen und Betriebsstätten.*

33. There may, however, be certain related physical "emergences" such as cold keys.

34. MünchKomm/*Leipold*, § 1922 BGB Rdn. 19.

Dennis Kunschke
Tel: +49 69 2648 5895 / Email: Dennis.Kunschke@allenovery.com

Dennis Kunschke, Counsel at Allen & Overy LLP, Frankfurt, specialises in financial supervisory law. His particular focus is on banking supervisory and investment law/asset management. He also covers the fintech sector, the Eurozone law of monetary policy and central banks as well as payment services law.

From mid-2013 to the beginning of 2014, he was seconded to the European Central Bank where he was – *inter alia* – invited to act as rapporteur for the legal committee. Before joining Allen & Overy, he was an advisor at the German Federal Financial Supervisory Authority (BaFin) and, prior to that, he worked at Clifford Chance, Munich.

Dennis regularly acts as publisher and author of academic standard reference works in the field of financial supervisory law and he regularly lectures in this field of law (e.g. University of Liechtenstein).

Dr Stefan Henkelmann
Tel: +49 69 2648 5997 / Email: Stefan.Henkelmann@allenovery.com

Stefan is a Partner at Allen & Overy LLP, Frankfurt with broad expertise advising on German and international capital markets transactions. Stefan specialises in advising on securitisations and other structured finance transactions (covering true sale, secured loan and synthetic structures across a broad range of asset classes) and on restructurings in the capital markets sector (including bond restructurings and restructurings of securitisations and related assets), also covering the fintech sector.

Another focus of his practice is the advice on bond transactions including *Pfandbriefe*, covered bonds, structured notes, hybrid and corporate bonds. Stefan has also broad experience in advising on all related regulatory and insolvency law matters.

He is a lecturer for capital markets law at the Institute for Law and Finance of the Goethe University Frankfurt.

Allen & Overy LLP

Bockenheimer Landstraße 2, 60306 Frankfurt am Main, Germany
Tel +49 69 2648 5000 / Fax +49 69 2648 5800 / URL: www.allenovery.de

Gibraltar

Joey Garcia & Jonathan Garcia
ISOLAS LLP

Government attitude and definition

The Government of Gibraltar has approached the growing cryptocurrency and wider blockchain and distributed ledger technology ("DLT") related sector with a uniquely receptive and progressive attitude. Financial regulators and policymakers in Gibraltar have understood the need for regulation in this sector, responding rapidly to such demand as far back as 2014, with the creation of the Cryptocurrency Working Group. This private sector initiative led to the development of the Distributed Ledger Technology framework ("DLT Framework"), which became effective on 1 January 2018, making Gibraltar the first jurisdiction in the world to deliver a framework of its kind that regulates businesses that use DLT. The DLT Framework includes nine principles that apply to DLT businesses operating in Gibraltar.

The response to this approach has been global and truly significant. Those who know nothing about Gibraltar may be surprised, but those who know the history of a small jurisdiction with a joined-up partnership between law-makers, regulator and industry, that is able to adapt and evolve to attract the right opportunities at the right level, with the speed and flexibility needed to accomplish such goals, will not be surprised at all. If the introduction of a framework such as the DLT Framework were proposed in other larger jurisdictions, there would have to be so much consultation and inbuilt self-interest in certain existing participants that it would take years to achieve the same result. Since the coming into force of the DLT Framework, the Gibraltar Government has been delivering on a detailed and strategically formulated activity schedule, created to proactively drive home Gibraltar's very strong DLT message, by researching and identifying key markets and audiences and focusing its marketing in these areas.

Legal status of cryptocurrencies

Cryptocurrencies are not considered legal tender in Gibraltar and accordingly, are not issued or guaranteed by the Gibraltar Government. However, cryptocurrencies may still qualify as electronic money ("E-Money") under certain circumstances. On a European level, the regulation of E-Money is based on the EU E-Money Directive. There, E-Money is defined as an electronically, including magnetically, stored monetary value as represented by a claim on the issuer, which is issued on receipt of funds for the purpose of making payment transactions, and accepted by a natural or legal person other than the electronic money-issuer. This definition is in line with the definition contained in the Financial Services (Electronic Money) Regulations 2011 which transpose the E-Money Directive into Gibraltar law. E-Money requires an issuer. Therefore, a cryptocurrency which comes into existence by way of mining (e.g. Bitcoin) without an issuer does not qualify as E-Money. Conversely, a cryptocurrency that is issued by an issuer at par value against fiat and furnished with the promise of the issuer to be redeemed in exchange for fiat, and therefore being accepted as means of payment by third parties, would qualify as E-Money.

Cryptocurrency regulation

Owing largely to the difficulty of regulating cryptocurrencies themselves, the DLT Framework has attempted not to enforce regulation of cryptocurrencies but instead to impose a regulatory regime for firms that carry on by way of business, in or from Gibraltar, the use of DLT for storing or transmitting value belonging to others. Accordingly, regulation will depend on what services a firm is providing customers in respect to their cryptocurrencies and whether this falls under the scope of regulation.

Supplementing the DLT Framework, on 13 March 2018, the Gibraltar Government published a consultation paper detailing proposals 'for the regulation of token sales, secondary token market platforms and investment services relating to tokens' ("Token Regulation Proposals"). Draft legislation is imminently expected, but at the time of writing, is not available. The Gibraltar Government hopes to have the legislation in place by October 2018. The scope of the proposals contained in the Token Regulation Proposals is set out in further detail below.

In keeping with the DLT Framework, the legislation proposed by the Token Regulation Proposals does not aim to directly regulate tokens (whether cryptocurrencies or otherwise) subject to a token sale, rather how the actual token sale itself is conducted and the persons appointed to supervise the sale and ensure that it complies with the legislation. Because cryptocurrencies vary widely in design and purpose, it should be kept in mind that these may represent transferable securities, and their promotion and sale would already be covered by existing securities legislation in Gibraltar such as the Prospectuses Act 2005. Its classification as a security triggers various consequences, in particular, regulatory consequences. The requirement to issue a prospectus when offering securities publicly is only one example of such a requirement. A distinction must be drawn between the concept of a security on the one hand and a financial instrument on the other, with the latter being the broader term.

"Securities" are one of several sub-categories of financial instruments. Regulatory requirements may therefore also arise for non-securities that are classified as financial instruments. This includes the requirements arising under MiFID II, transposed into Gibraltar law through the Financial Services (Markets in Financial Instruments) Act 2018, which, in addition to applying to businesses providing certain investment services or engagement in certain activities with clients in relation to financial instruments, also defines "financial instruments" in a wide form, including forms of commodity derivative contracts and arrangements that may apply to any asset or right of a fungible nature (under certain conditions).

Sales regulation

Most often, tokens do not qualify as securities under Gibraltar or EU legislation. In the event that they do constitute securities, there is currently an EU-wide framework dealing with this, as has been described above. Accordingly, Gibraltar is not looking to introduce a framework that will modify in any way, securities law or the EU Prospectus Directive requirements. That is to say, the public offering of tokens that constitute securities does not require further regulation from a Gibraltar perspective and will continue to fall under current frameworks governing issuance of securities. The Token Regulation Proposals will introduce legislation covering the promotion, sale and distribution of tokens that will serve some cryptocurrency or functional use, such as prepayment for access to a product or service. Cryptocurrencies that function solely as decentralised virtual currency (e.g. Bitcoin) or as central bank-issued digital currency will be excluded from the Token Regulation Proposals.

Even though we do not know the full extent of the Gibraltar Government's legislative proposals for the regulation of token sales, the Token Regulation Proposals provide a high-level outline of what lies in store. Amongst other things, it is proposed that new legislation will regulate the promotion and sale of tokens conducted in or from Gibraltar though the appointment of authorised sponsors of public token offerings, who themselves would be regulated.

The Token Regulation Proposals are proposing a requirement for adequate, accurate and balanced disclosure of information to enable anyone considering purchasing tokens to make an informed decision. The legislation may prescribe what, as a minimum, constitutes adequate disclosure, and in what form disclosures are made (*e.g.*, in a key facts document not exceeding two (2) pages). From time to time, guidance on disclosure rules may be published by Gibraltar Financial Services Commission ("GFSC"), the financial services regulator in Gibraltar.

The token industry often refers to the concept of "self-regulation", and best practice frameworks for token offerings have already been established. The key difference with the Token Regulation Proposals is that while being attractive in the sense that it may be said to decentralise certain standards and requirements, the concept of self-regulation is also, in many senses "voluntary", and does not necessarily raise the standards through any legally enforceable framework such as the one being proposed in Gibraltar. As a result, the GFSC can ensure and enforce their regulatory objectives through the implementation of the Token Regulation Proposals.

As outlined above, the GFSC intends to regulate authorised sponsors of public token offerings. It therefore appears that the onus of ensuring compliance with appropriate standards will be on the service providers. The GFSC does not intend to regulate token issuers, nor will it regulate the underlying technology or the tokens themselves.

The Token Regulation Proposals will establish a regime for the authorisation and supervision of authorised sponsors possessing appropriate relevant knowledge and experience, who will be responsible for compliance with various obligations. It is intended that an authorised sponsor will need to be appointed in respect of every public token offering promoted, sold or distributed in or from Gibraltar.

Authorised sponsors will be subject to an authorisation and supervision process by the GFSC and must possess suitable knowledge and experience of the industry to be admitted into the sponsorship regime. A critical component for authorised sponsors to be authorised, is to have a local presence in Gibraltar, with "mind and management" based in the jurisdiction. The onus will also be on the authorised sponsors to produce their own codes of conduct, setting out what they consider to be best practices relating to token offerings. These codes will form part of a prospective authorised sponsors' application for authorisation. The introduction of an authorised sponsors regime is comparable to what currently exists today in the UK in relation to regulated public market listings, where Sponsors and Nominated Advisors effectively act as listing agents that guide prospective issuers through the flotation process. It appears this same model is being adapted under the authorised sponsors regime to hand-hold prospective token-issuing entities through a compliant token sale process.

The GFSC will establish and maintain a public register of authorised sponsors and their respective past and present codes of practice.

It should also be noted that entities issuing tokens may separately have to comply with classic consumer protection law, depending on the design of the digital token. All relevant EU legislation covering e-commerce and consumer protection has been transposed into Gibraltar law via various Acts of Parliament or Regulations. The EU e-commerce and consumer protection rules (E-Commerce Directive, Consumer Rights Directive, Directive on Distance Marketing of Consumer Financial Services) all specify the information that should be disclosed.

Taxation

It should be noted that the treatment of cryptocurrencies is not specifically considered in current tax legislation in Gibraltar, nor in accounting standards that are generally accepted in Gibraltar; therefore, where relevant, general principles implicit in current legislation and accounting standards that are believed to be appropriate, are applied.

In Gibraltar there is no capital gains tax, value added tax, death duties, inheritance, wealth, capital transfer, gifts, or withholding tax levied at present. For companies, corporation tax is generally 10%, payable on profits that derive from income accrued in or derived from Gibraltar; that is to say, by reference to the location of the activities which give rise to the profits. Under tax legislation, the location of the activities which give rise to the profits of a business whose underlying activity that results in the income, requires a licence and regulation under any law of Gibraltar, shall automatically be considered to be Gibraltar.

Money transmission laws and anti-money laundering requirements

The EU Anti Money Laundering Directive has been transposed into Gibraltar law by the Proceeds of Crime Act ("POCA"). It should be noted that Section 9(1)(p) of the POCA now includes within the definition of "relevant financial business", "undertakings that receive, whether on their own account or on behalf of another person, proceeds in any form from the sale of tokenised digital assets involving the use of distributed ledger technology or a similar means of recording a digital representation of an asset". Essentially, the addition of the new definition of relevant financial business specifically brings sales of a digital asset clearly within existing anti-money laundering laws, which in turn have been very well received by other service providers in the industry.

The DLT Framework also requires, as part of its regulatory principles, for a firm to have systems in place to prevent, detect and disclose financial crime risks such as money laundering and terrorist financing.

These requirements devolve from the above sources, in addition to the GFSC's Anti-Money Laundering Guidance Notes.

These businesses must therefore adequately apply anti-money laundering and counter-terrorist financing preventive measures as prescribed by the above-mentioned Act and Guidance Notes.

These businesses are required to establish procedures to:

• apply customer due diligence procedures;

• appoint a Money Laundering Reporting Officer (MLRO) to whom money laundering reports must be made;

- establish systems and procedures to forestall and prevent money laundering;

- provide relevant individuals with training on money laundering and awareness of their procedures in relation to money laundering;

- screen relevant employees; and

- undertake an independent audit for the purposes of testing customer due diligence measures, ongoing monitoring, reporting, record-keeping, internal controls, risk assessment and management, compliance management and employee-screening. The frequency and extent of the audit shall be proportionate to the size and nature of the business.

Under POCA, these businesses would be required to undertake Customer Due Diligence ("CDD") procedures on their customers.

There will be differences as to how POCA applies to organisers of token sales and firms falling under the DLT Framework.

There are no exchange-control restrictions in Gibraltar, and there exists complete freedom to remit funds into and out of the territory and to convert funds into other currencies, subject always to compliance with the above anti-money laundering requirements.

Promotion and testing

Gibraltar has always maintained itself at the forefront of novel technological development. In fact, if you look in the small print for most online gambling businesses around the world, it is found that most are based in Gibraltar.

Gibraltar is hoping to replicate that philosophy in the blockchain space and follow the success of online gaming, and is doing so by stepping out of the regulatory "sandbox", in the same way as it did back in the gaming days. Rather than creating a "safe space" for businesses to test innovative financial products, services, business models and delivery mechanisms in a live environment without immediately incurring all the normal regulatory consequences of engaging in the activity in question, Gibraltar has instead chosen to provide legal certainty and allow businesses to operate within a purpose-built legislative framework. In doing so, it considers that a flexible, adaptive approach is required in the case of novel business activities, products and business models and that whilst regulatory outcomes remain central, these are better achieved through the application of principles rather than rigid rules. This is because, for businesses based on rapidly-evolving technology, such hard and fast rules can quickly become outdated and unfit for purpose. Accordingly, it has created a principles-based framework based on risk and proportionality, and an outcome-focused, yet robust approach.

The Gibraltar Government recognises that this is a nascent industry and whilst Gibraltar has shown leadership in this space, development is clearly an ongoing process and Gibraltar is aware of the importance as a jurisdiction, for it to invest in supporting the development of knowledge and skills, in tandem with generating economic results as Gibraltar continues to strive for excellence.

On 21 June 2018, an announcement was made by the Gibraltar Government regarding the creation of Gibraltar Association for New Technologies ("GANT"), an association to be formed with the private sector. GANT will serve several purposes, primarily to enhance the development in Gibraltar of the use of blockchain and DLT and other future developments, as considered appropriate, collectively referred to as "New Technology", with a view to enhancing the reputation, integrity and public trust in this sector. GANT will also be tasked to raise the profile of "New Technology" in Gibraltar across a spectrum not necessarily limited to financial services. This includes encouraging respective organisations to emphasise the high value of their reputation and interest in contributing to enhanced client and investor protection and remaining committed to safeguarding customer and jurisdictional interests. It is also expected to provide a forum for discussion on "New Technology" issues within the membership and to assist other sectors of the wider Gibraltar Finance Centre, whilst also assisting and advising the Gibraltar Government on all aspects of this sector.

Ownership and licensing requirements

If a firm is engaging in an activity for business purposes, which involves the storage or transmission of cryptocurrencies belonging to third parties, it will need to be licensed under the DLT Framework.

Providing investment and ancillary services relating to cryptocurrencies is not currently regulated in Gibraltar. The Gibraltar Government has proposed under the Token Regulation Proposals, to regulate the provision of investment and ancillary services in or from Gibraltar and, to the extent not otherwise caught by existing legislation, their derivatives. This is intended to cover advice on investment in tokens, virtual currencies, and central bank-issued digital currencies, including:

- generic advice (setting out fairly and in a neutral manner the facts relating to token investments and services);
- product-related advice (setting out in a selective and judgmental manner the advantages and disadvantages of a particular token investment and service); and
- personal recommendations (based on the particular needs and circumstances of the individual investor).

This will be proportionately modelled on provisions that currently exist under MiFID II with the aim of ensuring that such services are provided fairly, transparently, and professionally.

A person may hold and trade his own cryptocurrency without the need for authorisation.

Holdings in cryptocurrency by investment advisors or fund managers

If there is an intention to establish an arrangement that enables a number of investors to pool their assets and have these professionally managed by an independent manager, rather than buying investments directly as individuals, then collective investment scheme ("CIS") law is another relevant legal consideration.

The Financial Services (Collective Investment Schemes) Act 2011 defines a "collective investment scheme" as "any arrangement with respect to property, the purpose or effect of which is to enable persons taking part in the arrangement, whether by becoming owners of the property or any part of it or otherwise, to participate in or receive profits or income arising from the acquisition, holding, management or disposal of the property or sums paid out of such profits or income".

The arrangement referred to above must be such that the participants in the arrangement do not have day-to-day control over the management of the assets. Further, the investments and the profits/income arising from them must be pooled, and/or the property managed as a whole.

There are two popular structures for setting up a CIS in Gibraltar: the Experienced Investor Fund ("EIF"); and the Private Scheme ("PS"). These structures are agnostic to the underlying assets they govern for investors.

Typically, a CIS which is to focus on crypto-assets would best be established as an EIF. Only when such a CIS is set up for a small group of persons previously known to each other, and where there will be no promotion of the CIS, would it be suitable to set up a CIS of this nature as a PS. Indeed, the local Gibraltar Funds and Investment Association (GFIA) has recently published a draft code of conduct to this effect which also serves as a reference point of elements that should be kept in mind when establishing funds dealing with crypto-assets. Among other things, the code will cover custody of crypto-assets, valuation, corporate governance and security.

The EIF is designed for professional, high-net-worth or experienced investors. Each investor would need to invest at least €100,000 in the EIF – or its equivalent in an alternative fiat – or prove a net worth of at least €1m, excluding one's personal residence.

The EIF regime is reliant on EIF Directors and other licensed service providers.

A CIS of this nature will fall within the definition of an alternative investment fund ("AIF") under the Financial Services (Alternative Investment Fund Managers) Regulations 2013, which transposes the EU Alternative Investment Fund Managers Directive. Accordingly, there will be multiple considerations that become relevant, both in terms of the sale, promotion and management of that AIF, as well as the depositary arrangements for AIF units.

Mining

The mining of Bitcoin and other cryptocurrencies is not covered by any specific legal or regulatory framework. Accordingly, it is permitted. As set out above, a cryptocurrency such as Bitcoin, which comes into existence by way of mining without an issuer, does not qualify as E-Money and, as a cryptocurrency that functions solely as a decentralised virtual currency, is also excluded from the Token Regulation Proposals. However, this will ultimately depend on how the mining activity is conducted. For example, given the definition of an AIF, if the mining activities are conducted in a particular way which involves a collective group of people and shared infrastructure, an argument could certainly be made that the arrangement would qualify as a collective undertaking in the sense of the legal meaning.

Border restrictions and declaration

Presently, there are no border restrictions in place on declaring cryptocurrency holdings. Instead these restrictions are usually in place for issues such as transport of goods. Though there are no restrictions in this sense, several of the above authorisation processes required by the regulations will require "mind and management" to be in Gibraltar, comprising an office with registered employees.

Reporting requirements

No specific reporting requirements are triggered for cryptocurrency payments made in excess of a certain value. However, any threshold amounts may determine the record-keeping requirements that may apply to a business under POCA. Businesses under POCA must report suspicious activity of money laundering.

Estate planning and testamentary succession

The law of succession in Gibraltar is largely based upon the UK Wills Act 1837, which is amended by Gibraltar's Wills Act. Administration of estates is governed by Gibraltar's Administration of Estates Act 1933, consolidated in 1948 (as amended).

The law of Gibraltar as it relates to a deceased person who dies domiciled, closely resembles the laws of England & Wales. Moveable and immoveable property are treated differently. In the case of moveable property, the law of the country where the deceased died domiciled is applied.

There are no death duties to pay in Gibraltar.

Estate planning for cryptocurrency presents its own unique difficulties. Ordinarily, probate is a public process completed upon the presentation of various legal documents. Both of these concepts are in conflict with cryptocurrency.

Estate practitioners are going to have to be aware of the specific issues of cryptocurrency when drafting testaments, the aim being to ensure that the cryptocurrency property is accurately reflected, can be properly transferred upon the death of the holder, and also to ensure that the value of the property can be maintained.

As yet, there is no specific guidance issued in Gibraltar in relation to cryptocurrency and estate planning or succession.

Joey Garcia
Tel: +350 2000 1892 / Email: Joey.Garcia@isolas.gi
Deeply involved in shaping the regulatory environment in Gibraltar, Joey Garcia co-chaired the Government of Gibraltar working group on crypto-currencies, leading to the introduction of the consultation document on a regulatory framework for Distributed Ledger Technology in Gibraltar, published on 9 May 2017 which led to the framework coming into force on 1 January 2018. He spearheaded Gibraltar's first Initial Coin Offering, an offering which was fully subscribed within 12 minutes. He is an internationally recognised thought leader in the fintech/cryptocurrency and wider blockchain/distributed ledger technology space in Gibraltar, and one of only 12 lawyers around the world recognised by *Chambers & Partners* as leading global lawyers in blockchain and cryptocurrencies.

He has and continues to advise a large number of blockchain start-ups and businesses in the DLT financial services space and leads the fintech think-tank established by the firm, thinkfintech.gi. He contributes to leading blockchain podcasts, is invited as a regular speaker and panellist at conferences, and is a member of the prestigious global Wharton Reg@Tech think-tank. He has been quoted in numerous prominent media outlets, including the *Economist*.

Jonathan Garcia
Tel: +350 2000 1892 / Email: Jonathan.Garcia@isolas.gi
Jonathan Garcia was involved in shaping Gibraltar's company legislation, which led to a full-scale review and overhaul of the legislation, and advised the Government of Gibraltar on introducing a new business entity previously not in existence. He is currently advising various blockchain start-ups on raising finance through Initial Coin Offerings and on obtaining regulatory authorisations for carrying out their business activities, and part of the fintech think-tank established by the firm, thinkfintech.gi.

Jonathan was recently booked to speak at various blockchain events, including the European Commerce Registers' Forum 21st annual conference (http://www.ecrforum.org/), at a private event hosted by the Gibraltar Blockchain Exchange (https://www.gsx.gi/article/9445/gibraltar-house-london-exclusive-update-seminar-15th-january) and at Technische Universität Berlin on Token Regulation in the EU (https://www.bundesblock.de/2018/06/03/discussion-of-token-regulation-in-the-eu/). He recently participated in the Blockchain Bundesverband (Association for the Promotion of Blockchain Technology in Germany) working group on Token Regulation. Very recently, he has been elected to the executive committee of the Gibraltar Funds and Investments Association (GFIA) as it considers updates to legislative positions and innovative products in the crypto space.

ISOLAS LLP

Portland House, Glacis Road, GX11 1AA, Gibraltar
Tel: +350 2000 1892 / URL: www.gibraltarlawyers.com

Guernsey

David Crosland & Felicity White
Carey Olsen LLP

Government attitude and definition

The Bailiwick of Guernsey ("**Guernsey**"), as one of the world's leading financial centres, has always been an early adopter of financial innovation and has a reputation for expertise and stability. The first ever commercial deployment of blockchain technology for the private equity market in early 2017, which was pioneered in Guernsey by Northern Trust and IBM, demonstrates that Guernsey is very much open to new innovation and development.

The Guernsey Financial Services Commission (the "**Commission**") is the body responsible for the regulation of the finance sector. One of the founding objectives of the Commission is to protect the public, and to protect and enhance the reputation of Guernsey as a financial services centre, and one of the ways that the Commission seeks to fulfil this objective is to adhere the highest international standards of compliance and transparency and to adopt a policy of encouraging promoters of only the highest calibre. Accordingly, the Commission has issued advice calling for caution in the field of digital, virtual or cryptocurrencies ("**Virtual Currencies**") and initial coin offerings ("**ICOs**"). The Commission has indicated that whilst it has a broad policy of encouraging innovation, and is keen to liaise with firms or individuals to discuss potential applications, it believes that there are potential risks in the use of Virtual Currencies especially for retail customers. The Commission has indicated that it would be cautious about approving applications for ICOs which could then be traded on a secondary market, or the establishment of a digital currency exchange within Guernsey, due to the significant risk of fraud and/or money laundering, and has generally issued advice to investors that when investing in Virtual Currencies they should act with extreme caution – and be prepared to lose the entire value of their investment.

At present, there are no cryptocurrencies backed by Guernsey's government, the States of Guernsey, and Guernsey does not have a central bank. There have been no pronouncements from the States of Guernsey or the Commission which would indicate that Virtual Currencies are given any form of equal status as domestic currency, although it should be noted that there have similarly been no pronouncements that would indicate that Virtual Currencies will *not* be treated as a currency or foreign currency.

In general, funds seeking to invest in Virtual Currencies should be aware that whilst the Commission is generally cautious about the regulatory approach which should be taken in relation to Virtual Currencies and ICOs, Guernsey as a jurisdiction is keen to encourage financial innovation, and provided that an applicant can satisfy the Commission that key controls are in place for the protection of investors, there should be no reason why a responsible fund should not be regulated in Guernsey by the Commission.

Cryptocurrency regulation

Guernsey does not at present have any specific regulatory laws or guidance relating to any form of Virtual Currencies or ICOs, but the nature of Guernsey's existing regulatory laws is such that Virtual Currencies and ICOs could be capable of regulation in a number of ways. The Commission has indicated that it will assess any application for regulation by the same criteria that it uses for any other asset types or structure, and look to ensure that key controls around custody, liquidity, valuation of assets and investor information are in place.

A fund based on Virtual Currencies or the making of an ICO, if required to be regulated, is likely to fall under one of two regulatory regimes; that of the Protection of Investors (Bailiwick of Guernsey) Law, 1987 (as amended) (the "**POI Law**") or the Registration of Non-Regulated Financial Services Businesses (Bailiwick of Guernsey) Law, 2008 (the "**NRFSB Law**").

Regulatory position under the POI Law

Every "collective investment scheme" (a "**fund**") domiciled in Guernsey is subject to the provisions of Guernsey's principal funds legislation – the Protection of Investors (Bailiwick of Guernsey) Law, 1987, as amended (the "**POI Law**") – and regulated by the Commission.

Broadly speaking:

• Every fund domiciled in Guernsey (a "**Guernsey fund**") must be administered by a Guernsey company which holds an appropriate licence under the POI Law (a "**POI Licence**").[1] The administrator is responsible for ensuring that the fund is managed and administered in accordance with the fund documentation.

• Every open-ended Guernsey fund must also appoint a Guernsey company which holds a POI Licence to act as custodian (or trustee, where the Guernsey fund is structured as a unit trust). The trustee/custodian is (with limited exceptions) responsible for safeguarding the assets of the fund and, in some of the rules, to oversee the management and administration of the fund by the administrator.

The POI Law makes it a criminal offence, subject to certain exceptions, for any person to carry on or hold himself out as carrying on any controlled investment business in or from within the Bailiwick of Guernsey without a POI Licence. Additionally, it is an offence for a Bailiwick body to carry on or hold itself out as carrying on any controlled investment business in or from within a territory outside the Bailiwick of Guernsey unless that body is licensed to carry on that business in the Bailiwick and the business would be lawfully carried on if it were carried on in the Bailiwick.

Guernsey funds regulation only applies to "collective investment schemes" – arrangements relating to property of any description which involve:

• the pooling of contributions by investors;

• third party management of the assets; and

• a spread of risk.

Thus arrangements with a single investor or a single asset would not usually be classified as a fund.

The POI Law divides Guernsey funds into two categories:

• "**registered funds**", which are *registered with* the Commission; and

• "**authorised funds**", which are *authorised by* the Commission.

The difference between authorised funds and registered funds is essentially that authorised funds receive their authorisation following a substantive review of their suitability by the Commission, whereas registered funds receive their registration following a representation of suitability from a Guernsey body holding a POI Licence (the administrator, who scrutinises the fund and its promoter in lieu of the Commission and takes on the ongoing responsibility for monitoring the fund).

The POI Law grants the Commission the power to develop different classes of authorised and registered funds and determine the rules applicable to such classes.

Funds seeking authorisation or registration must therefore satisfy the requirements of the POI Law and (where applicable) the applicable rules specified by the Commission.

The rules governing the different classes of Guernsey funds state whether funds in each class may be open-ended or closed-ended (or whether they may choose from either).

A Guernsey fund is open-ended if the investors are entitled to have their units redeemed or repurchased by the fund at a price related to the value of the property to which they relate (i.e. the net asset value).

There is no prescribed period within which the redemption must occur or the moneys be paid.

Fund types in Guernsey include, but are not limited to:

- Registered Collective Investment Schemes (a registered open- or closed-ended fund governed by the Registered Collective Investment Schemes Rules 2015 and the Prospectus Rules 2008).

- Private Investment Funds (a registered open- or closed-ended fund governed by the Private Investment Fund Rules 2016).

- Class A Funds (an authorised open-ended fund governed by the Authorised Collective Investment Schemes (Class A) Rules 2008). Class A Funds are primarily designed for offering to retail investors.

- Class B Funds (an authorised open-ended fund governed by the Authorised Collective Investment Schemes (Class B) Rules 2013). Class B Funds are the most popular form of fund and are suitable for retail and institutional investors alike.

- Class Q Funds (an authorised open-ended fund governed by the Authorised Collective Investment Schemes (Qualifying Professional Investor Funds) (Class Q) Rules 1998). Class Q Funds benefit from a lighter regulatory regime and are therefore limited to Qualifying (sophisticated) Investors.

- Authorised closed-ended funds (an authorised closed-ended fund governed by the Authorised Closed-Ended Investment Schemes Rules 2008).

Regulatory position under the NRFSB Law

The NRFSB Law provides that if an entity carries out certain "financial services businesses" *in or from within the Bailiwick by way of business* then it must, subject to certain exceptions (see below), register with the Commission. A financial services business which is not registered is guilty of an offence.

The NRFSB Law provides that a business holds itself out as carrying on business in or from within the Bailiwick if:

1.1 by way of business, it occupies premises in the Bailiwick or makes it known by an advertisement or by an insertion in a directory or by means of letterheads that it may be contacted at a particular address in the Bailiwick;

1.2 it invites a person in the Bailiwick, by issuing an advertisement or otherwise, to enter into or to offer to enter into a contract or otherwise to undertake business; or

1.3 it is otherwise seen to be carrying on business in or from within the Bailiwick.

Financial services business

The NRFSB Law only applies to businesses specified in Schedule 1 of the NRFSB Law, the relevant parts of which are summarised as follows:

A) Facilitating or transmitting money or value through an informal money or value-transfer system or network.

B) Issuing, redeeming, managing or administering means of payment, including, without limitation, credit, charge and debit cards, cheques, travellers' cheques, money orders and bankers' drafts and electronic money.

For the purposes of the NRFSB Law, the activities listed will only constitute "financial services businesses" when carried on: (i) by way of business; and (ii) for or on behalf of a customer". "By way of business" is interpreted to mean charging some form of fee for the service provided.

A business will not constitute a "financial services business" for the purposes of the NRFSB Law if it is a "regulated business", meaning business carried on in accordance with a licence granted under: the Banking Supervision (Bailiwick of Guernsey) Law, 1994, as amended; the POI Law; the Insurance Business (Bailiwick of Guernsey) Law, 2002, as amended; or the Insurance Managers and Insurance Intermediaries (Bailiwick of Guernsey) Law, 2002, as amended.

Exceptions

Businesses undertaking "financial services business" on an incidental or occasional basis may not be required to register with the Commission. To be excluded, the business must meet *all of the criteria* below:

1. the total turnover of that business, plus that of any other financial services business carried on by the same person, does not exceed £50,000 per annum;

2. no occasional transactions are carried out in the course of such business, that is to say, any transaction involving more than £10,000, where no business relationship has been proposed or established, including such transactions carried out in a single operation or two or more operations that appear to be linked;

3. the turnover of such business does not exceed 5% of the total turnover of the person carrying on such business;

4. the business is ancillary, and directly related, to the main activity of the person carrying on the business;

5. in the course of such business, money or value is not transmitted or such transmission is not facilitated by any means;

6. the main activity of the person carrying on the business is not that of a financial services business;

7. the business is provided only to customers of the main activity of the person carrying on the business and is not offered to the public; and

8. the business is not carried on by a person who also carries on a business falling within Paragraphs 20 to 23A of Part I of Schedule 1 to the NRFSB Law.

In addition, activities that are merely "incidental and other activities", as listed in Part III of

Schedule I of the NRFSB Law, do not constitute "financial services businesses". In short, these relate to activities carried out in the course of carrying on the professions of a lawyer, accountant or actuary.

Requirement to register

This is still an evolving regulatory area in Guernsey, and there is some uncertainty as to whether cryptocurrency falls within the terms set out in B) above (and Schedule 1 of the NRFSB Law), but as these are not exhaustive, the cautious approach would be to assume that this section is wide enough to capture cryptocurrency. Further, A) also refers to transfer of money or value, which is wide enough to capture cryptocurrency.

Application to virtual currencies

A person is treated as carrying on controlled investment business if he engages by way of business in any of the "**restricted activities**" specified in Schedule 2 of the POI Law in connection with any "**controlled investment**" identified and described in Schedule 1 of the POI Law. The scope of this chapter does not permit a detailed look at either of these concepts, but generally "restricted activities" include the promotion of funds, dealings with investments (including buying, selling, subscribing for, borrowing, lending or underwriting an investment) or making arrangements for another person to do the same, or operating an investment exchange, each in connection with a controlled investment, which can include either open- or closed-ended collective investment schemes, or general securities and derivatives.

Whether a POI Licence is necessary in relation to an ICO or a fund engaged in any way with a Virtual Currency will largely turn on whether such a Virtual Currency can legitimately be defined as a security. This is likely to be tested on a case-by-case basis in practice, but consideration may be given to whether a Virtual Currency is asset-based or whether it is a more "pure" cryptocurrency.

Given the uncertainty surrounding the nature of Virtual Currencies in Guernsey, it would be prudent to assume that where an endeavour in Guernsey is not subject to regulation under the POI Law, it will be registrable under the NRFSB Law.

Sales regulation

At present, there are no securities laws or commodities laws in Guernsey regulating the sale of Bitcoin or tokens. The POI Law makes it a general offence to operate an investment exchange in relation to a controlled investment without an appropriate POI Licence, but it is generally unclear if any specific Virtual Currency would constitute a "security" for the purpose of the POI Law, and whilst the Commission have not yet adopted an official position on the matter, it would likely find guidance issued by the prominent financial regulators (the U.S. Securities Exchange Commission, the UK Financial Conduct Authority, etc.) persuasive. Given the general uncertainty in this area, it would be prudent for any individual or firm contemplating engaging in the business of running an investment exchange in relation to any Virtual Currency to consult with the Commission at the early stages.

Taxation

There are no specific laws in Guernsey regulating the taxation of Virtual Currencies, and it is therefore likely that they will be taxed in accordance with general Guernsey taxation principles and provisions.

Guernsey does not have a concept of value added, goods and services or consumption tax, capital gains tax, net wealth/net worth tax or inheritance tax (although there are registration fees and *ad valorem* duty for a Guernsey Grant of Representation where required). Similarly, apart from transfers of Guernsey real property or transfers of interest in certain unlisted entities (other than collective investment schemes) that have a direct or indirect interest in Guernsey real property, which may (subject to exemption) attract a document duty, no stamp or transfer taxes are applicable. Withholding taxes are payable at a rate of 20% solely in relation to the payment of dividends by a Guernsey company to a Guernsey resident individual (unless the company has exempt status), but are not payable in relation to the payment of dividends to non-residents, or on interest, royalties or service fees.

It would therefore be prudent to assume that any income arising from a Virtual Currency (whether in the form of a Virtual Currency or otherwise), or any income arising in the form of a Virtual Currency, will be taxable in line with Guernsey income tax provisions and valued at the appropriate spot rate on the date that the income arises, although the Guernsey Income Tax Office has not made a formal statement on the matter and may determine that another valuation method should be used.

Corporate Income Tax

Companies incorporated in Guernsey are treated as tax-resident in Guernsey. Companies resident in Guernsey are subject to income tax on their worldwide income (although certain reliefs are available to prevent double taxation). Most companies that are tax-resident in Guernsey are taxed at a standard rate of 0%, but income arising from certain activities is taxed at 10% or 20%. This includes (but is not limited to) income arising from fund administration, investment management (except in relation to funds) and fiduciary business (each of which are taxed at the 10% rate), and income arising from regulated trading activities such as telecommunications or the importation and/or supply of gas and hydrocarbon oil in Guernsey (which are taxed at the 20% rate).

Unit trusts are treated as companies for Guernsey income tax purposes and limited partnerships and limited liability partnerships are considered tax-transparent, and so are not taxable entities in Guernsey.

There is an exemption regime available for collective investment schemes, entities beneficially owned by collective investment schemes, and entities established for the purpose of certain specified activities relating to a specific collective investment scheme. Applications for this exemption must be made annually and attract a payment of an annual fee currently fixed at £1,200. Where an exemption is granted, the entity is treated as not being resident in Guernsey for tax purposes and is not liable for Guernsey tax on non-Guernsey source income (including Guernsey bank deposit interest).

Personal income tax

Individuals in Guernsey pay income tax at a flat rate of 20%. The personal income tax year is based on the calendar year, and income tax returns must be filed by 30 November of the year following the relevant tax year (which filing can be made electronically or on paper).

There are different classes of residence which may affect an individual's tax treatment. Individuals may be:

- "principally resident" – they are in Guernsey for 182 days or more in a tax year, or are in Guernsey for 91 days or more in a tax year and have spent 730 days or more in Guernsey over the four prior tax years;

- "solely resident" – they are in Guernsey for 91 days or more in a tax year, or are in Guernsey for 35 days or more in a tax year and have spent 365 days or more in Guernsey over the four prior tax years, and in either case have not spent 91 days or more in any other jurisdiction in the tax year; or

*   "resident only" – they would be treated as solely resident in a tax year, but they have spent 91 days or more in another jurisdiction for that tax year.

Individuals who fall within the scope of any of the above will pay Guernsey tax on their worldwide income, although foreign tax relief is available. Individuals who are "resident only" can elect to pay a standard charge of £30,000, which has the effect of exempting them from Guernsey income tax on their worldwide income (they will still have to pay tax on any Guernsey-source income).

A personal allowance is available for individuals of £10,500 (although earners of more than £142,896 have their allowance reduced by £1 for every £3 exceeding this limit. Certain reliefs are available for pension contributions and mortgage interest which are beyond the scope of this chapter. A Guernsey resident individual can elect for a cap on their income tax liability in relation to their worldwide income (but not in relation to income arising on Guernsey real property).

FATCA and CRS

Guernsey is party to an intergovernmental agreement with the United States regarding the Foreign Account Tax Compliance Act of 2009 ("**FATCA**") and implemented FATCA due diligence and reporting obligations in June 2014. Under FATCA legislation in Guernsey, Guernsey "financial institutions" are obliged to carry out due diligence on account holders and report on accounts held by persons who are, or are entities that are controlled by, one or more natural persons who are, residents or citizens of the United States, unless a relevant exemption applies.

Guernsey is also a party to an intergovernmental agreement with the United Kingdom in relation the United Kingdom's own version of FATCA, which it also implemented in June 2014. However, the United Kingdom's version of FATCA has now been superseded by the adoption by Guernsey (alongside numerous jurisdictions) of the much broader global Common Reporting Standard ("**CRS**").

Guernsey is a party to the OECD's Multilateral Competent Authority Agreement regarding the CRS and implemented the CRS into its domestic legislation with effect from 1 January 2016. Under CRS legislation in Guernsey, Guernsey "financial institutions" are obliged to carry out due diligence on account holders and report on accounts held by persons who are, or are entities that are controlled by, one or more natural persons who are residents of jurisdictions that have adopted the CRS, unless a relevant exemption applies.

Guernsey has implemented measures equivalent to the EU Savings Directive ("**EUSD**"), although these are in the process of being phased out following the repeal of the EUSD in order to make way for the CRS.

It is unclear at this stage what, if any, reporting should take place in relation to Virtual Currencies under FATCA or CRS, and much will turn on whether individual Virtual Currencies are "securities" for FATCA and CRS purposes. Until this point has been settled, it would be prudent to adopt a conservative approach.

Money transmission laws and anti-money laundering requirements

All Guernsey individuals and firms are subject to the Drug Trafficking (Bailiwick of Guernsey) Law, 2000 (as amended), the Terrorism and Crime (Bailiwick of Guernsey) Law, 2002 (as amended) and the Disclosure (Bailiwick of Guernsey) Law, 2007. These laws contain various offences which arise should a financial service business, a non-financial service business or a nominated officer in a financial service business fail to make a disclosure to Guernsey's Financial Intelligence Unit, the Financial Intelligence Service where they have knowledge or suspicion (or reasonable grounds for knowledge or suspicion) of money laundering or terrorist financing. It is also an offence to disclose information or any other matter which is likely to prejudice an investigation by law enforcement.

In addition, regulated entities in Guernsey are bound by various rules and regulations – in particular, Guernsey's anti-money laundering and counter-terrorist financing legislation, including the Criminal Justice (Proceeds of Crime) (Financial Services Businesses) (Bailiwick of Guernsey) Regulations, 2008 and the Handbook for Financial Services Businesses on Countering Financial Crime and Terrorist Financing (current edition June 2017) published by the Commission (the "**Handbook**").

The full scope of Guernsey's anti-money laundering regime, counter-terrorist financing legislation and of all of the applicable laws, rules and regulations applicable to an entity regulated under the POI Law or the NRFSB Law is beyond the scope of this chapter but the key points to consider are as follows:

- a regulated entity should appoint a money laundering reporting officer ("**MLRO**") resident in Guernsey;

- the board or equivalent of the entity will have effective responsibility for compliance with Guernsey's anti-money laundering regime and counter-terrorist financing legislation and must take responsibility for the policy on reviewing compliance, consider the appropriateness and effectiveness of compliance and the review of compliance at appropriate intervals, and take appropriate measures to keep abreast of and guard against the use of technological developments and new methodologies in money laundering and terrorist financing schemes. The board may delegate some or all of its duties but must retain responsibility for the review of overall compliance with Guernsey's anti-money laundering and counter-terrorist financing legislation requirements;

- the entity will require appropriate customer take-on policies; procedures and controls will need to be adopted to sufficiently identify and verify identity (to a depth appropriate to the assessed risk of the business relationship and occasional transaction) of all of its existing and new customers;

- all transactions and activity will need to be monitored on an ongoing basis to include all business relationships (on a risk-based approach), with high-risk relationships being subjected to an appropriate frequency of scrutiny, which must be greater than may be appropriate for low-risk relationships;

- appropriate and effective policies, procedures and controls must be established in order to facilitate compliance with the reporting requirements of the regulations; and

- appropriate employee screening and training policies will need to be in place.

The Handbook permits the use of technology for customer due diligence, and indeed as referenced above, Guernsey was one of the earliest adopters of blockchain technology in the private equity market for administration purposes. Other administrators have since adopted technologically backed systems for undertaking customer due diligence, and in particular, private equity fund administrator Ipes has set up the ID Register, an online platform for connected due diligence, FATCA and investor reporting.

Promotion and testing

The Commission has introduced the free "Innovation SoundBox" to serve as a hub for enquiries regarding innovative financial products and services, and encourages firms or individuals to use this facility to discuss potential applications in the field of Virtual Currencies at an early stage. No fees are charged for engaging with the Innovation SoundBox.

Ownership and licensing requirements

There are no specific restrictions in Guernsey on investment managers holding cryptocurrencies for investment purposes, and as the regulatory position is unclear, individuals should approach the Commission on a case-by-case basis to determine whether they are required to obtain a POI Licence in order to hold cryptocurrency as an investment advisor or fund manager. The above section, headed "Cryptocurrency regulation", provides more detail on when an individual or entity is required to be licensed under the POI Law, and the section headed "Money transmission laws and anti-money laundering requirements" provides further detail about applicable anti-money laundering and counter-terrorist financing requirements.

Mining

There are no specific restrictions on the mining of Virtual Currencies in Guernsey.

Border restrictions and declaration

There are no specific border restrictions or declarations which must be made on the ownership of Virtual Currencies in Guernsey. However, the Cash Controls (Bailiwick of Guernsey) Law, 2007 (as amended) (the "**Cash Controls Law**") does set out requirements for any person who is entering or leaving Guernsey who is carrying cash in any currency to the equivalent value of €10,000 or more to make a declaration to a Guernsey Border Agency Officer. The definition of "cash" under the Cash Controls Law is broad, including banknotes, bullion, ingots and coins (whether or not in circulation as a medium of exchange) and it is not clear whether Virtual Currencies would be caught under such a provision. Despite this, it is likely that the Cash Controls Law will not apply to the movement of Virtual Currencies, as to be caught under the Cash Controls Law the cash must be carried in baggage or on one's person and, given the purely digital nature of many Virtual Currencies, it is unclear whether it would be conceptually possible for it to be "carried".

Reporting requirements

There are no specific Guernsey reporting requirements for cryptocurrency payments made in excess of a certain value. However, any transactions should be monitored to ensure that they are compliant with anti-money laundering and countering the financing of terrorism procedures.

Estate planning and testamentary succession

At present, Virtual Currencies in Guernsey are not treated differently than any other asset on the death of the holder. In principle, therefore, if an estate is subject to Guernsey succession laws, Virtual Currencies would be treated in the same way as any other asset and distributed in accordance with the will or intestacy of the holder under Guernsey law. There may, however, be practical difficulties with both locating and distributing any Virtual Currencies which may be stored in virtual wallets or protected by other forms of security, and the means for transferring Virtual Currencies to a successor in title may largely depend on the relevant issuer or exchange.

* * *

Endnote

1. Under the POI Law, such an administrator is referred to as a "designated manager", but in the rules governing the various classes of funds in Guernsey, such an administrator is sometimes described as a "designated administrator". For the sake of convenience, we will refer to them as an "**administrator**" throughout this chapter.

David Crosland, Partner
Tel: +44 1481 741556 / Email: david.crosland@careyolsen.com
David undertakes a wide range of corporate transactions with a particular experience in the launch of investment funds.

He is regularly instructed by fund managers, UK and international law firms and other financial services firms on the launch, administration, restructuring and listing of both closed and open-ended investment funds. David was listed in the *International Who's Who of Private Funds Lawyers* 2018.

In addition to fund formation, David frequently advises on corporate real estate and general corporate matters, including those with a heavy regulatory content.

David trained at Clifford Chance in London, qualifying as an English solicitor in the Private Funds Group in 2004. While there, he specialised in the establishment of institutional closed-ended investment funds particularly private equity, real estate and infrastructure funds. In 2006, he spent nine months on secondment at ABN AMRO advising on the structuring and launch of institutional fund-linked investment products, before joining Carey Olsen in May 2007. David became a partner in 2013.

Felicity White, Associate
Tel: +44 1481 741535 / Email: felicity.white@careyolsen.com
Felicity is an associate in Carey Olsen's Guernsey Corporate team. She assists on a range of corporate, commercial, banking and finance matters.

Felicity joined Carey Olsen in 2016, having trained and qualified as a solicitor in the UK. Having initially read Modern History at Merton College, Oxford, she obtained her GDL (Commendation) at City Law School, London, before completing her LPC at the University of Law in Guildford (Distinction), where she was awarded prizes in Commercial Litigation and Commercial Dispute Resolution.

Felicity is a member of the Law Society of England and Wales.

Carey Olsen LLP

PO Box 98, Carey House, Les Banques, St Peter Port GY1 4BZ, Guernsey
Tel: +44 1481 727272 / Fax: +44 1481 711052 / URL: www.careyolsen.com

Hong Kong

Yu Pui Hang
L&Y Law Office / Henry Yu & Associates

Government attitude and definition

Cryptocurrencies (often called "**coins**" or "**tokens**", and collectively referred to in colloquial manner as "**crypto**") and blockchain technology (certain blockchain technologies may also be referred to as "**Distributed Ledger Technology**" or "**DLT**" for short) have, in their short life span of the past decade, created a new economy which to date stands at close to US$ 300bn.

The first cryptocurrency to enter the market was Bitcoin, and it has introduced an effective way to transfer value over the internet by relying on peer-to-peer and distributed verification. Ever since Bitcoin there have been other blockchain-based projects that have introduced new innovations to blockchain technology (these cryptocurrencies are often referred to as "**Altcoins**"), one of the most noteworthy being Ethereum, which allows for the deployment and execution of software on the blockchain called smart contracts. As a result of this growth, many private and public enterprises have formed in Hong Kong to take advantage of the opportunities this new technology can offer, and to leverage Hong Kong's unique position in business, technology and law.

Hong Kong is a unique jurisdiction, as it leverages the "one country, two systems principle" which gives it a high degree of autonomy. The Basic Law of Hong Kong enshrines various free market principles and its position as an international financial centre. Thus, given its free market foundations, the Hong Kong government has not taken any specific measures to restrict cryptocurrencies or cryptocurrency businesses (save to the extent for enforcing the existing legislation), nor has the government so far passed any new bespoke regulations to control the cryptocurrency economy.

As there are no new statutory instruments to directly regulate cryptocurrencies in Hong Kong, there is a certain degree of uncertainty on the legal definition within the statutory law. There are secondary sources of law, namely the designation set by the Secretary for the Financial Services and Treasury Bureau ("**FSTB**"), Professor K C Chan, who designated Bitcoin (specifically) as a "virtual commodity". In a press release, Hong Kong Monetary Authority ("**HKMA**") stated in 2015 that Bitcoin and other similar currencies were not legal tender but "virtual commodities", as Bitcoin has no backing – either in physical form or by the issuers – it cannot qualify as a means of payment or electronic money. The HKMA, which acts as Hong Kong's *de facto* central bank, has also stated that it has no plans to issue any central bank-backed cryptocurrency. For the purpose of this publication, references to "cryptocurrencies" shall mean "virtual commodities" as meant by the HKMA.

The most observable attitude made by government and the various regulatory authorities is to warn the public against the uncertainties in the cryptocurrency marketplace. The earliest observable public warning was made by the Hong Kong Police in 2014 which highlighted that Bitcoins are not money and are not regulated by the HKMA; the volatility of the prices of Bitcoin; the cybersecurity risks associated with dealing with Bitcoin; and potential fraud especially with "Bitcoin Mining Contracts". Any suspected proceeds of crime should be reported to the Joint Financial Intelligence Unit ("**JFIU**"), a joint unit composed of the Hong Kong Police Force and the Hong Kong Customs and Excise Department ("**CED**"). The press release issued by the HKMA contained a similar warning about the volatile nature of Bitcoins.

With the advent of Ethereum and other smart contract blockchain platforms, new applications of cryptocurrency such as initial coin offerings, or token sale (collectively "**ICO(s)**") became more widely popular in Hong Kong and globally. As many ICO issuers have established their base of operations in Hong Kong and have opened their campaigns to Hong Kong residents, the local securities regulator, the Securities and Futures Commission ("**SFC**") has issued various statements warning the public about: (i) the risk of participating in ICO campaigns; (ii) that ICO tokens that possess features of "securities" as defined under the Securities and Futures Ordinance (Cap. 571) would require to be authorised by the SFC; and (iii) that dealing and advising on "securities"-based ICOs would require the person dealing to obtain the appropriate licences.

In subsequent public communications, the SFC has stated that it is monitoring the cryptocurrency space and will enforce any relevant provision under the SFO if necessary. Aside from the statement given by the SFC, in early 2018 the Investor Education Centre and the FSTB launched an education campaign on ICOs and cryptocurrencies. The campaign's key message is to not buy something you do not understand. In conclusion, the Hong Kong government's view towards cryptocurrencies can be described as relatively passive.

The regulatory authorities have not called for new legislation to regulate cryptocurrencies, as current laws are still applicable. For now, it is observable that the government and the regulatory authorities aim to educate the public about the risk involved in the cryptocurrency economy. The Hong Kong government and several agencies have put in place initiatives to promote fintech development in Hong Kong, for example through regulatory "sandboxes" (as discussed below).

Cryptocurrency regulation

As mentioned above, HKMA and the SFC have recognised Bitcoins and other currencies like it as a "virtual commodity" (it is not clear if and how this extends to other Altcoins) and Hong Kong has not created new legislation or regulations to regulate this "virtual commodity". Certain businesses which are common in the cryptocurrency economy are ordinarily regulated in Hong Kong, and thus a cryptocurrency company that wishes to participate in such market must abide by such specific legislation.

Hong Kong does not regulate private possession or transfer of cryptocurrencies between private individuals, on the assumption that the cryptocurrency in question was obtained and is transferred in good faith (cryptocurrencies are subject to anti-money laundering laws which are discussed below).

The most noteworthy regulated industry that is quite pervasive in the cryptocurrency economy is the ICO space. ICOs are campaigns where issuers sell blockchain-based tokens to potential participants in exchange for other cryptocurrency such as Ether or Bitcoin. The purpose of conducting an ICO is to crowdsource funds for a specific project that the issuer aims to develop, and the tokens have certain "utility" within such project. One example is the OAX project (https://www.oax.org/en) which was considered as the first ICO in Hong Kong. The conventional ICO follows the ERC-20 Ethereum standard and the sale is conducted through a web portal. Aside from the technical elements, the issuers also circulate several documents to the public during the ICO period such as the white paper (or even technical white paper) and the token sale agreement, if any.

Nevertheless, if the tokens that are sold in ICO campaigns possess the features of "securities" under the SFO, e.g. the characteristics of equity, debt or collective investment scheme, such ICO tokens may be regarded as "securities" and the related advertisements, invitations or documents which involve securities, structured products and collective investment schemes would be subject to the provisions of the SFO.

In general, Hong Kong does not prohibit the possession or trading of cryptocurrencies, as Bitcoins and currencies similar to it are considered to be virtual commodities and not electronic money, provided the cryptocurrencies are possessed and traded in good faith. There are other regulatory considerations depending on the use of cryptocurrencies, such as the running of ICO campaigns or trading Bitcoin futures contracts.

Sales regulation

As remarked in the paragraph above, the government has a duty to safeguard the free flow of capital as enshrined under Article 112 of the Hong Kong Basic Law. Trade controls and consumer protection are predominantly controlled by the CED, and the basic trading of cryptocurrencies is subject to oversight by CED. The applicable legislation and regulations on the trading of cryptocurrencies will depend on the features of each particular cryptocurrency, as certain cryptocurrencies such as ICO tokens may take the form of or possess features that are common in other financial products such as shares, interests in a fund or securitisation of another asset or asset class, and they will be regulated by the applicable legislation such as the SFO.

Trading of Bitcoin in Hong Kong is commonly done on cryptocurrency exchanges, on over-the-counter ("**OTC**") desks and peer-to-peer ("**P2P**") platforms with both consumer and institutional participants; depending on the nature of the transaction, different legislation will apply. In most business-to-consumer transactions conducted on exchanges and OTC desks, general consumer protection laws such as the Sales of Goods Ordinance (Cap. 26) and the Trade Descriptions Ordinance (Cap. 362) apply, with the former specifying the procedures and rights of parties in the transaction, and the latter setting out rules on the prevention of unfair trade practices. Business-to-business transactions are not covered *per se* by the above statutes which are mostly aimed at protecting individual consumers.

Certain commodity exchanges are prohibited from establishing in Hong Kong, under the Commodity Exchanges (Prohibition) Ordinance (Cap. 82) with the list of prohibited commodities being specified in the Schedule of the above Ordinance, e.g. barley, cocoa, coffee, copper, cotton, gold, lead, maize, oats, platinum, rice, rubber, silver, oil seeds and vegetable oils, sugar, timber, tin, wheat, zinc, jute, frozen meat, poultry and fish and soybeans. To date, cryptocurrency (or "virtual commodity") has not been added to the Schedule, and therefore there are no statutory prohibitions on operating exchange in Hong Kong for trading of cryptocurrencies, which are classified as virtual commodities.

Cryptocurrency exchanges and OTC desks do also observe other legal requirements such as anti-money laundering and counter-terrorist financing and customer due diligence checks (further discussed below).

There are certain cryptocurrencies that will be restricted in trading on the abovementioned platforms. The first type of restricted cryptocurrency is the "security" token, which replicates features of securities and under Hong Kong law is the broadest category of restricted cryptocurrency given the broad definition of security under the SFO. This definition is contained under Schedule 1 of the SFO and can be broadly split into the following categories:

- *Shares* – shares are defined under the Companies Ordinance (Cap. 622) and in the common law relate to an equitable ownership interest of a company; such interest gives the holders certain rights, as stipulated in the company's articles of association. A cryptocurrency token can form a blockchain-based share certificate, if each token unit represents *inter alia* legal or beneficial ownership in the company, a right to vote in shareholders' meetings, and a right to receive a dividend or some kind of distribution. Public offerings of such cryptocurrencies via ICO would be restricted on the basis that in Hong Kong, under the Companies (Winding Up and Miscellaneous Provisions) Ordinance (Cap. 32), a person may not offer the sale of shares of a company to the public without registering a prospectus, unless the issuer elects to issue the tokenised shares in accordance with the "safe harbour" provisions under the SFO.

- *Debentures* – encompasses various debt-based instruments issued by a company. This category is quite broad as it is not necessary for a debenture to be expressly described as one; all that is required is that the instrument evidences a debt obligation by the company, whether or not the debt is charged against the company. Cryptocurrencies that could be considered as a debenture would be distributed in a similar manner as share tokens and would be subject to similar restrictions.

- *Collective Investment Schemes* ("**CIS**") – the provisions concerning CIS products aim to regulate investment products that are collective in nature; examples of such products include unit trusts and mutual funds. Unlike the definition of "share" above, a CIS may form if the definition under Schedule 1 of the SFO, which includes four components, is satisfied:

  1. There must be an "arrangement of property".
  2. The participating persons do not have day-to-day control over the management of the property, whether or not they have the right to be consulted or to give directions in respect of such management.
  3. The property is managed in whole or on behalf of the person operating the arrangements; and/or contributions and profits or income are pooled.
  4. The purpose or effect, or the pretended purpose or effect, is to enable the participating persons to receive: (a) profits, income or other returns represented to arise; or (b) payments from the acquisition or disposal of the property.

Given the broad nature of the CIS definition, it could be argued that many ICO campaigns could fall within the parameters of the CIS definition. If this is the case, the issuer may not make the ICO open to the public without prior authorisation from the SFC. In March 2018, the SFC halted the ICO operated by a company called Black Cell Technology Limited ("**Black Cell**"), which allowed token-holders to redeem their tokens into equity shares in Black Cell. The SFC has considered this arrangement to be a CIS under the circumstances. In the above case, Black Cell has undertaken not to proceed with the ICO. It is important to note that in light of SFC numerous statements to date, the regulators are closely observing the ICO and broader cryptocurrency economy to ensure that the relevant securities legislation is complied with. As with "shares" tokens, the trading of "CIS" tokens will be subject to similar restrictions, thus cryptocurrency exchange must conduct sufficient legal due diligence to ensure the cryptocurrencies they allow on their marketplace are not considered "securities".

Aside from securities, other types of financial instrument markets have also developed in the cryptocurrency economy. Bitcoin-based derivatives products have enjoyed considerable popularity, trading on exchanges such as Bitmex. Bitcoin futures gained even more popularity in late 2017 when CBOE and CME started offering Bitcoin futures contracts. The SFC stated in its announcement on 11 December 2017 that any intermediary in Hong Kong that offers brokerage services for the above Bitcoin futures will be required to obtain the appropriate licences from the SFC (namely "Type 2" when dealing with such futures contracts, and "Type 5" when advising on such futures contracts).

In the broad sense, trading of cryptocurrencies is not restricted in Hong Kong so long as they are classified as "virtual commodities" (and not "securities" for the purpose of SFO) and do not infringe on any applicable securities and futures legislation. Cryptocurrency exchanges are not subject to legislation that prohibits the operation of commodity exchanges.

Taxation

In general, there is no capital gains tax payable from the sale of financial instruments in Hong Kong. That being said, any Hong Kong-sourced income from frequent cryptocurrency trading in the ordinary course of business may be treated as income in case of individual clients, and profits in case of a corporation, and subject to income tax and profits tax respectively, regardless of whether the trading is made in exclusive cryptocurrency or fiat-to-cryptocurrency exchanges. To date, the Inland Revenue Department has not issued specific guidelines on how it would treat cryptocurrencies for the purposes of tax assessment.

Money transmission laws and anti-money laundering requirements

Many jurisdictions have implemented stringent anti-money laundering and counter-terrorist financing ("**AML/CTF**") laws and regulations, with the majority implementing recommendations set out by the Financial Action Task Force ("**FAFT**"), an international intergovernmental organisation that aims to standardise AML/CTF systems around the world.

In Hong Kong, the principal AML/CTF legislation is the Anti Money Laundering and Counter Terrorist Financing Ordinance (Cap. 615) ("**AMLO**") which applies to financial institutions (including HKMA-authorised institutions, i.e. banks, SFC-licensed corporations, licensed insurance companies, stored value facility issuers and money service operators) and "designated non-financial business and professions" ("**DNFBP**") (such professions being lawyers, public accountants, estate agents, and trust and company services agents), and also creates a licensing regime for money service operators, and trust and company services providers. Businesses that principally deal with cryptocurrencies such as exchanges and OTC desks are not directly subject to the provisions of AMLO, as such businesses do not fall within the definition of a financial institution or DNFBP unless the cryptocurrency business partially operates in a regulated business, for example, providing money services such as money changing and remittance services. Further to the rules set out in AMLO, each regulatory authority has formulated its own guidelines on dealing with AML/CTF issues.

As mentioned in the paragraph on the "Government Attitude" above, the Hong Kong regulatory authorities have maintained a cautious approach to cryptocurrencies. In 2014, both the HKMA and the SFC issued circulars to their respective supervised institutions warning of the anonymous nature of cryptocurrency transactions and their inherent money-laundering and terrorist-financing risks. These statements come around the same time as the most noteworthy cryptocurrency money-laundering case stemming from the apprehension and conviction of Ross Ulbricht, the operator of the deep-web marketplace, "Silk Road". Both regulators have clearly indicated the requirement for increased vigilance when dealing with cryptocurrency business, including inquiring into the internal controls on AML/CTF policies and procedures of the cryptocurrency businesses. In light of these requirements, many cryptocurrency businesses voluntarily apply the customer due diligence measures set out in Schedule 2 of AMLO as part of their AML/CFT policies.

While AMLO sets out specific guidelines applicable to financial institutions and DNFBPs, other business and individuals have a statutory duty to report any suspicious transactions under various criminal statutes, namely the Drug Tracking (Recovery of Proceeds) Ordinance (Cap. 405) ("**DTRPO**"), Organised and Serious Crimes Ordinance (Cap. 455) ("**OSCO**"), and the United Nations (Anti-Terrorism Measures) Ordinance (Cap. 575) ("**UNATMO**"). Any suspected transactions involving money laundering, terrorist financing or receipts of crime must be reported to the JFIU by submitting a suspicious transaction report ("**STR**"); failure to file an STR is a criminal offence which is liable to HK$ 50,000 fine and three-month imprisonment. As highlighted above, many cryptocurrency businesses implement AML/CTF measures to comply with the relevant suspicious transaction reporting provisions under the DTRPO, OSCO and UNATMO, and also the likely requests from their banks in Hong Kong.

Promotion and testing

Various regulatory bodies in Hong Kong have embraced the Hong Kong government's plan to promote fintech and financial innovation in the city. Currently the HKMA, SFC and the Insurance Authority are operating "sandbox" programs that allow innovative financial products to be tested in a limited regulatory environment.

The first regulatory sandbox was introduced by the HKMA on 6 September 2016. The sandbox provides HKMA-authorised institutions ("**AIs**"), e.g. banks, to allow for live testing of financial technologies before their formal launch. AIs must set applicable boundaries to conduct the trials on the client base and must offer appropriate customer-protection measures to resolve customer losses. On 28 November 2017, the HKMA introduced the Fintech Supervisory Sandbox 2.0 Chatroom that allows AIs to receive supervisory feedback through emails, video conferences and face-to-face meetings from the HKMA's Fintech Facilitation Office and Banking Department during the early stages when the new technological application is being contemplated by the AIs. As of July 2018, the HKMA has reported that it has supervised four distributed technology projects; this means that banks in Hong Kong are actively looking at rolling our blockchain technologies as part of their services. The one visible disadvantage of the HKMA sandbox is that it is only available to AIs or technology companies that are associated with an AI. Technology start-up companies that do not meet the above criteria are limited from accessing the HKMA sandbox.

The SFC sandbox was announced on 29 September 2017. The objective of the SFC sandbox is to allow firms to utilise innovative technologies and demonstrate a genuine commitment to carry out SFC authorised activities through the use of financial technology that may increase the quality of products and services for investors in Hong Kong. The SFC sandbox will be open to qualified firms who are 'fit and proper' and hold the applicable SFC licences and comply with the licensing requirements such as Financial Resources Rules. The SFC will impose licensing conditions on firms in the sandbox, which can be removed upon the firms' exit from the sandbox when the firm satisfies the requirements to operate outside of the sandbox. The guidelines from the SFC do not specify what technologies are permitted in the sandbox as they only require a genuine commitment to use financial technology in carrying out regulated activity, i.e. a cryptocurrency-based service that falls within the preview of regulated activity. Similar to the HKMA sandbox, access to the scheme is also limited to firms that hold SFC licences or who qualify for SFC licences, which may also limit access to the sandbox for start-up companies.

Aside from the sandbox initiatives by the various regulatory authorities in Hong Kong, the HKMA has, along with the Monetary Authority of Singapore, announced on 15 November 2017 its intent to launch the Global Trade Connectivity Network using DLT, and connecting the Hong Kong Trade Finance Platform and the National Trade Platform in Singapore. The Trade Finance Platform is scheduled to commence operation by the end of 2018.

Ownership and licensing requirements

Ownership of cryptocurrencies is currently not subject to any restrictions and regulations in Hong Kong, provided they are obtained in good faith. Possession of cryptocurrencies may be illegal when their sources originate, amongst others, from computer crime, which under Hong Kong laws are proscribed in section 161 of the Crimes Ordinance (Cap. 200), and section 27A of the Telecommunications Ordinance (Cap. 171) and other applicable Hong Kong legislation including the DTRPO and the OSCO which establish offences for handling the proceeds of crime.

There are no requirements to date to obtain any licence to own or trade cryptocurrencies which are classified as "virtual commodities". On the other hand, this statement is subject to exceptions when dealing with securities and futures involving cryptocurrencies, such as Bitcoin futures: a broker who wishes to offer such contract to their client will require the appropriate SFC licences.

Mining

Mining is the process of creating of new blocks on the blockchain; this process includes verifying transactions and collecting "block rewards" of cryptocurrencies. This type of activity is common to blockchain platforms that use the "proof-of-work" consensus algorithm, where the transaction is proved by the computing power used to process it. There are other consensus models such as "proof of stake", where the block producers stake their cryptocurrencies to gain the rights to process the transaction.

Assuming that 'mining' is considered as mining of "proof of work"-based cryptocurrencies (such as Bitcoin) to date, there are no specific regulations governing mining of cryptocurrencies in Hong Kong. Moreover, to date no Hong Kong governmental body has issued any guidance that discourages, restricts or prohibits Bitcoin mining activities. Whether cryptocurrency mining is legally permitted in Hong Kong is subject to other regulations in Hong Kong under certain circumstances, as discussed below.

Mining operations (especially for cryptocurrencies such as Bitcoin) can be highly industrialised operations, usually involving the use of hundreds of ASIC (application-specific integrated circuits) computers to mine cryptocurrencies. Such operations closely resemble large-scale data centre operations. Any regulations that apply to other similar applications such as data centres may also be applicable to cryptocurrency mining sites. In Hong Kong, data centre facilitation is overseen by the Office of the Government Chief Information Officer.

Businesses that intend to operate large-scale data centres should be aware of the relevant land-use rights stipulated under the laws of Hong Kong. Under the statutory Outline Zoning Plans prepared by the Town Planning Board under the Town Planning Ordinance ("**TPO**"), such data centres belong to "Information Technology and Telecommunications Industries for cryptocurrency mining purposes and would therefore require application for amendment to the OZP under Section 12A of TPO. Apart from zoning permission, it should be noted that development of a site is subject to *inter alia* the terms and conditions of the land lease governing the site; the usage set out in the occupation permit; and the deed of mutual covenants, if any.

The operation of a data centre involves mechanical and electrical installations which may be subject to statutory requirements in Hong Kong. The key statute in question is the Buildings Energy Efficiency Ordinance (Cap. 610) and, in order to comply with the ordinance, the owner or operator of a data centre in a prescribed building should engage a Registered Energy Assessor to certify that its building services installations have complied with the requirements under the above ordinance. The above rules would only be applicable to large-scale cryptocurrency mining operations and would not likely apply to domestic or small-scale mining operations.

Border restrictions and declaration

Prior to recent legislative changes there were no statutory declaration requirements on the import and export of large quantities of money in Hong Kong as advised by FATF Recommendation 32. As of 16 July 2018, with the commencement of the Cross-boundary Movement of Physical Currency and Bearer Negotiable Instruments Ordinance (Cap. 629) ("**CMPCBNIO**"), a person who physically imports or exports large amounts of currency or bearer-negotiable instruments ("**CBNIs**") through the designated checkpoints stated in the CMPCBNIO must now disclose and declare such movement to CED. The disclosure threshold is set at HK$120,000 (Schedule 4 of the CMPCBNIO).

The new CMPCBNIO is only applicable to CBNIs, which are defined as cash or negotiable instruments such as bearer cheques, promissory notes, bearer bonds, traveller's cheques, money orders or postal orders. As Bitcoin has so far been classified by the HKMA as a "virtual commodity", it should not fall within the definition of CBNI, but it is unclear how this would apply to other Altcoins. There also would be considerable difficulties in enforcing this provision, as CMPCBNIO requires the physical movement of CBNIs; thus to enforce the declaration requirements, the CED would have to prove that Bitcoins were physically moved across the border.

Reporting requirements

In Hong Kong, there is no requirement to report cryptocurrency transactions of any amount. Profits generated through cryptocurrency trading may be subject to declaration in a tax return under the applicable tax legislation, as discussed above. As cryptocurrencies are not defined as CBNIs, there is no obligation to declare them to CED when importing them to Hong Kong.

Estate planning and testamentary succession

In essence, any cryptocurrencies or cryptocurrency accounts would be treated as personal property and would fall into the estate of the deceased, which can be administered by the Executor named in the Will of the deceased or an Administrator appointed by the Probate Court. The Executor or the Administrator could apply for a "Grant of Probate" or a "Letter of Administration" before he is allowed to handle the cryptocurrencies or exchange accounts.

Ordinary access to cryptocurrencies requires the user to have access to the private key to make transactions on the blockchain, and if the private key is lost then the cryptocurrencies are irrecoverable. Thus when conducting estate planning, arrangements should be made to preserve the private key beyond the death of its owner, such as recording the recovery seed and storing in a safe environment (i.e. a bank safe deposit box). Cryptocurrency exchange accounts may be accessed by the Executor or the Administrator in accordance with the procedures of each exchange; like with many internet-based services, this may require the Executor or the Administrator to submit the certificate of death, the Grant of Probate and/or the Letter of Administration to the exchange.

Yu Pui Hang (Henry Yu)
Tel: +852 2115 9525 / Email: hyu@lylawoffice.com
Mr Yu is the founding partner of L&Y Law Office and Henry Yu & Associates.
He obtained his Bachelor of law degree in England and is qualified as a
solicitor in both England & Wales and Hong Kong.

Over recent years, Mr Yu has developed a strong interest in the blockchain
industry and his enthusiasm and insightful views have been affirmed
widely by various professional bodies. Mr Yu is a member of the Innotech
Committee (a.k.a. the Technology Committee) of the Law Society of Hong
Kong, and he has also been appointed as: Hon. Legal Advisor to the Hong
Kong Federation of Innovation and Invention; Hon. Legal Advisor to the
Institute of Financial Technologists of Asia; and Hon. Legal Advisor to the
GHM-Greater Bay Area TECHFIN Association. From time to time, Mr Yu
represents the Bitcoin community at meetings with the Legislative Council
Members, HKMA and the FTSB.

L&Y Law Office / Henry Yu & Associates

Suite 806, 8/F, Tower Two, Lippo Center, 89 Queensway, Admiralty, Hong Kong
Tel: +852 2115 9525 / URL: www.lylawoffice.com

India

Ashwin Ramanathan, Anu Tiwari & Rachana Rautray
AZB & Partners

Introduction

In India, cryptocurrencies have started gaining popularity since around 2013, when small-scale businesses began accepting Bitcoin as a form of payment. Since then, cryptocurrencies have grown into a means of investment, evidenced by the emergence of cryptocurrency exchanges in India.

The first regulatory response in the context of cryptocurrencies was when the Reserve Bank of India ("RBI") issued a press release – on December 24, 2013 ("Press Note 1"). The RBI (which is in charge of monetary policy, regulation of financial markets and exchange control related issues) was careful in terms of neither sanctioning, nor prohibiting, cryptocurrencies; rather, all that Press Note 1 constituted was a caution to users, holders and traders of 'virtual currency', of potential risks associated with cryptocurrencies.

Almost immediately after the issuance of Press Note 1, several Bitcoin exchanges such as 'Buysellbitco.in' and 'INRBTC' temporarily shut operations. The Enforcement Directorate ("ED", which enforces exchange control regulations) undertook raids on the proprietor of 'Buysellbitco.in' to examine if transactions being carried out on its platform violated foreign exchange control regulations.

While Press Note 1 and the ED's actions caused a setback in the popularity of cryptocurrency transactions, this was only temporary; ultimately, cryptocurrencies were not banned or prohibited, and India witnessed a steady rise in transactions in cryptocurrency, tracking the global increase in similar activities.

The RBI released warnings similar in scope to Press Note 1 on February 1, 2017 ("Press Note 2") and December 5, 2017 ("Press Note 3") reiterating its caution, and went one step further to clarify that it (i.e. the RBI) has not provided any entity with any licence or sanction to transact with cryptocurrency.

It should be noted that the government does distinguish between Bitcoin and its underlying technology, i.e. blockchain. Despite the issuance of the press notes cited above, the RBI has issued a White Paper on 'Applications of Block Chain Technology to the Banking and Financial Sector in India' in January 2017, which views the application of blockchain technology by banks favourably. The RBI has also indicated that it may create a domestic ledger platform involving National Payment Corporation of India similar to existing platforms (such as RTGS, NEFT and IMPS). Towards this end in particular, the RBI, in September 2017, announced that it had taken steps to create such a platform, and also filed three patent applications in this regard.

Along similar lines, the Indian Finance Minister, in his Budget Speech on February 1, 2018, stated that although the Indian government does not recognize Bitcoin as legal tender, it does encourage the use of blockchain technology in payment systems.

The Budget Speech has several times been cited as the precursor to the regulation of cryptocurrency in India, although it is certainly not the sole reflection of the Indian government's attitude to cryptocurrency. Since the RBI's press releases, the government has constituted an inter-disciplinary committee (which includes representatives from the RBI) to examine: (i) the present status of cryptocurrency in India and globally; (ii) the existing global regulatory and legal structures governing cryptocurrency; and (iii) measures to address issues relating to consumer protection and money laundering.

These developments initially suggested a positive approach towards the regulation of cryptocurrency, in that it was expected, in some quarters at least, that the RBI and the government would officially permit the use of cryptocurrencies.

All that changed with RBI's circular dated April 6, 2018 ("Circular"), as a result of which the dealing of cryptocurrency in India today has been substantially impeded. Through the Circular, the RBI banned all entities regulated by it (i.e., banks, financing institutions, non-banking financing institutions, payment system providers and the like) from dealing in, or facilitating any dealings in, cryptocurrencies. These entities were given a three-month period within which all accounts dealing with cryptocurrency would have to be shut down.

As a consequence, while the government has not banned cryptocurrency in India *per se*, it has certainly made it quite difficult for participants to conduct transactions using traditional banking channels.

No other regulator in India has issued any directions concerning cryptocurrencies.

Press releases as recent as July 2018 indicate that the government will clarify its stance on cryptocurrency and is working with various industry participants to issue detailed guidelines, although timing in this regard remains uncertain.

Indian Supreme Court on cryptocurrency

Along with the Executive contemplating regulation of cryptocurrency, several stakeholders have also approached the judiciary by filing petitions before the Indian Supreme Court ("SC") in order to compel the government to provide clarity.

The two primary petitions seeking to address the legality of cryptocurrency were filed by: (i) Vijay Pal Dalmia and Siddharth Dalmia through civil writ petition 1071 of 2017 on June 2, 2017 ("Dalmia Petition"); and (ii) Dwaipayan Bhowmick through civil writ petition 1076 of 2017 on November 3, 2017 ("Bhowmick Petition").

The Dalmia Petition was filed against the Union of India (through the cabinet secretary), Ministry of Home Affairs, Ministry of Finance and the RBI ("Respondents 1"), seeking an order to direct Respondents 1 to "restrain / ban the sale / purchase of or investment in, illegal cryptocurrencies and initiate investigation and prosecution against all parties which indulge in the sale / purchase of cryptocurrency".

The grounds for the stated petition, as available on public sources, was based on:

(i) the anonymous nature of cryptocurrency transactions which makes them well-suited for funding terrorism, corruption, money laundering, tax evasion, etc.;

(ii) production and introduction of new cryptocurrency being generated by private parties, without the intervention of the government, and hence violating the Constitution;

(iii) use of cryptocurrency being in contravention of several laws such as FEMA and Prevention of Money Laundering Act, 2002;

(iv) ransomware attacks having occurred through the use of Bitcoin;

(v) illegal cryptocurrency providing an outlet for personal wealth that is beyond restriction and confiscation;

(vi) cryptocurrency exchanges encouraging undeclared and anonymous transactions, making it difficult for government authorities to identify such transactions; and

(vii) the fact that trading of cryptocurrencies permits players to bypass prescribed KYC norms.

The Bhowmick Petition was filed against the Union of India, Ministry of Finance, Ministry of Law and Justice, Ministry of Electronic and Information Technology, SEBI, RBI, Income Tax Dept. (through its secretary) and Enforcement Directorate (through its joint director) seeking an "issuance of direction to regulate the flow of bitcoins as well as requiring the constitution of a committee of experts to consider prohibition/regulation of bitcoins and other cryptocurrencies".

The grounds for the petition, as reflected in public sources, *inter alia* include:

(i) Bitcoin trading/transactions, being unregulated, lack accountability;

(ii) investigators can only track Bitcoin holders who convert their Bitcoin to regular currency;

(iii) counterfeiting of cryptocurrency is not an issue so long as the miners keep the blockchain secure;

(iv) bitcoins may be used for trade and other financial activities without accountability, having an effect on the market value of other commodities;

(v) conversion of Bitcoin into foreign exchange does not fall under the purview of the RBI, making such transactions highly unsafe and vulnerable to cyber attacks;

(vi) presently, no regulator has the power to track, monitor and regulate cryptocurrency transfers;

(vii) cryptocurrency has the potential to support criminal, anti-social activities like money laundering, terrorist funding and tax evasion; and

(viii) use of cryptocurrency could result in widespread adverse financial implications if left unchecked.

Subsequent to the aforementioned petitions, certain industry participants have filed writ petitions challenging the constitutionality of the RBI's Circular and reiterated the need for clarity on regulation. Other stakeholders, such as the Internet and Mobile Association of India have filed intervention applications in the Bhowmick Petition in order to draw attention to the impact that any restrictive regulation on cryptocurrencies may have on their businesses.

To date, while the Supreme Court has admitted these petitions, the matters remain *sub judice*, offering limited insight on the judiciary's stance. Nevertheless, the arguments made (as publicly reported) indicate that there is a degree of acknowledgment that various risks are presented by the continuing lack of regulation around cryptocurrencies.

Is cryptocurrency valid currency in India?

The Indian Parliament has enacted the: (i) Reserve Bank of India Act, 1934 ("RBI Act") regulating *inter alia* bank notes; and (ii) Coinage Act, 2011 ("Coinage Act") regulating coins, and these remain the only statutes that define and recognise legal tender.

Per section 26 of the RBI Act, "*[E]very bank note shall be legal tender at any place in India for payment, or on account for the amount expressed therein, and shall be guaranteed by the Central Government.*" The central government specifies and approves the denomination value, form and material of such bank notes and the RBI has the sole right to issue bank notes in the country. Similarly, section 6 (1) of the Coinage Act provides legal sanction to coins that are made of any metal or other material as approved by the Central Government. Bank notes and coins therefore encompass the entire universe of physical legal tender available in India.

Under the existing framework therefore, there is no sanction for cryptocurrencies as legal tender.

Is cryptocurrency a valid payment system in India?

In India, prepaid instruments and payment systems are regulated by the Payments and Settlement Act, 2007 ("PSSA"). Prior to the enactment of PSSA, a working group on electronic money set up by the RBI, issued a report in July 11, 2002 ("Report"), which defined electronic money as "*an electronic store of monetary value on a technical device used for making payments to undertakings other than the issuer without necessarily involving bank accounts in the transaction, but acting as a prepaid bearer instrument*".

These products may be classified into two broad categories, that is: (a) pre-paid stored value card (sometimes called "electronic purse" or "e-wallet"); and (b) pre-paid, software-based product that uses computer networks (sometimes referred to as "digital cash" or "network money"). It was highlighted that the stored value card scheme typically uses a microprocessor chip embedded in a physical device (such as a plastic card) while software-based schemes typically use specialised software installed on a personal computer.

The aforementioned definition may seem wide enough to include cryptocurrency in its scope. However, this must be read in conjunction with the PSSA, which does not explicitly define electronic money, but regulates payment systems that effect electronic funds transfer. These payment systems include "systems that enable payment between a payer and beneficiary, involving clearing, payment or settlement service or all of them, but does not include a stock exchange". Such systems include credit cards, debit cards, smart cards, and money transfer operations.

In addition to the PSSA, the RBI has also issued the 'Master Direction on Issuance and Operation of Prepaid Payment Instruments' dated October 11, 2017 ("PPI Regulations") that regulate prepaid wallets. Prepaid wallets may be issued by bank or non-bank entities to facilitate the purchase of goods and services, including financial services, remittance facilities, etc., against the value stored on such instruments.

In order to fall under the purview of the above, the instrument in question must store some monetary value. Cryptocurrencies may not have any value stored on them and their value (if any) is contingent on market speculation. Consequently, their issuance is not likely to be construed as regulated electronic money, or a valid payment system, as is currently understood by Indian regulation. Consequently, associated compliance requirements such as obtaining RBI registration, the requirement to establish an entity incorporated in India, the requirement to comply with AML regulations etc., are not applicable.

Are cryptocurrency cross-border trades valid?

Cryptocurrencies are easily capable of being traded on a cross-border basis and are, generally speaking, exchangeable into fiat currency. Under the RBI Master Directions – Liberalised

Remittance Scheme dated January 1, 2016, an Indian-resident individual may remit up to US$ 250,000 per year towards a permissible current or capital account transaction, or both.

A permissible current account transaction includes *inter alia* remittance towards:

(i)   private visits, business travel, or remittance by tour operators;

(ii)   fees for participation in global conferences and specialised training;

(iii) remittance for participation in international events/competitions (towards training, sponsorship and prize money);

(iv)   film shooting;

(v)   medical treatment abroad;

(vi)   disbursement of crew wages, overseas education, remittance under educational tie-up arrangements with universities abroad;

(vii) remittance towards fees for examinations held in India and abroad and additional score sheets for GRE, TOEFL, etc;

(viii) employment and processing, assessment fees for overseas job applications;

(ix)   emigration and emigration consultancy fees;

(x)   skills/credential assessment fees for intending migrants;

(xi)   visa fees, or processing fees required for registration of documents with other governments; or

(xii) registration/subscription/membership fees to international organisations.

A permissible capital account transaction includes *inter alia* remittance towards: (i) investment in foreign securities; (ii) foreign currency loans; (iii) transfer of immovable property; (iv) guarantees; (v) export, import or holding of currency notes; (vi) loans and overdrafts; (vii) maintenance of foreign currency accounts overseas; (viii) insurance policies; (ix) capital assets; or (x) sale and purchase of foreign exchange derivatives.

As is evident from the above, payment for cryptocurrency is not *per se* listed as a permitted activity. Nevertheless, it may have been possible for an individual to broadly declare the remittance of funds towards investments, without specifying that the intent was to invest in cryptocurrency. At present, given the financial blockage imposed by RBI's Circular, if a banking institution were to examine the purpose of the remittance further or trace such remittance to its ultimate use, the individual may be held liable for violating foreign exchange regulations (at the very least, the banking institution in question would be unable to facilitate the transaction).

Closely associated with cross-border transactions are anti-money laundering regimes that require periodic reporting and declarations to be made prior to undertaking the transaction. While Indian money-laundering regulations only apply to specific regulated entities such as banks, financial institutions, securities market intermediaries, etc., as a means to address concerns relating to money laundering, several cryptocurrency participants, such as cryptocurrency exchanges, have imposed self-regulatory measures such as complying with standard 'know your customer' obligations.

Conclusion

Regulatory uncertainty does not seem to have hindered industry participants from applying creative alternatives to capitalise on the Indian cryptocurrency market. For instance, cryptocurrency exchanges are exploring the option of setting up a 'peer to peer' platform to act as an intermediary between entities trading in cryptocurrency. As a proof of concept, it can be argued that businesses in India are keen to adopt blockchain and cryptocurrency, evidenced by various banks exploring the use of blockchain to facilitate cross-border payments and large business houses contemplating issuing their own cryptocurrency.

Given the burgeoning market and technological potential, the Indian government is likely to seek to strike a balance in its approach. It will be interesting to witness whether the government recognises the need for such technology by providing for regulation similar to the United States or Singapore governments which have imposed their taxation regime on cryptocurrency or, in the alternative, choose to nip this disruptive technology in the bud, like China, which has banned cryptocurrency.

Ashwin Ramanathan
Tel: +91 22 6639 6880 / Email: ashwin.ramanathan@azbpartners.com
Ashwin Ramanthan is a partner at AZB & Partners, Mumbai. He graduated with a B.A. LL.B. (Hons.) degree from the National Law School of India University, Bangalore in 2000. He is registered as an advocate with the Bar Council of Maharashtra & Goa. Ashwin began his career with ICICI Limited (the development finance institution that later merged into ICICI Bank) and joined AZB & Partners in 2004. He has been a partner at the Firm since 2007. Although Ashwin's initial focus at the Firm was on banking and structured finance, his practice areas now include mergers and acquisitions, the distressed debt markets, Fintech and private equity transactions. Ashwin is also active in the derivatives and aviation finance space. In recent times, he has advised Fairfax in its acquisition of Thomas Cook in India, The Royal Bank of Scotland in the sale of its mortgage and credit card businesses to Ratnakar Bank, and ING Vysya Bank in relation to its proposed merger with Kotak Mahindra Bank, besides acting on a number of private equity growth investments in both publicly listed and privately held companies.

Anu Tiwari
Tel: +91 22 6639 6880 / Email: anu.tiwari@azbpartners.com
Anu Tiwari holds a Bachelor of Law degree from the National University of Juridical Sciences: 2007, and is a senior partner at AZB & Partners. Anu has over 11 years of experience in mergers and acquisitions, JVs, financial regulatory, asset management, emerging technology, i.e., blockchain, payment systems, cryptocurrency and general corporate advisory. Anu regularly advises banks, non-banks (NBFCs), asset managers/securities market intermediaries, global information technology (IT) and payments/fintech players on regulatory and mergers and acquisitions (both domestic and cross-border) aspects. His practice includes advising on cyber-security, financial crimes and regulatory investigations. He has actively participated in various policy initiatives, including as a Member of the Confederation of Indian Industries (CII) – Fintech Working Group, and as a Member of the Legal Advisory Sub-Committee, Reserve Bank India (RBI) Committee on Household Finance.

Rachana Rautray
Tel: +91 22 6639 6880 / Email: rachana.rautray@azbpartners.com
Rachana Rautray holds a Bachelor of Law degree from the National University of Juridical Sciences: 2016, and is an associate with AZB & Partners, having experience in various practice areas including mergers and acquisitions, general corporate and commercial laws. Rachana regularly advises banks, non-banks (NBFCs), securities market intermediaries, global information technology (IT) and payments/Fintech players on regulatory and mergers and acquisitions (both domestic and cross-border) aspects. Her practice includes advising on data protection/cyber-security, financial crimes and regulatory investigations involving the RBI, SEBI and Government of India. She is also a member of the Young Mumbai Centre for International Arbitration, launched in association with the Mumbai Centre for International Arbitration.

AZB & Partners

AZB House, Peninsula Corporate Park, Ganpatrao Kadam Marg, Lower Parel, Mumbai 400 013, India
Tel: +91 22 6639 6880 / Fax: +91 22 6639 6888

Ireland

Maura McLaughlin, Pearse Ryan & Caroline Devlin
Arthur Cox

Government attitude and definition

While the Irish Government has, to date, remained largely silent on its attitude towards cryptocurrencies, the Irish Department of Finance issued a Discussion Paper on Virtual Currencies and Blockchain Technology in March 2018. The Paper discusses various aspects of both, such as risks and benefits of currencies, but also gives examples and details of countries which are either proponents or opponents of cryptocurrencies and/or blockchain technology.

While the Discussion Paper does not outline or represent the attitude of the Irish Government on this topic, it states that no one policy measure or State agency has the ability to comprehensively address all the risks and opportunities in the area. Instead, it states that to evaluate each of these issues the Irish Government will require the expertise of multiple State agencies such as the Department of Finance, the Revenue Commissioner, the Data Protection Commission and the Department of Business, Enterprise and Innovation to allow for the development of holistic policy measures that encourage innovation while addressing risks to consumers, investors and businesses.

In order to facilitate this process, the Department of Finance is currently in the process of establishing an inter-departmental working group on blockchain and cryptocurrencies in order to, amongst other things, monitor international developments in the area, engage with other areas of Government, assess possible involvement, and consider if policy recommendations will be necessary.

In Ireland, cryptocurrencies are not regarded as either "money" or "currency". The Central Bank of Ireland (CBI) has issued a warning on its website that cryptocurrencies are not legal tender and are neither guaranteed nor regulated by the CBI. The dangers associated with such currencies, as mentioned by the CBI in its warning, include their extreme volatility, the absence of regulatory protection, and the risk of being given misleading or incomplete information.

The CBI also issued an "Alert on Initial Coin Offerings" in December 2017. The purpose of the alert is to warn against, amongst other things, the high risk of losing all invested capital due to the lack of regulation and the associated risk of becoming the victim of fraud or other illicit activities. Extreme price volatility was also mentioned as one of the risks.

There are currently no cryptocurrencies which are backed by either the Irish Government or the CBI. While other jurisdictions around the world are investigating the use of digital currencies, no such plans have been announced to date by either the Irish Government or the CBI.

Cryptocurrency regulation

There is no specific cryptocurrency regulation in Ireland, but there is also no specific prohibition in Ireland on any activities related to cryptocurrency.

The CBI is the competent authority in Ireland for the regulation of financial services including electronic money, payment services and securities law. The CBI has yet to indicate the extent to which existing financial regulation will apply. The CBI has issued warnings in relation to ICOs and cryptocurrencies and has also contributed to the European Securities and Markets Authority (ESMA)'s warnings to both consumers and to firms engaged in ICOs (see also "Government attitude and definition").

In respect of cryptocurrency regulation, we expect that the CBI will focus on securities law and the recognised EU concepts of "transferable security" and "financial instruments" as defined in the 2014 European Union Markets in Financial Instruments Directive (MiFID II) and the characteristics which they view as bringing cryptocurrencies or tokens within those definitions. Depending on their structure, cryptocurrencies could be classified as transferable securities, which would bring them within scope of a range of securities laws. For example, the issuer of a cryptocurrency may be required to publish a prospectus (or avail of an exemption) prior to their being offered to the public, or certain activities in respect of the cryptocurrency may require authorisation as an investment firm under MiFID II.

A pure, decentralised cryptocurrency is unlikely to be a transferable security, while a token with characteristics similar to a traditional share or bond may be. It is also possible that true "utility" tokens intended for exclusive use on a platform or service will not be transferable securities. The definition of transferable security is non-exhaustive and it is for each issuer and their advisers to determine whether their cryptocurrency or token is a transferable security.

As in many jurisdictions, the regulatory environment in relation to cryptocurrencies and their interaction with securities law is not yet settled and ESMA acknowledges that depending on how an ICO is structured, it may fall outside the regulated space entirely.

Sales regulation

Depending on the structure of an ICO or token, it may fall within the regulated space and require the publication of a prospectus (or availing of an exemption from that requirement, see above) prior to it being offered to the public.

Taxation

There are no specific rules for dealings in cryptocurrencies, and normal basic principles apply. The Irish Revenue confirmed this in a publication issued in May 2018. The taxation of dealings in cryptocurrencies will generally follow the underlying activities. Thus the receipt of cryptocurrency in lieu of cash for goods or services rendered will generally be taxed as income. Dealing in cryptocurrencies of themselves will depend on the nature and level of activity of the dealer. Occasional investment in and disposals of cryptocurrencies would likely be treated as a capital receipt, currently taxed at 33%. Where there is significant and regular dealing, this could be considered to be trading, which for a company would be taxed at 12.5%, or the marginal higher rates for individuals. The actual tax position will depend on an analysis of the specifics of each transaction, and would need a case-by-case consideration, as is normal in trading activity.

If it is assumed that the profit may be taxable under some heading, the next issue is valuing the profit generated. This is naturally a challenge, and indeed records of trades through various exchanges may be difficult, if not impossible to obtain. It is likely that this area will be the subject of further guidance from the Irish Revenue in due course, but in the interim, those dealings in cryptocurrencies should keep all relevant contemporaneous records to assist in the valuation.

No Irish VAT arises on the transfer of cryptocurrency. Irish stamp duty should not arise, although as stamp duty is a tax on documents, the manner in which the transfer takes place would be worth monitoring to ensure that a stampable document has not been inadvertently created.

The territoriality aspect of cryptocurrencies is still an involving area. In the case of an Irish resident (and for an individual ordinarily resident) person, they will usually be liable to tax in Ireland on their worldwide income and gains (subject to any reliefs or exemptions, including double tax treaty reliefs). A non-resident person will generally only be subject to tax on Irish-sourced income or gains, or profits of an Irish trade. (In the case of individuals, tax may also apply where amounts are remitted into Ireland.) It is evident therefore that understanding the source or situs of cryptocurrencies is of significance in international dealings. This is likely to be an area that will be developed further.

Money transmission laws and anti-money laundering requirements

There is a risk that certain ancillary services in connection with cryptocurrency could be subject to regulation as a form of money remittance or transmission under the Payment Services Directive (PSD) or, where PSD does not apply, under the Irish regulatory regime for money transmission. For example, the operator of a cryptocurrency platform who settles payments of fiat currency between the buyers and sellers of cryptocurrency could be viewed as being engaged in the regulated activity of money remittance/transmission. There are a number of exemptions which may be applicable, for example, where the platform operator is acting as a commercial agent or where the platform could be viewed as a securities settlement system. The application of the exemption would depend on the features of the trading platform.

The application of existing Irish anti-money laundering requirements to cryptocurrencies is unclear due to uncertainty surrounding the regulatory status of cryptocurrency. Where the cryptocurrency or any activity relating to it is subject to regulation (e.g. it has the characteristics of transferable security), then Irish anti-money laundering requirements will apply.

The 5th Anti-Money Laundering Directive (AMLD5) will impose new anti-money laundering requirements on cryptocurrency exchanges and custodians operating in Europe. AMLD5 has not yet been implemented in Ireland.

Promotion and testing

Ireland does not operate a regulatory sandbox, of which cryptocurrency or token issuers could avail themselves. The Irish Department of Finance is establishing an intra-departmental working group with a view to engaging with industry and overseeing developments in virtual currencies and blockchain technology. The Industrial Development Authority, the government agency tasked with attracting inward investment, has led efforts by the Irish Blockchain Expert Group to establish Blockchain Ireland, to help promote and share information on blockchain in Ireland. Further, the CBI recently announced that it was establishing an innovation hub to allow companies to engage directly with the CBI in the areas of Fintech and innovation, including a new dedicated page on its website.

Ownership and licensing requirements

In principle, there are no specific ownership and licensing requirement set out with regard to cryptocurrency. More specifically, while heavily regulated retail funds (e.g. UCITS funds) have specific restrictions on the type and diversity of assets they can hold, which restrictions would likely exclude cryptocurrencies, there are no generally applicable restrictions on investment managers owning cryptocurrencies for investment purposes. In addition, no specific licensing requirements are imposed on anyone who holds cryptocurrency as an investment advisor or fund manager.

However, in stating the above, it should be noted that the CBI has not, to date, confirmed its position on the status of cryptocurrencies as a security, a token or otherwise and as such, until such time as that position is clear, the precise treatment of cryptocurrencies, and any rules that might apply to advising on the issuance of or dealing in the same will ultimately depend on the CBI's determination of that analysis.

Particular areas that regulation might touch on include:

(a) Is the crypto currency itself a security, subject to securities regulations of all forms, or is it something else, a token, another form of right, etc.?

(b) The status of the issuer of a cryptocurrency – i.e. is it an issuer of a security, is it a collective investment scheme, or are the cryptocurrency and the issuer outside of these types of categories?

(c) Is a crypto currency an eligible asset for holding by certain regulated entities including UCITS, Insurance Company, Banks, etc.?

In relation to the last category above, this question is likely only to be answered by wider EU regulation, which is likely to follow only after an exhaustive analysis of the first two questions. As things stand, cryptocurrencies do not fall within the categories of eligible assets for the above.

In relation to the issuer status, the CBI has not yet provided any guidance as to their thoughts on whether certain coin offerings creating a crypto currency may effectively be structured to come within AIF or Investment Company definitions, i.e. be defined as a "Fund".

Applying Fund definitions to what is traditionally seen in ICOs, it would seem to be a difficult argument to make to suggest that the purpose of the undertaking was collective investment, and the entities do not usually seek to pool investors' funds to provide a pooled return, rather they are often a commercial undertaking. In addition, although it might be said that capital was being raised from a number of investors, it is not usually being invested in accordance with a defined investment policy, nor is that capital being invested for the benefit of those investors.

While tokens may ultimately be sold in a secondary market for profit, the schemes themselves do not seek to provide a pooled return as such and in addition, it does not appear that any eventual price for the token would be based on the value of the assets into which investors' capital was invested and, furthermore, there is a case to say that the underlying assets are those of a normal commercial business developing its own products and services, rather than assets being bought, held and sold primarily to provide a pooled return.

Therefore, while this has not been the subject of regulatory or other decision to date, traditional forms of initial coin offerings would not appear to be Funds (AIFs under the EU rules regarding same).

Finally, the analysis of cryptocurrencies as a security may well be undertaken on a case-by-case basis, with the specific characteristics of individual currencies being key to a determination of whether they are a security issued by a company, and as such subject to the relevant securities laws, or if they are something else.

Mining

There are no restrictions in Ireland on the mining of cryptocurrency. As noted above in the "Cryptocurrency regulation" section, the regulatory status of cryptocurrency in Ireland is uncertain. It is likely that the focus going forward will be on securities law.

Mining of cryptocurrency is a technical process relating to the release of new cryptocurrency and the tracking of cryptocurrency transactions on a blockchain. Where the cryptocurrency is a form of transferable security, the mining activity could be viewed as a form of securities settlement system. However, as the mining is carried out on a decentralised basis, it does not fit neatly into any existing regime for securities settlement. On that basis, we would view mining as an unregulated activity under Irish law.

Border restrictions and declaration

In Ireland, there are no border restrictions or obligations which are specifically aimed at cryptocurrencies. The traditional reporting requirements for "cash" (which is defined as currency, cheques and money orders or promissory notes) when entering or leaving the European Union do not apply to virtual or cryptocurrencies. This is because they are deemed to be neither "cash" nor "currency".

Reporting requirements

In respect of financial regulation, there are currently no specific reporting requirements relating to cryptocurrencies. (See "Money transmission laws and anti-money laundering requirements".) Where the cryptocurrency or any activity related to it is subject to regulation, then Irish anti-money laundering requirements will apply. This will include obligations to submit suspicious transaction reports to the Garda Síochana and the Revenue Commissioners.

Estate planning and testamentary succession

As a general rule, a person can devolve their assets by a will in any jurisdiction, although it is common to have a complementary will or similar document in jurisdictions in which significant assets are located. As mentioned above, the situs of cryptocurrencies remains an area of discussion, so this will be a matter that will evolve in time.

From an inheritance tax perspective, Irish inheritance tax can arise if any of the following are relevant:

- Irish disponer;
- Irish beneficiary; or
- Irish property.

In the case of individuals with a presence but perhaps not fully within the tax net in Ireland, the situs of cryptocurrencies will be an important consideration.

Acknowledgments

The authors acknowledge with thanks the contribution to this chapter by:

Ian Dillon
Tel: +353 1 920 1788 / Email: ian.dillon@arthurcox.com

Ian is a senior member of the firm's Asset Management & Investment Funds Group with experience in all aspects of Irish fund law and regulation. Ian's particular focus is on alternative investments including all aspects of AIFMD as well as hedge, real asset, credit, private equity and liquid fund formation. In addition, Ian has advised on the funding of initial coin offerings and issuers including in relation to their regulatory status.

Declan McBride
Tel: +353 1 920 1065 / Email: declan.mcbride@arthurcox.com

Declan is a senior member of the Financial Regulation Group. He advises a wide range of domestic and international financial institutions. Declan's experience includes providing advice on authorisation requirements, anti-money laundering, payment services, Central Bank of Ireland investigations and compliance with conduct of business rules.

Maura McLaughlin, Partner
Tel: +353 1 920 1182 / Email: maura.mclaughlin@arthurcox.com
Maura advises international and domestic listed, public and private companies, as well as public sector bodies, on all aspects of company law and a wide range of commercial matters, as well as advising listed companies on compliance and governance issues. She has extensive experience of advising on public and private mergers and acquisitions, with particular emphasis on takeovers, schemes of arrangement and mergers. Maura has employed this experience to achieve clients' strategic objectives, notably in the design and implementation of structures permitting the inversion or migration of holding companies to Ireland. Equity capital markets work is another area of focus: Maura regularly advises on Irish securities laws, and has acted for companies, investors and underwriters on listings and fundraisings. Prior to joining the firm, Maura worked for Linklaters' London office.

Pearse Ryan, Partner
Tel: +353 1 920 1180 / Email: pearse.ryan@arthurcox.com
Pearse is a partner in the Technology & Innovation Group and member of the firms cross-departmental FinTech Group and Cyber Security Group. Pearse specialises in the areas of digital transformation/cloud computing, commercialisation of technology innovation/technology related IPR, computer security/fraud, cyber insurance, e-commerce and Fintech. Pearse is a member of the Irish Blockchain Expert Group, as well as the new Lex Mundi Blockchain Group. Pearse is a frequent writer and speaker on Fintech and cyber security topics. This includes recurring speaking slots with the Incorporated Law Society of Ireland (PPCII and Diploma courses) and The Honorable Society of King's Inns (Advanced Diploma in White Collar Crime). Pearse was a part-time lecturer 2017/2018 on the National College of Ireland new MSc in Fintech.

Caroline Devlin, Partner
Tel: +353 1 920 1224 / Email: caroline.devlin@arthurcox.com
Caroline is Co Chair of the Arthur Cox Tax Group, and is an experienced partner in taxation in particular in financial services issues. She is a member of the Law Society Taxation Committee, and represents the Law Society in many of its dealings with the Irish Revenue Commissioners. She is editor and co-author of the Institute of Tax publication, *The Law and Practice of Stamp Duty*. Caroline advises domestic and international clients on tax planning, including in particular financial services, also involving cryptocurrencies and ICOs, along with other raising capital products for companies and financial institutions. She is very experienced in advising clients in the most efficient manner on establishing in Ireland.

Arthur Cox

Ten Earlsfort Terrace, Dublin 2, D02 T380, Ireland
Tel: +353 1 920 1000 / Fax: +353 1 920 1020 / URL: www.arthurcox.com

Japan

Taro Awataguchi
Anderson Mōri & Tomotsune

Government attitude and definition

General overview

With the steep rise of the Bitcoin price and increasing enthusiasm for initial coin offerings ("**ICO**"), the Japanese cryptocurrency market has seen explosive growth in 2017. It is often said that Japan has become one of the largest cryptocurrency markets in the world.

The Japanese government intends to support and encourage the sound growth of cryptocurrency business. Actually, Japan is the first country in the world to have enacted a law defining Virtual Currency as a legal term, and requires an entity to register as a Virtual Currency Exchange Service Provider in order to provide Virtual Currency Exchange Services to residents in Japan. The definition of these terms will be discussed in detail in "**Cryptocurrency regulation**".

The purpose of the Japanese government's immediate legislation above is to: (i) protect customers of cryptocurrency exchanges; and (ii) attend to anti-money laundering and combating the financing of terrorism ("**AML/CFT**").

Looking back on history, in February 2014, a Japanese company named MTGOX Co., Ltd ("**MTGOX**"), the world's largest exchange at that time providing convertible cryptocurrency exchange services between cryptocurrencies and fiat currencies, filed for civil rehabilitation proceedings with the Tokyo District Court. Through the proceedings, money (fiat currencies) and bitcoins which actually remained in the bankruptcy estate were found to be far less than the amount which had been escrowed by the customers. The refund claims of MTGOX customers were treated as bankruptcy claims (unsecured ordinary claims) in the bankruptcy proceedings, and hence the creditors were forced to incur loss in the proceedings. This particular case led the Japanese government to recognise the intense necessity to protect customers of cryptocurrency exchanges.

In addition, in 2015, following the Leaders' Declaration at the G7 Elmau Summit, the Financial Action Task Force ("**FATF**") published "Guidance for a Risk-based Approach to Virtual Currencies" ("**FATF Guidance**") in June 2015, which requested any virtual currency exchange to be registered and/or licensed, and to comply with regulations on money laundering and terrorist financing, including customer identification obligations.

Given these circumstances, a bill to amend the Payment Services Act and the Act on Prevention of Transfer of Criminal Proceeds was submitted to the Japanese Diet on March 4, 2016, and passed the Diet on May 25, 2016. The amended laws came into force on April 1, 2017.

Since the enforcement of the laws, 16 cryptocurrency exchanges have been registered with the Financial Services Agency of Japan (the "**FSA**") as Virtual Currency Exchange Service Providers by the end of 2017.

Recent developments

In January 2018, however, Coincheck, Inc. ("**Coincheck**"), one of the largest cryptocurrency exchanges in Japan, announced that it had lost approximately US$530 million worth of cryptocurrencies through a hacking attack on its systems.

As mentioned above, the purpose of the laws was to protect exchange customers from such an incident; however, a hacking incident occurred again in Japan after all. This incident became a social problem because the exchange had a number of users in Japan, and caused FSA to take stricter approach against the exchanges and applicants for registration. After the incident, FSA made intensive on-site and off-site inspections on the exchanges including Coincheck, and approval of new registration has been suspended for more than six months, although a number of applicants have filed and waited for registration. Coincheck was finally acquired by Monex Group Inc., one of the largest online brokerage companies in Japan, in April 2018.

Given the incident, on March 8, FSA formulated a study group on Virtual Currency Exchange Services, etc. in order to address outstanding issues including many findings through on-site inspections against the exchanges, and the circumstances surrounding cryptocurrencies being used for the purpose of speculation rather than settlement. As of June 30, 2018, four sessions have been held since April 10, 2018.

The incident also accelerated integration of the exchange industry. Japan Virtual Currency Exchange Association ("**JVCEA**") was established on March 29, 2018, and all the 16 Virtual Currency Exchange Services Providers have participated as members. JVCEA aims at being appointed by FSA as the self-regulatory organisation under the Payment Services Act.

Furthermore, on June 22, 2018, pursuant to the Payment Services Act, FSA took administrative actions against six Virtual Currency Exchange Service Providers, ordering improvement of their business operations based on the findings from FSA's on-site and off-site inspections, in which the entities were found to have failed to establish an effective management structure to ensure appropriate and reliable business operations.

June 22, 2018 was also an important date for Japanese cryptocurrency history because the Tokyo District Court commenced civil rehabilitation proceedings of MTGOX on that date. As mentioned above, MTGOX first filed for civil rehabilitation proceedings in February 2014, but at that time it was found to be impossible to formulate the rehabilitation plan and the proceeding was converted to liquidation-type bankruptcy in April 2014. However, under the Bankruptcy Act of Japan, a bankruptcy claim, including Bitcoin refund claims, must be evaluated in Japanese yen as of the commencement of the case, which is a much lower amount than the current market price of Bitcoin. In addition, there are some creditors who prefer distribution by Bitcoin than cash, the legality of which was questioned under the bankruptcy proceedings. Hence, a petition for commencement of the civil rehabilitation was filed by some creditors with the court in November 2017. The court, after appointment of the examiner and receipt of the examiner report, ordered commencement of the civil rehabilitation proceedings of MTGOX on June 22, 2018. The creditors, even if they have already filed a proof of claim in the previous bankruptcy proceedings, need to file it again in the new civil rehabilitation proceedings to make sure of their positions. The bar date of filing the proof of rehabilitation claim is October 22, 2018.

To sum up, after the Coincheck incident, FSA took a stringent approach towards the cryptocurrency industry. Given these circumstances, it is expected that mergers and acquisitions of the registered exchanges will be active in 2018 and going forward.

Very recently, on August 10, 2018, FSA published an interim report which outlines the problems found from the inspections of cryptocurrency exchanges. FSA uses the term "crypto-assets", which includes Virtual Currencies, for the first time in the report. The report points out that the total assets of the exchanges expanded rapidly to 533% on average in one year, but their internal control systems have not kept up with the rapid expansion. According to the report, through the inspections of the exchanges, there was found to be: insufficient evaluation of the risks of each's crypto-assets; improper sale of the crypto-assets; advertisement without establishment of internal control systems; insufficiency of countermeasures against AML/CFT; insufficiency of segregation of assets; insufficiency of security personnel; insufficiency of control over outsourcees; insufficiency of internal audit; insufficiency of corporate governance; and so forth.

FSA said in the report that, given the findings, it will deepen its monitoring of Virtual Currency Exchange Service Providers and substantialise the examination of applicants for registration. As of August 10, the number of Virtual Currency Exchange Service Providers is still 16, but recently FSA has resumed the examination of applicants. FSA reflected the findings to the examination, and broadened the contents of the questionnaire to applicants (the number of questions increased from 166 to approximately 400). It is expected that FSA's examination of the applicants will be tightened in the future for the purpose of sound growth of the cryptocurrency market.

Central Bank's thoughts toward cryptocurrencies

Under Japanese law, cryptocurrency is neither treated as "money" nor equated with fiat currency. There is no cryptocurrency that is backed by the Japanese government or the central bank of Japan (the Bank of Japan, "**BOJ**"). According to a speech on April 16, 2018 by the deputy governor of BOJ, BOJ does not have a plan to issue its own digital currency at this juncture because the issuance of central bank digital currencies for general use could be analogous to allowing households and firms to directly have accounts in the central bank and it may have a large impact on the two-tiered currency system and private banks' financial intermediation.

Cryptocurrency regulation

Under Japanese law, "Virtual Currency" is not listed as "Securities" defined in the Financial Instruments and Exchange Act (Please note, however, that a certain type of token may be subject to regulation of the Act, as discussed later in "**Sales regulation**"). The Payment Services Act defines "Virtual Currency", and requires a person who provides Virtual Currency Exchange Services to be registered with FSA. A person conducting Virtual Currency Exchange Services without registration will be subject to criminal proceedings and punishment.

Therefore, the definitions of Virtual Currency and Virtual Currency Exchange Services are very important.

Definition of Virtual Currency

The term "Virtual Currency" is defined in the Payment Services Act as:

(i)   proprietary value that may be used to pay an unspecified person the price of any goods purchased or borrowed or any services provided and which may be sold to or purchased from an unspecified person (limited to that recorded on electronic devices or other objects by electronic means and excluding Japanese and other foreign currencies and Currency Denominated Assets; the same applies in the following item) and that may be transferred using an electronic data processing system; or

(ii) proprietary value that may be exchanged reciprocally for proprietary value specified in the preceding item with an unspecified person and that may be transferred using an electronic data processing system.

Though the definition is complicated, in short, a cryptocurrency which is usable as a payment method to an unspecified person and not denominated in fiat currencies falls under Virtual Currency. For example, Bitcoin, Litecoin, Dogecoin, Ether and XRP fall under Virtual Currencies.

"Currency Denominated Assets" means any assets which are denominated in Japanese or other foreign currency, and which do not fall under the definition of Virtual Currency. For example, prepaid e-money cards usually fall under Currency Denominated Assets. If a coin issued by a bank is guaranteed to have a certain value of fiat currency, such a coin will likely be treated not as Virtual Currency but as Currency Denominated Assets. Tether (USDT), assuming that it is pegged with USD, is not likely to fall under the definition of Virtual Currency.

Definition of Virtual Currency Exchange Services

The term "Virtual Currency Exchange Services" means any of the following acts carried out as a business:

(i)   sale and purchase of Virtual Currency or exchange of Virtual Currency for other Virtual Currency;

(ii) intermediary (*bai-kai*), brokerage (*tori-tsugi*) or delegation (*dai-ri*) for the acts listed in (i) above; or

(iii) management of users' money or Virtual Currency in connection with the acts listed in (i) or (ii) above.

A person so registered with FSA is called a Virtual Currency Exchange Service Provider. Only Virtual Currency Exchange Service Providers may engage in Virtual Currency Exchange Services. A Foreign Virtual Currency Exchange Service Provider who has not obtained registration is prohibited from making solicitations of items (i) through (iii) above to a person in Japan. Advertisements on the websites of Foreign Virtual Currency Exchange Service Providers fall under solicitation except where reasonable measures (such as prevention of access from Japan by blocking Japanese IP addresses and disclaimer language cautioning that residents in Japan may not participate in the transaction) have been taken, so that the advertisements will not lead to transactions related to Virtual Currency Exchange Services with a person in Japan.

The applicant must be (i) a stock company (*kabushiki-kaisha*), or (ii) a Foreign Virtual Currency Exchange Service Provider which has an office(s) and representative in Japan. Accordingly, any foreign entity wishing to register as a Virtual Currency Exchange Service Provider must establish either a subsidiary (in the form of *kabushiki-kaisha*) or a branch in Japan.

In addition, the applicant must have: (a) a sufficient financial basis (minimum capital amount of JPY 10 million and positive minimum net assets); (b) a satisfactory organisational structure and certain systems to conduct the Virtual Currency Exchange Service appropriately and properly; and (c) certain systems to ensure compliance with relevant laws and regulations.

Registration process for the Virtual Currency Exchange Service Provider

The applicant must submit a registration application containing: (i) its trading name and address; (ii) capital amount; (iii) director's name; (iv) the name of the Virtual Currencies to be handled; (v) contents and means of Virtual Currency Exchange Services; (vi) name of outsourcee (if any) and its address; and (vii) method of segregation management and other particulars.

The registration application must be accompanied by documents including: (i) a document pledging that there are no circumstances constituting grounds for refusal of registration; (ii) extract of the certificate of residence of its directors, etc.; (iii) a resume of the directors etc.; (iv) a list of shareholders; (v) financial documents; (vi) documents containing particulars regarding the establishment of a system for ensuring the proper, secure provision/ performance of Virtual Currency Exchange Services; (vii) an organisational chart; (viii) internal rules; and (ix) a form of the contract to be entered into with users.

Practically, during the registration process, FSA requests applicants to fill in the checklist, which consists of approximately 400 questions, in order to confirm that the applicants have established systems to properly and securely perform the Virtual Currency Exchange Service. In addition, FSA separately prepares a detailed progress chart to confirm the checking process. The registration process is a kind of due diligence by FSA, and FSA is deliberate in approving the registration. In substance, the "registration" process is like issuing a "licence".

Upon registration, the registry of Virtual Currency Exchange Service Providers will be made available publicly.

Principal regulation on the Virtual Currency Exchange Service Provider

A Virtual Currency Exchange Service Provider must: (i) take measures necessary to ensure safe management of information; (ii) provide information to users (content of transactions, outline of each Virtual Currency handled by the provider, fees, the amount of cash or Virtual Currency which the provider has received from the user, the date of receipt, transaction records, etc.); (iii) take measures necessary for the protection of users and proper performance of its services; (iv) segregate users' property from its own property (with respect to cash, bank deposit or trust; with respect to Virtual Currency, clear distinction in a manner such that the user's Virtual Currency is immediately identifiable), and regularly undergo an audit of the status of such segregated management by a certified public accountant or audit firm; and (v) establish an internal management system to make fair and appropriate responses to customer complaints and take measures to resolve any disputes through financial ADR proceedings.

Principal supervision on the Virtual Currency Exchange Service Provider

A Virtual Currency Exchange Service Provider must: (i) prepare and maintain books and documents relating to Virtual Currency Exchange Services; (ii) prepare a report on its Virtual Currency Exchange Services for each business year and submit the same to FSA, which must be accompanied by financial documents and a certified public accountant's or audit firm's audit report on such documents; and (iii) prepare a report on the amount or quantity of users' money or Virtual Currency managed by the provider and submit the same to FSA.

When FSA finds it necessary for the proper and secure provision/performance of Virtual Currency Exchange Services, FSA may: (i) order the relevant Virtual Currency Exchange Service Provider to submit reports or materials; (ii) have officials enter its office or other facilities; or (iii) inquire about the status of its business or properties or inspect its books and documents.

FSA may order a Virtual Currency Exchange Service Provider to take necessary measures to improve its business operation or financial conditions, or other measures necessary for the purpose of supervision.

If a Virtual Currency Exchange Service Provider (i) becomes subject to any of the grounds for refusal of registration, (ii) obtains registration through fraudulent means, or (iii) violates the Payment Services Act or an order issued pursuant to the act or a disposition given pursuant thereto, FSA may revoke the registration or order the Virtual Currency Exchange Service Provider to suspend all or part of its services for a specified period of not more than six months. When FSA renders such disposition, it must give public notice to that effect.

Sales regulation

Overview

Cryptocurrencies (including Virtual Currencies) do not fall within the definition of "Securities" under the Financial Instruments and Exchange Act of Japan, and sale of Virtual Currencies or tokens (including ICO) are not specifically or directly regulated by the Financial Instruments and Exchange Act (Please note that a certain type of token may be subject to regulation of the Act as discussed below).

There are various types of tokens issued by way of ICO, and Japanese regulation applicable to ICO varies according to the respective schemes.

Main types of tokens and applicable regulations

1. *Virtual Currency type*

   If the token falls under the definition of Virtual Currency, the Virtual Currency regulation under the Payment Services Act is applicable. Hence, in this case, the token must be sold through a Virtual Currency Exchange Services Provider.

   According to a prevalent view under the current practice, (i) if the tokens issued via ICO are already dealt by Japanese or foreign exchanges, the tokens would fall within a Virtual Currency under the Payment Service Act because there must already exist exchange markets for the tokens, and (ii) even if the tokens are not yet dealt by Japanese or foreign exchanges, in the case where the token issuer does not give substantial restrictions so that they may not be exchanged for Japanese or foreign fiat currencies or Virtual Currencies, the tokens would likely fall within Virtual Currency under the Payment Services Act.

   The Virtual Currency-type tokens issued via ICO would fall within Virtual Currency at the time of issuance, and sale thereof would fall within sale of Virtual Currency. Hence, as a general rule, a token issuer itself must be registered as a Virtual Currency Exchange Service Provider if the token sale (ICO) is targeted to residents in Japan. However, there is a view that if the token issuer completely outsources the token issuance to a reliable ICO platformer which is registered as a Virtual Currency Exchange Service Provider, the token issuer may not need the registration.

2. *Securities (equity interest in an investment fund) type*

   If any distributions paid to token holders are based on the profits of the business conducted by the token issuer and are calculated based on the holder's ownership ratio of the tokens, this type of token may fall under equity interest in an investment fund (collective investment scheme) under the Financial Instruments and Exchange Act. In this case, the token issuer is subject to relevant regulations under the Financial Instruments and Exchange Act.

3. *Prepaid card type*

    If the tokens are similar in nature to prepaid cards and may be used as consideration for goods or services provided by token issuers, they may be regarded as "Prepaid Payment Instruments" (*maebarai-shiki-shiharai-shudan*) and subject to relevant regulation under the Payment Services Act (in this case, regulation on Virtual Currency under the same Act would not be applicable).

Recent developments

On October 27, 2017, FSA made a cautionary announcement on ICO. In the announcement, FSA warns token purchasers about the high-risk nature of a token, including the high volatility of a token price and potential risk of fraud. The announcement states: "You should transact in tokens at your own risk only after sufficiently understanding both the risks noted above and the other relevant details of the ICO. You should also pay careful attention to suspicious solicitation on ICOs."

The FSA announcement also warns token issuers that ICO may fall within the scope of the Payment Services Act or the Financial Instruments and Exchange Act, depending on how they are structured. FSA further warns that, if the ICO has an investment nature, even if the token is purchased by way of Virtual Currencies, the Financial Instruments and Exchange Act will be applicable to a scheme which could be deemed as if it were purchased by way of fiat currencies in substance. FSA also warns token issuers to adequately fulfil their duties required by related laws and regulations (such as making the relevant registrations when their services are regulated by those acts), and that delivering such services without registration is subject to criminal penalties.

Given the prudent attitude of FSA against ICO, there must be an established rule for ICO. In this context, a self-regulatory rule on ICO by the self-regulatory organisation of the Virtual Currency Exchange Service Providers (which is to be appointed by FSA pursuant to the Payment Service Act) is desirable.

In order to conduct ICO in Japan in the form of sale of Virtual Currencies, as a basic rule, the token issuer itself must be registered as Virtual Currency Exchange Service Provider. Although there have been some examples where ICO successfully completed in Japan, as FSA has become deliberate and slow in approving registrations, ICO in Japan have become temporarily slow.

Given the circumstances, there appear some different approaches. If reliable ICO platformers emerge in Japan, then token issuers would become able to outsource token sales to them. Another way is to attempt ICO outside Japan; however, in this case, the token issuer would be prohibited from soliciting residents in Japan unless the issuer is registered as a Virtual Currency Exchange Service Provider. The other way is to consider new funding schemes such as Simple Agreement for Future Tokens ("**SAFT**") and so forth. Mergers and acquisition of Virtual Currency Exchange Service Providers will also be an option.

Taxation

One of the most important issues in Japanese taxation of cryptocurrencies has been the treatment of consumption tax. Under Japanese tax law, sale of cryptocurrencies has been subject to consumption tax to the extent that the office of the transferor is located in Japan.

However, the relevant tax law was amended in 2017. If the sold cryptocurrency is Virtual Currency under the Payment Services Act such as Bitcoin, consumption tax is no longer imposed after July 1, 2017. The National Tax Agency of Japan also announced that gains realised by sale or use of Virtual Currency will be treated as "miscellaneous income" (*zatsu-shotoku*) where the taxpayer is unable to utilise losses elsewhere to offset gains realised by sale or use of the Virtual Currency. Furthermore, inheritance tax will be imposed upon the death of a person who has held the Virtual Currency.

Money transmission laws and anti-money laundering requirements

Money transmission

Under Japanese law, only licensed banks or fund transfer business operators may engage in the business of money remittance transactions. Money remittance transactions mean, according to the Supreme Court precedent, "to undertake the task of transferring funds requested by customers utilising the systems of fund transfer without transporting cash between distant parties, and/or to carry out such task". Technically speaking, Virtual Currency does not fall under the "fund"; however, if the remittance transaction of Virtual Currency contains exchange of fiat currencies in substance, such transaction will likely be deemed to be a money remittance transaction.

Anti-money laundering requirements

Under the Act on Prevention of Transfer of Criminal Proceeds, Virtual Currency Exchange Service Providers are obligated to: (i) verify identification data of the customer and a person who has substantial control over the customer's business for the purpose of conducting the transaction and occupation of business, (ii) prepare verification records and transaction records; (iii) maintain the records for seven years, (iv) report suspicious transactions to the relevant authority, and so forth.

Promotion and testing

On June 15, 2018, the "Basic policy of Regulatory Sandbox scheme in Japan" was announced by the Cabinet Office of Japan. The Regulatory Sandbox is a scheme to implement new outstanding technology such as AI, IoT, big data and blockchain, and is open to ideas for the "testing project" involving any industrial sector, inside and outside Japan.

Ownership and licensing requirements

There is no restriction on an entity simply owning cryptocurrencies for its own investment purpose, or investing in cryptocurrencies for its own dealing purpose. As a general rule, the Virtual Currency regulation under the Payment Services Act will not be applicable unless an entity conducts Virtual Currency Exchange Services as a business. Please note, however, that sale of certain types of tokens may be subject to regulation under the Payment Services Act or Financial Instruments and Exchange Act, as applicable, as discussed in **"Sales regulation"** above.

Mining

Mining of cryptocurrencies is not regulated. Mining in itself does not fall under the definition of a Virtual Currency Exchange Service. Please note, however, that if the mining scheme is formulated as the collective investment scheme and contains sale of equity interest in an investment fund, it is subject to relevant regulation by the Financial Instruments Exchange Act.

Border restrictions and declaration

Border restrictions

Under the Foreign Exchange and Foreign Trade Act of Japan, if a resident or a non-resident has received a payment exceeding JPY30 million made from Japan to a foreign country or made from a foreign country to Japan, the resident or non-resident must report it to the Minister of Finance. If a resident has made a payment exceeding JPY30 million to a non-resident either in Japan or in a foreign country, the same rule shall apply.

Recently, this rule extended to receiving or making payment via Virtual Currency. That is, on May 18, 2018, the Ministry of Japan announced that receipt of payment of Virtual Currency or payment of Virtual Currency, the market price of which exceeds JPY30 million as of the payment date, must be reported to the Minister of Finance.

Declaration

There is no obligation to declare cryptocurrency holdings when crossing Japanese Customs.

Reporting requirements

As explained above, a certain payment or receipt of payment exceeding JPY30 million, either by fiat currencies or Virtual Currencies, is subject to a reporting obligation to the Minister of Finance under the Foreign Exchange and Foreign Trade Act.

A Virtual Currency Exchange Service Provider must report to the relevant authority if it detects a suspicious transaction.

Estate planning and testamentary succession

There has been no established law or court precedent with respect to the treatment of cryptocurrencies under Japanese succession law. Under the Civil Code of Japan, inheritance (i.e., succession of assets to heir(s)) commences simultaneously upon death of the decedent. Theoretically, cryptocurrencies will be succeeded to heir(s), however, given the anonymous nature of cryptocurrencies, specification and collection of cryptocurrencies as the inherited property will be a material issue unless the relevant private key or password could be known to heir(s). On the other hand, even if the private key or password is unknown, to the extent that the inherited property can be specified, theoretically, inheritance tax may be imposed. An enclosed and notarised testament may be one of the solutions for these issues, but Japanese legal circumstances must be improved to attend to these new issues.

Taro Awataguchi
Tel: +81 3 6775 1104 / Email: taro.awataguchi@amt-law.com

Taro Awataguchi, a fintech partner at Anderson Mōri & Tomotsune ("AMT"), has extensive experience in advising clients, including Virtual Currency Exchange Service Providers (i.e., registered providers) and applicants for the registration, on various matters related to fintech and cryptocurrencies.

AMT is one of the largest legal firms (Big Four) in Japan, and Taro, as a member of AMT's fintech team which has one of the leading fintech practices in Japan, provides innovative, up-to-date legal advice to clients in this fast-growing and cutting-edge industry.

In addition, Taro was appointed by the Tokyo District Court as the trustee in bankruptcy proceedings of a Bitcoin-related company, where various legal issues and disputes related to Bitcoin were involved. He is a frequent speaker and author in the fintech field. For example, he made a speech on "Cryptocurrencies" at the American Bar Association ("ABA") Section of International Law 2016 Fall Meeting held in Tokyo, and he is a co-author of Japan Chapter of the *International Comparative Legal Guide to: Fintech 2017 and 2018*.

Taro already has extensive experience in the field of banking, financing, financial regulation and insolvency as well. He is one of the pioneers of Asset-Based Lending practice in Japan, and serves as the head of managing committee of the ABL Association. He is recognised by Best Lawyers (banking and financing law). He is noted for successful creditor representations in various cross-border insolvency matters, including representation of Japan's first-ever secured creditors' committee in getting full recovery from the corporate reorganisation proceedings of Spansion Japan Limited.

Anderson Mōri & Tomotsune

Otemachi Park Building, 1-1-1 Otemachi, Chiyoda-ku, Tokyo, 100-8136, Japan
Tel: +81 3 6775 1000 / URL: www.amt-law.com

Jersey

Christopher Griffin
Carey Olsen

Jersey's legal and regulatory framework in relation to blockchain and cryptocurrencies can be divided up into the following areas:

(a) investment funds;

(b) the regulation of managers;

(c) Initial Coin Offerings ("**ICOs**"); and

(d) Virtual Currency Exchanges ("**VCEs**").

Set out below is an overview of the regulatory framework for each of these areas.

Investment funds

Promoters of cryptocurrency funds can take advantage of Jersey's well established funds regulatory regime. Indeed, Jersey stole a march on its competitor jurisdictions as a crypto-friendly jurisdiction when the Island's regulator, the Jersey Financial Services Commission (the "**JFSC**"), approved the launch of the world's first regulated Bitcoin investment fund, GABI Plc. At the time, Bitcoin was far less well known and was regarded by the mainstream as a fringe asset class. GABI Plc's regulatory approval was regarded by many industry commentators as a statement of intent from the Island.

Cryptocurrency fund promoters typically make use of one of the following regulatory regimes to establish their investment funds:

(a) the Jersey Private Fund (up to 50 investors); or

(b) the Jersey Expert Fund (unlimited number of investors) – GABI Plc was approved as an Expert Fund.

A brief summary of each regime is set out below:

Jersey Private Fund – Key features

*   Maximum of 50 investors at any time and a maximum of 50 initial offers, and must not be listed on a stock exchange.

*   May be open or closed for redemptions by investors.

*   Investors must qualify as "professional' investors and/or subscribe for interests with a value of at least £250,000, and sign a simple investment warning (usually included in the subscription document).

*   No investment or borrowing restrictions.

*   A Jersey regulated administrator must be appointed as the fund's designated service provider ("**DSP**") to ensure that the necessary criteria and applicable anti-money laundering legislation are complied with, to carry out due diligence on the promoter

and to file an annual compliance statement.

- A non-Jersey administrator can be appointed to administer the fund (but not to act as the DSP).

- Jersey "special purpose" vehicles established to act as service providers (such as a general partner, trustee or investment manager/adviser) are generally not required to be regulated.

Due to requirements imposed on Jersey as conditions to its EU/EEA market access, additional requirements apply if the fund is actively "marketed" into the EU/EEA (as defined in the AIFMD):

- *Not actively marketed into the EU/EEA*

  Where the fund will not be marketed into the EU/EEA:

  - There is no need to prepare an offering memorandum.

  - There is no need for Jersey directors or service-providers, and no audit requirement.

  - The fund is not regulated by the JFSC on an ongoing basis.

- *Marketed into the EU/EEA (AIFM is sub-threshold)*

  Funds which are to be actively "marketed" into the EU/EEA in accordance with the AIFMD and which have appointed a sub-threshold AIFM:

  - For a Jersey AIFM, a simple JFSC consent is required (there is no ongoing regulation).

  - Minimal requirements will apply under the Code of Practice for Alternative Investment Funds and AIF Services Business published by the JFSC.

- *Marketed into the EU/EEA (AIFM is not sub-threshold)*

  Funds which are to be actively "marketed" into the EU/EEA in accordance with the AIFMD through national private placement regimes (or when available, through passporting):

  - JFSC consent obtained in 48 hours (draft PPM to be filed with the JFSC).

  - An "AIF Certificate" is needed to permit EU/EEA marketing. For the ongoing JFSC, regulation is limited to compliance with the limited applicable AIFMD provisions.

  - The JFSC assesses the suitability of the fund's promoter, having regard to its track record and relevant experience, reputation, financial resources and spread of ultimate ownership, in light of the level of sophistication of the target investor group.

  - Where the AIFM is a Jersey entity (such as a general partner or trustee or an external manager), it must be regulated by the JFSC, in accordance with the AIFMD.

Jersey Expert Fund – Key features

Expert Funds are attractive for non-retail schemes aimed at "Expert Investors". Expert Funds can be established quickly and cost-effectively and must comply with the Jersey Expert Fund Guide (the "**EF Guide**").

- *JFSC approval process*

  The JFSC does not need to review the fund structure, documentation or the promoter. Instead the fund administrator certifies to the JFSC that the fund complies with the EF Guide and, once the certification and the fund's offer document are filed, the JFSC aims for a three-day turnaround on the application for approval. The EF Guide provides fund promoters with certainty, efficiency and cost-effectiveness in the establishment of a new fund.

- *What is an Expert Fund?*

  The definition of "Expert Investor" is crucial. An investor must fall within any one of the 10 categories, which include a person or entity: in the business of buying or selling investments; with a net worth of more than US $1m, excluding principal place of residence; with at least US $1m available for investment; connected with the fund or a fund service provider (there is a flexible approach to carried-interest arrangements); or (the simplest category) making an investment or commitment of US $100,000 or more (or currency equivalent).

  The investment manager/adviser must be established in an OECD member or any other state or jurisdiction with which the JFSC has entered into a Memorandum of Understanding or equivalent; regulated in its home jurisdiction (or, if not required to be, approved by the JFSC, which usually occurs on an expedited basis); without convictions or disciplinary sanctions; solvent; and experienced in using similar investment strategies to those adopted by the Expert Fund. If the investment manager/adviser does not meet these requirements, it may approach the JFSC on a case-by-case basis. Of course, if permission is granted then, absent any material change, the investment manager/adviser will not need specific approval to establish further Expert Funds. An investment manager/adviser is not required for certain self-managed funds, such as direct real estate or feeder funds.

  A small number of additional requirements are imposed on Expert Funds:

  - Two Jersey-resident directors with appropriate experience must be appointed to the board of the general partner/trustee/fund company.
  - A licensed Jersey administrator or manager (which may be a special purpose vehicle) must be appointed (save in the case of a unit trust, where a trustee is often the only required Jersey service provider).
  - A Jersey custodian or (in the case of hedge funds) an international prime broker must be appointed for funds which are open for redemption at the option of investors.
  - The offer document must set out all material information in respect of the fund.
  - Investors must sign a prescribed form of investment warning (usually contained in the subscription document).
  - The fund must be audited.

- *Flexibility*

  There are no investment or borrowing restrictions imposed on the fund, nor is there any limitation on the number of investors such a fund may have.

  The EF Guide aims to provide a "safe harbour" available to the majority of non-retail funds. On occasion, where derogations from the EF Guide are required, these are considered on an expedited basis.

- *Ongoing requirements*

  Ongoing requirements are limited. Future changes to the fund generally do not require regulatory approval unless they are contrary to the EF Guide or there is a change to the fund's directors or service providers.

- *AIFMD*

  Expert Funds are eligible to be marketed into the EU/EEA in accordance with the AIFMD through national private placement regimes (and, when available, third country passporting).

Jersey fund managers

Subject to the requirements applicable to the fund's regulatory category, a manager/ investment manager of a Jersey fund can be: (i) an entity with proper physical presence in Jersey; or (ii) a "special purpose" Jersey vehicle.

AIFMD

Jersey entities which act as the manager of a fund (the "AIFM" as defined in the AIFMD) are subject to regulation by the JFSC.

- Managers which are already regulated (such as those acting for Expert Funds) need only comply with the applicable requirements of the AIFMD.

- For other managers (such as Jersey "special purpose" companies established to act for Jersey Private Funds):

   (a) a "light touch" approach applies where the AIFM will qualify as a "sub-threshold" manager (by reference to value of the funds under management);

   (b) otherwise, the usual 10-day application process applies, including prior submission of personal questionnaires (see paragraph headed, "Establishing a special purpose vehicle manager").

Manager of a Jersey Private Fund

Subject to any AIFMD related requirements (see "**AIFMD**" in this section, above), managers which are special purpose companies established in Jersey are usually exempt from regulation using an applicable exemption, for example:

- for services between "connected companies";

- an exemption for trustees and general partners; or

- where the fund is a "professional investor regulated scheme", which requires only that the investor sign a simple specified form of investment warning and either: (i) qualify as a "professional investor" (which includes "a person whose ordinary activities involve the person in acquiring, holding, managing or disposing of investments (as principal or agent) for the purposes of the person's business or who it is reasonable to expect will acquire, hold, arrange or dispose of investments (as principal or agent) for the purposes of that business"); or (ii) make a minimum investment of £250,000 or currency equivalent.

Please note that a regulated "designated service provider" (i.e. Jersey administrator) will also be needed.

Establishing a special purpose vehicle manager

Where a special purpose Jersey entity needs to be regulated as described above (for example, where acting for an Expert Fund or acting as an AIFM which is not "sub-threshold"), a simplified licensing regime applies:

- The entity is administered by a regulated Jersey administrator, which assumes responsibility for ongoing regulatory compliance and often provides one or more directors.

- Minimum capital requirement is usually £25,000 (or £10,000 where acting only for one or more related Expert Funds, other than for AIFMs where £125,000 is required (increasing where assets under management exceed £250,000)).

- Each director of the entity (and each of its beneficial owners with a 10% or greater interest) is required to be approved by the JFSC. As international regulatory checks often take three weeks or more to complete for individuals who have not already been approved by the JFSC, these should be completed and submitted as early as possible.

- The JFSC licensing process for a manager to an Expert Fund under the Financial Services law typically takes two weeks.

Initial Coin Offerings

There has been an explosion in the number of ICOs in the last year. Founded principally on the Ethereum blockchain, the use of the "smart contract" allows an ICO promoter to mint his own coin or token in exchange for Ether subscriptions. Tokens can be "utility" in nature, allowing the holder access to new software or to a particular platform, or they may give the holder certain economic rights. In essence, ICOs are cryptographic crowdfunding, and regulators are understandably nervous because they do not conform to traditional ways of raising capital, around which the word's capital markets and securities regulations have been crafted.

All jurisdictions have scrambled to get up to speed with ICOs, with varying degrees of risk appetite. While some regulators have prohibited ICOs entirely and others have given *carte blanche* to almost any ICO promoter, the JFSC has sensibly recognised that there is a middle ground; ICOs are here to stay and those ICOs with proper substance, and which are backed by a credible promoter, should be nurtured.

Against this backdrop, Carey Olsen advised on launch of Jersey's first ICO in December 2017, ARC Reserve Currency. ARC is an asset-backed "stablecoin" crypto-currency which is designed to act like a currency without the volatility spikes one sees in other cryptocurrencies such as Bitcoin. Against a very tight timeline, and with other competitor coins about to be launched, Carey Olsen worked closely with the JFSC to ensure that the ARC coin launched ahead of time and with a degree of regulatory scrutiny which should give prospective purchasers a degree of comfort that is not available in other jurisdictions. Very recently, Carey Olsen built on its ICO expertise by advising on AX1 token, an ICO designed to raise capital for investment in a crypto-currency mining operation based in the UK.

In both instances, the JFSC adopted a purposive and pragmatic approach to approving the ICOs, focusing on consumer protection and anti-money laundering and having regard to the fact that ICO promoters want to use a Jersey-incorporated issuer because of Jersey's reputation as a well-regulated and reputable jurisdiction.

In order to give prospective ICO investors a degree of disclosure and comfort that may not be available in many other jurisdictions – and being mindful of the guiding principle pursuant to which the JFSC discharges its functions as the Island's financial services regulator – the JFSC sets out certain requirements on an ICO issuer.

JFSC requirements on a Jersey ICO issuer

The ICO issuer is required to:

- be a Jersey company;
- receive consent from the JFSC before it undertakes any form of activity (see "Application process", below);
- comply with the JFSC's Sound Business Practice Policy (see below);
- apply relevant AML/CFT requirements to either purchase tokens from or sell tokens back to the issuer;
- appoint a Jersey-licensed administrator;
- appoint and maintain a Jersey-resident director on the board;
- be subject to an ongoing annual audit requirement;

- have procedures and processes in place to (i) mitigate and manage the risk of retail investors investing inappropriately in the ICO, and (ii) ensure retail investors understand the risks involved;
- prepare an information memorandum which complies with certain content requirements required under Jersey company law; and
- ensure that any marketing material is clear, fair and not misleading, and include in any such materials certain prescribed consumer warnings.

Security *vs.* non-security tokens

Before the issuer can undertake any activity, it requires a consent from the JFSC under the Island's statutory instrument governing the raising of capital, the Control of Borrowing (Jersey) Order 1958 ("**COBO**"). The type of COBO consent granted by the JFSC will depend on whether the token is categorised as a "security" under COBO.

While there is no precise definition of what constitutes a "security" under COBO, the Guidance Note stipulates that a token which has one or more of the following characteristics will be regarded by the JFSC as a "security":

- a right to participate in the profits/earnings of the issuer or a related entity;
- a claim on the issuer or a related party's assets;
- a general commitment from the issuer to redeem tokens in the future;
- a right to participate in the operation or management of the issuer or a related party; and
- an expectation of a return on the amount paid for the tokens.

Importantly and helpfully, there is an express statement in the Guidance Note that the JFSC will not treat a utility token (i.e. a token conferring a usage right and with no economic or voting rights) as a security token solely by reason of the fact that it might be traded in the secondary market (e.g. listed on the cryptocurrency exchange).

Whether or not a token is a "security" under COBO makes no difference as to the requirements imposed on an issuer by the JFSC.

Application process

Application for the issuer's COBO consent is to be accompanied by analysis prepared by the issuer's legal advisers outlining:

- the proposed activity including relevant timelines;
- details of the issuer and the ICO;
- rationale for the ICO, amount to be raised and use of proceeds;
- a summary of the features of the tokens;
- a summary of the token purchase and redemption processes;
- the service providers to the issuer;
- the relationship between issuer and holder of tokens;
- the management of underlying assets and security rights over such assets (if any) for holders of the tokens;
- how the activity will be wound up/dissolved and assets (if any) distributed to the holders of the tokens; and
- a Jersey legal and regulatory analysis, including consideration of relevant legislation or other regulatory laws (for example, whether the ICO is a "collective investment fund" under Jersey law).

Following grant of the COBO consent, the issuer must seek the prior consent of the JFSC to any material change to the matters contained in the application.

JFSC's Sound Business Practice Policy

The Guidance Note makes clear that an ICO is a "sensitive activity" under the JFSC's Sound Business Practice Policy.

The practical consequence of this is that certain AML/CFT obligations are imposed on the issuer, such as to carry out checks on: (i) the purchasers of the tokens who purchase coins directly from the issuer; and (ii) the holders of tokens issued by the issuer in the event they are sold back to the issuer. In such circumstances, the issuer will be required to obtain information to: (a) establish and obtain evidence to verify identity; and (b) establish and, depending on the level of risk, obtain evidence to verify the source of funds and source of wealth.

Ongoing requirements imposed on the issuer

- The JFSC's prior consent is required for any change of Jersey administrator or Jersey-resident director.

- The board of the issuer is required to advise the JFSC promptly if the issuer defaults on any token issued.

- The directors of the issuer are required to make an annual confirmation to the JFSC (at the same time as the normal company annual return) that, to the best of their knowledge and belief, there have been no breaches of the conditions set out on the issuer's COBO consent.

Virtual Currency Exchanges

At a very early stage, the JFSC saw that the volume and value of trading in crypto-currencies was increasing hugely, as people sought to convert their crypto into real-world 'fiat' currency and *vice versa*. Recognising that there was a regulatory gap, the JFSC brought those enterprises that provide so-called VCE services under Jersey's regulatory umbrella way back in 2016, requiring VCEs to comply with Jersey law and regulation aimed at preventing and detecting money laundering and terrorist financing.

The Proceeds of Crime (Miscellaneous Amendments) (Jersey) Regulations 2016 (the "**Regulations**") require VCEs to comply with the Island's laws, regulations, policies and procedures aimed at preventing and detecting money laundering and terrorist financing.

The Regulations also make virtual currency exchange a supervised business and require VCEs to register with and be subject to the supervision of the JFSC.

At the same time, the JFSC recognised that many promoters of VCEs need time to road-test their product without being burdened by the full weight of regulatory compliance. The JFSC therefore allowed VCEs with turnover of less than £150,000 per calendar year to test VCE delivery mechanisms in a live environment without the normal registration requirements and associated costs.

As such, Jersey's VCE regulation balances the need to provide robust regulation with a desire to foster the development of the Island's burgeoning crypto-credentials.

Christopher Griffin
Tel: +44 1534 822256 / Email: christopher.griffin@careyolsen.com
Christopher has broad experience of both general international corporate and funds work with particular expertise in private equity and hedge funds, having spent ten years in the City at Ashurst, RAB Capital plc and most recently at SJ Berwin.

Christopher spearheads Carey Olsen's crypto practice, advising on the launch in 2017 of Coinshares Fund I (a venture cap fund investing in crypto assets) and ARC Reserve Currency, Jersey's first initial coin offering or "ICO". Christopher also advises on all aspects of fund and corporate transactions, including the legal and regulatory aspects of fund launches, and joint ventures. He also has considerable experience in dealing with the Jersey Financial Services Commission in navigating investment vehicles through the Jersey regulatory approval process.

Carey Olsen

47 Esplanade, St Helier, Jersey JE1 0BD, Channel Islands
Tel: +44 1534 888900 / Fax: +44 1534 887744 / URL: www.careyolsen.com

Korea

Jung Min Lee, Samuel Yim & Joon Young Kim
Kim & Chang

Government attitude and definition

There is no statute or guidance from the Korean regulatory authorities that provides a coherent insight on how cryptocurrencies would be classified under Korean law. The Financial Supervisory Service (the "FSS") issued a press release on June 23, 2017 where it announced its views on what cryptocurrencies are *not* from a financial regulatory perspective. Namely, the FSS's position was that cryptocurrencies are not considered: (i) fiat currencies; (ii) prepaid electronic means or electronic currencies; or (iii) financial investment instruments. Unfortunately, the FSS press release did not provide any guidance on how cryptocurrencies *are* classified and in what legal form.

However, the Supreme Court of Korea ruled on May 30, 2018 that cryptocurrencies can be confiscated as criminal proceeds. This decision represents the first time the Supreme Court recognised cryptocurrency as property. However, given the narrow scope of its interpretation, it is unclear what impact this ruling will have on subsequent cryptocurrency regulations in Korea.

The classification of cryptocurrencies from a legal perspective has just begun in Korea and will likely develop in the near future. Other Korean regulatory authorities may have a different view from the FSS's announcement and the legal classification of cryptocurrencies. As a result, there is currently no law or clear guidance from any regulatory authority in Korea that provides clarity on the legal issues relating to cryptocurrencies and how they will be treated under Korean law.

Based on recent events, the Korean government has shown a mixed view on its attitude toward cryptocurrencies. Set forth below are key announcements by the Korean government regarding cryptocurrency.

Margin trading

On September 1, 2017, the Financial Services Commission ("FSC") banned individuals from borrowing funds or cryptocurrency from cryptocurrency exchanges in order to sell them. The FSC declared that such practice violated existing Korean lending/credit laws. The FSC also directed financial institutions to halt all transactions and partnerships that enabled these practices.

ICO ban

On September 4, 2017, the FSC issued a press release banning initial coin offerings ("ICOs") that violate the Financial Investment Services and Capital Markets Act ("FSCMA"), the main securities law in Korea. However, this press release did not explain how and in what context ICOs would be a violation of the FSCMA. The financial regulators' initial position was to penalise ICOs where the tokens are offered in the form of a securities issuance (i.e., the token is classified as a security). Thereafter, on September 29, 2017, the financial regulators announced through a press release that any type of ICOs, including those in the form of securities, would be prohibited.

If coins or tokens are classified as "securities" under the FSCMA, ICOs or token offerings will be subject to the offering restrictions in Korea under the FSCMA. Where the coins or tokens are not classified as "securities" under the FSCMA, though there are no legal grounds for the prohibition and/or enforcement unless there is a violation of existing Korean laws and regulations, there is a possibility that Korean regulators could challenge the legality of the ICO or token offering based on this press release.

Real name verification

On September 4, 2017, the FSC announced it would initiate an identification policy for accounts in cryptocurrency exchanges that required cross-checking user names and account numbers. Accordingly, a "Real Name Verification System" was introduced from January 30, 2018. Under this system, existing anonymous account users can only withdraw money and not make any further deposits. All new users would have to provide actual identification information to open cryptocurrency accounts.

Central bank-backed cryptocurrency

On January 9, 2018, the Bank of Korea ("BOK") launched a task force on cryptocurrency and is reviewing a central bank-backed cryptocurrency as part of the project. In addition, various local governments in Korea are exploring the option of issuing their own cryptocurrency.

Cryptocurrency regulation

There is no existing regulatory regime or statute that specifically regulates cryptocurrency. However, the Korean regulators are likely to apply and/or enforce the existing Korean laws and regulations for cryptocurrencies.

Existing laws

For example, in an ICO, if tokens are classified as "securities" under Korean law, the tokens will then be subject to the offering restrictions in Korea under the FSCMA. Or, even if the tokens are not classified as securities, if the marketing of the tokens in an ICO raises funds from the public with a promise to return the original investment amount, or an amount exceeding such investment in the future, the ICO could be regulated by the Act on the Regulation of Conducting Fundraising Business without Permission.

Pending bills

Currently, there are several cryptocurrency bills proposed at the National Assembly. These bills generally cover, among others, licensing requirements for cryptocurrency businesses, anti-money laundering requirements, consumer protection, cybersecurity requirements for cryptocurrency exchanges, and damage compensation for consumer losses. It is unclear when or if these pending bills, in their current form, will be enacted into law in Korea.

Sales regulation

As explained above, if tokens are classified as "securities", the tokens will be subject to the offering or sales restrictions in Korea under the FSCMA. Whether a token will be classified as a security will depend on the facts and circumstances of the offering of the tokens. Under the FSCMA, an offer or sale of securities (tokens) to 50 or more non-accredited investors (excluding professional investors) would be regarded as a public offering and be subject to offering restrictions under the FSCMA. In a public offering of securities (tokens) in Korea, an onshore or offshore issuer must file a securities registration statement for the securities (tokens) to be offered in Korea with the FSC.

However, cryptocurrencies such as Bitcoin have not been classified as securities at this time, and have not been subject to the FSCMA. Also, cryptocurrencies are not yet explicitly subject to the commodities laws in Korea. Therefore, it is unclear which laws would regulate the sale of Bitcoin or other tokens since there has not been any application of Korean laws thus far to the sale of Bitcoin or other tokens.

Taxation

The Ministry of Strategy and Finance has announced that plans for the taxation of cryptocurrency are being developed but no decisions have been made. Meanwhile, the National Tax Service ("NTS") published its preliminary assessment of taxation on cryptocurrency after its 2017 annual forum. This assessment is not official policy but is the only published position/research on cryptocurrency taxation by the Korean government.

NTS Preliminary Assessment on Cryptocurrency Tax

Type	Rate	Assessment
Corporate Income Tax	11%–27.5%	Taxable under current law
Corporate or Individual VAT	10%	Undecided
Income Tax	6.6%–46.2%	Taxable under current law
Capital Gains Tax	6.6%–46.2%	Undecided, but for retail investors, levying Capital Gains Tax is advisable
Inheritance and Gift Tax	10%–50%	Taxable under current law

Money transmission laws and anti-money laundering requirements

Cryptocurrency exchanges are not subject to Korea's anti-money requirements under the Act on Reporting and Use of Certain Financial Transaction Information ("AML Act"). There is, as discussed above, a pending bill at the National Assembly that would require anti-money laundering obligations for cryptocurrency exchanges under the AML Act. Currently, anti-money laundering obligations of cryptocurrencies are enforced through financial institutions linked with cryptocurrency exchanges.

From January 30, 2018, financial institutions doing business with companies that handle cryptocurrencies (e.g., cryptocurrency exchanges) must comply with the Anti-Money Laundering Guidelines for Cryptocurrencies ("AML Guidelines") issued by the Korea Financial Intelligence Unit. The notable requirements in the AML Guidelines are as follows:

1. Real-name verification required for fiat withdrawal from and deposit to cryptocurrency exchanges

    Fiat withdrawals from and deposits to a cryptocurrency exchange are available only if the exchange user's bank account is verified under the Real Name Verification System provided by financial institutions (e.g., banks), as explained above. Financial institutions may decline transactions with cryptocurrency exchanges that do not comply with this requirement. It also bans minors under the age of 18 and foreigners from opening new cryptocurrency accounts.

2.   Customer due diligence

Financial institutions must implement a due diligence process to confirm whether any of their customers is a cryptocurrency exchange. Financial institutions must verify certain additional information enumerated in the AML Guidelines by conducting due diligence of the cryptocurrency exchange at least every six months.

Examples of such additional information include whether the cryptocurrency exchange: (i) checks the identity of its users; (ii) maintains a separate transaction record for each user; and (iii) is in compliance with the cryptocurrency-related policies issued by the government.

3.   Suspicious transaction reports

If there is a transaction which falls under the suspicious transaction types, financial institutions must review and file a suspicious transaction report. Financial institutions must also appoint a staff member dedicated to monitoring suspicious cryptocurrency transactions. Suspicious transaction types include: (i) financial transactions between cryptocurrency exchanges and corporate entities or organisations; (ii) if the amount of financial transactions between a cryptocurrency exchange and a single user is KRW 10 million or more within one day or KRW 20 million or more within a seven-day period; and (iii) if the number of financial transactions between a cryptocurrency exchange and a single user is five times or more within a day, or seven times or more within a seven-day period.

Promotion and testing

The Korean government conceptually differentiates cryptocurrency from blockchain technology. While some regulations to curb speculative investment in cryptocurrency have been introduced, the Korean government has highlighted the innovative nature of blockchain technology in many different industries. The Korean government has also expressed its interest in fostering, promoting, and investing in blockchain technology as part of its strategic and economic plans for Korea to be a leader in the 4th Industrial Revolution.

Ownership and licensing requirements

Fund managers

Though there is no specific law that prohibits the registration of cryptocurrency-related investment funds, it is unclear whether the Korean financial regulators will be receptive to cryptocurrency-related investment funds. As a result, currently, there are no cryptocurrency-based investment vehicles and funds registered with the Korean financial regulatory agencies.

Investment advisors

Investment advisors need to be licensed in Korea to provide investment advice on financial investment products. Nevertheless, since the financial regulatory agencies have announced a position that cryptocurrencies are not financial investment products, there are currently no licensing requirements for investment advisors on cryptocurrency investments.

Licensing requirements

Korean financial authorities have taken the position that as cryptocurrency (or a cryptocurrency asset) is not a financial investment product, financial institutions (including fund managers and investment advisors) licensed under FSCMA may not invest in cryptocurrencies. If such regulatory position becomes law, a cryptocurrency investment fund will unlikely require a licence from the FSC under the FSCMA. However, the current regulatory perspective by the Korean regulatory agencies on such characterisation of cryptocurrency assets may change, or other agencies may announce contradicting views. Or, there may be court decisions that are contrary to the current views by the Korean regulatory agencies.

Mining

There are no explicit laws and regulations that regulate "mining" of bitcoins or other cryptocurrencies in Korea. However, based on an actual case in Korea, it is illegal for mining companies to move in and mine at industrial complexes to take advantage of discounted electricity fees for certain manufacturing companies.

Border restrictions and declaration

There are no explicit border restrictions or obligation to declare cryptocurrency holdings. However, for fiat currencies, remittance of funds out of Korea to an overseas account is governed under the Foreign Exchange Transaction Act (the "FETA") and the Foreign Exchange Transactions Regulations. As a general principle under the FETA, there must be a "legal basis" (e.g., loan repayment, dividend payments, sale proceeds payment, etc.) along with supporting documents as prescribed under the FETA to repatriate funds overseas. The FETA prescribes certain procedures and documents for each type of transaction listed in the FETA for both the remitter of funds and the bank handling the remittance. Each type of transaction has different procedures and requirements to remit funds overseas.

Nonetheless, there are no guidelines under the FETA for cryptocurrency transactions. As a result, it is not permitted to remit fiat currency funds from cryptocurrency transactions overseas. Generally, any person engaging in a cross-border capital transaction must file a foreign exchange report under the FETA with, and obtain approval from, the BOK or a designated foreign exchange bank for all remittances exceeding the limit of US$ 3,000 per transaction, or a yearly aggregate limit of US$ 50,000 from Korea to other countries. In practice, however, Korean banks have declined to process wire transfers overseas when they are related to cryptocurrency trading, even if the amounts do not exceed the monetary limits and would not trigger reporting requirements to the BOK/designated foreign exchange bank.

Reporting requirements

No. There are no explicit laws and regulations for cryptocurrency payments. For overseas payments using cryptocurrencies, there are no reporting requirements at this time to any Korean regulatory agency. However, there are requirements being developed by the Korean financial regulators that may require a filing requirement with the BOK for foreign exchange purposes.

Estate planning and testamentary succession

As discussed in the Taxation section above, cryptocurrency is taxable under current Korean law for inheritance and gift tax. The tax rate would be 10%–50%. The NTS, however, has indicated the need to develop accounting standards for cryptocurrencies to further develop their taxation.

Jung Min Lee
Tel: +82 2 3703 1671 / Email: jungmin.lee@kimchang.com

Mr Lee is the head of the fintech group at Kim & Chang. With expansive experience in areas spanning e-finance & fintech, blockchain and cryptocurrency, privacy and data security, banking, and finance disputes, he has acted for various private and public clients on the most cutting-edge fintech matters in the market.

As one of the leading experts in the field, Mr Lee has served on a number of government committees including the Legal Interpretation Committee Board (Korea Ministry of Government Legislation) and the Task Force on the P2P Loan Plan of the Financial Services Commission. He is trusted by the Korean government to advise on key fintech-related issues and to develop and implement key government initiatives in the field.

Samuel Yim
Tel: +82 2 3703 1543 / Email: samuel.yim@kimchang.com

Mr Yim is a senior foreign attorney in Kim & Chang's fintech group and his practice focuses primarily on blockchain and cryptocurrency matters. He regularly represents token sellers, cryptocurrency exchanges, venture, hedge and private equity funds and their portfolio companies, token marketers and broker-dealers, funds interested in trading digital assets, major global investment banks, financial institutions and asset managers, and others in the space.

He has advised foreign and domestic clients on major industry-defining matters such as, among others, ICOs and reverse ICOs, token private placements, listing Bitcoin ETFs on the Korean stock exchange, gaming licences for decentralised apps, establishing or acquiring cryptocurrency exchanges, cryptocurrency arbitrage, and establishing cryptocurrency not-for-profit foundations.

Joon Young Kim
Tel: +82 2 3703 1824 / Email: joonyoung.kim@kimchang.com

Mr Kim is one of the key members of the fintech practice group at the firm. In addition to e-finance & fintech, his practice focuses on insurance, non-bank financial companies, corporate governance, mergers & acquisitions and foreign direct investment. He has a strong reputation in the area and is praised by clients for his expertise and knowledge. Mr Kim regularly advises clients on legal issues relating to the latest innovations and technology such as blockchain technology, cryptocurrency and cloud computing.

As one of the leading experts in the field, Mr Kim has been actively involved in publishing on various Korean and international journals and conducting lectures related to e-finance & fintech, blockchain technology and cryptocurrency. Mr Kim has served as external expert member of the Financial Dispute Settlement Committee of the Financial Supervisory Service.

Kim & Chang

39, Sajik-ro 8-gil, Jongno-gu, Seoul 03170, South Korea
Tel: +82 2 3703 1114 / Fax: +82 2 737 9091/9092 / URL: www.kimchang.com

Liechtenstein

Dr Ralph Wanger & Laura Johann
BATLINER WANGER BATLINER Attorneys at Law Ltd.

Government attitude and definition

The Liechtenstein Government is very open to financial innovation and consequently also to cryptocurrencies. To demonstrate this, in the year 2016 the Government founded a working group that has developed a draft "Blockchain Act" over recent months. Despite the fact that the precise wording of the law has not yet been published, it is already apparent that the new law aims to offer the best-possible conditions for a token economy as an expression of trustworthy financial technologies. In this conjunction, the law is not limited merely to cryptocurrencies, but instead covers any possible tokenisation of assets as well as further innovations that go beyond blockchain technology. Within this context, the Liechtenstein Government is keen to create fertile conditions for cryptocurrencies as well as associated TGEs.

As in Austria and Switzerland, Liechtenstein defines money and monetary assets to mean not just legal tender (bank notes as well as coins in the respective currency), but also book-entry money. This legal definition of money does not cover cryptocurrencies, though.

Last year, however, following the amendment of the Liechtenstein Law on Professional Due Diligence to Combat Money Laundering, Organised Crime and Terrorist Financing (*Gesetz über berufliche Sorgfaltspflichten zur Bekämpfung von Geldwäscherei, organisierter Kriminalität und Terrorismus-finanzierung*, Due Diligence Act – *Sorgfaltspflichtgesetz*, "SPG", LGBl. 2017/161), Liechtenstein lawmakers attempted for the first time to formulate a legal definition of virtual currencies. Pursuant to Art. 2 Para. 1 lit. l SPG, virtual currencies (e.g. Bitcoin) are deemed to be digital monetary units that can be exchanged for legal tender, used to obtain goods or services or to store assets, meaning that they can assume the function of legal tender. As a consequence, this excludes those virtual currencies that can be redeemed or used to obtain goods or services only to a limited extent (e.g. bonus programmes). Against this backdrop, it is also clear that legal tender and cryptocurrencies are not to be treated equally, even though they serve the same purposes.

By contrast, the Liechtenstein Financial Market Authority (hereinafter called "FMA"), views cryptocurrencies essentially as "commodities", whereby other classifications may also be used, depending on the configuration of the token representing the cryptocurrency.

At the current time, there are no cryptocurrencies that are supported or backed by the Government or a bank in Liechtenstein.

Cryptocurrency regulation

Insofar as cryptocurrencies fulfil exclusively a payment function or are issued and used solely as a payment token, they are deemed to be commodities and are accordingly not regulated. However, as soon as additional functions are included, tokens may represent financial instruments that are covered by financial market law and can accordingly trigger FMA supervision as well as a corresponding licensing obligation (FMA Factsheet on the Initial Coin Offering of 10 September 2017, https://www.fma-li.li/files/fma/fma-faktenblatt-ico.pdf). This may, for example, include tokens that exhibit features of equity securities or have an investment character (e.g. security, asset or equity-backed tokens). Activities relating to financial instruments are generally subject to a special statutory licensing obligation by the FMA and may therefore be subject to the prospectus requirement.

This means that a special statutory licensing obligation may exist on a case-by-case basis, depending on the configuration of the specific business model (FMA Factsheet on Virtual Currencies of 16 February 2018, https://www.fma-li.li/files/fma/fma-faktenblatt-virtuelle-waehrungen.pdf). For this reason, it is necessary to clarify on an individual basis which licensing obligations need to be adhered to for each business model. The relevant criteria in each case are the specific configuration and the effective function of the token. At any rate, there is no general ban on cryptocurrencies.

Sales regulation

On the basis of the above assumption, tokens that are classified purely as a means of payment are not covered by the scope of statutory capital market provisions. This consequently means that, in general terms, the use of virtual currencies as a means of payment is not subject to any special statutory licensing obligation (FMA Factsheet on Virtual Currencies of 16 February 2018, https://www.fma-li.li/files/fma/fma-faktenblatt-virtuelle-waehrungen.pdf). A purchase or sale of cryptocurrencies is thus equivalent to a commercial transaction in goods and is covered by the General Civil Code (*Allgemeines Bürgerliches Gesetzbuch* – "ABGB") which is applicable in Liechtenstein.

Taxation

In Liechtenstein, the tax treatment of cryptocurrencies is such that every natural person subject to unlimited tax liability must declare their holdings of cryptocurrencies at the beginning of the respective tax year and convert them into Swiss francs (like foreign exchange). At the same time, speculative profits arising out of trade in cryptocurrencies are tax-exempt and do not need to be declared.

With regard to legal entities, changes in value realised through investments in cryptocurrencies must be declared for tax purposes. This consequently means that investments in cryptocurrencies are not covered by the tax exemptions provided by Art. 48 of the Liechtenstein Tax Act (*Steuergesetz* – "SteG"). In addition to the income tax rate of 12.5%, the effective tax amount also depends on the deductible equity interest rate, which reduces the assessment basis for income tax.

The equity interest deduction is calculated on the modified equity, whereby the interest rate is redefined annually and currently amounts to 4%. Insofar as the corporate purpose also includes the holding of cryptocurrencies and the investment in cryptocurrencies falls under the operating assets, the corresponding investment is subject to the equity interest deduction and thus leads to a reduction in the effective tax burden.

Money transmission laws and anti-money laundering requirements

In Liechtenstein, subjection to the Due Diligence Act (*Sorgfaltspflichtgesetz* – "SPG") focuses on financial intermediaries. In the absence of a connection of this nature, there is essentially no subordination to the Due Diligence Act. On a case-by-case basis, however, the Due Diligence Act may indeed be applicable. For this reason, individual clarification by the FMA in respect of a possible due diligence obligation is recommended (FMA Factsheet on Virtual Currencies of 16 February 2018, https://www.fma-li.li/files/fma/fma-faktenblatt-virtuelle-waehrungen.pdf).

An obligation to report to the FMA as a person subject to due diligence may arise, for example, if a commercial exchange from fiat funds to cryptocurrencies is performed. Against the backdrop of the current Liechtenstein legal situation, the corresponding activity would have to be qualified as a currency-exchange activity and would accordingly open up the scope of application of the Due Diligence Act. On the other hand, from a technical legal perspective, trade between cryptocurrencies is viewed as a normal exchange within the meaning of §§ 1045 *et seq.* ABGB, meaning that this is essentially not subject to the Due Diligence Act.

In principle, however, it is important to note that compliance with Anti Money Laundering Guidelines ("AML") and the Know-Your-Customer Principle ("KYC") is recommended in any case for reasons of practicability, as this facilitates cooperation with the financial institutions involved or is generally required by them. This means it is therefore advisable, within the context of a planned TGE, to discuss this in advance with the financial institution involved, in order to compare requirements in the AML/KYC field with the existing in-house guidelines that are confidently deemed to be sufficient on account of the fact that the financial institution is subject to the Due Diligence Act.

Promotion and testing

On account of the large number of enquiries received in the fintech field relative to the small size of the country (98 enquiries in the year 2018 to 28 June 2018), the FMA has established a dedicated unit called "Regulatory Laboratory/Financial Innovation" that collects know-how in this field, and also aims to promote these topics by organising corresponding workshops. All enquiries in the blockchain technology field (incl. ICOs) should be addressed to this unit.

Ownership and licensing requirements

There is currently no special law in Liechtenstein that would impose restrictions or supervisory obligations on investment advisors or fund managers when investing in cryptocurrencies. It would, however, be necessary to assess on a case-by-case basis whether the holding of cryptocurrencies by the corresponding professional groups might be subsumed under one of the classic statutory capital market laws. In particular, the Asset Management Act (*Gesetz über die Vermögensverwaltung / Vermögensverwaltungsgesetz*, "VVG") would need to be taken into account.

Mining

The production of virtual currencies as a means of payment (so-called "mining") is not currently subject to any specific statutory licensing obligation (FMA Factsheet on Virtual Currencies of 16 February 2018, https://www.fma-li.li/files/fma/fma-faktenblatt-virtuelle-waehrungen.pdf). This means the mining of Bitcoin or other cryptocurrencies is permitted. In February 2018, the Liechtenstein Tax Administration agreed that mining is regarded as a taxable gainful activity. This consequently means that mining is subject to income tax, whereby the associated overheads (e.g. IT costs, rent of business premises, etc.) are tax-deductible.

Border restrictions and declaration

As Liechtenstein forms a customs and currency union with Switzerland, reference may be made to the relevant passages in the Swiss chapter.

Reporting requirements

From a statutory supervisory perspective, as far as the authors are currently aware, there are no value-related limits that would entail a reporting obligation.

Estate planning and testamentary succession

Due to the novelty of cryptocurrencies as a heritable asset, it has yet to be clarified how to proceed with a testamentary disposition of virtual currencies. Practical and legal problems arise, for example, with regard to the associated private keys, since their availability at the time of inheritance is a key prerequisite for the transfer of ownership within the context of legal succession under inheritance law. The storage of cryptocurrencies (cold/warm storage), or the corresponding keys as access codes, will therefore play a crucial role when it comes to the transfer of virtual assets across generations. It remains to be hoped that the Blockchain Act, which is currently going through the process of consultation, will also address this issue and provide for corresponding regulations to establish the necessary legal certainty.

Dr Ralph Wanger, LL.M.
Tel: +423 239 78 78 / Email: ralph.wanger@bwb.li
Dr Ralph Wanger, LL.M., Attorney-at-Law, born 1969, Liechtenstein citizen.
He graduated in law at the University of Zurich (*lic. iur.*) in 1994. He
completed his doctorate (*Dr. iur.*) at the University of Zurich in the year
1997. He passed the bar exam in 1999. Two years later he completed post-
graduate studies at New York University, School of Law, with a Master in
Comparative Jurisprudence (LL.M.).
Having completed his studies, he performed various internships at the Princely
Court of Justice, at the Princely Government as well as in the fiduciary field,
and worked at a Liechtenstein law firm.
He began working as a self-employed attorney-at-law in the year 2000. In
2002 he joined and was made a partner at BATLINER WANGER BATLINER
Attorneys at Law, which was converted into a stock corporation in 2008. He
has been a member of the Board of Directors ever since.
From 2005 to 2015, he acted as a Substitute Judge at the Constitutional Court
of the Principality of Liechtenstein.
Dr Ralph Wanger is currently focusing on the topic of blockchain, and is
taking part in the first (Swiss) CAS Blockchain programme at the University
of Lucerne. In addition, Dr Ralph Wanger is also a founder and member of
the Board of Directors of the company Blockstar AG (http://www.blockstar.
li). He is head of the FinTech Department at BWB and advises clients in the
Distributed Ledger Technology and ICO fields.

Laura Johann, MLaw
Tel: +423 239 78 78 / Email: laura.johann@bwb.li
Laura Johann, MLaw, Attorney-at-Law, born 1989, Liechtenstein citizen,
grew up in Triesen, Principality of Liechtenstein.
She graduated in law from the University of Berne in 2010 (Bachelor of Law)
and at the University of Zurich in 2012 (Master of Law). She passed the Bar
exam in 2017.
Having completed her studies, she completed a number of internships at the
Office of the Public Prosecutor in Liechtenstein as well as at the Princely Court
of Justice, and worked as a trainee at BATLINER WANGER BATLINER
Attorneys at Law Ltd.
She has worked as an attorney-at-law at BATLINER WANGER BATLINER
Attorneys at Law Ltd. since 2017. She is a member of the FinTech Department
at BWB and provides advice in the field of distributed ledger technology,
specifically in conjunction with initial coin offerings.

BATLINER WANGER BATLINER Attorneys at Law Ltd.

Am Schrägen Weg 2, LI-9490 Vaduz, Liechtenstein
Tel: +423 239 78 78 / URL: www.bwb.li

Malta

Malcolm Falzon & Alexia Valenzia
Camilleri Preziosi Advocates

Government attitude and definition

Malta has positioned itself as a key player in the world of Distributed Ledger Technologies
("**DLTs**"). The Government of Malta, local regulators and other stakeholders have adopted
an open and collaborative approach towards this sphere, rooted in striking the right balance
between maintaining Malta's perception as a jurisdiction of repute, integrity and financial
stability, and the desire to foster a business and legal environment conducive towards
innovative technologies, products and services.

The first half of 2018 has been characterised by Malta's clear determination to promulgate
regulation that is a first of its kind. A collective effort, spearheaded by the Parliamentary
Secretariat for Financial Services, Digital Economy and Innovation together with the Malta
Financial Services Authority (the "**MFSA**"), has enabled Malta to carry out the necessary
reforms to formulate an innovative yet robust regulatory and legal framework designed to
meet the commercial, technical and technological peculiarities inherently characterising
blockchain and cryptocurrencies. The Government of Malta has led by example and has
expressly stated that it is resolute in establishing Malta as the "Blockchain Island". To this
end, it has set up a number of blockchain-related innovative projects with the intention of
attracting big industry players to the island (see "Promotion and testing", below).

Following a series of public consultations with the industry throughout the course of the
past year, the willingness of the Government of Malta to digitalise Malta's economy and
cement its position as a jurisdiction of choice for innovators has culminated in the formal
enactment of a comprehensive set of three complementary legislative acts at the beginning
of July 2018. These acts are:

(i)   the Malta Digital Innovation Authority Act (the "**MDIA**");

(ii) the Innovative Technology Arrangements and Services Act (the "**ITAS**"); and

(iii) the Virtual Financial Assets Act (the "**VFAA**"),

(collectively hereinafter referred to as the "**Digital Innovation Framework**").

In essence, this means that market participants in the blockchain and cryptocurrencies
industries may establish or operate in or from Malta, and benefit from a higher degree of
legal certainty – which will have a knock-on beneficial impact through enhanced trust,
marketability, legal certainty and consumer adoption.

Cryptocurrency is not treated as money or given equal recognition with domestic or foreign
fiat currency in Malta – or at least, not as yet. As at the date of writing, there are no
cryptocurrencies that are backed by the Government of Malta or the Central Bank of Malta.

Cryptocurrency regulation

Following the enactment of the VFAA, cryptocurrencies may be regulated under the VFAA or existing financial services legislation, including but not limited to the Markets in Financial Instruments Directive II ("**MiFID II**"), the Investment Services Act (Chapter 370 of the Laws of Malta) and the Financial Institutions Act (Chapter 376 of the Laws of Malta). Which regulatory regime (if any) will apply is dependent on the classification of the asset in question.

Malta's Digital Innovation Framework sets out four possible categories of Distributed Ledger Technology Assets ("**DLT Assets**"), which may include cryptocurrencies. These are:

(i)   Electronic Money;

(ii) Financial Instruments (albeit that are intrinsically dependent on, or utilise, Distributed Ledger Technology);

(iii) Virtual Tokens (more commonly referred to as Utility Tokens); or

(iv) Virtual Financial Assets ("**VFAs**").

The classification of the DLT Asset in question into one of the four categories listed above will be mutually exclusive therewith.

The VFAA introduces a mandatory regulatory regime that regulates DLT assets and related service providers, including, amongst others, Initial Virtual Financial Asset Offerings ("**IVFAOs**") issuers (more commonly known as ICOs), and Virtual Financial Asset Exchanges ("**VFA Exchanges**") (more commonly referred to as Crypto-Exchanges). The VFAA also introduces a new class of intermediaries, to be known as Virtual Financial Asset Agents ("**VFA Agents**").

The crux of the matter is determining whether the asset in question falls within the scope of the VFAA and is therefore prone to being regulated thereunder. In this respect, the VFAA empowers the MFSA to introduce a test, to be known as the Financial Instrument Test (the "**Test**"), for the purpose of classifying a DLT Asset as one of the aforementioned classes of DLT Assets and thereby determining whether the DLT Asset would be regulated under the VFAA, existing financial services laws or neither of the two (remaining unregulated). The Test was published in July 2018 along with a guidance note on how to interpret and apply its steps. The Test must be carried out on a case-by-case basis. The VFAA indicates that it will be the task of the VFA Agent (along with the VFA issuer if the Test is being carried out in relation to an IVFAO) to carry out this assessment with respect to a DLT Asset when:

(i)   an issuer intends to launch an IVFAO to the public in or from within Malta;

(ii) an issuer admits the VFA to trading; and/or

(iii) a service provider intends to conduct VFA-related services.

The Test will firstly determine whether the DLT Asset is to be classified as a Virtual Token and therefore fall outside the scope of regulation. A Virtual Token is defined as being a form of digital medium recordation whose utility, value or application is restricted solely to the acquisition of goods or services, either solely within the DLT platform on, or in relation to which, it was issued or within a limited network of DLT platforms (but not DLT exchanges).

If the DLT Asset is determined not to be a Virtual Token, one must move on to the second stage of the Test wherein it will be determined whether the DLT Asset falls within the scope of existing financial services legislation. If the VFA Agent determines that the DLT Asset does indeed fall within the scope of existing financial services legislation, then the issuer or service provider in question would be required to comply with the regulatory regime applicable to financial instruments or electronic money, depending on the characteristics of the asset. On the other hand, if it is determined that the DLT Asset does not fall within the scope of existing financial services laws (or would be considered a Utility Token as aforesaid), the token automatically falls into the last stage of the Test, whereby the token would be deemed to be a VFA, and therefore, due to be regulated by the VFAA.

If a DLT Asset is determined to be a VFA, VFA-related service providers will be required to adhere to the provisions of the VFAA. For example, an issuer of an IVFAO offered to the public in or from Malta must register its white paper with the MFSA, and the white paper must comply with the conditions set out in the First Schedule of the VFAA. Furthermore, a VFA service provider as listed in the Second Schedule of the VFAA (such as VFA exchanges) offering a VFA service in or from Malta will be required to obtain a licence from the MFSA before it may commence its operations.

Sales regulation

The sale of cryptocurrencies such as Bitcoin or other tokens may be regulated by securities laws. In order to determine whether the sale of tokens would be regulated by securities laws, according to the VFAA each DLT Asset must be assessed to determine whether the said DLT Asset falls within the scope of (i) existing securities laws or (ii) the VFAA, or be unregulated. Should the DLT Asset fall within the scope of existing securities laws by virtue of it being classified as a Financial Instrument following completion of the Test, then that token must comply with securities laws.

There are no commodities laws regulating the sale of cryptocurrencies or other tokens as at the date of writing.

Taxation

At present, there are no rules or guidance in place that specifically treat the taxation of cryptocurrency in Malta, whether from an income tax, duty or VAT perspective. In the absence of specific rules, the general rules and principles of Maltese tax legislation apply.

By way of background, the Income Tax Act (Cap. 123 of the laws of Malta) distinguishes between receipts that are of an income nature and receipts that are of a capital nature. Receipts that are of an income nature are in principle subject to Maltese income tax either: (i) at the rate of 35% if the recipient is a body of persons; or (ii) at progressive rates – up to the maximum level of 35% – if the recipient is a natural person. Gains that are of a capital nature are subject to Maltese income tax either: (i) at the fixed rate of 35%; or (ii) are not taxable at all. The Income Tax Act does not define "income", rather, it attempts to provide a meaning of the term by non-exhaustively listing several sources of revenue that are considered to be income, such as gains or profits from any trade, business, profession or vocation. On the contrary, the Income Tax Act exhaustively lists those capital gains that are within scope of income tax. Cryptocurrency is currently not listed as an asset that is subject to income tax on any capital gains.

Whether a receipt is considered to be of an income nature (that is, generally arising from a trade, business, profession or vocation) or of a capital nature depends on the so-called "badges of trade". These are indicators developed by UK jurisprudence and accepted by both the Maltese tax authorities and courts. The indicators point towards a profit or gain being derived from a trading activity and therefore having the nature of income, as opposed to capital. Important indicators of profits derived in the course of a trade (and therefore taxable as income) include, amongst others: the frequency of transactions; the existence of a profit-seeking motive; the nature of the asset; whether supplementary work and marketing has been conducted; and the length of the ownership.

In applying the above principles to transactions in cryptocurrency, profits derived from a transaction would be characterised as income of a trading nature or income of a capital nature dependent on subjective factors such as: (i) the intention of the acquiror when the cryptocurrency was bought; (ii) the period of time that the cryptocurrency was held; (iii) the price at which the acquiror entered the market and the price-trend at the moment of entry; and (iv) the price of disposal and the price-trend at the moment of exit.

For instance, if an individual acquired bitcoins in 2012 when the acquisition value was substantially lower than its price at the end of 2017 and has held the bitcoins through the currency's highs and lows but decides to dispose of the holding in 2018, it is likely that the cryptocurrency was held, and will be perceived to have been held, as a long-term investment. The receipt derived from the transfer of such cryptocurrency would likely be treated as income of a capital nature. As discussed above, capital gains from the disposal of cryptocurrency do not currently fall within scope of taxable capital gains and therefore no tax should be payable by the transferor. On the other hand, if an individual consistently trades in Bitcoin, on an ongoing basis, such activity is susceptible to having any receipts derived from the transfer of the cryptocurrency treated as income from a trading activity and taxable at the relevant rate. It is pertinent to note that there is currently no official position in Malta that sheds light on the period of time that should lapse for the holding of the cryptocurrency to be treated as being held for capital purposes as opposed to trading purposes. In view of the above, the nature of the income derived from cryptocurrency would therefore need to be assessed on a case-by-case basis.

Insofar as duty payable by the acquiror of the cryptocurrency is concerned, there are currently no provisions in the Duty on Documents and Transfers Act (Cap. 364 of the laws of Malta) which impose a duty charge on the transfer of cryptocurrency.

From a VAT perspective, we expect the Maltese tax authorities to follow the Court of Justice of the European Union's pronouncements in the *Hedqvist* case (C-264/14) should and if a similar domestic situation arise. Thus, the exchange of bitcoin for traditional currency and vice versa, which is effected for consideration, would likely be seen as a supply of a service but would ultimately be exempt from VAT.

In order to complement the recent domestic developments in blockchain regulation as discussed in the section "Cryptocurrency regulation" above, industry and practitioners expect the Maltese tax authorities to issue guidance on the income tax, duty and VAT treatment of transactions in cryptocurrency in the near future.

Money transmission laws and anti-money laundering requirements

Malta's main legislation regulating anti-money laundering and the countering of the funding of terrorism ("**AML/CFT**") are: (i) the Prevention of Money Laundering Act (Chapter 373 of the Laws of Malta) ("**PMLA**"); and (ii) the Prevention of Money Laundering and Funding of Terrorism Regulations (Subsidiary Legislation 373.01) ("**PMLFTR**"). These legislative instruments transpose the requirements of the Fourth Anti-Money Laundering Directive (Directive (EU) 2015/849).

Persons carrying out either a "relevant financial business" or "relevant activity" will be considered to be a subject persons under the PMLA and PMLFTR and, therefore, they must adhere to the obligations therein relating to subject persons. In addition, subject persons shall also comply with the Implementing Procedures, and other guidance, as issued and updated from time to time by the AML/CFT regulator in Malta, the Financial Intelligence and Analysis Unit ("**FIAU**").

With specific reference to issuers of cryptocurrencies and related service providers, the VFAA provides that: (i) an issuer; (ii) a VFA licence holder; and (iii) a VFA agent under the VFAA, shall be considered as a subject person. Finally, in the white paper required to be registered with the MFSA for the purposes of an IVFAO to the public, or the admission thereof on a DLT Exchange, the issuer is required to include a description of the issuer's adopted white-listing and anti-money laundering and counter financing of terrorism procedures in terms of the PMLA and any regulations made and rules issued thereunder. VFA issuers, licence-holders and agents are also required to abide by any sector-specific guidance that may be issued by the FIAU from time to time.

Promotion and testing

In March 2018, the Malta Gaming Authority ("**MGA**") released guidance on the use of DLTs and the acceptance of Virtual Currencies ("**VCs**") in the gaming sector through the implementation of a sandbox environment. The sandbox commenced early in Q2 2018 and will last for a period of six months. The principal objective of the MGA's sandbox is to consider allowing the use and implementation of DLTs and VCs by gaming and gambling operators licensed by the MGA.

In order to safeguard players and the gaming ecosystem, either of two distinct implementation scenarios is deemed acceptable:

(i)   a "single wallet system"– in the first scenario, the operator has a maximum of one wallet for every supported cryptocurrency. The players issue deposits to the address of that wallet and use their account with the operator to notify that they just made a deposit from a certain wallet's address. If the deposited amount respects the "maximum amount" and any deposit limit previously set by the player, the funds are kept in the operator's wallet and are made available to the player's account for gaming use. Otherwise, if the operator receives a transaction from a player's account without first being notified, the funds are sent back to the originating wallet. In this scenario, the operator does not assign an individual wallet to each player. Instead, every player is assigned ownership of a balance virtually segregated within one of the operator's holding wallets; and

(ii) a "multiple wallet system"– in the second scenario, the operator assigns a gaming wallet for each currency to every player's account. The MGA only accepts this case if the operator has an intermediate wallet structure comprised of one or more wallets. Such an intermediate setup is used to accept deposits from the player's personal external source of funds. However, in contrast to that scenario, if the deposited amount is within the "maximum amount", the funds are forwarded to the player's respective VC gaming wallet rather than allocating players a share of the operator's wallet. The intermediate wallet reverses incoming transactions if they exceed the "maximum amount" and/or if the funds come from a wallet that is not expected to make a deposit. The player uses the account with the operator to inform of an incoming deposit and get feedback from the operator of the deposit being awaited.

More recently, in June 2018, the Malta Stock Exchange announced its MSX Fintech Accelerator, an initiative endorsed by Binance and Thomson Reuters, which is an accelerator providing a programme designed to mentor and support start-ups and entrepreneurs in the crypto and blockchain space, matching them with international technology and business leaders.

From a broader perspective, Malta has also experienced a flurry of collaborative activity amongst various stakeholders, with a variety of associations and interest groups being formally established to further the development of the cryptocurrency community in Malta, sharing the common goal of providing a mutual educational and learning experience and fostering a business environment that is conducive to these innovations. Examples include:

• BitMalta;

• the Blockchain Malta Association;

• the Blockchain Research Group, University of Malta; and

• the Malta Information Technology Agency (MITA) – YouStartIT Accelerator.

Finally, in April 2018, Malta joined another 23 European Union Member States in establishing the European Blockchain Partnership ("**EBP**"). The EBP is intended to act as a vehicle for co-operation among 23 EU Member States in terms of exchanging experience and know-how in technical and regulatory fields.

Ownership and licensing requirements

Owning cryptocurrencies for investment management purposes

As set out above, according to the provisions of the VFAA, a licensing requirement is triggered under the VFAA where an entity provides a service set out in the second schedule of the VFAA in relation to a VFA, whether such services are provided in or from within Malta (note that the VFAA does not define the phrase '*in or from within Malta*'; however, we interpret this to mean: (i) the provision of a VFA service by an entity from within Malta; or (ii) the provision of services by an entity to clients in Malta on a cross-border basis).

Investment management is one of the services listed in the second schedule to the VFAA. Accordingly, where such service is provided in respect of VFAs in or from Malta, this would trigger a licensing requirement under the VFAA and such person would be required to obtain a licence under the VFAA to carry out this activity.

Please note that according to draft legislation (which has yet to be implemented) (the "**Draft Legislation**"), exemptions are available where the investment manager manages the investments for its own account (that is, on a proprietary basis) and does not: (i) receive, directly or indirectly, any remuneration or other benefit for the service; (ii) hold himself out as providing a VFA service; or (iii) solicit members of the public to take such services.

Licensing requirements for advisors and fund managers

Investment advice

Investment advice is also listed in the second schedule to the VFAA. Accordingly, a licensing requirement would be triggered under the VFAA where such service is provided in relation to one or more VFAs in or from Malta.

Fund management

As a preliminary matter, please note that, in terms of Maltese law, it is possible for a Maltese domiciled fund to be structured as: (i) a UCITS fund; (ii) an alternative investment fund ("**AIF**"); or (iii) a professional investor fund ("**PIF**"). At the time of writing, Maltese domiciled AIFs and UCITS are not permitted to invest in cryptocurrencies. Therefore, it is currently only possible for Malta-domiciled collective investment schemes to invest in cryptocurrencies when structured as PIFs (which are subset of AIFs available to managers which fall within the *de minimis* thresholds set out in the AIFMD (Directive 2011/61/EU)).

The licensing requirements for the management of a Malta-domiciled PIF will depend on whether the management company is established in or outside Malta.

Fund managers which manage PIFs investing in cryptocurrencies through a management company established in Malta are required to be licensed under the Investment Services Act (Chapter 370 of the Laws of Malta, the "**ISA**"). In line with the Draft Legislation, such fund manager would not require a separate licence under the VFAA to manage a PIF investing in cryptocurrencies.

Fund managers which manage PIFs investing in cryptocurrencies through a management company established outside Malta are not required to be licensed under the ISA. However, in order for the foreign-based entity to manage the PIF, the MFSA must be satisfied that such management company has the necessary skills, competence and expertise to manage the PIF. A fund manager domiciled overseas which is managing a Malta-domiciled PIF would not require a separate licence under the VFAA.

Mining

Cryptocurrency mining activities are permitted but are, at the time of writing, unregulated.

Border restrictions and declaration

At the time of writing, there are no border restrictions or obligations to declare cryptocurrency holdings.

Reporting requirements

As at the time of writing, there are no reporting requirements for cryptocurrency payments made in excess of a certain value.

Estate planning and testamentary succession

As at the date of writing, there are no laws regulating the treatment of cryptocurrencies for the purposes of estate planning and testamentary succession; general laws such as the relevant provisions found within the Civil Code (Chapter 16 of the Laws of Malta) would apply.

Malcolm Falzon
Tel: +356 2123 8989 / Email: malcolm.falzon@camilleripreziosi.com
Malcolm Falzon is the partner at Camilleri Preziosi responsible for the firm's
insurance, gaming and aviation practices. His areas of specialisation also
comprise corporate and M&A, capital markets, securitisation, asset finance
and pensions. He regularly advises local and international clients on legal,
regulatory, operational and licensing matters as well as related corporate and
commercial and dispute resolution issues across various industry sectors.
Malcolm also leads Camilleri Preziosi's Blockchain Taskforce, which was
set up in order to study the technology and its potential application to the
industry sectors serviced by the firm. He regularly acts as an examiner at the
University of Malta and lecturer at the Malta Stock Exchange Institute, and
is a speaker at seminars and conferences relating to his areas of expertise.
Following his traineeship at the firm and return from postgraduate studies at
University College, London, Malcolm returned to the firm as an associate in
2005, and was admitted to partnership in 2013.

Alexia Valenzia
Tel: +356 2123 8989 / Email: alexia.valenzia@camilleripreziosi.com
Alexia forms part of Camilleri Preziosi's Technology, Media and Telecoms
department and the firm's Blockchain Taskforce. Her areas of specialisation
include fintech regulation, technology, intellectual property and data
protection. She often works on DLT-related matters, specifically within the
field of cryptocurrencies, initial coin offerings and related services. Her
interests lie in the development of nascent technologies such as artificial
intelligence and the internet of things, and the legal implications which arise
as a result of their development. She frequently contributes to Camilleri
Preziosi's publications on the applicability of these technologies to various
industry sectors. She also regularly assists clients with data protection
and intellectual property-related matters. Alexia graduated from The City
Law School in London in 2016 after completing the Graduate Diploma in
Law course. Prior to this, Alexia obtained a First-class Honours degree in
Pharmacology from the University of Portsmouth in 2015.

Camilleri Preziosi Advocates

Level 3, Valletta Buildings, South Street, Valletta, VLT 1103, Malta
Tel: +356 2123 8989 / URL: www.camilleripreziosi.com

Mexico

Juan Carlos Tejado & Miguel Gallardo Guerra
Bello, Gallardo, Bonequi y García, S.C.

Introduction

This current March in Mexico, the financial authorities, the financial sector (traditional), and the fintech industry, took a great step forward with the enactment of the Law to Regulate Financial Technology Institutions (Fintech Law). Together with the enactment of this law, nine laws related to the financial sector were amended and, therefore, the focus is on publishing and amending several other secondary provisions issued by the financial and monetary authorities in the country.

Mexico is the first country to enact a specific compendium of legal provisions to govern different actors in the fintech industry (crowdfunding, e-money, cryptocurrency operators and experimental platforms – sand box), a fast-growing sector, either by: (1) improving the low levels of financial inclusion in Mexico; and/or (2) a radical change in the needs and customs of a growing generation of new bank service users; and/or (3) the technological advances, and specifically the use of mobile devices.

Fintech Law is the first step forward in acknowledging the importance and relevance that the fintech industry is gaining, providing legal certainty to its participants, foreseeing/mitigating risks and illegal operations of money laundering, and bringing financial services and solutions closer to unattended people and sectors.

The law is based on six principles:
- Financial inclusion and innovation.
- Promotion of competence.
- Consumer and user protection.
- Technology neutrality.
- Preserving financial stability.
- Preventing illegal operations.

Fintech Law sets forth the basis and a minimum regulation; it is a flexible and adaptable legal instrument that will be supported by more than 30 secondary provisions to be issued by the financial authorities (the Ministry of Finance [SHCP for its abbreviation in Spanish], Banco de México (Mexico's Central Bank), the National Banking and Securities Commission [CNBV for its abbreviation in Spanish], the National Commission for the Protection and Defence of Financial Service Users, the National Insurance and Bonding Commission and the National Retirement Savings System Commission) – these with terms of 6, 12 and 24 months for their publication. We believe this is a flexible and adaptable instrument because, when supported by secondary provisions, it does not require a long legislative process to be amended. Thus, the authorities may adapt them to the conditions established by both the sector and the new technologies.

Fintech Law governs services, organisation, operation and transactions rendered by Financial Technology Institutions (ITFs), such as: (1) Joint Funding Institutions [IFC, for its abbreviation in Spanish] (Crowdfunding); (2) Payment Funds Institutions [IFPE, for its abbreviation in Spanish] (e-wallets and cryptocurrency exchanges); and (3) novel models and sandboxes, which are those institutions using business models and/or technologies and/or tools and technology means which require a level of maturity or which are different from those currently existing in the market. Fintech Law also: (1) acknowledges and defines virtual assets (cryptocurrencies) and sets forth the operations that ITFs and some traditional financial entities (Banks) can make with these virtual assets (with prior authorisation by Banco de México and the CNBV); and (2) sets forth the rules to make ITFs work with programming interfaces and applications (APIs), which allow for connectivity of digital financial services. Finally, the law sets forth a regulatory framework for administrative and criminal sanctions for cases infringing the provisions thereof or secondary provisions.

Likewise, the law establishes rules to integrate cross-sector committees (which shall comprise representatives from SHCP, Banco de México and the CNBV), the creation of the *Grupo de Innovación Financiera* (the Financial Innovations Group, which shall comprise members of both the public and private sector) and the creation of trade associations for each ITF.

It is evident that the success of Fintech Law is linked to the issue of secondary provisions and to the authorities' awareness of the risk of generating unnecessary regulatory burdens that render sector growth impossible. However, to date, the willingness of all authorities to listen and to work together with everyone involved, the growth of capital investment in the sector, and the interest in new generations of clients/users of financial services, lead us to believe that we are on the right road to consolidate the fintech industry in Mexico, without setting aside cryptocurrencies and blockchain-based technology, which are of great importance to this process.

Goverment attitude and definition

As we described above, the Mexican authorities have given cryptocurrencies a formal acknowledgment and definition as a Virtual Asset in the Fintech Law. For regulatory purposes:[1]

> *"[...] Virtual asset is the representation of value electronically recorded and used among the public as payment means to any kind of legal acts and which transfer can solely be carried out by electronic means. In any case, a virtual asset will be of legal tender in the national territory, a foreign currency or any other asset denominated in a legal tender or foreign currency."*

That is, Virtual Assets have two functions according to the Mexican authorities:

- of investment (representing value); and
- to transfer value as a payment method (used among the public for all types of legal acts).

Banco de México shall be – by secondary provisions – the authority that will determine which Virtual Assets ITFs may operate (especially IFPE Exchange), and which banks.[2]

Banco de México shall consider <u>at least</u> the following aspects when determining which Virtual Assets are liable to operate in the country:

- The use made by the public of the digital units as a means of exchange and value-storage (investment), as well as the account unit (as means of payment).

- The treatment other jurisdictions give to special digital units like Virtual Assets.
- The mechanisms, rules or protocols allowing for generating, identifying, fractioning and controlling mirroring of digital units.

Mexican authorities, and in particular Banco de México as the authority responsible for the country's monetary system, do not consider Virtual Assets to be legal tender (fiat currency) in Mexico, as set forth in the second part of the definition of Virtual Assets above-mentioned.

> *"[...] In no case a virtual asset shall be the legal tender in the national territory, foreign currency or any other asset in legal tender or foreign currency.*
>
> *[...]"*

Likewise, Banco de México in two press releases (March 2014[3] and December 2017[4]) warns about the use of Virtual Assets and Initial Coin Offerings schemes. As Virtual Assets represent a significant difference in regard to fiat currencies in Mexico, Banco de México establishes in such releases the following:

- They are not legal tender in Mexico, as Banco de México neither issues nor backs them.
- They do not have the power to free debts from payment obligations; therefore, their function as payment means is not secured, as shops and people are not obliged to accept them.
- Banco de México neither regulates nor monitors them.
- Institutions governed by the Mexican financial system are not authorised to use them or to carry out transactions with them (unless they are previously authorised in terms of Fintech Law and the secondary provisions).
- In other jurisdictions, their use has been appointed for illegal operations, including fraud and money laundering.
- There is no guarantee or regulation assuring consumers or shops that by acquiring this type of asset, they may further recover their money. Moreover, as there is no identifiable organisation that issues these assets or a third party accepting obligations arising therefrom, a legal resource would hardly be upheld in case of loss.
- The price in Mexican pesos or in terms of other currencies, as determined by people accepting to trade this asset, has shown great volatility. This is a consequence of its highly speculative nature and of the high sensitivity of its price to changes in the trust of users (for example, technology changes, emergence of new virtual assets, legal restrictions, etc.). As a consequence, acquiring and using these assets involve a high depreciation risk and, thus, monetary losses.

Based on the above, Article 34 of Fintech Law sets forth that ITFs operating with Virtual Assets must inform customers that:

- the virtual asset is not legal tender and not backed by the Federal Government or by Banco de México;
- it is impossible to revert operations once executed, where applicable;
- Virtual Assets suffer from volatility of value; and
- technology, cybernetics and fraud risks are inherent to Virtual Assets.

Regulation of cryptocurrencies

As we mentioned in the introduction, in March 2018 Fintech Law was enacted. This Law **does not** attempt to govern the issue, procedure, circulation or quotation of technology supporting cryptocurrency, **but** the operation of operators or intermediaries, in this case Payment Fund Institutions [IFPE] and Banks previously authorised by Banco de México.

It is important to mention that Fintech Law does not aim at regulating the use individuals give to cryptocurrencies or to Virtual Assets.

Payment Fund Institutions [IFPE] and Banks that were previously authorised by Banco de México may solely operate cryptocurrencies or virtual assets that have been approved by Banco de México.

Sales regulation

As a consequence of the enactment of Fintech Law, some Articles of the Securities Market Law were amended to the effect that:

(a) the offer and intermediation of securities or instruments that ITFs operate with shall be regulated by Fintech Law instead of the Securities Market Law; and

(b) investment advisors' operation is updated in regard to automated investment counselling and management services.

These amendments allow Crowdfunding Institutions (IFC or crowdfunding) to network with individuals in order to participate in debt, capital or royalty schemes, without going through the process of an Initial Public Offering (IPO).

Therefore, selling cryptocurrencies, tokens linked to these latter or to derivative financial instruments owning Virtual Assets as underlying assets, are not regulated by the Securities Market Law or by the provisions related to derivatives (swaps or futures).

Fintech Law sets forth that ITFs can only participate in the operation, design or marketing of derivative financial instruments with Virtual Assets as underlying assets, in case Banco de México authorises secondary provisions. It is important to point out that financial authorities (SHCP, CNBV and Banco de México) issued a bulletin warning about the risks associated with virtual assets and ICOs in December 2017. This bulletin establishes that ICOs related to a Security Token can be considered as securities under the terms of the Securities Market Law. Therefore, ICOs should be subject to register with the National Securities Registry and when not meeting with the provisions, this could be considered an administrative fault and, in some instances, an offence.

Taxes

As of today, there are no specific rules in Mexico establishing the tax treatment arising from earnings from operations carried out using cryptocurrencies on income tax matters. As we mentioned above, Fintech Law does not govern cryptocurrencies, but regulates the exchanges [IFPE] and Banks authorised by Banco de México to operate with Virtual Assets. Thus, any provision on tax matters was amended. Tax treatment of cryptocurrencies, therefore, is subject to general tax regulations.

Tax experts have opined that regardless of the operation carried out, management of cryptocurrency involves an implicit effect of foreign exchange gain to accruals, whereas others suggest that this refers to gains from selling goods, which should not be subject to any exchange effect. In regard to the first assumption, the Income Tax Law sets forth that those exchange profits or losses caused by the fluctuation of foreign currency shall be treated as of interest. These will be determined based on the type of exchange published by Banco de México in the Federal Official Gazette.

This treatment would seem to acknowledge cryptocurrencies as foreign currency which, in our opinion, among other aspects, would be incorrect. There is no official exchange issued by Banco de México for the purpose of determining an exchange gain from operations carried out using such Virtual Assets.

Therefore, we believe that income from cryptocurrency should be acknowledged as gain on sale of assets. This, under the terms of the law under discussion, will be determined by individuals or bodies corporate, acknowledging the differences between the selling price and the income earned and the amount of acquisition or cost.

Such treatment shall allow for acknowledging an increased equity arising from operations using cryptocurrencies at the time of selling those virtual assets. Thus, in our opinion, this would be the best treatment applicable to operations under discussion.

In this connection, and in view of the increasing importance of operations using cryptocurrency, we should wait for regulations clearly establishing the tax treatment for these operations, as they are part of the current market.

Provisions in regard to laws against money laundering

By virtue of the enactment of Fintech Law, the **Federal Law to Forecast and Identify Operations Using Illicit Proceeds** was amended, so that the ITFs and, in particular, the exchanges (IFPS) may be considered financial entities that shall fully comply with the provisions set forth in the aforementioned Law.

Thus, the ITFs using Virtual Assets shall establish the measures and procedures to prevent and identify omissions or operations to finance operations with illicit proceeds, namely: identifying customer safeguarding information; internal training; use of automated systems; establishing structures and internal manuals; appointing compliance officers; and carrying out an annual audit. Likewise, the SHCP via the CNBV should receive reports about: (1) acts, financial operations or operations related to payments made and services rendered by their clients as well as by those allegedly carrying out operations financing terrorism or operations using illicit proceeds; and (2) acts, operations or services carried out by members of the Board of Directors, directors, officers, employees and true-and-lawful attorneys that may be allocated under the assumption of operations financing terrorism or operations using illicit proceeds.

The SHCP shall issue secondary provisions related to guidelines that need to be met by ITFs in regard to:

- Clients' proper knowledge.
- Information and documentation that shall be collected to carry out operations and render services.
- The terms and conditions on which personnel need to be trained.
- Characteristics of automated systems.
- Establishing communication and control committees.
- Characteristics and functions of the compliance officer.
- The terms of the annual audit.

ITFs shall be obliged to cooperate and share information among themselves and with other financial entities (traditional), to strengthen the detection of operations using resources from illicit proceeds.

Promotion and testing

Those involved in the process of preparing Fintech Law realised that legal standards and their secondary provisions will never adapt or change to the rhythm and speed with which technology advances and new and innovative business models constantly go public. Consequently, the law provides for a flexible legal framework that allows for the emergence, evolution and consolidation of new product and/or service-based business models, without complying with all regulatory burdens.

ITFs, financial entities (traditional) or any other individual may get authorisation by Financial Authorities to temporarily carry out operations or activities through "Novel Models" which exercise requires authorisation, registration or concession pursuant to Fintech Law or by any other financial law; that is, the law provides for a similar scheme to that sandbox established somewhere else.

The law sets forth that:

> [...] "Novel Model is that which in order to render financial services uses tools or technology means with different fashions to those already existing in the market at the time of temporarily authorising under the terms set forth in this Law" [...]

Thus, any individual – related to Fintech Law or not – shall submit before the authority any Novel Model, supported by Virtual Assets or cryptocurrencies.

In order to grant authorisations, authorities shall consider Novel Models to be those which:

(a) financial service/product uses tools or technologies different from those of the market;

(b) benefits clients receive for using the service/product are clear in regard to existing products in the market;

(c) product is in a condition to enter the market once authorisation is delivered;

(d) needs to be refined to a limited market; or

(e) considers the opinion of all the financial authorities that may be involved.

Authorisations may be temporarily granted:

- to unregulated individuals or bodies corporate for a period of two years (may be extended by one more year); and

- to ITFs and regulated entities for a period of one year (extendable for one more year).

Individuals receiving authorisation to operate Novel Models shall submit to the authorities reports related to their operations and comply with the provisions against money laundering.

Ownership and licensing requirements

Fintech Law does not provide for any limit, so investment managers may operate with Virtual Assets either on their own or on account of their clients.

There is no requirement by authorities for investment advisors or fund managers to operate with Virtual Values.

Nevertheless, Fintech Law establishes that Banco de México shall establish the conditions and restrictions for operations and other acts that may be carried out using Virtual Assets.

Likewise, ITFs are forbidden to sell, assign or transfer ownership, loan or to have as collateral Virtual Assets in custody, save in case of sale or allocation by express order by the client/user.

Mining

As we said in the introduction, Fintech Law **does not** attempt to govern the issue, process, circulation, quotation or technology by which cryptocurrencies are supported, **but** the performance of their operators and intermediaries. In this case, Payment Funds Institutions [IFPEs] and Banks need to be prior authorised by Banco de México. **Therefore, mining activities of cryptocurrencies are not subject to the law in effect in Mexico.**

Border restrictions and statements

Fintech Law does not provide for any restriction due to the origin or nationality of the issuer of cryptocurrencies, but Banco de México is the authority responsible for determining which Virtual Assets may be operated and marketed in the national territory.

It is important to point out that operations carried out by ITFs or Banks using cryptocurrencies not authorised by Banco de México will be considered as a vulnerable activity, which may have an administrative and criminal impact.

Reporting requirements

The regulatory framework to avoid money laundering for ITFs is the same as that for any financial entity in Mexico. Thus, ITFs shall submit to the CNBV or the SHCP as described above.

Due to the above, ITFs shall submit to the financial authorities at least the following reports related to operations classified as follows:

*   *Relevant* (for an amount in cash equal or over US$5,000.00).
*   *Unusual* (operations beyond the profile or regular behaviour of a client, taking into account the amount, frequency, type of operation, origin and allocation of funds).
*   *Internal concerns* (acts or omissions that ITFs' counsellors, directors or officers are involved in and which may contravene internal policies, secondary provisions or laws related to avoiding money laundering).

It is important to point out that secondary provisions eventually issued by the CNBV may establish ITFs' obligation to submit other reports and information to avoid money laundering.

Estate planning and intestate succession

IFPE (exchanges) clients may appoint beneficiaries in case of death of the account owner or holder and may replace them at any time as well as amend, where applicable, the relevant percentage to each beneficiary.

In the event no beneficiaries are appointed, the amount corresponding to electronic payment funds shall be delivered under the terms of the common legislation, in the event of the death of the account holder of the beneficiary.

Challenges and conclusions

Mexico took a decisive step to consolidate the fintech sector by enacting Fintech Law. However, there is a lot to do by each and every participant in the sector:

*   to make secondary provisions adapt to the needs, changes and evolution of the fintech sector and not to become a burden for participants;

- to continue with the principle of regulating activities by participants and not to try to regulate or to restrict technology or trends being uncontrollably presented in the world to lead to innovation for the benefit of clients/users;

- to give legal certainty or a clear regulatory framework to their vertical fintech sector (e.g. segtech, regtech, ICO, Tokens, etc.);

- to generate incentives for APIs' implementation by fintech and financial entities;

- to generate communication structures to inform clients/users of financial services about the advantages of the fintech sector; and

- to generate a financial ecosystem to allow for the use of technology advances to benefit other sectors (e.g. blockchain).

The purpose is that the country should benefit from an innovative and flexible regulatory framework and a fintech sector motivated to participate, aimed at:

- encouraging financial inclusion;

- reducing transaction costs and time for the benefit of clients/users who still do not have access to the financial system;

- achieving healthy competition in the financial sector; and

- generating and adopting innovative business technologies and models.

* * *

Endnotes

1. Article 30 of Fintech Law, http://www.diputados.gob.mx/LeyesBiblio/pdf/LRITF _090318.pdf.

2. Article 88 of Fintech Law.

3. http://www.banxico.org.mx/informacion-para-la-prensa/comunicados/miscelaneos/ boletines/%7B5D9E200E-2316-A4B8-92A9-3A5F74938B87%7D.pdf.

4. https://www.gob.mx/shcp/prensa/las-autoridades-financieras-advierten-de-los-riesgos-asociados-al-uso-de-activos-virtuales.

Juan Carlos Tejado
Tel: +52 55 5292 5232 / Email: jctejado@bgbg.mx
Attorney at Law from Universidad Iberoamericana, with a specialty in Commercial Law from Escuela Libre de Derecho; studied an MBA-MEDE and the Private Capital Administration Program (ADECAP), both from the *Instituto Americano de Altra Dirección de Empresas* (IPADE). With over 20 years' experience in the negotiation and operation of investment vehicles and projects related to private capital, Juan Carlos Tejado has worked as the legal director of Umbral Capital, of Grupo ICON, Grupo Irradius, and of Invexcor. Since 2015, he has been a partner at Bello, Gallardo, Bonequi y García S.C. ("BGBG") where he works as managing partner of the Venture Capital and Real Estate Area.

Miguel Gallardo Guerra
Tel: +52 55 5292 5232 / Email: mgallardo@bgbg.mx
Attorney at Law from Universidad Iberoamericana, with an LL.M. degree from New York University School of Law in Comparative Jurisprudence (Fulbright scholar, Funed scholar and Conacyt scholar, 2001). An Insurance Contract Expert certified by the National Insurance and Bonding Commission; AML Expert certified by the National Banking and Securities Commission, Miguel Gallardo Guerra has been appointed as: (i) a member of several boards of directors; and (ii) an external compliance officer by banking and financial institutions in Mexico. He is currently managing partner of the Banking and Financial area and of the Compliance Services Practice Group at Bello, Gallardo, Bonequi y García, S.C. ("BGBG").

Bello, Gallardo, Bonequi y García, S.C.

Agustin Manuel Chávez 1-101, Centro Ciudad Santa Fe, Ciudad de México, 01210, Mexico
Tel: +52 55 5292 5232 / URL: www.bgbg.mx

Netherlands

Björn Schep, Christian Godlieb & Willem Röell
De Brauw Blackstone Westbroek

Government attitude and definition

The focus of the Dutch government with regard to cryptocurrencies is two-pronged. On the one hand, it is eager to mitigate the risks associated with cryptocurrencies. According to the Dutch government, these risks include: (i) the use of cryptocurrencies for criminal purposes such as fraud and money laundering; and (ii) the lack of proper protection afforded to consumers who want to invest in cryptocurrencies. To mitigate these risks, the Financial Intelligence Unit (FIU) has hired experts to trace criminal crypto-activities while the Dutch Central Bank (DNB), the Dutch Authority for the Financial Markets (AFM) and the Authority for Consumers and Markets (ACM) have issued separate press releases to warn consumers against the potential risks of cryptocurrencies. On the other hand, the Dutch government is also keen to stimulate the innovation of blockchain technology. It sees the potential of the technology and is very interested in the possibilities it can offer. For example, the municipality of Groningen has, since 2016, successfully used a blockchain application to provide minimum-income households with "funds" that can be used when buying products or services from companies that are affiliated with the programme. In general, the Dutch government has a positive attitude towards blockchain technology.

Bitcoin and other cryptocurrencies are not formally treated as money in the Netherlands. Cryptocurrencies do not qualify as a legal currency (*wettig betaalmiddel*). This is also the position taken by the Dutch Minister of Finance, DNB and the ECB. The ECB stated that it "*does not regard virtual currencies, such as Bitcoin, as full forms of money as defined in economic literature. Virtual currency is also not money or currency from a legal perspective.*" A Dutch court decided in May 2014 that bitcoins should be treated as a "medium of exchange" and not as a legal currency. On appeal, the court did not rule on whether bitcoins qualify as money or not. The Dutch tax authority treats cryptocurrencies as assets. It is possible to pay with bitcoins in certain shops in the Netherlands; for example, at the Bitcoin Boulevard in The Hague.

DNB started experimenting with its own cryptocurrency in 2015, the DNBCoin. It is not yet the intention of DNB to put the DNBCoin into circulation, but it serves as an internal learning project to better understand blockchain technology. DNB is interested because blockchain technology may have implications for the overarching goal of financial stability and DNB's three primary tasks of: (i) promoting the smooth functioning of the payment system; (ii) prudential supervision and oversight; and (iii) monetary policy.

A motion on the topic of money creation was adopted by the Dutch Parliament during a debate on the citizen initiative, 'Our Money' ('*Ons Geld*'). As a consequence, the Dutch Minister of Finance formally requested the Netherlands Scientific Council for Government

Policy (WRR) for an advisory report on the functioning of the monetary system. The WRR looks at the different aspects of money creation and explores the pros and cons of alternative systems of money creation, and other more limited reforms. The WRR has confirmed to the Dutch Minister of Finance that the DNBCoin will be taken into account in its report.

Cryptocurrency regulation

Cryptocurrencies are not regulated in the Netherlands, and most fall outside of the scope of Dutch financial regulations. However, depending on its structure and specifics, a token may qualify as a security or investment object, in which case it is regulated under Dutch financial law.

A security is (in short) a transferable share, transferable bond or an equivalent instrument. If the token qualifies as a security, the offeror must publish a prospectus in line with the relevant prospectus rules. Whether a token qualifies as a security also impacts whether trading in these tokens is regulated under Dutch law.

If a token is asset-backed, it may qualify under Dutch law as an investment object. An investment object is defined *"as an object, a right to an object or a right to the full or complete return in cash or part of the proceeds of an object, (...) which is acquired for payment, at which acquisition the acquirer is promised a return in cash and where the management of the object is mainly carried out by someone other than the acquirer"*. An offeror of such a token would require a licence from the AFM and would need to comply with governance and information requirements.

The Dutch government has stated that it does not wish to prohibit cryptocurrencies; however, it does wish to regulate them. The intention is to regulate cryptocurrencies on the basis of the following four principles:

(i)   Where necessary, gaps in consumer and investor protection must be filled. These measures should be proportional in relation to the risks of the consumer and investor.

(ii) The integrity of the financial system must be guaranteed on a continuous basis. This means, for example, that risks with regard to money laundering must be mitigated.

(iii) The technology behind cryptocurrency must be maintained and further improved.

(iv) Due to the cross-border nature of cryptocurrency, the regulation must be created at an international level. The Netherlands prefers a coordinated international approach in relation to regulating cryptocurrency, and wishes to play a leading role in setting up a European and international strategy.

Alongside the Netherlands' preferred international strategy, the Dutch government is also looking into the possibility of regulating cryptocurrency at a national level. Currently the Dutch government is analysing legislation adopted in other countries, such as Japan, Germany and Switzerland, to see whether such a model would work in the Netherlands. However, as yet there are no concrete plans to adopt specific Dutch regulations in relation to cryptocurrencies.

The AFM, DNB and the ACM are not currently supervising cryptocurrencies, although they have been actively warning consumers of the risks associated with them.

Sales regulation

The sale of cryptocurrencies as such is not regulated in the Netherlands. However, an entity selling cryptocurrencies in the Netherlands may fall within the scope of Dutch regulation depending on which kind of token (security or investment object) is offered, and how it is offered (investment fund, payment in a fiat currency).

If the token that is sold qualifies as a security, the entity providing this service requires a licence as an investment firm from the AFM. Securities are financial instruments, and offering services with regard to financial instruments, such as executing orders on behalf of clients or receiving and transmitting orders, is a regulated activity. An investment firm must comply with specific ongoing regulations, including those related to governance (e.g. the fit and proper test for prospective board members), market conduct rules (e.g. best execution, know your customer regulations, informing consumers about the risk of the products and a sound and proper business operation) and prudential rules (minimum capital requirement).

If the token that is sold qualifies as an investment object, the act of selling the token qualifies as a regulated service in the Netherlands and a licence from the AFM is required (see 'Ownership and licensing requirements'). The entity selling the token would need to comply with ongoing regulations, including those concerning governance (e.g. fitness of board of directors and supervisory board) and market conduct rules (e.g. information requirements and a sound and proper business operation).

If the cryptocurrencies are offered through a fund structure, the manager of this fund requires a licence from the AFM as an alternative investment fund manager (AIFM) (see 'Ownership and licensing requirements'). For small funds (with assets under management below €100 million or, if no leverage is used and the fund is closed-ended for a period of at least five years, with assets under management below €500 million) which are offered only to professional investors, there is an exemption to the licence requirement and to certain rules applicable to a AIFM. In this case, however, such an AIFM must still be registered with the AFM. An AIFM with a licence must comply with specific ongoing obligations including those regarding governance (e.g. fitness of board of directors and supervisory board, appointment of a custodian), market conduct rules (e.g. a sound and proper business operation, risk management, information requirements) and prudential rules (minimum capital requirement).

Finally, the exchange of fiat currency into cryptocurrency is not currently regulated in the Netherlands. However, this will change following the adoption of the fifth Anti-Money Laundering (AML) Directive in April 2018. The fifth AML Directive includes certain cryptocurrency exchanges within its scope, and consequently these must comply with AML rules, such as customer due diligence and reporting unusual transactions. Please note that cryptocurrency exchanges that only provide services to exchange one cryptocurrency for another cryptocurrency do not fall under the fifth AML Directive. Only providers engaged in exchange services between cryptocurrencies and fiat currencies fall within the scope of the fifth AML Directive.

Taxation

The Dutch Secretary of State of the Ministry of Finance has indicated that it is unlikely that earnings from mining or trading cryptocurrencies by natural persons not acting in business or professional capacity will be qualified – for taxing purposes – as income.[1]

Cryptocurrencies are counted towards a person's assets. The market value as of 1 January of the taxed year is used to determine the taxable value of cryptocurrencies.

Dutch income tax due on assets is set at a rate of 30% of a fixed notional return, which in turn is calculated based on the value of the total assets. The notional return over the first

€70,800 of a person's total assets is fixed at 0.36% over the first 67%, and at 5.38% over the remaining 33%. For any amount between the first €70,800 and €978,000, the notional return is fixed at 0.36% for the first 21% and at 5.38% for the other 79%. Everything that exceeds €978,000 has been assigned a fixed notional return of 5.38%.

The percentages used to calculate the notional return are based on average returns, 0.36% being the average return on savings accounts in the Netherlands for the past five years and 5.38% being the average return on long-term investments, such as securities investments, over the past 15 years. This means these percentages are subject to change.

For legal entities residing in the Netherlands, any income resulting from dealings involving cryptocurrencies – including mining and trading – is allocated to the amount of profits liable to Dutch corporate income tax.

Money transmission laws and anti-money laundering requirements

The Netherlands has no overriding restrictions in place on transmissions or transactions in cryptocurrencies. Risks of money laundering and terrorism financing, however, have been signalled as a major issue by the Dutch regulators and government.

As part of the aim of preventing money laundering and the financing of terrorism, any undertaking or person that falls within the scope of the Dutch Money Laundering and Terrorist Financing (Prevention) Act (*Wet ter voorkoming van witwassen en financiering van terrorisme* (Wwft)) is required to perform client due diligence measures and to report any unusual transaction – or suspicion of such – to the FIU. However, parties providing services involving cryptocurrencies generally do not fall within the scope of the Wwft. Therefore, any party providing services involving cryptocurrencies is not in itself required to perform client due diligence measures. Furthermore, as these parties fall outside the scope of the Wwft, there are currently no hard requirements in place which demand that a suspicion of an unusual transaction in cryptocurrency be reported, provided that no undertaking or person that does fall within the scope of the Wwft is involved in the transaction.

Following the upcoming implementation of the Fifth AML Directive in 2020, the scope of the Wwft will be extended to include custodian wallet providers and parties providing exchange services between fiat currency and cryptocurrencies. These parties will then be required to apply the same client due diligence measures and reporting standards as, for example, banks. This means that, as of January 2020, custodian wallet providers and parties providing exchange services with respect to cryptocurrencies in Europe will need to have in place policies, controls and procedures which are considered appropriate in view of identified risks of money laundering and terrorism financing, and which mitigate and effectively manage those risks.

Promotion and testing

In 2016, the AFM launched its Innovation & Fintech programme to promote technological innovation, including blockchain-based applications, in the financial sector. Under the Innovation & Fintech programme, two initiatives have been launched jointly by the AFM and DNB: the InnovationHub and the Regulatory Sandbox.

InnovationHub[2]

The AFM and DNB set up the InnovationHub in June 2016 to support market parties with questions on the regulation of issues such as crowdfunding, automated advice and blockchain technology. The aim of the InnovationHub is to enable market parties that wish to bring an innovative service or product to the market, and that have questions regarding regulation, to have a single, straightforward and low-threshold single point of access to both regulators. Market parties can thus obtain an indication at an early stage of whether their concept falls under supervision, and if so, what type of supervisory regulation may apply. This support ranges from a single conversation clarifying existing regulation, to intensive processes to understand a complex concept and find an adequate application of legislation and regulation. At this point, more than three-quarters of the questions have concerned market access and authorisation policy, whereby innovations in payments services and blockchain technology were the major themes.

Following the successful introduction of the InnovationHub, to further facilitate innovation and to enable businesses to launch their innovative financial products without unnecessary (regulatory) hindrance, in January 2017 DNB and the AFM created a regulatory sandbox.

Regulatory sandbox

The goal of the Dutch regulatory sandbox is to provide an environment in which tailor-made solutions can be created in order to safely test innovative products and business models. In the context of the regulatory sandbox, the relevant regulator (either DNB or the AFM) will assess whether the applicants and their innovative concepts comply with the underlying purposes of applicable financial markets regulations, rather than the strict letter of the law.

The relevant regulator will assess whether the applicant can or cannot reasonably be held to comply with specific relevant policies, rules or regulations. As an example, the regulators describe a situation in which a financial institution has developed a superior method for complying with rules pertaining to sound and proper business operations using blockchain technology. By using this innovative method, however, the financial institution might deviate from standard or prescribed models or methods for ensuring sound and proper business operations. Within the regulatory sandbox framework, the relevant regulator may grant dispensation from these models or methods for a specified period of time and, if necessary, under specific tailor-made requirements. Similarly, financial institutions introducing an innovative business model for which the current policies, rules and regulations do not yet provide a fitting regulatory framework (e.g. a new form of investment management) may be allowed to test their business model as long as they comply with the underlying purpose of the applicable financial markets regulation.

In addition, DNB and the AFM invite businesses that are experimenting with innovative, non-regulated (e.g. by way of a regulatory exemption) financial activities to involve DNB or the AFM in the development of those operations. DNB and the AFM offer to help identify the risks and drawbacks of the innovative operations at an early stage. This would then add value when such operations are (eventually) brought into the financial regulatory framework following successful experimentation.

Partial authorisation

Finally, in addition to the InnovationHub and the regulatory sandbox, DNB and the AFM offer innovative businesses the possibility to apply for partial authorisation. A partial authorisation may be issued when a financial undertaking does not wish to engage in all operations governed by a full authorisation, or is not yet able to meet all eligibility requirements for such an authorisation. It can be granted on a temporary basis, but may also have a more permanent nature. As such, partial authorisation may be used by businesses to gradually develop a fully-fledged financial undertaking.

Ownership and licensing requirements

In the Netherlands, there are no restrictions on fund managers owning cryptocurrency. However, fund managers must be authorised to operate as an AIFM (by the AFM) if they manage an investment fund with assets under management above certain thresholds or if they offer participation rights to retail investors. This applies to managers of 'regular' investment funds and crypto investment funds alike (also see 'Sales regulation'). In June 2018, the AFM issued a communication on the management of crypto investment funds specifically, in which it highlights a number of requirements (based on European regulations) for authorisation and ongoing supervision that may present compliance difficulties for crypto fund managers; these requirements concern liquidity management, valuation, depositary, product approval and review processes, and anti-money laundering. When considering a licence application, the AFM is expected to pay special attention to these elements.

This varies when it comes to providing investment advice on cryptocurrency. Due to the fact that – currently – cryptocurrencies do not qualify as financial products as defined in the Dutch FMSA, advising investors on buying or selling cryptocurrencies as such is not regulated under the FMSA. If the investment advisor, however, advises on tokens that qualify as financial instruments (securities), that advisor will fall within the scope of the definition of an investment firm and will need to be authorised as such by the AFM. A licence is also required when advising on tokens that qualify as investment objects (also see 'Sales regulation'). In addition, if the investment advisor holds retail client funds (fiat currency) in order for this retail client to exchange the purchased cryptocurrency, the advisor will again fall under the scope of another regulatory rule, as it is prohibited under the Dutch FMSA, to attract, obtain or hold repayable funds from the public. There are several exceptions and exemptions to this prohibition, as well as the possibility of obtaining a dispensation, but these typically do not apply to an investment advisor that holds retail client funds.

Mining

Mining of bitcoin and other cryptocurrencies is unregulated and permitted in the Netherlands. Certain members of Parliament have recently shared their concerns with regard to the energy that is used to mine cryptocurrencies; however, at this stage, it seems unlikely that the Netherlands will prohibit or regulate mining of cryptocurrencies in the near future.

Border restrictions and declaration

If liquid assets with a value equivalent to an amount of €10,000 are brought into the European Union through the Netherlands, the bearer of those liquid assets is required to file a declaration with Dutch Customs. However, cryptocurrencies do not currently qualify as liquid assets as referred to in the Liquid Assets Regulation (i.e. (foreign) banknotes or coins that are in circulation as a means of payment, securities to bearer, not registered by name, such as shares and bonds and travellers cheques that are not registered by name). Therefore, bringing cryptocurrency into the Netherlands does not trigger any filing obligation for the bearer, regardless of whether the cryptocurrency is held by the bearer through online storage or is brought into the Netherlands 'physically' using cold storage devices or facilities.

Reporting requirements

See 'Money transmission laws and anti-money laundering requirements'.

* * *

Endnotes

1. This is, of course, different in the case where a natural person receives salary in the form of cryptocurrencies. In such cases, the cryptocurrencies' value in euro at the moment of payout is taxable as income.
2. The ACM has recently joined this initiative.

Björn Schep
Tel: +31 20 577 1358 / Email: Björn.Schep@debrauw.com
Björn Schep is a senior associate in the firm's Financial Markets Regulatory practice group and specialises in financial law and, in particular, investment management and financial markets regulation. Björn was seconded to Slaughter and May in London in 2012, where he worked in the Financial Regulation group. In October 2017, Björn completed the Executive Master Insurance Studies/Enterprise Risk Management at the Amsterdam Business School.
He regularly advises insurers, banks, investment firms and financial services providers on applicable financial regulatory requirements such as licence requirements, prudential requirements and market conduct requirements. Björn has assisted large established banks and insurers in the Netherlands with their discussions with DNB and the AFM in connection to new innovative ideas. Björn has worked with several fintech startups, mostly advising them on market access issues.

Christian Godlieb
Tel: +31 20 577 1474 / Email: Christian.Godlieb@debrauw.com
Christian is an associate in De Brauw Blackstone Westbroek's financial markets regulation practice group and focuses on banks, insurers, pension funds, investment funds and payment institutions. Christian further specialises in innovation in the financial sector – in which developments pertaining to blockchain and cryptocurrency play an important part. Christian regularly publishes on the topic of the development of regulation with regard to financial innovation.

Willem Röell
Tel: +31 20 577 1032 / Email: Willem.Roell@debrauw.com
Willem is an associate in De Brauw's Corporate Litigation department with previous experience in the firm's Financial Markets Regulatory practice group. Willem focuses on financial institutions and the financial markets as a whole. He is part of the firm's fintech team and has been researching blockchain developments and cryptocurrencies since 2014. Willem is frequently invited to speak about the legal aspects of working with new technologies such as distributed ledgers and payment solutions.
Willem is active in several charitable organisations with a focus on education, human rights and art.

De Brauw Blackstone Westbroek

Claude Debussylaan 80, 1082 MD Amsterdam / P.O. Box 75084, 1070 AB Amsterdam, The Netherlands
Tel: +31 20 577 1771 / URL: www.debrauw.com

Portugal

Filipe Lowndes Marques, Mariana Solá de Albuquerque
& João Lima da Silva – Morais Leitão, Galvão Teles, Soares da Silva &
Associados, Sociedade de Advogados, SP, RL

Government attitude and definition

Blockchain technology in general, and cryptocurrencies in particular, are some of the
most closely followed topics in the financial technology industry amongst the Portuguese
government and the relevant regulatory authorities, along with prevailing fintech trends
in other jurisdictions. In particular, in the last five years these technologies have been
brought to public attention largely due to the dramatic increase in the value of Bitcoin,
the rise in the number of ICOs globally, and their market capitalisation. This focus is also
driven by some significant developments that the Portuguese market has seen in recent
years in this sector, most notably the rise of tech-based companies and the steady increase
in the use of cryptocurrencies in the last decade.

Notwithstanding, in Portugal, blockchain technology has not been implemented in a
significant number of services and is yet to have a relevant impact on either private or
public organisations. In fact, to date in Portugal, most blockchain technology has been
used in the issuance of tokens, including in the context of initial coin offerings ("ICOs").
For these reasons, the government and regulatory authorities have been invested in
studying blockchain technology and cryptocurrencies with a view to creating favourable
conditions for the establishment and development of the sector, while protecting all
market participants' interests.

For the purpose of this chapter, cryptocurrencies can be broadly defined along the
European Central Bank's definition – to which the Portuguese authorities have largely
subscribed – as a "digital representation of value, not issued by a central bank, credit
institution or e-money institution, which in some circumstances can be used as an
alternative to money".[1]

In Portugal, cryptocurrencies do not have legal tender and thus do not qualify as fiat
currency, nor are they treated as "money" (whether physical or scriptural) or "electronic
money". Nonetheless, they are largely seen as an alternative payment method with
a contractual nature that results from private agreement between participants of
cryptocurrency transactions and with intrinsic characteristics that somewhat replicate
some of the core traits of traditional money: storage of value; unit of account; and medium
of exchange. Taking this into consideration, contrary to other countries that have been
developing trials for government-backed cryptocurrencies (e.g. Singapore), in Portugal
cryptocurrencies are not backed by the government or by *Banco de Portugal.*

Cryptocurrencies can also be seen under a different light concerning their functionality.
In this context, there has been recognition of other types of tokens, such as utility tokens
and security tokens, commonly marketed through ICOs. These may be differentiated

by their distinctive function, since the former are largely linked to consumption and the latter to investment. For this reason they encompass or give rise to many other rights, including, among others, the rights to receive a product or service or economic rights.

In light of the above, these new technologies have inevitably drawn the attention of the Portuguese government and the relevant regulatory authorities, most notably the Portuguese banking authority (*Banco de Portugal*), the Portuguese securities authority (*Comissão do Mercado de Valores Mobiliários* or CMVM) and the Portuguese insurance and pension funds authority (*Autoridade de Supervisão de Seguros e Fundos de Pensões* or ASF).

Banco de Portugal, in its capacity as both central bank and national competent authority for the supervision of credit and payment institutions, has shown a clear interest in cryptocurrencies, notably from the perspective of consumer/investor protection, but has otherwise clarified that it will not take any immediate steps to regulate cryptocurrencies, having adopted instead a watchdog approach to the phenomenon and its development.

Nevertheless, since 2013, *Banco de Portugal* has issued a number of public statements and warnings in relation to cryptocurrencies, in line with the regulatory practices of other central banks of the eurozone and European regulatory authorities, such as the European Central Bank (ECB) and the European Banking Authority (EBA). We highlight, *inter alia*, *Banco de Portugal*'s publications which have included a warning focused on Bitcoin (Nov. 2013), where it cited the European Central Bank's study, *Virtual Currency Schemes* (Oct. 2012) (in which the ECB noted that it would be closely monitoring this phenomenon with a view to studying any necessary regulatory responses[2]), and a warning to consumers regarding the potential risks in using cryptocurrencies (Oct. 2014).[3]

In the same manner, CMVM has published a warning to investors, in line with other European regulatory authorities, such as the European Securities and Markets Authority (ESMA), alerting investors to the potential risks of ICOs in order to raise awareness to these risks (Nov. 2017)[4] and has also issued a notice relating to a specific ICO for the issuance of Portuguese token Bityond (May 2018),[5] stating that it did not consider it a security and accordingly, Bityond was not subject to the CMVM's supervision or compliance with securities laws.

More recently, the CMVM has issued a formal notice addressed to all entities involved in ICOs,[6] regarding the legal qualification of tokens. The CMVM stressed the need for all entities involved in ICOs to assess the legal nature of the tokens being offered under the ICOs, in particular their possible qualification as securities with the application of securities laws as a consequence. In this context, the CMVM noted that tokens can represent very different rights and credits, and be traded in organised markets, thus concluding that tokens can be qualified, on a case-by-case basis, as (atypical) securities under Portuguese law, most notably considering the broad definition of securities provided under the Portuguese Securities Code, approved by Decree-Law no. 486/99, of November 13, as amended.

Finally, the Portuguese Government and Parliament have shown an interest in cryptocurrencies, having publicly discussed their potential regulation in the context of the transposition of Directive (EU) 2015/2366 of the European Parliament and of the Council of 25 November 2015 on payment services in the internal market (Payment Services Directive 2 or PSD2). Notwithstanding, neither the Government nor any other regulatory authority have yet issued specific laws or regulations in relation to cryptocurrencies, which therefore remain vastly unregulated.

Cryptocurrency regulation

As previously mentioned, at present, there are no specific laws and regulations applicable to cryptocurrencies in Portugal, including in relation to their issuance and transfer. Hence, cryptocurrencies are not prohibited and investors are allowed to purchase, hold and sell cryptocurrencies.

Nevertheless, on 10 March 2015, *Banco de Portugal* issued a recommendation urging banks and other credit institutions, payment institutions and electronic money institutions, to abstain from buying, holding or selling virtual currency due to the risks associated with the use of virtual currency schemes identified by the European Banking Authority (the Bank of Portugal's Recommendation).[7] Pursuant to this recommendation, most of the aforementioned institutions in Portugal have stopped accepting any orders to process payments made to and by cryptocurrency platforms and exchanges, such as Coinbase, which in practice have restricted its clients to purchasing or selling cryptocurrencies through these platforms and exchanges.

In relation to other types of tokens in Portugal, the same can be said as there are also no specific regulations applicable to other forms of virtual tokens.

However, one cannot say that there is a regulatory vacuum in this context, since existing laws will need to be assessed on a case-by-case basis to determine if they apply to a particular ICO, token or related activity. In this regard, the laws applicable to tokens will vary greatly depending on the specific characteristics of each token.

Thus, from a legal framework perspective, the main concern when analysing an ICO and the respective tokens, will be to determine whether the ICO represents a utility token or a security token.

ICOs that aim to offer tokens that represent rights and/or economic interests in a specific project's results, use of software, access to certain platforms or virtual communities or other goods or services, may hypothetically overlap with consumer matters and become subject to certain regulations regarding consumer protection.

ICOs that aim to offer tokens that represent rights and/or economic interests in a pre-determined venture, project or company, such as tokens granting the holder a right to take part in the profits of a venture, project or company or even currency-type tokens, may potentially be qualified as securities and cross over to securities' intensively regulated world, becoming subject to existing securities regulations, most notably regulations applicable to public offerings of securities and/or securities trading venues. In this respect, it should be noted that ESMA has highlighted that ICOs qualifying as financial instruments may be subject to regulation under the following EU law:[8]

- Regulation (EU) 2017/1129 (Prospectus Regulation);

- Directive 2011/61/EU (Alternative Investment Fund Managers Directive);

- Directive 2014/65/EU (Markets in Financial Instruments Directive) and Regulation (EU) 600/2014 (Markets in Financial Instruments Regulation); and

- Directive 2015/849/EU (Anti-Money Laundering Directive).

It is also worth noting that, within the context of the information published regarding Portuguese cryptocurrency Bityond, mentioned above, the CMVM has already publicly stated that a token which allows its users to (i) participate in surveys related to the development of an online platform, and (ii) further donate tokens to the online platform for the develop of new tools, is not qualified as a financial instrument, i.e. is not a security token, and therefore is not subject to securities law and the supervision of the CMVM.

Additionally, in its formal notice addressed to entities involved in ICOs, dated 23 July 2018, and mentioned above, the CMVM has further clarified the elements that may, in abstract, implicate the qualification of security tokens as securities, namely: (i) if they may be considered documents (whether in dematerialised or physical form) representative of one or more rights of private and economic nature; and (ii) if, given their particular characteristics, they are similar to typical securities under Portuguese law. For the purpose of verifying the second item, the CMVM will take into account any elements, including those made available to potential investors (which may include any information documents – e.g. white paper), that may entail the issuer's obligation to undertake any actions from which the investor may draw an expectation to have a return on its investment, such as: (a) to grant the right to any type of income (e.g. the right to receive earnings or interest); or (b) undertaking certain actions, by the issuer or a related entity, aimed at increasing the token's value.

The CMVM thus concludes that if a token is qualified as a security and the respective ICO is addressed to Portuguese investors, the relevant national and EU laws shall apply, including, *inter alia*, those related to: the issuance, representation and transmission of securities; public offerings (if applicable); marketing of financial instruments for the purposes of MiFID II; information quality requirements; and market abuse rules. Finally, should the ICO qualify as a public offering, the CMVM further clarifies that a prospectus should be drafted and submitted, along with any marketing materials for the ICO, to the CMVM for approval, provided that no exemption applies in relation to the obligation to draw a prospectus. Lastly, in this notice the CMVM also alerts that where a token does not qualify as a security, its issuer should avoid the use, including in the ICO's documentation, of any expressions that may be confused with expression commonly used in the context of public offerings of securities, such as "investor", "investment", "secondary market" and "admission to trading".

Sales regulation

Considering the lack of exclusive regulation in relation to cryptocurrencies in Portugal, as described under "Cryptocurrency regulation" above, the purchase and sale of cryptocurrencies *per se* is also not specifically regulated.

However, to the extent that a token sale may be qualified as, for example, an offer of consumer goods or services or an offer of securities to the public, the relevant existing laws and regulations on, respectively, consumer protection and securities and financial markets, may apply by default, including their sanctions regime, subject to, in any case, an individual assessment. In these cases, both consumer protection law and securities law provide a number of obligations that must be complied with during and after the sale process. Therefore existing regulations on the sale of consumers' goods or services and of securities can apply to certain types of tokens on a case-by-case basis, in accordance with an "as-applicable principle".

Taxation

In Portugal there is no specific regime that deals exclusively with the taxation of cryptocurrencies. Nonetheless, the Portuguese Tax Authority has published two official rulings in the context of certain requests for binding information relating to cryptocurrencies; one in the context of personal income tax (Dec. 2016[9]), and the other in the context of value added tax (Feb. 2018[10]). In the absence of other laws and regulations that may clarify the taxation regime of cryptocurrencies, these rulings have an important weight and will work as precedents in relation to how the Portuguese Tax Authority will look into cryptocurrency and cryptocurrency-related activities when interpreting existing tax provisions and deciding whether or not a certain fact or action should be subject to Portuguese tax (corporate, individual, VAT or stamp duty). In any event, as these were given in the context of requests for binding information, the Portuguese Tax Authority may revoke these rulings in the future.

In the 2016 official ruling, the Portuguese Tax Authority analysed the possible classification of cryptocurrencies within certain types of income that are subject to Portuguese tax, notably capital gains, capital income and income from business activities, and decided that, as a general rule, natural persons should not be taxed in respect of gains derived from the valuation of cryptocurrency or sale of cryptocurrencies, except that, in the case of sale of cryptocurrencies, if they correspond to the individual's main recurrent activity, income obtained from such activity could be subject to Portuguese tax. It should also be noted that this was only a partial decision that did not elaborate on other types of income derived from other cryptocurrency-related activities (e.g. mining and farming activities).

In the 2018 official ruling, the Portuguese Tax Authority received a request to issue an opinion on the application or exemption of value added tax (VAT) to cryptocurrencies exchanges. The Portuguese Tax Authority invoked precedent from the Court of Justice of the European Union (Case C-264/14, *Skatteverket v. David Hedqvist*) to argue that although cryptocurrencies, such as for example Bitcoin, were analogous to a 'means of payment' and therefore subject to VAT, they were exempt by application of VAT exemption rules, which should be consistent across EU Member States considering existing VAT EU harmonisation.

Money transmission laws and anti-money laundering requirements

The Portuguese law on anti-money laundering and combating terrorist financing[11] (AML Law) imposes a general undertaking to obliged entities of risk management in the use of new technologies or products which are prone to favour anonymity.[12] This means that, under Portuguese law, obliged entities are legally required to monitor the risks of money laundering and terrorist financing arising pursuant to the use of new technologies or developing technologies, whether for new products or existing ones,[13] and, before launching any new products, processes or technologies, they will have to analyse any specific risks of money laundering or terrorist financing related to it, and to document the specific procedures adopted for their risk mitigation.

In addition, obliged entities must undertake identification procedures and customer due diligence whenever there is an occasional transaction of more than €15,000, as well as reinforce their identification procedures and customer due diligence when they identify an additional risk of money laundering or terrorist financing in business relationships, in occasional transactions or in the usual operations of the customer. Pursuant to the AML Law, an additional risk is presumed to exist in products or operations that favour anonymity, in new products or commercial activities, in new distribution mechanisms and payment methods and in the use of new technologies or developing technologies, whether for new products or existing ones. This has obvious implications for cryptocurrencies and cryptocurrency-related activities (including cryptocurrencies exchanges) in case those operations intersect with the activities and operations of entities that are covered by obligations imposed by anti-money laundering and combating terrorist financing, since obliged entities should reinforce their identification procedures and customer due diligence when participating in any related operation.

In the banking sector, the Bank of Portugal's Recommendation, mentioned above, was driven also by concerns with the risks of money laundering, terrorist financing and other financial crime arising pursuant to the overall predominance of anonymity and lack of intermediaries that would communicate suspicious activities to the authorities.[14] This recommendation followed a previous warning to consumers issued in October 2014, as mentioned above, that was made in response to the fact that certain automated teller machines (ATMs) in Portugal, which were not integrated in the Portuguese payment system, were enabling exchange between bitcoins and euros.

Banco de Portugal's stance in respect of cryptocurrencies does not affect other market participants such as consumers, investors and other entities that wish to, respectively, hold, invest or develop cryptocurrencies, but it goes a long way towards reducing the participation of banks and other credit institutions, payment institutions and electronic money institutions that are traditional 'obliged entities' for the purposes of anti-money laundering and combating terrorist financing laws. It should be also noted that insofar as operations in cryptocurrencies are not undertaken by obliged entities (as legally defined), compliance with and enforcement of anti-money laundering and terrorist financing laws should be diluted, as cryptocurrencies and related activities are confined to virtual platforms and private relations.

Furthermore, considering the publication of AMLD 5[15], additional obligations in relation to cryptocurrencies exchanges and custodian wallet providers are expected to come into force after 10 January 2020, when Member States, including Portugal, are required to implement and bring into force laws transposing AMLD 5.

Promotion and testing

The Portuguese government has recently launched a think-tank with the objective of promoting and fostering fintech generally – mostly by identifying and targeting entry barriers. The ultimate aim of the think-tank is to implement a regulatory 'sandbox' with the aid of the Portuguese financial regulators. Within the objectives of the think-tank, cryptocurrencies have been listed as one of the priorities.

Additionally, both the CMVM and *Banco de Portugal* have developed specific spaces for fintech on their webpages, http://www.cmvm.pt/en/ and https://www.bportugal.pt/en/, respectively, which include, *inter alia*, information regarding distributed ledger technology, initial coin offerings and tokens.

These fintech spaces were created with the intent to facilitate the provision and exchange of information and dialogue between these regulators and developers or sponsors of new financial technologies which cross over with the areas of regulatory competence of the CMVM and *Banco de Portugal*, and also to clarify the regulatory framework applicable to the same. These objectives are obtained mainly by having a dedicated contact within the CMVM and *Banco de Portugal* that deals solely with issues relating to fintech, and by being active in promoting conferences and workshops aimed at investors and the public in general with a formative and educational goal.

Ownership and licensing requirements

As mentioned in "Cryptocurrency regulation" above, in Portugal there are no restrictions or licensing requirements when it comes to purchasing, holding or selling cryptocurrencies.

Furthermore, insofar as cryptocurrencies are not qualified as financial instruments, advisory services that are made exclusively in relation to and the exclusive management of cryptocurrency portfolios are not subject to the same investment services laws and regulations as those applicable to securities. Thus, these types of activities, when undertaken solely in relation to cryptocurrencies, are not subject to any licensing requirements.

However, traditional advisory services and management services require licensing and are subject to the CMVM's supervision.

One thing to note is that, given the relative novelty of some of these instruments, the overall regulatory uncertainty and even some regulatory pushback (e.g. the Bank of Portugal's Recommendation), underpinned by the already existing and overarching obligations applicable to the provision of investment services, it is not at all likely for the time being that traditional investment advisors, including, among others, credit institutions and fund managers, will recommend or invest in cryptocurrencies.

Mining

There are no restrictions in Portugal to develop mining of cryptocurrencies and the activity itself is not regulated.

Border restrictions and declaration

In Portugal there are no border restrictions or obligations to declare cryptocurrency holdings.

Reporting requirements

There is no standalone reporting obligation in case of cryptocurrency payments above a certain threshold, except in the case of transactions that may involve an obliged entity covered by anti-money laundering and terrorist financing laws, in which case such entity will have to report suspicious transactions or activities irrespective of the amounts involved.

Estate planning and testamentary succession

There is no precedent, specific rules or particular approach regarding the treatment of cryptocurrencies for the purposes of estate planning and testamentary succession in Portugal.

Notwithstanding, certain aspects of estate planning and testamentary succession should be highlighted. Inheritance tax does not exist in Portugal, but stamp duty may apply to certain transfers of certain assets (e.g. immovable property, movable assets, securities, negotiable instruments, provided they are located, or deemed to be located in Portugal) included in the deceased estate in case of succession.

However, in the absence of a legal amendment or binding information from the Portuguese tax authorities, it may be argued that the drafting of the relevant legal provisions does not expressly foresee assets such as cryptocurrencies, thus excluding the same from the scope of application of stamp duty, which *de facto* mitigates the need for estate planning with respect to cryptocurrencies. Estate planning and testamentary succession must therefore be analysed on a case-by-case basis, considering all variables involved.

* * *

Endnotes

1. *Cf.* EUROPEAN CENTRAL BANK, *Virtual currency schemes – a further analysis*, February 2015, available at https://www.ecb.europa.eu/pub/pdf/other/virtualcurrencyschemesen.pdf.

2. *Cf.* BANCO DE PORTUGAL's public statement regarding Bitcoin, dated 22 November 2013, available in Portuguese at https://www.bportugal.pt/comunicado/esclarecimento-do-banco-de-portugal-sobre-bitcoin.

3. *Cf.* BANCO DE PORTUGAL's warning regarding the risks associated with cryptocurrencies, dated 3 October 2014, available in Portuguese at https://www.bportugal.pt/comunicado/alerta-aos-consumidores-para-os-riscos-de-utilizacao-de-moedas-virtuais.

4. *Cf.* CMVM's warning regarding the risks associated with ICOs, dated 3 November 2017, available in English at http://www.cmvm.pt/en/Comunicados/Comunicados/Pages/20180119.aspx.

5. *Cf.* CMVM's notice regarding the cryptocurrency Bityond, dated 17 May 2018, available in Portuguese at http://www.cmvm.pt/pt/Comunicados/Comunicados/Pages/20180517a.aspx.

6. CMVM's notice addressed to all entities involved in ICOs, dated 23 July 2018, available in Portuguese at http://www.cmvm.pt/pt/Comunicados/Comunicados/Pages/20180723a.aspx?v=.

7. *Cf.* BANCO DE PORTUGAL's Circular Letter no. 11/2015/DPG, dated 10 March 2015, *Recommendation relating to the buying, holding and selling virtual currencies*, available in Portuguese at https://www.bportugal.pt/sites/default/files/anexos/cartas-circulares/11-2015-dpg.pdf.

8. *Cf.* EUROPEAN SECURITIES AND MARKETS AUTHORITY, Statement "ESMA alerts firms involved in *Initial Coin Offerings* (ICOs) to the need to meet relevant regulatory requirements", dated 13 November 2017, available at https://www.esma.europa.eu/sites/default/files/library/esma50-157-828_ico_statement_firms.pdf.

9. *Cf.* AUTORIDADE TRIBUTÁRIA E ADUANEIRA, Binding Information provided in process no. 5717/2015, dated 27 December 2016.

10. *Cf.* AUTORIDADE TRIBUTÁRIA E ADUANEIRA, Binding Information provided in process no. 12904, dated 15 February 2018.

11. Law no. 83/2017, of August 18, transposing Directives 2015/849/EU, of the European Parliament and of the Council, of May 20, and 2016/2258/EU, of the Council, of December 6.

12. *Cf.* Article 15 of Law no. 83/2017.

13. *Cf.* Article 36 (5) and Annex III of Law no. 83/2017.

14. *Cf.* EUROPEAN BANKING AUTHORITY, *EBA Opinion on 'virtual currencies'* (EBA/Op/2014/08), 4 July 2014, available at https://www.eba.europa.eu/.

15. Directive (EU) 2018/843 of the European Parliament and of the Council of 30 May 2018 amending Directive (EU) 2015/849 on the prevention of the use of the financial system for the purposes of money laundering or terrorist financing.

Filipe Lowndes Marques
Tel: +351 213 826 601 /Email: flmarques@mlgts.pt

Filipe Lowndes Marques is the coordinator of the Banking and Finance department and the Restructuring & Insolvency department.

Filipe has worked since 1995 in the area of loan and bond finance, representing lenders and borrowers, including restructurings of existing financings. In the project finance sector he has worked on several types of projects, including bridges, motorways, power plants, wind and solar farms, football stadia, LNG terminals and natural gas concessions.

He has also been active in the field of banking and financial regulation, on which he teaches several classes in postgraduate courses at the Faculty of Law of the University of Lisbon.

Mariana Solá de Albuquerque
Tel: +351 213 826 601 / Email: msalbuquerque@mlgts.pt

Mariana Albuquerque joined the firm in 2014. She is a member of the banking and finance team.

Mariana develops her work primarily in the area of banking and finance law, with special focus on compliance and providing legal advice and consultancy with regard to the regulation and supervision of banks and other financial institutions, in securitisation transactions, negotiating derivatives and other financial instruments, structured finance, corporate finance and project finance transactions and in negotiating the sale and purchase of non-performing loans portfolios.

She also works in debt restructurings, debt issues and other issues of hybrid financial instruments, also having experience in public offers and takeover bids.

João Lima da Silva
Tel: +351 213 826 601 / Email: jlsilva@mlgts.pt

João Lima da Silva is a member of the Banking and Finance department, as well as the Private Equity & Investment Funds department.

João develops his work primarily in the area of banking and finance law, with special focus on structured finance, project finance, debt restructuring, debt issues, credit facilities and non-performing loans transactions. João also regularly works in transactions involving investment funds and provides legal advice to management companies.

He has also been active in the fields of compliance, regulation and supervision of banks and other financial institutions, most notably in the investment and payment services sector.

Morais Leitão, Galvão Teles, Soares da Silva & Associados, Sociedade de Advogados, SP, RL

Rua Castilho 165, 1070-050 Lisbon, Portugal
Tel: +351 213 826 601 / URL: www.mlgts.pt

Russia

Vasilisa Strizh, Dmitry Dmitriev & Anastasia Kiseleva
Morgan, Lewis & Bockius LLP

Government attitude and definition

In sum, cryptocurrencies are used in Russia in various contexts including as payment for goods or services or as some instrument analogous to securities. Given the absence of laws which would directly govern cryptocurrency and the generally non-transparent nature of transactions with cryptocurrencies, the Russian authorities have an established negative attitude to their use. However, the Russian legislators have been working on a set of laws which would govern cryptocurrencies. As regards blockchain technology, there is no uniform approach, but in general it has already been used in Russia.

For several years, the Russian authorities have been giving attention to potential uses of blockchain technology and cryptocurrencies. The focus has been on compliance and anti-corruption and anti-money laundering measures. The Central Bank of the Russian Federation (The Bank of Russia) and the Ministry of Finance are the key regulators that have paid specific attention to these issues.

There is no law at present that would specifically address cryptocurrencies, and there is no legal definition of cryptocurrency. On the contrary, there are laws that might be viewed as prohibiting cryptocurrencies in Russia. For example, under the Russian Constitution, the *rouble* is the only means of payment in Russia. Further, under the Federal Law on the Central Bank of the Russian Federation of 2002, the *rouble* is the only national currency, and the introduction of other currencies or the issuance of currency surrogates on the Russian territory is prohibited. Cryptocurrencies may be such prohibited currency surrogates.

Further, there is a view that the use of cryptocurrencies is associated with illegal activities. In January 2014, The Bank of Russia issued an information letter[1] warning that the trading in goods or services for "virtual currencies", as well as the conversion of such currencies to *roubles* or foreign currencies, could be used for money laundering and terrorist financing. Therefore, any transactions involving cryptocurrencies are subject to heightened scrutiny.

In 2016, the Ministry of Finance proposed amendments to certain laws[2] that would impose large administrative fines and criminal penalties including imprisonment for up to seven years, for the issuance, purchase, or sale of bitcoins. Certain other Russian governmental bodies expressed support for these proposals, including the Ministry of Economic Development and the Investigative Committee, a federal agency with authority over criminal investigations. However, these proposed amendments have not been introduced.

Nevertheless, cryptocurrencies are used in Russia. Moreover, there are attempts to bring regulation to cryptocurrency. For example, the State Duma, the lower chamber of the Russian parliament, has adopted in the first reading a set of draft laws on cryptocurrency (*see* section "*Cryptocurrency regulation*" for further details). These draft laws propose definitions of a "token", "cryptocurrency", and an umbrella definition for both tokens and cryptocurrency – a "digital financial asset."

Cryptocurrency would be broadly defined as a variety of digital financial assets created and accounted for in the distributed ledger of financial transactions by the participants of that ledger and in accordance with its rules. In turn, the digital financial asset would be defined as property in electronic form, created using cryptographic means, and which includes cryptocurrency and tokens. "Digital money" would be defined as a digital code or enumeration in a decentralised information system that does not certify rights to any assets, but rather is used for making payments. It is proposed that digital money can be used as payment in Russia in certain circumstances and subject to conditions to be set forth in other laws.

Similarly to cryptocurrencies, there is no law at present specifically addressing blockchain technologies. However, the authorities do not view blockchain negatively. On the contrary, the use of blockchain technologies for the formation and implementation of "smart contracts" is of great interest in Russia and they have already been used in certain areas. In many respects, Russia remains a tradition-bound market in which physical documents are essential. In particular, the transition to distributed ledger systems and virtual contracts will conflict with existing, centralised registers that are now legally required for certain activities and transactions.

However, Russia is moving toward digitalisation of many services and functions that government agencies perform. Governmental authorities are in the process of modernising their operations, allowing filings and document exchange via online platforms – including, for example, filing of tax declarations, accounting reports and licence and patent applications. These include the Federal Tax Service, the Federal Service for Intellectual Property, and the Federal Service for Supervision of Communications, Information Technology and Mass Media. Notary filings may be submitted electronically, and the register of the companies is also accessible online. Still, legal reforms are needed to allow the use of these technologies, and there are various proposals for ways to achieve this.

Cryptocurrency regulation

There is no existing specific regulation of cryptocurrencies, and their use in Russia is currently subject to great legal uncertainty. However, over the last couple of years, different proposals for governing cryptocurrencies and related matters have been announced.

In May 2018, the State Duma (the lower chamber of the Russian parliament) approved in the first reading three draft laws that address the use of cryptocurrencies in respect of mining, token offerings, and crowdfunding:

1. A draft law "On Introduction of Changes to Parts One, Two and Four of the Civil Code of the Russian Federation", primarily aimed at amending the Civil Code, with core concepts related to cryptocurrencies: "digital rights" and "digital money".

2. A draft law "On Digital Financial Assets", that would introduce certain key rules with respect to issuance, offering or otherwise transacting with tokens including initial token offerings (also known as initial coin offerings or ICOs), the mining of cryptocurrency, and the use of digital wallets.

3. A draft law "On Attracting Investments with Use of Investment Platforms", that seeks to regulate the activities of crowdfunding platforms and related investment activities (collectively, the **Draft Laws**).

The Draft Laws appear to be the first comprehensive attempt to adopt regulations directly governing cryptocurrencies and related matters. However, prior to becoming the law, the Draft Laws would need to be approved by the State Duma in the second and third readings, then approved by the Council of Federation (the upper chamber of the Russian parliament), and signed into law by the Russian President. The second reading has not been scheduled. It appears likely that the Draft Laws will be further considered by the State Duma this autumn. We think that substantial revisions will be made before the second reading, especially because the current versions overlap or even contradict each other in many respects.

Sales regulation

Under the Draft Laws, digital assets may be exchanged only for traditional currencies (*roubles* or foreign currency) through the so-called "operators of digital financial assets trade". An operator of digital financial assets trade must be a Russian legal entity that is considered a broker, a dealer, or a securities manager pursuant to the Federal Law on Securities Market of 1996 or a trading organiser pursuant to the Federal Law on Organized Trading of 2011.

In addition, the Draft Laws introduce rules for issuing and offering tokens. It is proposed that a token offering would comprise two steps. First, the issuer of tokens disseminates via the Internet an investment memorandum ("white paper") containing a public offer to purchase tokens and such other documents as the issuer may determine. After the investment memorandum and other documents become public, the issuer can sell tokens to investors, including by means of smart contracts.

The Draft Laws propose certain mandatory requirements for the contents of the investment memorandum and the public offer, to make the process transparent. For example, the investment memorandum must include information on the issuer's shareholders, the purpose of issuing tokens, the planned use of proceeds (for example, it should contain a business plan for any projects being funded), and the description of rights associated with tokens. The public offer must include information on the issuer, the purchase price (or method of its determination), the rules for maintaining the register of transactions with tokens, and the procedure of opening and maintaining digital wallets. In essence, the proposed rules are similar to the existing rules on issuing and offering securities in Russia.

Taxation

Although there are no special rules on the taxation of transactions with cryptocurrencies, the Tax Code of the Russian Federation would apply.

Recently, the Ministry of Finance expressed a view that all profits from operations with cryptocurrencies should be subject to personal income tax, and issued two information letters in May[3] and July[4] 2018 (the **Letters**). In these Letters, the Ministry of Finance specifically noted, among other things, that any economic benefit derived from transactions with cryptocurrencies is taxable and taxpayers must pay income tax (the tax imposed by the Tax Code); the tax base from cryptocurrency sale and purchase transactions should be determined in *roubles* as a surplus of income received by the taxpayer from the sale of cryptocurrencies over the total amount of expenditures for the purchase of cryptocurrencies; and the taxpayer must calculate the amount of tax to be paid and file the tax declaration himself.

Reportedly,[5] the amendments to the Draft Laws that are now being prepared for the second reading at the State Duma (see section "*Cryptocurrency regulation*" for further details) will contain amendments to the Tax Code of the Russian Federation on taxation of digital rights.

Money transmission laws and anti-money laundering requirements

There is no express cryptocurrency-related anti-money laundering legislation.

In September 2017, The Bank of Russia issued yet another information letter[6] warning about possible illegality and associated risks of transactions with cryptocurrencies. The Bank of Russia noted that cryptocurrencies are issued by anonymous and unidentifiable persons and, therefore, in transacting with cryptocurrencies, persons may become involved in illegal activities, including money laundering and terrorist financing. The Bank of Russia warned that cryptocurrencies entail high-level risks, both when issuing cryptocurrency and tokens in initial token or coin offerings, as well as later, during exchange operations. The Bank of Russia further emphasised that it believes that "admission of cryptocurrencies and other financial instruments nominated in or related to cryptocurrencies, to circulation and use in organised trading as well as in clearing and settlement infrastructure for servicing transactions with cryptocurrencies and related derivatives in Russia", is premature.

Promotion and testing

The Russian Government and The Bank of Russia have launched or announced several initiatives to support the development of blockchain technologies while keeping a watchful eye on the cryptocurrency market.

In September 2015, The Bank of Russia established a working group[7] to study blockchain technologies and to explore potential practical applications, including in the financial markets. This has led to efforts to establish a prototype distributed database for financial messaging. In July 2016, a consortium including Qiwi, a provider of electronic payment and financial services in Russia and the CIS; Accenture, a global management consulting and professional services firm; and several Russian private banks, began testing[8] blockchain technologies, working together with The Bank of Russia. The work of the consortium has resulted in Masterchain,[9] an Ethereum-based blockchain prototype for the validation and exchange of client data and transactional information. In contrast to Ethereum, Masterchain is a permissioned (private) database of chained blocks of data. The Bank of Russia acts simultaneously as an ordinary user in payment processing and as a trusted administrator. The next step may be to develop further prototypes. The Bank of Russia is currently examining two other proposed versions of Masterchain.

Further, in 2017, the Russian President issued an order[10] for the Russian Government and The Bank of Russia to create a regulatory sandbox for testing various innovative financial technologies. The Bank of Russia created the sandbox in April 2018.[11] It allows innovative start-ups to test their technologies without running a risk of violating current legislative restrictions.

Another proposal is the establishment of a professional association called "FinTech",[12] which would assist in drafting legislation to regulate blockchain technologies. Representatives of various governmental agencies would also participate. The association would address various applications of blockchain technologies, such as electronic voting, notary systems, maintenance of shareholder, real estate and other statutory registers, and validation of client data and transactional information.

Several Russian organisations are also becoming active in the blockchain sphere. The National Settlement Depository, Russia's central securities depository, has initiated a pilot e-proxy shareholder voting[13] project using a blockchain solution, and has already serviced several blockchain-backed commercial bond offerings.[14]

Ownership and licensing requirements

The Draft Laws propose certain regulations regarding ownership and licensing requirements with respect to cryptocurrencies (see section "*Cryptocurrency regulation*" for further details on the status of the Draft Laws).

Under the Draft Laws, ownership of cryptocurrencies would not be specifically restricted, and would be based on a person's having access to a "digital right" recorded in a decentralised information system, as well as the related recordals made in the register of digital transactions.

The Draft Laws propose to define a "digital right" as a digital code or enumeration in a decentralised information system that: (a) certifies that a person having "unique access" to such code or enumeration will also have rights to certain assets (other than intangible assets); and (b) allows such person to obtain information on these assets at any time. An owner of a digital right would be a person with "unique access" to such code or enumeration that would allow such person to dispose of the digital right. The Draft Laws also propose that in certain cases, an owner of a digital right could also be a person recorded as such by the person with "unique access" to the code or enumeration.

As regards investments, the Draft Laws propose to introduce a concept of the "investment platform." An investment platform would be defined as an information system in the information-telecommunication network the Internet, that is used for concluding contracts with the use of information technologies and technical features of the investment platform by means of which investments are attracted, and which is also available as a mobile application. Only a Russian legal entity included by The Bank of Russia into a register of operators of investment platforms may be the operator of an investment platform.

The Draft Laws would also limit investments by individuals who are not considered "qualified investors" under Russian securities laws. Qualified investors are deemed to have sufficient experience in the investment market and include so-called professional participants in the securities market such as broker-dealers, clearing organisations, banks and other financial institutions, securities investment funds, management companies of investment and pension funds, non-state pension funds, The Bank of Russia and other persons which are considered to be, or could be qualified as, "qualified investors" under the securities laws. These could include individuals who meet certain eligibility criteria established by the securities laws. Individuals who are not qualified investors would not be able to invest above certain thresholds to be further determined by The Bank of Russia. At present, similar rules apply for non-qualified investors investing via stock exchanges and otherwise in securities and other financial instruments.

The Draft Laws contain no specific licensing requirements to be imposed on the holders of cryptocurrency.

Mining

The Draft Laws would introduce the definitions of "mining" and "digital record validation".

"Mining" would be defined as actions aimed at creating cryptocurrency, and/or digital record validation for the purpose of obtaining cryptocurrency reward.

"Digital record validation" would be defined as an action of legal significance aimed at verifying the validity of digital records in the register of digital transactions. The validation is supposed to be performed in accordance with the rules on maintaining the register of digital transactions.

The Draft Laws also contemplate that mining of cryptocurrencies would become a taxable business activity when it exceeds, for three months in a row, certain electricity consumption thresholds to be determined by the Russian Government.

As regards the existing legislation that may be applicable to mining activities, certain hardware used in mining activities may be currently recognised as devices containing encryption and cryptographic tools. Under the applicable laws, the use and distribution of such devices may be subject to import restrictions as well as licensing by the Federal Security Service or the Ministry of Industries and Trade.

Border restrictions and declaration

At the moment, the existing laws and initiatives do not provide for any border restrictions or obligations to declare cryptocurrency holdings when entering or exiting Russia.

Reporting requirements

At present, there is no specific regulation with respect to cryptocurrency reporting requirements for individuals or legal entities. However, the issue of reporting has been discussed in the context of Russian anti-corruption laws, requiring public and governmental officials to report on their property and other holdings. These discussions are also associated with another important legal issue: whether cryptocurrency is property.

In May 2016, the Ministry of Labour and Social Security of the Russian Federation issued the reporting guidelines.[15] Notably, in these guidelines the Ministry of Labour specifically advised that public and government officials are not obliged to disclose ownership of "*virtual currencies*", in contrast to rather strict reporting obligations in relation to their assets and funds on bank accounts. In other words, these guidelines assume that *virtual currencies* are not property.

However, in other spheres cryptocurrency is viewed as property, at least in the insolvency context. For example, Russian courts are already facing difficult questions regarding the nature of cryptocurrencies and their exposure against creditor claims. Recently, the Moscow appellate court has ruled[16] that the concept of "*other property*" as set forth by the Civil Code of the Russian Federation could be interpreted to include cryptocurrency. Therefore, cryptocurrency should be included into the insolvency estate of the debtor along with other property. The court obliged the debtor to disclose his password to give the insolvency manager access to the debtor's cryptocurrency wallet.

Estate planning and testamentary succession

At present, there are no special rules on succession of cryptocurrency. Still, the rules on succession of the Civil Code of the Russian Federation generally apply, subject to the below considerations.

It is possible that, under the general rules of the Civil Code of the Russian Federation, cryptocurrency could be recognised as an estate property (asset or other property). This has already been supported in court (see section "*Reporting requirements*", for further details). However, given that access to cryptocurrency assets is restricted to persons having a code or specific "unique access", certain steps should be taken by a person to ensure that the cryptocurrency will be passed to heirs.

Cryptocurrency has two crucial features that prevent existing legal structures from being applicable to the succession of cryptocurrency: (1) that the identity of a cryptocurrency owner is not generally revealed to third parties; and (2) that the cryptocurrency owner is neither shown in any certificate or other document nor listed in any register.

Therefore, one needs to create an action plan to enable to include a person's cryptocurrency assets to the estate (as it is recognised by the Civil Code of the Russian Federation). In essence, a person needs to set up a structure allowing heirs to inherit tangible media (a piece of property) containing the information allowing access to a cryptocurrency wallet and to transact with the cryptocurrencies stored in it. For example, the person can do as follows. First, determine what information is required to get access to the wallet and transactions with the cryptocurrencies such as, for example, a login and password to a website, a secret question or a key (code). Secondly, fix such information on a physical storage device such as, for example, a USB flash drive, a compact disk, a paper note. A physical storage device would be a piece of property that could be inherited too, including by default. Under the Civil Code of the Russian Federation, estate includes assets and other property, including property rights and liabilities owned by the deceased as of the date of opening of the inheritance.

These steps are relevant only if there are no laws addressing the issue. It is possible that once the cryptocurrency is expressly allowed in Russia, inheritance laws might be amended to deal with cryptocurrencies directly.

* * *

Endnotes

1. https://www.cbr.ru/press/PR/?file=27012014_1825052.htm.
2. https://iz.ru/news/607066.
3. Letter of the Ministry of Finance No. 03-04-07/33234 of 17 May 2018, https://www.nalog.ru/html/sites/www.new.nalog.ru/docs/minfin/03040733234.pdf.
4. Letter of the Ministry of Finance No. 03-04-05/48714 of 12 July 2018, https://normativ.kontur.ru/document?moduleId=8&documentId=317281.
5. https://ru.insider.pro/topnews/2018-06-13/iz-rossijskih-zakonoproektov-uberut-ponyatiya-kriptovalyuta-i-cifrovye-dengi/.
6. Information Letter of The Bank of Russia "On Using Private 'Virtual Currencies' (Cryptocurrency)" of 4 September 2017, https://www.cbr.ru/press/pr/?file=04092017_183512if2017-09-04T18_31_05.htm.
7. https://www.vedomosti.ru/finance/news/2015/09/18/609329-tsb-blockchain.
8. https://www.vedomosti.ru/finance/articles/2016/07/04/647759-tsb-rasprobuet-blockchain.
9. http://masterchain.rbc.ru/.
10. https://lenta.ru/news/2017/10/24/crypto/ and http://kremlin.ru/acts/assignments/orders/55899.
11. https://www.cbr.ru/fintech/regulatory_platform/.
12. https://forklog.com/tag/assotsiatsiya-fintech/.
13. https://www.nsd.ru/common/img/uploaded/files/gm_proxy_voting.pdf.
14. https://www.nsd.ru/en/press/ndcnews/index.php?id36=633749.
15. Methodical Recommendations on Issues of Reporting Information on Income, Expenditures, Property and Property Liabilities and on Filling out of the Respective Type of Certificate, of 16 May 2017.
16. Decision of the 9th Arbitrazh Appellate Court in Case No. A40-124668/2017, dated 15 May 2018.

Vasilisa Strizh, Partner
Tel: +7 495 212 2540 / Email: vasilisa.strizh@morganlewis.com
Vasilisa represents global and domestic strategic and financial investors across multiple industries, including financial services, mass media and telecommunications, energy, and pharmaceuticals and life sciences. Vasilisa's practice focuses on cross-border investment, joint venture, and merger and acquisition transactions. Vasilisa also counsels on corporate governance and compliance and advises on capital market transactions and related regulatory matters. She has served as lead lawyer on complex corporate projects, including acquisitions, divestitures and joint ventures, public and private equity offerings, financing, and structured settlements. She participated in a project for the Russian central securities depository on the Russian corporate reform to allow paperless shareholder meetings, electronic voting, settlements through the CSD and disclosures via the Center of Corporate Information. Vasilisa serves as the Managing Partner of the Moscow office.

Dmitry Dmitriev, Associate
Tel: +7 495 212 2574 / Email: dmitry.dmitriev@morganlewis.com
Dmitry represents domestic and international companies across multiple industries, such as media, energy, retail, and financial services in mergers, acquisitions, and joint venture transactions as well as in general corporate matters and real estate transactions. On an ongoing basis, he also counsels clients on virtually all regulatory aspects of employment relations, including issues of personnel mobility, executive compensation, long-term incentive (LTI) programs and a variety of personnel issues arising in M&A transactions. He is also actively involved in the global Fintech industry working group at Morgan Lewis and frequently co-authors publications related to legal developments in the blockchain and cryptocurrency industries in Russia.

Anastasia Kiseleva, Associate
Tel: +7 495 212 2568 / Email: anastasia.kiseleva@morganlewis.com
With a focus on telecommunications, media, entertainment, and technology industries, Anastasia represents international and Russian companies in transactions relating to joint ventures, mergers and acquisitions, technology and IP licensing, distribution arrangements, as well as in general corporate and commercial matters. Anastasia also advises on various regulatory aspects of mass media and IT businesses; use and protection of intellectual property; production and distribution of motion pictures in Russia; corporate governance and compliance matters; e-commerce, advertising and outsourcing. Anastasia actively follows new initiatives in media and technology industries, including related to cryptocurrency and blockchain matters, and regularly participates in the firm's related activities, such as publications on the Morgan Lewis tech & sourcing blog. Anastasia's experience also includes a wide spectrum of data privacy issues, including personal data protection and related regulatory matters, website privacy policies, consent requirements, cross-border transfers of personal data and audits of data processing activities.

Morgan, Lewis & Bockius LLP

Legend Business Center, Tsvetnoy Bulvar, 2, Moscow 127051, Russia
Tel: +7 495 212 2500 / Fax: +7 495 212 2400 / URL: www.morganlewis.com

Singapore

Franca Ciambella, En-Lai Chong & YingXin Lin
Consilium Law Corporation

Government attitude and definition

Singapore is commonly referred to as one of the world's "cryptohavens", not only because it is a world financial centre, but also as a result of its balanced legal and regulatory regime fostered by the Monetary Authority of Singapore ("MAS"). Acting as the central bank and as the financial regulating body, MAS' approach is to regulate the space to prevent stifling innovation, while simultaneously protecting investors and the public at large.

The government has not defined a virtual currency (used interchangeably with "cryptocurrency" or "token" or "coin" unless otherwise specified) to be one exclusive thing, but instead has stated the following: (a) they are not a currency or legal tender issued by any government; (b) they are to be encouraged as a means of paying for goods or services to someone who is willing to accept them as a mode of payment, and are a means of making payments; (c) they cannot be a store of value, as their prices fluctuate (in this regard, the government attitude is to not encourage people to use them as an investment tool as they are risky); and (d) they are recognised as assets and personal property, with more and more people trading in them.

Regarding blockchain technology, the government encourages its development, but says that this positive attitude does not mean it is necessarily encouraging cryptocurrencies. Cryptocurrencies are not the only application of blockchain technology; it has many other uses. Government confidence in blockchain technology is shown through its development of "Project Ubin".

Backed by MAS, Project Ubin is aimed at creating a digital token for the Singapore dollar on the Ethereum blockchain. Each ledger is supported by the equivalent amount of Singapore dollars held by the government, which will ensure that the overall money supply is not impacted by the token and has full redemption possibilities. The project is intended to make financial transactions cheaper and more efficient. Although the project is still in its early stages, it is a prime example of one of the ways that Singapore is seeking to have digital tokens backed by the government and central banks.

Cryptocurrency regulation

A virtual currency itself is not regulated in Singapore; however, the activities surrounding it or its characterisation resulting from its activity are what determine whether it will be regulated under securities or other legislation. This leaves the door wide open for tokens, for example, of a payment nature only, to be unlicensed, non-security tokens that can be sold to the public without any licensing or MAS oversight using a simple set of sale terms and conditions. Moreover, in the analysis of the characterisation of a token, a key difference with other major jurisdictions is that it will not be considered a security simply because there will be some sort of crowd-funding or capital-raising activity. Instead, an in-depth analysis of whether it falls within the scope of securities law is required to determine its characterisation as a security or not, and any ensuing or other licensing or regulatory requirements.

A "legal opinion" on the characterisation of the token as falling within securities legislation, and any other licences that may be required, should be a first step. One reason for this is that unlike some other jurisdictions, regulators such as MAS will not get involved in this exercise and do not provide opinions or specific guidance on a particular situation.

This section will deal with the regulations surrounding Initial Coin Offerings ("ICOs") and Exchanges.

ICOs – Are they securities?

An ICO refers to the fund-raising process whereby digital tokens (or coins) are offered for sale online to the public in return for payment in a specified cryptocurrency or fiat. The tokens may or may not have utility functions. Some tokens serve as both fund-raising tools and tools that enable access and usage of the issuer's platform or eco-system, while some other tokens are solely fund-raising tools.

As will be examined below, some tokens may resemble securities, which raises the issue of whether Singapore's securities laws apply to certain ICOs. The implications of this issue are significant, as there are extensive laws and regulations governing the issuing of securities to the public, such as the registration of a prospectus, making conducting an ICO an onerous and costly endeavour to embark on.

MAS announced on 1 August 2017 that the offer or issue of digital tokens in Singapore will be regulated by MAS if the digital tokens constitute products regulated under the Securities and Futures Act (Cap.289, Rev. Ed), (hereinafter "SFA") or other securities legislation.

Where digital tokens fall within the definition of securities in the SFA, the offeror of the tokens would be required to lodge and register a prospectus with MAS prior to offering such tokens, unless otherwise exempted from such requirement.

In the analysis, the first issue to look into is the definition of securities, which may be found in the SFA. The term "Securities" is defined in Section 2(1) and Section 239(1) of the SFA. As follows:

Section 2(1)

"securities" means —

(a) *debentures or stocks issued or proposed to be issued by a government;*

(b) *debentures, stocks or shares issued or proposed to be issued by a corporation or body unincorporate;*

(c) *any right, option or derivative in respect of any such debentures, stocks or shares;*

(d) *any right under a contract for differences or under any other contract the purpose or pretended purpose of which is to secure a profit or avoid a loss by reference to fluctuations in —*

(i) *the value or price of any such debentures, stocks or shares;*

(ii) *the value or price of any group of any such debentures, stocks or shares; or*

(iii) *an index of any such debentures, stocks or shares;*

(e) *any unit in a collective investment scheme;*

(f) *any unit in a business trust;*

(g) *any derivative of a unit in a business trust; or*

(h) *such other product or class of products as the Authority may prescribe, but does not include —*

    (i) *futures contracts which are traded on a futures market;*

    (ii) *bills of exchange;*

    (iii) *promissory notes;*

    (iv) *certificates of deposit issued by a bank or finance company whether situated in Singapore or elsewhere; or*

    (v) *such other product or class of products as the Authority may prescribe as not being securities;*

Section 239 (1)

'"securities" means —

(a) *shares or units of shares of a corporation;*

(b) *debentures or units of debentures of an entity;*

(c) *interests in a limited partnership or limited liability partnership formed in Singapore or elsewhere; or*

(d) *such other product or class of products as the Authority may prescribe, but does not include such other product or class of products as the Authority may prescribe as not being securities.*

There are some exemptions from the requirement in Section 240(1) SFA, and Section 272B(1) SFA provides an exemption for being a private placement, if certain requirements are met. Such exemptions can be one of the following:

(a) the offers are made to no more than 50 persons within any period of 12 months;

(b) none of the offers is accompanied by an advertisement making or calling attention to the offer or intended offer;

(c) no selling or promotion expenses are incurred in connection with each offer other than those incurred for administrative or professional services, or by way of commission or fee for services rendered thereby; and

(d) no prospectus in respect of any of the offers has been registered by the Authority or where a prospectus has been registered.

While ICOs are typically offerings to the public, some issuers limit the sale of their tokens to private or institutional investors. Some issuers carry out both the private and public sale, with the former at an earlier stage, before proceeding with the latter.

There is a new piece of legislation, the Payment Services Bill ("PSB") that is being prepared by the Singapore Government. The PSB, when enacted, will regulate the purchase and sale of virtual currencies. Under the PSB, entities that carry out any of the following activities need to hold a licence and be subject to regulation:

(a) account sale services;

(b) domestic money transfer services;

(c) cross-border money transfer services;

(d) merchant acquisition services;

(e) e-money sale;

(f) virtual currency services; and

(g) money-changing services.

It is possible that the activities of ICO companies may fall under the categories of "e-money sale" and/or "virtual currency services", and it would be important to look into the application of the PSB after it has been enacted.

Exchanges

Once a coin is offered, it is typically traded on the market via an exchange. Markets, as defined in the SFA, are regulated according to Section 6 of the SFA:

> "6.
>
> — (1) No person shall establish or operate a market, or hold himself out as operating a market, unless the person is —
>
> (a) an approved exchange; or
>
> (b) a recognised market operator."

A party would have to obtain the requisite approvals or licences from MAS in order to set up and operate an exchange. However, this is a costly process with no guarantee that MAS would grant such an approval or licence.

Section 2(1) SFA, read with Paragraph 1 of Part I of the First Schedule of the SFA, defines "market" in the SFA as a securities market or futures market.

Paragraph 2 of the First Schedule of the SFA defines futures markets. They are described as a place where offers or invitations to sell, purchase, or exchange are made or may reasonably be intended to lead to results.

Further, futures contracts are defined in Section 2(1)(a) of the SFA, which states that a contract that creates the effect where one party agrees to deliver a specific commodity by a specified future time at a specified price payable at that time. Or it can be where a specified quantity of a specified commodity is agreed at the time of the making of the contract and at a specified future time.

Hence, the issue of whether or not a token is a futures contract could be affected by: whether it is paid for and delivered at or around the time of entering into the ICO contract instead of at a specified future time; whether there is any difference between the value of the token at different points of time that has to be settled between the issuer and the purchaser; whether the potential profits or losses that a purchaser may make on the token will be as against the issuer; and whether the tokens are interests in or contractual rights against the issuer that may be realised or enforced in the future.

Paragraph 3 of Part I of the First Schedule of the SFA defines securities market, which describes it as being a place or a facility by means of which offers or invitations to sell, purchase or exchange issues securities are regularly made on a centralised basis, that are intended or expected to result in the sale, purchase or exchange of issues securities or prescribed securities.

Overall, it appears that as long as the virtual currency is not a "security" under the SFA, its virtual currency exchange would currently not be regulated and no licence is currently required, however, if even one token is a security, then the exchange would be regulated under the SFA.

On 24 May 2018, MAS issued a warning to eight cryptocurrency exchanges who were found to have permitted trading of coins that were securities in Singapore. It is clear that MAS is taking a firm stance on these exchanges. As set out above, cryptocurrencies that are securities may only be listed on approved exchanges or recognised market operators.

Besides regulating exchanges on which security tokens are listed, MAS will also regulate cryptocurrency exchanges in general through anticipated legislation tabled in the PSB.

Sales regulation

Sales of virtual currencies can occur through: (a) private sale when created; (b) ICO; or (c) trading.

Private sale at creation

This could occur as part of a pre-ICO or sale and purchase in the context of a newly created token. Generally, these are by a private agreement. However, if a token is deemed a security under the SFA, then licences need to be applied for and obtained (as discussed above).

ICOs

Please refer to the above section on the rules pertaining to the sale of a token pursuant to an ICO.

Trading

There are no regulations for retail investors specifically governing their trading of cryptocurrencies. Nonetheless, MAS has issued a statement to advise the public to "act with extreme caution and understand the significant risks they take on if they choose to invest in cryptocurrencies".

However, there are regulations governing certain activities that are related to trading. There is a list of activities that are regulated and licensed under the SFA and some of them may be related to trading. Section 82 of the SFA states:

> Any person carrying on or holding himself out as carrying on business in any "regulated activity" in Singapore must hold a Capital Markets Services Licence (CMS licence) for that "regulated activity".

Sub-section 82(1) of the SFA states:

> *"Subject to subsection (2) and section 99, no person shall, whether as principal or agent, carry on business in any regulated activity or hold himself out as carrying on such business unless he is the holder of a capital markets services licence for that regulated activity."*

Section 2(1) and the Second Schedule of the SFA define the regulated activities as:

"(a) dealing in securities;

(b) trading in futures contracts;

(c) leveraged foreign exchange trading;

(d) advising on corporate finance;

(e) fund management;

(ea) real estate investment trust management;

(f) securities financing;

(fa) providing credit rating services;

(g) providing custodial services for securities."

Section 2(1) and Part II of the Second Schedule of the SFA states:

> *"'dealing in securities" means (whether as principal or agent) making or offering to make with any person, or inducing or attempting to induce any person to enter into or to offer to enter into any agreement for or with a view to acquiring, disposing of, subscribing for, or underwriting securities'.*

Hence, if a person is trading as part of their business, then they would be regulated under the SFA and require a Capital Markets Services licence.

Fund management is defined in the Second Schedule as:

> *""fund management" means undertaking on behalf of a customer (whether on a discretionary authority granted by the customer or otherwise) —*
>
> *(a) the management of a portfolio of securities or futures contracts; or*
>
> *(b) foreign exchange trading or leveraged foreign exchange trading for the purpose of managing the customer's funds,*
>
> *but does not include real estate investment trust management."*

Therefore, if a person trades on behalf of a customer, then he/she would be regulated under the SFA and require a Capital Markets Services licence.

Taxation

(a) Revenue for goods or services using virtual currencies: Businesses that choose to accept virtual currencies for consideration for goods or services are subject to normal income tax rules found in the Income Tax Act (Cap.134), hereinafter, ITA. For example, if a business accepts payment in Ether, then it will be considered as revenue just as it would be if paid in fiat. The value given would be the value of the services (or goods) on the date of the transaction, or the parties could choose a mutually acceptable date for valuation. Taxation would be based on the net profits (after deducting allowable expenses under the ITA). The general current tax rate for businesses is 17% of taxable income.

(b) Capital gains tax: Individuals or businesses that buy virtual currencies for long-term investment purposes may enjoy a capital gain from the disposal of these virtual currencies. However, there are no capital gains taxes in Singapore, and as a result, these gains are not subject to tax. However, individuals or businesses that buy and sell virtual currencies in the ordinary course of their business will be **taxed on the profit derived from trading in the virtual currency**. Profits derived by businesses which mine and trade virtual currencies in exchange for money are also subject to tax, as these would be considered "revenue". Whether gains from disposal of virtual currencies are subject to capital gains tax depends on the facts and circumstances of each case. Factors such as purpose, frequency of transactions, and holding periods are considered when determining if such gains are taxable.

(c) Tax on proceeds from an ICO: The issue is whether the proceeds from an ICO are recorded as revenue and taxable in Singapore. As time evolves, more guidance is being given by the Inland Revenue Authority of Singapore (hereinafter "IRAS"), however, the position is not yet definitive. According to the ITA, revenue is taxable in Singapore if: (i) it is accrued or derived from Singapore; or (ii) if it is foreign-derived income, it is received in Singapore. In the situation of (i), following Par.10(1)(a) of the ITA which states that revenue by a trade or business carried on by a taxpayer (as the entity usually used for an ICO is registered in Singapore, it would qualify as a taxpayer), are taxable. While still not clear, some taxpayers have therefore deemed income derived outside of Singapore (i.e. in the case where a token purchaser is outside of Singapore) as not subject to tax. It is for this reason that some ICO terms and conditions stipulate that Singaporeans may not purchase tokens. In scenario (ii), proceeds would not be taxable if not received in Singapore. This territorial criterion is based on an analysis of the facts, such as where the founders of the ICO are based, if the ICO is marketed outside of Singapore through promotional "hypathons" or via the cloud, and if the participants are based outside of Singapore. Even for those ICO proceeds that fall within (i) or (ii), tax planning such as imputing proceeds over a period of time and offsetting qualifying expenses, can serve to minimise taxes payable. In addition, it should be remembered that only the income that falls within (i) or (ii) is taxable, and not the totality of the proceeds. It is advisable to seek tax advice prior to embarking on an ICO.

(d) <u>Goods and Services Tax ("GST") on sale of virtual currencies</u>: IRAS has confirmed the sale of tokens as a sale of a "supply of services". Under the <u>Goods and Services Act</u> ("<u>GSTA</u>"), GST is imposed on the supply of services. However, if the sale of a token is to purchasers who do not have any connection to Singapore, then this could be viewed as an international supply of services, which has a zero rate of tax under the GSTA. The current rate of tax under the GSTA is 7%; however, this is expected to increase to 9% some time between 2021 and 2025.

Money transmission laws, Know Your Client and anti-money laundering requirements

With respect to money transmission laws, please refer to above discussion on PSB.

In this section, the following will be examined:

1. Know Your Client "<u>KYC</u>" requirements (including source of income requirements).
2. Anti-Money Laundering ("<u>AML</u>") requirements.
3. Combating of Financing of Terrorism ("<u>CFT</u>") requirements.

The standards an issuer of a cryptocurrency token must comply with depend on whether or not the token is a security. If the token is a security as defined in the SFA, the MAS guidelines on KYC, AML and CFT will apply.

MAS requires that financial institutions must:

1. verify the customer's identity including name, unique identification number, date of birth, nationality and residential address;
2. if the customer is not a natural person, verify the identities of the natural persons who have the authority to act for the customer;
3. ascertain whether there are any beneficial persons and if so, the identities of those beneficial persons;
4. determine the nature and purpose of the business relations with the customer;
5. visit the place of business if it is considered necessary;
6. obtain information about source of the funds;
7. after business relations are established, conduct ongoing monitoring of the business relations; and
8. conduct periodic reviewing of the adequacy of the customer information.

When the business is not done on a face-to-face basis, MAS suggests the following measures:

1. holding real-time video conferencing that is comparable to face-to-face communication in addition to obtaining electronic copies of identification documents;
2. verifying the identity of a customer through a document the customer has signed with a secure digital signature using a set of Public Key Infrastructure-based credentials issued by a certified Certificate Authority; and
3. using biometric data such as fingerprints, iris scans or facial recognition.

Regarding the KYC process, in order to determine if someone is a Politically Exposed Person ("<u>PEP</u>"), it is possible to refer to databases compiled commercially or by the authorities. It is also beneficial to look at the customer themselves including details of their occupation, name of their employer, and non-public information.

MAS publishes lists of entities who are suspected of terrorist activities and all potential token purchasers must be screened to ensure they are not dealing with suspected terrorists (part of CFT requirements). Additionally, MAS maintains a list of countries which are subject to sanctions and customers must also not be from these countries. These should also be consulted.

In the event of a suspicious transaction, the Suspicious Transaction Reporting Office should be notified within 15 days.

Examples of suspicious transactions include:

1.   transactions which do not make economic sense;
2.   transactions involving large amounts of cash;
3.   transactions involving a high velocity of transactions through a bank account;
4.   transactions involving transfers abroad;
5.   investment-related transactions that are suspicious;
6.   merchants acquired for the purpose of credit or charge card transactions; and
7.   transactions involving unidentified parties;
8.   transactions related to tax crimes; and
9.   trade-based related transactions with significant discrepancies.

For tokens that do not fall within the definition of securities set out in the SFA, the MAS Guidelines on KYC, AML and CFT do not, strictly speaking, apply. However, it is a good business practice to follow these Guidelines nevertheless.

Personal data protection laws

The Singapore Personal Data Protection Act ("PDPA") and the European Union's General Data Protection Regulations ("GDPR") are discussed in this section.

The protection of a customer's personal data is governed by the PDPA. When an individual's personal data is collected, consent must be obtained and the individual must be informed of the purpose for which it is collected. Consent is deemed to have been given in circumstances where the individual volunteers the personal data and it is reasonable that the personal data would be provided. An individual may withdraw consent to the collection of personal data at any time.

An organisation must ensure that personal data cannot be accessed by implementing reasonable security arrangements. Security would include measures such as encryption and requiring that personal data can only be accessed with passwords of a sufficient length. When personal data is transferred out of Singapore, the organisation must ensure that it is afforded the same level of protection as required by the PDPA.

Under the PDPA, an individual may request access to and the correction of personal data. While an organisation may charge a reasonable fee to comply with such requests, it must provide a written estimate of the fee before complying with a request for access.

Singapore's PDPA is well aligned with the European Union's GDPR. However, the GDPR further provides that, in relation to citizens or residents of the European Union, the owner of personal data may request that his or her personal data be erased. The GDPR also requires that an organisation's privacy policy must be readily understood by a layperson.

The Personal Data Protection Commission ("Commission") has jurisdiction over complaints made by individuals in respect of breaches of the PDPA. The Commission has the power to order that an organisation cease collecting or destroy personal data, and also to impose a fine of up to S$1 million.

Ownership and licensing requirements

In this section, ownership and investment licences under MAS, as well as licensing, are discussed by asking the following questions:

1. Can investment managers use virtual currencies for investment purposes? Are they required to have the same licences as if they were using fiat? What could these licences be?

2. What are the types of licences needed by someone who uses virtual currencies as an investment advisor or fund manager or capital markets advisor? What is the process for obtaining these?

MAS has not provided any guidance on whether virtual currencies may be used for investment purposes. Therefore it would be advisable for investment managers to enquire with MAS before using virtual currencies.

Under the Second Schedule of the SFA, MAS requires companies engaged in fund management or advising on corporate finance to hold a Capital Markets Services Licence. If the assets under management are less than S$250 million and the number of qualified investors is 30 or less, the company would need to be a Registered Fund Management Company.

MAS estimates that applications for a licence or registration will take approximately two to four months to process.

The General Criteria for the grant of a CMS licence are set out in the MAS Guidelines on Criteria for the Grant of a Capital Markets Services Licence:

1. must be a corporation;
2. must be a reputable entity with an established track record in the proposed activity to be conducted in Singapore or in a related field for at least the past five years;
3. the applicant and its holding company or related corporation must have a good ranking in their home country;
4. must be subject to proper regulation by the authority in its home country, if applicable;
5. must satisfy MAS that it will discharge its duties efficiently, honestly and fairly;
6. must establish and operate out of a physical office situated in Singapore;
7. must be primarily engaged in conducting one of the regulated activities under the SFA; and
8. its officers, employees, representatives and substantial shareholders are fit and proper, in accordance with the criteria set out by MAS.

In order for the Board of Directors, Chief Executive Officer and Representatives to hold a CMS licence they are required to comply with additional criteria.

Investment advisors would be required to have a financial advisor's licence pursuant to the Second Schedule of the Financial Advisors Act.

The MAS Guidelines on Criteria for the Grant of a Financial Advisor's Licence specify a minimum paid-up capital of S$150,000 or the equivalent in a foreign currency. Other relevant criteria include:

1. whether at least two individuals are employed or appointed for financial advisory services;

2. whether the Chief Executive Officer and all Executive Directors have at least five years of relevant working experience in financial advisory services, with a minimum of three years in management, as well as acceptable academic and professional qualifications;

3. whether the Board of Directors has at least two members one of whom is resident in Singapore;

4. whether the Chief Executive Officer is resident in Singapore; and

5. whether the Chief Executive Officer or Executive Directors are placed in a position of conflict of interest.

Mining

Cryptocurrency mining is the process of using computers to verify transactions on the blockchain and add a new block to the blockchain, in return for an amount of cryptocurrency. Cryptocurrency miners need to compete against each other in order to be the first to verify the transaction and earn the amount of cryptocurrency, using the Proof-of-Work ("PoW") method. In order to sustain a mining business, large amounts of computational power and electricity are required. This is the same process as is used in most other jurisdictions.

Currently, there are no regulations specifically governing the mining of cryptocurrency in Singapore. A miner would require specialised hardware with adequate cooling systems and large amounts of electricity. Hence, the miner should ensure that he is allowed to carry out mining at his chosen venue following local regulations on emissions and noise.

A miner should also be conscious of his tax liabilities arising from his income from mining. IRAS states on its website that: "Profits derived by businesses which mine and trade virtual currencies in exchange for money are also subject to tax." The current business tax rate is 17% on net profits pursuant to the ITA.

As mining is considered work, a foreigner would be required to have the requisite work permit to be able to work in Singapore. In addition, businesses who employ miners need to respect Singapore employment law.

In any case, mining is likely to become less prevalent in the future in Singapore given the high electricity costs, tropical temperatures, and premium on space. Blockchain projects initially relied on PoW to validate transactions. However, in Singapore, there are now more blockchain projects using the Proof-of-Stake ("PoS") method of validating transactions on the blockchain. The PoS method does not require mining in the way that the PoW method does, because, under the PoS method, whether a transaction on the blockchain may be verified by a person depends on the number of coins that he/she holds. The said person would earn an amount of cryptocurrency by verifying the transaction on the blockchain, but there is no competition in doing so, and minimal computational power is required, thereby saving on electricity.

Border restrictions and declaration

There are currently no border restrictions or declarations required with respect to virtual currencies, other than complying with the regulatory regime as described above. Virtual currencies are borderless.

The IRAS treats virtual currencies as the supply of services. While this usually means virtual currencies are a service provided to the purchaser when the currency is first issued, there is some uncertainty as to whether a virtual currency must be declared when it is imported into Singapore.

Arguably, importing cryptocurrencies stored on USB flash drives or similar hardware wallets into Singapore need not be declared to the customs authorities as only the private keys are being transported, while the blockchain remains decentralised and not situated in any particular location. Further, cryptocurrencies are not one of the categories of goods subject to import duty under the <u>Customs Act (Chapter 70)</u>. That said, to err on the side of caution, it would be advisable to declare the value of goods or services which exceed SGD $600.00 when entering Singapore. The <u>Goods and Services Tax (Imports Relief) Order</u> provides that a *bona fide* traveller may import goods worth up to SGD $600 if the traveller has been outside Singapore for at least 48 hours, or up to SGD $150 if the traveller has been outside Singapore for less than 48 hours.

Reporting requirements

Virtual currencies are meant to be decentralised and anonymous. There are currently no reporting requirements for the ownership, use or sale of virtual currencies other than for tax purposes as described above.

Everyone is required under the law to report suspicious transactions, which they come across in the course of their trade, profession, business or employment, to the Suspicious Transaction Reporting Office ("<u>STRO</u>") in the Commercial Affairs Department of the police. All suspicious transaction reports, including those involving cryptocurrencies and digital tokens, are analysed by STRO. Where there are indications of an offence, STRO will refer the matter to the enforcement agencies, such as IRAS for possible tax crimes, and the Capital Adequacy Directive ("<u>CAD</u>") for possible money laundering.

Estate planning and testamentary succession

This section will discuss how virtual currencies can be included as an asset in estate planning and succession, including issues of confidentiality or security and valuation.

The main pieces of legislation, the <u>Intestate Succession Act (Cap.146)</u>, the <u>Wills Act (Cap.352)</u>, and the <u>Probate and Administration Act (Cap.251)</u> have no specific laws dealing with estate planning and succession relating to virtual currencies. Wallets containing virtual currencies, and even value-stored cards, can be transferred in much the same way as other personal property is transferred.

The security of a cryptocurrency is a major concern. Virtual currencies are typically stored in wallets where their ownership is anonymous, and where there are no designated beneficiaries. If no-one has details of a wallet, it will not generally be possible to have access to its contents. For estate planning or testamentary purposes, methods are being devised to make the wallet accessible through an executor or trustee by providing details of the service provider, the user details and the private key. As wills have to be in writing in Singapore, and witnessed by two persons, and often sent to a central registry, it is not recommended that these details be written in a will or trust or other estate document, as whoever has access to these details will be able to access the wallet.

With respect to valuation, since there is no capital gains tax in Singapore, the differences in valuations from the time a cryptocurrency is acquired by a testator, bequeathed, inherited and converted to fiat are not relevant. Valuations may, however, be relevant for practical purposes when trying to bequeath specific sums to heirs or beneficiaries, as their value changes over time.

Franca Ciambella
Tel: +65 6235 2700 / Email: fciambella@consiliumlaw.com.sg
Trained in law and business in Canada, New York and Singapore, Franca was amongst the first foreigners admitted to the Singapore Bar. She has been the Managing Director of Consilium Law Corporation since 2010, and prior to that was a partner at an international Canadian law firm, and General Counsel for Asia for a US based Fortune 500 multinational. She practises corporate & commercial law, contracts, mergers & acquisitions, blockchain/ICOs and acts as a mediator. Franca sits on the Board of a number of chambers of commerce, does *pro bono* for non-profit organisations, mentors students and was recently awarded the Sovereign Medal by Canada's Governor General for her volunteerism and leadership. She is often called to speak on the topic of virtual currencies, blockchain and ICOs at conferences.

En-Lai Chong
Tel: +65 6235 2700 / Email: enlai@consiliumlaw.com.sg
Graduated from the National University of Singapore in 2005, En-Lai Chong has a broad range of experience from civil litigation to corporate & commercial law. From working with a multinational corporation as a legal counsel, he also gained practical commercial experience. He has a keen interest in blockchain technology and cryptocurrencies.

YingXin Lin
Tel: +65 6235 2700 / Email: yingxin@consiliumlaw.com.sg
YingXin Lin's practice encompasses Corporate & Commercial Law as well as Commercial Litigation. He specialises in general corporate advisory work as well as the drafting of commercial contracts and other legal documentation. He has advised and assisted clients on regulatory compliance, trade mark applications, capital raising, securities regulation, disputes and employment law matters. He has assisted clients in a variety of industries and sectors, including fintech, construction, aviation, software and technology. He has also advised and assisted blockchain technology companies on the structuring of their operations, regulatory compliance issues, structuring of their token sales and cryptocurrency exchanges, as well as legal documentation, in accordance with Singapore law. He has handled a variety of contentious cases, including shareholder disputes, employment disputes, securities disputes, property disputes and contractual disputes.

Consilium Law Corporation

1 Scotts Road, #16-02, Shaw Centre, Singapore 228208
Tel: +65 6235 2700 / URL: www.consiliumlaw.com.sg

South Africa

Angela Itzikowitz, Ina Meiring & Era Gunning
ENSafrica

Government attitude and definition

In March 2014, the South African Reserve Bank ("**SARB**") issued the virtual currency position paper ("**VC Position Paper**"), which distinguishes virtual currency ("**VC**") from e-money. E-money, as defined in the National Payment System Department Paper on Electronic Money 01/2009, is electronically stored monetary value issued on receipt of funds and represented by a claim on the issuer. E-money is generally accepted as a means of payment by persons other than the issuer and is redeemable for physical cash or a deposit into a bank account on demand.

A VC is a digital representation of value that can be digitally traded and functions as a medium of exchange, a unit of account and/or a store of value, but does not have legal tender status. VCs are either centralised or decentralised, and convertible or non-convertible. Convertible VCs have an equivalent value in real currency and can be exchanged back-and-forth for a real currency.

Decentralised VCs, such as Bitcoin, are distributed, open-source, math-based peer-to-peer virtual currencies without a central administrating authority, monitoring and oversight authority. On the other hand, non-convertible VCs, such as Q Coins, are intended for a particular virtual domain and cannot be exchanged for real currency. All non-convertible VCs are centralised, as they are issued by a central authority that establishes rules, making them non-convertible. As such, non-convertible (centralised) VCs pose fewer risks to the public than decentralised VCs, which are "on the radar" of many financial regulators. The emerging VC regulatory proposals are thus directed at managing the risks associated with decentralised VCs, which is hence the main focus of the VC Position Paper.

The VC Position Paper provides that decentralised VCs do not constitute legal tender in South Africa, as they are not "*generally accepted*" as payment by persons other than the issuer. The paper cautions that decentralised VCs should not be used as payment for the discharge of any obligation in a manner that suggests that they are a perfect substitute for legal tender. Therefore, there is a clear distinction between decentralised VCs and e-money, as decentralised VCs are tradable for cash while e-money is redeemable for physical cash or a deposit into a bank account on demand.

The VC Position Paper highlights several risks which are posed by decentralised VCs, such as those relating to: payment systems; price stability; anti-money laundering; consumer risk; circumvention of Exchange Control Regulations; and financial stability. The SARB does <u>not</u> oversee, supervise or regulate the VC landscape, systems or intermediaries for effectiveness, soundness, integrity or robustness. Consequently, any and all activities related to the acquisition, trading or use of VCs are performed at the end-user's risk and without recourse to the SARB.

The SARB has also established a Fintech Unit to assess the emergence of Fintech in a structured and organised manner, and to consider its regulatory and strategic implications. This Unit has been tasked to review the approach to policy and regulation of cryptocurrencies and to investigate innovation structures like innovation accelerators, innovation hubs and regulatory sandboxes.

The Fintech Unit of the SARB initiated Project Khokha in the latter part of 2017, with the project team consisting of seven banking industry participants, a technical service provider (ConsenSys), and consulting practice, PricewaterhouseCoopers Inc. The scope of Project Khokha was to trial interbank wholesale settlement using distributed ledger technology ("**DLT**").

It was reported by the SARB that the results of Project Khokha show that the typical daily volume of the South African payment system could be processed in less than two hours, with full confidentiality of transactions and settlement finality. The SARB was also satisfied that it was able to view the detail of all the transactions to allow for regulatory oversight.

Although this project laid the foundations for future collaborative work, the report published by the SARB notes that there are several issues to consider before the decision to take a DLT-based system into production can be taken. These issues include the practicalities of implementation, legal and regulatory factors, and the impact on the economy. A fully live DLT-based payments system is therefore not currently planned in South Africa.

Cryptocurrency regulation

Cryptocurrencies are not currently regulated, and are also not prohibited.

Sales regulation

The Financial Markets Act 19 of 2012 ("**FMA**") regulates the provision of securities services in South Africa. Central to the meaning of "securities services" is the definition of "securities" (given that "securities services" are rendered in respect of securities). The definition of securities does not contain any reference to cryptocurrencies and the Registrar of Securities Services ("**Registrar**") has not prescribed cryptocurrencies to be instruments similar to any of the securities listed in the FMA. Furthermore, the type of securities listed in the FMA all have one common feature: there is an issuer against whom the holder of the securities will have a claim. A cryptocurrency lacks this feature, as it is not issued by any central authority or person; rather, it comes into existence through the process of "mining".

While it could be argued that cryptocurrencies have certain features in common with securities, namely that they could be, or are, treated as investments (i.e. a capital outlay or an expenditure to acquire property or assets to produce revenue), there are many other products which share this feature and it would be implausible to categorise all such products as securities as contemplated in the FMA.

The Financial Advisory and Intermediary Services Act 37 of 2002 ("**FAIS**") regulates the rendering of financial services in South Africa. "Financial service" is defined to mean the furnishing of "advice" and/or the rendering of "intermediary services" in respect of a financial product.

The first enquiry is whether a financial product is involved and if the answer is in the affirmative, then the enquiry that follows is whether advice and/or intermediary services are rendered in respect of that financial product. If there is no financial product, that is the end of the enquiry. The definition of a "financial product" in FAIS contains no reference to cryptocurrencies. We also point out that the Registrar of Financial Services Providers has not declared cryptocurrencies to be financial products in terms of FAIS. Since cryptocurrencies are not "financial products", FAIS will not apply to any such product offerings.

Taxation

A draft Taxation Laws Amendment Bill ("**TLAB**") has been published and proposes various amendments to the Income Tax Act 58 of 1962 ("**Income Tax Act**") and the Value Added Tax Act 89 of 1991 ("**VAT Act**"), which (amongst others) seeks to clarify the existing provisions dealing with cryptocurrencies in the South African tax law.

Under the Value Added Tax Act 89 of 1991 ("**VAT Act**"), it is proposed to amend section 2 to include in the description of "financial services", the issue, acquisition, collection, buying or selling or transfer of ownership of any cryptocurrency. In the result, if the proposal in respect of the VAT Act is accepted, all dealings in cryptocurrencies will be exempt from VAT in terms of section 12 of the VAT Act.

Under the Income Tax Act, it is proposed to insert cryptocurrency in the definition of "financial instrument". Moreover, it is also proposed to amend section 20A of the Income Tax Act, to include the acquisition or disposal of any cryptocurrency under the ring-fencing of assessed loss provisions. If this proposal is accepted, cryptocurrency dealers will not be able to offset the losses incurred from the dealing in cryptocurrencies from any other trade. These losses are therefore ring-fenced to be used only against income earned from cryptocurrency trade.

Money transmission laws and anti-money laundering requirements

The Financial Intelligence Centre Act 38 of 2001 ("**FICA**"), one of South Africa's anti-money laundering statutes, imposes various duties on "accountable institutions". These include the duty to identify and verify clients; to keep records; and to report certain transactions to the Financial Intelligence Centre ("**FIC**").

"Accountable institutions" are listed in schedule 1 to FICA and include banks and money remitters. Importantly, the duty to report suspicious or unusual transactions is more widely cast and applies not only to accountable institutions but to all persons who carry on business in South Africa.

In terms of section 29 of FICA, any person (including an accountable institution) who carries on a business, or is in charge of, or manages a business, or who is employed by a business, who knows or suspects that:

(a) the business has received or is about to receive the proceeds of unlawful activities or property connected to an offence relating to the financing of terrorism;

(b) a transaction or series of transactions to which the business is a party, facilitated or is likely to facilitate the transfer of the proceeds of unlawful activity or property relating to the financing of terrorist activities; has no apparent business or lawful business; may be relevant to the investigation of tax evasion or relates generally to the financing of terrorism; or

(c) the business has been used, or is about to be used for money-laundering purposes, or the financing of terrorism,

must report within a prescribed period to the FIC. These provisions could be interpreted to apply to cryptocurrencies where such cryptocurrencies are involved in unlawful activities or the proceeds of unlawful activities.

Promotion and testing

A collaborative initiative has been set up in which regulators and policymakers have engaged with industry to develop key considerations and a more harmonised approach to Fintech-driven innovations. This initiative is known as the Intergovernmental Fintech Working Group and includes four financial regulators, namely: the Financial Intelligence Centre; the Financial Sector Conduct Authority; the National Treasury; and the SARB. The purpose of the initiative is to identify the risks and benefits of financial innovation driven by Fintech, so that regulators and policymakers can develop appropriate policies and implement effective frameworks that allow for responsible innovation.

Ownership and licensing requirements

There are currently no restrictions on investment managers owning cryptocurrencies for investment purposes. As a result, there are also no licensing requirements imposed on anyone holding cryptocurrency as an investment advisor.

The Financial Institutions (Protection of Funds) Act 28 of 2001 ("**FI Act**") imposes certain duties on persons dealing with funds of clients, and with trust property controlled by financial institutions and nominee companies. 'Trust property' is defined in the FI Act to mean:

> '*[A]ny corporeal or incorporeal, movable or immovable asset invested, <u>held, kept in safe custody, controlled</u>, administered or alienated by any person, partnership, company or trust for, or on behalf of, another person, partnership, company or trust, and such other person, partnership, company or trust is hereinafter referred to as the principal.*'

This definition is sufficiently wide to encompass money – and arguably also a cryptocurrency – as an incorporeal asset. If an asset manager as a financial institution holds cryptocurrencies on behalf of clients, this may amount to holding trust property for purposes of the FI Act. The FI Act imposes duties on financial institutions which deal with trust property.

Section 2 of the FI Act provides that a financial institution which invests, holds, keeps in safe custody, controls, administers or alienates any funds of the financial institution or any trust property:

- must, with regard to such funds, observe the utmost good faith and exercise proper care and diligence;

- must, with regard to the trust property and the terms of the instrument or agreement by which the trust or agency in question has been created, observe the utmost good faith and exercise the care and diligence required of a trustee in the exercise or discharge of his or her powers and duties; and

- may not alienate, invest, pledge, hypothecate or otherwise encumber or make use of the funds or trust property, or furnish any guarantee in a manner calculated to gain, directly or indirectly, any improper advantage for any person to the prejudice of the financial institution or principal concerned.

Other duties imposed by the FI Act on financial institutions (or the directors, members, partners, officials, employees or agents of the financial institution) include:

- a requirement for all parties who take part in investment decisions to declare any direct financial interest in a company in which trust property will be invested to the board of management of the company prior to the investment being made (section 3);

- investing the trust property only in such manner as directed by agreement (with the client) or, in the absence of such an agreement, as directed by the FI Act; and
- keeping its assets separate from the trust property (which separation must be visible in its books of accounts).

The FI Act, however, does not impose a regulatory approval or registration requirement on financial institutions.

Mining

Cryptocurrency "mining" is not regulated in South Africa and is therefore permissible.

Border restrictions and declaration

Exchange Control in South Africa is mainly governed by the Currency and Exchanges Act 9 of 1933 (as amended) and the Exchange Control Regulations issued under this Act. The SARB also publishes Exchange Manuals and guidelines ("**Manuals**").

Any person wishing to move funds offshore for the purposes of buying cryptocurrencies has to make an application for exchange approval through authorised dealers in foreign exchange. "Authorised Dealers" are South African commercial and merchant banks, appointed by the Minister of Finance, to buy and sell foreign exchange, within the limits and subject to conditions prescribed by the Treasury and the SARB. Authorised dealers act on behalf of their customers and they are not agents of the SARB.

The basic principle applicable in terms of the Exchange Control Regulations is that no exchange commitment may, in terms of the Exchange Control Regulations, be entered into by South Africans without prior approval. In certain instances, Authorised Dealers are empowered to approve applications themselves (i.e. without reference to the SARB). The Manuals contain the conditions and limits applicable to transactions in foreign exchange which may be undertaken by Authorised Dealers. For all other applications involving foreign exchange that fall outside the scope of the Manuals, the Authorised Dealer must forward such application to the Financial Surveillance Department of the SARB.

Reporting requirements

The reporting requirements under FICA require certain cash transactions to be reported. However, FICA defines cash as: (a) coin and paper money of South Africa or of another country that is designated as legal tender and that circulates as, and is customarily used and accepted as, a medium of exchange in the country of issue; and (b) travellers' cheques. This definition clearly does not include cryptocurrencies and such reporting obligations will therefore not be imposed under FICA. Other reporting obligations under FICA relate to electronic transfers of money to and from South Africa. Since it is not possible to transfer cryptocurrencies via an electronic funds transfer, these reporting obligations will also not apply.

Estate planning and testamentary succession

Cryptocurrency is not regulated for purposes of estate planning and succession.

Angela Itzikowitz
Tel: +27 11 269 7600 / Email: aitzikowitz@ENSafrica.com
Professor Angela Itzikowitz is an executive in ENSafrica's banking and finance department. She specialises in banking and financial market regulation, including finance and regulatory reform, card and related electronic payment instruments, derivatives, loan agreements, collective investment schemes, insurance, money laundering and debt origination and securitisation. She has done a significant amount of work in South African Development Community (SADC) countries such as Uganda, Kenya and Zambia including regulatory law reform through capacity-building projects. More recently, she drafted and advised on the Finance and Development Protocol for SADC in her capacity as a senior legal expert. She has also advised the World Bank on deposit insurance and bank insolvencies. Angela has participated in a number of financial market initiatives in Asia in collaboration with colleagues from Beijing, Shanghai, Hong Kong and India. She also acts for a number of European banks.

Ina Meiring
Tel: +27 11 269 7600 / Email: imeiring@ENSafrica.com
Ina Meiring is an executive in ENSafrica's banking and finance department. Ina is regarded as one of the top finance regulatory experts in South Africa and her clients include leading local and international financial institutions. Her experience includes advising on banking and financial services regulation and consumer law matters, including: the South African Consumer Protection Act, 2008; the National Credit Act, 2005; and the Protection of Personal Information Act, 2013. Her expertise further includes advising on corporate governance, exchange control, securitisations, payment instruments and payment methods. Ina is a member of the expert group appointed by the South African Reserve Bank for the review of the National Payment System Act, 1998. She has authored chapters on South African banking regulation for a number of legal publications, and has lectured at the University of Johannesburg and the University of South Africa.

Era Gunning
Tel: +27 11 269 7600 / Email: egunning@ENSafrica.com
Era Gunning is a director in ENSafrica's banking and finance department. She is an admitted solicitor of the Supreme Court of New South Wales, Australia and has advised various clients, including leading banks, on the practical application of international anti-money laundering initiatives and statutory compliance issues. Era's experience also includes the drafting and perusal of all legal documents such as commercial leases, as well as advising on consumer and data protection. Era has conducted numerous workshops and seminars in respect of data and consumer protection for clients, including banks, insurers, credit providers, pharmaceutical companies, medical schemes, government agencies, parastatals and direct marketers. She has drafted numerous opinions on data and consumer protection, as well as "Do's and Do nots" policies for many institutions.

ENSafrica

The MARC | Tower 1, 129 Rivonia Road, Sandton, Johannesburg 2196, South Africa
Tel: +27 11 269 7600 / URL: www.ENSafrica.com

Spain

Alfonso López-Ibor, Pablo Stöger & Zhongbo Jin
Ventura Garcés López-Ibor Abogados

Government attitude and definition

The Spanish government has been very cautious and conservative with regard to cryptocurrencies, since Spanish law is highly protective of the rights of investors and consumers, and because during the recession there has been a large number of cases of financial and securities fraud.

Cryptocurrency cannot be legally treated as money for legal tender. The Law 46/1998 of 17th December, on the introduction of the euro as the national currency, provides that from 1st January 1999 the national currency of Spain shall be the euro. This law cross-refers to Council Regulation (EC) Nº 974/98 of 3rd May 1998. Under article 10 of this Regulation, only banknotes and coins denominated in euros and valid in other Eurozone countries shall have the status of legal tender in Spain and, more generally, the euro shall be the sole unit of account in legal instruments, whether under private or public law.

On 8th February 2018 the Bank of Spain and the Spanish Stock Market Regulator (CNMV) issued a joint communiqué about the perils of investing and dealing in cryptocurrencies, and emphasises that small investors should avoid these investments. The communiqué does not contain a normative definition of cryptocurrencies, although it describes accurately concepts such "initial coin offering" (ICO) and "tokens" by differentiating between "security tokens" and "utility tokens", using terms in Spanish which can be easily understood and are accessible to the layman. The communiqué is not part of Spanish true legal order as such, but certain parts could be considered as "soft law" in as much they signal the Spanish government's attitude.

Regarding blockchain technology, it is fair to say that a technology which allows digital information to be distributed but not to be copied, will have many uses in the Spanish legal environment. In Spain, notaries have a monopoly on certifying the authenticity of legal documents, so that blockchain platforms could be an alternative to notaries for the documentation of certain legal documents. A recent example has been a syndicated financing carried out by a major bank (BBVA) based on a blockchain platform.

Cryptocurrency regulation

There is no specific regulation on cryptocurrencies in Spain, except that they cannot be treated as legal tender, which is exclusively reserved for the euro as national currency. The mentioned joint communiqué also points out that there are no issues of cryptocurrency or ICO which have been approved or verified by any regulatory authority such as the Bank of Spain or the CNMV. In Spanish law, cryptocurrency cannot be considered as a financial instrument (promissory note, derivative, etc.) either, nor a currency (domestic or foreign), but we consider that they could be assimilated to securities in the case of public offerings, or to chattels or commodities when they are traded individually.

To the extent that they can be considered as securities, ICOs may fall within the prospectus-filing requirements of the Spanish stock market law (LMV), as the definition of financial instruments and negotiable securities is very wide (article 2 LMV), and the Spanish government can add new types of securities by its own fiat without an amendment of the law being necessary, provided this has been agreed under EU regulations. A communiqué of the CNMV dated 8th February 2018 has also confirmed this view and therefore been ratified by a notice, dated 6th July 2018. Under article 38 of Royal Decree 1310/2005, as amended from time to time, offerings addressed exclusively to professional investors or to fewer than 150 persons, or with a minimum investment of at least €100,000 per investor, or in the case of securities having a face value of at least €100,000, would not be subject to the prospectus-filing requirements (CNMV).

As discussed, the Spanish regulator (CNMV) is highly protective of small investors' rights. This may have had an impact on the non-advertisement of ICOs in the Spanish market so far. On the other hand, the CNMV is also sensitive to the benefits of ICOs, to the extent that they bring technological innovation and may promote entrepreneurial business.

The current position of CNMV and Bank of Spain is that specific regulation of cryptocurrency and ICOs is necessary, but such regulation can only be made at European Union level and after consultation with certain third countries such as the U.S., which play a major role in world financial markets (see statement to the press by Sebastian Albella, Chairman of the CNMV, *El Economista*, dated 9th June 2018).

Sales regulation

To the extent that cryptocurrencies are considered commodities, they will be traded under the general rules of the Civil Code and the Code of Commerce, and in particular, those applicable to the contract of barter (*permute*). Aside from Spanish law that would allow the parties freedom of choice of the governing law, applicable to the transaction (article 3 of Regulation Rome I, Regulation (EC) 593/2008 on the law applicable to contractual), small investors qualify for treatment as consumers and therefore even if a law other than Spain has been chosen, mandatory Spanish law on consumer or investment protection will apply to the trade in order to benefit the Spanish party (article 6.2 of Regulation Rome I), which expressly refers to the "protection afforded by legal provisions that cannot be derogated from by agreement" (…).

Depending on the type of tokens (security or utility), the Spanish rules on title transfer may be more easy or difficult to apply. Broadly speaking, Spanish law requires a contractual agreement plus the delivery of the object, so that title is passed from the seller to the purchaser. This would be non-controversial if the security token comprised only membership rights within the meaning of corporate law, but would be different and more complicated in the case of dematerialised claims such as payment claims via the internet.

Thus, much depends on how Spanish law would characterise cryptocurrencies. The Bank of Spain and the CNMV seem to consider them as "securities" based on the position adopted by the SEC (see the SEC Chairman's communiqué dated 11th December 2017, which has been extensively quoted by Spanish regulators). This view is based on the fact of the purchase of a financial instrument, there being a profit expectation, and also the confidence in other people's efforts to generate an economic revenue. However, in Spanish law, in certain cases, cryptocurrency has been simply categorised as an electronic product, which is intangible, and which is certainly similar to the information stored in computer hardware. The Spanish Mercantile Register has already followed this approach in late 2017 when it accepted that the corporate capital of a limited company could be contributed in bitcoins (although the capital was denominated in its euro counter value).

Aside from the foregoing, the judgment of the European Court of Justice (ECJ) of 22nd October 2015, which treated bitcoins as foreign exchange, could also have a future bearing in Spain, even though there is the serious objection that there is no state authority or central bank supporting bitcoins and they cannot be legal tender, which creates legal uncertainty. Finally, utility tokens which can be assimilated to vouchers entitling the selling entities to discounts, would not be treated as securities or commodities and would only be subject to consumer protection legislation.

Aside from the foregoing, token sales of bitcoins against euros could lead to a risk of criminal prosecution to the extent that the bitcoins' seller purports to the buyer to be selling or exchanging "money", hiding the risk of bitcoins' depreciation, as under Spanish law the payment of debts must be done in the agreed currency or in euros as the currency of legal tender in Spain (article 248 CP in relation with section 1170 CC).

Taxation

Capital gains from the sale of cryptocurrencies by a person resident in Spain will be taxed according to a rate of 23%. If they have been acquired and sold within 12 months, the tax rate may vary from 24.75% to 52%. If the capital gains have been obtained by a company, there is a flat tax rate of 25%.

VAT treatment

The exchange of cryptocurrencies into euros or vice versa is VAT-exempt (ECJ, 22nd October 2015-C-264/14, Hedqvist). This judgment establishes that such exchange is a provision of a service and not the delivery of a good, and that bitcoins can be assimilated as to a type of foreign exchange, which has been voluntarily accepted by the parties to the relevant transaction, and therefore enjoys the VAT exemption provided under article 135, 1 subsequently e) of Directive 2006/112/CE on VAT.

Money transmission laws and anti-money laundering requirements

Law 10/2010 dated 28th April, on the prevention of money-laundering, is widely drafted regarding the parties which are subject to it. Article 2 expressly mentions entities of electronic money, foreign exchange or money transfer companies, depositors or custodians or funds or payment means, all of which may trade or deal in one way or another in cryptocurrencies, and therefore become subject to money laundering supervision. On top of this, the new EU Directive (2015/849/EU) will also extend the requirements to entities providing services to safeguard private cryptographic keys to hold, stake or transfer virtual currencies. In addition to this, it is clear that purchase, conversion or transfer of cryptocurrencies that have originated in a crime will fall within the scope of the Spanish Criminal Code (Article 301 *seq*) which imposes very serious penalties on this activity.

Promotion and testing

There is new draft legislation currently before Parliament which will allow the introduction of new technologies to the Spanish market through a "controlled testing environment". In this, Spanish law seems to be drawing its inspiration from the UK Financial Authority (FA) which grants licences for sandboxes, but it is still at a very incipient stage and the Ministry of Economy has drafted preliminary legislation that will be subject to open consultation.

Ownership and licensing requirements

To the extent that cryptocurrencies are considered to be technological products, there are no licence requirements. If they are used as financial instruments, they will be subject to stock market regulation with regard to the issue and the ICO of cryptocurrencies. There is no published guidance about investments in cryptocurrencies by funds except that alternative investment funds may invest in cryptocurrencies when dealing with the money of qualified investors.

Mining

Many bitcoin and other cryptocurrencies are not yet regulated, and this is permitted except as discussed in 'Cryptocurrency regulation', above.

Border restrictions and declaration

There are no frontier restrictions or obligations to report cryptocurrency holdings at the border which are only applicable to "cash" as defined by article 2 of regulation (EU) 1889/2005, which does not include electronic means of payment.

Reporting requirements

Under article 34.2 of law 34.2 of law 10/2010 of 28th April on the prevention of money laundering, electronic payments which can be used to make payments to an unidentified beneficiary (payments to the bearer) are treated as physical money (banknotes, cheques, etc.) and therefore subject to a limit of €2,500 per payment, or €15,000 per payment if the party making the payment is not resident in Spain. This limitation is not applicable if the payment is made through banks.

Estate planning and testamentary succession

Cryptocurrency for the purposes of wills and intestate succession will be treated as any other ordinary assets of the deceased person.

Alfonso López-Ibor
Tel: +34 91 521 78 18 / Email: alfonso.lopezibor@vg-li.com
Alfonso López-Ibor is Managing Partner of the Madrid office. He had previously been Managing Partner of the Madrid office of Allen & Overy for 10 years. He has extensive experience of corporate law, finance and banking. Alfonso López-Ibor is also widely known for his expertise in litigation, arbitration and air transport.

In the corporate field, he regularly advises clients on the acquisition and sale of Spanish and foreign companies, venture capital and private equity transactions, management buy-outs and corporate restructuring processes. He has extensive experience advising multinationals setting up in Spain, whether through subsidiaries, branches or the acquisition of existing companies.

In banking and finance, he has developed extensive experience of syndicated loan operations, guarantees and asset finance and dealing with the Spanish stock market regulator (CNMV).

He leads a department that has gained wide recognition for its expertise in providing legal advice to the air transport industry in areas such as domestic and international commercial agreements, handling agreements and financing structures, including operational leasing arrangements, guarantees, acquisition finance, licences, authorisation and registration.

He is one of Spain's foremost legal experts on the aviation sector. His litigation work includes advising on international disputes and arbitration processes, with a focus on highly complex issues.

Pablo Stöger
Tel: +34 91 521 78 18 / Email: pablo.stoger@vg-li.com
Pablo Stöger Pérez has spent most of his legal career with Ventura Garcés López-Ibor.

Pablo is a specialist in Corporate Law and Litigation (contracts, company agreements, mergers and acquisitions and bankruptcy law, among other areas). He has extensive experience of forming subsidiaries, branches and representative offices for foreign companies in Spain, and has advised clients in sectors such as banking and financing, private equity, air transport, real estate and construction, insurance, automation and control, high-tech and food and agriculture.

Zhongbo Jin
Tel: +34 91 521 78 18 / Email: zhongbo.jin@vg-li.com
Zhongbo specialises in aviation law representing airlines, aircraft leasing companies and financiers in a broad variety of commercial aviation transactions. His practice also includes general corporate and business law.

Zhongbo is a member of our China Desk, coordinating legal services for Chinese companies in the Spanish market. He is a Chinese native speaker, was born in Dalian, China and is fluent in English and Spanish.

Ventura Garcés López-Ibor Abogados

López de Hoyos, 35, 3º A 28002 Madrid / Freixa, 26-28, Baixos 08021 Barcelona, Spain
Tel: +34 91 521 78 18 (Madrid) / +34 93 241 97 40 (Barcelona) / URL: www.venturagarceslopezibor.com

Switzerland

Daniel Haeberli, Stefan Oesterhelt & Urs Meier
Homburger

Government attitude and definition

In Switzerland, the government's general attitude towards cryptocurrencies, and in particular towards the technology underlying cryptocurrencies, is very positive.

Both the Swiss federal government as well as the Swiss Financial Market Supervisory Authority FINMA ("FINMA") recognise the potential that blockchain/distributed ledger technology may offer to the financial services industry as well as various other areas of the economy. Switzerland sees an opportunity to take a global lead in this sector, and officials and authorities are generally open *vis-à-vis* new developments. This is particularly true for cantonal, *i.e.* state authorities, namely in the Canton of Zug.

Accounting for some of the first and the largest initial coin offerings ("ICOs"), Switzerland has had success in attracting developers and investors, largely due to its business-friendly regulations and digital expertise. This has led to the creation of the so-called "Crypto Valley" in the Zug-Zurich area, considered to be one of the world's leading blockchain/distributed ledger ecosystems.

Cryptocurrencies and ICOs give rise to various fundamental legal questions. In January 2018, the Swiss federal government therefore set up a "blockchain/ICO working group",[1] which aims at analysing the current legal framework and identifying the need for action by Swiss lawmakers and regulators. Results are expected to be presented to the Swiss federal government by the end of 2018. Whether, or to what extent, Swiss laws will then be amended is currently not yet clear. Amendments could range from rather simple changes such as removing "written form"/"wet ink signature" requirements, to more profound changes such as the introduction of a new statutory asset class regulating the various forms of cryptocurrencies.

Swiss financial market regulator's position

Due to the sharp increase of ICOs in 2017, FINMA – like financial market regulators in other jurisdictions – issued a series of statements:

- On September 19, 2017, FINMA warned investors about a "fake cryptocurrency", communicating that an issuer of so-called e-coins, as well as a related trading platform, have been closed down. The reason for this enforcement action was that these e-coins were, according to FINMA, unlike "real cryptocurrencies", not based on "distributed networks" using blockchain technology. Instead, these e-coins were completely under the issuers' control and created/stored locally on the issuers' servers.

- On September 29, 2017, *i.e.*, a few days later, FINMA published a brief note addressing regulatory aspects of ICOs conducted in Switzerland. FINMA highlighted some potentially applicable regulations, and furthermore mentioned that there are no specific laws in Switzerland governing ICOs or blockchain/distributed ledger technology specifically. FINMA made it clear, however, that market participants are required to comply with all existing law, in particular potentially applicable banking, securities dealer, anti-money laundering and prospectus laws and regulations.[2]

- On February 16, 2018, FINMA then published a detailed guidance entitled "Regulatory Treatment of Initial Coin Offerings" ("ICO Guidelines").[3] In these guidelines, basic elements of ICOs were set out and it was mentioned that, even though no typical or standard ICO exists, most of these fundraising processes share two common elements: (A) investors transfer funds, often in the form of cryptocurrencies, to an ICO organiser/issuer; and (B) in return they receive tokens which are created and stored in a decentralised form, either on a blockchain infrastructure, which was specifically created for the ICO, or through an existing blockchain infrastructure (e.g. Ethereum blockchain). The ICO Guidelines affirmed FINMA's view that ICOs are a way to raise funds digitally, for entrepreneurial purposes. Furthermore, FINMA clarified some regulatory aspects, in particular regarding the qualification of tokens as securities (see below, "Sales regulation") and anti-money laundering requirements (see below, "Money transmission laws and anti-money laundering requirements").

Definition of cryptocurrencies

Swiss law does not define the term cryptocurrency or virtual currency.

However, the Swiss federal government had to address the topic of virtual currencies in a special report dated June 25, 2014.[4] In this report, the following definition was used:

> "*A virtual currency is a digital representation of a value which can be traded on the Internet and although it takes on the role of money – it can be used as means of payment for real goods and services – it is not accepted as legal tender anywhere. (...) Virtual currencies exist only as a digital code and therefore do not have a physical counterpart for example in the form of coins or notes. Given their tradability, virtual currencies should be classified as an asset.*"

The same definition was later used by FINMA, when anti-money laundering regulations were being amended,[5] and the term virtual currency has been mentioned in the Swiss anti-money laundering ordinance ("AMLO") since January 1, 2016.[6]

However, given that there is no statutory definition and no case law, probably the best approach currently is to rely on the definitions used by FINMA. In its ICO Guidelines, it defined three basic categories of cryptocurrencies, *i.e.*, tokens:

- *Payment tokens* (according to FINMA, synonymous with pure "cryptocurrencies"; henceforth named "native payment tokens"), are tokens which are intended to be used, now or in the future, as a means of payment for acquiring goods or services or as a means of money or value transfer. Pure "cryptocurrencies" do not give rise to any claims towards an issuer or a third party. Examples of such native payment tokens are Bitcoin or Ether.
- *Utility tokens* are tokens, which are intended to provide access digitally to an application or service by means of a blockchain-based infrastructure.
- *Asset tokens* represent assets such as a debt or an equity claim on the issuer. Asset tokens promise, for example, a share in future company earnings or future capital flows. In terms of their economic function, therefore, such tokens are analogous to equities, bonds or derivatives. Tokens, which enable physical assets to be traded on a blockchain-infrastructure, according to FINMA, also fall into this category.

FINMA points out that tokens may also fall into more than one of these three basic categories. Such *hybrid tokens* are, for example, asset tokens or utility tokens, which at the same time also qualify as payment tokens.

Cryptocurrencies are not legal tender

In Switzerland, cryptocurrencies are not legal tender.[7] Consequently, cryptocurrencies are not "money" in a narrow sense. However, some legal scholars argue that cryptocurrencies, provided they are widely used, accepted by the public and have adopted the typical functions of money, qualify as "money" in a broader sense.[8]

There is currently not any form of "state-backed" cryptocurrency available in Switzerland. In particular, the Swiss national bank, *i.e.*, the country's central bank, has not issued any cryptocurrencies, nor are there any indications that it intends to do so in the near future.[9]

Cryptocurrency regulation

In Switzerland, cryptocurrency-related activities are not prohibited and there are (apart from the provision in the anti-money laundering ordinance mentioned under "Government attitude and definition", above) no Swiss statutes or regulations which are tailor-made to the phenomenon of cryptocurrencies.

Sales regulation

While offering and selling native payment tokens is not subject to specific Swiss sales regulations, an offer and sale of utility tokens and asset tokens may become subject to offer/sales regulations, if the relevant sold tokens constitute *securities*.

Under Swiss law, securities (*Effekten*) are financial instruments, which are: (i) standardised; (ii) suitable for mass trading; and (iii) either certificated securities (*Wertpapiere*), uncertificated securities (*Wertrechte*), derivatives or intermediated securities (*Bucheffekten*). Whether, or which, cryptocurrencies are securities is currently not absolutely clear, *i.e.*, there is neither any statutory guidance nor is there any case law regarding this question.

However, in its ICO Guidelines FINMA indicated that generally speaking, it does not intend to classify native payment tokens as securities. According to FINMA, utility tokens are not treated as securities if their sole purpose is to confer digital access rights to an application or service, and if the utility tokens can already be used in this way at the point of issue.

Currently,[10] FINMA has the following view on whether tokens may qualify as securities or not:

- Native payment tokens such as Bitcoin or Ether are currently not treated as securities by FINMA. In our opinion, this assessment of the Swiss regulator is correct. Pure "cryptocurrencies", sometimes also referred to as native tokens or native payment tokens, do not grant their holders or users any relative or absolute rights *vis-à-vis* an issuer or a third party. They serve as mediums of exchange and (arguably) also as units of account and stores of value. Whether native payment tokens are "financial instruments" as defined in the recently adopted Swiss Financial Services Act ("FinSA"), which will enter into force most likely on January 1, 2020, is unclear. Given the wording of the FinSA, we are of the opinion that pure "cryptocurrencies" are not "financial instruments" in the sense of this act (see also "Money transmission laws and anti-money laundering requirements", below). It remains to be seen whether the legal definition of "financial instrument" will be amended to explicitly include cryptocurrencies.

- Utility tokens are currently not treated as securities by FINMA, provided: (i) their sole purpose is to confer digital access rights to an application or service; and (ii) the tokens can actually already be used in this way when they are being issued. If these two conditions are met, the typical "connection with capital markets" inherent to securities does, according to FINMA, not exist. In its Annual Economic Report 2018, the Bank for International Settlement seems to follow this approach and acknowledge that the mere promise of future access to software does not constitute investment activity, but instead calls for the application of consumer protection laws.[11] FINMA points out that it will qualify utility tokens as securities if they fully or partially "have the economic function of an investment".

- Asset tokens shall, according to FINMA, generally be treated as securities, for example if they represent uncertified securities or derivatives and are standardised as well as suitable for mass trading. As FINMA points out, uncertificated securities may also be created in so-called pre-financing and pre-sale scenarios, if claims to purchase tokens in the future are granted in the course of such processes. Such uncertified securities will also be treated as securities provided they are standardised and suitable for mass trading.

Securities dealer licence

Sales activities relating to tokens, which qualify as securities, may in particular trigger: (i) Swiss securities dealer licence requirements under the Swiss Stock Exchange and Securities Trading Act ("SESTA");[12] (ii) Swiss trading platform regulations under the Financial Market Infrastructure Act ("FMIA");[13] or (iii) Swiss prospectus requirements.

- Persons creating securities tokens in a professional capacity may become a so-called issuing house or derivate firm and therefore require a securities dealer licence. For example, issuing asset tokens, which are linked to the performance of a share or a project may, under certain circumstances, qualify as regulated securities dealer activity. Such licensing requirements do, however, not apply as long as the person engaging in such activities has no physical presence (*i.e.*, no personnel and no branch) in Switzerland. Acting on a mere cross-border basis does not trigger any duty to obtain a securities dealer licence.

- Operating a platform in Switzerland which enables trading of cryptocurrencies may trigger licensing requirements under the FMIA. For example, so-called "organised trading facilities" may only be operated by licensed banks, licensed securities dealers or recognised (foreign) trading venues. Organised trading facilities are establishments for: (i) multilateral trading in securities or other financial instruments whose purpose is the exchange of bids and the conclusion of contracts based on discretionary rules; (ii) multilateral trading in financial instruments other than securities whose purpose is the exchange of bids and the conclusion of contracts based on non-discretionary rules; and (iii) bilateral trading in securities or other financial instruments whose purpose is the exchange of bids. Even if the types of cryptocurrencies traded are limited to such that do not qualify as securities under Swiss law, a platform may still be regulated as an "organised trading facility" if the types of cryptocurrencies traded are "other financial instrument". Unlike for "securities", FINMA to date has not yet offered any public guidance on whether they consider native payment tokens to be such "other financial instruments".

  As mentioned, the FinSA will provide for a definition of the term "financial instrument" (see above, "Sales regulation"), which is commonly held to also be relevant for "organised trading facilities". This definition of "financial instrument" is wider than the definition of securities. However, in our view, the current wording of the legal definition suggests that native payment tokens do not qualify as financial instruments. This view is shared by the – however scarce – Swiss legal doctrine to date. Should this view be followed, a platform allowing for the trading of native payment tokens such as Bitcoin or Ether would not be considered an "organised trading facility" and fall outside the scope of the Swiss financial regulations.

Taxation of cryptocurrencies (currency token)

Cryptocurrencies held by individuals

*   *Wealth tax*

    For the purpose of the tax assessment, cryptocurrencies must be converted into Swiss francs.[14] The Federal Tax Administration provides year-end conversion rates for certain cryptocurrencies such as Bitcoin, Ethereum, Ripple, Bitcoin Cash or Litecoin. According to the understanding of different cantonal tax authorities, cryptocurrencies are considered to be assets, comparable with bank deposits and are therefore subject to wealth taxes. If the FTA does not determine a year-end market value, the cryptocurrencies must be declared at the year-end price of the trading platform via which the buying and selling transactions are executed. If no current valuation rate can be determined, the cryptocurrency must be declared at the original purchase price in Swiss francs (cost of acquisition). Because the rules for declaring the cryptocurrencies can vary, the rules must first be checked in the canton of residence.

*   *Income tax*

    In general, capital gains on assets of individuals such as cryptocurrencies are exempt from income tax.

    However, if cryptocurrencies are held as part of the business assets of an individual (e.g. because the individual is classified as a professional securities dealer based on the principles laid out in circular no. 36 of the Swiss Federal Tax Administration), capital gains of cryptocurrencies are subject to income tax.

Cryptocurrencies held by legal entities

*   *Capital tax*

    Legal entities are subject to annual capital tax. Therefore, legal entities have to declare cryptocurrencies in their tax assessment at cost of acquisition or, if this value is lower, converted at the year-end exchange rate provided by the Federal Tax Administration. Therefore, cryptocurrencies with no market value provided by the FTA are to be declared at acquisition costs.

*   *Corporate income tax*

    Corporations are subject to Swiss corporate income tax on any net taxable earnings from the sale of cryptocurrencies. Non-realised gains on cryptocurrencies are only subject to Swiss corporate income tax in case of a mark-to-market accounting in the Swiss GAAP accounts of the corporate investor.

*   *VAT*

    For the purpose of VAT, cryptocurrencies are treated the same way as legal tender, meaning that the trading or exchange activities of cryptocurrencies and additional services related to such trading or exchange activities are exempt from VAT.[15]

Money transmission laws and anti-money laundering requirements

Under Swiss law, both the initial offering of certain cryptocurrencies as well as the subsequent sales and trading activities may be subject to anti-money laundering requirements.

The relevant starting point is to ask whether a person/company engages in any activities which constitute so-called financial intermediation and hence is considered a financial intermediary for purposes of the Swiss Anti-Money Laundering Act ("AMLA").[16]

There are two main groups of financial intermediaries. First, regulated financial intermediaries belonging to the "banking sector", and second, other financial intermediaries belonging to the "non-banking sector".

- Financial intermediaries belonging to the "banking sector" are companies, which are subject to comprehensive, prudential regulation under special legislation, covering the whole range of their activities. Such financial intermediaries are, for example, banks or securities dealers.

- Financial intermediaries belonging to the "nonbanking sector" are any persons/ companies, which on a professional basis: (i) accept or hold on deposit assets belonging to third parties; (ii) assist in the investment of such assets; or (iii) assist in the transfer of such assets. This general definition covers, for example, persons/companies that provide services related to payment transactions, hold securities on deposit or manage securities. Whether such activity is carried out in a professional capacity or not must be assessed based on quantitative benchmarks (e.g. gross margin of CHF 50,000 p.a., business relationships with more than 20 parties p.a., unlimited control over third-party assets exceeding CHF 5m at any time, or transaction volume exceeding CHF 2m per calendar year). Prior to engaging in financial intermediation, such persons/companies must either join a Swiss self-regulatory organisation ("SRO") or request a licence from FINMA in order to become a so-called directly supervised financial intermediary ("DSFI").

The AMLA and implementing regulations provide for a series of obligations that financial intermediaries must adhere to, *e.g.*, regarding the verification of the identity of customers/ contracting parties as well as the beneficial owners of funds held.

With regard to cryptocurrencies, the following is important with regard to anti-money laundering regulations:

- *Primary market/ICOs*: According to FINMA, it is the initial offering of native payment tokens that constitutes financial intermediation. An ICO of a utility token, however, is not subject to anti-money laundering regulations as long as the main feature of the token is to provide access to rights to a non-financial application of blockchain technology. Therefore, provided the payment functions of the utility token only constitute an "accessory service", no means of payment is issued according to FINMA, and hence no anti-money laundering requirements apply. Also, ICOs of asset tokens are not subject to anti-money laundering regulations. It must be noted, however, that organisers of ICOs generally opt to follow Swiss anti-money laundering requirements in any case, *i.e.*, even if there would be no need to do so. The main reason for this is that applying a higher standard to terms of KYC/AML is deemed to be helpful for future operations after the ICO. For example, blockchain/distributed ledger related activities and companies engaging in such activities currently only have a few options when it comes to opening a bank account for the company with a Swiss bank. Being "overly compliant" is viewed as best practice and will help to facilitate future dealings with Swiss or foreign banks or other financial intermediaries.

- *Secondary market/sales and trading*: Merely selling native payment tokens such as Bitcoin to another party, or using such pure "cryptocurrencies" as means of payment for the sale or purchase of goods and services, does not constitute financial intermediation. However, specific rules may apply with regard to cryptocurrencies qualifying as securities (see "Sales regulation", above). Also, depending on the services offered by the relevant person/company, activities relating to sales and trading may constitute financial intermediation, whenever a person/company on a professional basis: (i) accepts or holds on deposit cryptocurrencies belonging to third parties; (ii) assists in the investment of cryptocurrencies; or (iii) assists in the transfer of cryptocurrencies.

Promotion and testing

Switzerland has not established any "sandbox" exemptions or similar arrangements, which specifically focus on fintech companies active in the blockchain/cryptocurrency sector.

However, there are specific rules in place, which aim at generally promoting fintech developments in Switzerland.

In 2016, the Swiss Government announced that it plans on reducing barriers to market entry for fintech businesses[17] and on August 1, 2017, two of the three planned pillars entered into force: the innovation area/"sandbox", as well as the revised settlement account exemption. The third pillar, a fintech-specific licence sometimes also referred to as "banking licence light", has yet to be implemented.

- The first pillar, the Swiss "sandbox" exemption, will allow companies to engage in activities which, under the former regulation, would have triggered bank licensing requirements. According to the Swiss Banking Act ("BA"),[18] only licensed banks are allowed to accept deposits from the public in a professional capacity. Any person or entity continuously accepting more than 20 deposits from the public or publicly advertising to accept deposits is deemed to be acting in a professional capacity.[19] Under the sandbox exemption, companies accepting deposits are not considered to be acting in a professional capacity, if: (i) the deposits accepted do not exceed the threshold of CHF 1m; (ii) the deposits accepted are neither invested nor interest-bearing; and (iii) the investors are informed in advanced that the funds are not supervised by FINMA and that the funds are not protected by the Swiss deposit insurance regime (article 6 para 2 BO). If the threshold of CHF 1m is exceeded, the company must notify FINMA within 10 days and file for a banking licence.

- The second pillar provides that funds held in customer accounts of asset managers, securities dealers, dealers of precious metals or similar companies, which exclusively serve the purpose of settling customer transactions, do not qualify as deposits and therefore do not trigger bank licensing requirements, provided the funds are not interest-bearing and provided that they are forwarded within a relatively short time. This amended "settlement accounts exemption" now allows for the funds to be processed within up to 60 days. However, FINMA clarified that these exceptions will not apply to cryptocurrency-traders which execute a similar activity as foreign exchange traders by maintaining accounts for their clients for investments in different currencies. Under what circumstances a particular activity is considered to be similar to the activities of "foreign exchange traders" is currently not clear. FINMA to date has not yet offered any public guidance regarding this question.

To date, the scope and content of the planned fintech licence, *i.e.*, the third pillar of Swiss fintech regulation, have not yet been defined.

In addition to the official efforts to promote fintech developments in Switzerland, there are private initiatives with certain blockchain-specific suggestions.

For example, the Blockchain Task Force[20] recently published ideas regarding additional regulatory sandboxes. It proposes establishing a specific sandbox for blockchain projects. This sandbox would provide for lower standards as far as financial market infrastructure, securities dealing and banking activities are concerned. However, anti-money laundering regulations, as well as prospectus requirements set out in the FinSA and currently applicable law, shall continue to apply to the full extent.[21] The Blockchain Task Force furthermore suggests creating a "token map", which would be used to assess whether a particular cryptocurrency/token will likely qualify as a security or not. The map will consist of three elements: (i) a regulatory map to refine FINMA token categories and provide guidance as to regulatory requirements; (ii) a design map with a focus on the design of the tokens and their legal and tax effects; as well as (iii) an investor map to assess and evaluate the risks of tokens.[22]

Ownership and licensing requirements

Whether tokens may actually be "owned" or not depends, in particular, on the question whether they qualify as securities or not. Under Swiss law, it is undisputed that securities may be legally owned. With regard to tokens, which do not qualify as securities, *i.e.*, native payment tokens such as Bitcoin, the ownership question is currently unresolved. The majority of Swiss scholars currently are of the view that, due to their lack of tangibility and for other reasons, native payment tokens are not a "thing" (*Sache*) in the sense of Swiss civil law.[23] Some Swiss scholars have even suggested that native payment tokens such as Bitcoin may be considered data.

There are no licences/authorisations specifically relating to cryptocurrencies in Switzerland and, therefore, a variety of regulatory licences may be relevant in the area of cryptocurrencies, in particular (but not limited to) the banking licence and the securities dealer licence (see above, "Sales regulation").

Under Swiss law, only banks are allowed to take deposits from the public on a professional basis (see above, "Promotion and testing"). Regulated deposit-taking may become an issue for service providers offering to store customers' native payment tokens, in particular. It is currently not clear under what circumstances such service providers qualify as banks. This depends, in particular, on how the native currency tokens are being stored, and the technical details of how such storage occurs. One possible way to avoid bank licence requirements might be to cumulatively ensure that: (i) each token is allocated to the relevant client all the time, possibly in a client-specific wallet, so that these native currency tokens can be properly segregated in the event of the services provider's insolvency; and (ii) that the service provider does not have the possibility to freely dispose over such native currency tokens without the involvement of the relevant client. However, this view is untested and technical details of such a set-up would need to be discussed with FINMA prior to engaging in any such activities, which might constitute regulated deposit-taking under Swiss banking regulation.

With regard to further licensing requirements, it must be kept in mind that Switzerland will implement the new Financial Institutions Act along with the FinSA in 2020. These new acts will set forth a new licensing requirement for individual asset managers, and a registration requirement for client advisors. Such registration will be subject to certain requirements such as proof of proper education, training and professional experience.

Mining

Switzerland has no laws or regulations which are tailor-made to the phenomenon of cryptocurrencies or mining of cryptocurrencies. Hence, mining of cryptocurrencies is permitted and the activity is not subject to particular laws and regulations.

Since the mere use of cryptocurrencies is not considered as financial intermediation (see above, "Money transmission laws and anti-money laundering requirements"), mining does not constitute financial intermediation, as far as it is for personal use.

Border restrictions and declaration

In Switzerland, there are no particular border restrictions or declaration requirements, which would apply to cryptocurrencies.

Reporting requirements

In Switzerland, making payments with cryptocurrencies is not a regulated activity and there are no reporting requirements to be met when such payments are made.

Estate planning and testamentary succession

In Switzerland, there are no particular estate planning or testamentary succession aspects concerning cryptocurrencies.

Under Swiss law, heirs acquire the inheritance as a whole upon death of the testator by operation of law. Therefore, all possessions with an inheritable value are transferred to the heirs by universal succession.

Cryptocurrencies such as Bitcoins are considered as having an inheritable value.[24] They are part of the inheritance and therefore shall be transferable. Bitcoins that are recorded on a blockchain are attached to the latter. It is recommended to determine the heir of the cryptocurrency assets, thereby taking into account the value of these assets for calculating the recipient's share. Problems arise when the heir does not possess the necessary elements to obtain the cryptocurrencies directly. The heir has to claim the accession data from the online provider, which might prove difficult in reality.[25]

Acknowledgment

The authors acknowledge with thanks the contributions of Manuel Dubach and Livia Kappeler to this chapter.

* * *

Endnotes

1. Cf. https://www.admin.ch/gov/en/start/documentation/media-releases.msg-id-69539.html.
2. FINMA Guidance 04/2017, Regulatory Treatment of Initial Coin Offerings, September 29, 2017, p. 4.
3. FINMA Guidance 04/2017, Regulatory Treatment of Initial Coin Offerings, September 29, 2017, p. 4.
4. Cf. https://www.newsd.admin.ch/newsd/message/attachments/35355.pdf.
5. Cf. https://www.finma.ch/en/news/2015/06/mm-gwv-finma-20150623/.
6. Cf. article 4 paragraph 2 of the Swiss Anti-Money Laundering Ordinance: "Money or

asset transfer transactions are deemed to be the transfer of assets through the acceptance of cash, precious metals, virtual currencies (...)."

7. The Swiss Federal Act on Currency and Payment Instruments determines Switzerland's legal tender. To date only (i) coins issued by the Federal Government, (ii) banknotes issued by the Swiss National Bank and (iii) Swiss franc sight deposits at the Swiss National Bank qualify as legal tender. Legal tender is considered as "money" in the narrow sense and as legal tender are an official means of payment.

8. *Cf.* HAUSER-SPUEHLER/MEISSER, Eingenschaften der Kryptowährung Bitcoin, in: digma 2018, p. 7; MÜLLER/REUTLINGER/KAISER, Entwicklungen in der Regulierung von virtuellen Währungen in der Schweiz und in der Europäischen Union, in EuZ 2018, p. 80.

9. https://www.snb.ch/en/mmr/speeches/id/ref_20180405_amr.

10. It must be noted that this is a novel and rapidly developing field of law and different views can be taken as to the classification of crypto assets as securities under Swiss law. In light of this, it cannot be excluded that FINMA will come to a different conclusion in the future, in particular also with regard to native payment tokens. FINMA noted that they would reconsider their conclusion in light of the views taken in any future case law or any new legislation in this area.

11. Bank for International Settlement, Annual Economic Report 2018, p. 107.

12. Federal Act on Stock Exchanges and Securities Trading of March 24, 1995, SR 954.1 (SESTA).

13. Federal Act on Financial Market Infrastructures and Market Conduct in Securities and Derivatives Trading of June 19, 2015, SR 958.1 (FMIA).

14. *Cf.* Swiss Legal Tech Association (SLTA), *Regulatory Task Force Report*, p. 33; the Federal Tax Administration publishes every year end an exchange list (official exchange rate) for Bitcoin, Ethereum, Ripple, Bitcoin Cash, Litecoin, Cardano, NEM, Stellar, IOTA and Tron.

15. *Cf.* Swiss Legal Tech Association (SLTA), Regulatory Task Force Report, p. 33.

16. Federal Act on Anti-Money Laundering of October 10, 1997, SR 955.0 (AMLA).

17. *Cf.* https://www.sif.admin.ch/sif/en/home/dokumentation/medienmitteilungen/medien mitteilungen.msg-id-64356.html.

18. Federal Act on Banks of November 8, 1934, SR 952.0 (BA).

19. *v.* articles 2 and 6 of the Swiss Banking Ordinance ("BO").

20. http://blockchaintaskforce.ch/.

21. *Cf.* Blockchain Task Force, White Paper, p. 10.

22. *Cf.* Blockchain Task Force, White Paper, p. 11 *et seq.*

23. *Cf.* MUELLER/REUTLINGER/KAISER, p. 86 *et seq.*; MAURENBRECHER/MEIER, Insolvenzrechtlicher Schutz der Nutzer virtueller Währungen; EGGEN, Chain of Contracts – Eine privatrechtliche Auseinandersetzung mit Distributed Ledgers, AJP 2017, p. 14; BÄRTSCHI/MEISSER, Virtuelle Währungen aus finanzmarkt- und zivilrechtlicher Sicht, in: WEBER/THOUVENIN (Hrsg.), Rechtliche Herausforderungen durch webbasierte und mobile Zahlungssysteme, Zurich 2015, p. 141.

24. *Cf.* EIGENMANN/FANTI, Successions, Données Personnelles, Numériques et Renseignements, in: SJ 2017 II, p. 198.

25. *Cf.* EIGENMANN/FANTI, p. 203.

Daniel Haeberli
Tel: +41 43 222 16 33 / Email: daniel.haeberli@homburger.ch
Daniel Haeberli is a banking and finance as well as a capital markets transactions and financial market regulations specialist. He is particularly focused on secured lending, syndicated debt and structured financing as well as derivatives, securitised structured products, investment funds and bond offerings. Daniel regularly advises clients on initial coin offerings (ICOs) and on cryptocurrency matters.
Daniel Haeberli is heading the working group "Legal & Regulation" of the Swiss Structured Products Association (SSPA).

Stefan Oesterhelt
Tel: +41 43 222 12 65 / Email: stefan.oesterhelt@homburger.ch
Stefan Oesterhelt's practice focuses on tax law, in particular international tax law, mergers and acquisitions, capital market transactions and tax litigation. He is a lecturer on tax law at the University of Sankt Gallen and regularly speaks at seminars on tax law.

Urs Meier
Tel: +41 43 222 13 29 / Email: urs.meier@homburger.ch
Urs Meier's practice focuses on financial markets and banking law. Additionally, he advises and represents companies on white collar crime matters. He is a member of Homburger's White Collar | Investigations working group.

Homburger

Hardstrasse 201, 8005 Zurich, Switzerland
Tel: +41 43 222 10 00 / URL: www.homburger.ch

Taiwan

Robin Chang & Eddie Hsiung
Lee and Li, Attorneys-at-Law

Government attitude and definition

While Taiwan has not promulgated any laws or regulations specifically dealing with the rise of certain applications of blockchain technology such as so-called "virtual currencies" or "cryptocurrencies", Taiwan's financial regulators have issued several press releases to announce their positions and attitude towards such developments, as well as to educate and warn the general public in Taiwan.

On 30 December 2013, both the Central Bank of the Republic of China (Taiwan) ("CBC") and Taiwan's Financial Supervisory Commission ("FSC") first expressed the government's position toward Bitcoin by issuing a joint press release ("2013 Release"). According to the 2013 Release, the two authorities held that Bitcoin should not be considered a "currency", but highly speculative digital "virtual commodity". In another FSC press release in 2014 ("2014 Release"), the FSC ordered that local banks must not accept Bitcoin or provide any other services related to Bitcoin (such as exchange Bitcoin for fiat currency). Recently, the FSC further issued a press release on 19 December 2017 ("2017 Release"), in which the FSC reiterated the government's positions as specified in the 2013 Release and 2014 Release.

Given the above, in light of the authorities' attitude, "Bitcoin" is not considered "legal tender", "currency" or a generally accepted "medium of exchange" under the current regulatory regime in Taiwan; instead, Bitcoin is deemed as a digital "virtual commodity". Please note that the government's attitude stated in the abovementioned press releases only covers "Bitcoin", instead of any other types of virtual currencies/cryptocurrencies (except for "ICOs" as further explained below). But we tend to think that any other virtual currencies/cryptocurrencies, if having the same nature and characteristics as Bitcoin, should also be considered as digital "virtual commodities".

Cryptocurrency regulation

Please see our reply to "Government attitude and definition" above. So far no Taiwanese laws or regulations have been promulgated or amended to formally regulate "virtual currencies" or "cryptocurrencies"; therefore, currently, virtual currencies/cryptocurrencies cannot be considered "legal tender", "currencies" or a generally accepted "medium of exchange" in Taiwan.

Further, currently there exists no required licence in Taiwan for (a) operating the services of exchange between virtual currencies or virtual currencies with fiat currencies, or (b) acting as a "money transmitter" and the like in Taiwan.

Sale regulation

Sale of Bitcoin or any other virtual currencies/cryptocurrencies of the same nature and characteristics

So far there exist no laws or regulations specifically dealing with sale of virtual currencies/cryptocurrencies. Sale of Bitcoin, currently considered by the FSC as sale of a digital "virtual commodity" but not "currency", should generally be fine from a Taiwan regulatory perspective, and the general principles and rules governing "purchase and sale" under the Civil Code would apply if the consideration is cash. Also, we tend to think that the above would apply to the sale of other virtual currencies/cryptocurrencies of the same nature and characteristics as Bitcoin.

Please note that the above are subject to "ICO and token offering" as described below.

ICO and token offering

In response to the rising amount of Initial Coins Offerings ("ICOs") and other investment activities regarding virtual currencies/cryptocurrencies, the FSC also expressed the following view on ICO through the 2017 Release as mentioned above:

(1) An ICO refers to the issue and sale of "virtual commodities" (such as digital interests, digital assets, or digital virtual currencies) to investors. The classification of an ICO should be determined on a case-by-case basis. For example, if an ICO involves offer and issue of "securities", it should be subject to Taiwan's Securities and Exchange Act ("SEA"). The issue of whether tokens in an ICO would be deemed "securities" under the SEA would depend on the facts of each individual case.

(2) If any misrepresentations with respect to technologies or their outcomes and/or promises of unreasonably high returns are used by the issuer of virtual currencies or an ICO to attract investors, the issuer would be deemed as committing fraud or illegal fund-raising.

Given the above, in an ICO (or other types of token offering, such as private token pre-sale before the ICO stage), the core issue in this regard is whether an ICO would be considered issuing "securities" under Taiwan's securities regulations. Under current Taiwan law, the offer and sale of "securities" in Taiwan, whether through public offering or private placement, are regulated activities and shall be governed in accordance with the SEA, its related regulations as well as relevant rulings issued from time to time by the FSC.

The term "securities" has a very broad (but maybe not clear enough) definition in Taiwan. According to Article 6 of the SEA, "securities" could mean government bonds, corporate stocks, corporate bonds, and other securities approved by the competent authority, and any stock warrant certificate, certificate of entitlement to new shares, and certificate of payment or document of title representing any of the above securities shall be deemed securities. Additionally, according to a recent Taiwan Supreme Court opinion, a contract or agreement would be considered securities under the SEA if it has monetary value, the nature of investment and transferability.

Taxation

There is currently no express interpretation or regulation governing the taxation of Bitcoin or other cryptocurrencies. Given that Bitcoin is currently classified as a digital "virtual commodity" by the FSC and the CBC, it is possible that the tax authorities might take the following stances on Bitcoin:

(1) Business Tax

In general, sales of goods and services in Taiwan are subject to Taiwan's business tax. Given this, a legal entity selling cryptocurrencies in Taiwan should be subject to Taiwan's business tax.

Individuals should refer to the standards for "online personal sale of goods" for guidance on tax liability. Specifically, an individual with online monthly sales of goods (including virtual commodities) reaching NT$80,000 on average for the past six months should apply for taxation registration with Taiwan's tax authority and pay applicable business tax.

(2) Income Tax

Taiwanese legal entities are subject to Taiwan income tax for their worldwide income. Accordingly, for a Taiwanese legal entity, its income from sale of cryptocurrencies should be subject to income tax in Taiwan. As to a foreign legal entity, if its income is generated from the sale of cryptocurrencies to Taiwanese persons, it should be subject to Taiwan's income tax.

As for Taiwanese individuals, it depends on whether the cryptocurrency trading is conducted on an offshore platform. If the trading is conducted on a local platform, the trader (individual) should consolidate the income from trading Bitcoin into his/her personal consolidated income, on which a consolidated income tax shall be levied and the current highest progressive tax rate applicable is 40%. If the trading is conducted on an offshore platform, then the income should be classified as "non-Taiwan-sourced income", which is not included in the calculation of personal consolidated income tax. However, such non-Taiwan-sourced income is subject to alternative minimum tax ("AMT"), currently at a flat rate of 20%.

Money transmission laws and anti-money laundering requirements

As advised under "Cryptocurrency regulation" above, currently there exists no required licence for (a) operating the services of exchange between virtual currencies or virtual currencies with fiat currencies, or (b) acting as a "money transmitter" and the like in Taiwan.

As for anti-money laundering ("AML"), Taiwan's Ministry of Justice issued a press release on 10 April 2018 about bringing virtual currencies exchange/platform operators under Taiwan's AML regulatory regime. According to the press release, the details on cryptocurrency and AML compliance are still under discussion and should be subject to further discussion and decision by local regulators.

Promotion and testing

Taiwan's law for the fintech regulatory sandbox, the "FinTech Development and Innovation and Experiment Act" ("Sandbox Act"), was promulgated on 31 January 2018 and took effect on 30 April 2018. The Sandbox Act was enacted to enable fintech businesses to test their financial technologies. In April 2018, the FSC promulgated the enforcement rules for the regulatory sandbox. As of the date of this article, the FSC has not started accepting applications for entering the sandbox, but it is generally expected that it would start from the second quarter of 2018.

According to the Sandbox Act, an applicant (which can be an entity or individual) needs to obtain approval from the FSC before entering the sandbox. Once the experiment begins, the experimental activities may enjoy exemptions from certain laws and regulations (such as FSC licensing requirements and certain legal liability exemptions).

After completion of the approved experiments, the FSC will analyse the results of the experiments. If the result is positive, the FSC would actively examine the existing financial laws and regulations to explore the possibility of amending them, after which the business model or activities previously tested in the sandbox could become feasible under law. Please note, however, that the sandbox entity or individual might still be required to apply for a relevant licence or approval from the FSC in order to formally conduct the activities as previously tested in the sandbox.

It is possible that the relevant market players of some controversial fintech business models and activities (e.g., ICOs) would wish to apply to the FSC to enter the sandbox. However, according to the Sandbox Act, any experimental activity needs to be "innovative". Therefore, (a) whether or not the commonly seen cryptocurrency-related activities (such as ICOs) would enter the sandbox, and (b) if yes, whether the result of the experiment would be considered "positive", would still depend on the FSC's then-effective policies and final decision.

Ownership and licensing requirements

As mentioned above, Taiwan has not promulgated any laws or regulations specifically dealing with "virtual currencies" or "cryptocurrencies", so there exists no ownership or licensing requirements under Taiwanese law, except for "ICO and token offering" as advised under "Sale regulation" above. Under current Taiwanese law, the offer and sale of "securities" in Taiwan are regulated activities. In other words, theoretically speaking, any offer or sale of ICOs or tokens in Taiwan needs to obtain the FSC's approval beforehand if such ICOs or tokens are considered "securities" under the SEA. However, currently such approval is not available under the SEA and its related regulations.

Mining

So far no Taiwanese laws or regulations have been promulgated or amended to regulate the "mining" of Bitcoin or any other types of cryptocurrencies. The mining activities should generally be permitted.

Border restrictions and declaration

So far no Taiwanese laws or regulations have been specifically promulgated or amended to impose any border restrictions on or requirements for declaration of holdings of cryptocurrencies.

Reporting requirements

So far no Taiwanese laws or regulations have been specifically promulgated or amended to impose any reporting requirement for cryptocurrencies.

Estate planning and testamentary succession

So far, Taiwan's laws and regulations have not addressed this topic. Since cryptocurrencies have value, we tend to think they would be considered as "property" or "assets" from the perspective of Taiwan estate and succession law, unless they are confiscated by the government due to, for example, the commission of a criminal offence violating the prohibition of "securities" offering without prior approval from or registration with the FSC as required under the SEA (see under "Sale regulation", above).

Robin Chang
Tel: +886 2 2715 3300 ext. 2208 / Email: robinchang@leeandli.com
Robin Chang is a partner at Lee and Li and the head of the firm's banking practice group. His practice focuses on banking, IPOs, capital markets, mergers and acquisitions, project financing, financial consumer protection law, personal data protection law, securitisation and antitrust law.

Mr Chang advises major international commercial banks and investment banks on their operations in Taiwan, including providing advice on compliance and regulatory issues, setting up a banking branch or bank subsidiary in Taiwan and customer complaints. He has been involved in many M&A transactions of financial institutions. He has also been involved in government projects in e-payment regulations in Taiwan.

Eddie Hsiung
Tel: +886 2 2715 3300 ext. 2162 / Email: eddiehsiung@leeandli.com
Mr Eddie Hsiung is licensed to practise law in Taiwan and New York, and is also a CPA in Washington State, U.S.A. His practice focuses on securities, M&A, banking, finance, asset and fund management, cross-border investments, general corporate and commercial, fintech, startups, etc.

He regularly advises leading banks, securities firms, payment/credit cards and other financial services companies on transactional, licensing and regulatory/compliance matters as well as internal investigation. He is experienced in advising asset management companies and issuers on sale of offshore funds and other investment products in Taiwan. He is familiar with derivatives and fintech issues (ICOs, cryptocurrencies, platform operators, e-payment, digital financial services, regulatory sandbox, etc.).

Lee and Li, Attorneys-at-Law

7F, 201, Tun Hua N. Road, Taipei, Taiwan 10508, R.O.C.
Tel: +886 2 2715 3300 ext. 2208 / Fax: +886 2 2514 9841 / URL: www.leeandli.com

UAE

Joby Beretta
The Bench

Government attitude and definition

<u>Blockchain</u>

The United Arab Emirates ("**UAE**") is a staunch supporter of blockchain technology. The Emirates Blockchain Strategy 2021 was launched in April 2018 and aims to handle 50% of all federal government transactions over the blockchain platform within three years. The initiative is expected to result in some impressive savings of AED 11bn, 398 million printed documents, 1.6 billion kilometres of driving and 77 million work hours annually.

In Dubai (one of the seven Emirates of the UAE), His Highness Sheikh Hamdan Bin Mohammed Al Maktoum launched the Dubai Blockchain Strategy back in October 2016 with the intention that Dubai should be the first city fully powered by Blockchain by 2020. The Dubai Blockchain Strategy is a collaboration between Smart Dubai Office and the Dubai Future Foundation, and has three pillars:

1. Government Efficiency: The intention is to increase efficiency by enabling a paperless digital layer for transactions such as visa applications, bill payments and licence renewals.

2. Industry Creation: This will introduce a system to enable citizens and partners to create new business using the technology across multiple sectors such as real estate, fintech, banking, healthcare, transportation, urban planning, smart energy, digital commerce and tourism.

3. International Leadership: Dubai will open its blockchain platform for global partners to enhance safety, security and convenience for international travellers to Dubai. Visitors will benefit from faster entry, pre-approved passport and security clearance and visas, easier mobility by way of approved driver's licence and car rental, wireless connectivity and pre-authenticated digital wallets and payments.

As highlighted by the third pillar above, Dubai is playing an integral role in the international development of blockchain, with the creation of the Global Blockchain Council. It was founded by the Dubai Future Foundation and consists of 46 members including government entities, international private companies, leading UAE banks, freezones and international blockchain technology firms.

There are already a number of private and public sector blockchain initiatives in the UAE including: Emirates NBD which is developing a service for validating bank cheques; the Dubai Roads and Transport Authority which is launching a vehicle lifecycle management system; and the Dubai Land Department which is in the process of migrating to a blockchain system.

Cryptocurrency

Whereas the underlying blockchain technology has clearly been welcomed in the UAE with open arms, cryptocurrencies are experiencing more of a mixed reception here – at least from the regulators.

Generally speaking, there is currently a lacuna of specific legislation covering cryptocurrencies. Most of the financial regulatory authorities in the UAE have taken the position of issuing warnings of the risks inherent in certain cryptocurrencies and initial coin offerings ("**ICO**") and are considering draft regulations. The position of the UAE Central Bank is somewhat uncertain because, as we look at in more detail below, the digital payment regulations expressly prohibit 'virtual currencies', but there was a subsequent statement made clarifying that these regulations do not apply to cryptocurrencies such as Bitcoin. Only a few of the freezones (out of the 45+ in the UAE) are known to have granted licences to cryptocurrency companies, and only one of the financial freezones has taken the 'bull by the horns' and issued a regulatory regime for cryptocurrencies and ICOs.

What is clear is that the UAE Government is committed to develop its own cryptocurrency. In October 2017, Dubai announced that it was developing emCash, a cryptocurrency which can be used as part of a payment system to pay for school fees and governmental services. It was launched in partnership with Emcredit Limited and UK-based Object Tech Group Limited. A couple of months later, in Dec 2017, the UAE Central Bank also announced it had been testing a new cryptocurrency for cross-border payments to Saudi Arabia. With the Government itself driving these initiatives, there is no doubt that the regulatory regime will be developed accordingly.

Cryptocurrency regulation

In the UAE, the financial regulatory framework can essentially be divided between: (i) the financial freezones (being the Abu Dhabi Global Markets ("**ADGM**") and Dubai International Financial Centre ("**DIFC**")) ("**Financial Freezones**"); and (ii) the rest of the UAE including onshore and the non-financial freezones ("**Rest of the UAE**"). The Financial Freezones essentially have their own laws, courts and jurisdiction and are only subject to a few federal-level laws such as criminal and anti-money laundering ("**AML**") laws.

The exact treatment of cryptocurrencies will therefore depend upon: (i) the geographical location; and (ii) how they are categorised or viewed by the applicable regulator in that location.

In the Financial Freezones, the activities are regulated by their own regulator, i.e. Dubai Financial Services Authority ("**DFSA**") in DIFC, and the Financial Services Regulatory Authority ("**FSRA**") in ADGM. Accordingly, they will have discretion how to categorise and regulate cryptocurrency.

In the Rest of the UAE, if cryptocurrencies are deemed to be a commodity (such as oil or gold) or a security (such as equity in a company), they could fall within the remit of the UAE Securities and Commodities Authority ("**SCA**"), whereas if they are deemed to be a currency (such as AED or USD) they could fall under the UAE Central Bank ("**Central Bank**"). That said, there is always potential for an overlap in responsibilities and collaboration between the two regulators.

UAE Securities and Commodities Authority

The UAE's federal financial services and securities regulator issued a warning on 4 February 2018 in relation to ICOs, stating:

"*At present, SCA does not regulate or mandate or recognise any ICO. ICOs involve the issuance of digital tokens created using distributed ledger technology and sold to investors by action or through subscription in return for cryptocurrency. The terms and features of ICOs differ in each case, as does the nature of the rights or interest (if any) that is acquired by the investor. ICOs are highly speculative and characterised by high volatility in the prices of tokens,*" the statement said. The SCA went on to warn that "*no legal protection is currently offered and investors are entering into these investments at their own risk.*"

The warning from the SCA followed a similar warning by the International Organisation of Securities Commissions ("**IOSCO**"), which sets global securities regulation standards. One example of the international reach of this organisation was the case taken by one of its members, the US Securities and Exchange Commission ("**SEC**"), which obtained an order to freeze assets of AriseBank in the USA during their ongoing ICO in January 2018. This case has a Dubai connection because one of the founders lived in Dubai. AriseBank was alleged to have illegally raised up to US$ 600m from investors without registering with the regulators.

This highlights the willingness of financial regulators around the world to intervene to protect investors where the cryptocurrencies fall within the category of securities.

UAE Central Bank

The Central Bank issued the Regulatory Framework for Stored Values and Electronic Payment Systems on 1 January 2017 ("**E-Payment Regs**"). The stated objective of the E-Payment Regs is to facilitate the adoption of digital payments across the UAE in a secure manner.

The E-Payment Regs acknowledge and define a 'virtual currency' as "*any type of digital unit used as a medium of exchange, a unit of account, or a form of stored value*". The definition then goes on to state that "*virtual currency is not recognised by this regulation except digital units that (a) can be redeemed for goods, services and discounts for goods, services and discounts as part of a user loyalty or rewards program with the issuer and (b) cannot be converted into a fiat currency or a virtual currency*".

The E-Payment Regs then go on to expressly state that "*all virtual currencies (and all transactions thereof) are prohibited*".

This obviously raised some major concerns about the general legality of cryptocurrencies in the UAE. However, a month later, the Central Bank Governor, His Excellency Mubarak Rashed Khamis Al Mansouri, issued a statement that "*these regulations do not apply to bitcoin or other cryptocurrencies, currency exchanges or underlying technology such as blockchain*". Some commentators have questioned the enforceability of these informal statements by the Governor, whereas others point to provisions in the E-Payment Regs stating that "*the Central Bank's interpretation of this regulation shall be deemed final*". Either way, we anticipate that there will be some more formal statement or regulation soon. In fact, the Governor commented that "*the area is currently under review by the Central Bank and new regulations will be issued as appropriate*".

Later that year in October, the Governor issued a warning against cryptocurrencies. At the Islamic Financial Services Board Summit he was quoted as saying, "*[S]ome nations have announced that they are not using Bitcoin, and consequently its value sharply plummeted. In addition, it can be easily used in money laundering and in funding terror activities*".

The regulatory regime for cryptocurrencies in the UAE from a Central Bank perspective is therefore somewhat of a grey area at present, with some commentators suggesting that whilst the use of cryptocurrencies as a currency or for digital payments by licensed payment service providers ("**PSP**") may be prohibited under the E-Payments Regs, the ownership or trading of cryptocurrency appears to be tolerated.

Dubai Financial Services Authority

The DFSA, the regulator of the DIFC issued a 'General Investor Statement on Cryptocurrencies' on 13 September 2017. The statement concluded that:

"The DFSA wishes to highlight that these types of product offerings, and the systems and technology that support them, are complex. They have their own unique risks, which may not be easy to identify or understand; such risks may increase where offerings are made on a cross-border basis. These offerings should be regarded as high-risk investments. The DFSA would like to make it clear that it does not currently regulate these types of product offerings or license firms in the Dubai International Financial Centre (DIFC) to undertake such activities. Accordingly, before engaging with any persons promoting such offerings in the DIFC, or making any financial contribution toward such offerings, the DFSA urges potential investors to exercise caution and undertake due diligence to understand the risks involved."

We understand that the DFSA is considering the regulation of cryptocurrencies and we expect that we may see regulatory developments in due course.

The Financial Services Regulatory Authority (FSRA)

The FSRA is the only regulator in the UAE that has issued a regulatory framework specifically dealing with cryptocurrencies. It went through a consultation exercise in May 2018 and then issued the Guidance on Regulation of Crypto Asset Activities on 25 June 2018 ("**Crypto Regs**"). The Crypto Regs regulate spot crypto-assets activities including those undertaken by exchanges, custodians and other intermediaries in the ADGM.

Amendments to a key piece of legislation, the *Financial Services and Market Regulations 2015*, introduced the definition of a 'Crypto Asset' as:

"a digital representation of value that can be digitally traded and functions as (1) a medium of exchange; and/or (2) a unit of account; and/or (3) a store of value, but does not have legal tender status in any jurisdiction. A Crypto Asset is (a) neither issued nor guaranteed by any jurisdiction, and fulfils the above functions only by agreement within the community of users of the Crypto Asset; and (b) distinguished from Fiat Currency and E-money."

The Crypto Regs make a clear distinction between:

1. 'Security Tokens' e.g. virtual tokens which have the characteristics of a Security, such as shares, which are regulated as Securities by the FSRA;

2. 'Crypto Assets' e.g. no fiat virtual currencies which are treated as commodities and therefore not regulated by the FSRA as Specified Investments (although market intermediaries and those dealing in or managing Crypto Assets will need to be approved);

3. 'Utility Tokens' e.g. virtual tokens that do not have the characteristics of a regulated instrument, which are treatment as commodities and therefore not regulated by the FSRA as Specified Investments; and

4. 'Derivatives and Collective Investment Funds', which are regulated as Specified Investments.

Not all Crypto Assets will be able to be dealt with from the ADGM. Only those deemed to be 'Accepted Crypto Assets' by the FSRA will be allowed. It is understood that this is to protect against higher-risk crypto activities. Although the ADGM has stated it does not intend to make a list of Accepted Crypto Assets publicly available, it will however provide information to applicants, and it has a non-exclusive list of factors that it will take into consideration. These include security, traceability, exchange connectivity, market demand/ volatility, type of distributed ledger, innovation and practical application.

The ADGM also issued a Guidance on the Regulation of Initial Coin / Token Offerings and Crypto Assets on 9 October 2017 (which was updated on 25 June 2018 in line with the new Crypto Regs).

The ADGM therefore appears to offer an attractive option for a cryptocurrency business in the UAE, as it has the framework in place to provide regulatory compliance comfort to the company and its investors.

Sales regulation

DIFC

Pursuant to DFSA's statement above, no companies in the DIFC are licensed to sell cryptocurrencies in the DIFC.

ADGM

Under the Crypto Regs, a new Regulated Activity of 'Operating a Crypto Asset Business' ("**OCAB**") has also been introduced. As a Regulated Activity, OCAB is widely drafted and includes:

- buying, selling or exercising any right in Accepted Crypto Assets (whether as principal or agent);
- managing Accepted Crypto Assets belonging to another person;
- making arrangements with a view to another person (whether as principal or agent) buying, selling or providing custody of Accepted Crypto Assets;
- marketing of Accepted Crypto Assets;
- advising on the merits of buying or selling Accepted Crypto Assets or any rights conferred by such buying or selling; and
- operating a "Crypto Asset Exchange" or operating as a "Crypto Asset Custodian".

Accordingly, any entities wishing to sell cryptocurrencies or carry out any of the other OCAB activities in ADGM may do so provided that they obtain an OCAB licence from the FSRA.

Rest of the UAE

Other than the provision in the E-Payment Regs discussed above, there are no express regulations prohibiting or regulating the sale of cryptocurrencies in the Rest of the UAE.

Indeed, the use of cryptocurrencies appears to be a tolerated practice and there are a number of companies in the UAE reportedly accepting payment in Bitcoin or other cryptocurrencies. These apparently include properties in City Walk that accept Bitcoin for rental payments and a real estate project in Dubai Science Park where you can purchase property with Bitcoin. There were even claims of an ATM in Dubai Media City which allowed you to withdraw cash in exchange for Bitcoins, but the location remains elusive.

There have also been a couple of Bitcoin exchanges set up in the UAE such as Igot and BitOasis in 2014. BitOasis commenced operating from Dubai Silicon Oasis freezone but in May 2018 it was reported that a number of banks (including Emirates NBD, Noor Bank and

Mashreq) blocked AED deposits and withdrawals from BitOasis accounts. We understand that subsequently BitOasis moved its platform to the British Virgin Islands, which may have resolved some of the payment issues with UAE bank accounts. However, the BitOasis website terms and conditions still anticipate and cover what happens if customers face issues with banks processing fiat withdrawals in the UAE or GCC.

There have also been a number of ICOs in the UAE such as the Islamic financial services and technology company OneGram in partnership with GoldGuard, a gold trading platform licensed by the Dubai Airport Free Zone. OneGram's coin is backed by one gram of gold and claimed to be the world's first *Sharia*-compliant cryptocurrency. Other ICOs include Afterschool which, in October 2017, voluntarily suspended sale of the tokens (of which it had sold 11 million by that time).

Taxation

VAT

The value added tax ("**VAT**") regime was only recently introduced into the UAE on 1 January 2018. As such, the current position on taxation of cryptocurrencies is untested and it will depend on the view the UAE Federal Tax Authority ("**FTA**") takes on cryptocurrencies pursuant to the Federal Law No. 8 of 2017 ("**VAT Law**") and the implementing regulations.

If cryptocurrencies are deemed to be 'Goods' or 'Services' for the purposes of the VAT Law, then the value of the purchase would be subject to VAT. It is unlikely that cryptocurrencies would fall within the definition of 'Goods', which is *"physical property that can be supplied including real estate, water and all forms of energy"*. The definition of 'Services', on the other hand, is extremely wide and covers *"anything that can be supplied other than 'Goods'"*, which would obviously enable the FTA to catch cryptocurrency if it so desired.

If, however, the FTA takes the view that cryptocurrencies are 'financial services' or a currency, then the purchase value of the crypto is likely to be exempt from VAT. Financial services are defined in the VAT Law as *'services connected to dealings in money (or its equivalent)'*. In relation to such financial services, where there are express transaction fees (such as a commission), those fees in relation to the financial service provided may still be subject to VAT. This means any transaction fees in relation to buying or selling cryptocurrencies could be subject to VAT.

In any event, it seems fairly certain that if cryptocurrencies are used to purchase goods and services in the UAE, then VAT will be payable on such goods or services to the same extent that they would if payment had been made in UAE dirhams or other fiat currency.

Other taxes

Currently in the UAE corporation tax is only levied on oil and gas companies and foreign banks. To the extent that such corporations make a profit from cryptocurrencies, one would assume the normal treatment of corporation tax would apply equally to such profits.

There are currently no personal income, capital gains or inheritance taxes in the UAE, so none of these would be applicable in any event on any gains in the value of cryptocurrencies.

Money transmission laws and anti-money laundering requirements

Money transmission

Under the Crypto Regs, the FSRA requires OCAB licensees to have adequate controls in place which include setting appropriate daily limits, e.g. on cash deposits, and to have adequate technology to meet their regulatory obligations (e.g. KYC, transaction identification and reporting) and risk management requirements (e.g. margin limits, large exposure monitoring).

In the Rest of the UAE there are both individual transaction limits and maximum daily limits for retail PSPs set out in the E-Payment Regs but, as stated above, these expressly do not apply to cryptocurrencies.

AML

There are numerous anti-money laundering laws in the UAE including Federal Law No. 4 of 2002 combating money laundering and financial terrorism (as amended by Federal Law No.9 of 2014) ("**AML Law**") and Cabinet Resolution No 38 of 2014 ("**AML Regs**").

The AML Law has a wide definition of 'Property' used in the commission of an offence, which is *"assets of every kind, whether corporeal or incorporeal, movable or immovable, including the national currency and foreign currencies and the documents or instruments, of whatever kind, whether in electronic or digital format, evidencing title to those assets or any right attached thereto"*.

In our view, the definition is therefore wide enough to cover cryptocurrencies. Indeed, there have been a number of cases in the UAE where financial institutions have suspended payments from cryptocurrency accounts due to suspected non-compliance with the AML Law or AML Regs. If convicted of a money laundering offence, the AML Law provides punitive measures including fines ranging from AED 10,000 to AED 1m and imprisonment of up to 10 years.

There are also additional AML regulations depending on the location of the company – such as the SCA Decision 2010, the AML Module of the DFSA Rulebook and the AML Rules of the FSRA. For OCAB licensees, the FSRA supplements its normal AML Rules with requirements to adopt international best practices (including the Financial Action Task Force recommendations) for cryptocurrency activities.

Promotion and testing

There are a number of private sector fintech collaborations such as the Emirates NBD Future Lab (which has provided AED 500m over three years to support digital innovation) and hackathons (such as Emirates Islamic Banks 'appathon' to create the next banking app). In addition, the key financial regulators have developed promotion and testing programmes and schemes; however, they are more generic 'fintech' sandboxes rather than blockchain- or cryptocurrency-specific.

SCA

In January 2017, the SCA announced its initiative to support innovation-based fintech. The general idea is to offer an appropriate environment for the testing and launch of fintech services and products, and to provide regulatory support and advice. The SCA requested comments and suggestions from various market participants on how to best formulate the initiative.

ADGM

ADGM launched RegLab in 2016 which offers a 'Developing Financial Technology Services' licence to start-ups for up to two years. ADGM provides support in terms of co-working spaces and a network of collaborators and mentors. Applicants must establish a company in the ADGM and pass certain tests and milestones within the two-year period.

DIFC

The DIFC initiative is called the Fintech Hive and was launched in January 2017. It offers an 'Innovation Testing Licence' for a period of 6–12 months. The initiative provides similar support such as workspace, mentoring, workshops, etc. The requirements are similar to ADGM's and applicants have to have a business model and a product or service that uses new, emerging or existing tech in an innovative way.

Ownership and licensing requirements

ADGM

The licensing and ownership requirements for the OCAB licence under the Cyber Regs are essentially the same as any other Authorised Person under the FSRA regulation, i.e. to be authorised as an OCAB, the applicant must satisfy FSRA that all applicable requirements of FSMR and the relevant FSRA Rulebooks have been, and will continue to be, complied with. This includes the FSRA General Rulebook, the FSRA Anti-Money Laundering and Sanctions Rules and Guidance, and the FSRA Rules of Market Conduct. The definition of OCAB is drafted such that investment advisors or fund managers dealing in cryptocurrencies from the ADGM are likely to be caught by the definition and require appropriate licensing as well.

At the date of writing this article we are not aware of any companies that have received an OCAB licence, although the regulations are only a month old. This is a development which will be monitored with interest, going forward.

DIFC

As stated above, the DFSA has not yet issued any licences to cryptocurrency companies.

Rest of the UAE

As mentioned above, cryptocurrencies are currently unregulated by the Central Bank and SCA so there are no applicable ownership or licensing requirements from those federal-level regulators.

In addition to the Financial Freezones, there are a number of freezones in the Rest of the UAE that fall under the umbrella of the Central Bank and SCA but are free to set their own rules and regulations in relation to areas such as company licensing, foreign ownership restrictions, etc. One of these freezones, the Dubai Multi Commodities Centre ("**DMCC**") serves as a global marketplace for commodities to drive trade flows through Dubai, and is also a member of the Global Blockchain Council.

In February 2018, DMCC licensed Regal RA DMCC (a gold trader and storage provider) as the first company in the DMCC free zone to expressly trade in cryptocurrencies. The company apparently offers storage of Bitcoin, Ethereum and other cryptocurrencies in a vault located at DMCC. At the time of the announcement, it was stated that *"DMCC is the only Free Zone in the Middle East to have a government-issued license to trade in crypto-commodities and offers unparalleled full market value insurance on such investments."*

The DMCC Authority appears to have taken the view that these specific activities are trading in commodities rather than currencies or securities. We understand that the licence is available for proprietary trading in crypto commodities only, and that no ICOs or exchanges are permitted. Other than the innovative licence category, we understand that DMCC's normal corporate ownership and licensing regulations apply.

The DMCC is considered by many to be fintech-friendly as it has a wide range of categories of company licences and takes a flexible approach to licensing. In addition, companies in the DMCC would not need to meet the requirements of the Crypto Regs that they would have to if they set up in the ADGM.

Mining

ADGM mentioned in the circular in October 2017 that it did not view mining of cryptocurrencies as a regulated activity, whereas DIFC remains silent on the matter.

There are no regulations in the Rest of the UAE specifically regulating the activity of mining cryptocurrencies but, due to the uncertainty and unavailability of licences, we would caution against it. If the mining is on a sufficiently large scale (which nowadays requires substantial sophisticated hardware), it could be deemed to be 'carrying out business in the UAE' without a business licence.

Border restrictions and declaration

As with many countries around the world, the UAE has regulations requiring the declaration of cash (aptly entitled 'Regulations regarding declaration by travellers entering or leaving the UAE carrying cash and monetary or financial bearer instruments'), which came into effect on 1 September 2011.

Under the regulations, any cash money (inclusive of currencies and travellers' cheques) above AED 100,000 or the equivalent in other currencies, needs to be declared. In our view, it is unlikely that this is intended to cover cryptocurrencies held in a digital wallet, although we are unaware of any clarification of this by the Federal Customs Authority to date.

Reporting requirements

As mentioned above, under the Crypto Regs, the FSRA requires OCAB licensees to have adequate controls in place, which include meeting their regulatory obligations in relation to reporting. Again, no specific regulation in DIFC.

We are not aware of any reporting requirements in the Rest of the UAE for cryptocurrency payments made in excess of a certain value.

Estate planning and testamentary succession

We are not aware of any regulations or cases of how cryptocurrencies will be treated for the purposes of estate planning in the UAE. The treatment will depend on a number of factors such as whether the owner is a Muslim, whether there is a will in place, and whether the will has been registered with one of the Financial Freezones such as the DIFC Courts Wills Registry (available for non-Muslims in Dubai and Ras Al Khaimah) or is subject to *Sharia* rules.

In practice, whoever knows the unique password/private key for the cryptocurrency will effectively have control over the asset, therefore succession planning will need to take this into consideration.

Joby Beretta
Tel: +971 56 683 0775 / Email: joby@thebenchlaw.com

Joby Beretta is the Founder of The Bench, an award-winning innovative legal services provider offering cost-effective legal services. Joby is recognised as one of the leading TMT lawyers in the UAE by *Chambers & Partners* (Band 1), *The Legal 500* (Leading Individual), and *Who's Who Legal*. Prior to establishing The Bench, Joby was a Partner and Head of TMT for the Middle East at Dentons, the world's largest law firm. He was advising financial institutions on technology projects long before the recent fintech frenzy. *Who's Who Legal* 2016 described Joby as a "standout" lawyer in the Middle East and noted he is "incredibly gifted". Clients appreciate his "industry insight" gained while working in-house, and having been based in Dubai since 2003, he has a "great appreciation for the cultural nuances of the region".

The Bench

Fujairah Creative Zone, Fujairah, UAE
Tel: +971 56 683 0775 / URL: www.thebenchlaw.com

United Kingdom

Simon Lovegrove & Albert Weatherill
Norton Rose Fulbright LLP

Introduction

In this chapter we discuss the UK regulatory approach to cryptocurrencies. As in other jurisdictions, the treatment and characterisation of cryptocurrency has not yet been fully clarified, although the UK regulatory authorities are working on this issue, forming a task force to explore issues related to crypto-assets and working closely with market participants under various other initiatives. This work has become particularly pertinent given the increasing media and market focus on cryptocurrencies in the UK, coupled with the reality that the UK's existing regulatory framework, like many other national regulatory frameworks, was not designed with this new asset class in mind.

Government attitude and definition

Responsibility for the supervision of financial services in the UK rests with the Prudential Regulation Authority (**PRA**), which is part of the Bank of England (**BoE**), and the Financial Conduct Authority (**FCA**). Financial services legislation and policy is also driven by HM Treasury (**HMT**), which is a ministerial department of the UK Government. The PRA, BoE and FCA operate independently of, but in close cooperation with, HMT to maintain and develop the UK's financial services legislative and regulatory framework, including in relation to cryptocurrency and the activities performed by market participants in relation to cryptocurrency.

The legal status of cryptocurrency in the UK

It is a common assessment, both in the context of English law and more broadly in terms of economic theory, that money generally possesses three necessary properties: it is a store of value; it is a medium of exchange; and it is a unit of account. Whilst cryptocurrencies, particularly those with larger market capitalisations such as Bitcoin and Ether, certainly possess characteristics that are akin to those three core elements of money, the prevailing view is that cryptocurrencies should not be characterised as money within the UK financial system. In a 2014 paper on this point,[1] the BoE concluded that cryptocurrencies are unlikely to be considered money due to their relatively limited adoption within the UK financial system and their seeming inability to form a reliable unit of account, given a lack of inherent value and high volatility, marking them as a relatively immature asset class by comparison. Whilst the adoption and use of cryptocurrency has undoubtedly increased since that BoE paper, the assessment that cryptocurrency should not be seen as money for the time being remains persuasive.

What then is the legal status of cryptocurrencies under English law? It is likely that an answer can be reached by considering the UK's common law. In this sense, cryptocurrency is generally considered to be a digital form of personal property referred to as a *chose* in possession,[2] whereby the rights of the owner of that property derive from the ability to physically possess it and transfer title to it to others, albeit that cryptocurrencies themselves are intangible. The legal status of cryptocurrencies and crypto-assets continues to remain in a degree of flux, so it cannot be ruled out that legal concepts of property may change to reflect the changing nature and characteristics of our personal property.

Definition of cryptocurrency

There is as yet no formal, statutory definition of a cryptocurrency under English law. In responding to a question raised in Parliament, the UK Government confirmed that, in defining its approach to any possible regulation of cryptocurrency, it is principally guided by the amendments to the Fourth Anti-Money Laundering Directive (**MLD5**) which must be transposed into English law by 10 January 2020.

Under MLD5, we have for the first time a statutory definition of a "virtual currency", which is "*a digital representation of value that is not issued or guaranteed by a central bank or a public authority, is not necessarily attached to a legally established currency, but is accepted by natural or legal persons as a means of exchange, and which can be transferred, stored or traded electronically*". The definition does not require for the digital representation of value to be encrypted using cryptographic techniques, and it should therefore be considered to include a variety of digital representations of value, including, but not limited to, cryptocurrencies. Barring any change to the Government's position in the intervening period, this will be the basis upon which cryptocurrencies are defined in English law both up to and following the implementation of MLD5.

Initiatives relating to cryptocurrency and blockchain

The UK authorities have been particularly vocal in the last few years on Fintech matters generally, including in their discussions of cryptocurrencies and crypto-assets. The UK Government has assembled a Cryptoassets Task Force comprising senior representatives from HMT, the BoE and the FCA, who are collectively tasked with plotting the way forward for cryptocurrencies and crypto-assets in the context of UK legislation and regulation. Holding its first meeting in May 2018, the Cryptoassets Task Force is working to publish its initial report in Q3 2018, which will hopefully provide a greater degree of insight as to how the three bodies view the benefits and risk factors presented by cryptocurrencies and other forms of crypto-assets, as well as a proposed approach, if any, to the regulation of cryptocurrencies (discussed further in the "*Cryptocurrency regulation*" section, below). The establishment of the Cryptoassets Task Force flows from HMT's Fintech Sector Strategy paper published in March 2018 which, amongst other things, highlights the potential benefit to the UK economy of crypto-assets and blockchain and distributed ledger technology, particularly within the financial services sector.

The work of the Cryptoassets Task Force builds on the existing experience that the BoE and the FCA have gathered via their own respective initiatives. The FCA launched its Project Innovate initiative in October 2014 and, since that time, it has interacted with a range of firms via its Regulatory Sandbox, which allows firms to deploy products and test business models in a controlled testing environment with live customers under a restricted authorisation, with the ability to obtain individual guidance and no enforcement action letters (see "*Promotion and Testing*" later in this chapter). The FCA's initiative has been well received by startups and financial institutions alike, particularly those with business models and product offerings related to crypto, blockchain and distributed ledger technology.

For instance, 36% of firms who have participated in the Regulatory Sandbox since its first cohort in July 2016 fall within this category of firms, demonstrating that the FCA recognises the benefits that the Sandbox, and Project Innovate more broadly, can contribute to nascent business models and products in this space.

In addition to the activities of the FCA and HMT, the BoE has itself been exploring crypto-assets and blockchain and distributed ledger technology. The BoE's approach has principally focused on three main areas: (a) whether or not cryptocurrencies and other forms of virtual currencies can be regarded as money; (b) exploring the possible use cases of blockchain and distributed ledger technology in the context of settlement and market infrastructure (including in terms of access to central bank money); and (c) assessing the basis for a central-bank issued digital currency.

This exploratory work has resulted in a range of extensive working papers drafted by the BoE's economists as to the status of cryptocurrencies,[3] the content of which informs the views expressed earlier in this chapter. On a practical level, the BoE has worked closely with a range of firms as part of its proof-of-concepts programme, which is an element of its broader Fintech Accelerator initiative. The programme involves the BoE working with firms across a range of areas, including in relation to blockchain and distributed ledger technology, to test the viability and usability of a range of products and services that are relevant to financial market infrastructure and the operability of the UK financial services framework.

Despite the BoE's economists considering the economics and functionality of central bank-issued digital currencies at length,[4] the UK does not currently have a central bank-issued cryptocurrency or digital currency, although the possibility of such an arrangement being established cannot be ruled out, as the BoE continues to explore how best to ensure that both financial institutions and start-ups have the opportunity and the technical capability to access central bank money and settle a range of transactions through the BoE's Real Time Gross Settlement System.

Cryptocurrency regulation

A brief summary of the UK's regulatory framework

The UK's regulatory framework consists of a range of different individual frameworks, certain of which flow down from European legislation, whilst others represent evolution in legal and regulatory thinking over many years at a national level. The two key considerations that arise in connection with determining whether or not cryptocurrencies are within the scope of the UK's regulatory perimeter are: (i) whether or not the performance of activities by a firm in relation to those cryptocurrencies results in that person performing a regulated activity requiring either authorisation or registration with the FCA, and potentially also the PRA; and (ii) whether or not there are any restrictions on how those cryptocurrencies can be marketed and distributed in the UK. As the latter question is addressed in the "Sales Regulation" section of this chapter, we will focus on the former question for the time being.

At the heart of the UK's regulatory framework is the Financial Services and Markets Act 2000 as amended (**FSMA**),which incorporates the so-called general prohibition that provides that a person may not carry on a regulated activity in the UK unless they are authorised to do so, or exempt. Beyond FSMA, the UK also has two separate frameworks for payment services and electronic money, which are governed by the Payment Services Regulations 2017 (**PSRs 2017**) and the Electronic Money Regulations 2011 (**EMRs 2011**) respectively. Given the primary use cases of cryptocurrencies as a means of exchange across certain underlying protocols, these two regimes are particularly relevant when assessing the regulatory status of cryptocurrencies under English law.

Separately to the regulatory status of cryptocurrencies, the UK has implemented the Fourth Anti-Money Laundering Directive into English law via the Money Laundering, Terrorist Financing and Transfer of Funds (Information on the Payer) Regulations 2017 (**MLRs 2017**)[5] and, as discussed above, is currently considering the implementing legislation to incorporate the provisions of MLD5 into English law. The provisions of MLD5 in particular will impact certain operators in the crypto sector, and we explore these requirements in further detail in the *Money Transmission Laws and Anti-Money Laundering Requirements* section of this chapter below.

Regulatory status of cryptocurrency

A crucial element of the UK's regulatory regime is whether or not activities are being undertaken in relation to certain types of financial instrument. A person may arrange a transaction in many contexts without falling within the scope of the UK regulatory perimeter, but the arranging of a transaction in relation to certain types of financial instrument that have been designated as such under English law places that person, barring any exclusions, firmly in scope of the UK regime. Whether or not a financial instrument is a specified instrument for the purposes of English law is determined by Part III of the Financial Services and Markets Act (Regulated Activities) Order 2001 as amended (**RAO**). The RAO designates certain forms of financial instrument, such as shares, debt instruments and a range of contractually-based instruments (such as options, futures and contracts for differences) as within scope of the regulatory regime, such that performing certain types of activities in relation to those instruments results in the carrying-on of a regulated activity if such activities are carried on in the UK by way of business.

Despite the ongoing debate regarding the legal and regulatory status of cryptocurrency under English law, there is currently no legislative or regulatory provision that specifically designates whether or not cryptocurrencies, or other forms of virtual currency, are specified investments. This is largely reflective of three considerations. The first is that the primary-use case of cryptocurrencies continues to be as a means of exchange (albeit that many holders undoubtedly hold them in the hope of capital appreciation); the second is that the nature and scope of cryptocurrencies from a legal and regulatory perspective is not immediately obvious in the same way as other asset classes (it is, after all, hard to regulate something if you do not know how to characterise it); and the third is because the adoption of cryptocurrencies has remained, until recently, relatively limited.

In determining what a cryptocurrency is from a regulatory perspective, it is helpful to approach the matter in the inverse, and consider what we know it is not. The FCA has expressly confirmed that it does not consider cryptocurrencies to be commodities or currencies in the traditional sense.[6] Given their nature and form, cryptocurrencies are not what one would typically consider as contractually based instruments, and so it is not appropriate to consider a cryptocurrency to be, in and of itself, a derivative contract such as an option or a future. Given the decentralised nature of cryptocurrencies, it is also clear that cryptocurrencies do not amount to shares or other forms of debt instrument, given the absence of any centralised issuer and the corresponding rights that one typically obtains by holding such instruments.

Given that many of the more mainstream cryptocurrencies are listed on various centralised and decentralised exchanges, there is a question as to whether or not cryptocurrencies should be considered transferable securities, with the consequence that an offer to the public of such transferable securities is governed by the UK's prospectus regime (discussed in further detail in 'Sales regulation', below). A full and detailed analysis as to what constitutes a security under English law could fill a textbook all by itself, but generally speaking the English courts have typically interpreted a security to constitute either an investment (largely speaking a form of property in which an income or profit is expected to be derived in the ordinary course of trade or business as distinguished from pure speculation) or an obligation created by an instrument. Whether or not something is transferable largely depends on whether or not the security in question is negotiable on the capital markets, which itself requires the satisfaction of certain conditions – which it is not yet clear that the increasing number of centralised and decentralised cryptocurrency exchanges satisfy.

In the absence of any further guidance from the FCA, cryptocurrency itself will likely remain outside the scope of the regulatory perimeter, with persons engaging in spot crypto transactions unlikely to be performing regulated activities in the UK for the time being. However, the FCA has stated[7] that it considers that derivative contracts with cryptocurrency underlyings will be specified investments and, therefore, any entities engaging in certain types of activities in relation to such instruments should seek authorisation with the FCA. Firms will, therefore, need to consider the exact nature of the instruments in which they are performing activities to determine whether those instruments fall within the scope of the regulatory perimeter.

How does the position differ for other crypto-assets, including tokens?

The position with regard to other forms of crypto-assets, including tokens, is significantly less clear than with more "conventional" cryptocurrencies. Whilst the use cases of the latter are often relatively easy to identify (primarily to act as a means of exchange for transactions occurring on the underlying blockchain), the use cases of tokens, and the regulatory implications of such tokens, often requires significant analysis, with the outcome of that analysis heavily fact-dependent. Whilst other national regulators have sought to clarify their understanding of tokens and implement a form of taxonomy, the FCA continues to consider its position on tokens more generally.

That is not to say, however, that the FCA has been silent in respect of tokens and their issuance and sale via initial coin offerings (**ICOs**). After initially confirming that it would continue to assess tokens and ICOs,[8] the FCA subsequently issued a notice warning consumers of the risks associated with tokens and ICOs. That notice also cautioned that ICOs may involve the performance of regulated activities requiring FCA authorisation given that, in the FCA's view, certain tokens that the FCA has encountered were effectively specified investments under the RAO.

As with cryptocurrencies, the regulatory assessment of tokens remains in flux until further guidance is received from the FCA, but any firm considering an ICO or seeking to perform activities in relation to tokens or other forms of crypto-assets needs to carefully consider whether or not the nature of their activities and the functionality of their tokens is, when compared against the UK's regulatory framework, something that would fall within the regulatory perimeter.

Sales regulation

As discussed above, whether or not cryptocurrencies and other forms of crypto-asset are within the scope of the regulatory perimeter will also impact how, and to whom, they can be marketed and sold. The regulation of the sale of financial instruments under English law consists of two distinct, but not mutually exclusive, frameworks: the financial promotions regime; and the prospectus and public offer regime.

With respect to the financial promotions regime, FSMA imposes a general prohibition on the communication of an invitation or inducement to engage in investment activity which is made from the UK, to UK persons, or is otherwise capable of having an effect in the UK, unless the person making such communications is an FCA-authorised person or the communication is approved by an FCA-authorised person. The financial promotions regime only applies to "controlled investments",[9] and for these purposes cryptocurrency is not currently designated as a controlled investment under English law. Nevertheless, firms providing activities in relation to cryptocurrencies will need to exercise a degree of caution when marketing such assets in or to persons in the UK, particularly where those persons are the general public and, as a matter of good practice, ensure that their communications are at least fair, clear and not misleading.

As with other prospectus regimes throughout the European Union, the UK's prospectus rules apply in instances where an offer of transferable securities is made to the public in the UK or an admission of transferable securities is sought to a regulated market in the UK. Given that no cryptocurrencies are admitted to trading on a regulated market in the UK, the primary consideration is whether the ongoing offer or sale of cryptocurrencies via centralised and decentralised exchanges results in a public offer of transferable securities. As noted above, whether or not cryptocurrencies are securities, as well as whether they are in fact transferable in a manner as described under English law, remains open to debate, albeit the UK market thus far has seemingly concluded that ongoing trading of cryptocurrencies via such infrastructure does not result in the need for the publication of a prospectus.

However, the prospectus regime poses harder questions for tokens than it does for cryptocurrencies. Given the vast majority of tokens are issued via an ICO, coupled with the increased regulatory uncertainty as to the nature of tokens, the question as to whether or not a prospectus is required in relation to that offer is arguably more pertinent than with cryptocurrencies. How firms proceed on this point will largely depend on the conclusions they draw from their assessment of the tokens, their use cases and whether or not they are comparable to existing forms of specific investments under the RAO.

Taxation

Whilst taxation authorities have been challenged by cryptocurrencies and crypto-assets, the first response of the taxman is to bring them into the fold of taxable activities. This has typically been done by applying the existing tax framework – which has led to a number of practical questions as to how such assets fit within such framework. One particular difficulty with the taxation of cryptocurrencies and crypto-assets results from the fact that their value can fluctuate enormously. How cryptocurrencies and crypto-assets will be taxed will typically depend upon the precise nature of the cryptocurrency or crypto-asset.

Her Majesty's Revenue and Customs (**HMRC**) was among the first of the global taxation authorities to deal with the concept of a cryptocurrency, publishing a business brief[10] which covers the way in which transactions with Bitcoin should be treated for tax purposes. In addition, the European Court considered how the services provided by a Bitcoin exchange in exchanging Bitcoin for fiat currency should be treated for VAT purposes (see *Skatteverket v David Hedqvist* Case (C-264/14)). At a high level, the UK and European Court's approach has been to treat Bitcoin as being akin to a fiat currency other than sterling. It should be noted that HMRC's published guidance pre-dates the increased volumes and advancement of cryptocurrencies, and so largely focuses on Bitcoin. Given the variety in the nature of different types of cryptocurrencies being developed, whether the approach adopted by

HMRC in relation to Bitcoin will apply to another cryptocurrency will depend on the exact features of the cryptocurrency in question.

Money transmission laws and anti-money laundering requirements

The concept of money transmission under English law is principally governed by the PRSs 2017 and the EMRs 2011, and the extent to which either will apply depends on the activities being performed and the nature of the instruments in question. Whilst cryptocurrencies are not currently considered to be a form of payment instrument, and nor are they considered electronic money, firms should consider whether any ancillary activities in fiat currency connected to any cryptocurrency-related activities, such as remittance of fiat currency between wallets, constitutes payment services under English law for which authorisation or registration may be required.

As to anti-money laundering requirements, the UK regime comprises two pieces of legislation, one applying specifically to certain types of firms; the other applying generally. The MLRs 2017 apply only to certain types of firms, which includes credit institutions and a range of firms performing financial services collectively referred to as "financial institutions". At present, firms engaging in activities solely in relation to cryptocurrencies, such as cryptocurrency exchanges, are not subject to the MLRs 2017 and are not strictly required as a matter of law to undertake customer due diligence on their customers as prescribed under the MLRs 2017.

It is the general applicability of the UK's anti-money laundering regime under the Proceeds of Crime Act 2002 (**POCA**) that has resulted in many crypto businesses voluntarily engaging in customer due diligence to a standard as laid down under the MLRs 2017. POCA, amongst other things, lays down a number of criminal offences which any person, regardless of their status and the nature of their activities, can commit if they are involved with criminal property and so, whilst the concept of identity verification is anathema to many crypto enthusiasts, the largely anonymous nature of cryptocurrencies is often a risk too far for cryptocurrency businesses operating in the UK.

Promotion and testing

As we mentioned earlier, the FCA's Regulatory Sandbox provides selected firms with an ability to test product offerings, services and business models in a controlled environment. Applications for the Sandbox are competitive, and successful firms may take the benefit of some or all of the four key available resources: restricted authorisation; individual guidance; waivers or modifications to the FCA's rules; and no-enforcement action letters. The benefits gained to firms from these tools is significant, particularly in the early stages of a particular product offering, business model or service, when the prospects of success are unclear and the cost of regulatory compliance in order to explore those prospects further are significant.

Ownership and licensing requirements

The essence of cryptocurrencies is that they are decentralised, such that there is no central, governing or controlling authority that claims ownership of any one cryptocurrency. As is commonplace in the crypto space more generally, the underlying protocols that govern cryptocurrencies are typically open-sourced, thereby supporting the collaborative nature of cryptocurrencies. It is entirely possible that creators of cryptocurrencies may have sought to protect their brands through trademark registrations, but it would likely defeat the purpose of cryptocurrencies if participants required a licence to utilise any particular cryptocurrency to effect transactions on a particular blockchain, or to acquire cryptocurrency via an exchange.

Mining

Mining is a fundamental underlying activity for many cryptocurrencies, as miners play a key role in obtaining consensus on the underlying blockchains by validating transactions, collating those transactions into blocks and hashing the new blocks to the blockchain. In a proof-of-work system, such as Bitcoin, miners will compete to solve mathematical problems which, once solved, will entail that the block is valid and capable of being recorded to the public blockchain. In exchange for their efforts, miners receive an amount of the relevant cryptocurrency which, in the absence of a central authority issuing new batches of cryptocurrency, is a primary influencer of the overall supply of the cryptocurrency in question. This is, in part, why mining is so resource-intensive – if it were easy, then the supply of a particular cryptocurrency could be significantly greater than that which is needed, leading to deflationary pressures on the cryptocurrency.

For the time being, mining remains outside the scope of the UK regulatory framework and, even if cryptocurrencies were to fall within the regulatory perimeter, it remains to be seen whether the activities of miners in validating transactions via proof-of-work or proof-of-stake would constitute a form of regulated activity under English law.

Border restrictions and declaration

Like most jurisdictions, the UK has implemented rules and restrictions on certain types of goods and other substances that can be transported within its borders. The current UK rules on disclosures relating to financial matters relate solely to cash, albeit that, for the time being at least, where a person is entering the UK from another EU Member State, there is no requirement to declare cash holdings. When entering from a non-EU Member State, a person must declare cash holdings of €10,000 or more (or the equivalent in another currency). The current rules do not provide that cryptocurrencies are cash for these purposes.

Reporting requirements

For firms performing activities and services solely in connection with cryptocurrencies outside of the regulatory perimeter, the reporting obligations that typically flow down from existing financial services legislation will largely be inapplicable. The expansion of transparency and transaction reporting requirements under EU Directive 2014/65/EU (**MiFID II**) and Regulation No 600/2014 (**MiFIR**) and their delegated legislation, may impact firms in the crypto space in two ways. First, to the extent that firms are themselves engaging in investment activities or providing investment services under MiFID II, such as through the provision of derivative contracts with cryptocurrencies as the underlying assets, those firms will need to consider whether the transparency and transaction reporting requirements in MiFIR will apply to them. The transparency requirements will be particularly relevant where firms are engaging in over-the-counter trading in cryptocurrency derivatives, and it remains to be seen how various cryptocurrency exchanges are to be categorised for these purposes – the definition of a trading venue under MiFID II only captures regulated markets, multilateral trading facilities and organised trading facilities, with many centralised and decentralised cryptocurrency exchanges falling outside the scope as a result.

Secondly, to the extent that firms operating in the crypto space engage in cryptocurrency derivatives trading with other parties who themselves are subject to MiFID II, for hedging purposes, for example, then such firms may find that they need to provide certain information to those parties to allow them to comply with their own reporting obligations.

As previously discussed, the provisions of POCA and the MLRs 2017 impose reporting obligations on firms in instances where money laundering or terrorist financing is suspected. Under POCA, it is typically a defence to the relevant offences under Part 7 for a person to report their suspicions to the appropriate authority, which in the UK is the National Crime Agency (**NCA**). Anyone who suspects money laundering or terrorist financing can file a Suspicious Activity Report with the NCA and it remains in a person's interest to do so in such circumstances.

* * *

Endnotes

1. *The economics of digital currencies*, Q3 2014.
2. See, for instance, the paper prepared by the Financial Markets Law Committee dated July 2016, entitled *Issues of legal uncertainty arising in the context of virtual currencies.*
3. See, for instance, *The economics of digital currencies,* and *Innovations in payment technologies and the emergence of digital currencies.*
4. See, for instance, the working papers, *The macroeconomics of central bank issued digital currencies,* and *Central bank digital currencies – design principles and balance sheet implications.*
5. The Joint Money Laundering Steering Group's published guidance is also highly influential in this context.
6. FCA statement, *Cryptocurrency derivatives*, 6 April 2018.
7. FCA statement, *Cryptocurrency derivatives*, 6 April 2018.
8. See the FCA's response to Discussion Paper 17/3 on the use of distributed ledger technology in financial services.
9. Whilst broadly similar, there are slight differences between controlled investments and specified investments. By way of example, electronic money is a specified investment but not a controlled investment.
10. *Revenue and Customs Brief 9: Bitcoin and other cryptocurrency* (3 March 2014), and *Capital Gains Manual – Introduction and computation: chargeable assets: intangible assets: cryptocurrencies.*

Simon Lovegrove
Tel: +44 20 7444 3110 / Email: simon.lovegrove@nortonrosefulbright.com
Simon Lovegrove is global head of financial services knowledge at Norton Rose Fulbright LLP. He specialises in knowledge management and financial services regulation. Simon has led a number of knowledge initiatives including designing a training programme for a regulator. Simon is also widely published in the financial services field: *Practitioners Guide to MiFID II* (co-editor); *Practitioners Guide to Individual Accountability* (co-editor); *Financial Services Law* (OUP) (third edition) (chapters on money laundering and individual accountability); and *Global Legal Insights – Banking Regulation* 2018 (UK chapter). Since 2008 he has also written the financial regulation update that appears in *Butterworth's Journal of International Banking and Financial Law*.

Albert Weatherill
Tel: +44 20 7444 5583 / Email: albert.weatherill@nortonrosefulbright.com
Albert is an associate in the financial services group at Norton Rose Fulbright LLP, advising clients on a wide-range of regulatory issues under English and European law. Albert's particular specialism is the development and regulation of innovative financial services and products, advising financial institutions, regulatory authorities, governments and start-ups in areas such as payments and payment infrastructure, online brokerage platforms, cryptocurrencies and initial coin offerings, robo-advice, RegTech, blockchain and distributed ledger technology, crowdfunding, and cybersecurity. Albert has previously been seconded to the trade association of the UK payments industry, gaining experience working closely with the UK's payment schemes, member banks and payment infrastructure providers.

Norton Rose Fulbright LLP

3 More London Riverside, London, SE1 2AQ, United Kingdom
Tel +44 20 7444 6000 / Fax +44 20 7283 6500 / URL: www.nortonrosefulbright.com

USA

Josias Dewey
Holland & Knight LLP

Government attitude and definition

In the United States, cryptocurrencies have been the focus of much attention by both Federal and state governments. Within the Federal government, most of the focus has been at the administrative and agency level, including the Securities and Exchange Commission (the "**SEC**"), the Commodities and Futures Trading Commission (the "**CFTC**"), the Federal Trade Commission (the "**FTC**") and the Department of the Treasury, through both the Internal Revenue Service (the "**IRS**") and the Financial Crimes Enforcement Network ("**FinCEN**"). While there has been significant engagement by these agencies, little formal rulemaking has occurred. Generally speaking, Federal agencies and policymakers have praised the technology as being an important part of the U.S.'s future infrastructure, and stressed the need for the U.S. to maintain a leading role in the development of the technology. Some agencies have acknowledged the risk of over-regulating, and cautioned policymakers from passing legislation that would drive investment in the technology overseas.

Several state governments have proposed and/or passed laws affecting cryptocurrencies and blockchain technology, with most of the activity taking place in the legislative branch. There have generally been two approaches to regulation at the state level. Some states have tried to promote the technology by passing very favorable regulations, often by exempting cryptocurrencies from state securities laws and/or money transmission statutes. These states hope to leverage investment in the technology to stimulate local economies and improve public services.

One example, Wyoming, recently passed a bill exempting cryptocurrencies from property taxation. The state has been praised for becoming the most crypto-friendly jurisdiction in the country. Another state, Colorado, passed a bipartisan bill promoting the use of blockchain for government record-keeping. Two other states have taken steps to legalize Bitcoin as a payment option for taxation purposes. Arizona has pledged to become the first U.S. state to start accepting taxes in cryptocurrency. Georgia may also provide its residents with the option to pay taxes in Bitcoin. On the other hand, authorities in at least ten other states, like California and New Mexico, have issued warnings about investing in cryptocurrencies. Others, like New York, have passed laws generally considered restrictive, and as a result, have seen a number of cryptocurrency-based companies exit the New York market.

There is no uniform definition of "cryptocurrency", which is often referred to as "virtual currency", "digital assets", "digital tokens", "cryptoassets" or simply "crypto". While some jurisdictions have attempted to formulate a detailed definition for the asset class, most have wisely opted for broader, more technology-agnostic definitions. Those taking the latter approach will be better positioned to regulate as and when the technology evolves.

Sales regulation

The sale of cryptocurrency is generally only regulated if the sale (i) constitutes the sale of a security under state or Federal law, or (ii) is considered money transmission under state law or conduct otherwise making the person a money services business ("**MSB**") under Federal law. In addition, futures, options, swaps and other derivative contracts that make reference to the price of Bitcoin or another virtual currency that is considered a commodity, are subject to regulation by the CFTC under the Commodity Exchange Act. In addition, the CFTC has jurisdiction over attempts to engage in market manipulation with respect to those virtual currencies that are considered commodities. The likelihood of the CFTC asserting its authority to prevent market manipulation is much higher today as a result of Chicago's two largest derivatives exchanges, CBEO and the CME, both offering futures linked to the price of Bitcoin.

Securities laws

The SEC generally has regulatory authority over the issuance or resale of any token or other digital asset that constitutes a security. Under U.S. law, a security includes "an investment contract" which has been defined by the U.S. Supreme Court as an investment of money in a common enterprise with a reasonable expectation of profits to be derived from the entrepreneurial or managerial efforts of others. *SEC v. W.J. Howey Co.*, 328 U.S. 293, 301 (1946).

In determining whether a token or other digital asset is an "investment contract", both the SEC and the courts look at all the facts and circumstances to determine the substance of the transaction, instead of its form. In 1943, the U.S. Supreme Court determined that "the reach of the [Securities] Act does not stop with the obvious and commonplace. Novel, uncommon, or irregular devices, whatever they appear to be, are also reached if it be proved as matter of fact that they were widely offered or dealt in under terms or courses of dealing which established their character in commerce as 'investment contracts,' or as 'any interest or instrument commonly known as a 'security'." *SEC v. C.M. Joiner Leasing Corp.*, 320 U.S. 344, 351 (1943). It has also been said that "Congress' purpose in enacting the securities laws was to regulate investments, in whatever form they are made and by whatever name they are called." *Reves v. Ernst & Young*, 494 U.S. 56, 61 (1990).

The SEC has been clear on its position that even if a token issued in an initial coin offering ("**ICO**") has "utility", the token will still be deemed to be a security that is regulated under the Securities Act if it meets the elements of the *Howey* test. On February 6, 2018, in written testimony to the U.S. Senate Banking Committee, the Chairman of the SEC stated as follows:

> "Certain market professionals have attempted to highlight the utility or voucher-like characteristics of their proposed ICOs in an effort to claim that their proposed tokens or coins are not securities. Many of these assertions that the federal securities laws do not apply to a particular ICO appear to elevate form over substance. The rise of these form-based arguments is a disturbing trend that deprives investors of mandatory protections that clearly are required as a result of the structure of the transaction. Merely calling a token a 'utility' token, or structuring it to provide some utility, does not prevent the token from being a security."

In a more nuanced speech delivered in June, 2018, William Hinman, the SEC's Director of Corporate Finance, stated:

"Returning to the ICOs I am seeing, strictly speaking, the token – or coin or whatever the digital information packet is called – all by itself is not a security, just as the orange groves in *Howey* were not. Central to determining whether a security is being sold is *how* it is being sold and the reasonable expectations of purchasers. When someone buys a housing unit to live in, it is probably not a security. But under certain circumstances, the same asset can be offered and sold in a way that causes investors to have a reasonable expectation of profits based on the efforts of others. For example, if the housing unit is offered with a management contract or other services, it can be a security."

Later in the same speech, Mr Hinman made clear that a digital token that might initially be sold in a transaction constituting the sale of a security, might thereafter be sold as a non-security where the facts and circumstances have changed over time, such that the Howey test is no longer met. While such comments are not official policy of the SEC, they are a good indicator of the positions staff will take in formulating such policies.

If a digital asset is determined to be a security, then the issuer must register the security with the SEC or offer it pursuant to an exemption from the registration requirements. For offerings that are being made under a federal exemption from securities registration, the SEC places fewer restrictions on the sale of securities to "accredited investors". An individual investor is an "accredited investor" only if he or she: (i) is a director or executive officer of the company issuing the securities; (ii) has an individual net worth (or joint net worth with a spouse) that exceeds $1 million, excluding the value of the investor's primary residence; (iii) has an individual income that exceeds $200,000 in each of the two most recent years, and has a reasonable expectation of reaching the same individual income level in the current year; or (iv) has a joint income that exceeds $300,000 in each of the two most recent years, and has a reasonable expectation of reaching the same joint income level in the current year. See SEC Rule 501(a)(5).

In addition to Federal securities laws, most states have their own laws, referred to as blue sky laws, which are not always pre-empted by Federal law. Anyone selling digital assets likely to constitute a security should check with counsel about the applicability of blue sky laws. Of particular importance, there are certain exemptions from registration under Federal law that do not pre-empt the application of state blue sky laws.

Two other implications for a token constituting a security are: (i) the requirement that a person be a broker-dealer licensed with the SEC and a member of FINRA in order to facilitate the sale of securities or act as a market maker or otherwise constitute a dealer in the asset; and (ii) the asset can only trade on a licensed securities exchange or alternative trading system ("**ATS**") approved by the SEC. As of June, 2018, several exchanges were seeking approval as an ATS and several firms were seeking registration as a broker-dealer; in each case, with the intent to deal in cryptocurrencies that are considered securities.

Money transmission laws and anti-money laundering requirements

Under the Bank Secrecy Act (the "**BSA**"), FinCEN regulates MSBs. On March 18, 2013, FinCEN issued guidance that stated the following would be considered MSBs: (i) a virtual currency exchange; and (ii) an administrator of a centralized repository of virtual currency who has the authority to both issue and redeem the virtual currency. FinCEN issued guidance that stated as follows: "An administrator or exchanger that (i) accepts and transmits a convertible virtual currency, or (ii) buys or sells convertible virtual currency for any reason is a money transmitter under FinCEN's regulations, unless a limitation to or exemption from the definition applies to the person." See FIN-2013-G001, Application of FinCEN's Regulations to Person's Administering, Exchanging or Using Virtual Currencies (March 18, 2013).

An MSB is required to conduct a comprehensive risk assessment of its exposure to money laundering and implement an anti-money laundering ("**AML**") program based on such risk assessment. FinCEN regulations require MSBs to develop, implement, and maintain a written program that is reasonably designed to prevent the MSB from being used to facilitate money laundering and the financing of terrorist activities. The AML program must: (i) incorporate written policies, procedures and internal controls reasonably designed to assure ongoing compliance; (ii) designate an individual compliance officer responsible for assuring day-to-day compliance with the program and Bank Secrecy Act requirements; (iii) provide training for appropriate personnel, which specifically includes training in the detection of suspicious transactions; and (iv) provide for independent review to monitor and maintain an adequate program.

All U.S. persons are prohibited from doing business with foreign nationals who are on the Specially Designated Nationals and Blocked Entities List ("**SDN List**") of the U.S. Department of the Treasury's Office of Foreign Assets Control ("**OFAC**"). OFAC provides an updated and searchable version of its SDN List at: sanctionssearch.ofac.treas.gov. OFAC requires all U.S. citizens to "block" (i.e., freeze) the assets of individuals and companies who are engaging in transactions with: (i) countries that are subject to U.S. economic sanctions ("blocked countries"); (ii) certain companies and entities that act as agents for such countries ("blocked parties"); and (iii) certain individuals that act as agents for such countries ("specially designated individuals" or "**SDNs**"). It is important to have a compliance program in place to avoid (or mitigate) receiving civil and criminal penalties from OFAC for non-compliance. See 31 C.F.R. Part 501 (OFAC Reporting Regulations); OFAC Economic Sanctions Enforcement Guidelines (November 9, 2009).

On February 13, 2018, in response to a letter from Senator Ron Wyden, an official within the Treasury Department issued a correspondence that called into question whether ICO issuers were *de facto* a MSB that was required to register with FinCEN. While there were several flaws in the logic set forth in the letter, it remains an area of concern for anyone considering a token sale.

State laws on money transmission vary widely but can generally be grouped into a few categories. Most states define money transmission as including some or all of three types of activities: (i) money transmission; (ii) issuing and/or selling payment instruments; and (iii) issuing and/or selling stored value. A few states only regulate these activities when "money" is involved, and define money as "a medium of exchange that is authorized or adopted by a domestic or foreign government". Other states regulate substitutes for money and consider virtual currency within the scope of their money transmission statutes. Generally, state money transmission laws apply to any entity that is either located in the state or is located outside of the state (including in a foreign jurisdiction) but does business with residents of the state.

Taxation

In March 2014, the IRS declared that "virtual currency", such as Bitcoin and other cryptocurrency, will be taxed by the IRS as "property" and not currency. See IRS Notice 2014–21, Guidance on Virtual Currency (March 25, 2014). Consequently, every individual or business that owns cryptocurrency will generally need to, among other things: (i) keep detailed records of cryptocurrency purchases and sales; (ii) pay taxes on any gains that may have been made upon the sale of cryptocurrency for cash; (iii) pay taxes on any gains that may have been made upon the purchase of a good or service with cryptocurrency; and (iv) pay taxes on the fair market value of any mined cryptocurrency, as of the date of receipt.

For an individual filing a federal income tax return, the gains or losses from a sale of virtual currency that was held as a "capital asset" (i.e., for investment purposes) are reported on: (i) Schedule D of IRS Form 1040; and (ii) IRS Form 8949 (Sales and Other Dispositions of Capital Assets). Any realized gains on virtual currency held for more than one year as a capital asset by an individual are subject to capital gains tax rates. Any realized gains on virtual currency held for one year or less as a capital asset by an individual are subject to ordinary income tax rates. The IRS requires, on Form 8949, for each virtual currency transaction, the following information be disclosed: (i) a description of the amount and type of virtual currency sold; (ii) the date acquired; (iii) the date the virtual currency was sold; (iv) the amount of proceeds from the sale; (v) the cost (or other basis); and (vi) the amount of the gain or loss. It should be noted that the record-keeping requirements of IRS Form 8949 can be particularly onerous for those who have used cryptocurrency to make numerous small purchases of goods or services throughout the year.

Prior to January 1, 2018, Section 1031(a)(1) of the Internal Revenue Code states the following: "No gain or loss shall be recognized on the exchange of property held for productive use in a trade or business or for investment if such property is exchanged solely for property of like kind which is to be held either for productive use in a trade or business or for investment." In 26 C.F.R. 1.1031(a)-2(b), "like kind" is defined as follows: "As used in section 1031(a), the words like kind have reference to the nature or character of the property and not to its grade or quality. One kind or class of property may not, under that section, be exchanged for property of a different kind or class." It should be noted that, in order to attempt to utilize the tax treatment of Section 1031(a) for transactions done on or prior to December 31, 2017, (i) each transaction must comply with certain requirements set forth in IRS regulations (such as the use, in certain instances, of a "qualified intermediary"); and (ii) the taxpayer must file a Form 8824 with the IRS.

For transactions completed on or prior to December 31, 2017, the IRS has not issued any guidance on whether different cryptocurrencies are "property of like kind" that would qualify for non-recognition of gain under Section 1031(a).

There is a risk that the IRS could use its prior revenue rulings on gold bullion as a basis for taking the position that, for transactions completed on or prior to December 31, 2017, different cryptocurrencies are not "property of like kind" under Section 1031(a). In Rev. Rul. 82-166 (October 4, 1982), the IRS ruled that an exchange of gold bullion for silver bullion does not qualify for non-recognition of gain under Section 1031(a). The IRS stated: "Although the metals have some similar qualities and uses, silver and gold are intrinsically different metals and primarily are used in different ways. Silver is essentially an industrial commodity. Gold is primarily utilized as an investment in itself. An investment in one of the metals is fundamentally different from an investment in the other metal. Therefore, the silver bullion and the gold bullion are not property of like kind." The IRS also stated in Rev. Rul. 79-143 (January 5, 1979) that an exchange of $20 U.S. gold numismatic-type coins and South African Krugerrand gold coins does not qualify for non-recognition of gain under Section 1031(a). The IRS stated: "The bullion-type coins, unlike the numismatic-type coins, represent an investment in gold on world markets rather than in the coins themselves. Therefore, the bullion-type coins and the numismatic-type coins are not property of like kind."

For transactions completed on or after January 1, 2018, the Internal Revenue Code now clearly prohibits the use of Section 1031(a) for cryptocurrency transactions, and requires a taxpayer to recognize taxable gain or loss at the time that any cryptocurrency is converted into another cryptocurrency. Section 13303 of P.L. 115-97 (the tax act signed into law on December 22, 2017) changes Section 1031(a) to state as follows: "No gain or loss shall be recognized on the exchange of real property held for productive use in a trade or business or for investment if such real property is exchanged solely for real property of like kind which is to be held either for productive use in a trade or business or for investment."

Promotion and testing

Arizona has become the first state in the U.S. to adopt a "regulatory sandbox" to shepherd the development of new emerging industries like fintech, blockchain and cryptocurrencies within its borders. The law will grant regulatory relief for innovators in these sectors who desire to bring new products to market within the state. Under the program, which will take effect later this year, companies will be able to test their products for up to two years and serve as many as 10,000 customers before needing to apply for formal licensure.

Ownership and licensing requirements

Cryptocurrency fund managers that invest in cryptocurrency futures contracts, as opposed to "spot transactions" in cryptocurrencies, are required to register as a CTA and CPO with the CFTC and with the National Futures Association ("**NFA**"), or satisfy an exemption. Also, because of additions to the Dodd-Frank Act, cryptocurrency hedge fund managers that use leverage or margin may also need to register with the CFTC and NFA. The Dodd-Frank Act amended the Commodities Act to add new authority over certain leveraged, margined, or financed retail commodity transactions. The CFTC exercised this jurisdiction in an action against BFXNA INC. d/b/a BITFINEX in 2016. Fund managers should be cautious when using margin/leverage, as it may require them to register as a CTA and CPO with the CFTC, and to register with the NFA.

The Investment Company Act of 1940 (the "**Company Act**"), the Investment Advisers Act of 1940 (the "**Advisers Act**"), as well as state investment advisor laws, impose regulations on investment funds that invest in securities. The Company Act generally requires investment companies to register with the SEC as mutual funds unless they meet an exemption. Cryptocurrency funds, and hedge funds generally, can be structured under one of two exemptions from registration under the Investment Company Act. Section 3(c)(1) allows a fund to have up to 100 investors. Alternatively, Section 3(c)(7) allows a fund to have an unlimited number of investors (but practically, it should be limited to 2,000 to avoid being deemed a publicly traded partnership under the Securities Exchange Act), but requires a significantly higher net worth suitability requirement for each investor (roughly $5 million for individuals, $25 million for entities). As a general rule, most startup funds are structured as 3(c)(1) funds because of the lower investor suitability requirements.

Until the SEC provides more guidance on classifying individual cryptocurrencies as securities or commodities, the likelihood of many cryptocurrencies being deemed securities is high. As such, we recommend that cryptocurrency funds that invest in anything other than Bitcoin, ether, Litecoin, and the handful of other clearly commodity coins, comply with the Company Act pre-emptively. For most startup funds, this would mean limiting investors within a given fund to fewer than 100 beneficial owners.

Regardless of whether a startup cryptocurrency fund manager is required to register as a CPO/CTA with the CFTC under the Commodities Act, register or seek exemption from the SEC as an investment advisor (under the Adviser's Act), or investment company (under the Company Act), every cryptocurrency fund manager will be subject to the fraud provisions of the CFTC and/or the SEC. In September, 2017, the CFTC announced its first anti-fraud enforcement action involving Bitcoin. These anti-fraud actions can be taken by the SEC and CFTC regardless of the cryptocurrency fund's exempt status.

Mining

The general rule of thumb regarding Bitcoin mining remains relatively straightforward. If you are able to own and use cryptocurrency where you live, you should also be able to mine cryptocurrency in that location as well. If owning cryptocurrency is illegal where you live, mining is most likely also illegal. There are few, if any, jurisdictions in the U.S. where possession of cryptocurrency is illegal. Plattsburgh, New York, however, is likely the only city in the U.S. to impose a ban (temporary) on cryptocurrency mining.

Border restrictions and declaration

A group of U.S. lawmakers have proposed a requirement that individuals declare their cryptocurrency holdings when entering the U.S., but to date no such requirement has gone into effect.

Reporting requirements

We are not aware of any broadly applicable reporting requirements specific to cryptocurrency in the U.S.

Estate planning and testamentary succession

Cryptocurrency, such as Bitcoin, has value and therefore is increasingly likely to become an estate asset. While there are few, if any laws, specific to cryptocurrency, due to the nature of cryptocurrencies, typical wills and revocable living trusts may not be well suited to efficiently transfer this new type of asset. Consequently, new estate planning questions and clauses may be needed.

While cryptocurrency is not sufficiently mature to allow existing legal structures to promulgate a complete set of rules and regulations, cryptocurrency's technological character allows estate planning to protect the intent of clients holding cryptocurrency. However, the lack of statutory structure necessitates proactive steps. Accordingly, if you want greater certainty of bequeathing cryptocurrency to your heirs, you will need to provide specific and detailed written instructions in your estate planning documents. The information that you will need to include will depend upon the type of virtual currency wallet that you have.

There are a wide range of cryptocurrency wallets that are available at this time. The most common types of cryptocurrency wallets include: (i) a non-hosted software wallet in which you hold the private keys (example: Bitpay wallet); (ii) a hosted software wallet in which you do not hold the private keys (example: Coinbase wallet); (iii) a hardware wallet in which you hold the private keys (example: Trezor wallet); and (iv) a "paper wallet" in which the private keys are written down on paper (which can be later loaded into a software wallet to be spent) and securely stored.

The instructions that you provide in a will (for your personal representative) or in a declaration of trust (for the successor trustee of a testamentary trust) should be written in a manner that is easy to understand for individuals who are not familiar with cryptocurrency. For example, in the case of an unhosted software wallet in which the person holds the private keys, instructions could include: (i) a description of the name and version of the wallet software; (ii) a description of the name and version of the operating software system of the wallet device (i.e., iOS, Android, MacOS, Windows or Linux); (iii) a description of the types of virtual currency held by the wallet; (iv) either the long-form private and public keys for the wallet or the 12-word "seed" BIP39 or BiP44 recovery phrase for the wallet; and (v) step-by-step instructions (which may include screenshots) showing how the wallet can be restored on to a new device, if the current wallet device cannot be accessed.

In addition, care must be taken to ensure that virtual currency that arises from "hard forks", "air drops", or other subsequent events not anticipated at the time a will or trust is prepared, is addressed and the intended beneficiary of such assets is clearly identified.

As transfers from a Bitcoin wallet and most other wallets are irrevocable, private key information about your cryptocurrency accounts will need to be kept in a secure manner. Security can be enhanced by storing the private key information in a safe-deposit box or vault, which could only be accessed after your death by the personal representative designated in your will (or the successor trustee designated in your trust).

Josias N. Dewey
Tel: +1 305 374 8500 / Email: joe.dewey@hklaw.com

Joe Dewey is a financial services and real estate partner in Holland & Knight's Miami office and is considered a thought leader on blockchain technology. Mr Dewey regularly represents banks and other financial institutions across the entire spectrum as measured by assets and scale, from community to global money center banks. Mr Dewey spends a considerable amount of time at the convergence of human prose legal contracts, as well as computational contracts, based primarily on computer code. This includes smart contracts that can be implemented on Hyperledger Fabric (or IBM's Blockchain service), Ethereum (both public and permissioned versions) and R3's Corda platform. Dewey spends a considerable amount of his practice in this space assisting clients in identifying optimal distributed ledger use cases and developing proof of concept applications. He can assist in the transition from proof of concepts (PoCs) to production systems built by our clients' primary technology solutions providers.

Holland & Knight

701 Brickell Avenue, Suite 3300, Miami, FL 33131, USA
Tel: +1 305 374 8500 / Fax: +1 305 789 7799 / URL: www.hklaw.com

Venezuela

Luisa Lepervanche
Mendoza, Palacios, Acedo, Borjas, Páez Pumar & Cía. (Menpa)

Government attitude and definition

The Venezuelan government has had an ambivalent attitude towards cryptocurrency.

On the one hand, it has taken on obligations to promote the use of cryptocurrency, both in the public and private spheres; it has created its own cryptocurrency, called the Petro; it has taken additional steps to promote cryptocurrencies (such as the creation of special zones for paying with petros and other cryptocurrencies, granting special authorisations to ensure that contracts may be paid in petros, etc.). On the other hand, the government has, from time to time, imprisoned miners and threatened to close cryptocurrency operations that deal with foreign exchange transactions.

Further to the creation of the petro, recent statements made by President Maduro and instruments enacted by the Constitutional Assembly[1] suggest the government's intention is now to link its value to that of the official currency, the bolivar.[2]

<u>Promotion of cryptocurrencies</u>

As an introduction, a little background on the rules regulating money in Venezuela.

Article 318 of the Constitution provides that the bolivar is the "monetary unit" of Venezuela. This is ratified by Article 106 of the Law on the Central Bank of Venezuela (*Ley del Banco Central de Venezuela*). So, the legal tender in Venezuela is the bolivar. There are two exceptions to this rule: the possibility of issuing common monetary units issued in the context of integration agreements regarding Latin America and the Caribbean; and the possibility of issuing communal money (*monedas comunales*) issued by *comunas*, which is a complicated concept that refers to basic social groups. None of these exceptions apply currently to cryptocurrency.

Due to hyperinflation, amounts expressed in bolivars are huge. Whether the amounts refer to prices, to salaries, to the value of goods, etc., they have become extremely high amounts – sometimes so high that systems do not recognise them. As a solution, the President has ordered a monetary conversion, that is, to create a "new" bolivar (called sovereign bolivar, *bolívar soberano*), which would be represented by dividing the current bolivar value by 100,000. In theory, this will enter into force on August 20, 2018, but so far the conversion has been delayed twice.

Pursuant to the Constitution and the law, only bolivars (soon to be sovereign bolivars) represent legal tender. Cryptocurrencies do not represent legal tender.

However, Venezuela – particularly the Executive Branch and the Constitutional Assembly – have made important efforts to promote the use of cryptocurrency.

In April 2018, the Constitutional Assembly issued a constitutional decree, regulating cryptocurrencies.[3] It mandates, under Article 9, that Venezuela must promote, protect and guarantee the use of cryptocurrencies as means of payment of obligations, both by the public sector and the private sector, not only in Venezuela but also abroad. Other instruments referred to below also reflect similar obligations.

Accordingly, Venezuela is making efforts, at least theoretically, to promote cryptocurrencies. However, these efforts may extend beyond its legal powers and may even be impossible to achieve in practice.

First, Venezuela is, in theory, bound to promote, protect and guarantee the use of cryptocurrencies by the public and private sectors. The obligation to promote may prove both possible and legal. Venezuela may create incentives, benefits, discounts, etc. But it cannot guarantee the use of cryptocurrencies because, as indicated, only bolivars are legal tender in Venezuela, so forcing (by guaranteeing) the use of cryptocurrencies would violate both the Constitution and the law.

Second, Venezuela bound itself not only to promote, protect and guarantee the use of cryptocurrencies in Venezuela, but it also bound itself to do it abroad. Needless to say, even in practical terms, complying with such obligation is going to prove difficult (if not impossible).

Launch of the petro

In December 2017, by Presidential Decree, the government authorised the issuance of the petro, a cryptocurrency "backed" (*respaldada*) by Venezuelan oil reserves.[4] In January 2018, it published the first petro whitepaper,[5] which it then modified in March.[6] In February, the Executive earmarked a portion of the oil reserves in the Orinoco Belt for potential development to "back" (*respaldar*) the issuance of petros.[7] In April, the Constitutional Assembly issued the Constitutional Decree, further regulating petros and approving the decision to dedicate the oil reserves to serve as "backing for the creation and issuance of the Venezuelan cryptocurrency Petro" (*como respaldo para la creación y emisión de la criptomoneda venezolana Petro*).[8]

However, even if the petro is a cryptocurrency, in our opinion, it also qualifies as public debt – even if an atypical one. And because it qualifies as such, its issuance breaches the Constitution and the law. The petro qualifies as public debt under the Law on the Financial Administration of the Public Sector (*Decreto con Rango, Valor y Fuerza de Ley Orgánica de la Administración Financiera del Sector Público*). Article 80 provides that the issuance of securities and the granting of guarantees, *inter alia,* qualify as public debt transactions. Petros fall within both categories.

First, petros qualify as securities under Venezuelan law. This assertion probably requires a paper of its own, but for the purposes of this analysis let us state that they constitute a unilateral promise by the issuer – Venezuela – represented in dematerialised documents issued *en masse*, which grant their holders certain rights (*e.g.* the right to benefit from the eventual exploitation of a portion of oil reserves, the right to pay debts to the Republic at a certain rate determined by oil prices, etc.). Other Venezuelan authors have also categorised petros as securities.[9]

Second, when issuing petros, the government set aside part of the reserves of the Orinoco Belt to back the cryptocurrency. It did so by means of the Presidential Decree issued in February, confirmed by the Constitutional Decree issued in April. Further, both the Presidential Decree creating petros in December and the white paper published in January refer to petros being backed by oil. The efficiency of the guarantee has been questioned in economic terms,[10] as well in legal ones – these are addressed below. Yet, its inefficiency or illegality does not change the fact that a guarantee was granted regarding petros. Again, Venezuelan authors share this point of view.[11]

Accordingly, since petros qualify as securities under Venezuelan law, and guarantees were granted regarding their issuance, petros would fall within the scope of the definition of Article 80 of the Law on the Financial Administration of the Public Sector, thus being public debt. A very unusual type, but still public debt. The National Assembly – the Venezuelan equivalent of Congress – has taken this position.[12] This was also the initial position of the government of the United States of America, through the Office of Foreign Assets Control, which on its website regarding Frequently Asked Questions on Venezuela-Related Sanctions indicated the following: "A currency with this characteristics would appear to be an extension of credit to the Venezuelan government…"[13]

<u>Petros – the issuance of public debt?</u>

There is an argument to be made that the petro is both illegal and unconstitutional.

First, pursuant to Article 312 of the Constitution and Article 98 of the Law on the Financial Administration of the Public Sector, public debt must be approved by law. Laws in Venezuela are issued by the National Assembly, by mandate of Article 202 of the Constitution. The National Assembly did not enact a law approving the issuance of petros. Further, the National Assembly has denounced its unconstitutionality and illegality on such grounds.[14]

Second, Article 12 of the Constitution and Article 3 of the Organic Law on Hydrocarbons (*Ley Orgánica de Hidrocarburos*) prohibit encumbering oil reserves. Further, the Law on the Financial Administration of the Public Sector also prohibits guaranteeing public debt transactions with public assets. Accordingly, the granting of the guarantee violates the Constitution and the law.

Pursuant to Article 25 of the Constitution and Article 19 of the Organic Law on Administrative Proceedings (*Ley Orgánica de Procedimientos Administrativos*), acts that violate rights constitutionally vested are null and void.

Therefore, the issuance of petros is null and void pursuant to Venezuelan law.

Regulations and agreements governing cryptocurrencies

The two most relevant regulations are both dated April 9, 2018: the Constitutional Decree on Cryptoassets and the Sovereign Cryptocurrency Petro, referred to above; and Presidential Decree N° 3.355,[15] which created the Superintendence on Cryptocurrency and Connected Activities (*Superintendencia de Criptoactivos and Actividades Conexas,* SUPCACVEN).[16]

Additional regulations and agreements have also been enacted, executed or negotiated. A few examples:

(a) The SUPCACVEN and the Zamora Municipality, Miranda State, have executed agreements to grant certain benefits to taxpayers who cancel their taxes in petros and other cryptocurrencies, as well as authorising virtual mining.

(b) The President has created special zones for mining and negotiating with petros and other cryptocurrencies, which it has called "Petro Zones".

(c) Resolutions N° 36 and 37 enacted by the Ministry of Transport, which refer to payment of certain obligations due to the National Institute of Civil Aviation (*Instituto Nacional de Aeronaútica Civil*, INAC), Institute of the International Airport of Maiquetía (*Instituto Aeropuerto Internacional de Maiquetía*, IAIM) and Bolivarian Airports

Company (*Empresa del Estado Bolivariana de Aeropuertos*, BAER), provide that these may be paid in cryptocurrencies.

(d) In the context of promotion of youth employment (*Gran Misión Chamba Segura*), the President imposed an obligation to create conditions to develop and strengthen a cryptocurrency "ecosystem", which would allow young people to be instructed regarding blockchain technology, digital mining, virtual trading, virtual exchanges, digital wallets, etc.

(e) In the context of the economic emergency, the President has been granted powers to incorporate cryptoassets to the economy.

(f) The Ministry of Economy and Finance (*Ministerio de Economía y Finanzas*) authorised the Superintendence of Insurance Activities (*Superintendencia de la Actividad Aseguradora*) to, in turn, authorise the issuance of bonds to guarantee certain obligations derived from public contracts paid in petros.

(g) Venezuela tried – and failed – to negotiate with India payment of its oil exports in petros.

The validity of some of these instruments may be questionable. But, at least rhetorically, Venezuela has shown a positive attitude towards cryptocurrencies, which have not necessarily been translated into practice. However, the government is not always consistent with this promotion.

First, in the past few years, different police forces (including the anti-money laundering tasks force) have apprehended virtual miners.

Second, certain government officials have also criticised and threatened persons dealing in cryptocurrencies. For instance, the Executive Vice-President of Venezuela (now Vice-President for the Economic Area) issued a statement in June 2018 criticising the "imposition" of "speculative cryptocurrencies' prices", and threatening to "severely punish" the culprits. This needs to be understood in the current local context: a foreign currency exchange control system has been in place in Venezuela since 2003, which has given rise to a parallel foreign currency market (which at times has been illegal) that the government has heavily criticised and sometimes tried to control. Cryptocurrency transactions have been used to circumvent the exchange controls regime. Therefore, the former Vice-President's threats, based on the exchange controls considerations, incidentally affected cryptocurrency ones.

Yet, the Executive parlance changed in the last days of July 2018 regarding exchange controls, and there is now a more tolerant approach towards activities involving foreign currency, including the parallel market. In fact, after statements to that effect by the President and Vice-President of the Economic Area, the Constitutional Assembly issued the Constitutional Decree which establishes the Abrogation of the Currency Exchange Regime and its Crimes (*Decreto Constituyente mediante el cual se establece la Derogatoria del Régimen Cambiario y sus Ilícitos*).[17] The preamble of this decree refers to the need to allow currency exchange transactions between private parties (*"que los particulares puedan realizar transacciones cambiarias entre privados propias en divisas"*), and the need to provide security-productive foreign investment (*"máximas seguridades para la inversión extranjera productiva"*).

Based on such premises, Article 2 thereof abrogates the Law on the Exchange Regime and its Crimes (*Ley de Régimen Cambiario y sus Ilícitos*). The latter contained important sanctions regarding different crimes and infractions related to the exchange controls regime – including considerable prison terms – some of which we address below. Please note that, based on strict legal considerations, we question the validity of this decree.[18] However, the stance of the authorities regarding the exchange controls regime has been far from consistent over the years, which makes it difficult to foresee what will happen in this area in the future.

Based on the above, we can argue that Venezuela has taken a positive view of cryptocurrencies – even promoting them – to the extent of issuing its own, illegal and unconstitutional, cryptocurrency, the petro. Yet, from time to time, it has also shown a negative attitude towards certain activities connected to cryptocurrencies.

Cryptocurrency regulation

Venezuela has issued regulations specific to cryptocurrencies. Instead of taking the more conservative approach of other jurisdictions, which have applied existing rules on commodities, capital markets, etc., to cryptocurrency transactions, Venezuela has issued regulations applicable specifically to cryptocurrencies, and has even created a controlling body to supervise and control them: SUPCACVEN.

As indicated above, the most relevant regulations are the Constitutional Decree on Cryptoassets and the Sovereign Cryptocurrency Petro, and the Presidential Decree N° 3.355,[19] which "created" SUPCACVEN.[20]

Specific rules under these instruments shall be addressed below, in each relevant section. However, two general ideas are important at this point:

(i)   The regulations contain both explicit and implicit controls and limitations. For instance, on the one hand, the Presidential Decree explicitly imposes, under Article 17, a registration obligation on all individuals and corporations who conduct activities related – directly or by connection – to cryptoassets. On the other hand, the same decree establishes, among the powers vested in SUPCACVEN under Article 9 (numbers 5, 6 and 7), the power to authorise and grant permits in connection with cryptoasset-related activities. Thus, although prior authorisation or permission is not expressly required by the rules, an implicit obligation to obtain such authorisation or permit is inferred from the rules. However, the rules detailing registration, and authorisation or permission, have not been specified in the Presidential Decree or elsewhere.

(ii) Regulating cryptocurrencies via the Constitutional Decree and the Presidential Decree violates the Constitution for two reasons.
      First, the Constitution provides, under Article 112, the right to economic freedom, that is, the right of every person to pursue the economic activities of choice, without limitation other than the ones provided by Constitution or law. The Constitution (which dates from 1999) establishes no limitation regarding cryptoassets. The law – which must be understood, as indicated above, as the one enacted by the National Assembly – does not provide limitations regarding this subject either.
      Second, Article 156 (32) of the Constitution limits legislation of certain matters (including commercial issues) to the national authorities; and Article 187 (1) mandates that the National Assembly legislate regarding matters reserved to the National authorities. This is known as *reserva legal*. Accordingly, commercial matters are part of the *reserva legal*, that is, only subject to regulation by law enacted by the National Assembly.

Therefore, a law is needed both to establish limitations to the right to economic freedom and to regulate commercial matters. Regulating cryptoassets qualifies as both and, thus, may only be done by law, and not by Constitutional Decree nor by Presidential Decree.

Accordingly, even if the regulations regarding cryptoassets exist, they are unconstitutional and, thus, null and void.

Apart from these regulations, which, as indicated, are targeted directly to cryptocurrency, the Law on the Exchange Regime and its Crimes – theoretically abrogated by the Constitutional Assembly – was also applicable. Due to the nullity of its abrogation, we shall still address the interaction of this law with cryptocurrency activities.

For the purposes of its own interpretation and application, Article 3 established the following definition of foreign currency (*divisas*): money other than bolivar, which includes "deposits in foreign or national banks or financial institutions, transfers, bank checks, promissory notes, securities and credit instruments, as well as <u>any other asset or obligation that is denominated or may be liquidated in foreign currency</u>..." (our emphasis).

Pursuant to this definition, cryptocurrencies – which are assets that may be liquidated in foreign currency – would probably qualify as "foreign currency". Accordingly, in the context of the Law on the Exchange Regime and its Crimes, activities involving cryptocurrencies would have been subject to the prohibitions, limitations and restrictions contained therein, including restrictions regarding exchange transactions, obligations to declare such transactions, obligations to sell export prices, obligations not to publish non-official exchange rates, among others.

Sales regulation

As indicated below, all activities related – directly or by connection – to cryptoassets are regulated by the decrees enacted on April 9, 2018, pursuant to which both registration and authorisation requirements are applicable to individuals and corporations that conduct activities related to cryptocurrencies.

Article 16, which creates the Registration System, refers to the registration requirement extending to virtual miners, virtual exchanges, entities dedicated to saving or intermediation with cryptoassets.

The implicit authorisation requirement provided for under Article 9 (5, 6 and 7), refers to: (i) persons regulated by SUPCACVEN; (ii) corporations dedicated to intermediation and "capital markets" of national cryptoassets; (iii) corporations dedicated to virtual wallets; (iv) corporations dedicated to mining activities; and (v) persons that conduct activities regulated by the decree.

To understand numbers (i) and (v) above, please note the following:

(a) The Presidential Decree indicates, under Article 2, that SUPCACVEN's object is to regulate activities conducted by corporations and individuals related to cryptoassets, such as commodities agreements, virtual exchanges, mining activities, virtual intermediation, among others.

(b) Pursuant to Article 4, the function of SUPCACVEN is to coordinate and control activities conducted by individuals or corporations related to commerce, circulation and possession of Venezuelan cryptoassets, including international exchanges, virtual miners, entities dedicated to saving and intermediation.

(c) Article 17 includes, within the scope of the registration obligation, two additional categories, not referred to above: (i) suppliers of goods for any of the phases of activities regulated by SUPCACVEN (a broad concept, which we believe must be interpreted considering goods that are relevant to cryptocurrency, for instance, mining equipment, and not unrelated goods); and (ii) individuals and corporations that conduct studies for mineral reserves' certification (which, except for the relationship of petros with oil, seems to be an odd category to include. Thus, we believe this category would be subject to registration only when the certification is to be related to cryptocurrencies).

Articles 2, 4, 9 and 16 have a residual category: activities related directly or by connection to cryptoassets. To summarise, there are authorisation and registration requirements which apply to any individual or corporation that conducts activities related directly or indirectly to cryptoassets.

Additionally, we believe that it may be possible that the Capital Markets Law (*Ley del Mercado de Valores*) also applies. Indeed, to the extent that a particular cryptocurrency qualifies also as a security under such law, it may become applicable too. Other jurisdictions have taken the position that in order to determine whether cryptocurrencies qualify as securities, the particular characteristics of each cryptocurrency must be analysed. Further, they have defended that in such case, capital markets rules and controls would apply.

We believe this may be the case in Venezuela too. In fact, as explained above, certain cryptocurrencies – the petro being a good example – may qualify as securities too. Further, the Capital Markets Law, under Article 46, mandates that, in case of doubt, the National Superintendence of Securities (*Superintendencia Nacional de Valores*, SUNAVAL) shall have the final right to determine if a particular asset qualifies as a security. If SUNAVAL were to determine that a certain cryptocurrency qualifies as a security, then all the capital markets rules would be applicable to the particular ICO and/or related activities.

We believe the authorities are not interpreting this matter from the perspective of dual control or regulations. There is no evidence of a joint approach by SUPCACVEN and SUNAVAL. However, from a strict legal point of view, this would be, in our opinion, the correct approach.

Finally, to the extent that cryptocurrency transactions qualified as implicit exchange transactions, limitations under the Law on the Exchange Regime and its Crimes would have been applicable too. For instance, the transactions would have had to be reported to the National Foreign Trade Center (*Centro Nacional de Commercio Exterior*, CENCOEX) pursuant to Article 16 thereof; or the transaction would have had to be conducted at a particular rate, pursuant to Article 11, jointly with Articles 28 and 30 of Exchange Agreement N° 39 (*Convenio Cambiario N° 39*). Again, these rules were abrogated by the Constitutional Assembly; however, such abrogation is unconstitutional.

Taxation

Except as detailed below, the tax authorities and regulators have not issued tax rules regarding cryptocurrencies in particular. Accordingly, transactions relating to cryptocurrencies would be regulated by general rules on the matter.

However, the following tax-related issues are relevant:

(a) Venezuela has assumed a general obligation to promote the use of cryptocurrencies. It has also taken on a specific obligation to accept payment of taxes by means of cryptocurrencies in the agreements between SUPCACVEN and the Zamora Municipality. Further, it has assumed such obligations particularly with respect to petros in the petros whitepaper.

(b) Article 7 of the Presidential Decree which creates the "Petro Zones" provides an exception regarding customs duties for the import of goods related to electronic equipment, computer equipment, software licences, hardware, electric power plants, air conditioning units, support equipment, etc. used in connection with virtual mining. Such exceptions would apply in Margarita Island, Los Roques, Territorio Insular Francisco de Miranda, Paraguaná and Ureña – San Antonio; and would last for two years, beginning on March 22, 2018.

Money transmission laws and anti-money laundering requirements

No specific rules regarding these matters have been formally enacted in connection with cryptocurrencies. So general rules on money transmission and anti-money laundering apply.

However, two very vague documents regarding anti-money laundering have been published on the petros website: http://www.elpetro.gob.ve/#docs. Such documents are: (i) Guidelines for the manual on internal control regarding prevention of money-laundering and financing of terrorism (*Lineamientos para el manual de control interno para la prevención del lavado de activos y financiamiento del terrorismo*); and (ii) an Orientation Guide for prevention of laundering of cryptoassets, financing of terrorism and "Know Your Customer" policies (*Guía de Orientación para la Prevención de Lavado de Criptoactivos, Financiamiento de Terrorismo y Políticas de "Conoce a tu Cliente"*).

From a formal point of view, such documents: (i) are not signed or issued by a particular public official or authority, yet they are included in the website; and (ii) have not been published in the Official Gazette. Accordingly, their validity is questionable.

From a substantive point of view, the documents: (i) are very vague – and sometimes technically defective; and (ii) contain obligations and recommendations applicable to the virtual exchanges. The main obligation refers to the need to submit to SUPCACVEN, for approval, any project regarding mechanisms to avoid criminal activities being conducted in connection with cryptoassets. Such projects must address issues such as the implementation of KYC procedures, the obligation of reporting criminal activities, the appointment of a Compliance Officer, etc.

In any case, as indicated, we believe that general rules on anti-money laundering and related activities would be applicable to cryptocurrencies and, in the case of cryptocurrencies which also qualify as securities, the specific rules on the matter enacted in connection with the capital market would also be applicable.

Promotion and testing

As already indicated, Venezuela is, in principle, bound to promote the use of cryptocurrencies.

Also, as referred to above, Venezuela has created two types of special "environments" for the promotion and development of cryptocurrencies.

First, the Zamora Municipality has in theory created a special space for: (i) virtual mining; and (ii) payment of taxes in cryptocurrency.

Second, the President has created the "Petro Zones", which also have benefits from the point of view of mining (including the customs tax benefits referred above) and payment in cryptocurrencies (e.g. gas prices).

Ownership and licensing requirements

Activities related – either directly or by connection – to cryptoassets are subject to prior authorisation, and individuals and corporations conducting them are subject to registration. However, in our opinion, this would not extend to ownership.

As evidenced from the joint analysis of Articles 2, 4, 9, 16 and 17 detailed above, the regulatory scope would not seem to extend to mere owners of cryptocurrency. Indeed, as evidenced from the above lists, the only reference to possession (*tenencia*) is under Article 4, but it seems to refer to players in the intermediation field, rather than to individuals and corporations who merely own cryptocurrency.

Accordingly, in our opinion, ownership is not subject to requirements or controls.

Mining

As indicated, mining cryptocurrency in Venezuela is permitted, subject to prior authorisation, pursuant to Article 9 of the Presidential Decree; and registration, pursuant to Articles 16 and 17 thereof.

Border restrictions and declaration

No specific rules regarding these matters have been enacted in connection to cryptocurrencies. General rules contained in the Law on the Central Bank of Venezuela and the Organic Law Against Organised Crime and Financing of Terrorism (*Ley Orgánica Contra la Delincuencia Organizada y Financiamiento al Terrorismo*) contain limitations regarding import and export of fiat money, under Articles 118 and 137 in the case of the first law, and import and export of money or securities by individuals entering or leaving the country, under Article 22 in the second one. We believe none of these is extensible to cryptocurrency transactions.

Finally, Article 15 of the Law on Exchange Regime and its Crimes established an obligation to notify CENCOEX of any import, export, entry or exit of foreign currency in amounts that exceed US$ 10,000. Since the term *foreign currency* was so broadly defined – and may have been deemed to include cryptocurrency – the authorities may have argued that cryptocurrency transactions were subject to this requirement. However, we believe that this makes no sense, in practical terms, because cryptocurrencies are not properly imported or exported. We believe for an obligation of this kind to be applicable to cryptocurrency, it would probably have to be imposed regarding the owner, that is, it would have to refer to the holdings of the person entering or exiting the country, rather than to the transactions themselves. In any case, as indicated, the law in reference was abrogated by the Constitutional Assembly, but we question the validity of the abrogation.

Reporting requirements

No rules regarding these matters have been formally enacted specifically in connection to cryptocurrencies. General rules may be extensible to cryptocurrencies.

Estate planning and testamentary succession

There are no special rules regarding this matter. We have not been privy to any estate planning or succession by testament containing cryptocurrency holdings in Venezuela.

* * *

Endnotes

1. The Constitutional Assembly is a body elected in 2017 to enact a new Constitution. References to its validity and functions are made below.

2. At the time of submission of this paper, the only regulation published in this regard was a constitutional decree issued by the Constitutional Assembly, which merely stated that the sovereign bolivar would have a reference of value linked to the petro, which in turn is associated with the price of Venezuelan oil (*cuyo valor referencial, estará anclado al valor del Petro, el cual estará asociado al precio del barril de petróleo venezolano*). But how this link would work was unknown as of this date.

3. The validity of this decree is highly questionable. First, the Constitutional Assembly was elected amidst very controversial circumstances (which included the technical company hired to conduct the election having stated that the electoral authority announced more votes than those actually cast), which may render its appointment null and void. Yet, we shall refer to only one of those circumstances: the basis for the election violated the principle of universal vote, which is a right recognised under Article 63 of the Constitution. Such violation occurred because the principle of one person–one vote was not respected, since certain categories (workers, women, natives, etc.) had the right to cast more than one vote, while other persons did not. Accordingly, the election of the Constitutional Assembly is null and void. Second, the Constitutional Assembly – even setting aside the nullity of the election – was elected to enact a new Constitution, not to enact other regulations. Some may argue that the Constitution, under Article 347, empowers the Constitutional Assembly to enact a new legal system (*ordenamiento jurídico*). However, that must be understood in the context of its mandate: The Constitutional Assembly would be allowed to enact new regulations only to the extent necessary to make the legal system compatible with the new Constitution. This is not the case. Further, the Constitutional Assembly has not even enacted the new Constitution.

4. President. <u>Decreto N° 3.196, mediante el cual se autoriza la creación de la Superintendencia de los Criptoactivos y actividades conexas venezolana</u>. Official Gazette N° 6.346 (E), December 8, 2017, Preamble.

5. Venezuela. "Petro. Papel Blanco. Versión Beta 0.9. Propuesta Financiera. 30 de enero 2018." Available at <u>http://pandectasdigital.blogspot.com/2018/01/whitepaper-libro-blanco-del-petro.html</u> (Last visit 7/20/2018).

6. Venezuela. "Petro. Papel Blanco. Beta 1.0. Propuesta Financiera y Tecnológica. 15 de marzo 2018". Available at <u>http://www.elpetro.gob.ve/pdf/esp/Whitepaper_Petro_es.pdf</u>. (Last visit 7/20/2018).

7. President. <u>Decreto N° 3.292 mediante el cual se determina como respaldo para la implementación de operaciones de intercambio financiero y comercial a través de criptoactivos, el desarrollo potencial de 5.342 MMBN de Petróleo Original en Sitio (POES) pesado y extrapesado, de acuerdo a una certificadora internacional independiente, localizado en el Bloque Ayacucho 01, de la Faja Petrolífera del Orinoco Hugo Chávez Frías</u>. Official Gazette N° 41.347. February 23, 2018.

8. Constitutional Assembly. <u>Decreto Constituyente sobre Criptoactivos y la Criptomoneda Soberana Petro</u>. Official Gazette N° 6.370 (E), April 9, 2018, Articles 5 and 12.

9. Lepervanche, Luisa & Acedo Sucre, Manuel. <u>A few ideas on Petros and other cryptocurrency transactions in Venezuela</u>. Available at <u>http://www.menpa.com/serve/file/assets%2Fuploads%2FEFEE5A71CC346147C.pdf</u> (Last visit: 7/20/ 2018). CAPRILES BAENA, Gonzalo. <u>Petro, la "moneda virtual" del gobierno venezolano.</u> Available at <u>http://www.cavecol.org/wp-content/uploads/2018/02/BDE-5-PETRO.pdf</u> (Last visit: 7/20/2018). HERNÁNDEZ, José Ignacio. ¿Es el petro una operación de crédito público? Available at <u>https://prodavinci.com/es-el-petro-una-operacion-de-credito-publico/</u> (Last visit: 7/20/2018).

10. Monaldi, Francisco J. <u>Is the Petro Truly Backed by Oil Reserves?</u> February 27, 2018. Available at <u>https://www.caracaschronicles.com/2018/02/27/petro-truly-backed-oil-reserves/</u> (Last visit: 7/20/2018).

11. Lepervanche, Luisa y Acedo Sucre, Manuel, *op. cit.*. Capriles Baena, Gonzalo, *op.cit.* Hernández, José Ignacio, *op.cit.*

12. National Assembly. Acuerdo sobre la emisión de la criptomoneda Petro. 9 de enero de 2018. Available at https://es.scribd.com/document/368773539/Acuerdo-sobre-la-emision-de-la-criptomoneda-Petro#from_embed (Last visit 7/20/2018).

13. However, this version of the FAQs was eliminated when the new Executive Order 13827, dated March 19, 2018, was issued. Such order prohibits transactions on any "digital currency, digital coin, or digital token". After the issuance of said order, the position of the OFAC changed, and now reflects that petros are forbidden under the new Executive Order, as evidenced in https://www.treasury.gov/resource-center/faqs/Sanctions/Pages/faq_other.aspx#venezuela, question N° 564 (Last visit: 7/20/2018).

14. National Assembly. Acuerdo sobre la emisión de la criptomoneda Petro. 9, see Endnote 12 above.

15. Presidente de la República. Decreto N° 3.355, mediante el cual se crea la Superintendencia de los Criptoactivos y Actividades Conexas Venezolana (SUPCACVEN), como servicio desconcentrado sin personalidad jurídica, administrado, supervisado e integrado a la Vicepresidencia de la República Bolivariana de Venezuela, con capacidad de gestión presupuestaria, administrativa y financiera sobre los recursos que correspondan. Official Gazette N° 6.371 (E). April 9, 2018.

16. Please note that although SUPCACVEN was, according to Decree 3.355, "created" on April 9, 2018, although it had already been operating for five months. Indeed, the appointment of the corresponding Superintendent was published in the Official Gazette in December 8, 2018 and such Superintendent has been acting, even jointly with other public officials, since that date. Further, SUPCACVEN's Twitter account indicates that it was created in December 2018.

17. Constitutional Assembly. Decreto Constituyente mediante el cual se establece la Derogatoria del Régimen Cambiario y sus Ilícitos. Official Gazette N° 41.452, dated August 2, 2018.

18. There are two reasons that lead us to argue that this decree is null and void. First, as indicated above, the Constitutional Assembly's election violated the Constitution and, thus, is null and void. Second, laws may only be abrogated by other laws, as established under Article 218 of the Constitution and Article 7 of the Civil Code. The Law on the Exchange Regime and its Crimes is a decree issued by the President, under legislative delegation (*habilitación legislativa*) pursuant Articles 236.8 and 203 of the Constitution. Thus, it is considered to be a law and, therefore, it may only be abrogated by another law. A decree issued by the Constitutional Assembly does not qualify as a law and, thus, may not abrogate one. We have also expressed above our position against the argument that the Constitutional Assembly is empowered with legislative powers.

19. Presidente de la República. Decreto N° 3.355, mediante el cual se crea la Superintendencia de los Criptoactivos y Actividades Conexas Venezolana (SUPCACVEN), como servicio desconcentrado sin personalidad jurídica, administrado, supervisado e integrado a la Vicepresidencia de la República Bolivariana de Venezuela, con capacidad de gestión presupuestaria, administrativa y financiera sobre los recursos que correspondan. Official Gazette N° 6.371 (E). April 9, 2018.

20. Please note that although SUPCACVEN was, according to Decree 3.355, "created" on April 9, 2018, although it had already been operating for five months. Indeed, the appointment of the corresponding Superintendent was published in the Official Gazette in December 8, 2018 and such Superintendent has been acting, even jointly with other public officials, since that date. Further, SUPCACVEN's Twitter account indicates that it was created in December 2018.

Luisa Lepervanche
Tel: +58 212 909 1611 / Email: llepervanche@menpa.com

Luisa Lepervanche graduated from Law School at Universidad Católica Andrés Bello, *cum laude;* and later specialised in Corporate Law, at Universidad Metropolitana. She has been a Junior Partner at Menpa since 2017, when she rejoined the firm after being Legal Counsel to The Coca-Cola Company for Venezuela and the Caribbean. She taught Legal Analysis and Human Rights and worked on human rights issues. Her practice is focused on corporate law, mergers and acquisitions, banking and finance, project financing and debt restructuring, real estate issues and public law, and it includes an important *pro bono* component. Luisa has written articles on corporate matters, cryptocurrencies, insurance and exchange controls. She is a member of the Legal Committee of the *Cámara Venezolana Americana de Comercio e Industria (Venamcham)*. Luisa is fluent in Spanish and English.

Mendoza, Palacios, Acedo, Borjas, Páez Pumar & Cía. (Menpa)

Urb. Las Mercedes, Calle Veracruz con Calle Cali, Torre Aba, Piso 1 y 2, Caracas 1060, Venezuela
Tel: +58 212 909 1611 / URL: www.menpa.com